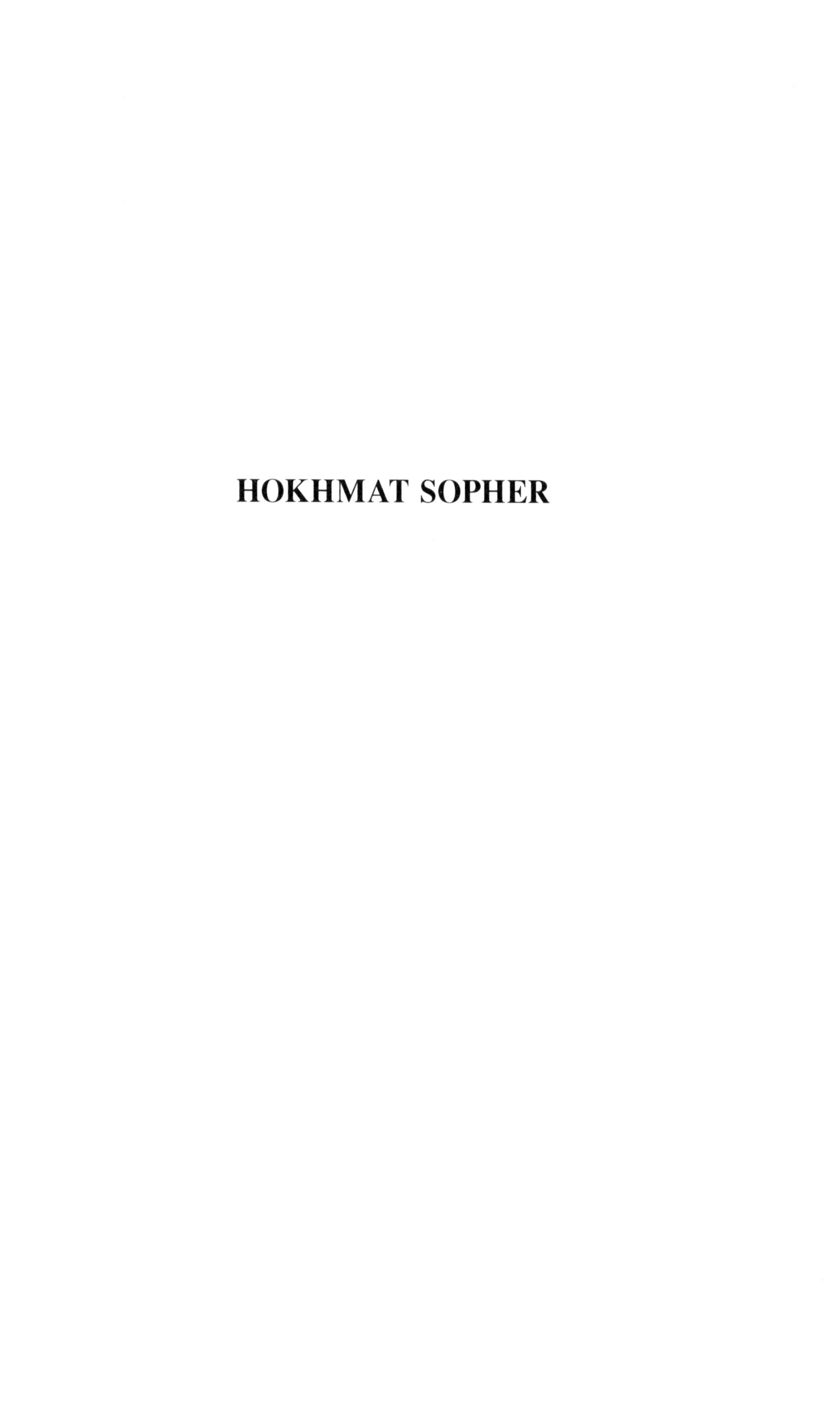

HOKHMAT SOPHER

ÉTUDES BIBLIQUES

(Nouvelle série. N° 88)

HOKHMAT SOPHER

Mélanges offerts au Professeur Émile Puech en l'honneur de son quatre-vingtième anniversaire

éditées par

Jean-Sébastien REY et Martin STASZAK

PEETERS
LEUVEN – PARIS – BRISTOL, CT
2021

ISBN 978-90-429-4575-3
eISBN 978-90-429-4576-0
D/2021/0602/102

A catalogue record for this book is available from the Library of Congress.

ÉMILE PUECH – NOTES SUR UNE VIE AU SERVICE DE L'ÉPIGRAPHIE

Il n'est pas difficile de s'apercevoir que la vie de nos contemporains est plus fluctuante qu'autrefois. Grâce à une mobilité plus grande et à la globalisation, elle se compose souvent d'éléments hétérogènes. Personne ne niera que c'est un immense bénéfice : la flexibilité et la diversité, la connaissance d'autres champs de travail, d'autres pays et cultures enrichissent la vie et contribuent à la construction d'une nouvelle identité. Néanmoins, la diversité postmoderne amène le danger d'une dispersion qui a du mal à arriver à la synthèse. La multiplicité, qu'elle soit antique ou moderne, pour ne pas sombrer dans une multitude de monologues, doit être maîtrisée pour faire émerger des conclusions signifiantes.

Émile Puech, pour sa part, a pratiqué la cohérence. À l'occasion de son quatre-vingtième anniversaire et après quarante ans de présence à l'École biblique et archéologique française de Jérusalem, on s'émerveille devant une recherche qui tire sa richesse extraordinaire d'une cohésion thématique fidèlement centrée sur l'épigraphie du Proche-Orient ancien. Le cœur de son travail scientifique reste les écrits qumraniens dont il a patiemment déchiffré nombre de manuscrits, corrigé des lectures et profondément illuminé l'interprétation de ces textes fragmentaires.

À côté de ce travail, Émile Puech a publié sur de nombreuses inscriptions anciennes, hébraïques, araméennes, phéniciennes, cananéennes, protosinaïtiques, etc., ainsi que sur des objets archéologiques de l'époque paléochrétienne. C'est toujours l'écriture et ses dérivés, les œuvres littéraires courtes ou longues, qui ont attiré l'attention du jubilaire. L'écriture, contrairement aux images, est capable de transporter une terminologie abstraite, de décrire et interpréter notre monde existant et de concevoir un autre qui n'existe pas (encore). On trouve ici certainement le point commun du judaïsme, du christianisme et des idées élaborées et transmises à Qumrân. Ainsi, on n'est pas étonné que les thèmes de l'eschatologie et de la résurrection apparaissent à de nombreuses reprises parmi les publications d'Émile Puech.

Sa biographie académique reflète cette cohérence productive : né le 9 mai 1941 à Cazelles de Sébrazac (Aveyron), il a étudié la philosophie et la théologie, les langues orientales, l'histoire des religions, l'épigraphie sémitique et la sigillographie mésopotamienne.

En 1971 il est boursier de l'Académie des Inscriptions et Belles-Lettres à l'École biblique, puis attaché de recherche au CNRS en 1980, chargé de recherche en 1983, puis directeur de recherche au CNRS en 1996. Il obtient une double thèse de doctorat (ès Lettres et Théologie) en 1992 à Paris, puis une habilitation à diriger les recherches en 2001 à Strasbourg. Ses premières publications débutent en 1971 et se poursuivent jusqu'aujourd'hui.[1]

La direction de l'École Biblique et Archéologique Française de Jérusalem, ses collègues et amis partout dans le monde, les contributeurs et éditeurs de cette Festschrift lui souhaitent encore des années productives au service de l'épigraphie hébraïque et araméenne.

Jean Jacques PÉRENNÈS, O.P.
Martin STASZAK, O.P.
EBAF, Jérusalem

[1] Pour plus de détails sur la biographie et les premières publications d'Émile Puech, voir Florentino GARCÍA MARTÍNEZ, Annette STEUDEL and Eibert TIGCHELAAR, *From 4QMMT to Resurrection. Mélanges qumraniens en hommage à Émile Puech* (StTDJ 61) Leiden, Boston, Brill, 2006, vii-ix.

LEXICAL NOTES ON *MUSAR LAMEVIN*: מחסור, אוט

Jonathan BEN-DOV

The vocabulary of *Musar Lamevin* (Henceforth MLM) keeps baffling interpreters of this difficult text.[1] This previously unknown wisdom composition uses words not attested elsewhere in the Dead Sea Scrolls or other related literature, and assigns novel meanings to previously known words. In some cases the meanings of these words may be deduced from the context, but in such a difficult scroll, with such fragmentary preservation, the context remains necessarily opaque. In the present article I wish to examine two such terms, whose general meaning in context was more or less understood, but scholars remained at odds in elucidating the etymology or the semantic shifts that lead to their idiosyncratic usage.[2] The following lexical discussion will first employ a close reading of the pertinent terms in selected contexts, and will then suggest an etymology or derivation for them, describing the semantic shifts that led to their present use in MLM.

A similar move of crafting philosophical vocabulary is attested in the 3rd-century BCE Book of Qohelet (Ecclesiastes). Martin Hengel and Peter

[1] This study is funded by a grant from the DIP foundation (Deutsche-Israelische Projektkooperation), Grant Number BE 5916/1-1, as part of the project *Scripta Qumranica Electronica*. It was previously presented at the annual conference in memorial of Moshe Held, Ben-Gurion University 2010, with the kind of invitation of the late Prof. Chaim H. Cohen. It benefitted from many discussions with the team at the University of Haifa, especially Asaf Gayer and Shlomi Efrati, as well as from correspondence with Matthew Goff. I would like to thank Tamar Sovran (Tel-Aviv) and Christian Stadel (Beer Sheva) for their helpful comments on semantic theory. Thanks are due to Antony Perrot for the French translation of the abstract.

Daniel Vos (Boston College) has independently developed similar ideas with regard to the word אוט, in a paper presented at the Annual Meeting of the SBL, Denver, 19 November 2018. I am grateful to him and to Jeff Cooley (Boston College) for positively discussing the matter with me.

[2] Previous studies and commentaries of MLM cited here are: John STRUGNELL, Daniel HARRINGTON and Torleif ELGVIN, *Qumran Cave 4 XXIV. Sapiential Texts, Part Two* (DJD, 34), Oxford, Clarendon Press, 1999; Matthew GOFF, *4QInstruction* (SBL Wisdom Literature from the Ancient World, 2) Atlanta, SBL, 2013; Jean-Sébastien REY, *4QInstruction: Sagesse et eschatology* (STDJ, 81) Leiden, Brill, 2009. There is a section on vocabulary in DJD 34, pp. 22-32, as well as in Eibert TIGCHELAAR, *To Increase Learning for the Understanding Ones. Reading and Reconstructing the Fragmentary Early Jewish Sapiential Text 4QInstruction* (STDJ, 44) Leiden, Brill, 2001, 237-244.

Machinist have shown how the author of Qohelet, in the lack of adequate vocabulary to express new philosophical (Greek) ideas, adopted rare terms from elsewhere or invented novel linguistic creations for that purpose.[3] The Israeli scholar Nili Samet has recently carried this notion forward, coining the concept of "semantic availability". According to her, the author of Qohelet chose words that are either very rare or of foreign origin, or for some other reason become available for accruing novel semantic loads. These words are taken over and loaded with concrete philosophical meanings that perfectly matched the idiosyncratic interest of that philosopher, in the specific case of Qohelet being mainly ideas on one's share in life in the face of death.[4] A similar phenomenon, I submit, pertains to the author of MLM, who has chosen rare Hebrew or foreign words and fashioned them to fit his unique interests. In this case, the author's interest lies in the metaphysical share of individuals in the world, and the way to use this share as a commodity in interpersonal encounters.

The discussion departs from a general notion about the aim of MLM. While most scholarly attention was given to the – equally enigmatic – term רז נהיה and the concepts of eschatology and revelation, it is important to underscore another, earthly message of this composition.[5] A large portion of MLM is dedicated to interpersonal, financial or vocational interactions. More than earlier wisdom literature, MLM stresses that every individual has a share in the world, and that he should be conscientious to retain that share for himself, not exceed it, and not let others take part in it.[6] Problems would rise, for example, if one takes a loan or sold into slavery, or accepts the property of a neighbor for repair. From another angle, problems arise if one accepts other individuals into his household, rendering a situation of dependence. For the author of MLM these are not mere social-economic situations, but rather religious-metaphysical events which must

[3] Martin HENGEL, *Judaism and Hellenism: Studies in their Encounter in Palestine during the Early Hellenistic Period*, London, SCM, 1974, 117-121; Peter MACHINIST, "Fate, miqreh and Reason: Some Reflections on Qohelet and Biblical Thought", in: Z. ZEVIT et al. (eds.), *Solving Riddles and Untying Knots. Biblical, Epigraphic and Semitic Studies in Honor of Jonas C. Greenfield*, Winona Lake, IN, Eisenbrauns, 1995, 159-175.

[4] Nili SAMET, "Qohelet's Idiolect and Its Cultural Context", *Harvard Theological Review* (forthcoming). I thank the author for kindly sharing her manuscript with me.

[5] For example, the section on "Teaching" in the introduction to DJD 34, 32-33, does not even mention the theme of private property and economic conduct, and their metaphysical counterparts.

[6] This insight was initially formulated by Menahem KISTER, "Wisdom Literature at Qumran", in: M. Kister (ed.), *The Qumran Scrolls and Their World*, Jerusalem, Yad Ben Tzvi, 2009, 313-316 (Hebrew). See now Jonathan Ben-Dov, "Family Relations and the Economic-Metaphysical Message of Instruction", *JSP* 30 (2020), 87-100.

be accounted for, and which dictate specific regulations for the actors in each of these scenes. Most of the large fragment 4Q416 2 is dedicated to these matters, catalogued by Elisha Qimron as בין אדם לחברו, "interpersonal matters". In order to convey the unique message of MLM about these interactions, the author was in need of new terms, such that were not previously used in similar literature. Given this author's unique poetry and linguistic brilliance, these terms remained exceptionally difficult to unravel. Yet with the general ideological argument in mind, the linguistic investigation is now possible to a greater extent.

1. מחסור

The word מחסור appears 13 times in Biblical Hebrew with the quite clear meaning "lack", as indicated in the dictionaries (HALOT, BDB). For example, the meaning can be seen when contrasted with surplus or riches: Prov 21:5 מחשבות חרוץ אך למותר / וכל אץ רק למחסור, "The plans of the diligent make only for gain; All rash haste makes only for loss" (NJPS). Similarly in Judg 19:19, where the speaker recounts the ample supplies at his disposal, claiming that אין מחסור כל דבר, "we lack nothing". A rather frequent component of the sapiential vocabulary, the term מחסור appears eight times in the Book of Proverbs and once more in the wisdom psalm 34:10. A suggestive occurrence for our purposes comes in Prov 24:34 ובא מתהלך רישך / ומחסריך כאיש מגן "poverty will come to you like a vagrant, and want like a beggar".[7] This verse is important for MLM, where the word ריש "poverty" is rather frequent. Note that in this verse, מחסור parallels ריש, both denoting a state of lack or poverty.

The editors of DJD 34 claim with regard to the term מחסור (4Q415 9 9) that "Rather than 'deficiency, lack' the more general sense 'poverty, need' is more likely here" (DJD XXXIV, 56). Rey defines this term as "indigence, manque, besoin" (p. 36). Indeed, some occurrences of the term in MLM seem on an initial examination to support this meaning, for example:

(1) 4Q417 2 i 21 אם הוֺן אנש[י]ם תֿלוה למחסורכֿה

which is usually rendered "Si tu empruntes l'argent des homm[e]s à cause de ton indigence" (Rey, p. 47), or more freely by Goff (p. 185): "If you borrow the money of m[e]n for what you need". Both these readings understand the term מחסור as denoting a state of need.

[7] Translation follows William McKane, *Proverbs* (OTL), London, SCM, 1970, 250. For מגן see Menahem Z. Kadari, *A Dictionary of Biblical Hebrew* (Ramat Gan: Bar Ilan University Press, 2006), 579 (Hebrew).

This unequivocal biblical meaning, however, requires a more attenuated analysis since it often points to a positive entity rather than to lack. In MLM מחסור denotes a positive content, some kind of wealth or commodity that can be shared with others or withheld. Consider the following examples:

(2) 4Q418 81 18 הוצא מחסורכה לכול דורשי חפץ

Offer out your *mḥswr* for all those who seek sustenance

(3) 4Q418 127 1 [כי יד]ל̊ מׄקורכה ומחסורכה לא תמצא

[if] your source [is impoverished] and you shall not find your *mḥswr*

In (2), *mḥswr* is clearly something positive that can be pulled out and offered to others. Goff's translation (p. 241) "Bring forth what you need to all who seek business" thus misses the point of the statement. The main linguistic mechanism in (3) is the parallelism, which, though fragmentary is still clear enough for our purposes. The second hemistich describes how the addressee will not find his *mḥswr*; this must be a reference to him not being able to find sustenance. "Not finding lack" – such a translation fails to account for the message. Similarly so:

(4) 4Q418 97 2 מ]חסור̊ׄיכה קח מידו̊[

Take your [*m*]*ḥswr* (pl.), i.e., [p]rovisions, from his (His?) hand

Other passages in MLM will yield an improved sense when read with this meaning in mind. See for example the following quote:

(5) 4Q416 2 ii 20 אל תתכבד במחסורכה ואׄתה רׄי̊ש (4Q417 2 ii 25 במׄחסוריכׄה)

This clause is often rendered "Do not glorify yourself with what you lack while you are poor" (Goff; similarly Rey p. 69); or in other words "do not be lavish (lit. honor yourself) in your poverty when you are in fact poor" (cp. however Sir 10:31 ms A). This translation, however, produces an awkward duplicity with regard to the addressee's poverty. A better translation would be "do not use *your provision* lavishly while you are in fact poor".

Such a reading gives a better sense also for source (1) above. That sentence does not mean "if you borrow the wealth of people when in state of need", but rather "if you borrow the wealth of people for your sustenance".

Another occurrence of this word, in the prologue of MLM (4Q416 1 and 4Q418* 1), can now be better understood:

(6) לפי מֹחסור צבאם] ומשפט כולם לו

… according to the provision of their multitudes, and the portion of them all lies with Him.

This verse explicitly refers to the supply or provision required for maintaining a working squad.[8] The meaning of the term מחסור thus shifted from "need" to that which fulfills the need, i.e., provision.[9] Accordingly, the word משפט denotes "ratio, assigned portion", as in Deut 18:3.

Two more occurrences of the noun מחסור appear in consecutive lines of 4Q417 in a notoriously difficult context, with a somewhat ambiguous meaning. The ambiguity of these sentences makes it difficult to determine the meaning of this slippery noun in them. That is, these sentences are difficult regardless of the ambiguity of the term מחסור.

(7) 4Q417 2 i 17 and parallel ואתה אם תחסר טרף מחסוֹרֿכֿה ומותריכה [ה]בֹא [ביחד]

You, if you lack food, your mḥswr and your surplus bring together

(8) 4Q417 2 i 18-19 (וֹאֹם) תחסר לוא מבֹלֹי הוֹן מחסורכה

… if you are in need, your *mḥswr* is not without capital

The apodosis of the condition in (7) is notoriously difficult with regard to the meaning of יחד, whether noun or adverb.[10] Even the syntactic analysis of the sentence is unclear, as several scholars see the protasis extending to include the word מחסורכה: "if you lack the food that you need", with the apodosis beginning only with the word ומותריכה.[11] I cannot agree, however, to such parsing because an apodosis cannot begin with *vav*, and due to the integrity of the word pair מחסור-מותר. Regardless of these exegetical questions, and even if they are resolved, it remains unclear what the author offers to the addressee as solution for his dire situation.[12] The pair

[8] The word צבא denotes "term of work", "assembly of workers" without any military connotation (see e.g. Job 7:1, 14:14; Num 4:3, 23; 1QSa 1:17-18). This meaning is noted in the translation of Job by Ed GREENSTEIN, *Job. A New Translation* (New Haven: Yale University Press, 2019), *pace* HALOT and BDB who stress the military meaning.

[9] The translation "the poverty of their hosts" is thus off the mark: Catherine MURPHY, *Wealth in the Dead Sea Scrolls and in the Qumran Community* (STDJ 40) Leiden, Brill, 2002, 168. For this section see Ben-Dov, "Family Relations", 90-91.

[10] REY, *4QInstruction*, 47, 51, reads this sentence as a command to collect the surplus into a community pool. GOFF, *4QInstruction*, 205, rightly opposes it, adopting instead an adverbial sense of the word, as translated here. This understanding follows Eibert TIGCHELAAR, "הבא ביחד in *4QInstruction* (4Q418 64+199+66 par 4Q417 1 i 17-19)", *RQ* 18 (1998) 589-593, and DJD 34, p. 186.

[11] Thus GOFF, *4QInstruction*, 185; REY, *4QInstruction*, 47.

[12] I do admit that the verbal use of חסר follows the usual meaning "lack".

מחסור – מותר seems to be antithetic, as in Prov 14:23, 21:5. According to my reading, the word pair does not mean here "need vs. surplus" but rather "due provision vs. surplus" (cf. the verb תותיר immediately below, line 18). The addressee should take both his required daily provision (מחסור) and his exceeding wealth (מותר) and balance them together.[13]

With regard to (8), the difficulty arises from the double negation לוא מבלי.[14] However, I follow Kister and Qimron who read this sentence with a single negation, carrying the reasonable sense: "your provision will not be found from wealth", promising a divine source of sustenance of some sort. Such a reading works well if מחסור is understood as "provision", as indicated here.

Other passages in MLM use the graphically similar term מסחור (e.g. 4Q418 103 ii 6; 122 i 5). While it is sometimes suggested that this term involves a pun with מחסור,[15] I see no reason to claim so. מסחור stands for the Hebrew term מסחר, "commerce, merchandise", as claimed by Rey (p. 30, 36).

A final case in point is:

(9) 4Q418 126 ii 13 ואם לא ת<ס>שיג ידו למחסורכה ומחסור אוטו[

If he cannot afford (lit. his hand does not reach), by your *ʾwṭ* and his *mḥswr ʾwṭ*[

This sentence borders on the discussion of the term אוט in the next section of this article. The term *mḥswr* appears here twice, the second time being in the construct מחסור אוטו. Due to the bad preservation of this sentence, it is hard to determine where to place the comma in it. It presumably reads: "If he cannot afford (lit. his hand does not reach), by your provision and by his *ʾwṭ*-provision[". Further clarification will appear below.

Having deduced the meaning of מחסור in MLM based on the context, its derivation must be accounted for. How can a term which usually means "lack" shift its meaning to the entirely opposite meaning "resource, supply"? A twofold answer can be given to this query: from the point of view

[13] TIGCHELAAR, "הבא ביחד", 592.

[14] Many readers consider the word לוא as the imperative of the root לוה, hence "borrow" (GOFF, *4QInstruction*, 185, 206 n. 69; DJD 34, 187; Rey, *4QInstruction*, 51-52). However, I follow KISTER, "Wisdom Literature", 315, in reading this double negation as a single one. Similarly QIMRON, quoted in DJD 34, p. 188. See further Ben-Dov, "Family Relations", 91.

[15] See e.g. TIGCHELAAR, *To Increase Learning for the Understanding Ones*, 179; cf. the response by Benjamin G. WOLD, *Women, Men, and Angels. The Qumran Wisdom Composition* Musar leMevin *and its Allusions to Genesis Creation Traditions* (WUNT 201), Tübingen, Mohr Siebeck, 2005, 89 n. 20.

of semantics, and from a close reading of some biblical phrases. The textbooks for semantics describe a regular shift dubbed "enantiosemy", in which the meaning of a word shifts to neighboring meanings, sometimes even to its opposite.[16] Thus for example the English word "fast", which can mean both "moving rapidly" and "unmoving"; or the word "sanction", which means both "permit" and "penalize". In fact, such a semantic flip can be deduced from several occurrences of the noun in Biblical Hebrew, for example Judges 19:20 כל מחסורך עלי. While this verse probably originally meant "whatever you lack I shall provide", an equally valid reading would be "All your provision is on me", with *mḥswr* indicating a positive content rather than "lack".[17]

While the meaning "lack" was the original one, I can see how later readers, who had profound interest in regulating the world's provisions as indicating metaphysical shares, developed a different meaning, more attuned to their interests. Such a reading appears not only in MLM but rather also in a rabbinic liturgical text with similar interest. Consider the interesting analogy from the Jewish short blessing after the consumption of food: ברוך אתה ה׳ ... בורא נפשות רבות וחסרונן, "Blessed are You O Lord... who creates many living beings and their חסרון" (m.Ber 6:8). Since there is little sense in praising God for creating lack for the living beings, this epithet must relate to God's creation of *provision* to fulfill the needs of those beings.

To conclude this section, the noun מחסור in MLM should be rendered "provision, sustenance" rather than "need". Accordingly, this noun should not be seen as part of the language of poverty in MLM.[18] It is not about lack or misery but rather about normal human provision.

2. אוט

In contrast to the previous term, the word אוט is a very rare one. Some scholars would connect it with BH אט (see below), but this connection is not intuitive. The word is attested fifteen times in MLM, many of them in

[16] For a recent discussion and some examples see Serguei SAKHNO and Nicole TERSIS, "Is a 'Friend' an 'Enemy'? Between 'Proximity' and 'Opposition'", in: M. VANHOVE (ed.), *From Polysemy to Semantic Change* (Studies in Language Companion Series 106), Amsterdam, John Benjamins, 2008, 317-339. I thank Christian Stadel (Ben Gurion University) for this reference.

[17] Similarly in Deut 15:8: והעבט תעביטנו די מחסורו אשר יחסר לו. The original verse maintained the same meaning for both the noun מחסור and the verb יחסר, as in the NRSV translation "willingly lending enough to meet the need, whatever it may be". However, the verse can also be understood with the noun meaning "provision" rather than "need", hence: "Lend him sufficient for whatever he needs" (NJPS).

[18] *Pace* WOLD, *Women, Men, and Angels*, 3-4, 24.

fragmentary contexts, as well as once more – in the defective spelling אט – in 4Q424 "Instruction-Like composition B". In the absence of previous attestations, readers sought to establish its meaning by means of the context, alongside educated guesses about derivation and semantics.[19]

One attempt, since disproven, relies on the quote from 4Q424:

(10) 4Q424 1 6 ביד עצל אל תפקיד אט כי לא יצניע מלאכתך

In the hand of a lazy man do not deposit *ʾṭ*, for he shall not *ṣnʿ* your business

This advice is part of a series of similar sapiential advices, ordering to abstain from interacting with precarious personalities, in this case a lazy man. But what is it that should not be deposited with the lazy man? Sarah Tanzer in DJD 36 relied on the verb יצניע in the second hemistich, understanding it as "will not keep private", hence the translation: "Into the hand of one who is stupid do not entrust a secret, for he will not keep private your affairs".[20] Tanzer connects the term with BH בלט and לאט, yielding the meaning "secret". Novick has noted, however, following earlier scholars, that the root צנע in Second Temple literature means "caution and craftiness" (see Prov 11:2; Sir 16:25).[21] Thus the meaning "secret" for אט is not valid, and so is the proposed derivation from the root אטט, "slowly, quietly". Novick further calls attention to the next statement in 4Q424 1 6-7 ואל תשלח דב[ר] לקח כי לא יפלס כל ארחתיך "and do not send (him) on a purchase matter, because he will not measure out your paths". This translation was suggested by Novick, based on the noun פלס in Isa 40:12 (‖ מאזנים "scale"). The two adjacent proverbs convey the message that work should be entrusted to a trustworthy worker, who would be crafty and run the business in a trustworthy manner. The meaning of אט should therefore be related to "property, affairs". But how so? I would like to point out the connection with measuring and scale, which will arise again later on in the discussion.

[19] See the prudent statement by WOLD, *Women, Men, and Angels*, 215 n. 90: "It is better not to translate אוט in order to reflect the level of uncertainty surrounding the word". Cp. Ibid. 219 n. 106.

[20] Sarah TANZER "424. 4QInstruction-Like Composition B", in: S.J. Pfann et al. (eds.), *Qumran Cave 4 XXVI Cryptic texts and Miscellanea part 1* (DJD 36) Oxford, Clarendon, 2001, 337-339. Similarly Daniel J. HARRINGTON, *Wisdom Texts from Qumran*, New York, Routledge, 1996, 61. See earlier bibliography in Tzvi NOVICK, "The Meaning and Etymology of אוט", *JBL* 127 (2008) 339-343, fn 4.

[21] See further references and bibliography in NOVICK, "The Meaning and Etymology", 340-341. Further Menahem KISTER, "A Contribution to the Interpretation of Ben Sira", *Tarbiz* 59 (1990): 303-378 at 351-352 (Hebrew).

Another attempt was recently carried out by Ingo Kottsieper, who sees אוט as a Qumranic spelling of the BH word אט, considering also the defective spelling אט twice in the Qumran literature (4Q424 1 6; 4Q418 8 13 [in the parallel line 4Q416 2 ii 12 the plene spelling is employed).[22] This word usually appears in BH in such combinations as לאט (2 Sam 18:5; Isa 8:6), לאטי (Gen 33:14) but also אט (1 Kgs 21:27). Also notable is the fact that in 1QIsa[a] the word לאט (Isa 8:6) is spelled לאוט. According to Kottsieper, the biblical meaning of the word was "Sanftheit", i.e. "gentleness"; the meaning then gradually developed into "Amngemessenheit", i.e., "appropriateness, adequacy", the latter meaning being used in MLM. He quotes the occurrences of the word in MLM and claims that "an allen Stellen die Konnotation 'Angemessenehit' insbesondere auch im sinn von 'angemessener Bedarf' sinnvoll ist".[23] However, as I read these quotes from MLM, in my mind they do not match the suggested meanings "adequacy" or "adequate requirements", as suggested by Kottsieper. I shall presently explore a different interpretation of the word in its various contexts.

From the context of the occurrences in MLM, Novick justly concludes that the term אוט means something like "property". This meaning is apparent from the vicinity of אוט with terms such as חפץ, טרף, עבודה, as in:

(11) 4Q416 2 ii 1-2 +4Q417 2 ii 3 למל]א כל מחסורי אוטו ולתת טרף לכל חי

to fill all of his *'wṭ*-provisions and to give food for all the living

Novick renders the construct phrase מחסורי אוטו as "all of his material needs". As always in the verbiage of MLM there seems to be much redundancy in the parallelism, as many words denote "provision" with meager semantic variation. The general context seems clear, yet some awkwardness remains in the construct phrase, which seems pleonastic. Novick further suggests a derivation for the noun, positing a semantic shift (that occurred in learned circles) for the word אוט, from "leisure" to "property". He suggests that this word underwent a similar process to that of the noun הון. The latter noun means "gentleness, ease" in cognate

[22] Ingo KOTTSIEPER, "'Was du erbert von deinen Vätern…': Eine Randbemerkung zur hebräischen Lexicographie", in: E. Bons, J. Joosten and R. Hunziker-Rodewald (eds.), *Biblical Lexicology: Hebrew and Greek* (BZAW, 443) Berlin, de Gruyter, 2015, 33-69, esp. 59-69; Reinhard KRATZ, Annete STEUDEL, and Ingo KOTTSIEPER (eds.), *Hebräisches und Aramäisches Wörterbuch ze den Texten vom Toten Meer*, Berlin, de Gruyter, 2017, vol I, 34.

[23] KOTTSIEPER, "Was du erbert", 62. In fn 96 Kottsieper acknowledges the proximity of his interpretation with that of NOVICK, yet rejects the latter's derivation in analogy with the word הון (see below).

languages (Arabic, Aramaic), and has developed to mean "that which affords opportunity for ease", hence "capital, property".[24] One may still raise some objection, however, since the Arabic-Aramaic meaning of הון as "ease, gentleness" is a very marginal one in Hebrew, if at all, while the term הון is quite common both in BH and at Qumran in the later, fully developed sense. With doubts about this original shift, I am reluctant to apply the same shift to yet another word, and an exceptionally rare one at that.

While Strugnell and Harrington follow the meaning "secret",[25] later interpreters of MLM have generally accepted Novick's proposal. Thus Goff (p. 64 and n. 8) states that the term "while enigmatic, likely has a material sense as well, denoting assets of resources". Goff also notes the disparity with the biblical meaning of **אט** as "softly, gently". Already before Novick, Puech suggested the meaning "ressources" but did not offer an etymology.[26] This meaning was adopted also by Rey (p. 33), who has equally abstained from explaining the derivation.

I would like to note that the occurrences of **אוט** in MLM are often strongly linked with the vocabulary of weights and measurements, a fact that may bear on the exact meaning of this term. Thus in the following examples:

(12) 4Q418 126 ii 2-3

5 וא]תה מב]י̊ן באמת מוד כל אוט אנשים א[
6 כי באי̊[פ]ת̊ אמת ומשקל צדק תכן אל כול מ̊[עשיו

5 You, Mevin, truly measure all the *ʾwṭ* of men [
6 for in a true measure and a just weigh has God measured all of his d[eeds

אוט is measured here in various ways, and similarly so in the following:

(13) 4Q418 127 5-6

5 ... כי אל עשה כול חפצי אוט ויתכנם באמת
6 ... ו̊במוזני צדק שקל כול תכונם ובאמת̇[

5 ... for God made all the requirements of *ʾwṭ*, and measured them truly
6 ... and in just scales He weighed all their measure, and truly[

Sources (12-13) show that the term **אוט**, beyond denoting property in general, carries a special connotation of weighing and measuring. Let us

[24] NOVICK, ibid., 342. In fact, the word הון is used in the Targumin to translate the Hebrew **אט**.

[25] But see HARRINGRON and STRUGNELL, DJD 34, pp. 3-32 where they suggest the meaning "matter, business".

[26] Émile PUECH, "Les fragments eschatologiques de *4QInstruction* (4Q416 1 et 4Q418 69 ii, 81-81a, 127)", *RQ* 22 (2005) 89-119, here p. 105.

recall that a similar sense arises from its mention in 4Q424, due to the verb לפלס. While weights and measures play a central role in the entire argumentation of MLM,[27] the application of this idea with regard to one term in particular raises the possibility that this term is more closely connected with measurements. In fact, the various contexts in which the word אוט is used rather point to the meaning "measured share, assigned share", relating to the portion assigned by God to each person. Thus the phrase מחסורי אוטו quoted above (11) would mean "The provisions of his appointed share", or more simply "his measured provisions".[28] The sapiential advice in (10) warns the addressee not to deposit his assigned portion with a lazy man, who would not handle it properly.[29] In the worldview of MLM, as mentioned above following Kister, this assigned portion is a primary metaphysical category, which in many ways dictates the argument in the entire economic section of MLM.[30] It is quite fitting therefore that this metaphysical concept be expressed by means of a dedicated philosophical term.[31]

Consider now again the example quoted above:

(14) 4Q126 ii 12 ובידכה אוט<ה>ו ומטנאכה ידרוש חפצו

His (=the person who seeks sustenance) assigned share is in your hand, and from your basket he seeks sustenance

The addressee, being a proprietor, holds the means for sustaining other individuals who depend on him. The term אוט parallels the term חפץ, which squarely belongs in the same semantic field. Equally so:

(15) 4Q417 2 ii 2-3 and parallels[32]

[מא]ל שאל טרפכה כי הוא פתח רחמיו[... למל]א כל מחסורי אוטו ולתת טרף לכל חי

[27] For this theme see Menahem KISTER, "Physical and Metaphysical Measurements Ordained by God in the Literature of the Second Temple Period", in: E.G. Chazon, D. Dimant and R. Clements (eds.), *Reworking the Bible. Apocryphal and Related Texts at Qumran* (STDJ 58) Leiden, Brill, 2005, 153-176. The forthcoming dissertation by Asaf Gayer will give a comprehensive treatment of this theme in MLM and related literature.

[28] The translation "deficiencies of his secrets" (MURPHY, *Wealth in the Dead Sea Scrolls*, 170) is thus unwarranted.

[29] Following NOVICK, it is important to mention the similar statement in 4Q416 2 ii 4-5 (and parallels): כי כיס צפונכה פק]דתה לנושה בכה].

[30] See Ben-Dov, "Family Relations".

[31] A similar concept is essential for the philosophical message of Qohelet, where it is expressed by means of the term חלק. See SAMET, "Qohelet's Idiolect".

[32] For the full score see Elisha QIMRON, *The Dead Sea Scrolls. The Hebrew Writings*, Vol. II, Jerusalem, Yad Ben Tzvi, 2003, 154.

> Ask your food [from Go]d, for He has opened his mercy[... to fulfi]l all of his (=the individual's) *measured provisions* and to provide food for all the living.

If the reconstructed word למל]א is indeed true, this will give further credence to the sense of a measured portion, which should be fulfilled.

The meaning of "shared portion" can be further substantiated with an etymology. Somewhat surprisingly, the answer in this case should be sought in Akkadian, where one finds the unit of length *ūṭu* (occasionally also *rūṭu*) denoting "span, half-cubit".[33] This unit is attested through all layers of the Akkadian language, from Old Akkadian in the third millennium, through Old Assyrian and until Neo Babylonian in the late first millennium BCE. For our purposes it is also important to note that the word was accepted also in west-semitic languages, attested in Ugaritic.[34] Accordingly, I suggest the following semantic process for the term אוט: from a concrete unit of length > to the abstract meaning "measure" > and then by way of metonymy to the wider metaphysical sense of "assigned share". Metaphorical use of weights and measures is a conspicuous feature of MLM, as for example in 4Q415 11, when the groom is ordered to weigh his bride, assessing her spiritual or horoscopic qualities.

Such a shift from the concrete to the abstract is universally attested, but may be exemplified by one word attested in Qumran in a close semantic field. The Aramaic word מלוש is attested in Syriac and Mandaic in the sense of "zodiacal sign" or "horoscope". As noted in the dictionaries, it originates with the Akkadian ^{MUL}*lumāšu*, "star, constellation". Surprisingly it also turns up in Qumran Hebrew (4Q439 1 i 2) carrying the meaning "fate", in proximity to the better-known term נחלה.[35]

That Akkadian words appear in the Hebrew of Qumran should come as no surprise. Thus the late Victor Hurowitz has demonstrated how the word רוקמה in D relates to the Akkadian *rugummû*, "legal claim".[36] Another famous example is the calque אוחזי אבות, "intercessors" (1QS 2:9), cognate

[33] Jeremy BLACK et al, *A Concise Dictionary of Akkadian* (SANTAG, 5) Wiesbaden, Harassowitz, 2000, 431; further CAD U-W, page 358. The latter dictionary mentions only the meaning "half-cubit".

[34] Gregorio del Olmo Lete and Joaquín Sanmartín, *A Dictionary of the Ugaritic Language in the Alphabetic Tradition* (HdO I, 67) Leiden, Brill, 2003, 120. For measurement terms crossing borders in the ancient Near East see Wilfred G.E. Watson, "Measure for Measure", *N.A.B.U.* 2010/10.

[35] See Menahem KISTER, "Three Unknown Hebrew Words in Newly-Published Texts from Qumran", *Lešonénu* 63 (2000-2001) 35-40 (Hebrew).

[36] Victor A. HUROWITZ, "Rwqmah in Damascus Document 4QD^{e} (4Q270) 7", *DSD* 9 (2002) 34-37.

to the Akkadian *āḫiz abbūti* or *ṣābit abbūti*. One cannot outright claim that these terms were borrowed directly from Akkadian into Hebrew, as they may have found wider circulation in other Semitic languages too. Note that the latter two examples are also attested in Aramaic. While the length-measure *ūṭu* is not attested outside Akkadian in the first millennium BCE, its wider circulation cannot be overruled, keeping in mind that such administrative terms as weights and measures are prone to transfer from one language to another by means of commercial relations.

The reason for pointing out *ūṭu* as a possible etymology, despite the geographical and stemmatic distance, is the emphasis laid in MLM on אוט as a measurable unit, and the general emphasis placed on measures in this composition. Earlier derivations of the word, learned as they are, do not give full justification for this meaning. In this case etymology may share forces with the lucid meaning required by the context, yielding an improved sense for the enigmatic term at hand.

Focusing on the metaphysics of economy in MLM, one may use the same method to elucidate more accurate meanings and derivations for additional terms beyond the two terms discussed here.

THE "PESHER ON THE PERIODS" (4Q180): NEW READINGS AND PERSPECTIVES

Devorah Dimant

4Q180 was one of the earliest Qumran manuscripts to be published and therefore it earned a long history of scholarly discussion. Included in the fifth DJD volume, it was first edited by John Allegro with minimal comments.[1] This editor labeled the work "Ages of Creation," a title still used sporadically today. However, this name should be replaced by the title offered by the text itself, "Pesher on the Periods" (4Q180 1 1), now adopted by most of its commentators. From the outset, it was noticed that 4Q180 1 5–9 resemble 4Q181 2 1–4. In the few comments John Strugnell devoted to 4Q180 as part of his long review on DJD V, he suggested that 4Q180 comments on 4Q181.[2] However, it was the late Józef Milik, the scholar who devoted most attention to this manuscript, who went as far as to argue that 4Q180 and 4Q181 are copies of the same work. Consequently, he produced a single composite text from the two manuscripts.[3] His thesis received wide acclaim and is still current today.[4] Unfortunately, the detailed criticism I have launched of Milik's thesis has received less attention than it merits.[5] Nonetheless, recent infrared photographs and better copies of the older PAM photographs produced by the Israel Antiquities Authority (IAA), enable today an amelioration of the readings of 4Q180, especially those of frags. 2–4, 8. This improves the understanding of the composition to such an extent that its content and relation to 4Q181

[1] John M. Allegro, *Qumran Cave 4.I (4Q158–4Q186)*, DJD V (Oxford: Clarendon, 1969), 77–79 (pl. XXVII).

[2] Cf. John Strugnell, "Notes en marge du volume V des "Discoveries in the Judaean Desert of Jordan," *RevQ* 7 (1970): 252–54 (252).

[3] Józef T. Milik, "Milkî-ṣedeq et Milkî-reša' dans les anciens écrits juifs et chrétiens," *JJS* 23 (1972): 112–24; idem, *The Books of Enoch* (Oxford: Clarendon, 1976), 248–52.

[4] Including the most recent edition and comments by Chanan Ariel, Alexey (Eliyahu) Yuditsky, and Elisha Qimron, "The Pesher on the Periods A–B (4Q180–4Q181): Editing, Language, and Interpretation," *Meghillot* 11–12 (2014–2015): 3–39 (Heb.). Their edition follows closely that of Elisha Qimron, *The Dead Sea Scrolls: The Hebrew Writings* (Jerusalem: Yad Ben-Zvi Press, 2013), 2:296–97 (Heb.).

[5] Cf. Devorah Dimant, "The 'Pesher on the Periods' (4Q180) and 4Q181," *IOS* 9 (1979): 77–102; eadem, "The *Pesher on the Periods* (4Q180) and 4Q181," in *History, Ideology and Bible Interpretation in the Dead Sea Scrolls*, FAT 90 (Tübingen: Mohr Siebeck, 2014), 385–404; eadem, "On Righteous and Sinners: 4Q181 Reconsidered," ibid., 403–21.

merit a fresh evaluation.[6] For this purpose, the manuscript is reedited below with the help of the new photographs, accompanied by a fresh commentary.[7]

Eight decipherable fragments have been associated with this work. However, only frags. 1, 2–4, and 8 may be attributed with certainty to the composition. The provenance of frags. 5–6, 7, and 9 is uncertain and their content does not accord with that of the main pieces. Therefore they are not discussed here. The remaining fragments, 1, 2–4, 8, display similar physical characteristics and the same content and therefore they belong together. The script of 4Q180 is written in a late Herodian formal hand.[8] Frag. 1 is the best-preserved piece. The surviving sections of the badly preserved frags. 2–4 produce the same size and number of lines. If the other columns were of the same size, the present document was written in a small format.[9] Some scholars have therefore labelled it a pocket scroll.[10] From the content point of view, the lost columns, probably containing the story of the flood, would have been placed between frag. 1 and frags. 2–4. So the small size of the copied columns may also be due to the limited scope of its subject matter. The scribe left an uninscribed line (4Q180 1 6) or a blank space of a word or two (4Q180 2–4 ii 3; [2–4 i 6?]) to mark distinct literary units, a scribal practice well known from other Qumran manuscripts.[11] Another scribal convention used in the Qumran nonsectarian texts that appears also in this work is the writing of the divine names in paleo-Hebrew characters (4Q180 1 1; 2–4 1–2, 8).[12]

Frags. 1, 2–4, and 8 present a coherent structure and style. The exposition of the events surrounding the flood and the punishment of Sodom

[6] The paper, dealing as it does with 4Q180, is dedicated to Émile Puech, a colleague of long standing, who himself wrote about this manuscript in his, *La croyance des Esséniens de la vie future: immortalité, résurrection, vie éternelle?: Histoire d'une croyance dans le Judaïsme ancien*, *EBib* 22 (Paris: Gabalda, 1993), 2:526–31.

[7] The 4Q180 fragments are found on Museum Inventory Plate no. 468 at the Israel Museum in Jerusalem. The photographs used for establishing the present edition are the following: PAM 41.506, 41.819, 42.624, 43.425, 44.193, 59.433, 59.444; IAA B-295794 (infrared), B-295225 (full-spectrum color image). The complete editions and commentaries of 4Q180 and 4Q181 are scheduled to appear in the forthcoming reedition of DJD V, edited by Moshe BERNSTEIN and George BROOKE.

[8] Cf. STRUGNELL, "Notes en marge," 252.

[9] TOV, *Scribal Practices*, 85, 143–49 (see n. 13 below) provides lists of Qumran documents of a similar size.

[10] Cf. BROOKE, "Some Scribal Features," 131 (see n. 16 below). Cf. n. 13 below. ARIEL – YUDITSKY – QIMRON, "Pesher on the Periods," 6. Brooke, ibid. 132, n. 23, 140 (cf. n. 16 below) suggests that scrolls of this size were perhaps produced for the use of itinerant instructors of the community.

[11] See TOV, *Scribal Practices*, 218.

[12] See TOV, *Scribal Practices*, 242. BROOKE, "Some Scribal Features," 132 notes that this practice differs from the usage of other thematic commentaries from Qumran.

and Gomorrah are encapsulated in the introduction (frag. 1 1–5) and conclusion (frags. 2–4, 8 9–10), which are ideological in nature, spelling out the idea of the pre-established historical periods. Appearing to constitute a logical and self-contained sequence, those fragments may contain the entire original work. If so, the composition may have been written on a single sheet of four columns.[13] In terminology, style, and themes, the composition is linked to other works belonging to the particular literature of the Yahad community.

The title Pesher on the Periods defines the work as an interpretation of a general topic rather than that of a particular biblical text or texts, as known from other types of pesharim. However, the exposition of the details of the topic is accomplished through the exegesis of specific biblical passages, but always in relation to the overall theme of periods; in this way, the particular biblical interpretations serve the main theme as is illustrated in frags. 2–4 9–10. Thus, the pesher is still a work devoted to a theme rather than to particular biblical passages. Preserved in a single copy, it is difficult to determine whether the Pesher on the Periods is an autograph or a copy of an earlier original. However, its use of traditions known from other sources, sectarian as well as nonsectarian, suggests that it draws on earlier compilations or at least has knowledge of such sources.[14] The similarity between 4Q180 1 5–9 and 4Q181 2 1–4, referring to the birth of giants, may represent one of these sources.[15]

Frag. 1

This is the best-preserved fragment. The surface is wrinkled due to the shrinking of the skin and at places the top layer of the skin has peeled

[13] This is the normal number of columns per sheet in the Qumran manuscripts. Cf. Emanuel Tov, *Scribal Practices and Approaches Reflected in the Texts Found in the Judean Desert*, STDJ 54 (Leiden: Brill, 2004), 80–81.

[14] As suggested by Brooke, "Some Scribal Features," 132–33.

[15] The edition of frags. 2–4 owes much to the improved readings offered by reeditions by Elisha Qimron, The *Dead Sea Scrolls*, and that by Ariel – Yuditsky – Qimron, "The Pesher on the Periods." Both editions have been checked anew against the new advanced IAA photographs and the better copies of the older PAM photographs. I thank Pnina Shor, the outgoing Curator and Head of the Dead Sea Scrolls Projects at the Israel Antiquities Authority, and Orit Rosengarten, Assistant to the Director of the Dead Sea Scrolls Projects, for placing at my disposal a set of the new high-quality IAA photographs, taken with spectral imaging technology, and the improved versions of the older PAM photographs. My thanks are also owed to the team of the Dead Sea Scrolls Conservation Laboratory at the Israel Museum for hosting me on November 12, 2018, which enabled me to check the museum inventory plates with the fragments. Special thanks are due to Shai Halevi of the IAA for providing me with multispectral photography imaging of frag. 1 of 4Q180.

away. The piece comes from the right section of a column and holds the top and bottom margins, both of which measure 2 cm.[16] It thus produces the entire height of the column, containing ten lines of script, with its margins, as well as its entire width. The writing block is 10.5 cm in height.[17] In lines 1–2, the upper section of the right margin is also preserved. This suggests that all the lines of the column have survived. The context of lines 1–2 and 7 indicates that only two or three words are missing at the end of the lines, so it is a very short and narrow column. In all, it contains only ten lines, nine inscribed and one blank in the middle of the column (4Q180 1 6).

1 פשר על הקצים אשר עשה אל קץׄ להתׄם֯[כל הויה]
2 ו֯נׄהיה בטרם בראם הכין פעולותׄ[יהם לפרוש קציהם]
3 [ק֯ץ לקצו והוא חרות על לחות[השמים לכל בני איש]
[]לׄ
4 [כ] קצי ממשלותם זה סרך פ[עולותיהם מאדם לאברהם]
5 [ע]דׄ הוליד ישחק את עשרו֯תׄ ה[דורות]
6 *vac*
7 פ֯שׄר על עזאׄל והמלאכים אש[ר באו אל בנות האדם]
8 [וי]לׄדו להם גברים ועל עזאל[ ]
9 [ ]עולה ולהנחיל רשעה כל ◦[ ]
10 [בהמ]ה֯ משפטים ומשפט סודׄ א֯[ ]

Notes on Readings

L. 1 אל – Written in paleo-Hebrew script, as also in frags. 2–4 ii 1, 2.

L. 4 פ[עולותיהם – The *pe* is clear in PAM 41.506, B-295794, and B-295225, and so should be read instead of a *bet*, as read by Strugnell, Milik 1972, and Dimant 1979 and 2014. Qimron has בׄ[ני] שׁ֯[ם], noting that the *shin* is a new reading, but there is no evidence for this letter in the photographs or on the actual fragment. Ariel – Yuditsky – Qimron, who essentially follow Qimron's edition (cf. *Meghillot* 11–12, 3 n. 4), read here only פׄ[and discard the reading of a *shin* in their note (*Meghillot* 11–12, 9).

L. 5 עשרו֯תׄ – This is a new reading. The last letter has been damaged due to the partial peeling of the skin[18] and some displaced fibers stuck to the bottom of the letter. Allegro read עשריׄם with a *yod* and final *mem*,

[16] Top and bottom margins of the same size are noted in other Qumran scrolls. See Tov, *Scribal Practices*, 101. See also George J. Brooke, "Some Scribal Features of the Thematic Commentaries from Qumran," in *Writing the Bible: Scribes, Scribalism and Script*, ed. P. R. Davies and T. Römer (London: Routledge, 2014), 124–43 (132).

[17] Noted by Brooke. "Some Scribal Features," 131.

[18] Observed also by Puech, *La Croyance*, 2:527.

followed by others,[19] while Milik 1972, Dimant 1979, and Qimron read עשרה. A close examination of the old and recent photographs (PAM 41.506, 41.819, B-295794, and B-295225), as well as the fragment, reveals that the penultimate letter is physically disconnected from the final one and so should be read as *yod* (as did Ariel – Yuditsky – Qimron) or a *vav*, but certainly not as *he*. Reading a *vav* is preferable as it fits with the reading of the following *tav*. Of the last letter, two parallel vertical strokes are seen clearly in the early photographs. Of the right one, even some of the slightly wavy top and a piece of the connected horizontal roof are seen in PAM 41.819. A short butt, protruding leftwards from the bottom edge of the left leg, is also observable; it is particularly clear in PAM 41.506. The remains of this butt are still noticeable in B-295794 and in several multispectral photographic images.[20] These traces match a *tav* rather than a final *mem*.

L. 10]אׄ – Two arms of an *aleph* have survived and are seen clearly in PAM 41.819 and B-295794. In PAM 41.506, even some of the slanted stroke that continues the left arm may be seen. It is perhaps written in paleo-Hebrew script, as is this word in line 1.

Translation

1. Pesher concerning the periods made by God,[21] (each) period in order to terminate[all that exist]
2. and come into being. Before he created them he established [their] activi[ties according to the exact meaning of their periods]
3. one period after another, and it is engraved on the [heavenly] tablets[for all the sons of man]
4. [al]l the periods of their dominions. This is the order of [their] ac[tivities from Adam to Abraham]
5. [un]til the birth of Isaac, the decades [of generations]
6. *vacat*
7. Pesher concerning 'Azaz'el and the angels wh[o came to the daughters of men]
8. [and] they [bo]re to them giants, and concerning 'Azaz'el[ ]
9. [ ]iniquity and to cause to inherit wickedness, all [ ]
10. [upon the]m judgments and the judgment of a council[ ]

[19] Cf. André Caquot, "Hébreu et Araméen," *Annuaire du Collège de France* 73 (1973): 377–95 (390 n. 5), and Dimant 2014. To justify the reading of a final *mem*, Puech (*La Croyance*, 2:527, n. 24) claims that its base horizontal stroke disappeared due to the peeling and shrinking of the skin. However, the protruding left bottom extremity does not accord with *mem* but with *tav*, and therefore a horizontal base never existed.

[20] Compare, for instance, photograph PAM 42.624, 43.425 and B-295794 (infrared).

[21] Understanding the expression אשר עשה אל to be part of the title.

Comments

Ll. 1–4 – The four opening lines introduce the title and define the subject matter of either the entire work or the section in question.

Ll. 1–2 פשר על הקצים אשר עשה אל קץ̇ להתם̇̊]   כל הויה] ונ̇היה – This is the title of the entire work or of a particular section within a larger composition. Its structure is parallel to lines 7–8, which introduce the pesher on the first specific period. This parallelism argues against disconnecting the expression פשר על הקצים from the rest of the sentence, as argued by Ariel – Yuditsky – Qimron.

L. 1 פשר על הקצים – The term pesher, "interpretation," which opens the line, is well documented in continuous and thematic pesharim that expound various biblical texts. However, the combination "pesher concerning" (פשר על) is rare.[22] The usual combination, occurring in other pesharim is פשרו על (e.g., 1QpHab 3:4; 7:4; 4Q164 1:7; 4Q169 3–5 ii 4). However, the case here is special in that the term "pesher" is applies to a topic, the periods, rather than to specific biblical texts. The use of the term in relation to a theme is repeated in line 7, where it refers to Azazel and the angels. The comments on particular verses in the body of the pesher belong to the elaboration of the general topics. Since 4Q180 avoids the historical symbolic-allusive commentary typical of the sectarian pesharim, its repeated use of the term "pesher" seems to indicate a general interpretation, at times even a literal one.[23]

L. 1 הקצים – This is a definite plural of the noun קץ. In the biblical parlance, the singular קץ designates "end" (*HALOT*, 1118–19), but in Daniel it also marks a span of time (e.g., 8:19; 11:27). The temporal sense is also recorded in Qumran documents (e.g., 4Q252 1 12) in addition to its use in its spatial meaning (e.g., 1QH^{a} 14:34; 4Q169 4 ii 6). However, the more frequent use is that of the plural in the sense of temporal periods (e.g., 1QS 1:14, 4:13; 1QM 1:8; 1QH^{a} 9:26; cf. *DCH* 7:276). The plural refers, in particular, to the notion of a string of periods that constitute the temporal sequence, which was divinely established before creation (cf. e.g., 1QS 10:1; 1QpHab 7:13; 1QH^{a} 9:17–18, 26), a notion adopted also by the so-called Pesher on the Apocalypse of Weeks (4Q247) and ancient Jewish apocalypses (e.g., Dan 9:24–27; the Animal Apocalypse

[22] It possibly occurs also in 4Q464 3 ii 7 (פשר ע̇]ל) but here the expression lacks context.

[23] Compare 4Q252 4:5, where the term "pesher" introduces a literal explanation of Gen 49:5. The same literal meaning may be intended also in the fragmentary reference in 1Q30 1 6 ופשריהם, "their interpretations." This sense may also be implied in the imperative of the verb ופש]ור, used to command Moses to interpret the Torah for the leaders of the people (1Q30 1 6).

[1 Enoch 85–90]; the Apocalypse of Weeks [1 En. 91:11–17, 93:1–10]). Therefore, the fact that the plural "periods" stands here in the definite state, defined by the following subordinate clause, indicates it was a well-established term. These periods are the subject of the first five lines, for the term also appears in singular and plural forms in lines 3–4. They belong to the cluster of notions regarding the divine predetermined creation of the temporal sequence.[24]

L. 1 אשר עשה אל – This clause specifies that the periods are made by God, a notion spelled out in the sectarian texts (e.g., 1QS 10:1, 5; 1QM 10:15–16; 1QH[a] 9:23–26; CD 2:7–10). The word אשר is understood here as introducing a subordinate clause עשה אל, defining the term "periods." The structure of lines 1–2a parallels that of lines 7–8a and thus validates the integrity of the introductory phrase, ending in ונהיה, and confirms the understanding of the line as a single title.

L. 1]להתֿםֿ – A *hiphil* infinitive of the verb תמם in the sense "to complete, to accomplish," stressing the active aspect of the action.

L. 1 [כל הויה] – The length of the line, indicated by line 7, requires some small additional word at the beginning of the lacuna.

Ll. 1–2 ונֿהיה [כל הויה] – The restoration was made originally by Strugnell, creating the hendiadys הויה ונהיה. The phrase designates the entire range of created entities (compare, e.g., 1QS 11:11; CD 2:10; 1QH[a] 20:12).

L. 2 בטרם בראם הכין – This clause affirms that God created the periods according to a predetermined plan, conceived before creation, a formulation of the well-known sectarian teaching of predestination. See the similar formulations in 1QH[a] 5:24–25, 9:9, 20:12–14; 1QS 3:15. The locution בטרם בראם is reintroduced in frags. 2–4 10 in a repeated expression of the same sectarian outlook on predetermination. Compare 3:15; 1QH[a] 5:25, 7:18, 9:9; 4Q215a 1 ii 9. The temporal preposition טרם, here with the prepositional *bet*, means "before." It is used here and in frags. 2–4, 8 ii 10 to define the moment before creation, and appears frequently in the sectarian texts. Cf., e.g., CD 2:7; 1QH[a] 5:25, 7:27. The plural suffix of בראם refers to the previous pair, הויה ונהיה, denoting the totality of the created entities. הכין is a *hiphil* 3rd sg. masc. pf. form of the verb כון, "to prepare, establish" (*DCH*, 4:374), referring to God. The verb is often used in the sectarian texts to designate the premeditated

[24] For this notion, see Devorah Dimant, "Exegesis and Time in the Pesharim from Qumran," in *History, Ideology and Bible Interpretation*, 315–32; eadem, "Election and Laws of History in the Apocalyptic Literature," in *From Enoch to Tobit: Collected Studies in Ancient Jewish Literature*, FAT 114 (Göttingen: Mohr Siebeck, 2017), 19–30.

preparations for the created beings. Cf., e.g., CD 2:7; 1QS 3:15; 1QH[a] 5:27, 7:28, 9:9.

L. 2 פעולוֹתֹ]יהם – The surviving letters suggest a plural of the noun פעולה. It is translated here as "work, deed" (*DCH*, 6:730), with the general meaning of "activities." The restoration of a plural masculine possessive suffix is proposed here to match the previous suffix of בראם and the plural of הויה ונהיה, both of which seem to refer to the periods in line 1. Two aspects of the creative act are specified here: the initial creation of entities and the manner in which they function as created beings. Both aspects are divinely determined before the creative act itself. This double distinction is spelled out in other sectarian works as part of the overall notion of predetermined creation (e.g., 1QS 3:16, 4:25; 1QH[a] 7:35; 4Q215a 1 ii 9). Since the terminology here concerns the general characteristics of the creative process, Milik's 1972 and 1976 restoration applying the terms to angels is inappropriate.

L. 2 [לפרוש קציהם] – The restoration reproduces the locution that appears in CD 2:9, 16:2 in a similar context (note especially CD 2:9–10). It thus provides an antecedent to the beginning of the following line 3 קץ לקצו.

L. 3 קׄץ לקצו – The expression depicts the sequence of the periods. Compare Ps 19:3 יום ליום ... לילה ללילה.

L. 3 והוא חרות על לחוֹת] השמים – הוא is a pronoun that may be used in the neuter, possibly alluding to the sequence of the periods indicated by the preceding expression קץ לקצו. That the entire sequence of the periods is inscribed on heavenly tablets is a notion mentioned in 4Q177 1–4 12 (הנה הכול כתוב בלוחות, "behold everything is written on the tablets").[25] The phrase והוא חרות על לחוֹת is close to the Torah description of the tablets written by God and given to Moses on Mount Sinai: הוא חרות על הלחת (Exod 32:16). However, the similarity hardly suggests the identity of the Mosaic tablets and the heavenly tablets,[26] but appears to be stylistic rather than an actual citation.

L. 3 לחות] השמים –The term is known from ancient as well as contemporary sources. See 1 En. 81:1–2, 93:2, 102:2, 106:19; Jub. 16:3, 19:9, 30:19–20; T. Levi 5:4.[27]

[25] Note that לחות is written in a defective way whereas in 4Q177 the word appears in a full orthography (לוחות). Cf. Elisha QIMRON, *A Grammar of the Hebrew of the Dead Sea Scrolls* (Jerusalem: Yad Ben-Zvi, 2018), 321–22 (n. 211).

[26] As argued by Armin LANGE, "Wisdom and Predestination," *DSD* 2 (1995): 340–54 (353).

[27] Cf. Shalom M. PAUL, "Heavenly Tablets and the Book of Life," *JANESCU* 5 (1973): 345–53; Michael SEGAL, *The Book of Jubilees*, JSJSup 117 (Leiden: Brill, 2007), 313–16.

L. 3 [לכל בני איש] –The restoration of Dimant 1979 and 2014 is followed here, taking up the terminology of 1QS 3:13. Qimron has [לבני האדם]. Most of the editors restored terms that refer to the entirety of humanity, assuming that the following ממשלותם concerns mankind in general.

L. 4 [כ]ל̇[] קצי ממשלותם – The restoration proposed above follows Qimron's suggestion that the superlinear *lamed* is a correction of a letter omitted by mistake.

L. 4 קצי ממשלותם – The construct pair "the periods of their dominions" connects the periods to the term ממשלות, "dominions," the plural of ממשלה, "dominion, rule, authority" (cf. *DCH*, 5:334–35). The sectarian texts use it to specify the domain of authority or rule of God (e.g., 1QH[a] 5:28), of angels (e.g., 1QS 1:18; 1QM 13:10; 4Q405 23 i 8), of humans (e.g., 1QM 1:6, 17:7–8), and of natural phenomena such as light, darkness, and the luminaries (e.g., 1QS 10:1; 1QH[a] 20:8–9; 4Q408 3 8). So its semantic field is broader than "rule" in the narrow sense. The following line clarifies that mankind is the intended subject, outlined here by the main active figures. The idea that human history was pre-established according to each period is spelled out in more detail in CD 2:9–12 and 16:2–4 (compare 1QS 3:12–18).

L. 4 זה סרך פ[עולותיהם מאדם לאברהם] – The formula זה סרך has the character of a title that introduces a list of details. Such a formula is common in the sectarian rules and frequently opens series of regulations concerning various subjects (e.g., CD 10:4, 12:22–23; 1QS 5:1, 6:8; 1QSa 1:1, 6). The subject of the list has not been preserved here but evidently it fleshes out the details of the broad outline in the preceding introduction. However, older as well as recent photographs show that the last preserved letter is a *pe* (see NOTES ON READINGS) and therefore the restoration פ[עולותיהם is proposed. Ariel – Yuditsky – Qimron restore זה סרך פ̇[רוש קציהם מאדם לאברהם], "this is the ex[planation of their periods from Adam to Abraham]." However, the expression פרוש קציהם is never linked with the term סרך.

L. 4 [מאדם לאברהם] – The restoration of the name Abraham is suggested by the genealogies of Genesis 5, 11. The biblical tradition is epitomized in the twenty generations listed from Adam to Abraham in m. 'Abot 5:2.[28] It also provides an antecedent to the following line 5.

[28] The supposed mention of Abraham in 4Q181 2 1 is, in fact, based on a conjectured restoration, for only a final *mem* is actually seen on the skin. Thus, it cannot provide a valid parallel to 4Q180 1 4. Cf. the discussion below on the relation between 4Q180 and 4Q181.

The combination "from Adam to Abraham" indicates that the pesher concerns the temporal span of early humanity until Abraham. According to the Animal Apocalypse (1 En. 89:12), Abraham is the last of the primordial generations and ushers in the era of the biblical patriarchs.[29]

L. 4 מאדם – The reading עשרוׄת requires the beginning of the temporal span from Adam.

L. 5 [ע]ד הוליד ישחק את עשרוׄת הׄ[דורות – Previous editors read הוליד as a *hiphil* sg. masc. pf. (e.g., Milik 1972 and 1976, Dimant 1979 and 2014) but it involves lexical difficulties as noted by Ariel – Yuditsky – Qimron. Therefore, following their note, it is parsed here as the *niphal* infinitive (cf. Gen 21:5), and translated thus above. Adopting this understanding implies viewing the remaining words,]את עשרוׄת הׄ[, as the start of a new sentence. However, if the reading עשרוׄת is adopted, it fits with the genealogies laid down in Genesis. Ten generations are counted from Adam to Noah (Genesis 5) while another ten are enumerated from Shem to Abraham (Genesis 11). Thus, the biblical tradition specifies twenty generations from Adam to the birth of Isaac, undoubtedly the source of the present pesher. Based on the biblical account, it became the traditional calculation of generations, as is suggested by m. 'Abot 5:2. In the present pesher, the twenty generations mark the temporal span expounded in the entire work. In fact, other fragments of the manuscript deal with episodes that fall within this span of time, Noah's speech (frags. 2–4 i 10–ii 3a), the angels who visited Abram (frags. 2–4 ii 3b–4), and the iniquity of Sodom and Gomorrah (frags. 2–4 ii 5–8).

L. 6 *vacat* – An entire line has been left blank, marking the end of the introduction and transition to another section.

Ll. 7–8 פׄשׄר על ... ועל – The introductory formula presenting a pesher interpretation reproduces the format of the first section in line 1. Still, it is obviously a subunit of the pesher as a whole, since it deals with a specific episode from the temporal sequence defined by the introductory lines 4–5. This particular pesher concerns two topics, each introduced by the preposition על. The first part concerns Azazel and the angels, while the second part is related solely to Azazel. It seems that the part pairing Azazel with the angels speaks of the sinful angels taking Azazel as their leader, on the basis of Gen 6:1–2, 4, whereas the second part involves an additional evil peculiar to Azazel, perhaps the nefarious practices he taught humans, as related in 1 En. 8:1.

[29] Cf. my analysis of the relevant passage in Devorah DIMANT, "Ideology and History in the *Animal Apocalypse* (1 Enoch 85–90)," in *From Enoch to Tobit*, 91–118 (96–97).

Ll. 7–8 פשׂר על ... להם גברים – The sentence introduces the first subject of the following interpretation. Structurally it runs parallel to the general introduction in lines 1–2a.

L. 7 פשׂר על – Standing as it does after the blank line, and opening with a formal introduction, פשר על, it expounds the first period. As at the beginning, the term here introduces a double topic rather than a specific biblical citation, although it is followed by a reference to the well-known story of Gen 6:1–2, 4. An example of a concise reference to a biblical episode is also observed in col. ii 3–4.

L. 7 עזזאל והמלאכים אש]ר באו אל בנות האדם] – This is the first topic addressed, restored to fit with the surviving text in the following line 8, [וי]לדו להם גברים. The explanation consists of a concise version of Gen 6:1–2, 4 regarding the sons of God who went to the daughters of men and fathered heroes. However, the nonbiblical Azazel is inserted into the scriptural reference, suggesting the recourse to external traditions recorded for instance, in the Book of Watchers (1 Enoch 6–8) and Jubilees (5:1–10). In these sources, the sons of God are angels. Various different names are given for their leader. According to one tradition (embedded in 1 En. 6:3), he is Shemihaza, while an angel named Azael leads antediluvian humans astray by revealing to them unlawful knowledge (1 En. 8:1–2). But in the tradition of the Book of Parables (=1 Enoch 37-71), it is Azazel who heads the sinful angels (1 Enoch 54–55), as he does here.[30] Perhaps this version of the tradition lies at the background of the second reference to Azazel here. Alternatively, 4Q180 may reflect the combination of the two originally distinct traditions into a single story, in which the single evil leader of the angels is Azazel.

L. 7 על עזזאל והמלאכים – This is the first topic specified by the title, introduced by the term על. The orthography of the name עזזאל standing here occurs also in 11QT^{a} 26:13. The form is also reflected in Tg. Ps.-J. to Lev 16:10; Sipra, *Aharei Mot* II, 8; b. Yoma 67b. Leviticus 16 in MT has עזאזל (an orthography reflected in the LXX and Symmachus to Lev 16:10), adopted also by the Qumran Aramaic Book of Giants (4Q203 7 6). In the Qumran Aramaic copies of the Enochic Book of Watchers, the corresponding figure is named עסאל (4Q201 1 iii 9) or עשאל (4Q202 1 ii 26; 4Q203 1 ii 26).

[30] The various traditions embedded in 1 Enoch 6–11 have been analyzed by Devorah DIMANT, "The 'Fallen Angels' in the Dead Sea Scrolls and in the Apocryphal and Pseudepigraphic Books Related to Them," (PhD diss., Hebrew University of Jerusalem, 1974), 23–72 (Heb.). See also Philip S. ALEXANDER, "The Targumim and Early Exegesis of the 'Sons of God' in Genesis 6," *JJS* 23 (1972): 60–71; Annette Yoshiko Reed, *Fallen Angels and the History of Judaism and Christianity: The Reception of Enochic Literature* (Cambridge: Cambridge University Press, 1973).

L. 8 [וי]לׄדׄו להם גברים – Taking up Gen 6:4 in a slightly abbreviated form.[31] A similar quotation method is observed in frags. 2–4 i 3–4.

L. 8 [וי]לׄדׄו – The orthography suggests a vocalization וְיָלְדוּ, as that in MT 6:4, rather than וילִדו, a variant attested by the LXX and the Samaritan Pentateuch (ויולידו).

L. 8 גברים – Note the defective orthography. Compare Gen 10:8-9 where the singular form of the same noun is also written defectively (גבר). Perhaps this particular orthography plays on the root גבר in allusion to the giants' violent deeds, a well-known episode cited in other Qumran texts (4Q370 i 6[32] and CD 2:9) as well as in non-Qumranic works (1 En. 10:9; Jub. 5:7–9; Sir 16:8 [LXX]).[33] 4Q370 stresses that the giants perished in the flood,[34] whereas 1 En. 10:9 alludes to their death by internal strife.

L. 8 ועל עזזאל] – This is the second topic of the pesher, introduced by a second על. While the first one refers to the collective sin of Azazel and the angels, this theme appears to deal with the particular evils committed by Azazel.

L. 9 עולה ולהנחיל רשעה[– The present broken line appears to be connected to the previous pesher and therefore it pertains to Azazel, his character, and his activities. If so, he is described as partaking in two of the attributes of the dark evil hosts, as described in other sectarian texts, עולה, "iniquity" (e.g., 1QS 4:9, 19; 1QH^{a} 6:37; 1Q27 1 i 5) and רשעה, "wickedness" (e.g., 1QS 5:11; 1QH^{a} 7:37; 1QM 1:6).

L. 9 להנחיל – The *hiphil* form of נחל stresses the causative aspect of the evil angelic activities and that it was they who induced the corruption of humanity.[35]

L. 10 [בהמ]ה̊ משפטים – Reading this broken line in the light of the predestination notion spelled out in line 2, it suggests that the sin as well as its punishment were predetermined before creation and the sequence of periods is being unfolded according to the preconceived divine plan.

[31] The episode is mentioned in similar words in 4Q181 2 2 but without reference to Azazel.

[32] The term ג[בור]ים is created by the two pieces composing frag. 1 of 4Q370. Previous editions restored the word in full orthography with a *vav*. However, an examination of the recent photographs B-295763 and B-295197 suggests that the space between the two pieces can accommodate only two letters, so this line should be restored ג[בר]ים. It thus may provide another example of defective orthography in the writing of this term.

[33] A similar play on the same root in connection to the גברים, namely the giants, is evident in 1 En. 10:9, according to which the angel Gabriel (גבריאל) is sent to instigate war among the giants and so to bring about their annihilation.

[34] Gabriel BARZILAI argues that in this detail 4Q370 implies a rejection of the tradition that the giants, or some of them, survived the flood (cf., e.g., Tg. Ps.-J. to Deut 3:11; b. Nid. 61a; Gen. Rab. 42:8). Cf. idem, "Incidental Biblical Exegesis in the Qumran Scrolls and Its Importance for the Study of the Second Temple Period," *DSD* 14 (2007): 1–24.

[35] Noted by CAQUOT, "Hébreu et Araméen," 390.

L. 10 [בהמ]ה̊ – "Upon them"; the restoration fits the lacuna of three letters. It restores the long form of the 3rd per. pl. preposition -ב, alluding to the group mentioned in lines 7–8.

L. 10 משפטים – For משפט in the sense of judgment, see e.g., CD 1:2; 1QS 2:15, 4:20. For the idea of the punishment of death by burning inflicted on the wicked, see 1QS 2:8; 1QpHab 10:5, 13; 1QH[a] 14:21–22; 4Q228 1 i 6. The judgments in question are perhaps the punishments awaiting Azazel and his followers. However, since the general context is that of the antediluvian events, it may also refer to the flood as punishment on humanity corrupted by the wicked angels and their offspring. Indeed, m. 'Abot 5:2 describes the first ten human generations as the rebellious antediluvians punished by the flood. Viewed from the divine foreknowledge perspective, both sinners and their punishment were predetermined. Compare 4Q181 1 1.

L. 10 ומשפט סוד א̊[– The judgment here continues the idea of the punishment to be meted out to the sinful group, so סוד appears here with the sense of "council, company," apparently alluding to the group that is the subject of the pericope. Ariel – Yuditsky – Qimron restor the line ומשפט סוד א̊[שמה. אשמה ("guilt") is indeed one of the attributes of the evil hosts (e.g., 1QM 13:4; 1QH[a] 14:22). Compare 4Q181 2 4.

Frags. 2–4, 8

The fragment consists of three smaller pieces, 2, 3, and 4, already combined by John Allegro.[36] Frag. 4, which supplies lines 9–10, was also joined at an early stage (see Notes on Readings below). However, doubts have been expressed regarding its attribution to frags. 2–3.[37] Yet frag. 4 shows scribal and ideological features similar to those of frags. 2–3 and therefore their combination should be retained.[38] Frag. 8, showing the edges of lines 6–8 in col. ii, was later identified and attached by John Strugnell. The composite fragment preserves remains of two columns, the intercolumn margin, the top margin and part of the bottom margin. The second

[36] See DJD V, 78–79 and pl. XXVII, reproducing PAM 43.425.

[37] Casting doubt on the connecting of frag. 4 to frags. 2–3, Ariel – Yuditsky – Qimron printed the last two lines in a different font. In this respect, they follow Raphael Weiss, "Fragments of a Midrash on Genesis from Qumran Cave 4," *Textus* 7 (1969): 132–34 (133) and Eibert Tigchelaar, "Sodom and Gomorrah in the Dead Sea Scrolls," in *Sodom's Sin: Genesis 18–19 and Its Interpretation*, ed. E. Noort and E. Tigchelaar, TBN 7 (Leiden: Brill, 2004), 47–62 (55). However, this position does not take into account the clear links between frag. 4 and frags. 2–3 elaborated in the Comments on col. ii 9–10.

[38] The fragment itself is now lost so no new photographs were made of it. Nor was it possible to verify Strugnell's statement (*RevQ* 7, 253) that the join of frag. 4 with frag. 2 is based on the stitch seen on both pieces.

column shows several features resembling those on frag. 1. It displays the same script as frag. 1, the same narrow column of ten lines, and the same scribal practice of leaving vacant spaces to mark new sections (line 2). In addition, it applies paleo-Hebrew script to the divine name אל (lines 2, 8), as does frag. 1 1. These features confirm that frags. 2–3 belong with frag. 1 and that the two came from the same scroll.[39] However, the script of the combined fragment has suffered badly from the shrinking of the skin, the fading of the ink, and at places the peeling away of the upper layer of the skin. Today, the fragment is so blackened that hardly any letter can be read with the naked eye.[40] The decipherment has been achieved with the help of recent infrared photographs and the better copies of the older PAM photographs.[41]

Col. i

1]]ר֯כׄן֯ כי֯[ ]ת֯∘∘ם֯
2]]ו֯ לקׄצ֯[ ]ל֯בׄן֯∘∘∘∘ בׄדרך
3]]∘ל גורלו ל֯ה֯תׄה֯ל֯ךׄ לפניו
4]]∘בׄה זכרון קצמ֯ה֯ הוא
5]]מ֯ה כמׄח֯שבותׄ ל֯בׄמ֯ה
6] *vacat* [
7]]ל֯בוׄא
8]]םׄ
9]]∘∘
10] ואש]ר֯ אמר נוחׄ

Notes on Readings

L. 2]ו֯ לקׄצ֯[– This is a new reading. The *vav* is clear in B-295795. The *qoph* has been fully preserved only in PAM 41.965, in which the piece attached subsequently to the top right section of the fragment is

[39] As noted by ARIEL – YUDITSKY – QIMRON, "Pesher on the Periods," 22 n. 92. In the NOTES ON READINGS on col. ii 9–10 below are listed the scribal, contextual, and terminological links that connect frag. 4 to frags. 2–3. But note the doubts expressed by other scholars cited in n. 37 above.

[40] Jimmy J. M. ROBERTS, "Wicked and Holy (4Q180–4Q181)," in *Damascus Document, War Scroll and Related Texts The Dead Sea Scrolls*, PTSDSSP (Tübingen: J.C.B. Mohr; Louisville: Westminster John Knox Press, 1995), 2:204–13 gave up editing col. i. QIMRON, *The Dead Sea Scrolls*, did not decipher lines 1, 7, and 9 of that column.

[41] J. STRUGNELL concluded his notes on this fragment by noting that "un déchiffrememt doit attendre la magie d'une photographie meilleure" (*RevQ* 7 [1970]: 254). Indeed, such "magic" has been achieved by the new advanced photographic techniques applied by the Israel Antiquities Authority for rephotographing all the Scrolls. 4Q180 2–3 has benefitted particularly from this enterprise. The present edition is based on the following photographs: PAM 41.719, 41.643, 41.972, 41.965, 42.052, 42.624, 43.425, 44.183, 44.193; IAA B-295795 (infrared), B-295222 (full-spectrum color image).

still detached. Also the next trace is the clearest on this piece, and may constitute the top section of the right arm of a medial *tsade*.

L. 2 לבׄן – The initial *lamed* is clear in B-295795 (a new reading). It is shorter than the following letters, reaching only the middle of the letter-line and curving slightly downwards. The remains are characteristic of a *lamed* and not of a *vav* as read by other editors. At the very top, a tip of the flag of the *lamed* may be seen in B-295795.

L. 6 *vacat* – An empty area of a few centimetres was left at the end of the line (not noted in previous editions).[42] That a blank was indeed left there is suggested also by the surviving remains in line 6 of the second column. The blank points to an intentional empty space, perhaps the edge of a blank line, as in frag. 1 6, or the blank space left in the second half of the line, as in line 3 of col. ii, marking new sections.

L. 7]לׄבוא – The three last letters, as well as the flag of the initial *lamed*, are clear in B-295795. However, the *he* read by Qimron (לׄהׄביא) is unsubstantiated. Ariel – Yuditsk y –Qimron read]ביא.

L. 10 נוׄח – With Allegro, Qimron, Ariel – Yuditsky – Qimron, rather than נוה (Dimant 2014).

Translation

1.] for[
2.] for the perio[d]to a son ….in the/a way
3.] his fate to walk before him
4.]a memory of their period is
5.] as the thoughts of their heart
6. *vacat* [
7.]to come
8.].
9.]..
10. and (as for) what] Noah said

Comments

Ll. 1–5 – It is uncertain to whom these lines refer. The key expression is להתהלך לפניו in line 3. The biblical account relates this locution to three persons: Enoch (Gen 5:22), Noah (Gen 6:9), and Abraham (Gen 17:1) and collectively to Abraham and Isaac (Gen 48:15). Given the biblical sequence of the entire work, Abraham is discarded for he could not be situated before Noah.[43] The locution may accommodate Enoch, but his

[42] Due to the blackened state of the fragment it has been impossible to verify the presence of a blank space on the actual piece.

[43] Dimant 1979 and 2014 suggested Abraham as the subject of the passage because she read נוה instead of נוח in col. i 10. Once the reading נוח is established, Abraham is excluded.

figure is difficult to reconcile with the mention of a son in line 2. Noah appears to be the most suitable candidate for both the specific expression להתהלך לפניו and the mention of a son, which would apply to Noah himself. The assumption that frags. 2–4 i 1–5 refer to the early career of Noah would fit with the mention in col. i 10 of his speech during his final stage of life (Gen 9:25–27).

L. 2 ל֯בן[– If Noah is the subject of the passage, the reference may concern his birth (Gen 5:28). Noah's miraculous birth is the subject of several Qumran texts and other ancient sources.[44]

L. 2 בׄדרך – The fragmentary state of the line does not permit a determination of the sense of the word דרך as it stands here. Above, it is translated as "manner, way."

L. 3 ל֯ה֯תׄהׄלׄך לפניו – See COMMENTS on lines 1–5 above.

Ll. 4–5 – If Noah's birth and early life are referred to in col. i 2–3 and if his pronouncement at the end of his life appears in col. i 10 and col. ii 1–2, col. i 4–5 may refer to the flood. This is also suggested by the possible references to Gen 6:5, 13 in these lines. This would place the present section in close relationship to frag. 1 7–10, which concerns the evil wrought by Azazel and the angels that finally brought the flood.

L. 4 זכרון קצמ֯ה֯ – A construct pair in which the first word זכרון is the *nomen regens* while קצמה is the *nomen rectum*. קצמה is the noun קץ that stands here with a 3rd per. masc. pl. possessive pronoun; קץ means "end, period." In frag. 1 1 the noun appears with the sense "period." However, perhaps the sense "end" is more appropriate here, obtaining the meaning "their end" in allusion to the annihilation of humanity in the flood. In this case, the pronoun may echo the biblical wording of Gen 6:13, also קץ כל בשר לפני, alluded to also in 4Q252 1:1 בא קצם לנוח. This understanding is supported by the parallel לבמה in the following line, also with a 3rd per. masc. pl. pronoun, "their heart," which appears to echo Gen 6:5.

L. 4 הוא – This sg. masc. personal pronoun may constitute part of a nominal clause, perhaps identifying the previous construct pair with some part of a biblical quotation that was included in the lost section. The same exegetical technique is used in col. ii 1, 4.

L. 5 מ֯ה כמׄח֯שבותׄ ל֯בׄמ֯ה[– The word לב is a 3rd per. masc. pl. pronoun. It is parallel to קצמה in the previous line. Perhaps this is a reference to mankind's evil inclination, defined by the biblical account מחשבות לבו

[44] Cf. 1Q19 3; 1QGenApoc 2–5; 1 En. 106–107. For the edition of 1Q19 1, see QIMRON, *The Dead Sea Scrolls*, 3:1. For a discussion, see Ariel FELDMAN, "1Q19–1Q19bis," in *Scripture and Interpretation: Qumran Texts that Rework the Bible*, ed. D. DIMANT, BZAW 449 (Berlin: De Gruyter, 2014), 22–26.

(Gen 6:5). In light of this connection, Ariel – Yuditsky – Qimron restore וישפט]מה כמ[ח]שבות לבמה following 4Q370 1 3. Qimron proposes לה[מה כמחשבות לבמה. The echoes of the biblical story of the flood suggest that it is the main subject of this damaged column, a theme that was perhaps fully treated in the preceding lost column.

L. 10 ואש]ר אמר נוח – Introducing a quotation of Noah's words in Gen 9:26–27, cited in the following col. ii 1–2. Compare the similar introductory formula in CD 8:14 ואשר אמר משה.

L. 10 ואש]ר אמר – A formula introducing a biblical quotation, appearing also in frags. 2–4 2 and similarly restored in frags. 2–4 9. The initial *vav* has been restored, connecting it to a previous interpretation. Compare the use of this formula for introducing a secondary or additional interpretation within a larger pesher (e.g., 1QpHab 7:3, 12:6; 4Q162 1:3). In the present case, the formula introduces a portion of Noah's blessing from Gen 9:27. The reference to this detail, which concludes the scriptural narrative of the flood, further supports the assumption that this major catastrophe was detailed in the preceding sections. The flood is then the judgment referred to at the end of frag. 1, probably presented from the perspective of God's predetermined plan.

Col. ii

1 באהלי שם ישכון הוא אשר שכן א[ל ב]ארץ[שם]
2 ואשר אמר נוח יפת אל [ל]יפת אשר ירש את
3 ארץ פורין[ ]ת *vacat* שלושת האנשים
4 הנרא[ים] אל [אבר]ם באלוני ממרה מלאכים המה[ ]
5 [זע]קת סדום ועמורה כי ר[בה ו]חטאתמה
6 כיכבדה מאדה ארדה נא ואראה כזעקת[מ]ה הבאה[]
7 [אלי אע]שה כלה ואם לא אדע[ה]הדבר[ ]
8 בעב[ור] אשר גבה[לבם על]אל[ ]על כו[ל]
9 דובר[שקר ואמר] ואראה כיא הכול[חקוק לקצי]
10 תע[ודותם כיא] בטרם בראם ידע מחשב[ותיהם]

Notes on Readings

L. 1 א[ל ב]ארץ[שם] – With Qimron.

L. 1 א[ל – Written in paleo-Hebrew script, as in the next line of col. ii and in frag. 1 1.

L. 2 אל – Written in paleo-Hebrew script.

L. 3 פורין[ ]ת – The reading is that of Elisha Qimron, in a revision of his published one (personal communication), and confirmed by photograph B-295795. The *tav* is clear on the left side of a tear in PAM 41.972 and B-295795 (a new reading).

L. 4 [הׄנׄרׄאׄ]ים] – Traces of the four first letter are visible in B-295795. However, the reading of the first letter is doubtful.

L. 4 ם[אבר] – With Qimron. Ariel – Yuditsky – Qimron read ם֯ר֯[אב] but no evidence of the *resh* is discernible.

L. 4 [ ]המׄהׄ – Here the left margin has not survived.

Ll. 6–8 – The last words in these lines (הבאׄהׄ, הׄדבר,]על כוׄן] appear on frag. 8, identified by Strugnell and attached by him to the left edge of frags. 2–4, on the basis of the word הבאה, which continues the citation from Gen 18:21 in line 6 (*RevQ* 7, 253–54). The fragment is seen as a separate piece on Mus. Inv. 468 and has been photographed thus in PAM 44.183, 44.193, IAA B-295223, and B-295796.

L. 6 כׄיׄכבדה – The two words are written without an intervening space.

L. 7 אע[שה – Strugnell and Milik 1972 propose ע[שה, influenced by MT Gen12:81 ועשה. However, from the point of view of space, the two surviving letters are better restored with two more in order to obtain a 1st sg. masc. future tense form of the verb עשה, referring to God.

L. 7 כלה – The reading is certain, as seen clearly in B-295795 as well as in the older PAM 41.719. So the reading offered by Armin Lange, כללה, is untenable.[45]

L. 8]אׄלׄ[ ]בעׄבׄ[ור] אשר גׄבׄהׄ – These traces are observed on a small fragment that has been incorporated into lines 9–10, as seen in PAM 44.183 (but not incorporated into Strugnell's presentation in *RevQ* 7). The photograph shows that the fragment has been attached to the final lines 9–10 of frags. 2–4, probably on the basis of the word ואראה, picked up from the previous citation of Gen 18:21.

L. 8 בעׄבׄ[ור] – With Qimron and Ariel – Yuditsky – Qimron. Of the second letter, an angular left arm has survived, which resembles that of an *ayin* rather than a *shin* (read by Strugnell, Milik 1972, Dimant 1979). Of the third letter, only a bottom horizontal stroke has survived, which precludes reading a *resh* (as did Milik 1972 and Dimant 1979, producing בשר).

L. 8 גׄבׄהׄ[– Read chiefly on the basis of PAM 41.972, 44.193, and B-295795 (with Qimron). Ariel – Yuditsky – Qimron read גׄבׄ]ה. However, traces of the top stroke of a third letter are seen in PAM 41.972. Other traces have been preserved at the top of frag. 4, but besides the *aleph* of אל they cannot be read. Even those seen at the corresponding section at the bottom of frags. 2–3 are barely legible.

[45] Cf. Armin LANGE, "Eine neue Lesart zu 4Q180: *kllh* vice *klh*. Die Vernichtung von Sodom and Gomorrah als Ganzopfer," *ZAH* 6 (1993): (232–34). The error is noted by E. TIGCHELAAR, "Sodom and Gomorrah," 54.

L. 8]אׄל֯[– The bottom section of the slanted stroke of the *aleph* and part of its right arm, as well as the bottom tip of the *lamed*, are seen on the top edge of frag. 4, written in paleo-Hebrew, as may be observed in PAM 41.506.

L. 8 כׄו֯]ל[– Strugnell read כול֯] but none of the available photographs (PAM 43.174, 43.425, B-295796, B-295223) show a final *lamed*.

Ll. 9–10 – These lines appear on frag. 4 and were attached to the bottom of frags. 2–3 early on, as attested by PAM 41.819 and Allegro's edition. However, the fragment is now lost and therefore it was not photographed anew, neither could it be examined in the museum.[46] However, the quotation in line 9 of the word ואראה from Gen 18:21, cited in col. ii line 6, the similarity of the script, the writing of אל in paleo-Hebrew, as well as the close affinity between frag. 4's terminology and ideas and those of frag. 1 1–4 secure the belonging of frag. 4 with frags. 2–3 (contra Ariel – Yuditsky – Qimron[47]). It is therefore deciphered according to PAM 41.506, 41.819, 41.972, 42.624, 43.425, and 44.183. See COMMENTS below.

L. 10 – The bottom margin is seen below the right edge of the line as well as below the second line of frag. 4.

Translation

1. "in the tents of Shem let him live," is (meant) that G[od] dwelt [in] the land of [Shem]
2. and as for what Noah said "may Go[d] enlarge [J]aphet" is (meant) that he will inherit the

[46] It was already missing when I checked the pertinent museum inventory plate 468 in November 2012. Cf. DIMANT, "Pesher on the Periods," (2014), 396–97. So the material data for supporting or rejecting the combination could not be verified with the actual fragment.

[47] Doubting the association of frag. 4 with frags. 2–3, ARIEL – YUDITSKY – QIMRON printed the last two lines in a different font. In this respect, they follow Raphael WEISS, "Fragments of a Midrash on Genesis from Qumran Cave 4," *Textus* 7 (1969): 132–34. WEISS thought that frags. 2–3 are not connected to frags.1 and 4, and one of the arguments he adduced for this claim is that frag. 4's state of preservation is much better than that of frags. 2–3. However, the differences in their state of preservation may stem from their different storage positions in the cache of scrolls. TIGCHELAAR just states that "it is not certain whether frag. 4 should indeed be placed here" (idem, "Sodom and Gomorrah," 55) without further explanation. However, the thematic links between frags. 2–3 and frag. 4, as indeed with frag. 1, are made amply clear through their elaboration of the idea of predestination, as noted by DIMANT, "Pesher on the Periods" (1979), 78. In support of ALLEGRO's and STRUGNELL's decision to attach frag. 4 to frags. 2–3 are also Milik, "Milkî-ṣedeq et Milkî-rešaʿ, 121 and later Menahem KISTER, "Aggadot and Midrash Procedures in the Apocryphal Literature and in the Rabbinic Literature," in *Higayon L'Yona: New Aspects in the Study of Midrash, Aggadah and Piyut in Honor of Professor Yona Fraenkel*, ed. J. LEVINSON, J. ELBAUM, and G. HASAN-ROKEM (Jerusalem: Magnes, 2007), 231–59 (251–52) (Heb.).

3. land of fertil[it]y. *vacat* The three men,
4. appeari[ng] to [Abra]m at Alonei Mamre, are angels.
5. ["the out]cry of Sodom and Gomorrah is so g[reat and] their sin
6. is so grave. I will go down and see according to their out[c]ry that has reached
7. [me I will wre]ak destruction, and if not I will kno[w."] the thing[ ]
8. on acco[unt] of the arrogance [of their heart against]God[ ] on eve[ry]
9. speaker [of lies. And he said] "and I will see" for everything [is engraved according to the periods of]
10. [their] de[signations for] before he created them he knew [their] desi[gns.]

Comments

Ll. 1–3a – This is the continuation and conclusion of a unit started in the previous column (see col. i 1) concerning the interpretation of Noah's blessing in Gen 9:27. Two quotations are cited from the biblical passage and are followed by interpretations.

L. 1 בֿאֹהלי שֿׁם ישכֿון – A reworked quotation of Gen 9:27 with a reverse word order of MT's וישכן באהלי שם. Also the order of the units in the verse is reversed. In the biblical passage, this phrase follows the one referring to Japhet, but here Shem is brought up first. This reversal enables the author to connect the phrase about Shem to the previous statement "Yahwe the God of Shem" and interpret both as God dwelling in the land of Shem. Jub. 8:18 makes the same connection. Obviously both the present pesher and Jubilees understood Noah's blessing as a forecast of the future. A similar understanding is put forward by 4Q252 2:7–8, which produces the citation in the same reversed order, in addition to the statement that the land alluded to in Noah's words is that assigned to Abraham, namely to Shem's descendant.[48]

L. 1 שכן א]ל ב[אֹרֹץ] שם] – The author thus understands the blessing in Gen 9:27b as alluding to the divine presence dwelling in the land assigned to Shem in the future, probably referring to the erection of the temple in Eretz Israel. The same interpretation of the verse is recorded in 4Q252 2:7–8, Jub. 8:18–19, and the rabbinic midrash (e.g., b. Yoma 10a; Gen. Rab. 36,

[48] Menahem KISTER remarks that in the Second Temple period the curse of Canaan became a justification for uprooting the Canaanites. In this connection, he discusses 4Q252 2:5–8, Philo, *QG* 2.65, and Gen. Rab. 1, 2 among others. See idem, "The Fate of the Canaanites and the Despoliation of the Egyptians," in *The Gift of the Land and the Fate of the Canaanites in Jewish Thought*, ed. K. BERTHELOT, J. E. DAVID, and M. HIRSHMAN (Oxford: Oxford University Press, 2014), 66–111.

26–27). However, in the present pesher, this perception is viewed as part of the prefixed sequence of events embedded in the string of periods.

L. 1 הוא אשר֯ – The phrase is formulated as a nominal clause that identifies the cited biblical phrase with the following subordinate clause. For this exegetical technique, see, e.g., 1QpHab 3:2; 4Q252 4:1; 4Q274 1 i 3. See COMMENTS on col. ii 4 below.

L. 1 ב]א֯ר֗ץ [שם] – The restoration of Shem at the end of the line (with Qimron and Ariel – Yuditsky – Qimron) is required by the preceding quotation and interpretation.

L. 2 ואשר א֯מ֯ר֯ – A formula introducing a biblical quotation, followed by an interpretation, employed also in frags. 2–4 i 10. In a pesher commentary it usually opens a secondary unit . Cf. COMMENTS on frags. 2–4 i 10.

L. 2 יפת אל֯ [ל]יפת – A second quotation from Noah's blessing to Japhet in Gen 9:27.

L. 3a פו֗ר֗י֯[ ]ת֗ – See NOTES ON READINGS. The phrase ירש את ארץ פו֗ר֗י֯[ ]ת֗ interprets Gen 9:27 to mean that Japhet received a particularly good piece of land. Compare Jub. 10:35–36, which states that Japhet did not like his original inheritance and was settled in the land of Madai, assigned to the sons of Shem. Ariel – Yuditsky – Qimron read here בי֗ד֗מ֯ה֯ and understand it as the name of a place in Japhet's inheritance. But both their reading and interpretation are awkward.

Ll. 3b–7 – This section is separated from the previous pericope by a blank space (in line 3), indicating that a new subject is broached in the following text. In terms of the different periods, the reference to Noah and his sons concludes the first period, namely the first ten generations alluded to in frag. 1 5, while the three angels who visited Abraham and the fate of immoral Sodom (Gen 18:2, 20–21) belong probably to the second period of ten generations. Both are considered to be part of the overall predetermined plan of events.

L. 3b שלושת האנשים – Taking up the formulation of Gen 18:2 שלשה אנשים. Note, however, MT's indefinite expression, שלשה אנשים, indicating their unknown identity, which is changed in 4Q180 2–4 to a definite expression, שלושת האנשים, signifying they are known figures as made clear by the following reference to the Genesis story. The definite status of the nouns and the mention of Elonei Mamre function as an explicit citation, since the biblical scene referred to is assumed to be well known. The interpretation important to the author, namely the identification with angels, is incorporated into the concise allusion to the biblical account.

L. 4 ה֯נר֗א[ים] אל֯ [אבר]ם באלו֯נ֯י֯ ממרה – The plural participle הנרא[ים] functions as the adjective of the preceding definite nouns referring to the biblical episode of the visit of the men to Elonei Mamre (Gen 18:1), rendering definite the entire string of nouns. The episode is presented with a few characteristic details that identify them as references to the story in Genesis 18. Thus, they function as a quotation, in a manner similar to frag. 1 7–8. The explanation of this biblical extract consists of the identification "they are angels." A similar method is observed in frag. 1 7–8.

L. 4 באלוׄנׄיׄ – MT באלני.

L. 4 ממרה – MT has ממרא.

L. 4 [ ]מלאכׄים המׄה – A nominal clause, consisting of the noun מלאכים and the 3rd. per. pl. personal pronoun המה, which identifies the three men who visited Abram (Genesis 18) as angels, based on the description of two of them as angels in the biblical episode about Sodom and Gomorrah (MT to Gen 19:1, 15).[49] Thus, the two words interpret the preceding noun. The method of explaining a biblical noun by equating it with a nonbiblical noun through a nominal clause is a technique familiar from other Qumran pesharim (see, e.g., CD 1:13, 4:2; 1QpHab 12:9; 4Q169 3–4 ii 9). However, here the proposed identification of the men with angels is not particularly sectarian but is suggested by the biblical text itself and espoused by most of the postbiblical sources.[50] The adjacency of the angels' visit to the intended penalty of the two cities denotes that the interest of the pesher lies in the divine judgment of the sinners, executed by the angelic emissaries (Genesis 19), that is, originated in God himself. Although the tidings the angels brought to Abram about a future son are not mentioned explicitly, they are engrained in the reference itself, for the entire nexus of Genesis 18–19 seems to underlie the sequence of the pesher. So the identification of the men as angels is not only a literal interpretation of the biblical detail, but also an allusion to the divinely intended birth of Isaac, thus connecting the angelic visit to the mention of Isaac's birth in the introduction to the pesher (frag. 1 5). The author may have seen in the fact that the angels came to Abram before the divine utterance regarding

[49] A fluctuation between "men"/"angels" in the Genesis story is recorded also in the ancient versions. LXX Gen 19:16 has "angels" instead of MT's "men." SP Gen 19:12 and Syr. Gen 19:16 display the same interchange.

[50] The biblical sequence opens with the statement that God appeared to Abram (Gen 18:1), immediately followed by the arrival of the three men, suggesting an equation of the two. Two of these visitors who went to Sodom are actually called "angels" (MT Gen 19:1). The identification of the men who came to Abram with angels is common in much of the postbiblical literature. See Tg. Neof. and Tg. Ps.-J. to Gen 18:2: תלתא מלאכין בדמות גברין. Compare Philo, *Abr.* 107; Heb 13:2; Josephus, *A.J.*, 1.196; Gen. Rab. 25, 2. See the detailed discussion of Gabriel BARZILAI, "Offhand Exegesis: Passing Allusions to Interpretation of the Book of Genesis, as Found in the Dead Sea Scrolls" (PhD diss., Bar Ilan University, 2002), 232–36 (Heb.).

the two cities a hint at the predetermined character of the punishment of the two cities, just as was the birth of Isaac, a theme elaborated in the interpretation of אראה in lines 9–10. Also the juxtaposition of Abram's promised progeny and the destruction of Sodom and Gomorrah, with the survival of Noah's chosen lineage from among the wicked antediluvians is not accidental. It suggests the basic parallelism between the two occasions. See Discussion below.

Ll. 4–5 זע[קת סדׂוׂם]הׂמׂה – Dimant 1979 and 2014 proposes the restoration הׂמׂה]ואשר אמר זע[קת סדׂוׂם. Although the restoration itself is hypothetical, it brings forth the explicit exegetical purpose of the quotation.

Ll. 5–7 – A quotation of Gen 18:20–21.

L. 6 מאדה – This adverbial form (MT מאד) is typical in the Qumran scrolls.[51]

L. 6 כׂזועקׂתׂ[מ]הׂ – The noun זעקה stands here with a 3rd pl. masc. pronoun ("their outcry") without the interrogative *he* provided by the MT version (הכצעקתה). This plural pronoun applies the outcry to the inhabitants of the two cities, as does the pronoun of חטאתמה in the previous line.[52] The same variant ("their outcry") is reflected in the LXX, Tg. Onk., and Frg. Tg. to Gen 18:21, as well as in Gen. Rab. 45, 8. MT's הכצעקתה with a 3rd fem. sg. pronoun ("her outcry") relates the outcry to the cities.[53]

L. 7 אע[שה כלה – The change from MT's עשו to אע[שה introduces a significant modification, for instead of MT's application of the noun כלה, "destruction," to the sin of the inhabitants of the two cities, the formulation here relates it to the divine punishment meted out to them.[54] The MT version involves a problem since the reader may have puzzled over the statement that God was not aware of the crimes of the cities.[55] The targumim solved it by stating that God went down to see whether the iniquitous inhabitants repented (Tg. Onk.; Tg. Neof.; Frg. Tg.; Tg. Ps.-J.). However, from the predestination viewpoint so dear to the author, this answer would be inadequate, for God should have foreknown if repentance

[51] Cf. QIMRON, *A Grammar of the Hebrew of the Dead Sea Scrolls*, § G 2.2.1 (p. 363).

[52] זעק is a by-form of the biblical צעק, used in Mishnaic Hebrew, Samaritan Hebrew, and Aramaic (*HALOT* 1:277). The Qumran documents use זעק exclusively. The rare cases in which צעק/צעקה appear (1Q19 1 4; 4Q365 7 i 3) are, in fact, restorations offered by various editors that should be replaced by זעק/זעקה. 1Q19 was indeed corrected in this way by Qimron, *The Dead Sea Scrolls*, 3:1.

[53] Apparently to conform with Gen 18:20 זעקת, "the outcry," standing in the singular.

[54] As noted by BARZILAI, "Offhand Exegesis," 237. See the similar formulation in Jer 46:28 ואתך לא אעשה כלה (observed by Ariel – Yuditsky – Qimron).

[55] As formulated clearly by James L. KUGEL, *Traditions of the Bible* (Cambridge: Harvard University Press, 1998), 347–48.

took place. It appears that 4Q180 affirms that the annihilation will be inflicted on the cities in accordance with their outcry. Such an understanding would also account for the dropping of the interrogative *he* in כֿזעקׄתׄ[מ]הׄ in line 6.[56]

L. 7 אע]שה – Strugnell and Milik 1972 propose ע]שה, influenced by MT 12:81 ועשה. Ariel – Yuditsky – Qimron point also to the possibility of reading ע]שה as an infinitive absolute, current in Second Temple Hebrew.[57] However, from the point of view of space, the two surviving letters are better restored with two additional letters to obtain a 1st sg. per. masc. future tense form of the verb עשה, referring to God. Also, the form obtained, אעשה, fits with the string of four similar verbs applying to God, אדעה, אעשה, אראה, ארדה, used in the present text to represent God's intentional acts. The restoration was proposed by Dimant 1979 and 2014 and followed by Qimron and Ariel – Yuditsky – Qimron. Thus, אעשה is a textual variant, differing from MT's ועשו,[58] a 3rd pl. masc. of the perfect, referring to the inhabitants of the two sinful cities. Note that Tg. Onk. to Gen 18:21 has a double translation, one reflects the MT and the other assumes the form אעשה.

L. 7 כלה – The word stands here as a noun with the sense "destruction" (see 1QM 1:5 כלה לכול גוי רשעה).[59]

L. 7]הׄדבר[– Milik 1972 and Dimant 2014 restored פשר]הדבר. Ariel – Yuditsky – Qimron reject this restoration arguing that in the Scrolls this locution is always followed by "about/on which" (על/אשר). Instead they suggest that the word may have been preceded by a verb.

Ll. 8–9 על כוׄ[ל] דובר[– Milik 1972, Dimant 1979 and 2014 restore ועל כוׄ[ל פה] דובר[. Cf. Isa 9:16.

[56] So the form lacking the interrogative *he* adopted in line 6 may have been intended, and not the result of a haplography or error, as suggested by ARIEL – YUDITSKY – QIMRON, "Pesher on the Periods," 29.

[57] It is particularly frequent in the Qumran Hebrew copy of Tobit, 4Q200.

[58] The MT version is recorded in a Qumran Genesis manuscript, 8QGen 2 21.

[59] On the basis of his reading כללה instead of כלה, LANGE argued that 4Q180 viewed the punishment of Sodom and Gomorrah as that inflicted upon the idolatrous city (Deut 13:13–18). See idem, "Eine neue Lesart." While his reading is erroneous (see NOTES ON READINGS above), and the application of this legal principle to 4Q180 is not substantiated by explicit references, it may not be entirely out of place. For it has been suggested that this rule was applied to Sodom and Gomorrah in another Qumran interpretative text, namely 4Q252 3 2–6. Cf. George J. BROOKE, "The Genre of 4Q252: From Poetry to Pesher," *DSD* 1 (1994): 160–79 (170). This is noteworthy since 4Q252 has other points of contact with 4Q180. Therefore, the application of the principle of the idolatrous city to the two cities may have been known to the author of 4Q180 and may underlay his reference to the sinful cities, although the author's interest lay in reading the episode from the divine foreknowledge perspective.

L. 8 בעֲבֿ[ור] אשר – A prepositional expression meaning "on account of" (cf. *DCH* 2:234–35), used in the sectarian texts also referring to sins committed in the past (cf. CD 1:18; 1QpHab 9:11–12), as seems to be the case here.

L. 8 בעֲבֿ[ור] אשר גֿבֿהֿ] לבם – Ariel – Yuditsky – Qimron propose that the term גבה refers to God. However, since the preposition בעב]ור suggests here a causal nexus, the word should be linked to the entire context. So גבה is better parsed as a verb in the past tense, applied to the two cities, for they are the subject of the preceding quotation and for the following sin. Perhaps this is a reference to the tradition attributing to the Sodomites the sin of arrogance, and therefore the restoration גבה] לבם is offered; for the expression, see, e.g., Ezek 28:2; Ps 131:1, Prov 16:5. The arrogance of Sodom and Gomorrah is already elaborated in Ezek 16:49 and has been taken up by interpretations to Gen 18:21. See Sir 16:8; t. Soṭah 3:11, 13; b. Sanh. 109a. If the first column does mention the flood (col. i 4–5), it suggests a parallel to the sin of the Sodomites, a parallelism well known from other sources. A tradition condemning antediluvian mankind of arrogance and revolt against the divine because of its excesses is recorded in Qumran documents (4Q370 i 1–3[60]) and in rabbinic midrashim (see b. Sanh. 108a.). The Sodomites are said to rebel against God for the same reason (e.g., Sir 16:8; Midr. Tana'im to Deut 32:15; Sipre, Eqev, Deuteronomy 43). Another correspondence between the two episodes concerns the outcry that went up from Sodom and Gomorrah, and the outcry that, according to 1 En. 7:10; 9:2 (compare 1Q19 1 4), was emitted by the land because of the evils committed by the sinful angels and their giant offspring. Both antediluvian humanity and the inhabitants of Sodom and Gomorrah figure in the traditional lists of sinners (cf. Sir 16:7–8; m. Sanh. 10:10; Mek. *beshalach*, *vayehi* 4; Mek. de Rashbi, 14, 21).[61]

Ll. 9–10 – The two lines, documented by frag. 4, reformulate the principles of the sectarian notion of predestination and thus join the statement of the same idea in frag. 1 1–4a. Accordingly they enclose the details elucidated in the body of the pesher in the framework of predestination, providing a sort of *inclusio* with the introduction.

L. 9 דובר] שקר – The restoration follows the locution in Prov 101:7 דֹבר שקרים. Milk 1972 restored דובר] נבלה on the basis of Isa 9:16. Qimron and Ariel – Yuditsky – Qimron propose דובר] רע.

[60] See the comments of A. FELDMAN, "4Q370 (Admonition on the Flood)," in *Scripture and Interpretation*, 48–51.

[61] On the historical list of this type, see the survey of Atar LIVNEH, "Abraham in the Second Temple Historical Summaries," *Meghillot* 13 (2017): 119–58 (Heb.).

L. 9 ואמר] ואראה – The restoration (with Qimron and Ariel – Yuditsky – Qimron) is based on the understanding that the following ואראה is a quotation from Gen 18:21 fully cited in the preceding lines 5–7 of the same column. The formula ואמר is typical of the present work, employed to introduce a citation, as in frags. 2–4 i 10 and ii 2.

L. 9 ואראה – A quotation from Gen 18:21 functioning as a lemma, followed by an interpretation applying it to the idea of predestination, namely, that God had a foreknowledge of the events in question. The repeated citation here, attested by frag. 4, clearly connects it to frags. 2–3, which contain the full quotation of Gen 18:21. The word calls for a particular explanation due to the underlying exegetical problem embedded in the entire biblical passage. Why would God wish to go down and see what was going on? Did he not already know?[62] This is an awkward question for an author who subscribes to the predestination notion.[63] The interpretation offered by our pesher consists of understanding the word "and I will see" in the sense of "see beforehand."[64] A repeated citation of a detail extracted from a previously quoted biblical text in order to elaborate an additional aspect of the citation is typical of the pesharim procedure.

L. 9 כיא הכול] חקוק לקצי[– Following the restoration proposed by Dimant 1979, adopted by Qimron and Ariel – Yuditsky – Qimron. The restoration of קצי in the plural (instead of the singular קץ of Milik 1972) fits better with the antecedent plural suffix of the following בראם.

L. 10 תעׄו]דותם [– The restoration follows the locution in 1QS 3:16; 1QH[a] 9:21. Dimant 1979, Qimron, and Ariel – Yuditsky – Qimron have תעׄו]דתם [. Milik 1972 has תעׄו]דתו. The term belongs to the sectarian teaching about creation according to a predetermined designated plan. See, e.g., 1QH[a] 20:12, 25:13.

L. 10 כיא] בטרם – Following the restoration of Dimant 1979, which provides a link to the previous words. It is followed by Qimron and Ariel – Yuditsky – Qimron; similarly García Martínez–Tigchelaar.

[62] The problem is thus formulated by KUGEL, *Traditions of the Bible*, 347.

[63] As noted by TIGCHELAAR, "Sodom and Gomorrah," 57; Roman VIELHAUER, "Sodom and Gomorrah: From the Bible to Qumran," in *Rewriting and Interpreting the Hebrew Bible: The Biblical Patriarchs in the Light of the Dead Sea Scrolls*, ed. D. DIMANT and R. G. KRATZ, BZAW 439 (Berlin: De Gruyter, 2013), 147–69 (160–61).

[64] In this connection, Menahem KISTER notes that biblical expressions of divine "seeing" (ראייה) are interpreted by rabbinic midrashim as God's ability to see the future (e.g., Mek. de Rashbi to Exod 19:1). See idem, "Aggadot and Midrash procedures," 251–52.

L. 10 בטרם בראם – The terms appear in the introductory section in frag. 1 2. See COMMENT ad loc.

L. 10 ידע – The use of this verb to express the divine foreknowledge before creation is found elsewhere in the sectarian literature (compare CD 2:7–9 and 1QS 4:25).

L. 10 מחשב̊[ותיהם] – The word is employed here in the sense of foreknowledge of the designs of everything. Compare 1QS 3:15 ולפני היותם הכין כל מחשבתם, "and before they came into being he established all their designs."

Discussion

Seen as an ensemble, the 4Q180 fragments present a coherent and well-constructed work that features an introduction (frag. 1 1–5) and conclusion (frags. 2–4 ii 9–10), outlining the ideological framework of the notion of predestination. The body of the composition enumerates the major episodes along the span of the first twenty generations of human history, introducing them with the pertinent biblical citations and references. Since the events are introduced according to the biblical sequence, the lost section between frags. 1 and 2–4 must have dealt with the preamble to the flood and the flood itself, followed by the pericope about Noah in the next surviving columns (frags. 2–4 i–ii). In the temporal scheme laid out in 4Q180, two intertwined events are subjected to commentary: antediluvian sin and its punishment (the flood) is paired with the survival of Noah and the election of his son Shem, marking the highlights of the first ten generations. The second span of ten generations is marked by the three angels announcing to Abram the birth of Isaac, paired with the destruction of the wicked Sodom and Gomorrah. The two clusters are structurally parallel: the righteous Noah living amid evil mankind is saved from the flood and fathers Shem, and Abram is to father Isaac while the wicked dwellers of the two evil cities are annihilated. So an analogy is drawn between the righteous Noah and his son Shem and their descendant Abraham. On the other hand, a connection is drawn between the antediluvians and the corrupted inhabitants of the two cities and between their respective punishments, the devastation brought by the flood and the destruction by fire. Both episodes concern the eradication of evil. They stand in contrast to the durability and longevity of Noah's offspring, especially these of the chosen Shem.

From a literary point of view, both the introduction and the first detailed period are introduced by the term "pesher" (frag. 1 1, 7). This means that the term "pesher" is a marker of a major expositional section. Indeed, in commenting on the various biblical segments, typical pesher terminology is used, for instance, the formula "as for what he said" (frags. 2–4 i 10; ii 2).

From the structural perspective, the work is clearly an exegetical oeuvre. Although the overall theme is a broad doctrinal one, it is presented via the use of biblical materials and quotations from Genesis. This interpretative character is evident not only in the recourse to the biblical sources, but also in the choice of introductory terms that are used in other exegetical works that resemble the pesharim. In this respect, the carefully crafted framework of the pesher is notable. The term pesher is used at the beginning of major exegetical units (frag. 1 1, 7) whereas the formulas "and as for what (X) said" or just "and he said" are reserved for explaining details subordinate to the main exegetical framework (frags. 2–4 i 10; ii 2, 9). However, it is worth noting that, within these sectarian parameters, 4Q180 does not resort to the peculiar type of symbolic explanations typical of other sectarian pesharim. It adheres to clarifications of various exegetical difficulties, solving them with sundry nonsectarian traditions. This exegetical strategy is engaged in order to view certain biblical episodes through the lens of the divine predetermination notion. Since all the verses treated are examined from this ideological perspective, the pesher as a whole is a systematic interpretation of a single notion.[65] The thematic and structural coherence of 4Q180 presents it as a unified, self-contained work that is not to be fused with 4Q181.

The events alluded to in the surviving fragments concern episodes well known from the traditional historical lists of ancient sinners, transmitted by both Qumran and non-Qumranic documents. Sirach (16:7–8), for instance, positions the giants and the people of Sodom at the head of his list. A sequence of historical sinners and righteous people stands at the base of the Apocalypse of Weeks (1 En. 91:11–17; 93:1–10). The Qumran Damascus Document opens its list with the angels and their giant offspring (CD 2:17–21). Interestingly, the next item in the Damascus Document list concerns the sons of Noah (CD 3:1). Perhaps it provides a parallel to the sequence in 4Q180. Thematically speaking, the flood, its preamble, and its aftermath were favourite subjects among the Qumran documents, both

[65] Ariel – Yuditsky – Qimron argue that it is not a pesher on a subject but a pesher on biblical verses, similar to other pesharim (eidem, "Pesher on the Periods," 30). But the presence of biblical verses does not exclude the thematic character of the pesher since all of them obviously serve the exposition of a single theme.

of sectarian and nonsectarian character. This is evident by the number of texts that treat the subject: 1Q19 1 and 2; 4Q370 i; 4Q422 ii; 4Q577 4.[66] Also relevant are lines 2–3 of 1Q34bis 3 ii, probably referring to the flood,[67] and 5Q13 1 7–8 referring to Noah,[68] not to mention the Aramaic Book of Giants, which is devoted entirely to the giants and the imminent flood.

However, the Commentary on Genesis, preserved in 4Q252, has a particular affinity with 4Q180. The Commentary opens a section with the story of the flood (4Q252 1–2:5) and concludes it with Noah's curse of Canaan and the blessing of Shem of Gen 9:26–27 (4Q252 2:5–8), a nexus found in 4Q180 2–4 ii 1. As in 4Q180, 4Q252 also addresses the episode of Sodom and Gomorrah (frag. 3 1–6). However, it is concerned with the exchange Abram had with God related to the imminent destruction (Gen 18:23–32), a scene not addressed in 4Q180. Both 4Q180 and 4Q252 share the selective choice of biblical sources on which they comment, presented in the biblical order. Both provide interpretation by recourse to manifold sources, some of nonsectarian provenance. The interpretations of both mostly lack the particular pesher-like symbolic exegesis. At the same time, both are clearly of sectarian authorship. So a combination of literal interpretation and sectarian ideology is present in both 4Q252 and 4Q180. However, unlike the coherent structure and theme of 4Q180, 4Q252 is a compendium of disparate comments.[69] Since 4Q180 does not resort to the symbolic-allusive exegesis typical of the sectarian

[66] These four works are reedited and discussed by A. FELDMAN, *Scripture and Interpretation*, 15–129.

[67] Discussed by Devorah DIMANT, "The Flood as a Preamble to the Lives of the Patriarchs: The Perspective of Qumran Hebrew Texts," in *Rewriting and Interpreting the Hebrew Bible: The Biblical Patriarch in Light of the Dead Sea Scrolls*, ed. D. DIMANT and R. G. KRATZ, BZAW 439 (Berlin: De Gruyter, 2013), 102–34 (110–12).

[68] Cf. Menahem Kister, "5Q13 and the 'Avodah': A Historical Survey and Its Significance," *DSD* 8 (2001): 136–48. It is interpreted differently by DIMANT, "The Flood as a Preamble,"106–9.

[69] Analyzed by George J. BROOKE, "The Thematic Content of 4Q252," *JQR* 85 (1994): 33–59. See also idem, "The Genre of 4Q252: From Poetry to Pesher," *DSD* 1 (1999): 160–79; Moshe J. BERNSTEIN, "4Q252: From Re-written Bible to Biblical Commentary," in *Reading and Re-Reading Scripture at Qumran*, STDJ 107 (Leiden: Brill, 2013), 1:92–125; Shani TZOREF, "4Q252: Listenwissenschaft and Covenantal Patriarchal Blessings," in *"Go Out and Study the Land" (Judges 18:2): Archeological, Historical and Textual Studies in Honor of Hanan Eshel*, ed. A. M. MAEIR, J. MAGNESS, and L. H. SCHIFFMAN, JSJSup 148 (Leiden: Brill, 2012), 335–57. Given the distinct character of 4Q180 and 4Q252, the attempt of ARIEL – YUDITSKY – QIMRON to assign them to a single "new genre of scrolls dealing with the Bible – a genre of nonsequential pesharim and interpretations" is fortuitous. Cf. eidem, "Pesher on the Periods," 31.

pesharim, its repeated use of the term "pesher" may convey a general interpretative genre. [70] Indeed, George Brooke has labelled 4Q180 a thematic commentary.[71]

The Relationship between 4Q180 and 4Q181[72]

In light of the new readings and new perception of 4Q180 proposed above, the character and structure of the work emerge more clearly and more comprehensibly. Hence, its relationship to 4Q181 may now be better assessed. Józef Milik is responsible for the influential theory that 4Q180 and 4Q181 are two copies of the same work, accepted by many scholars. However, the weighty arguments refuting his construction have not earned the consideration they merit.[73] Therefore, a short review of Milik's older arguments in favor of his thesis is in order: a) The similarity of 4Q181 2 1–4 to 4Q180 1 5–9 led Milik to claim that they may be integrated materially to create a single reconstructed text. In Milik's opinion, the Pesher on Melchizedek (11QMelch = 11Q13) constituted a third copy of the same work; b) He assumes that the pesher genre is present in 4Q180 as well as in 4Q181; c) In Milik's opinion, the chronology of seventy weeks of years, referred to in 4Q181 2 3, underlies both 4Q181 and 4Q180; d) Milik estimated that both texts deal with angelic activities and show priestly concerns; e) Milik judged that the main theme of the composed work 4Q180–181 is angelic activities.[74]

These arguments are unwarranted for the following reasons: 1) A connection between 4Q180–181 and 11QMelch should be discarded on material as well as contextual grounds.[75] As for the relationship between 4Q180 and 4Q181, 4Q180 1 5, 7–8 and 4Q181 2 1–2 show some affinity but they

[70] The characterization of 4Q180 as thematic pesher, proposed by some scholars (e.g., PUECH, *La Croyance*, 2:527; DIMANT, "Pesher on the Periods," [2014], 399) should therefore be qualified, since the term "thematic pesharim" designates expositions assembled around certain subjects, and formulated in the particular symbolic-historical interpretation cultivated by the sectaries. Cf. n. 23 above.

[71] BROOKE, "Some Scribal Features," passim.

[72] See the version of 4Q181 in the Appendix.

[73] These arguments have been submitted repeatedly. Cf. DIMANT, "Pesher on the Periods" (1979), 89–90; eadem, "Pesher on the Periods" (2014), 402–4, 420–21; Ronald V. HUGGINS, "A Canonical 'Book of Periods' at Qumran?" *RevQ* 15 (1992): 421–36. ARIEL – YUDITSKY – QIMRON, recently dismissed the claim that 4Q180 and 4Q181 are distinct works with one sentence, without considering the weighty arguments in its favor. Cf. eidem, "Pesher on the Periods," 6.

[74] Cf. MILIK, "Milkî-ṣedeq," 110, 122–23; idem, *The Books of Enoch*, 248–53.

[75] As noted by Émile PUECH, the two differ in the concept of history. Cf. idem, "Notes sur le manuscript de XIQMelkîsédeq," *RevQ* 12 (1987): 483–513 (509).

can hardly be fitted into each other. Milik does not stress sufficiently the fact that the similar lines are not entirely identical. Compare 4Q181 1 9]עולה ולהנחיל רשעה with 4Q181 2 4 ואוהבי עולה ומנחילי רשעה. Also notable is the lack of reference to Azazel in 4Q181, while he is mentioned twice in 4Q180. Moreover, the citation from Genesis 6, the mention of the angels, the allusion to their punishment, and the reference to Isaac are an integral part of 4Q180 and its structure, whereas their connection to the ideological and stylistic fabric of 4Q181 is not clear. Perhaps they stood as a historical prototype of the wickedness of Israel; 2) While the label "pesher" may apply to 4Q180, it is not at all the case with 4Q181. Even the lines in 4Q181 that resemble those in 4Q180 have not preserved the structure of a pesher or the use of the term "pesher." In fact, most of the lines that survived in 4Q181 display thematic and vocabulary links to thanksgiving hymns and not to the pesharim; 3) As for the chronology of seventy weeks, alluded to in 4Q181 2 3, it is not mentioned in the remaining text of 4Q180, and it is not required for the understanding of 4Q180. In fact, the chronology of seventy weeks of years or ten jubilees is widely attested in Second Temple Jewish writings, particularly in pseudepigraphic and Qumran compositions, and thus its presence in a given work cannot be taken in itself as evidence of literary dependence. At most, such scattered references point to a widespread notion that was reworked in various ways in many contemporary writings;[76] 4) Milik's claim that priestly interests are shared by 4Q180 and 4Q181 is also unsubstantiated;[77] 5) Also his claim that angelic activities are the main theme of the composed work is too general to be taken as a particular mark of affinity between 4Q180 and 4Q181. Firstly, not all the episodes reworked in 4Q180 concern angels. Noah's blessing, for instance, has no such connection. Secondly, angelic activities appeared in many compositions, Qumranic as well as non-Qumranic, and so are not exclusive to 4Q180 and 4Q181

Milik's thesis was revived recently by Ariel, Yuditsky, and Qimron, who merge 4Q180 and 4Q181 into a single version and argue in favor of the thesis that they reflect one and the same work. However, their composite text, like that of Milik, is an artificial creation that appears to be harmonious but in fact blurs the distinct character of the two manuscripts. Thus, the authors claim that their combined oeuvre produces "a

[76] Cf. Devorah DIMANT, *Qumran Cave 4.XXI: Parabiblical Texts, Part 4: Pseudo-Prophetic texts*, DJD XXX (Oxford: Clarendon, 2001), 113–14. See the review of James C. VANDERKAM, *Calendars in the Dead Sea Scrolls: Measuring Time* (London: Routledge, 1998), 97–109.

[77] As remarked by PUECH, *La Croyance*, 2:531.

homogenous text that concerns Israel in history and the role of Azazel."[78] However, they omit to mention that the attribution of both Israel and Azazel to the work exists only in their artificial composite text. In fact, 4Q180 does not mention Israel while 4Q181 does not mention Azazel, one of the significant disparities between the two. Aware of some discrepancies even in their similar lines, Ariel, Yuditsky, and Qimron proposed that 4Q180 is a shorter version of the work, while 4Q181 holds a longer version of the same composition.[79] To support this far-fetched thesis, Ariel, Yuditsky, and Qimron adduce the Community Rule and the Damascus Document as documents that survived in shorter and longer copies, which, they argue, show that "a difference between short texts does not necessarily indicate different compositions."[80] However, this is obviously an inappropriate and misleading comparison. For the Community Rule and the Damascus Document are consistent and cohesive works and their copies display substantial similarity, even identity, in most of their components. In their shorter and longer copies they basically attest to the same text. This is not at all the case with 4Q180 and 4Q181. The similarity between the two is reduced to a few lines while most of the remaining sections are completely different.[81] The theme of 4Q180 is a pesher on the periods and the divine foreknowledge of their details, whereas 4Q181 is a composition describing the respective punishment for the wicked and reward for the righteous from a dualistic point of view. Also their ideological orbits stand in contrast. 4Q180 is interested in the early history of humanity and the patriarchs as laid down in the periods established before creation. In contradistinction, the surviving fragments of 4Q181 are concerned with the eschatological fate of the wicked and the righteous probably in relation to the people of Israel. The disparity between 4Q180 and 4Q181 is seen even more clearly when the focus is placed on their distinct literary backgrounds and characters. 4Q180 is a pesher composition expounding segments from Genesis in light of the predetermined periods, using terminology and procedures typical of other pesharim, whereas 4Q181 is a poetic composition expressing dualistic and eschatological ideas with a strong affinity to Hodayot and Hodayot-like texts.[82] Hence, we cannot speak of 4Q180 and 4Q181 as copies of a

[78] ARIEL – YUDITSKY – QIMRON, "Pesher on the Periods," 14.

[79] ARIEL – YUDITSKY – QIMRON, "Pesher on the Periods," 6.

[80] ARIEL – YUDITSKY – QIMRON, "Pesher on the Periods," 7.

[81] The comparative table of the similar lines in 4Q180 and 4Q181 proposed by Ariel – Yuditsky – Qimron, "Pesher on the Periods," 8 illustrates this literary fact very well.

[82] Note that in the table compiled by QIMRON, ARIEL, AND YUDITSKY to compare their combined "Pesher on the Periods" to other sources, all the listed similarities to the

single work. The the two texts may be independently citing a well-known tradition.[83] 4Q180 presents a tightly constructed consistent work, whereas 4Q181 is fragmentary and incomplete and therefore remains somewhat obscure.

APPENDIX

4Q181[84]

Frag. 2

1]]ם̊ [ ]ד̊ י̊שחק [[
2 [בנות]האדם וילד[ו] להמה גבור֯[ים [
3 [א]ת֯ ישראל בשבעים השבוע ל[[
4 ו̊אוהב֯י֯ עולה ומנחילי אשמה ו̊[[
5 לעינ֯י֯ כול יודעיו ◦◦ש֯[[
6 ולטובו אין חקר̊[[
7 .[marg אלה נפלאו מדע֯[ת [
8 [ת֯כנם באמתו ו̊[[
9 [בכול קצותם̊[[
10 [בריאותיהם̊[[
11 [◦[[

Frag. 1

Col. i — Col. ii

1 [ם̊ לאשמה ביחד עם סו̊[ד] עפ̊[ר ו]ל֯ה̊ת̊ג̊ל֯ל בחטאת בני אדם ולמשפטים גדולים ומחלים רעים
2 בבשר לפי גבורות אל ולעומת רשעם לפי סודנ͏ͯדתם מסוד בני ש̊[מים] וארץ ליחד רשעה עד
3 קצה לעומת רחמי אל לפי טובו והפלא כבודו הגיש מבני תבל vac[ ]vac להתחשב עמו֯ ב̊ס̊[וד]
4 [א]ל֯ים לעדת קודש במעמד לחיי עולם ובגורל עם קדושיו כ̊ [ ]
5 [רזי פ]לאו איש לפי גורלו אשר ה̊פ̊[י]ל ל[ו [
6]]ל֯ח֯יי ע̊[ו]ל֯[ם [

Community Rule 11 and Hodayot 11 are found in 4Q181 and not in 4Q180. Cf. eidem, "Pesher on the Periods," 21.

[83] The option proposed by STRUGNELL (in *RevQ* 7, 252), namely, that 4Q180 comments on 4Q181 is less plausible given the abbreviated version of the common material offered by 4Q181.

[84] The unusual width of the surviving right margin suggests that the fragment stood at the beginning of the work, whereas the piece initially designated as frag. 1 came in one of the following columns. My detailed fresh edition of 4Q181 is scheduled to appear in the forthcoming reedition of DJD V.

AN INQUIRY INTO THE WORK OF THE HEAVEN AND EARTH A LITERARY STUDY OF THE ARAMAIC TEXT OF 1 EN. 2:1–5:2*

Henryk DRAWNEL, SDB

The introductory part of the Book of the Watchers, chapters 1–5 of 1 Enoch, is a composite text that depicts Enoch as the main narrative voice and a visionary (1:1–3a), describing God's coming for judgment (1:3b–9), exhortation to observe the earthly and heavenly phenomena (2:1–5:3), and rebuking sinners subject to judgment who, having viciously changed their behaviour, are subject to wrath and condemnation (5:4–6). When interpreting the first five chapters of 1 Enoch, scholars construct their opinions on the literary form and structure of 1 Enoch mostly on its Greek and Ethiopic versions with some references to the Aramaic text preserved in 4Q201 frgs. 3 i and 4 together with 4Q204 frgs. 1, 2, and 3 i. There exists, however, some disagreement, especially about the literary form and setting of 1 En. 2:1–5:3 interpreted together with 5:4 as one literary unit.

Lars Hartman, who dedicated a whole monograph to the opening chapters of the Book of the Watchers, considers the exhortation of 2:1–5:3 as the first section of chapters 2–5, labelling their literary form as a "denouncement speech."[1] Since the exhortation can hardly be considered a "denouncement speech," he treats verse 5:4 (accusation of the disorderly and sinful conduct of the sinners), attested in 4Q201 3 i 12–14 as well as in the versions, as part of the literary structure of 2:1–5:3,[2] although

* I dedicate this study to Prof. Émile Puech who introduced me to ancient Semitic epigraphy as well as to the vast field of Qumran studies at the École Biblique et Archéologique Française in Jerusalem, Israel. Throughout many years of ensuing friendship and sharing scholarly interests, his keen epigraphic eye and a good deal of sound judgment, not to mention his cordiality and an uplifting sense of humor, have accompanied and sometimes directed my solitary drifting through the distant seas of Aramaic studies and Enochic astronomy *usque ad imperfectum*.

[1] Lars HARTMAN, *Asking for a Meaning. A Study of 1 Enoch 1–5*, Lund, CWK Gleerup, 1979, 11.

[2] Ibid., 17–18. His translation of the exhortation is composite, based on different textual witnesses. He cites the translation of 4Q201 3 i 12b (the beginning of 5:4) without actually

in other places he argues for 5:4–9 as an independent unit.[3] Setting chapters 2–5 in the Jewish literary and religious context, he claims that their literary form can be termed "a covenant formulary text" or "rîb-patterned text" rooted in Old Testament Deuteronomic and prophetic literature and found in later Jewish traditions, such as 1 En. 100:4–13; 101–104, etc.[4] Concerning a possible setting in life for the introductory chapters of the Book of the Watchers, Hartman proposes a cultic context on the Day of Atonement.[5] Linking 5:4 with 5:3, Georges Nickelsburg closely follows Hartman, but he finds the proper background for the Enochic section in the wisdom traditions about the obedience of nature and man's disobedience in texts like Sir 16:24–30; 1QS III, 15–IV, 26; T. Naph. 3:2–4:1, etc.[6]

When setting out to analyse the created order in the Enochic books of wisdom, Argall begins with 1 Enoch 2:1–5:4 by pointing out that the vocabulary and *topoi* of 2:1–5:4 are characteristic of the nature of a creation hymn, such as Ps 104 in its treatment of the works of God in heaven, earth and sea (1 En. 2:1; 2:2; 5:3/ Ps 104:1–4. 5–23, 25–26); the watering of the trees and the marking of the seasons (1 En. 2:3–5:1/ Ps 104:16, 19) as well as the destruction of the wicked (1 En. 5:4/

acknowledging the fact: "But you, you have changed your *works*." Surprisingly, on p. 18 he translates the beginning of the *Greek* text of 5:4 (G^{C-1}) as part of 5:4–9: "But you have not been steadfast."

[3] See ibid., 30–38.

[4] See ibid., 49–95.

[5] See ibid., 101–120. In this chapter he is unable to show any direct thematic connection between 1 En. 2:1–5:2[3] and Old Testament cultic texts that celebrate the covenant between God and his people.

[6] George W.E. NICKELSBURG, *1 Enoch 1. A Commentary on the Book of 1 Enoch, Chapters 1–36; 81–108* (Hermeneia), Minneapolis, MN, Fortress, 2001, 150–158. In the heading of the section on p. 150, Nickelsburg calls 2:1–5:4 "the indictment," a label that can hardly be applied to the section without 5:4. Note that all the texts adduced by Nickelsburg are later than the generally accepted date for the composition of the Book of the Watchers, namely the 3rd c. BCE. It is therefore unseemly that they might in any way bear any influence on the Enochic text. The departure from 5:4 in the interpretation of 2:1–5:2[3] leads Nickelsburg (*1 Enoch 1*, 134) to an all-encompassing statement about 2:1–5:4 as containing the accusations "that the sinners are revisionists who have changed God's commandments." This conclusion can only be applied to 5:4 for 2:1–5:2[3] does not contain accusations against sinners. Matthew BLACK, *The Book of Enoch or I Enoch. A New English Edition with Commentary and Textual Notes* (SVTP, 7), Leiden, Brill, 1985, 109, considers chapters 2–5 to be a nature homily in which the order of nature is contrasted with the disorder of human life. His intuition about the literary genre considerably departs from Harman, Argall and Nickelsburg's approach and is worth pursuing. Note, however, that he does not attach any importance to the literary structure of 2:1–5:2[3] and to the redactional framework within which the exhortation has been positioned.

Ps 104:35).[7] He further classifies the Enochic pericope as an expanded "reproach" or "accusation" section, the first element of the late prophetic form known as the "salvation–judgment oracle."[8] The "topoi" of the creation hymn in 2:1–5:5 serve for the sinners to understand the message of creation before it is too late.[9] Argall's proposal sounds strangely distant from both the literary form and content of 1 En. 2:1–5:2[3], where neither reproach nor accusation is found.

From the literary point of view, the main problem with the opinions discussed above is that they do not seriously take into consideration the distinction between the Aramaic text and the Greek and Ethiopic versions, which are based on a reworked Aramaic *Vorlage*.[10] The Aramaic technical vocabulary about the movement of the stars and the earth has often been omitted in the base text of the versions. Additionally, it is not clear why they interpret verse 5:4 together with the preceding context that evidently has a different literary form. Without verse 5:4 that seems not to belong to the literary structure of 2:1–5:2[3] and evidently presents a distinct form in the Aramaic and Greek/Ethiopic texts, the pericope under consideration can hardly be called a "denouncement speech" or an "accusation" or "indictment" section, part of a salvation-judgment oracle. It is also methodologically questionable to read, understand, and explain the *whole* content of the exhortation and its literary form in the light of *one* verse of the text.

[7] Randal A. ARGALL, *1 Enoch and Sirach. A Comparative Literary and Conceptual Analysis of the Themes of Revelation, Creation and Judgment* (EJL, 8), Atlanta, GA, Scholars, 1995, 101.

[8] Ibid., 101, n. 240, directs the reader to Eckhard RAU, "Kosmologie, Eschatologie und die Lehrautorität Henochs: Traditions- und formgeschichtliche Untersuchungen zum äth. Henochbuch und zu verwandten Schriften," Ph.D. diss., Universität Hamburg, 1974, 106–24, esp. 115, 121. As the heading of the section 2:1–5:4 and 5:5–9 indicates ("oracle of judgment"), G. W. E. NICKELSBURG, *1 Enoch 1*, 150, 159 follows Rau and Argall.

[9] The second element of the "Salvation-judgment oracle" that Argall discusses later in the monograph where the author speaks about the "Divine Warrior" motifs, such as combat and victory over the enemies, victory shout, theophany, salvation of the nations, fertility, universal reign, that are detectable in 1:3c–9 and 5:5–9; see R. A. ARGALL, *1 Enoch and Sirach*, 168–174. The Divine Warrior hymns in late prophetic books tend to adapt and fuse there with the Salvation-Judgment oracles so that in the Enochic text 5:5–9 the attested literary form is that of the second part of the Salvation-Judgment oracle, namely "the announcement of salvation and judgment." Note that any reference to 2:1–5:2[3] is lacking.

[10] For an exemplary distinction between different text witnesses in the interpretation of 1 Enoch 91–108, see Loren T. STUCKENBRUCK, *1 Enoch 91–108* (CEJL, 1), Berlin, de Gruyter, 2007.

The starting point for any qualification concerning the literary genre and setting in life is the Aramaic text from Qumran where the substantial part of the exhortation has been preserved. An analysis of the immediate context of 1 En. 2:1–5:2 on the pages that follow explains 1:9 and 5:4 as a literary and redactional framework for the exhortatory section, which disproves the earlier proposals concerning the literary form of the analyzed text read in conjunction with 5:4. The explanation of the literary structure inherent in the Aramaic text allows the reader to consider the inner dynamics of the exhortation and shows its coherence in the narrative thread of the text. Finally, a closer look at the Aramaic vocabulary of 2:1–5:2 in comparison with other parts of Enochic literature does not point toward biblical texts suggested by the scholars as to its proper background and setting in life, but it rather demonstrates a dependence on the Enochic astronomic tradition attested in the Aramaic/Ethiopic Book of Enoch.[11]

1. Translation

As is the case with some parts of the Book of the Watchers (1 Enoch 1–36), the exhortatory composition is fragmentarily attested in the Aramaic Qumran manuscripts, the full text being preserved in the Greek Panopolitanus Codex,[12] dated to the sixth c. CE, and the much later ancient Ethiopic version that mostly agrees with the Greek. There are five fragments from Qumran cave 4[13] that provide the reader with the Aramaic text that preserves most of the exhortation to observe and contemplate the works of nature. The manuscript 4Q201, the oldest witness of Aramaic Enoch dated to the first half of the second century BCE, if not earlier, contains two fragments. Frg. 3 i preserves the left part of a column where our text begins in line 1 with the last clause of 2:2 and ends in l. 12a with 5:2. Containing one word only, "cloud," frg. 4 supplements frg. 3 i in line 4, standing at its beginning. Verses 1–3 of chapter 2 have been partially preserved in 4Q204 frg. 1 4–8 that makes part of the

[11] See § 4 in this research.

[12] The text of the codex here bears the siglum "G^{C-1}."

[13] All the Aramaic fragments of 1 Enoch are subsumed under the siglum "A." The Ethiopic readings bear the siglum "E." For the readings cited in original languages in this paper, see Henryk Drawnel, *Qumran Cave 4. The Aramaic Books of Enoch. 4Q201, 4Q202, 4Q204, 4Q205, 4Q206, 4Q207, 4Q212*, Oxford, Oxford University Press, 2019, *s.l.*

manuscript dated to the last third of the first century BCE. Finally, frgs. 2 and 3 i (3:1–5:1) of the same manuscript overlap in some places with 4Q201 frg. 3 i, providing thus the Aramaic text with some supplementary material.

The Aramaic fragments contain a text that is shorter in comparison with the Aramaic *Vorlage* of the Panopolitanus manuscript and the Ethiopic version. The Greek version reads only the beginning of 2:3 and 3:1, omitting by parablepsis the whole 4:1 and the beginning of 5:1.[14] The wording of the two versions is oftentimes different from the Aramaic, making it clear that their Aramaic underlying text was not identical with the one preserved at Qumran. One clause in 4Q201 frg. 3 i 3 ("[that] its whole work [pa]sses over it") is absent in the two versions. The Panopolitanus, usually followed by the Ethiopic, sometimes omits the literary structure marker "see!" together with the important interpretative term "signs." The redactor of the Aramaic text that underlies the Greek version evidently adapts 2:1–5:2 to its new context with the considerable reworking and expansion of 5:2 (4 clauses speak about obedience of all God's works),[15] the addition of 5:3 (seas and rivers follow God's command), and the accent laid on the lack of the observance of God's commandments by the sinners in 5:4.

The notes that follow are based on the Aramaic text whose most part has been preserved in the Qumran fragments. The text in square brackets has been tentatively retranslated on the basis of the Greek or Ethiopic versions, in accordance with the size of the lacuna; it is not taken into consideration in the proposed analyses. If needed, the Greek or Ethiopic lexeme is adduced for consideration where the Aramaic is missing. Table 1 contains the English translation of the composite Aramaic text divided into strophes in accordance with its literary markers, syntactic division, and content as expounded in § 3.1.

[14] The omission is caused by an error in copying the text and as such does not bear on the textual relationship with the Aramaic text.

[15] The size of a lacuna has some bearing on the interpretation of the text, as is the case in 1 En. 5:2, where the Greek text evidently does not fit into the short missing space in 4Q201 3 i 11–12.

Table 1. Translation of the composite Aramaic text of 1 En. 2:1–5:2[16]

4Q201 frg. 3 i + 4 1–12a (2:1–5:3)
4Q204 frg. 1 3–8 (2:1–2:3)
4Q204 frgs. 2–3 i 1–7 (3:1–5:1)

Strophe	Text[17]	
I.	a. [2:1] [Consider] **every sig[n,]**	b. **[and ob]serve the work of the sk[y,]**
	c. [how they do not change their paths] **in the positions of their [lumi]naries,**	d. **that all of them [a]ri[se and set,]**
	e. [and during their appointed times they appe]ar	f. and do not transgre[ss] in their course.
II.	a. [2:2] **Obser[ve] the earth**	b. **and consider** its **work**
	c. [that is executed, from the begin]ning to the end,	d. without being changed,
	e. and **everything is vi[si]b**le **to you**.	
III.	a. [2:3] Observe the signs [of summer]	b. [that] its whole work [pa]sses over it,
	c. and the signs of win**ter**	d. **that** the **wh**ole earth [fills with water]
	e. [as] the clouds and d[ew] and rain pour upon it.	
IV.	a. [3:1] Observe that all the tre[es] are as withered	b. [and all their leaves are falling,]
	c. [except] for fourteen trees whose leaves are long-lasting	d. [because they are not renewed]
	e. [unt]il two or three years pass.[18]	

[16] The longest and best preserved is the text of 4Q201 frg. 3 i + 4 1–12a (2:1–5:2). Its comparison with the Aramaic base of the Greek Panopolitanus shows a shorter textual form found in the Qumran manuscript. The changes include not only involuntary scribal errors but also deliberate, that is literary interventions. There exists a discernible tendency to adjust the base text of the Panopolitanus in 1 En. 2:1–5:3 to the context of 1:3b–9 and 5:4–9 in which the section now stands.

[17] For the Aramaic text of 4Q201 frg. 3 i 1–12a, 4Q204 1 3–8, 4Q204 2–3 i 1–7, see H. DRAWNEL, *Qumran Cave 4*, 87 (reconstruction: 91–92), 204 (reconstruction: 205), 210–11 (reconstruction: 212).

[18] The G-stem suffix periphrastic conjugation ה֯ו֯י֯ה֯ ע֯ב֯ר֯ן in the temporal clause (עד ד[י֯; 4Q201 frg. 3 i 6) is at first sight unusual. Its relative valence has most probably to be interpreted in relation to the preceding context where several participles express the durative or iterative aspect denoting the general present. It seems that the perfect expresses here the anteriority of the action (passing of two or three years) before the arrival of new foliage; the periphrastic conjugation stresses the durative character of the action. For the *futurum*

Strophe	Text	
V.	a. 4:1 Observe the signs [of summer] c. and you seek shade and shelter from it [upon the burning earth,]	b. [whereby[19] the sun bu]rns and scorches[20]; d. [and] you are not able [to tre]ad on the soil and on the stones because of [the burning.]
VI.	[a. 5:1a Consider all] the [t]rees, (c) and cover [the trees]	b. their leaves on them are beautiful green d. [and all their fruit is (brought forth) for spl]endor of praise.
VII.	a. 5:1b Examine [and] consider all these works, c. [that God who lives] for ever and ever fashioned all these works. d. 5:2 Year [after year they do not change their work,]	b. [and understand] e. [but] all of them do his bidding.

Notes[21]

I.a. דג[ל] "sig[n"] **A** | τὰ ἔργα **G**$^{\text{C-1}}$ | > **E** •
I.b. וחז]וא לכון] ["and ob]serve" **A** | > **G**$^{\text{C-1}}$ **E** •
I.b. לעובד "the work" **A E** | > **G**$^{\text{C-1}}$ (hmt.) •
I.b ש]מיא] "sk[y"] **A** | ἐν τῷ οὐρανῷ **G**$^{\text{C-1}}$ •
I.c. במסורת "in the positions" **A** | > **G**$^{\text{C-1}}$ **E** •
I.c. נה]יריהון] ["lumi]naries" **A** | foll τοὺς ἐν τῷ οὐρανῷ **G**$^{\text{C-1}}$ **E** •
I.e. Probably om. 4Q204 1 6 •
I.e. [מעדיהן] ["their appointed times"] **A** | ταῖς ἑορταῖς αὐτῶν **G**$^{\text{C-1}}$ | > **E** •

exactum in Official Aramaic and in the Aramaic of Daniel, see Holger GZELLA, *Tempus, Aspekt und Modalität im Reichsaramäischen* (VOK, 48), Wiesbaden, Harrassowitz, 2004, 232–36. For the future anterior expressed by the verb in perfect in BH, see 2 Kgs 7:3; cf. Paul JOÜON, Takamitsu MURAOKA, *A Grammar of Biblical Hebrew* (SubBi, 27), 2nd ed., Rome, Gregorian and Biblical Press, 2011, 335, § 112i.

[19] The interpretation of the prepositional expression בהון (4Q204 2 2 [4:1]) depends on the debated meaning of דגלי "signs" to which the pronominal suffix anaphorically refers. In 1 En. 82:16 the signs of spring are, among others, sweat and heat, while the signs of summer in 82:19 include heat and drought. Read in that context, the preposition -ב in בהון should be interpreted instrumentally: the signs of summer (especially heat and burning [cf. "burning" *wəʿyā* in **E**, 4:1]) are the means with which the sun sears and boils, the two verbs being used intransitively, the results of the burning sun upon humanity and the earth being described in the rest of 4:1. The Comprehensive Aramaic Lexicon (cal.huc.edu, under כוי) considers the prepositional expression בהון to be an object of the two following verbs: "[the su]n sears and cooks them." In light of the whole context of the clause and the meaning of the "signs of summer," the CAL understanding is unuual: the sun cannot "cook" the signs of summer.

[20] Lit. "boils," 4Q201 3 i 7, see H. DRAWNEL, *Qumran Cave 4*, 96.

[21] For more detailed notes, see ibid., 93–98, 208–9.

II.c. לסופה “to the end” **A** | foll ὥς εἶσιν φθαρτά **G**$^{C-1}$ | > **E** •

II.d. משתנא “changes” **A** | foll οὐδὲν τῶν ἐπὶ γῆς **G**$^{C-1}$ | > **E** •

II.e. כלה “everything” **A** | foll ἔργα θεοῦ **G**$^{C-1}$ **E** •

III.a. לדגלי “the signs” **A** | > **G**$^{C-1}$ **E** •

III.b. om. (parabl.) **G**$^{C-1}$ **E** •

III.c. לדגלי “the signs” **A** | > **G**$^{C-1}$ **E** •

III.d.–e. **A E** | om. (parabl.) **G**$^{C-1}$ •

IV.a. חזו “Observe” **A** | prec καταμάθετε καὶ **G**$^{C-1}$ **E** •

IV.a. כיבישין “as withered” **A** | prec **እሬ፡ ያስተርእዩ፡ E** | om until VI.a. (parabl.) **G**$^{C-1}$ •

IV.b. Reconstructed on the basis of **E** •

IV.d Reconstructed on the basis of 4Q204 frg. 2 5 (5:1) | **አላ፡ ይጸንሑ፡ እምብሉይ ፡ E** •

IV. e עד ד[י] [un]til A | foll **ይመጽእ፡ ኃዲስ፡ E** •

V.a חזו “Observe” **A** | prec **ወዳግመ፡** E •

V.a לדגלי “the signs” **A** | **መዋዕለ፡ E** •

V.b [כוי]ה ושלקה [“bu]rns and scorches” **A** | > **E** •

V.b ושלקה “and scorches” **A** | foll **በቀዳሚሃ፡ E** •

V.b לא תשכחון “you are not able” **A** | order; prec **ወአንትሙሰ፡ E** •

VI.b ישפרון “are beautiful” 4Q201 3 i 9 | יתח[דתון] 4Q204 2 5 | > **G**$^{C-1}$ **E** •

VI.c עליהן “their leaves” **A** | τὰ φύλλα **G**$^{C-1}$ **E** •

VI.d לה]דר תשבוחה “for] splendor of praise” **A** (**G**$^{C-1}$) | > **E** •

VII.a. דרשו “examine!” 4Q201 frg. 3 i 10 | διανοήθητε (?) **G**$^{C-1}$ | הל]לו 4Q204 frg. 2 6 | > **E** •

VII.a. אתבוננו “consider!” **A** | γνῶτε (?) **G**$^{C-1}$ | **ሉበዉ፡ E** •

VII.a. אלין “these” **A** | αὐτοῦ **G**$^{C-1}$ | > **E** •

VII.b. [אסתכלו] [“understand”]; reconstruction based on νοήσατε **G**$^{C-1}$ = **አእምሩ፡ E** •

VII.c. כל עבדיה אלין “all these works” **A** | **G**$^{C-1}$ αὐτὰ οὕτως | > **E** •

VII.d Reconstruction hypothetical; **G**$^{C-1}$ **E** expand **A** •

VII.d.–e. **G**$^{C-1}$ **E** rework and expand •

VII.e > **G**$^{C-1}$ **E** •

VII.e. foll 1 En. 5:3 **G**$^{C-1}$ **E** | 1 En. 5:3 > 4Q201 3 i •

2. The Context of 1 En. 2:1–5:2

In his commentary on 1 Enoch Dillmann distinguishes between God’s theophany and judgment described in 1:3b–9 and the following literary section 2:1–5:3 that speaks about the works of the heaven and earth.[22]

[22] August Dillmann, *Das Buch Henoch*, Leipzig, Vogel, 1853, 90–91. Some early exegetes followed Dillmann, seeing 2:1–5:3 as a literary unit, see Georg Beer, “Das Buch Henoch,” in: Emil Kautzsch (ed.), *Die Apokryphen und Pseudepigraphen des Alten Testaments. Zweiter Band: Die Pseudepigraphen des Alten Testaments*, Tübingen, Mohr Siebeck, 1900,

The latter begins, quite unexpectedly, with an address formulated in the 2nd person plural to an unspecified audience and being exhortatory in tone attracts the attention to the working of the heaven and earth. Since in 1:9 the description of God's theophany abruptly ends, the beginning of the new section where the form and content are different seems to be neither properly introduced nor prepared.

On the other hand, in the proclamation of God's coming for judgment against the ungodly and sinners in 1:9, His wrath comes on account of all works of their impiety (περὶ πάντων ἔργων τῆς ἀσεβείας αὐτῶν). Since behind the Greek ἔργων[23] there stands the Aramaic **עבדי** "works" (4Q204 1 2), the term is a catchword that introduces the main topic of the following section 2:1–5:2, which is the work of the heaven and earth, cf. **לעבד ש]מיא]** "work of the sk[y]" (4Q204 1 4 [2:1]) and **בעבד]ה]** "[its] work" (4Q204 frg. 1 6 [2:2]). The parallelism is, however, formal for in 1:9 and 5:4 the noun **עבד** "work" denotes human godless behavior, while in 2:1–5:2 – the harmonious work of the universe.

The same catchword **עבד** stands in 5:4a (4Q201 3 i 12b) connecting the clause with 1:9 and with the immediately preceding 5:1b–2. In a similar manner, verse 5:4b where the disobedience of the hard-hearted who speak arrogant and harsh words (**רברבן וקשין** 4Q201 3 i 13) against God's majesty takes up the same expression from 1:9 (**רברבן וקשין** 4Q204 1 3; **G**[C-1] σκληρῶν ὧν ἐλάλησαν λόγων). Thus, it shows the continuation of the theme of judgment against the sinners and ungodly that begins in 1:3b–9 and continues in 5:5–6.[24] One can therefore conclude that the same vocabulary and expressions used in 1:9 and 5:4a–b form an inclusion that enshrines 2:1–5:2 within its immediate literary context.[25]

217–310, esp. 221, and Robert Henry CHARLES, *The Book of Enoch or 1 Enoch. Translated from the Editor's Ethiopic Text*, Oxford, Clarendon, 1912, 8, n. to 2:1–5:3. Adolphe LODS, *Le livre d'Hénoch. Fragments grecs découverts à Akhmîm (Haute-Égypte) publiés avec les variantes du texte éthiopien traduits et annotés*, Paris, Ernest Leroux, 1892, 104–5 is probably the first to read 1 En. 5:4 together with the preceding context.

[23] G[C-1] adds πάντων.

[24] G. W. E. NICKELSBURG, *1 Enoch 1*, 152, 157 considers 5:4 to be in part a doublet of 1:9 and as a "closing bracket" of 2:1–5:3, where 1:9 is an "opening bracket." From the literary point of view the two verses are indeed "brackets" but serve as redactional catchwords within which the exhortation has been placed. They therefore do not "open" or "close" the poem for they do not make part of its thematic or literary structure. Following in the same vein, he affirms that in 5:4 "the author now explicates the conclusion to which the whole section [2:1–5:3, HD] has been leading" (ibid., 157) From the literary analysis of the poem there results that 5:1b–2 (strophe VII) concludes 2:1–5:2, see § 3.1 below.

[25] Thus 5:4 it does not close the literary unit 2:1–5:4, as claimed by R. A. ARGALL, *1 Enoch and Sirach*, 101, n. 239.

In the Aramaic text the end of the literary section 2:1–5:2 is marked off in 5:1b–2 (strophe VII) with an exhortation to consider all God's works in order to apprehend and understand Him as their maker. The Aramaic line that concludes the section in 5:2 (4Q201 3 i 11–12) is shorter than the Greek and Ethiopic versions, the latter two containing a redactional reworking and expansion of the attested Aramaic.[26] While it assumes no more than two short clauses, the second one being actually attested in the Aramaic manuscript, the Greek text reads four clauses, the last one bearing some resemblance to the Aramaic (4Q201 frg. 3 i 12), while the last but one being taken from 2:1 and 2:2 in order to create an inclusion with the beginning of the literary section.[27]

The first clause preserved in Aramaic at the beginning of 5:4 directed to the sinners is a mere statement, not an exhortation, and introduces a different topic from the one debated in 2:1–5:2. The new verse does not exhort to do the intellectual work of observing, researching and understanding the heavenly and earthly phenomena but chastises an unspecified group of listeners for a lack of moral incoherence. The adversative *waw* and the emphatically placed independent pronoun introduce a new literary and thematic unit: ואנתן שניתן עבדכן "but you, you have changed you work" (4Q201 frg. 3 i 12). The second person plural applied in the imperative throughout 2:1–5:2 constitutes a rhetorical device convenient to the redactor who in 5:4 can continue addressing the sinners changing the tone to accusatory.[28] The imperative, however, that plays the constitutive literary role in the exhortation is not used anymore.

By the recourse to the noun עבד "work, deed" the text in 5:4 shows the connection with the main topic of 2:1–5:2, perhaps especially with 2:2 (עבדה "its work" 4Q201 frg. 3 i 1) and with the concluding section 5:1b–2 (4Q201 frg. 3 i 10–12) where the same term "work" is frequent. In addition to that, the verb שניתן "you have changed" directly opposes the rebellious behavior of the targeted group with the work of the earth that

[26] **G**$^{C-1}$ καὶ τὰ ἔργα αὐτοῦ πάντα ὅσα ἐποίησεν εἰς τοὺς αἰῶνας ἀπὸ ἐνιαυτοῦ εἰς ἐνιαυτὸν γινόμενα πάντα οὕτως, καὶ πάντα ὅσα ἀποτελοῦσιν αὐτῷ τὰ ἔργα, καὶ οὐκ ἀλλοιοῦνται αὐτῶν τὰ ἔργα, ἀλλ᾽ ὡσπερεὶ κατὰ ἐπιταγὴν τὰ πάντα γίνεται.

[27] **G**$^{C-1}$ καὶ οὐκ ἀλλοιοῦνται αὐτῶν τὰ ἔργα; cf. 2:1: **G**$^{C-1}$ πῶς οὐκ ἠλλοίωσαν τὰς ὁδοὺς αὐτῶν; 2:2: ὡς οὐκ ἀλλοιοῦνται; for a discussion of the changes in 5:2, see H. Drawnel, *Qumran Cave 4*, 98.

[28] G. W. E. NICKELSBURG, *1 Enoch 1*, 157 affirms that the theme of the wicked deeds and harsh words that appears in 1:9 and 5:4 constitutes two parallel units that not only bracket the exposition of 2:1–5:3 but also determine its meaning. His is rather a reductionist opinion for the discussed passage has its meaning on its own, quite different from what precedes and follows. The redactional work seen in 5:4 proves that point clearly enough.

לא משתנא "does not change" (4Q201 frg. 3 i 2 [2:2]).[29] Thus the redactor does not refer to the central conclusion of the whole exhortation in 5:1b (God as the maker of all these works, strophe VII.c) but selectively chooses a topic convenient for pursuing the condemnation of the sinners announced in 1:9, reintroduced in 5:4 and developed in 5:5–6.

To the same redactional work in the Aramaic base text of the Greek, as well as in the Ethiopic, version there must be ascribed the inclusion of 5:3, absent in Aramaic (4Q201 frg. 3 i 12), that exhorts to consider the obedient working of the sea and rivers. Its insertion between 5:2 and 5:4 is secondary for the examples taken from the world of nature end in 5:1a (strophe VI.d) while verse 5:3 evidently reuses the phrases from 5:2 (G^{C-1}).[30] All these data allow us to consider the shorter version of 5:2 attested in 4Q201 frg. 3 i 11–12 as the original conclusion of the exhortation that begins in 2:1. The apostrophe concerning the sinners who have changed their works and do not God's bidding (5:4, 5–6b) followed by the praise of the righteous elect (5:6c–8) are two pieces of the same diptych characterized by different themes and different literary form.

Taking into account all the redactional work in 5:3–4, the content of the Aramaic line in 5:4a and the following accusation of apostasy in 5:4b, it is necessary to conclude that the Aramaic redactor considers 5:4 as transitory from 2:1–5:2 to the next part of the new literary section that begins in 5:5.[31] Except for the first sentence attested in Aramaic in 5:4a, the rest of 5:4–9 does not share its vocabulary with 2:1–5:2, an additional argument for considering 2:1–5:2 as an independent literary unit.

3. Literary Structure and Genre

The pericope 2:1–5:2 has a well-defined literary structure that marks its inner division and thematic development. The accent laid in the text on the exhortatory tone implied in all the seven strophes of the composition

[29] The Panopolitanus version reads two different verbs that make the relationship with the preceding context much less evident: "you have neither abided by, nor acted according to His commandments," G^{C-1} οὐκ ἐνεμείνατε οὐδὲ ἐποιήσατε κατὰ τὰς ἐντολὰς αὐτοῦ. The noun τὰς ἐντολὰς assumes פקוד rather than עבד.

[30] G^{C-1} ἀποτελοῦσιν καὶ οὐκ ἀλλοιοῦσιν αὐτῶν τὰ ἔργα. The example of seas and rivers appears as out of context here where cyclic astronomical and meteorological phenomena are discussed. Perhaps to the inclusion of these two items has contributed 1 En. 17:5, where in an "astronomical" context the river of fire flows into the sea of the west; cf. also 1 En. 32:2. In light of evident redactional work in 5:3, it is unlikely to claim with G. W. E. Nickelsburg, *1 Enoch 1*, 157, that the verse belongs to the original text and may have been displaced from between 2:2 and 2:3 or 5:1a and 5:1b.

[31] Note the literary marker אדין (4Q201 3 i 14) / τοιγὰρ (G^{C-1}) at the beginning of 5:5.

determines the qualification of its literary genre distinct from the preceding and following sections.

3.1. Structure

In stark contrast with the preceding and following context, the pericope 2:1–5:2 exhorts listeners to contemplate the celestial and earthly phenomena observable on the sky and on the earth. The author of this short composition written in the balanced prose style[32] has marked off each "stanza" or strophe with one or two verbs in imperative that open up the subsequent literary unit dedicated to a different topic.[33] The exhortation to scrutinize כול דג[ל] "all sign" (4Q204 1 4; G^{C-1} "all the works") in the opening sentence (I.a) introduces the main topic, namely the steady and regular movement of the heavenly and earthly phenomena produced by the heaven and earth and legible in their "signs."

The two verbs "to see" and to "consider" open up each literary section, marking thus the inner division of the text. The *peal* verb "to see" from the root ḤZY and the *ithpolel* "to watch, to consider" or "to investigate" from the root BYN are used interchangeably at the beginning of the strophes, whether in one or two successive clauses. The verb הללו "to extoll, to praise" in 4Q204 2 6 (5:1b) used instead of דרשו "to examine, to inquire"[34] (4Q201 3 i 10) is not attested in the versions. It was introduced

[32] L. HARTMAN, *Asking for a Meaning*, 13, recognizes 2:1–5:3 as "something like a rhytmical or poetic prose, which, in addition, is artistically built." His later presentation of its structure (pp. 16–18) is marred by the inclusion of 5:3 (his 4th part aa–cc) and 5:4 (4th part, bb–cc) and by the lack of distinction between the Aramaic text on the one hand and the Greek/Ethiopic version on the other. He bases his structure on the work of E. RAU, "Kosmologie, Eschatologie und die Lehrautorität Henochs," 68–70, who, however, had no access to the Aramaic form of the text. Hartman was in a better position for Milik's book with the Aramaic fragments was published in 1976, well before the publication of Hartman's monograph.

[33] R. A. ARGALL, *1 Enoch and Sirach*, 103, noted the verbs in imperative but since he did not study the literary structure of the passage, he did not note their literary function. G. W. E. NICKELSBURG, *1 Enoch 1*, 152, prefers to see the structure of 2:1–5:2[3] in conjunction with 1:8–9 and 5:5–6. He explains the whole as having a chiastic structure, where 2:1b–5:1c constitute its central part enshrined by 2:1a (part C: "contemplate the works") and 5:1d (part C': "contemplate all these works"). The inclusion of 1:8 and 5:5–6 in the literary structure is rather unwarranted by the analysis for these two texts make part of independent literary sections different in style and discussed themes (judgment over the sinners), just as the verses 1:9 (B) and 5:4 (B'). His parts C and C' based on a partial parallelism between 2:1a and 5:1d unduly separate the two verses from the rest of the composition in 2:1–5:2. The American exegete leaves the inner structure of the "central" section 2:1b–5:1c without an additional comment.

[34] For the reading דרשו, see H. DRAWNEL, *Qumran Cave 4*, 87, and note to l. 10 on p. 89. The reading חק[רו] by M. BLACK, *The Book of Enoch or I Enoch*, 328, is paleographically untenable and should rather be abandoned.

in the former manuscript under the influence of the preceding context (VI.d, 5:1a) with its terminology of glory and praise that assumes God as its referent.[35] An expansion of the literary pattern occurs in strophe IV of the composition where the Panopolitanus followed by the Ethiopic version adds the imperative καταμάθετε καὶ "perceive and" (G^{C-1} 3:1) not attested in Aramaic (4Q201 frg. 3 i 4).

The *peal* imperative חזו begins strophes II–V,[36] while, judging from versional evidence,[37] the *ithpolel* imperative אתבוננו probably begins strophe I (2:1)[38] and VI (5:1a); it is attested at the beginning of strophe VII (5:1b) accompanied by דרשו "to examine."

Table 2. Literary structure markers in 2:1–5:2

Strophe	Lexeme	Qumran reference (A)	Verse	Ms. Panopolitanus (G^{C-1})	*G ə'əz* (E)
I.a.	[אתבוננו]	4Q204 frg. 1 3	2:1	Κατανοήσατε	ጠይቁ፡
I.b.	[ח]זוא לכון	4Q204 frg. 1 4	2:1	———	———
II.a.	חז̊[ו]	4Q201 frg. 3 i 1 and 4Q204 frg. 1 6 (2:2)	2:2	ἴδετε	ርእይዋ፡
II.b.	אׄתׄבׄוׄננו	4Q201 frg. 3 i 1 and 4Q204 frg. 1 6 (2:2)	2:2	διανοήθητε	ለብዉ፡
III.a.	חזו	4Q201 frg. 3 i 2–3	2:3	ἴδετε	ርእይዎ፡
IV.a.	חזו	4Q201 frg. 3 i 4	3:1	(καταμάθετε καὶ) ἴδετε	(ጠይቁ፡ ወ)ርእዩ፡
V.a.	חזו לכן	4Q201 3 i 6	4:1	———	ጠይቁ፡
VI.a.	[אתבוננו]	4Q201 3 i 9	5:1a	———	ጠይቁ፡

[35] Cf. Józef T. MILIK, with the collaboration of Matthew Black, *The Books of Enoch. Aramaic Fragments of Qumrân Cave 4*, Oxford, Clarendon, 1976, 149.

[36] 4Q201 3 i 1 (2:2 = 4Q204 1 6), 2 (2:3), 4 (3:1), 6 (4:1).

[37] See H. DRAWNEL, *Qumran Cave 4*, 96, 208.

[38] Note that after the first, missing verb, there follows in synonymous parallelism the imperative of חזי, see 4Q204 1 4 (2:1). The opposite situation is found at the beginning of strophe II (2:2) opened by the imperative of חזי (II.a) and supplemented by אתבוננו (II.b), see 4Q204 1 6 (2:2).

Strophe	Lexeme	Qumran reference (A)	Verse	Ms. Panopolitanus (G^{C-1})	*G ə'əz* (E)
VII.a.	דרשו	4Q201 3 i 10	5:1b	(γνῶτε?)	———
VII.a.	ה̊[ל]ל̇[ו]	4Q204 frg. 2 6		———	———
VII.a.	ו̇א̊תבוננו	4Q201 3 i 10	5:1b	διανοήθητε	ለብዉ :
VII.b.	[אסתכלו̇]	4Q201 3 i 11	5:1b	νοήσατε	አእምሩ :

The last strophe of the speech (VII) diverts the eyes and mind of the observers from the heavenly and earthly phenomena to eternal God who as living for ever is the only responsible for the existence of these works. The verse that concludes the whole poem in 5:2 (4Q201 frg. 1 3 i 11–12a) conveying its most important point adds the last note to this theological perspective by stressing the cyclic, yearly character of the work of the heaven and earth and its obedience to God's word or command. It also reminds the reader of the unchangeable character of the heavenly and earthly works, forming thus and *inclusio* with 2:1c that discusses the unchangeable nature of the work of the heavenly luminaries.

The verbs in imperative that open each strophe are followed by subordinate object or relative clauses (I.c–f; II.c–e; III.b–e; IVaα–c; V.b; VIIb) or by paratactic sentences (I. e–f; V.c–d; VI.b–d; VII.c–d); in both cases these clauses give examples of what is subject to observation to which the main clauses exhort. In strophe VII the last two sentences construed paratactically do not depend on the imperatives in VII.a–b. Strophe I contains six clauses, strophes II, III,[39] IV, VII – 5 clauses, while strophes V and VI – 4 clauses.

Table 3. Literary structure of 1 En. 2:1–5:2

	Part 1: Observation of the work of the sky and earth		
Strophe	**1.1. Work of the sky**		
I.	Every sign and work of heaven	2:1	4Q204 1 4–5; 4Q201 3 i 1
	1.2. Work of the earth		
II.	The earth and all its work	2:2	4Q201 3 i 1–2; 4Q204 1 6–7

[39] At the beginning of strophe IIIc, the verb is absent but the preposition ב in ובדגלי "and the signs" (4Q201 3 i 3 [2:3]) signals the verb [אתבוננוא] just as in 4Q201 3 i 1 and 4Q204 1 6. The verb, however, is absent in Aramaic and in the versions, which is unusual because the imperative חזו "observe" at the beginning of strophe III (4Q201 3 i 2 [2:2] introduces its object with a *lamed* and thus it can hardly govern ובדגלי. One perhaps may consider the omission of the verb as an example of ellipsis that signals the presence of אתבוננוא with the preposition *beth*.

	Part 2: Observation of the signs of summer and winter		
	2.1 Signs of summer and winter		
III.	Signs of summer and winter	2:3	4Q201 3–4 i 2–4; 4Q204 1 8
	2.2 Signs of winter		
IV.	All the trees withered	3:1	4Q201 3 i 4; 4Q204 2–3 i 1–2
	2.3 Signs of summer		
V.	Signs of summer	4:1	4Q201 3 i 6–7; 4Q204 2–3 i 3–4
VI.	All the trees beautiful and green	5:1a	4Q201 3 i 9–10; 4Q204 2–3 i 5–6
	Part 3 (Conclusion): Living God as the maker of all these works		
VII.	All these works	5:1b–2	4Q201 3 i 10–12; 4Q204 2–3 i 6–7

The formal elements in the exhortatory speech structure it into seven strophes divided into three parts in accordance with the change of the debated theme. Part 1 contains two strophes whose main topic is the work of the sky (strophe I) and of the earth (strophe II). Strophe II is parallel to strophe I for it discusses in a general mode the regular and unchangeable work of the earth stressing that the earthly phenomena are all perceptible to the observers. On the other hand, it introduces strophes III–VI that discuss in more detail the earthly phenomena: signs of the seasons, meteorology and trees. The concluding part 3 is composed of one strophe only in which the regular work of the sky and earth is given for consideration together with eternal God as its maker to whose commanding word it remains faithful (strophe VII). The concept of עבד "work" in strophes I and II and the theme of not transgressing/changing the course/ link the beginning with the conclusion (strophe VII). In the second part of the composition (strophes III–VI) the composer focuses on the perception of the sings of the earth that is the two seasons, summer and winter, accompanying agricultural and meteorological phenomena, and the trees.

The vocabulary of the first part of strophe III (a+b) ("signs," "work") links it with the preceding context (Ia+b; IIb) but at the same time prepares the main topic of strophe V ("signs of summer"). The second part of strophe III (c–e) speaks about the "sings of winter" and the observation of the leaves falling off the trees in strophe IV evidently has to be read in connection with its preceding context. In a similar vein, the "signs of summer," mostly expressed by the burning sun in strophe V and human reaction to it, are followed in strophe VI by the observation of the beauty of the trees and their fruits. The "signs of winter" consist in the meteorological phenomena such as clouds, rain, dew that bring water on the earth (IIIc–e). In contradistinction to strophe III, the "signs of summer" are limited to the sun that burns and scorches, which has rather negative impact on the human beings. Any meteorological phenomenon such as "burning" is not directly cited, yet the two verbs "to burn" and "to scorch" signal about what kind of signs of summer the author intends to speak. The description of the human reaction to the heat of the sun in strophe V.c–d is evidently directed to the listeners of the exhortation and it rather cannot be included into the concept of the "signs of summer."

The theme of the eternal God who made these works and to whose command they are obedient appears in the concluding strophe only, constituting thus the focal point in the narrative thread of the composition. The reasoning proceeds from the perception and understanding of the cyclic works of the heaven and earth to the intellectual perception and understanding that the living God made these works. The central statement in strophe VII is clause VII.c that speaks about the ever-living God who brought the perceptible world with its cyclic phenomena into existence.[40]

3.2. Genre

As even a cursory reading makes it rather evident, the literary unit 2:1–5:2 is an exhortatory speech in which the speaker invites his audience to scrutinize and understand the regular and cyclic work of the heavenly and earthly phenomena in order to arrive in the last resort at the understanding of the ever-living God as their maker. In the rest of 1:1–5:9 the exhortation as a literary form is not attested and a different topic of the coming judgment of the sinners is dominant.

An exhortation with a well-defined literary structure such as in 2:1–5:2 and with the consideration of the work of the heaven and earth is not present in 1 Enoch. The exhortatory section 1 En. 101:1–9 whose text is

[40] By including 5:4 into the structure of 2:1–5:2[3] and concentrating on its interpretation, neither Hartman nor Nickelsburg and Argall recognized the importance of strophe VII, especially VII.c (God as creator of all these works) for the argumentation presented in the whole poem. G. W. E. NICKELSBURG, *1 Enoch 1*, 157 stresses 5:2 as the basic point of the whole section: "nature's faithful obedience to God's command" so that he may affirm that in 5:4 the author explains "the conclusion to which the whole section has been leading," namely the judgment on the sinners. For a similar perspective, see L. HARTMAN, *Asking for a Meaning*, 80–90; R. A. ARGALL, *1 Enoch and Sirach*, 101–107, mostly follows Nickelsburg's translation of the text and his general approach.

later that 2:1–5:2 opens in v. 1 with a similar call to observe the deeds of the Most High,[41] but the second part of the verse introduces the motif of fear[42] necessary for avoiding God's wrath. The rest of the section adduces examples showing that the world of nature is part of God's judgment against rebellious humanity,[43] but the motif of the signs of the heaven and earth that demonstrates their cyclic movement is absent. Except for the first verse the verbs in imperative are not attested and the structure of the passage is completely different from 1 En. 2:1–5:2. In a similar way, the exhortation to the righteous dead in 1 En. 102:4–11 opens up with verbs in the imperative in the first two verses only (4–5), while the motif of the signs of the heaven and earth are absent there altogether. In both cases the literary or thematic similarities with 1 En. 2:1–5:2 are rather insignificant.[44]

The exhortatory form chosen for such a presentation is something new in relation to what we know about Enochic astronomy. Its application to what we find in Enochic tradition should perhaps be considered as a pedagogical or didactic attempt to instil into the listeners/students the ability to attentively observe the regular and cyclic motion of the work of the heaven and the earth. The main purpose, though, is theological, namely the perception of God's creating presence which keeps the heaven and earth moving through His commanding word. The pedagogical thrust in Enochic astronomy is especially seen in 1 En. 81:5–6 where the angels leave Enoch on the earth to teach his son Methuselah and other Enoch's children.[45] Yet the exhortation focuses on the observation of the heavenly and earthly phenomena and has evidently a broader character, being directed to an unspecified audience, most probably adepts of Enochic astronomy, that only a later redactor in 5:4 identified with the sinners. From this perspective, the intended goal of 2:1–5:2 is not the chastisement for the sins committed

[41] G^{CM} κατανοήσατε; see also 1 En. 101:4: "Look (G^{CM} [ὁρᾶ]τε) at the captains who sail the sea." These are the only two places where the formal resemblance to 1 En. 2:1–5:2 may be noted.

[42] See 1 En. 101:1, 5, 7, 9.

[43] Speaking proud and hard things against God's majesty in 101:3 recalls 1:9 and 5:4, but not 2:1–5:2. L. T. STUCKENBRUCK, *1 Enoch 91–108*, 474, n. 822 proposes to see the influence of 1 En. 2:1–5:3 on 101:6a–7a, but the only possible point of contact is the relation of 101:6a (the sea and its waters and its movement are the work of the Most High) with 5:3 (the seas and the rivers do not change their work), the latter being a later redactional addition.

[44] See also 1 En. 91:2–4 (exhortatory speech of Enoch directed to his sons); 94:1–5 (moral exhortation of the two ways); 94:1–5 (exhortation to the righteous); 96:1–3 (exhortation to the righteous); 97:1–2 (exhortation to the righteous); 98:3–5 (preparation of the righteous for the last judgment); 104:9 (exhortation to the sinners not to err in the heart and lie).

[45] See 1 En. 82:1; 83:1; 85:1–2; cf. 91:1–3.

but an invitation to a reasoning which from the observation of the empirically verifiable data leads to the apprehension of empirically unverifiable theological assertion: God's creating and upholding power at work in the observable periodic laws governing the universe.

4. Relationship with Enochic Astronomy

The following sketchy notes attempt to point out the existing relationship of 1 En. 2:1–5:2 to the Enochic astronomical tradition.[46] The available material stemming from that tradition has been preserved in the Ethiopic Astronomical Book (EAB), in the fragmentary Aramaic manuscripts from Qumran (4Q208–4Q211; AAB) that partially overlap with Ethiopic evidence. Although most of Enochic astronomy is composed of schematic computations based on arithmetic calculations rather than actual observation,[47] it cannot function without the basic interest and inquiry into the cyclic movement of the universe to which the exhortation politely invites.[48]

4.1 The Regular Work of the Heavenly Luminaries and the Earth[49]

The two expressions "work of the sky" ([עובד ש[מיא, 4Q204 1 4 [2:1]) and work of the earth (עבדה, 4Q201 3 i 1 [2:2]) are the main object of

[46] Considering 1 Enoch 1–5 to be an introduction to the whole book, R. H. Charles, *The Book of Enoch or 1 Enoch*, 2, affirms that the phraseology of these introductory chapters connects them with every section of 1 Enoch except for 1 Enoch 72–82. In the adduced examples he is not able to find any parallel to 1 En. 2:1–5:3 with any part of 1 Enoch at all, which is rather strange for 1 En. 82:9–20 do speak about the seasons and the "luminaries that are in the sky" (2:1, G^{C-1}) dominate in 1 Enoch 72–82. See also idem, *The Apocrypha and Pseudepigrapha of the Old Testament. Vol. II. Pseudepigrapha*, Oxford, Clarendon, 1913, 169. The relationship between 2:1–5:2 and Enochic astronomy comes clearly to the fore only with the discovery and publication of the Aramaic fragments of 1 Enoch from Qumran.

[47] However schematic and perhaps not very precise for modern astronomical standards, Enochic astronomy does seem to reflect the real movement of the celestial bodies, see Dennis Duke, Matthew Goff, "The Astronomy of the Qumran Fragments 4Q208 and 4Q209," *DSD* 21 (2014) 176–210. Since, however, the manuscript evidence remains fragmentary and sketchy, much remains unknown, though.

[48] In an extremely interesting contribution to this volume, Paul Tavardon ("Un complexe scientifique à Qumran: Le disque de pierre, les jarres à conduit d'écoulement et les *mišmarot*") shows the way time was measured at Qumran with clay jars (four of them actually found at the site) serving as a water, or rather, sand clock. He additionally explains the use of this type of clock with the Qumran stone disc used for astronomical measurements.

[49] In scholarly literature, the relationship of 1 En. 2:1–5:2 to 1 Enoch 72–82 and 4Q208–4Q211 has only rarely been discussed. For example, Matthias Albani, *Astronomie und Schöpfungsglaube. Untersuchungen zum Astronomischen Henochbuch* (WMANT, 68), Neukirchen-Vluyn, Neukirchener, 1994, 43, n. 4, cites 5:1 only *en passant*. When discussing the judgment over the righteous and sinners in 1 En. 81:1–4; 82:4; 83:11, he makes a reference to

scrutiny in the exhortation. In both cases the term עבד "work" denotes the movement of the heavenly luminaries[50] and the signs of the earth in a regular manner that "does not change" (דלא משתנא, 4Q201 3 i 2 [2:2]) and that is repeated year after year.[51] Thus, the Enochic text has as its scope the consideration of the periodicity of the heavenly and earthly phenomena, which is the main topic of Enochic astronomy as expounded in the Aramaic (4Q208–4Q211) and Ethiopic (1 En. 72–82) text and which is succinctly expressed in the latter with the term *śərʿat* "law" or "order."[52] The scrutiny of מסורת "positions"[53] and הלך "path"[54] of the luminaries stresses the astronomical character of the "work of the sky."

The exhortation to observe (חזי)[55] the work of the heaven and earth in 1 En. 2:1–5:2 is an invitation to participate in the same inquisitive process found in Enochic astronomical tradition, but without the intermediary of an angel.[56] The observation the movement of the heaven and earth is thus

1 En. 5:2, 4, 7, see pp. 124, n. 89 (2–5); 131 (2–5); 99, 106, 320 (2:1); (4:1). The noteworthy exception is 1 En. 4:1 (p. 230) where the sings of summer and the scorching sun are interpreted in light of the cuneiform MUL.APIN astronomical composition. Albani usually cites the translation of the Ethiopic text by Eckhard Rau ("Kosmologie, Eschatologie und die Lehrautorität Henochs") and attaches little attention to the Aramaic text of 1 En. 2:1–5:2 from Qumran cave 4. Jonathan Ben-Dov, *Head of All Years. Astronomy and Calendars at Qumran in their Ancient Context* (STDJ, 78), Leiden, Brill, 2008, does not discuss the latter at all.

50 The partially preserved term נהיר "luminary" in 2:1 (4Q204 1 5 [2:1, G^{C-1} φωστῆρας]) denotes any kind of the heavenly bodies; for *bərhānāt* "luminaries" in ancient Ethiopic in the EAB, see 1 En. 72:2, 2, 4, 35, 36; 73:1; 75:2; 79:6; for the fragmentary Aramaic expression "heavenly luminaries," see 4Q205 1 6 (23:4, G^{C-1} τοὺς φωστῆρας τοῦ οὐρανοῦ); in ancient Ethiopic: *bərhānāta samāy*, see 1 En. 72:1; 75:3; 77:2.

51 [בשנה] שנה, 4Q201 3 i 11 (5:2). See G^{C-1} ἀπὸ ἐνιαυτοῦ εἰς ἐνιαυτὸν γινόμενα πάντα οὕτως, "year after year they all ('works' [HD]) behave in such a manner."

52 See, e.g., 1 En. 79:1 "the order of all the stars of the sky"; 82:9, "the order of the stars"' see also 79:5; 80:7; 82:4, 11, 13, 14, 20; cf. James C. VanderKam, "1 Enoch 72–82: The Book of the Luminaries," in: George W.E. Nickelsburg, James C. VanderKam, *1 Enoch 2. A Critical Commentary on the Book of 1 Enoch, Chapters 37–82*, Minneapolis, MN, Fortress, 2011, 333–569, esp. 516. In 1 En. 2:1 when speaking about the heavenly luminaries, the Panopolitanus speaks about τὴν ἰδίαν τάξιν "their own order." 4Q201 3 i 1 has here הלכ<<ה>>ן "their course"; the Greek text may here properly render the Aramaic term, see H. Drawnel, *Qumran Cave 4*, 93.

53 4Q204 1 5 (2:1). For the term in the AAB in relation to the order of the stars, see 4Q209 28 2 (82:10). For a general presentation of the discussion concerning the meaning of the term, see J. C. VanderKam, "1 Enoch 72–82," 559–60.

54 4Q201 3 i 1 (2:1). For the paleographic reading of the term and its meaning, see, H. Drawnel, *Qumran Cave 4*, 88 and 93. For the semantically corresponding term *məḥwār* "path" for the course of the luminaries in the EAB, see 1 En. 72:33, 34, 35; 74:1.

55 See § 3.1 in this research.

56 The intervention of angel Uriel as the one who "shows" astronomical knowledge to Enoch in the Ethiopic Astronomical Book (chs. 72–82) is found in its redactional parts

not presented as a revelation but as an intellectual scrutiny[57]of the "signs"[58] of the heaven and earth that "appear"[59] upon the earth.

The plural expression כל עבדיא אלין "all these works" (4Q201 3 i 10 [5:1]) in the concluding strophe VII refers to the work of the heaven and earth debated in the preceding context. Thus it rather denotes the regular and cyclic movement of the universe as visible in the phenomena, and not the objects "heaven, earth, heavenly luminaries" that are source of the former.[60] In the same concluding strophe VII the statement about the creation by God of "all these works" (כל עבדיא אלין, 4Q201 3 i 11 [5:1]) that are doing His commanding word (ממרה, 4Q201 3 i 12 [5:2])[61] denotes the regular movement of the phenomena, an all-encompassing declaration concerning God as the creator of them all.[62]

only, see 1 En. 72:1; 74:2; 75:3, 4; 78:10; 79:6; 80:1; 82:7; for the didactic approach to knowledge transmission in the Visions of Levi and in the AAB, see Henryk DRAWNEL, "Priestly Education in the *Aramaic Levi Document* (*Visions of Levi*) and *Aramaic Astronomical Book* (4Q208–211)," *RevQ* 22 (2006) 547–74. In the AAB (4Q208–4Q211) dominated by the calculation of lunar visibility periods, angel Uriel is absent. Note, however, that the Qumran manuscripts are fragmentary so that the angelic presence there is rather impossible to exclude altogether.

57 דרש, 4Q201 3 i 10 (5:1); νοήσατε G^{C-1} (5:1). The *peal* verb of דרש expresses here the action of researching the works of the heaven and earth through their attentive scrutiny. See Qoh 1:13: "And I applied my mind to seek (לדרוש, LXX τοῦ ἐκζητῆσαι) and to search out by wisdom all that is done under heaven"; cf. Judg 6:29; Deut 13:15; 17:4, 9; 19:18.

58 דגל, 4Q204 1 4 (2:1); 4Q201 3 i 2 (2:3), 3 (2:3), 6 (4:1). In the AAB the term is used in 4Q209 28 1 (82:9) in relation to the stars: "This is the law of the stars that set according to their places, to their appointed times, to their months, to their signs (לדגליהון)"; for the text see Henryk DRAWNEL, *The Aramaic Astronomical Book (4Q208–4Q211) from Qumran. Text, Translation, and Commentary*, Oxford, Oxford University Press, 2011, 198–99, commentary: 400–1.

59 מתחזי]ן, 4Q201 3 i 1 (2:1); מתח[ז]א, 4Q201 3 i 2 = 4Q204 1 7 (2:2). This general statement concerning the appearance of the heavenly bodies during their appointed times corresponds to 4Q209 28 1 (82:9) in the AAB that speaks about the order of the stars which set in their places, according to their appointed times (מעדיהון), months and signs (דגליהון), see ibid., 398–9. For the explanation of the Greek ταῖς ἑορταῖς (2:1e) as translating מעד "appointed time," see H. DRAWNEL, *Qumran Cave 4*, 93.

60 In the Panopolitanus the Greek text reads περὶ πάντων τῶν ἔργων αὐτοῦ "about all His works," stressing the theological perspective (αὐτοῦ) legible later in 5:1b (strophe VII.c)

61 In 4Q212 3 i 11 (93:2) the term ממר "word" denotes the revelation received by Enoch through the intermediary of the Holy Watchers.

62 At the end of the Book of Luminaries in his exploration of the horizon Enoch states that אחזית עבדין רבר[בין] "I was shown great works" (4Q206 6 6 [34:1]). The term "works" evidently encompasses the astronomical activities in the gates for the winds and meteorological phenomena (34:2–36:2), and the movement of the stars (36:3). The concluding praise of God for his work recalls the last strophe of the exhortation in 5:1a–2.

4.2. Signs of Winter and Summer

The central part of the exhortation, strophes III–VI, depends in its vocabulary and partly in its structure on the EAB and the fragmentary 4Q211 1 i that makes part of the Aramaic Astronomical Book (4Q208–4Q211).[63] The last section of the EAB, 82:9–20 contains the "order of the stars" (v. 9) divided into four 91-day parts of the year guided by the four leaders of the stars (82:10–14). Subsequently, the first part of the year is described (82:15–17) with its accompanying "signs (*tə'mərta*)[64] of the days that are to be seen on the earth" (82:16).[65] Then the Ethiopic text deals with the second season, presumably the summer, with the description of its "signs (*tə'mərta*) of the days on the earth" (82:19). This second season of the schematic year is also made of a period of 91 days presided over by Helememelek (82:18–20) whose name is also "the shining sun." The Ethiopic text breaks off here, the last two parts of the schematic year (fall and winter) being lost in the course of text transmission. 4Q211 1 i that contains a fragmentary description of winter may have originally continued the Ethiopic text although any direct relationship remains unclear.

Meteorological phenomena are also part of the presentation of the rose of winds in chapter 76 of the EAB where they are associated with the wind gates as propitious or harmful. The comparison of what constitutes the signs of summer and winter in 1 En. 2:3–5:1a with the aforementioned texts shows an overlapping in meteorological vocabulary as well as in general approach to the signs of the seasons. The description of the seasons and meteorological vocabulary in the aforementioned astronomical texts seem to have served as the building material in 1 En. 2:3–5:1, as shown in Table 4.

[63] Referring to the work of Rau ("Kosmologie, Eschatologie und die Lehrautorität Henochs," 73–75) and Milik (*The Books of Enoch*, 148), G. W. E. NICKELSBURG, *1 Enoch 1*, 156, notes the relationship of 2:3–5:1a to chapters 76 and 82 of the Astronomical Book but leaves the point without further elaboration concerning the impact of the connection on the interpretation of the exhortation. The same relationship was briefly noted by M. BLACK, *The Book of Enoch or I Enoch*, 109 and Otto NEUGEBAUER, "The 'Astronomical' Chapters of the Ethiopic Book of Enoch (72–82): With Additional Notes on the Aramaic Fragments by Matthew Black," in: Matthew BLACK, *The Book of Enoch or I Enoch. A New English Edition with Commentary and Textual Notes* (SVTP, 7), Leiden, E. J. Brill, 1985, 386–419, esp. 418–19.

[64] Behind the Ethiopic term for "sign" in 82:16 and 19 that denotes meteorological phenomena later in the same two verses there must have stood the Aramaic term דגל. Unfortunately, uncertainty about the translational equivalency of the Aramaic term will remain for the Greek and Ethiopic versions of 1 Enoch omit it wherever it appears in the Aramaic manuscripts.

[65] 1 En. 75:3 shows the relationship between the "signs" and "seasons" on the one hand and the year and day on the other, as an element of Uriel's teaching "shown" to Enoch.

Table 4. Signs of winter and summer in 1 En. 2:3–5:1a (strophes III–VI)

Strophe	1 En. 2:3–5:1a	Parallel phrases	Reference
III.c	Signs of winter	And winter comes	4Q211 1 i 4
III.d	water	———	———
III.e	clouds	———	———
III.e	dew and rain	dew, rain	76:6, 8, 11, 13; 76:9, 10
IV.a	trees as withered	Winter trees are dried up	82:16 (spring)
IV.b	[falling leaves]	Leaves of all the trees	4Q211 1 i 4 (winter)
IV.c	14 trees	14 trees	4Q211 1 i 5 (winter)
IV.c	long-lasting leaves	[thei]r[leave[s] remain	4Q211 1 i 6 (winter)
IV.d–e	renewed after 2–3 years	———	———
III.a/V.a	Signs of summer	Signs of the days	82:16: spring; 82:19: summer
V.b	the sun burns	burning	76:13
V.b	the sun scorches	(heat)	76:5; 82:16 (spring), 19 (summer);
V.c	Seeking shade/shelter	———	———
V.c	burning earth	burning	76:13
V.d	Not able to tread on soil/ stones	———	———
V.d	[burning]	burning	76:13
VI.a	[all the [t]rees	all the trees	82:16: spring)
VI.b	leaves beautiful green	leaves	82:16 (spring)
VI.c	and cover the trees	leaves come out on the trees	82:16 (spring)
VI.d	[all their fruit]	all the trees bear fruit.	82:16: spring)
		trees bearing their fruit ripe and yielding all their fruit ripe and ready.	82:19 (summer)

In the fragmentary 4Q211 1 i the thematic motifs of the leaves of all the trees, together with the leaves of 14 trees that remain closely match strophe IV (3:1) of the exhortation where the same topics are discussed. Winter (שתוא) as the main season mentioned in the Aramaic fragment

(4Q211 1 i 4) reappears in 4Q201 3 i 3 (2:3, strophe III.c) as an introduction to the description of the signs of this season. However, the motif of an abundance of water on the earth in strophe III.d–e (2:3) seems to be a development independent from Enochic astronomy. Note, however, that the word pair טל "dew" and מטר "rain" (4Q201 3 i 4; 2:3) are often mentioned as meteorological phenomena exiting different gates in the rose of winds (chapter 76).[66]

The signs of summer in strophe VI are a reworked version of the spring in 82:16 with the motif of the trees bearing fruit also present during the summer (82:19). Strophe V uses the motif of burning present in 1 En. 76:13, indicating the summer sun that burns[67] and scorches.[68] The motif of seeking shelter and being not able to tread on the soil/stones in the same strophe is an independent development of the author of the exhortation. It does not have any direct connection with the signs of summer and its presence here is most probably an element of rhetoric strategy intending to attract the attention of the listeners.[69]

[66] See H. DRAWNEL, *The Aramaic Astronomical Book*, 322–23; for the same word pair in the Hebrew Bible, see Deut 32:2; 2 Sam 1:21; 1 Kgs 17:1. In 1 En. 100:11 cloud, mist, dew, and rain testify against the sinners, an example of using meteorological phenomena in the upcoming divine judgment, cf. the following 100:12–13. In 101:2 the situation is contrary to 2:3: God withholds the rain and the dew from descending on the earth. The case of 1 En, 100:11 and 101:2 may be an example of the influence of 2:3 on the Epistle of Enoch read through the lenses of 5:4, not *vice versa*.

[67] In 1 En. 76:13 the ancient Ethiopic term for "burning" is *wāʿy*. The ancient Ethiopic verb semantically corresponding to the f. sg. participle כוייה "burns" (4Q201 3 i 7 and 4Q204 2 3 [4:1]) is omitted in in 4:1 in E (G^{C-1} is missing here), but it appears later in the verse: *mədrəsa təwwəʾi* "the earth burns." M. ALBANI, *Astronomie und Schöpfungsglaube*, 230 links 4:1 with MUL.APIN II Gap A 3 where the sun in the fourfold division of the year stands in the path of the Enlil stars, and this three-month period is characterized by prevailing weather conditions: *ebūru u uššu* "summer (or "harvest") and heat," see Hermann HUNGER, John STEELE, *The Babylonian Astronomical Compendium MUL.APIN*, (Scientific Writings from the Ancient and Medieval WORLD, London and New York, NY, Routledge, 2019, 84–85, 150–51, 209. Note that the semantic correspondence of this Mesopotamian line with the Enochic text is rather far from clear for 1 En. 4:1 speaks about "burning," not "heat" (in Eth. *moq*, cf. 1 En. 76:13). Additionally, the author of the Enochic text speaks about two seasons only and the accent is laid on the seasonal phenomena, not on the motion of the sun in the paths of Anu, Ea, and Enlil through the schematic year in MUL.APIN II Gap A 1–7. The division of the schematic year in Enochic astronomy is found in 1 En. 82:9–20. G. W. E. NICKELSBURG, *1 Enoch 1*, 156 draws attention to Sir 43:2–4, a description of sun heat and its bearing on the earth, as a text parallel to 4:1. Note that the Hebrew vocabulary in Sir 43:2–3 seems also to be different: heat of the sun (חמה Ms. B; 43:2); the next verse uses the synonymous noun חרב "heat" (Sir 43:3, Ms. B; Mas V, 19).

[68] The f.sg. participle שלקה 4Q201 3 i 7 (4:1; IVb), lit. "boils," cf. H. DRAWNEL, *The Aramaic Astronomical Book*, 96; cf. Sir 43:3, "the sun makes the earth boil" (ms. B; fragm. in Mas V, 19) with the verb in the imperfect *hiphil* from the root √*rtḥ* ; cf. Job 41:23.

[69] When commenting on the scorching heat of the sun in 1 En. 4:1, R. A. ARGALL, *1 Enoch and Sirach*, 106, states that "the reader intuits the meaning: one must escape the heat of wrath poured out in the final judgment." This seems to be an overstatement for neither

5. Conclusion

The intended goal of the exhortation is first of all the understanding of God as the maker of all the works of the heaven and earth, the central statement of the last strophe of the composition (VII.c, 1 En. 5:1b). The intellectual apprehension of this theological truth (VII.b, 1 En. 5:1b) results from the observation and intelligent scrutiny of the signs of the heaven and earth (strophes I–VI). Thus, the regular and unchanged work of the heaven and earth (strophe I.c and f, 1 En 2:1; II.d, 1 En 2:2; VII.d[?], 1 En 5:2) is not the central theme of the composition but it serves as a means for the discovery of the main point expressed in strophe VII.c, to which the last clause is the most convenient comment: "all of them do His word" (VII.e, 5:2, 4Q201 3 i 12). The setting of the exhortation in the different literary and thematic context of 1:3–9 and 5:4–9 did not change its message but linked it with the judgment of the sinners that have changed their "work" as stated in 5:4. The whole composition grew out of personal experience of busying oneself with Enochic type of horizon-based astronomy and presenting it as an ideal to follow in the quest for the apprehension of God through the creation that incessantly moves, upheld by His commanding word. As such, it is a unique document both in the Enochic tradition and Jewish texts of the Second Temple period.

The accusatory clause in 1 En. 5:4 against those who change their human activity is not an exhortation and does not make part of the literary form and structure of 1 En. 2:1–5:2. It results from the redactional attempt to include the exhortation within the larger literary unit of 1 En. 1:3b–9; 5:5–9 that announces the coming judgment on all the earth. The use of the expression "you changed your work (עבד)" in singular does not link the whole verse 5:4 to the overarching conclusion of the exhortation (intellectual apprehension of God's creative power) but rather to the collateral argument of the regular and unchanged work of the earth (II.d, 2:2; 4Q201 3 i 2. This thematic connection demonstrates the interest of the redactor(s) in linking the exhortation with a reason for subjecting the sinners to judgment, a rhetorical strategy whose function was not the change of the meaning or literary form of 1 En. 2:1–5:2.

The invitation to the inquiry into the work of the heaven and earth links the introductory section of the Book of the Watchers with its conclusion where in chapters 34–36 Enoch learns the principles of horizon-based

the content of the Enochic verse nor the immediate context set the "burning" in the context of judgment. In a similar way, Argall's intuitive connection of the trees that blossom and bear fruit (5:1) with the elect that will flourish at the time of judgment is rather distant from the plain meaning of the Enochic text.

astronomy.[70] Thus, the ideal of astronomical observation proposed at the beginning of the book finds its exemplary fulfilment in the person of Enoch, an ideal student of astronomy who acquires wisdom that surpasses human understanding (1 En. 82:2).

[70] See Henryk DRAWNEL, "Enoch at the Ends of the Earth: Horizon-Based Astronomy and the Stars in 1 Enoch 33–36," in: FRÖHLICH, Ida (ed.), *Proceedings from the Conference "Aramaic Science at Qumran," Budapest, Péter Pázmány Catholic University, 15–16 May 2018*, forthcoming.

OÙ DOIT-ON CAPTURER LES FUGITIFS ? UNE NOUVELLE LECTURE DE SFIRÉ III,6*

Jan DUŠEK

Le travail d'Émile Puech a considérablement marqué non seulement les études qumrâniennes, mais également le domaine plus large de l'épigraphie nord-ouest sémitique. Dans certaines de ses études, il a analysé les inscriptions araméennes de l'âge de fer, telles que l'inscription sur un ivoire d'Arslan-Tash, l'inscription sur la base d'une pyxide en ivoire de Nimrud, les fragments araméens trouvés à Tel Dan et l'inscription de Bar-Hadad sur une stèle dédiée à Melqart trouvée à Breidj.[1] Ses analyses ont en outre aidé à élucider le sens de certains passages obscurs des inscriptions araméennes de Sfiré, qu'il avait également traduites en français.[2] C'est donc un honneur pour moi de publier cet article sur une nouvelle interprétation d'un passage de Sfiré III, 6 à l'occasion de son anniversaire.

Un orthostate en basalte acquis par le Musée national de Beyrouth en 1956 porte une inscription araméenne qui s'étale sur 29 lignes ; c'est l'inscription traditionnellement désignée « Sfiré III ». L'origine exacte de cet objet et la date de sa découverte sont inconnus, mais l'écriture et le style de l'inscription ainsi que son contenu indiquent que l'orthostate a très probablement été découvert dans les fouilles clandestines du tell de

* Cet article est le résultat d'une recherche soutenue par la Fondation pour la Science de la République tchèque (*Czech Science Foundation*), projet GA ČR 20-26324S « Les traditions scribales dans les territoires araméens du Levant à l'âge de fer : les centres des cultures scribales et leur diffusion ».

[1] Émile PUECH, « Un ivoire de Bît-Guši (Arpad) à Nimrud », *Syria* 55 (1978), 163-169 ; É. PUECH, « L'ivoire inscrit d'Arslan Tash et les rois de Damas », *Revue biblique* 88 (1981), 544-562 ; É. PUECH, « La stèle de Bar-Hadad à Melqart et les rois d'Arpad », *Revue biblique* 99 (1992), 311-334 ; É. PUECH, « La stèle araméenne de Dan : Bar-Hadad II et la coalition des Omrides et de la maison de David », *Revue biblique* 101 (1994), 215-241 ; É. PUECH, « La stèle araméenne de Dan revisitée et le fragment de stèle d'Afis », dans : Innocent HIMBAZA, Clemens LOCHER (éd.), *La Bible en face. Études textuelles et littéraires offertes en hommage à Adrian Schenker, à l'occasion de ses quatre-vingts ans* (Cahiers de la Revue biblique, 95), Leuven – Paris – Bristol CT, Peeters, 2020, 331-345.

[2] É. PUECH, « Les inscriptions araméennes I et III de Sfiré : nouvelles lectures », *Revue biblique* 89 (1982) 576-587 ; É. PUECH, « La racine śyṭ - š'ṭ en araméen et en hébreu. À propos de Sfiré I A 24, I Q H[a] III, 30 et 36 (= XI, 31 et 37) et Ézéchiel », *Revue de Qumrân* 11 (1982-1984), 367-378 ; É. PUECH, « Les traités araméens de Sfiré », dans : Jacques BRIEND et al. (éd.), *Traités et serments dans le Proche-Orient ancien* (Supplément au Cahier Evangile, 81), Paris, Service biblique Évangile et vie – Éditions du Cerf, 1992, 88-107.

Sfiré, de même que les deux stèles dites de Sfiré, numérotées Sfiré I et Sfiré II, connues déjà depuis 1930.[3] Toutes ces inscriptions, Sfiré I-III, semblent avoir été écrites vers la fin du règne d'Aššur-dān III, autour de 754 av. J.-C.[4]

L'*editio princeps* de Sfiré III a été publiée par André Dupont-Sommer et Jean Starcky en 1956.[5] Comme les inscriptions Sfiré I et II, l'inscription Sfiré III contient également une partie d'un traité du type *adê*, bien connu des documents néo-assyriens.[6] Ce traité de Sfiré III a été conclu entre deux rois dont ni les noms ni les royaumes ne sont mentionnés dans le texte préservé. Dans le traité, un roi (nous le désignons « roi X ») impose à un autre roi (« roi Y ») des obligations dont l'objectif est de protéger l'intégrité du pouvoir et du territoire du premier. Le second, le roi Y à qui les obligations sont imposées, est probablement Matiʿʾel, roi d'Arpad/Bīt-Agūsi, un royaume qui était situé aux IXe et VIIIe siècles av. J.-C. autour de la ville d'Alep dans la Syrie du nord.[7] C'est le même roi à qui Bar-Ga'yah, roi de KTK, impose des obligations dans les traités préservés dans les inscriptions Sfiré I et II.

Mon analyse porte sur le paragraphe de Sfiré III, lignes 4b-7, qui stipule les obligations du roi Y, probablement Matiʿʾel d'Arpad, concernant les fugitifs qui quittent le territoire du roi X. Voici la traduction de ce texte selon l'*editio princeps* :

> (4b) Et si s'enfuit de chez moi l'un de mes officiers ou l'un de mes frères ou l'un (5) de mes eunuques ou l'un des gens qui sont dans ma main et qu'ils aillent à Alep, tu ne [l]eur ver[se]ras pas de vivres et tu ne leur diras pas : « Restez

[3] Sébastien RONZEVALLE, « Fragments d'inscriptions araméennes des environs d'Alep », *Mélanges de l'Université Saint-Joseph* 15 (1930-1931), 237-260, fac-similés Soudjîn I-V, planches XXXIX-XLV.

[4] Concernant la datation de Sfiré I B en 754 av. J.-C., voir Jan DUŠEK, « Dating the Aramaic Stele Sefire I », *Aramaic Studies* 17 (2019), 1-14.

[5] André DUPONT-SOMMER, Jean STARCKY, « Une inscription araméene inédite de Sfiré », *Bulletin du Musée de Beyrouth* 13 (1956), p. 23-41. L'*editio princeps* des inscriptions Sfiré I et II, publiée quatre ans plus tard, contient seulement une transcription et une traduction de Sfiré III, sans commentaire ; voir A. DUPONT-SOMMER, J. STARCKY, « Les inscriptions araméennes de Sfiré », *Mémoires présentés par divers savants à l'Académie des inscriptions et belles-lettres de l'Institut de France*, Tome XI, première partie, Paris, Imprimerie nationale 1960, 197-352, planches I-XXIX. L'inscription Sfiré III y est publiée dans l'appendice 1, pages 323-328.

[6] Simo PARPOLA, Kazuko WATANABE, *Neo-Assyrian Treaties and Loyalty Oaths* (State Archives of Assyria, 2), Winona Lake, Eisenbrauns, 2014.

[7] Jan DUŠEK, « The Kingdom of Arpad/Bīt-Agūsi : Its Capital, and Its Borders », dans : Jan DUŠEK, Jana MYNÁŘOVÁ (éd.), *Aramaean Borders. Defining Aramaean Territories in the 10th-8th Centuries B.C.E.* (Culture & History of the Ancient Near East, 101), Leiden – Boston, Brill, 2019, 172-202.

tranquillement à l'endroit où vous êtes », et tu ne me soustrairas pas (6) leur âme : tu devras les capturer et me les restituer. Et s'ils ne [résid]ent pas dans ton pays, capturez(-les) là-bas, jusqu'à ce que j'(y) aille moi-même et que je les capture. Mais si tu me soustrais leur âme (7) et que tu leur verses des vivres et que tu leur dises : « Résidez au lieu où vo[us] êtes et ne retournez pas à l'endroit où il est », vous aurez trahi ces pactes-ci.[8]

Le paragraphe contient des stipulations concernant deux cas différents pour lesquels le roi Y doit capturer les fugitifs et les rendre au roi X.

Le premier cas (lignes 4b-6a) concerne les fugitifs qui s'enfuient de chez le roi X et vont à Alep (le verbe הלך « aller », ligne 5), apparemment en traversant le territoire dominé par le roi Y. Ce dernier ne peut ni les nourrir ni leur donner asile. Le roi Y doit les capturer et les rendre au roi X. Au VIIIe siècle av. J.-C., la ville d'Alep était probablement entourée de territoires dominés par les rois d'Arpad, sans être elle-même soumise à ces rois araméens.[9] Par conséquent, au milieu du VIIIe siècle, les gens se rendant à Alep devaient traverser les territoires dominés par Matiʿʾel. Cela signifie que le premier cas correspond très probablement à celui des refugiés du royaume du roi X, qui doivent traverser le territoire d'Arpad/Bīt-Agūsi pour aller ailleurs, dans la ville d'Alep. Dans ce cas, la destination des fugitifs n'est pas le territoire d'Arpad/Bīt-Agūsi ; ce royaume n'est pour eux qu'un pays de transition.

Le deuxième cas selon l'*editio princeps*, et sa première stipulation en particulier (ligne 6b), sont beaucoup moins clairs : « Et s'ils ne [résid]ent pas dans ton pays, capturez(-les) là-bas, jusqu'à ce que j'(y) aille moi-même et que je les capture ». Cette stipulation traduit le texte araméen והן לי[שב]ן̇ ב̇א̇ר̇קך ר̇קו שם ע̇ד אהך אנה וארק הם.[10] Les autres interprètes qui

[8] A. DUPONT-SOMMER, J. STARCKY, « Une inscription araméenne inédite », 28.

[9] Voir J. DUŠEK, «The Kingdom of Arpad/Bīt-Agūsi », 192. La ville d'Alep est parfois associée au royaume d'Arpad ; voir par exemple Edward LIPIŃSKI, *The Aramaeans, Their Ancient History, Culture, Religion* (Orientalia Lovaniensia Analecta, 100), Leuven, Peeters, 207 ; John D. HAWKINS, « Ḫalab », dans *Reallexikon der Assyriologie und Vorderasiatischen Archäologie 4 : Ḫa-a-a – Hystaspes*, 1972-1975, 53. Cependant, Alep n'est mentionnée parmi les villes d'Arpad ni dans la liste de Sfiré I A, 34-35, ni dans la liste de Tiglath-pileser III (Hayim TADMOR, Shiego YAMADA, *The Royal Inscriptions of Tiglath-pileser III (744-727 BC) and Shalmaneser V (726-722), Kings of Assyria* [The Royal Inscriptions of the Neo-Assyrian Period, 1], Winona Lake, Eisenbrauns, 2011, inscription Tiglath-pileser III 43, i 25 – ii 7 [p. 109]). « Hadad d'Alep » qu'on peut reconstruire dans la liste de divinités en Sfiré I A, 10-11, y est très probablement mentionné en tant qu'une divinité assyrienne, non pas araméenne, et ne semble pas représenter le royaume d'Arpad ; voir Michael L. BARRÉ, « The First Pair of Deities in the Sefîre I God-List », *Journal of Near Eastern Studies* 44/3 (1985), 205-210, 209-210. Les inscriptions des rois néo-assyriens ne mentionnent jamais la ville d'Alep en rapport avec le royaume d'Arpad/Bīt-Agūsi.

[10] A. DUPONT-SOMMER, J. STARCKY, « Une inscription araméenne inédite », 26, ligne 6b.

ont édité le texte de cette inscription après la publication de l'*editio princeps* ont généralement suivi la traduction proposée par ses auteurs, Dupont-Sommer et Starcky. Mentionnons quelques exemples :

- « Und wenn sie sich nicht in deinem Territorium auf[hal]ten, (dann) *gewinne* dort über sie *die Oberhand*, bis ich selbst komme und sie *gefangensetze*. »[11]
- « If they will not [remain] in your land, be conciliatory (and keep them) there, until I come in person and make reconciliation with them. »[12]
- « Et s'*ils* n'*ha*[*bite*]*nt* pas dans ton pays, apaisez-(les) là jusqu'à ce que j'aille moi-même et que je les apaise. »[13]
- « Et s'ils ne se trouvent pas sur ton territoire, capturez-(les) là-bas jusqu'à ce que je vienne moi et que je les capture. »[14]
- « And if they [do] not [dwell] in your land, *placate* (them) there, until I come and *placate* them. »[15]

Une telle interprétation semble indiquer que le roi Y, probablement Mati''el d'Arpad, a l'obligation de capturer les fugitifs en dehors de sa juridiction, en dehors du territoire qu'il est lui-même capable de contrôler, et qu'il doit les retenir là-bas jusqu'à ce que le roi X vienne et les prenne lui-même. Une telle obligation semble absurde : quel roi accepterait volontairement de capturer les fugitifs d'un autre royaume sur un territoire qui n'est pas le sien ? Et pourquoi le roi X ne demande-t-il pas plutôt ce service au maître des lieux qui n'appartiennent pas au roi Y ?

La traduction proposée par Edward Lipiński semble résoudre cette difficulté : « And if they do not intend to r[emai]n in your land, make (them) harmless there, until I come and make them harmless ».[16] Cependant, il

[11] Herbert DONNER, Wolfgang RÖLLIG, *Kanaanäische und aramäische Inschriften. Band II: Kommentar*, Wiesbaden, Harrassowitz, 1973 (dritte unveränderte Auflage), 264 (no. 224). Selon leur commentaire (page 268), les auteurs traduisent le verbe ישב par « sitzen, wohnen, sich aufhalten ».

[12] John C. L. GIBSON, *Textbook of Syriac Semitic Inscriptions*. Volume 2 : *Aramaic Inscriptions Including Inscriptions in the Dialect of Zenjirli*, Oxford, University Press, 1975, 47.

[13] André LEMAIRE, Jean-Marie DURAND, *Les inscriptions araméennes de Sfiré et l'Assyrie de Shamshi-ilu* (Hautes études orientales, 20), Genève – Paris, Droz, 1984, 129.

[14] Hélène SADER, *Les états araméens de Syrie depuis leur fondation jusqu'à leur transformation en provinces assyriennes* (Beiruter Texte und Studien, 36), Beirut, in Kommission bei Franz Steiner Verlag, Wiesbaden, 1987, 135.

[15] Joseph A. FITZMYER, *The Aramaic Inscriptions of Sefire* (Biblica et Orientalia, 19/A), Roma, Editrice Pontificio Instituto Biblico, 1995 (revised edition), 137.

[16] Edward LIPIŃSKI, « Re-reading the Inscriptions from Sefire », dans : Edward LIPIŃSKI, *Studies in Aramaic Inscriptions and Onomastics I* (Orientalia Lovaniensia Analecta, 1), Leuven, University Press, 1975, 24-57, 55.

est difficile de l'adopter. Il n'est pas clair à quoi dans le texte araméen correspondrait le mot « intend », et Lipiński laisse sa traduction sans commentaire.

Si l'on ne parvient pas à trouver une solution convenable en se basant sur la lecture du texte araméen selon l'*editio princeps*, il faut en chercher une autre au niveau épigraphique, en examinant l'inscription elle-même. Au milieu de la ligne 6, Dupont-Sommer et Starcky ont reconstruit le texte והן לי[שב]ן ב̇ארקך « et s'ils ne [résid]ent pas dans ton pays ».[17] La collation de mes propres photographies de l'inscription Sfiré III, ainsi qu'une vérification des anciennes photographies de Jean Starcky,[18] montrent que, au vu des traces de lettres préservées dans la pierre, la reconstruction d'un autre verbe semble préférable. Je propose de lire והן לי[שב]ק̇ן א̇רקך « et s'ils ne [quitt]ent pas ton pays » (**Fig. 1**).

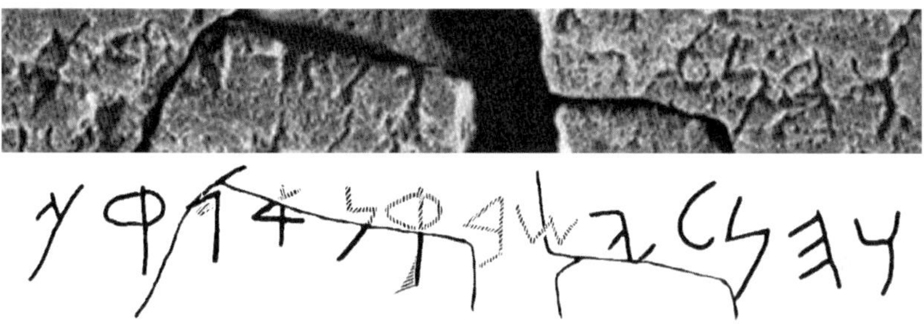

Fig. 1 : והן לי[שב]ק̇ן א̇רקך dans Sfiré III, 6. Photographie Jean Starcky ; dessin Jan Dušek.

Une telle reconstruction change le sens de la stipulation, et c'est ainsi que je la comprends : « Et s'ils ne [quitt]ent pas ton pays, capturez(-les) là-bas, jusqu'à ce que j'(y) aille moi-même et que je les capture ».

Ainsi, la première partie du paragraphe sur l'extradition des fugitifs (Sfiré III, lignes 4b-6a) concerne le cas de fugitifs de chez le roi X qui traversent le territoire de Matiʿʾel, roi d'Arpad/Bīt-Agūsi, pour se rendre à Alep. Le traité interdit à Matiʿʾel de leur faciliter ce passage (interdiction de les nourrir) et de leur accorder asile. Ces fugitifs, dont la destination n'est pas le royaume d'Arpad/Bīt-Agūsi mais la ville d'Alep, doivent être capturés sur le territoire d'Arpad/Bīt-Agūsi et rendus au roi X.

[17] A. Dupont-Sommer, J. Starcky, « Une inscription araméenne inédite », 26 (transcription), 28 (traduction).

[18] Je suis très reconnaissant à André Lemaire qui m'a donné ces photographies.

La deuxième partie du paragraphe (Sfiré III, lignes 6b-7) concerne les fugitifs de chez le roi X qui arrivent sur le territoire de Matiʿʾel, roi d'Arpad/Bīt-Agūsi, et souhaitent y rester, probablement pour y demander l'asile. Les gens de Matiʿʾel doivent les y capturer et les garder dans le pays de Matiʿʾel jusqu'à ce que le roi Y vienne pour les capturer lui-même.

Pour répondre à la question indiquée dans le titre de cet article : c'est très probablement dans le territoire du royaume d'Arpad/Bīt-Agūsi, dont le territoire était contrôlé par le roi Matiʿʾel, que les fugitifs de chez le roi X devaient être capturés, et non pas en dehors du pays de Matiʿʾel.

THE MEANING OF חק חסד IN 4Q521: A NEGLECTED ELEMENT OF APOCALYPTIC MESSIANISM[1]

Anthony GIAMBRONE, O.P.

Especially for New Testament scholars, one of the most fascinating and tantalizing of the Dead Sea Scrolls is certainly 4Q521 (4QApocalypse messianique). The mention in a very short space of the messiah alongside the coming resurrection, with a use of Isaiah 61 and list of signs paralleled almost exactly by Jesus' words in the Gospels (Matt 11:4–5 ǁ Luke 7:22), makes the fragment an extraordinary point of comparison and reference. It also means that interest in this dense and unfortunately quite lacunary text has focused almost exclusively upon these important messianic and eschatological themes. As a consequence, a very interesting and rather obscure motif has effectively been ignored: the חק חסד in the first line of Fragment 2, column iii.

In this short contribution, I suggest twinned interpretations of חק חסד, drawing upon several sources. After a succinct introduction to the well-known text, with special attention to the conjectural reading of the crucial phrase, I will pursue a pair of distinct but related readings, each activating different elements in the scroll and its wider context. To this end, I turn to recent lexicographical work on semantic shifts in the Hebrew of the period to propose that the notion of חסד in this passage should be heard as carrying a strong connotation of charity/mercy. I then contextualize this specific understanding within the wider rhetoric of 4Q521, highlighting its thematic links with a series of other structuring ideas, especially resurrection and reward. Finally, I fit this broad reading within the larger horizon of Second Temple thinking, as represented both in the scrolls and other materials, notably 4QpsEzek, 11Q13, and Luke's Gospel. As a conclusion, I will suggest that the חסד theology discernable in 4Q521 stands fully integrated into a larger eschatological vision, which might be imagined in several related configurations, all of serious interest for the study of Jewish apocalyptic messianism and New Testament theology.

[1] I would like to thank Nicolò Rizzolo, an able Puech *Schüler*, for his helpful comments on an earlier version of this paper.

It is a great joy for me to dedicate this study to Émile Puech, one of the honored *seniores* at the École biblique, whose remarkable career studying the texts of Qumran commenced with the editing of this very scroll, leading him to his landmark work on the resurrection.[2]

1. The Text of 4Q521

The text of 4Q521 is preserved on a leather scroll extending across six small (8.4 cm) columns, surviving in sixteen separate, poorly conserved fragments.[3] Most of these are damaged so severely that only isolated words are (*à peine*) decipherable; but Fragments 2, 5, and 7 all contain relatively significant chunks of text, dated paleographically to the Hasmonean period, c. 100–80 BCE.

The key fragment for our purposes is Fragment 2, which survives only in three columns, though column i is effectively destroyed, with only six or seven unconnected words legible. The first line of column ii – the most complete portion of the text – contains the famous mention of משחיו, unfortunately after a lacuna and thus without adequate context. After hesitating, Puech ultimately determined that this expression should probably be taken in the singular, i.e. "his messiah/anointed," referring to an eschatological high priest figure. The column continues with the equally celebrated list of the eschatological benefits and deeds accomplished by the Lord (lines 5–8, 10–13). Here mention of the resurrection corresponds to ideas echoed in Fragment 7.

The less well-preserved column iii of Fragment 2 contains seven lines of partial text (but little more than a single letter from the seventh line). Line 1 includes the phrase presently in question (ואת חק חסד-), which terminates a sentence begun in the lost, preceding line carried over from the bottom of column ii. Consultation of high definition and infrared images of the text makes very plain that the word חסד is a conjecture – albeit a good one ("lecture certaine") – as the upper portions of both the ח and the ס are effaced and a small hole in the leather disturbs the reading. The final letter is also very severely damaged, due in part to normal flaking on the surface and in part to faded and smudged ink. Puech suggests a correction

[2] Émile Puech, "Une apocalypse messianique (*4Q521*)," *RevQ* 15/60 (1992) 475–522; and É. Puech, *La croyance des Esséniens en la vie future : immortalité, résurrection, vie éternelle? Histoire d'une croyance dans le Judaïsme ancien*, I-II. Paris, Lecoffre, 1992.

[3] See É. Puech, *Qumrân Grotte 4, XVIII : textes hébreux (4Q521–4Q528, 4Q576–4Q579)* (DJD XXV) Oxford, Clarendon, 1998, 1–38.

introduced by the scribe, who grated off a final *caf* and then transformed a *yod* to be a *caf*, thus correcting from the plural חסדיך to the singular חסדך.

The scribe has introduced other (supralinear) corrections to the text (e.g. Frag. 2 ii 11; Frag. 8 10a, 11a), so mistakes are certainly possible; though one might ask why if the scribe went to the trouble of erasing his error, he would not have erased the faulty *yod* as well. The resemblance of the pointed, up-down stroke to a *yod* is unmistakable, however. What is more difficult to confirm is the corrected *caf*. Indeed, sadly, the lost letter that seemingly incorporated the *yod*-shaped mark sits half within the flaked-off portion of parchment. In this space, part of a very clear downstroke is visible, however. Blown-up digital images reveal with increased clarity the traces of ink neatly aligning this stroke with the *yod* and the early photos already show the gentle curve of this stroke, which angles in towards a faded vertical line. The suggestion of a wide horned head is also evident, though faded. A correction of חסדיך is certainly an expert suggestion and not to be discounted. Another possibility might also be entertained, however. When the clearly visible portion of the *curving* downstroke descending from the *yod* is compared with the scribe's usual, perfectly straight and very long downstroke in his final *caf* (cf. Frag. 2 i 9), the quite ample space before the following word might be understood to conserve the remnants of a lost final *mem*. Indeed, the final *caf* and the leftmost portion of the scribe's final mem are nearly identical in practice, so that one might imagine the faded portion to form the left half of a partially lost letter, met at the base by the broken-off, inward curving right leg. When checked against measurements of the preserved examples, the conjecture of a slightly awkward final *mem* (the scribe's final *mem*'s show some variability) that has perhaps corrected and absorbed part of a false transcription becomes intriguing. That a common word such as חסדים might well have been in the copyist's head would make an erroneous *yod* understandable – particularly since the expression חסדם with a third personal plural ending is somewhat unexpected.[4] If the question is asked, why the left-hand portion of the definitive, corrected letter is nearly lost, material factors related to the deterioration of the parchment would have to be invoked. Given the state of the scroll, this must be allowed: other similar discolorations and effacing of ink can be observed, even if this particular case is grave. Ultimately, of course, while entertaining this reading, it is

[4] The form חסדים appears frequently, including in many texts from cave 4: e.g. 4Q286 1 ii 8; 4Q377 2 ii 12; 4Q378 26,6; 4Q398 14–17 ii 1; 4Q491 8–10,6; 4Q502 16,2.

prudent (especially for amateur epigraphers) to defer to Puech's experienced eye, even if the tail of the corrected *caf* would diverge considerably from the norm. Still, rather than firmly insisting upon on purely paleographical grounds – the text is very damaged – it is useful to adjudicate with the help of other considerations. Indeed, indulging the exercise of playing with both senses will prove illuminating, bring diverse possibilities to the surface, and finally lead to some quite interesting theological perspectives and questions.

Pursuing the reading helps widen the view and the presence of אותם in the second half of the same line (Frag. 2 iii 1) could offer a first clue, hinting that a third person plural ending might perhaps be in the deictic context and correct. If a sequence of coordinate endings would be quite reasonable to imagine, however, the relation of the first to the second half of this fragmentary line is unfortunately not transparent. Without further analysis (see §2 below), no conclusion can therefore be drawn on this account.

Usage is a more revealing angle, though it also leaves the options open. Quite frequently in the scrolls, especially in the Hodayoth, God's חסד is spoken of in the second person singular, חסדך (e.g. 1QS 1,22). It is thus understandable to expect this common expression also in 4Q521. At the same time, the notion of "their hesed" (חסדם), though much less common, is not unknown, strikingly appearing in 4QpsEzek[a,b,d]: "They will be repaid for their *hesed* (ישתלמו חסדם)." The formula in the Hodayoth essentially belongs to confessional and liturgical discourse, which does not precisely fit 4Q521, a non-liturgical text where the voice is quite different, where God-talk is consistently in the third person, and where the rare second person pronouns are otherwise all exhortations and admonitions addressed to human actors (Frag. 1 ii 4; Frag. 2 ii 3-4; Frag. 5 i 6; Frag. 7 ii 7; Frag. 9 1). The expression חסדם in the cave 4 pseudo-Ezekiel texts, by contrast, belongs to the very suggestive resurrection context of Ezekiel 37, forging an obvious link with the rhetoric and content of 4Q521. Here a shared notion of eschatological reward is a point of major significance that will be further explored below. All of this obviously inclines towards seeing in 4QpsEzek[a,b,d] a case of analogous usage.

An additional argument may also be added. The text of 4Q521 2 ii 9 significantly uses the form חסדו, with the third person singular suffix. Although this isolated word is very clear, a rather sizable hole in the parchment has unfortunately destroyed almost the entire rest of the line, along with much of line 10, so it is difficult to be certain who exactly is in view. If the Lord's חסד is understood here, however, we would be confronted again with the consistently third person God-talk of the text. If another is in view, perhaps the איש proposed in the reconstruction of line 10, we would have reason to support a similar reference to non-divine חסד in column iii. Either way the locution חסדך would create a certain tension within the text, eased by adopting the reading חסדם. Accepting this reading would permit us finally to wonder if perhaps the twice repeated title חסידים (Frag. 2 ii 5, 7) is in this text not simply a moniker for the generically "pious," but more specifically a way to denote those characterized by their own proper concrete חסד.[5] Indeed, as will be seen, a case can be made that these righteous persons may well be understood precisely as the doers of *gemîlût ḥăsādîm*.

In sum, the statistically marginal and more paleographically adventurous reading חסדם would harmonize better with the broad rhetoric and themes of 4Q521, while the accepted and quite conventional חסדך is oddly disruptive at this level, yet stands to gain new interest precisely through its curious contextualization in a singular formula and application.

2. The Semantics of חק חסד

While both the words חק and חסד are enormously common throughout the Dead Sea Scrolls, the conjunction of the two in a construct chain is unique to 4Q521. This is interesting as both terms belong to multiple stereotyped pairings and even gravitate towards such rhetorical usage (e.g. חוק ומשפט, אהבת חסד, חסד ואמת, etc.). A first question is thus finding the lexical conditions under which these two specific ideas might come into contact in this way. Here it is very significant that both members of the phrase, חק and חסד, can be individually linked to distinct semantic developments underway during the period, converging on the shared meaning of "charity" as the prototypical form of *piety*.

The first development can be approached by observing the closest direct parallels in the scrolls to the expression חק חסד. These parallels are found in several other construct chains built with חק as the *nomen regens*, clustered together in CD 20: חקי הצדק, חקי קדשו, and חקי הברית (cf. 1QH[a] 8.24; 4Q249, etc.) Within this chapter of the Damascus Document these varied expressions all indicate the commandments of the Torah as interpreted and observed by the community, but rejected or imperfectly fulfilled by outsiders. In that sense the various formulae refer to the binding mode of life

[5] The wider role of 4Q521 in determining the sense of this surprisingly rare name חסידים should not be underestimated. Together with 11QPs[a], it is one of but two texts among the DSS that use the title more than once (11QPs[a] 18.10; 19.7; 22.3, 6).

enjoined by the statutes of the Community Rule itself (ספר סרכ היחד), viewed under a diversity of aspects: its justice, its divine holiness, and its covenantal character. In each case, the definitive article or pronomial suffix of the *nomen rectum* is attached to the governing noun in the construct state, though in the last case the definite article evidently belongs to both. Thus, "the laws of justice" (or "the just laws") and "his holy laws"; but "the laws of the covenant."[6]

While in CD the meaning of חק, which is frequently used in the document, is almost always explicitly linked with the covenant and the community's rule of life (1.20; 2.6; 5.12; 12.20; 15.5; 19.6, 14; 20.11, 29, 30, 33), alternative usages of the term are also found. One of these instances simply transfers the same sense of the "laws" to the gentiles (חוקי הגוים, 1.9; cf. 4Q270 6 iii 16); but one case (CD 4.12) carries a genuinely different meaning that will be invoked below.

Both singular and plural forms of חק are employed in CD, but significantly the singular never appears as in construct with a *nomen rectum*, as we find in 4Q521 (cf. 2 ii 2). The adjectival phrase חוק עולם does appear in CD 15.5 in reference to the specific and somehow all-embracing ordinance of taking the oath of the covenant (cf. 11Q19 39.8; and חוקי עולמים 4Q401 12.2). Otherwise the singular חק is reserved in CD for two passages where God's ברית or דרך is rejected (1.20; 2.6). Thus, whereas the "statutes" of Torah, when expressly qualified by their positive character or divine origin, are typically imagined in the plural in CD, the locution in 4Q521 works in a different way. The expression either functions as a collective, gesturing to a whole legal assemblage, or else it serves to single out one concrete law – perhaps of some metonymic significance, not entirely unlike CD 15.5. Context alone can determine what this specific commandment might be, of course – though context in 4Q521 is, unfortunately, prohibitively spotty.

One possibility meriting attention is that we are dealing in 4Q521 with essentially the same lexical phenomenon seen with the Greek term ἐντολή, which in Jewish and Christian sources, beginning around the time of Ben Sira, came to express the notion of *the* paradigmatic commandment, somehow representative of the entire Law: namely, "charity" or "mercy."[7] The normal LXX equivalence of ἐντολή is admittedly מצוה, not חק, which is

[6] See J. WEINGREEN, "The Construct-Genitive Relation in Hebrew Syntax," *VT* 4 (1954) 50–59.

[7] On this philological phenomenon, see Anthony GIAMBRONE, "'According to the Commandment' (Did 1.5): Lexical Reflections on Almsgiving as 'The Commandment,'" *NTS* 60 (2014) 1–18.

rendered instead with a diversity of other Greek words, very often nominalized neuters formed in -μα: e.g. δικαίωμα, πρόσταγμα, νόμιμα. It is clear that a rhetorical range of essentially exchangeable terms with very considerable semantic overlap is, nevertheless, here in play.[8] The development of ἐντολή in the sense of "charity" thus remains revealing for the meaning of this singular חק. Still, the syntagm in 4Q521 is distinct. Rather than speaking nakedly of "the commandment," 4Q521 has specified the contents or character of this particular חק by adding the notion of חסד.

The most straightforward rendering of the composite phrase and that followed by various translations (in line with Puech's reading) is simply to follow the schoolbook gloss: "The law of Your lovingkindness" (Wise, Abegg, Cook, and Gordon). If this innocuous rendering dutifully accommodates the sense of a "law" characterized by God's "loving kindness" (objective genitive), it has done nothing to inquire if some new semantic creation has been forged by the strange fusion of these two hefty concepts. The compendious, but inevitably dated Hebrew lexica are not of great help here unfortunately. In the light of the sense just evoked for חק, however, more contemporary research on the important biblical term חסד opens up an alluring possibility.

In an important study on Hos 6:6, Jan Joosten has recently demonstrated the semantic migration of the Hebrew category of חסד during the Second Temple period.[9] While in an earlier linguistic stratum the word might already mean "proofs of mercy" (HALOT), by the time of the LXX translation it had come to mean more concretely "charity" or "alms." A similar resonance in 4Q521 is thus to be considered. One need not overtranslate, but simply recognize that at the time prototypical "piety" had taken specific shape in works of mercy (as in the book of Tobit) and that this charitable behavior was an expression of the culture of supererogation closely connected to the חסידים. The two distinct elements in the phrase in 4Q521 in any case strikingly converge on a single semantic idea and חק חסד might justifiably be rendered "the commandment to practice mercy" or perhaps simply "the precept of mercy." This interpretation would effectively make the expression an epexegetical expansion of the more compact and common המצוה, "alms."

[8] The example of a text such as Neh 10:30 LXX demonstrates the proximity and stereotypical character of all these terms (cf. 1 Chron 29:19; 2 Chron 19:10).

[9] Jan JOOSTEN, « חסד "bienveillance" et ἔλεος "pitié". Réflexions sur une équivalence lexicale dans la Septante », in : Eberhard BONS (éd.), *« Car c'est l'amour qui me plaît, non le sacrifice ... ». Recherches sur Osée 6 :6 et son interprétation juive et chrétienne* (JSJ.S 88), Leiden, Brill, 2004, 23–42.

If this sense is attractive, one must simply hold on to charity/mercy (in the multifaceted sense of ἐλεημοσύνη) as part of the semantic coloratura invested in these collocated words. Each new addition to the syntax complexifies the philological difficulty of deciphering the phrase, however, while planting us more solidly in the specific grammatical context of 4Q521. In this precise syntactical environment, the problem that must presently be faced is thus how to handle the pronomial suffix along with the direct object marker – while regrettably lacking the all-important verb. The initial *waw* should also be borne in mind, for the phrase must be imagined to stand in conjunction with another idea.

The sole case in the Dead Sea Scrolls in which חק appears with the direct object marker is CD 20.32–33, where the men of the community are advised "not to reject the righteous statutes (ולא ישיבו את חקי הצדק) when they hear them" (cf. 4Q266?). Clearly these are *God*'s righteous statues and in 4Q521, on the model of חקי קדשו (i.e. the personal pronoun applied to the *nomen regens*), a second person "your commandment of mercy" would be commodious. A verb of fulfilling or observing (or *not rejecting*) would be the presumptive missing complement. Taken this way, the continuation of the line in 4Q521 2 iii 1b – "and I will liberate them…" – might be understood in a resultative sense. They have observed (or not rejected) God's commandment of showing mercy; *therefore* God will deliver them from eschatological danger. The infelicity here would be the jarring shift in person: from a liturgical, Hodayoth-style direct address ("you") to a first- and third-person perspective ("I" and "them"). The clumsiness is not easily resolved unless we suppose that the first-person subject in line 1b is also the subject of the lost verb preceding line 1a. Thus: "I have observed/will fulfill/accomplish [… something] and your precept of mercy and I will liberate them…" One would, of course, expect God himself to be the liberator and thus speaker, especially given the direct echo in line 1b of Ps 146:8, cited in Frag. 2 ii 8 and his first person speech in following line. This makes nonsense of חסדך, however.

To address this, perhaps one might imagine not the voice of God but rather of God's agent: the messiah or eschatological prophet (who right on cue comes obligingly into view in the following line, Frag. 2 iii 2). We know from Frag 9, 2–3 that something significant is to occur ביד משיח and בעבד אדני. It is very possible, moreover, that (as Puech contends) the proclamation of good news in Frag. 2 ii 12 is spoken, not by God directly, but by his eschatological agent. Perhaps, then, the evangelical message includes precisely this saving figure's announcement of his fulfillment of God's commandment of mercy and the freeing of those eschatologically bound. In this scenario the חק חסד would carry some sense of an epic divine decree realized and accomplished in the Lord's agent's very act of liberation. In the *Serekh ha-Yahad* column 10, an unidentified speaker suddenly proclaims, "By a prayer I shall bless him – a חוק forever engraved. When each new year begins... when weeks of years begin, Jubilee by Jubilee, while I live, on my tongue shall the חוק be inscribed" (1QS 10.6,8). Perhaps this mysterious first-person voice, who sings out the ordained seasons and Jubilees, might help us visualize the role of the eschatological speaker in 4Q521. He is the one who announces the arrival of the ordained moment of God's mercy – not unlike another similar voice in 4Q256 19.3–5, who also marks the appointed times, when "the precept is fulfilled" (בהשלם חוק) with an "offering of the lips according to the precept engraved forever" (חרות לעד כחוק), when the "everlasting mercies" are inaugurated (למפתח חסדי עולם). As I will suggest in §4 below, reading חוק חסד in this way, as the proclamation of the decree of mercy, would strongly align 4Q521 with 11Q13, where Melchizedek serves as the executor of God's merciful charity by freeing Israel from the debt bondage of sin.

The prospect of this messianic spin is rather attractive. There is another way around the clumsiness of the shifting persons, however. If one simply entertains the reading חסדם the awkwardness is *tout d'un coup* quite elegantly resolved. In this case, however, the interpretation of the phrase as *God*'s precept or decree of mercy no longer works. An option would accordingly be to rethink חק. Possibly it has the sense here not of a "law" at all, but rather of a prescribed "portion" as Prov 30:8 (לחם חקי) and Ezek 16:27 (חקך ואגרע). The phrase חק חסדם could then be understood as "the portion prescribed/stipulated by their works of mercy."[10] Here the חק could equally signify the "portion" of food/money that they in their mercy distributed or else, more like the payment/legacy in Gen 47:22, it would signify the fate allotted the just as a reward for their deeds of mercy, similar to the expression in Sir^{M} 41:3 or the sense of assigned inheritance found in the חוק of later Hebrew (e.g. *b. Erub.* 54a). This meaning of a "portion" or "measure" is not unknown in the scrolls, albeit through the citation of biblical verses like Mic 7:11 and Isa 5:14 (cf. CD 4,12; 4QpIsa^{b} ii 5; cf. 11Q19 39.8). The currency of the usage should hence not

[10] Syntactically, the construction משפט אלהיהם communicates a very similar notion to חק חסדם (Jer 5:4–5; cf. Ps 37:31; Neh 9:3; Hos 4:6; also, Ezra 7:14, 26; Dan 6:6). In this light, the possessive should be attached to the *nomen rectum*, so that the sense would not be "their portion of חסד" (perhaps reduced adjectively to "their *hesed*-like portion"), but rather "the portion of their חסד." The phrase then supports an instrumental sense and might thus be analyzed as a *genitivus auctoris*, "the portion prescribed by their mercy."

be impugned. Whether the peculiarity of the expression חק חסד supports or argues against such non-normative usage might be debated, on the other hand. Regardless, in the former case, made the direct object of a sentence about offering some measure of material mercy, the missing verb might be imagined to come from the lexicon of charitable giving; while in the second case one would expect some verb of recompense.

In the absence of the verb and simply at the level of syntax it is not clear how to decide between such options. While no direct object marker appears after the verb שלם in the important parallel seen in 4QpsEzek above, the naked construction is proper to this verb (cf. Ruth 2:12; 1 Sam 24:20): "They will be repaid [for] their piety/mercy (חסדם)." This basic sense is compelling, for the parallel fits within a shared eschatological context, closely binding these two scrolls together. Indeed, given 4Q521's similar interest in resurrection, something semantically similar to the ישתלמו חסדם of 4QpsEzek would perfectly complete the half phrase ואת חק חסדם. God will grant to the merciful the portion they have earned by their charitable works.

It can be noted that this last interpretation and the interpretation offered of חק חסדך above – the execution of a divine decree of חסד, resulting in eschatological liberation from some evil – reflect the same essential conceptual field, but seen from two differing angles. Namely, the alternative pronomial suffixes map onto a corresponding reorientation in the subject of the missing verb. Either a savior figure enacts God's eschatological precept of mercy, or God himself repays the pious for their works of mercy according to his command. In both instances, though, the consequence of enacting mercy is eschatological freedom from some great misfortune. The concrete dynamics of this liberating agency and the concrete character of the binding evil remain open questions, but it is in this conceptual context that one should understand the phrase. In other words, if it means anything more or other than simply "law of loving kindness" – whatever that means – the expression חק חסד in the immediate grammatical environment of 4Q521 concerns a concrete realization of mercy resulting in some massively important eschatological blessing.

3. 4Q521 and the Resurrection of the Doers of חסד

In approaching the next stage of this study, in which the horizon is widened and some coherent conceptual context is sought for the internal rhetoric of 4Q521, an important methodological remark must be made. The scrolls are in such a fragmentary state and riddled with so many lacunae that cautious guesswork is an inescapable part of interpretation. We accordingly cross here into a different aspect of the reconstruction: no longer the philological analysis of the existing textual remains – where controlled guesswork is already required, as seen – but rather a still more liberal exercise of historical imagination. Naturally, as a rule, "the difficulty of restoration increases with the originality of the document" and the scroll in question is certainly difficult on this measure.[11]

Significantly, in the *editio princeps* of 4Q521, Puech has found a place for the specific language of almsdeeds within a small textual gap. The location is in column ii, line 10, where he offers the following reading:

ופרי מעשה טוב לאיש לוא יתאחר

et le fruit d'une bonne œuvre ne sera différé pour personne

While this *ad sensum* proposal obviously cannot be confirmed and the lacuna is larger than the editorial brackets might betray, the spacing of the letters in the line is correctly reckoned and the phrasing is appropriate to the time and place of composition. The supplied expressions are thus a useful, disciplined guess and in line with the freer, more tentative Meritt-McGregor epigraphical school. More importantly, as an effort to revitalize the author's thought, the reconstruction resonates with a variety of recurrent themes perceptible in the text at different levels.

The technical expression מעשה טוב is commonly used specifically to denote almsdeeds, being largely synonymous with *gemîlût ḥăsādîm*. In Frag. 5 i 5, there is possibly another echo of the language of doing good, having as its object a man's "neighbor," an idea ostensibly drawn from Leviticus 19, though here again the text allows no absolute certainty. If present, however, an allusion to the prescription of Lev 19:18 would recall the very significant interpretation of that text in the Damascus Document as a commandment specifically to help the poor (see §4 below). Again, in Frag. 7 ii 4, there is a similar expression.

[11] Louis ROBERT, "Les épigraphies et l'épigraphie grecque et romaine" in: *Opera minora selecta : Epigraphie et antiquités grecques, volume 5*, Amsterdam, 1990, 65–101, 98. Roger Bagnall's caution is also here in order: "A restored text is… a means of clarifying an interpretation. But the historian who would use such texts must always keep in mind that reconstructions are a form of presentation of an argument, not simply another form of primary evidence messed up with some funny brackets" Roger S. BAGNALL, *Reading Papyri, Writing Ancient History* (Approaching the Ancient World) London, Routledge, 2020, 28. This perspective on reconstructions as compact arguments helps put a more positive spin on the justifiable concerns of Matthew MORGENSTERN, "A 'Reconstructionist' Approach to the Dead Sea Scrolls: E. Puech's Edition of Discoveries in the Judean Desert XXV," *JJS* 55 (2004) 347–53.

Returning to column ii, line 10, the collocation of "good works" with the notion of פרי, literally "fruit," calls directly to mind the evocative constellation of themes explored by Gary Anderson and Eliezer Diamond and arguably means "reward" and more specifically something like the "interest" earned on an investment: namely, the heavenly treasure stored up by the supererogatory performance of *gemîlût ḥăsādîm* – a eschatological reward quite explicitly *not yet* tasted here below.[12] This general notion would perfectly suit the circumstance evoked in the preceding lines (7–9):

> [7]Car Il honorera les pieux (חסידים) sur un trône de royauté éternelle,
> [8]Libérant (מתיר) les prisonniers, rendant la vue aux aveugles, redressant les cour[bés].
> [9]Aussi pour [to]jours je m'attacherai [a ceux qui] espèrent et dans son amour Il [*récompensera*/*jugera*/ ?]

Several significant connections link this concentrated rhetoric of reward and salvation in column ii, lines 7-10, with the broken off language of column iii, line 1. Above all, in column iii, the sentence beginning immediately after the half-sentence -ואת חק חסד contains the incomplete announcement of a promise:

ואתר אותם ב]

I shall set them free with/by…

As already mentioned above, this promise of "setting free" points directly back to the earlier use of the same verb just seen in column ii, line 8, where, in the words of Ps 146:7c–8ab, it is said that the Lord will honor the חסידים by enthroning them, *freeing them*, and raising them up. The text of Psalm 146:8c itself continues and summarizes the foregoing by saying that "the Lord loves *the righteous* (צדיקים)." The sense of this title, replaced here in 4Q521 by חסידים, resonates very directly with Second Temple charity discourse and supplies a hint at the concrete character of these "Pious" people: they are the Psalm's "doers of צדקה," thus "workers of mercy," saved and rewarded by the Lord.[13] The basic equivalence

[12] See Gary ANDERSON, *Charity: The Place of the Poor in the Biblical Tradition*, Yale, New Haven, 2013; and Eliezer DIAMOND, *Holy Men and Hunger Artists: Fasting and Asceticism in Rabbinic Culture*, New York, Oxford, 2004.

[13] On this meaning of צדקה in the DSS and Second Temple texts, see Francesco ZANELLA, "Between 'Righteousness' and 'Alms': A Semantic Study of the Lexeme צדקה in the Dead Sea Scrolls" in: Steven FASSBERG, Moshe BAR-ASHER, and Ruth CLEMENTS (eds.), *Hebrew in the Second Temple Period: The Hebrew of the Dead Sea Scrolls and of Other Contemporary Sources* (STDJ 108) Leiden, Brill, 2013, 269–88.

of these two titles for the scroll is clear from the parallelism in column ii, line 5: "the Lord seeks the חסידים and calls the צדיקים by name" (cf. Frag. 1 ii 6).[14]

The first-person reiteration in column iii of the eschatological deeds promised in the third-person language of Psalm 146 in column ii helpfully illuminates the pious party behind the אותם of line 1b and/or embedded in the third plural suffix, if we accept חסדם. The "they" here is precisely the group glorified and saved a few lines before.[15] Arguably, then, the direct object marker and missing verb in line 1a together represent an idea conceptually parallel to the royal glorification of the חסידים, which introduced the quotation of Psalm 146 in its earlier iteration.

The title חסידים is surprisingly rare in the texts of Qumran. 4Q521 and 11QPs[a] are the two most important texts. In 11QPs[a] 22, interestingly, God (or rather Zion as a metonym) is glorified במעשי חסידים, "by the works of the Pious," while these works become the principle by which the חסידים also receive their own reward (אניש כמעשיו ישתלם). Is it possible in 4Q521 to be any more precise about the specific eschatological blessing conferred upon these חסידים, whether for each man's works or because the Lord's decree of חסד is now being accomplished? The series of saving deeds recounted in Ps 146:7–8 and the Psalm's poetic characterization of these righteous חסידים as prisoners, blind, and bent could hold at least two precious clues.

First of all, the concept of liberating the אסורים has a critical echo in Isa 61:1, where the proclamation of דרור for these captives represents an amnesty, understood in the Second Temple context as the release of Israel from its debt bondage of sin (cf. 11Q13).[16] The citation of Isa 61:1 in 4Q521 (2 ii 12) only a few lines after Psalm 146 makes it very plausible that some such Jubilee of forgiveness is also a live idea for the author

[14] In the structure of the parallelism, one might perhaps detect a subtle preference for the overachieving חסידים intoned in the suggestive verb בקר. These are the rare ones that God so desires that he actively searches to find them.

[15] A contrast between an in- and an out-group is also theoretically envisageable: "Wicked men reject your precept of mercy, but (contrastive *waw*) I will free *them*, i.e. the pious..., etc." If אותם has an emphatic sense such a reconstruction might be correct. The preserved text of 4Q521 is not occupied with this sort of "sons of light vs. sons of darkness" dualism, however, though a tiny hint of the fate of the ארורים appears in Frag. 7 ii 13 and a distinction between the צדיק and רשע is present in Frag. 14, 2. Generally, though, from Frag. 2 ii 3 through the very end of Fragment 3, every indication is of benefits for the in-group. A variant on this out-group rendering, would be to imagine that the righteous themselves in the past transgressed against God's חק חסד, but that now he will liberate them from their iniquity and sins (cf. Frag. 1 ii 4).

[16] See the very useful study of Bradley GREGORY, "The Post-Exilic Exile in Third Isaiah: Isaiah 61:1–3 in Light of Second Temple Hermeneutics," *JBL* 126 (2007) 475–96.

of this scroll. Secondly, the promise of raising up the bowed down (זוקף כפופים) might contain a specific reference to the reward of resurrection, if as Benjamin Wold contends the citation of Ps 146:8 in both 4Q521 and 4QpsEzek encodes an image of raising the dead.[17] This would certainly accord with the general tenor of these two remarkable texts, so unusually interested in resurrection.

In 4QPsEzek the concrete recompense for חסדם is matter of open interrogation:

> These things, when will they come to pass and *how will they be rewarded for their pious mercy* (והכה ישתלמו חסדם)?

The Lord's direct answer to this question – which is our own question as well – is to command Ezekiel to prophesy over the dry bones. Linking resurrection to personal reward, as a specific and direct recompense for righteousness (חסדם), is an important development in this rewritten Bible passage that moves beyond the base text of Ezekiel 37.[18] Personal responsibility for reward and punishment is a clear teaching elsewhere in the prophetic book, of course, and it seems that 4QpsEzek has simply applied this notion to the prophecy of resurrection. If Ezekiel's prophetic gesture over the bones is missing from the preserved fragments of 4Q521, the graphic opening of graves appears to be present (Frag. 7 ii 8–9; cf. Ezek 37:12–13), and of the resurrection motif in general there can be no doubt. That column iii, line 2 evokes the eschatological coming of Elijah puts the חק חסד in immediate proximity to the biblical figure most known for reviving the dead, moreover.[19] Perhaps, then, personal reward is again asserting itself in the eschatology of 4Q521 and those raised by "the one who revives the dead of his people" (i.e., העושים את הטוב, Frag. 7 ii 4), are simply the חסידים receiving the portion merited for their pious practice of חסד, as in rewritten Ezekiel. Or perhaps, the scene in 4Q521 remains more corporate, as in the canonical book, focused on the merciful mission of God's end-time agent (or God himself?) to raise up the righteous dead.

[17] Benjamin WOLD, "Agency and Raising the Dead in 4QPseudo-Ezekiel and 4Q521 2 ii," *ZNWKAK* 103 (2012) 1–19, esp. 10–11.

[18] The limiting of resurrection to those who have shown חסד is one of the indications that 4QPsEzek, unlike the canonical book, envisions an individual resurrection, not simply the corporate resurrection of all Israel. See Devorah DIMANT, *Qumran Cave 4, XXI: Parabiblical Texts, Part 4 : Pseudo-Prophetic Texts* (DJD XXX) Oxford, Clarendon, 2001, 33.

[19] On the figure of Elijah as eschatological prophet in 4Q521 (and 4Q558), see Émile PUECH, "L'attente du retour d'Élie dans l'Ancient Testament et les écrits péritestamentaires : 4Q558 et 4Q521," *RevQ* 30/111 (2018) 3–26.

4. Reading 4Q521 as Second Temple Charity Theology

In this last part of the study, as one final step, I wish simply to highlight briefly the broader Second Temple context in which the preceding reconstruction(s) of 4Q521 2 iii 1 might be profitably read. Both the advantages and risks of this concluding move should be clear. Stitching together a coherent theological fabric from the bare threads of thought preserved in 4Q521 cannot be achieved without borrowing patches from more complete materials. The distinctive patterns and color of the original scroll must not thereby be lost, however.

The extraordinary significance of charitable giving as a pious exercise might first be mentioned. This obtains, moreover, not merely in the broader Judaism of the period, but for the Essene community in a very particular way. Josephus says that only two things were left to the personal discretion of individual Essenes: ἐπικουρία καὶ ἔλεος, helping the deserving poor when they begged for alms and handing out food to the destitute (*B.J.* 2.8.6). Such a statement is naturally exaggerated but quite revealing of the extraordinarily high place accorded to virtuoso acts of charitable giving within the eschatological worldview of this group. In this context, the Damascus Document innovatively interprets Lev 19:18 as a command to love one's brother specifically by "supporting the hand of the poor and needy" (CD 6.20–21).[20] This stipulation is bound through the citation of Ezek 16:49 to a well-developed section at the end of the document in CD 14.12–17, where a community wealth ethic is described in which two days' wages are offered each month to the Overseer for the benefit of orphans, the aged, the dying, captives, virgins with no dowry, and for "all the works of the community."[21] This concrete ethos of ἔλεος prevailing among the Essenes, which found practical expression in both private and corporately organized ways, could naturally be described at length, but this is enough to intone and amplify the importance of actual charitable praxis as the lived world of the חסידים who produced 4Q521.[22]

Debate, of course, exists over whether 4Q521 originated in the community or not and a certain circularity is hard to avoid in defining the texts that were produced by the Yahad. Still, if several motifs stand out in 4Q521

[20] See A. Giambrone, *Sacramental Charity, Creditor Christology, and the Economy of Salvation in Luke's Gospel* (WUNT 439) Tübingen, Mohr Siebeck, 2017, 143–50.

[21] On the extreme importance of charity in the context of the Essene community, see Brian Capper, "Essene Community Houses and Jesus' Early Community" in: James Charlesworth (ed.), *Jesus and Archeology*, Grand Rapids, Eerdmans, 2006, 472–502.

[22] See, for instance, Catherine M. Murphy, *Wealth in the Dead Sea Scrolls and in the Qumran Community* (STDJ 40) Leiden, Brill.

as being distinctive, notably resurrection, other themes and expressions are very familiar and widespread in the scrolls. The presence of charity motifs in 4Q521 would align this scroll with the Essenes as we know them, without thereby ruling out alternative reconstructions. In any event, it would be a text sympathetic to their behavior. Like the parallel expressions in CD 20, the notion of a divine חק חסד would have spoken directly to the Essene rule of life.

At the level of the ideas behind the praxis, 4Q521 is not an outlier in the soteriological value that it invests in חסד as somehow closely linked to the resurrection. The personal recompense theology of 4QpsEzek has already been invoked at several reprises. One may naturally debate how חסדם should specifically be understood in that context. If the lexical background advanced here for 4Q521 holds water, however, a similar semantic resonance might certainly be detected in 4QpsEzek. As a support for understanding חסד in the specific sense of charity/mercy in 4QpsEzek, moreover, it can be observed that the author's exegetical operation binding the principle of personal responsibility with the concrete reward of resurrection has an explicit source in the biblical base text. In Ezek 18:7 and 16 it is repeatedly said that the upright man who "gives his bread to the hungry and clothes the naked" will escape death: "he shall not die for his father's iniquity; he shall surely live" (18:17). Heard in the right eschatological light (i.e. Ezekiel 37), it is thus easy to see what has informed the thought of 4QpsEzek. Practicing charity means that one will enjoy an eschatological life stronger than death. In light of 4Q521 2 ii 7–10 it is entirely plausible that these two closely connected scrolls share the same basic perspective on just how the just will be rewarded for their works of חסד.

There is an additional important background for this resurrection-charity nexus, however. The entire, supererogatory framework of Second Temple merit soteriology is very closely bound up with a *sin-as-debt* and *charity-as-merit* paradigm, as Anderson has shown.[23] In this context, Prov 10:2b, a passage with a significant *Nachleben*, makes an unusually powerful claim: צדקה תציל ממות.[24] It is clear that as the semantic value of צדקה developed in the Second Temple period and came to mean specifically "alms" the verse inevitably came to be understood to mean that "almsgiving" had

[23] See above all G. ANDERSON, *Sin: A History*, Yale, New Haven, 2009.

[24] See G. ANDERSON, "A Treasury in Heaven: The Exegesis of Proverbs 10:2 in the Second Temple Period," *Hebrew Bible and Ancient Israel* 1 (2012) 351–67.

the power to save from death.[25] In the right eschatological environment, the jump to charity empowering a share in the resurrection was easily made. As I have argued elsewhere, one of the key witnesses to this precise notion is the Gospel of Luke.[26] It is not unreasonable to imagine that the worldview of 4Q521 (and 4QpsEzek) endorsed a similar conception. As Luke arguably also knows an interpretation of Ps 146:8 in reference to the resurrection, the proximity of the traditions is all the more impressive.

In the Lukan context, of course, the promise of participating in the resurrection through personal works of mercy has assumed a strong Christological shape. Luke's Christology, however, is very closely bound to the proclamation of the eschatological Jubilee. The Messiah announces a great amnesty, cancelling the debt of sin in the name of God (cf. Luke 4); while sinners receive and participate in the pardon of this "year of favor" by, in their turn, showing mercy to their neighbor. The citation of Isa 61:1–2 as the founding act of this gracious proclamation naturally binds the Gospel closely to 4Q521 Frag. 2 ii 12, where the same text is cited. Disagreement exists about who precisely makes this proclamation in 4Q521, whether the messiah (Frag. 2 ii 1), the eschatological prophet (Frag. 2 iii 2; Elijah?) – if he represents a distinct figure from the messiah – or perhaps the Lord himself. The speaker is either complicated or clarified, according to one's presuppositions, by the further link of Isa 60:1–2 to 11Q13, where Melchizedek proclaims the Jubilee. While both Luke and 11Q13 are clearly influenced strongly by a *sin-as-debt* and *release-of-debt-prisoners* soteriology, the shape of Melchizedek's amnesty is a more one-sided, divine act of *remission*, while Luke's messianic vision retains this element, similarly foregrounding the intervention of an Anointed One, but making more place alongside him for personal, pious *repayment* through works of mercy.

A spectrum of apocalyptic scenarios must thus be acknowledged, with greater or lesser attention to human involvement in redemption. A place within this field should be found for 4Q521, moreover, that respects its own specific interests and mechanics. Perhaps the first and most fundamental question to pose in this connection is whether the motif of liberating prisoners, present at least twice in this scroll and so closely linked to

[25] On this development, besides F. ZANELLA, *Between 'Righteousness' and 'Alms'*, see Franz ROSENTHAL, "Ṣĕdāqâh, Charity," *HUCA* 23 (1950–51) 411–30.

[26] GIAMBRONE, *Sacramental Charity*, 209–81.

the חק חסד, does not also, like these other traditions, owe something significant to the notion of sin as debt. And if it does, just how does this scroll think that that eschatological debt is cancelled? Various possibilities exist and it seems important at the end of this study to add a third player into the mix in the ongoing debate over the specific agency behind the eschatological benefits in 4Q521. Perhaps one must envision or at least entertain the possibility of a *double* coworking with God's sovereign power. Just as the Lord's own glorious deeds might be revealed through the hand of his anointed eschatological agent and/or prophet; so, perhaps, those raised up from the grave also have their own ethical part to play, in cooperation with the Lord and משיחו.

Conclusion

Patient paleographic and philological analysis of the widely neglected phrase חק חסד in 4Q521 2 iii 1 has opened up new perspectives on both the messianism and eschatology of this famous scroll. Namely, charity appears to hold a significant, not previously recognized place in the conceptual framework and resurrection emerges as a reward apportioned to the righteous, either by their own pious deeds of mercy or by some towering intervention of divine חסד. While it is important not to exaggerate the centrality charity holds in the rhetoric of the extant fragments, it is also important not to underestimate this subtle and incomplete allusion. Viewed within a wider Second Temple context, a soteriological grammar of immense influence is being invoked. The deep links to 4QpsEzek are obviously profoundly suggestive. Read in conjunction with this closely-related text, the resurrection theology of 4Q521 inclines toward an eschatological doctrine of personal reward. The contacts with 11Q13 are also revealing; and here the mediation of some chosen agent who accomplishes God's determined act of mercy would push the messianic perspective of 4Q521 in a different direction. Luke's Gospel, finally, blends these contrasting soteriological configurations in a single participative charity Christology. Perhaps, ultimately, the evocative fragments of 4Q521 represent a precursor to the synthesized Lukan vision. Such radiating theological relationships naturally in no way exhaust the significance or uniqueness of these very diverse texts. Still, the contacts and patterns invite recognition and reflection upon a kind of common eschatological messianism, ordered to resurrection and let loose by some decisive action of mercy. The Lord's prophets and messiahs have their proper apocalyptic roles to play in the eschatological drama of the resurrection – and so perhaps do the charitable חסידים.

So: Can agonizing over fragments of letters and the meaning of broken-off lines in poorly preserved, but tantalizing ancient scrolls yield any appreciable or solid theological fruit? Undoubtedly. It is a great challenge, however, to know just when to insist and when to give room to historical imagination and its reconstructions. If the present essay has tried to respect this infinitely delicate and hard-won scholarly balance, keenly conscious of the fragility of the source material, but inevitably making disputable judgments in its regard all the same, it is a rewarding effort and exercise only made possible by the extraordinary work and earlier similar efforts of Émile Puech.

QUEL EST LE SENS DE ΠΑ͂ΣΑ ΣΟΦΊΑ EN *SIRACIDE* 1,1A? NOTES PHILOLOGIQUES ET EXÉGÉTIQUES

Maurice GILBERT S.J.

Ces quelques pages, je les offre à un ami, Émile Puech, dont l'acribie est bien connue quand il s'agit de textes anciens, en particulier en hébreu ou en araméen: quel sens donner au premier distique du livre de Ben Sira dans sa version grecque?

1. UNE QUESTION DISPUTÉE

En 1989, Pancratius C. Beentjes a proposé de traduire en anglais les premiers mots de *Si* 1,1 par *Full wisdom,* comme en *Si* 19,20[1]. En 2004, il reprenait ses explications de 1989[2]. Le point principal de Beentjes consiste à voir un rapport entre l'expression πᾶσα σοφία en *Si* 19,20 et en *Si* 1,1. En outre, il observait aussi bien en 1989 qu'en 2004 un certain parallélisme entre *Si* 19,20-24 et *Si* 1,1-10.25-27. Enfin, en 2004, il justifiait sa traduction de πᾶσα par *Full* et expliquait que, pour Ben Sira, ce n'est pas n'importe quelle sorte de sagesse qui peut être identifiée (*equated*) à la crainte du Seigneur, mais seul un concept vraiment spécifique de la sagesse. Dès lors, selon Beentjes, le πᾶσα de *Si* 19,20 doit avoir une signification totalisante (*elative*). Il s'appuyait alors sur ce que Bo REICKE écrivait en 1954 dans le *TWNT* sur le sens de l'adjectif πᾶς sans article dans le Nouveau Testament[3] : « *Elative Bedeutung:* völlig, höchst, all, lauter » ; Bo Reicke renvoyait à Mt 28,18 (« Tout pouvoir... »); Ac 4,29 (« en

[1] Pancratius C. BEENTJES, « *Full Wisdom is Fear of the Lord* ». *Ben Sira 19,20-24,31: Context, Composition and Concept*, in *EstBib* 47 (1989) 27-45, spéc. 39-40, repris dans son recueil « *Happy the One who Meditates on Wisdom* » *(Sir 14,20). Collected Essays on the Book of Ben Sira* (BE&T, 43), Leuven, Peeters, 2006, 87-106, spéc. p. 99.

[2] P. C. BEENTJES, « *Full Wisdom is from the Lord* ». *Sir 1:1-10 and its place in Israel's Wisdom literature* », in A. PASSARO – G. BELLIA (eds.), *The Wisdom of Ben Sira. Studies on Tradition, Redaction, and Theology* (DLCS, 1), Berlin – New Yok, de Gruyter, 2008, p.147-148, repris dans son recueil « *Happy the One* », 19-34, spéc. p. 28-29. Conférence donnée à Palerme en 2004.

[3] Bo REICKE, πᾶς, ἅπας, in *TWNT*, 5, 885-889 et 890-895, spéc. p. 886, ligne 14. P. C. BEENTJES cite la version anglaise *TDNT V*, Grand Rapids, Eerdmans, 1977, 888.

toute assurance »); 2 Co 4,2; 9,8; etc. Beentjes ajoutait qu'il n'excluait pas que le πᾶσα de *Si* 1,1 ait le même sens.

Puis-je me permettre de mettre en doute cette interprétation de *Si* 1,1 et de *Si* 19,29?

2. Une question de grammaire

Pourquoi privilégier le sens *elative*, totalisant, alors que Bo Reicke mentionnait aussi le sens distributif (« chaque ») pour l'adjectif πᾶς sans article dans le Nouveau Testament? Ben Sira et son traducteur grec font partie de l'Ancien Testament. Commençons par cette version grecque. Le *Dictionnaire Bailly*[4] distingue, pour πᾶς au singulier, suivi d'un substantif sans article soit un sens partitif (« chaque homme »), soit le sens de « tout entier » (πᾶσαν ἀληθείην κατάλεξον, « à dire toute la vérité »: Homère, *Iliade*, 24, 407; πᾶν κράτος, « la plus haute puissance »: Sophocle, *Philoctète*, 142).

Dans la Septante, πᾶσα σοφία n'apparaît que trois autres fois. En Jb^{LXX} 26,3, on lit τίνι συμβεβούλευσαι ; οὐχ ᾧ πᾶσα σοφία ; « À qui donnes-tu des conseils? N'est-ce pas à qui est toute sagesse? » Il s'agit de Dieu qui est lui-même la sagesse dans sa totalité (cf. Si 1,8), mais le texte hébreu donne: ... ללא חכמה, « Quels bons conseils tu donnes à qui n'a pas de sagesse »: il s'agit alors de Job. En *Si*^{Gr} 37,21, texte qui n'a pas d'équivalent en hébreu, on lit, à propos du beau parleur: « Le Seigneur ne lui accorde pas [sa] faveur, car il est dépourvu de toute sagesse »: il en manque totalement. Enfin, en Dn 1,4, aussi bien dans la Septante que chez Théodotion, les enfants juifs que Nabuchodonosor veut à sa cour « devaient être [...] instruits *en toute sagesse*, savants en science et subtils en savoir »; le sens de *en toute sagesse* semble plutôt distributif: A. Crampon, dans sa *Sainte Bible* de 1905, traduisait משׂכלים בכל חכמה, « doués de toutes sortes de talents » et, en 1970, la *New English Bible*: *in all branches of knowledge*.

Qu'en est-il en *Si* 1,1 et 19,20 ?

Dans le Siracide grec, on trouve une cinquantaine d'emplois de πᾶς suivi d'un substantif sans article dans des phrases positives, mais aussi négatives. On relève en particulier treize emplois de πᾶσα σάρξ et six de πᾶς ἄνθρωπος. Dans la majorité des cas où le grec donne πᾶς suivi d'un substantif sans article, le texte hébreu donnait de même כל suivi d'un substantif sans article.

[4] Anatole Bailly, *Dictionnaire grec-français rédigé avec le concours de E. Egger. Édition revue par L. Séchan et P. Chantraine*, Paris, Hachette, 1950, p. 1495.

Or, mis à part *Si* 1,1 et 19,20 en discussion, dans cinq cas le grec et l'hébreu donnent à πᾶς ou à כל non pas un sens distributif, mais une nuance de totalité. Voici ces cinq cas:

Si 3,13b: ἐν πάσῃ ἰσχύι σου, « toi qui es en pleine forme ». Manque l'hébreu.
Si 30,15a: παντὸς χρυσίου, « plutôt que tout l'or du monde »: מפז, « plutôt que l'or ».
Si 47,8c: ἐν πάσῃ καρδίᾳ αὐτοῦ, « de tout son cœur »: בכל לבו.
Si 50,13c: ἔναντι πάσης ἐκκλησίας, « devant toute l'assemblée »: נגד כל קהל.
Si 50,20b: ἐπὶ πᾶσαν ἐκκλησίαν, « sur toute l'assemblée »: על כל קהל.

En hébreu, en effet, כל suivi d'un substantif sans article peut avoir deux sens[5]. Le premier, le plus fréquent, est distributif; le second, particulièrement en poésie, indique une totalité. En Si 1,1 et 19,20, quel est le sens? Pour Beentjes, ce doit être celui d'une totalité: *Full Wisdom*. Qu'en penser?

3. Discussion

Je propose de partir de *Si* 19,20, le premier texte pour lequel Beentjes a avancé sa proposition nouvelle de πᾶσα σοφία. Le titre de l'article dans lequel il s'en explique traduit le premier stique de ce verset: « Full Wisdom is Fear of the Lord »[6]. Est-ce bien la pensée de Ben Sira? L'absence du verbe *is* en grec, comme probablement dans l'hébreu qui manque, rend l'interprétation difficile. Il me semble que *Si* 19,20a doit être compris de la façon suivante: « c'est la crainte du Seigneur [le sujet] qui est πᾶσα σοφία [le prédicat]. Notons immédiatement qu'en Si 1,1a, par contre, πᾶσα σοφία est le sujet de la phrase: elle vient du Seigneur. En *Si* 19,20a, le sens de πᾶσα σοφία doit être déterminé en tenant compte des quelques faits littéraires que voici:

3.1. Crainte du Seigneur et accomplissement de la Loi

En grec, *Si* 19,20 s'énonce comme suit:

πᾶσα σοφία φόβος κυρίου
καὶ ἐν πάσῃ σοφίᾳ ποίησις νόμου

Crainte du Seigneur, voilà πᾶσα σοφία
et en toute sagesse [il y a] pratique de la Loi.

[5] Cf. Paul Joüon, *Grammaire de l'hébreu biblique*, Rome, Institut Biblique Pontifical, 1923, §139e = Paul Joüon – Takamitsu Muraoka, *A Grammar of Biblical Hebrew* (Subsidia Biblica 27), Roma, PIB, 2006, §139e. Franciscus Zorell, *Lexicon hebraicum Veteris Testamenti*, Romae, PIB, 1984, p. 356, III.
[6] Cf. note 1.

Beentjes renvoie, à *Si* 21,11:

Ὁ φυλάσσων νόμον κατακρατεῖ τοῦ ἐννοήματος αὐτοῦ
καὶ συντέλεια τοῦ φόβου κυρίου σοφία.

Qui garde la Loi maîtrise sa réflexion
et la perfection de la crainte du Seigneur [voilà] la sagesse.

Si 19,20 et 21,11 sont les seuls distiques du livre à rapprocher crainte du Seigneur et pratique de la Loi à propos de sagesse[7].

En grec, συντέλεια signifie « accomplissement », soit dans le sens de perfection (*Si* 38,28; 43,7; 45,8a; 47,10b; 50,11b) soit de terme, de fin (*Si* 11,27; 16,3; etc.) et le mot grec traduit différents mots hébreux. Quant au mot ἐννόημα il désigne une pensée[8].

En *Si* 21,11, il n'est pas question de πᾶσα σοφία mais simplement de σοφία. Si bien qu'en *Si* 19,20, πᾶσα σοφία pourrait signifier *Full wisdom*, mais pas nécessairement; le sens pourrait être distributif: « Il n'est pas de sagesse sans accomplissement de la Loi » ou « en toute forme de sagesse [même inchoative, comme en *Si* 1,26b], il y a accomplissement de la Loi ».

3.2. Un rapport progressif

Ce paragraphe entend montrer que le rapport entre crainte du Seigneur et sagesse peut être progressif et non pas *full* dès le début. De ce point de vue, Si 1,14-20 est éclairant. Cet ensemble procède selon une structure claire:

Si 1,14: Ἀρχὴ σοφίας
Si 1,16: πλησμονὴ σοφίας
Si 1,18: στέφανος σοφίας
Si 1,20: ῥίζα σοφίας ... καὶ οἱ κλάδοι αὐτῆς

Ce dernier distique reprend les deux extrêmes, le commencement et la plénitude; la racine, en terre, est invisible et la frondaison en est l'apothéose. Or, à côté de chacun des termes qui ouvre ces quatre versets, on trouve toujours la crainte du Seigneur, exprimée par un verbe à l'infinitif en 1,14.16.20 ou par un substantif en 1,18. On notera que la version syriaque n'a retenu pour chaque verset que le commencement.

« Commencement de la sagesse: craindre le Seigneur » (*Si* 1,14): « craindre le Seigneur » est le sujet et « commencement de la sagesse »,

[7] Cf. note 2, son article sur Si 1,1-10, p. 29 (2006) ou p. 148 (2008).

[8] Cf. Michelangelo PRIOTTO – Severino BUSSINO – Renato DE ZAN - Maurice GILBERT, *Sir 21,1–22,26: successo e insuccesso esistenziale. Parte I: Sir 21,1-28,* in *RivBib* 66 (2018) 101-123, spéc. p. 113-114.

l'attribut. Il en est de même dans les formules analogues de l'Ancien Testament: Pr 1,7a; 9,10a; 15,33a; Ps 111[110],10a; Jb 28,28a. On observe que chacun de ces textes, en hébreu comme un grec, formule de manière différente ce principe de comportement. Or, en grec, le mot ἀρχή est classique (Pr 1,7; 9,10; Ps 110[111],10), alors qu'en hébreu on a des mots différents (ראשית en Pr 1,7 et Ps 111,10; תחלה en Pr 9,10). Aillcurs chez Ben Sira, le mot ἀρχή de sa version grecque recouvre encore soit תחלה en *Si* 10,12a et 51,20e, soit ראש en *Si* 11,3; 16,26; 36,15; 37,16; 39,25.32, soit ראשית en *Si* 15,14; on lit même ימי קדם, « les jours d'antan », en *Si* 36,11b(16).

À la vue de ces données, il me semble que la crainte du Seigneur est présente chez le sage ou chez son disciple dès le début de son engagement à suivre la sagesse. Donc avant que la sagesse ne le remplisse tout entier. Dès lors, en *Si* 19,20, la traduction *Full wisdom* me paraît réductrice et donc abusive.

3.3. Si 1,9-10

Si 1,9-10 conforte cette conclusion:

C'est [le Seigneur] qui l'a créée [la Sagesse],
l'a vue et dénombrée,
et l'a répandue sur toutes ses œuvres,
sur toute chair, selon ce qu'il donne,
et l'a prodiguée à ceux qui l'aiment.

La deuxième ligne reprend ce que Jb 28,27 écrivait de la Sagesse. Les stiques de 1,9b appliquent à la Sagesse ce que Jl 3,1-2 disait de l'Esprit que le Seigneur promettait: il y a ici assimilation de la Sagesse de Dieu à son Esprit[9]. L'expression « toutes ses œuvres » est une insertion dans la citation de Joël: elle vise le monde créé dans toutes ses composantes. *Si* 24,3-6a, à la suite de Pr 8,31a rappelle la présence de la Sagesse au monde, de même que *Sg* 7,22–8,1; 14,5 (« les œuvres de ta sagesse »). En outre *Sg* 12,1a redit la même chose à propos de l'Esprit (« Ton Esprit incorruptible est en toutes choses »).

À cette Présence au monde se précise en *Si* 1,10a, en écho à Jl 3,1-2, le don de l'Esprit à « toute chair »: cette expression, treize fois présente chez le Siracide, doit avoir un sens distributif: chaque être de chair, c'est-à-dire chaque être humain à la mesure du don que Dieu lui accorde. Avec cette affirmation, le Siracide fait un pas de plus: les œuvres du Seigneur,

[9] Cf. Patrick W. SKEHAN – Alexander A. DI LELLA, *The Wisdom of Ben Sira* (AncB, 39) New York, Doubleday, 1987, p. 139.

toute chair et chacune d'elles reçoit la Sagesse selon la diversité du don de Dieu.

Plus encore, à ceux qui l'aiment – ou le craignent[10] – il a donné la Sagesse à profusion: aux fils d'Israël, il l'a prodiguée. Le verbe χορηγέω doit recouvrir le verbe hébreu ספק au qal ou au l'hifil, comme en *Si* 39,16.33[11].

Bref, chaque créature reçoit la Sagesse à sa mesure: ce n'est pas toujours *full wisdom*[12].

3.4. L'énigme de Si^{Gr} 1,26

Arrêtons-nous au texte de *Si*^{Gr} 1,26, étonnant pour notre thème:

ἐπιθυμήσας σοφίαν διατήρησον ἐντολάς
καὶ κύριος χορηγήσει σοι αὐτήν.

Désires-tu la sagesse? Garde les préceptes
et le Seigneur te la prodiguera.

Ce verset s'insère au centre de trois distiques (*Si*^{Gr} 1,25-27) consacré au thème de la docilité. Celui-ci, à son tour, fait partie d'un ensemble indiquant trois conditions pour devenir disciple de Ben Sira: maîtrise de soi (*Si* 1,22-24), docilité (*Si* 1,25-27) et enfin sincérité (*Si* 1,28-30). En *Si* 1,26b, on retrouve le verbe χορηγέω de *Si* 1,10b, avec de nouveau le Seigneur comme sujet. Mais le mot grec au pluriel ἐντολάς pose problème: s'agit-il des préceptes de la Tôrâh, opinion probablement majoritaire, ou des préceptes de la Sagesse?

Ce tercet de *Si*^{Gr} 1,25-27 concerne la sagesse, mentionnée à chaque verset. Or, en *Si* 1,25, on lit:

Ἐν θησαυροῖς σοφίας παραβολαὶ ἐπιστήμης
βδέλυγμα δὲ ἁμαρτωλῷ θεοσέβεια

Dans les trésors de la sagesse, maximes de savoir
mais abomination pour le pécheur que la piété.

[10] Sur cette différence entre le grec et le syriaque, en l'absence du texte hébreu, cf. P. W. SKEHAN – A. A. DI LELLA, *The Wisdom of Ben Sira*, p. 137. J'ai pris la même position en 1999 et P.C. BEENTJES, dans son article sur Si 1-10, mentionné *supra*, note 2, p. 27 (2006) ou p. 146 (2008), l'a refusée. Toutefois, il faut noter que le rapport entre aimer le Seigneur et le craindre est classique (cf. Ps 145,19-20); Nuria CALDUCH-BENAGES, *En el crisol de la prueba. Estudio exegético de Sir 2,1-18* (Asociación Bíblica Española, 32), Estella (Navarra), Verbo Divino, 1997, p. 192-208, avec bibliographie, p. 193, note 12.

[11] Cf. Jan LIESEN, *Full of Praise. An Exegetical Study of Sir 39,12-35* (JStJ.S, 64), Leiden, Brill, 2000, p. 190-191.

[12] Cf. *infra* sur l'autre emploi de χορηγέω en *Si* 1,26.

Et le troisième distique, *Si* 1,27, termine ainsi le tercet:

> σοφία γὰρ καὶ παιδεία φόβος κυρίου
> καὶ ἡ εὐδοκία αὐτοῦ πίστις καὶ πραΰτης.
>
> Car sagesse et éducation que la crainte du Seigneur
> et ce qu'il apprécie, c'est la confiance et la douceur.

En *Si*^{Gr} 1,26a, de quels préceptes s'agit-il? Il me semble que ce sont les préceptes, les commandements que l'on trouve dans « les maximes de savoir », celles qui font partie de l'éducation offerte par Ben Sira, comme le proposaient ses prédécesseurs[13]. Il y a, certes, inclusion entre θεοσέβεια du v. 25b et φόβος κυρίου du v. 27a, mais précisément au stique 1,25b, le traducteur grec évite la formule φόβος κυρίου[14], si bien que les ἐντολάς peuvent être ceux des « maximes de savoir »: le livre des Proverbes et celui de Ben Sira en sont remplis.

Mais *Si*^{Gr} 1,25-27 pose un autre problème: est-ce la version grecque d'un texte hébreu authentique de Ben Sira? Si oui, alors le verset 26 concerne notre sujet: le désir de la sagesse précède son abondante réception, mais son octroi exige antérieurement la pratique des préceptes de sagesse. En ce sens, cette pratique docile est déjà un premier pas de sagesse (cf. *Sg* 6,17-18).

Toutefois l'authenticité textuelle de *Si*^{Gr} 1,25-27 n'est pas garantie. Le texte hébreu de 1,1 à 3,6 n'a pas encore été retrouvé. La version syriaque omet Si 1,21-27 et le remplace par un beau texte cohérent à saveur eschatologique. La version *Vetus Latina* de la fin du IIe siècle de notre ère, passée dans la Vulgate probablement déjà à la fin du Ve siècle, insère *Si* 1,21a.22-24 à l'intérieur de nos trois distiques pour former ainsi Si 1,25.21a.22-24.26-27. En outre, cette version latine termine le v. 25 non pas par une traduction du grec θεοσέβεια, mais par *sapientia* et elle termine le stique 1,26a(33a^{VL-Vg}) non pas par la traduction du mot grec ἐντολάς, mais par le mot *iustitia*. C'est comme si le traducteur avait voulu éviter de traduire θεοσέβεια, seul emploi du mot chez le Siracide, et lever l'ambiguïté de ἐντολάς, préceptes divins ou sapientiaux. Le latin a donc compris ainsi:

> *In thesauris sapientiae intellectus et scientiae religiositas*
> *execratio autem peccatoribus sapientia.*
>
> Dans les trésors de la sagesse, intelligence et piété savante,
> mais la sagesse est honnie des pécheurs (*Si*$^{VL-Vg}$ 1,26).

[13] Ce sont surtout en hébreu comme en grec Pr 2,1; 4,4(5); 7,1-2; 10,8a; 13,13b; 19,16a.

[14] Le mot θεοσέβεια est un hapax dans la version grecque du livre de Ben Sira et, dans la Septante, il ne vient en version d'un texte hébreu, qu'en Gn 20,11 pour rendre l'expression hébraïque de « crainte de Dieu » et en Jb 28,28, pour celle de « crainte du Seigneur ».

Concupiscens sapientia conserva iustitiam
et Deus praebebit illam tibi.

Si tu désires la sagesse, garde la justice
et Dieu te la donnera ($Si^{VL\text{-}Vg}$ 1,33).

Qui a raison? Le grec ou le latin? En *Si* 23,1.5, c'est le latin qui a raison contre le grec, mais le latin est conforté par la version syriaque. Ici en *Si* 1,25-27, le latin est seul et le grec est mieux structuré, tant et si bien qu'un certain nombre de manuscrits de la *Vetus Latina*-Vulgate ont repris le verset latin de Si 1,26 en Si 1,31-32, traduit directement sur le grec! Mieux vaut donc s'appuyer ici sur la version grecque du Siracide.

3.5. La pédagogie de la Sagesse

À présent, voici une série de textes sur la pédagogie de la figure de la Sagesse vis-à-vis de son disciple. Les trois premiers textes sont en hébreu.

En Si^{Hb} 4,15-19, la Sagesse parle à la première personne[15]:

Qui m'écoute habitera dans mes chambres. [...]
Sous un déguisement, je marcherai avec lui
et d'abord je l'éprouverai par des tentations.
Mais quand son cœur sera rempli de moi,
je reviendrai vers lui et lui ouvrirai mes secrets (4,15b.17-18)[16].

La Sagesse donc ne se dévoile que progressivement. Quand elle a la preuve que le disciple est devenu fou d'amour, à ce moment-là elle lui ouvre ses « chambres » et lui donne accès à ses « secrets »: on peut alors parler du don que fait de soi la *full Wisdom*. Pas avant, pas lorsqu'elle se déguise, précisément pour ne pas apparaître dans sa *fullness*.

En *Si* 6,18-31, ce n'est plus la Sagesse qui parle de sa tactique pédagogique, mais Ben Sira, s'adressant à son disciple. Il se sert de trois comparaisons: les semailles (6,18-19), le joug (6,23-25) et la chasse (6,26-28). Le texte hébreu du manuscrit A est incomplet: manquent les versets 23-24.26, que l'on emprunte aux versions grecque et syriaque. L'idée de base est partout la même: « qui sème dans les larmes moissonne en chantant »,

[15] Cf. N. CALDUCH-BENAGES, *La Sabiduría y la prueba en Sir 4,11-19*, in *EstBib* 49 (1991) 25-48, repris dans son recueil intitulé *Pan de sensatez y agua de sabiduría. Estudios sobre il libro de Ben Sira* (Asociación Bíblica Española. Articulos selectos, 1), Estella (Navarra), Divino, 2019, 173-199.

[16] Dans la version *Vetus Latina*-Vulgate de *Si* 4,18b, à savoir en $Si^{VL\text{-}Vg}$ 4,21b, on lit: *et thesaurizat super illum scientiam et intellectum iustitiae*, « elle thésaurise sur lui science et intelligence de la justice ». C'est un ajout latin: il manque en hébreu, en grec et en syriaque, mais s'inspire de la traduction en $Si^{VL\text{-}VG}$ 1,26.33 de Si^{Gr} 1,25a.26a.

comme dit le Ps 126,5, surtout quand le cultivateur est pauvre. Le joug pèse et coince, mais bien mis, il permet d'avancer sûrement (cf. *Si* 51,26; Mt 11,29-30). À la chasse, c'est le gibier qui mène la danse, mais, une fois pris, il régale (cf. *Si* 14,22). C'est toujours la Sagesse qui, dans sa *fullness*, attire, mais celui qu'elle fascine est encore loin de la posséder.

Il en est de même en *Si* 14,20–15,8. Les huit premiers distiques décrivent avec force d'images tout l'effort de qui veut atteindre la Sagesse (*Si* 14,20-27). Son effort, c'est de craindre le Seigneur et de s'en tenir à la Tôrâh (*Si* 15,1). Sa récompense, c'est de voir la Sagesse venir à sa rencontre comme une mère et l'accueillir comme une jeune épouse (*Si* 15,2). De nouveau, la *fullness* de la Sagesse attire sans qu'elle soit perçue avant qu'elle-même ne se révèle au terme de tout un itinéraire.

Cette pédagogie, Ben Sira l'a lui aussi expérimentée. Dans le texte alphabétique qui achève son livre, le maître de sagesse confesse, si l'on comprend bien, que, dit-il, « pour moi, elle n'a cessé de croître » (v. 17a); il disait avant cela que « même si la fleur s'étiole à la maturation, les raisins réjouissent le cœur » (v. 15): un progrès de la nature se manifeste entre la floraison printanière, qui charme et envoûte, et la saison des fruits. Au terme, le sage avoue qu'il a compris les secrets de la Sagesse quand finalement il ouvrit ses portes (v. 19cd). C'est donc qu'auparavant il ne percevait pas la *fullness* de la Sagesse. La *full Wisdom* était bien là mais elle ne se laissait pas percevoir dans toute sa plénitude[17].

3.6. La croissance de la Sagesse en Si 24

Un dernier pas encore. En *Si* 24, dont manque encore l'original hébreu, le Siracide, du verset 12 au verset 21, utilise encore, à propos de la Sagesse qui parle, les images de la croissance végétale. Elle s'est « enracinée dans un peuple plein de gloire » (v. 12); elle a « grandi comme le cèdre du Liban » (v. 13a), « grandi comme le palmier d'Engaddi » (v. 14a), « grandi comme un platane » (v. 14d). Elle a « donné du parfum », elle a « embaumé » (v. 15ab); elle a « étendu ses rameaux » (v. 16a). Puis elle invite ceux qui la désirent à venir se rassasier de ses produits, les fruits qu'elle engendre (v. 19), que l'ajout du v. 18 explicite sans image.

[17] Cf. M. GILBERT, *Venez à mon école (Si 51,13-30)*, in Irmtraud FISCHER – Ursula RAPP – Johannes SCHILLER (eds.), *Auf den Spuren der schriftgelehrten Weisen. FS J. Marböck* (BZAW, 331), Berlin - New York, de Gruyter, 2003, 283-290, repris dans mon recueil intitulé *Ben Sira. Recueil d'études – Collected Essays* (BETL, 264), Leuven, Peeters, 2014, 191-199. É. PUECH, *La Sagesse dans les Béatitudes de Ben Sira. Étude de Si 51,13-30 et de Si 14,20–15,10*, in Jean-Sébastien REY – Jan JOOSTEN (eds.), *The Texts and Versions of the Book of Ben Sira. Transmission and Interpretation* (JStJ.S, 150), Leiden - Boston, Brill, 2011, 297-329, spéc. p. 297-317.

Comme le disait déjà *Si* 1,9b, la Sagesse a été répandue sur toutes les œuvres du Seigneur: *Si* 24,3-6a la montre parcourant l'univers et dominant le cosmos. *Si* 1,10a la voyait, telle l'Esprit du Seigneur (Jl 3,1-2), répandue « en toute chair » et *Si* 24,6b affirme qu'elle a « régné sur tous les peuples et toutes les nations ». La profusion des dons de la Sagesse à Israël, dont parle *Si* 1,10b, le Siracide le répète en *Si* 24, mais pour en décrire la croissance. Celle-ci culmine dans l'offre de fruits qu'elle produit (v. 19). C'est alors qu'on pourrait parler de *full Wisdom*. Avant cela, elle est elle-même en croissance. Pr 8, 22-31 la voyait aussi en croissance: engendrée, tissée dans le sein du Seigneur, enfantée et, enfin, jeune enfant au jeu.

4. Conclusion

Toutefois le premier mot du discours de la Sagesse en *Si* 24: « Je suis issue de la bouche du Très-Haut » (v. 3a), sa Parole, renvoie au premier mot du livre du Siracide: « Toute sagesse vient du Seigneur » et cette observation nous ramène à la question fondamentale: comment comprendre l'expression « toute sagesse »? S'il s'agit de la figure personnalisée de la Sagesse, alors le sens de *Full Wisdom*, proposé par Beentjes, est acceptable, sauf que sa manifestation ou sa reconnaissance par l'homme semble être, pour Ben Sira, progressive: la Sagesse ne se révèle pas totalement à toute créature ni dès les premières approches à ceux à qui elle ouvrira ses secrets. Elle-même avoue qu'elle a vécu en Israël une véritable croissance. On pourrait donc comprendre *Si* 1,1a comme ceci: chaque fois qu'elle se manifeste, sous quelques forme que ce soit, la Sagesse, de toute façon, vient du Seigneur

Il s'ensuit que la traduction de *Si* 1,1a par *Full Wisdom* ne correspond pas à la pensée de Ben Sira ni de celle de son traducteur grec, le Siracide.

Pour les auteurs de l'Ancien Testament, « toute sagesse vient du Seigneur » (*Si* 1,1a). Et cela vaut autant de la figure personnalisée de la Sagesse que de la sagesse humaine non personnalisée. D'où l'ambiguïté de la formule de *Si* 1,1a.

Que la Sagesse personnifiée trouve sa source dans le Seigneur, il suffit de renvoyer à Pr 8,22 et à *Si* 24,3a. Qu'elle soit un don de Dieu offert à l'humanité, on le sait par Pr 8; 9,1-6; *Si* 24,19-21; 51,17b grec; *Sg* 7,22a; 8,1.21; 9,4.10.17ab. Mais cette offre divine peut être refusée, comme le montre Pr 1,20-32; *Si* 4,19.

Non personnifiée, la sagesse est encore un don de Dieu: Dn 2,21; Pr 2,6; *Si* 43,33b; *Sg* 7,15, mais il peut être rejeté: *Si* 6,20-21. Pourtant elle est accessible: *Sg* 6,12, bien que, pour les pécheurs, elle devienne inaccessible: Pr 14,6; *Si* 15,7-8.

En *Si* 1,1a, la formule πᾶσα σοφία désigne-t-elle la Sagesse personnifiée ou la sagesse non personnifiée? En *Si* 1,9-10, on assiste à une diversification de l'offre que le Seigneur fait à ses créatures. Les renvois implicites à Jb 28,27 et à Jl 3,1-2 me conduisent à penser qu'en *Si* 1,1a il s'agit de la figure personnifiée de la Sagesse, mais, comme le Seigneur l'accorde de façon diversifiée, il me paraît difficile de comprendre πᾶσα σοφία, « Toute sagesse », dans le sens de *Full Wisdom*, car elle n'est donnée totalement qu'à ceux qui aiment – ou craignent le Seigneur, c'est-à-dire à ceux qui croient en lui.

En outre nous avons vu que, dans sa pédagogie, la Sagesse se manifeste au disciple de façon également diversifiée, procédant par étapes. Enfin en *Si* 24, la figure personnifiée de la Sagesse reconnaît sa propre croissance. Il est donc difficile de traduire πᾶσα σοφία de *Si* 1,1a par *Full Wisdom*. Mieux vaut garder l'ambiguïté en traduisant: « Toute sagesse ».

A TALE OF TWO SCRIBES: ENCOUNTERS WITH AN AVANT-GARDE MANUSCRIPT OF THE COMMUNITY RULES (4Q259)

Charlotte HEMPEL

Of the twelve manuscripts of the Rules of the Community 4Q259 (4QS^{e}) is a particularly idiosyncratic and fascinating exemplar. Its palaeography, content and character are learned and intriguing. It is not surprising, therefore, that this manuscript has attracted the attention of Professor PUECH – himself a renowned scribe with a beautiful hand – on several occasions.[1] The honouree of this volume has played a leading role in the analysis of the cryptic writing in 4Q259 as well as the manuscript's palaeographical analysis.[2] It is his expertise as a palaeographer-scribe that inspired the title of this tribute to a fine scholar and generous colleague.

In an earlier study[3] on the character of 4Q259 I described this manuscript as "avant-garde" based on the presence of two phrases in cryptic script in 4Q259 3:3-4 as well as the calendrical anthology that closes this manuscript. The latter was published separately by Jonathan BEN-DOV under the siglum 4Q319 (Otot).[4] In my recent Commentary on the Community

[1] Émile PUECH, "L'alphabet cryptique A en *4QSe (4Q259)*", *RevQ* 18, 1998, 429–35; Émile PUECH, "La paléographie des manuscrits de la mer Morte", in: Marcello FIDANZIO (ed.), *The Caves of Qumran. Proceedings of the International Conference, Lugano 2014* (STDJ, 118), Leiden, Brill, 2017, 96-105, 102; É. PUECH, "Remarques sur l'écriture de 1QS VII–VIII", *RevQ* 10, 1979, 35–43; É. PUECH, "Review of *The Textual Development of the Qumran Community Rule* by Sarianna METSO", *RevQ* 18, 1998, 448–453.

[2] É. PUECH, "L'alphabet cryptique A."

[3] Charlotte HEMPEL, "The Profile and Character of Qumran Cave 4Q: The Community Rule Manuscripts as a Test Case", in: M. FIDANZIO (ed.) *The Caves of Qumran*, 74–80.

[4] Jonathan BEN-DOV, "4Q319 (Otot)", in: Shemaryahu TALMON, Jonathan BEN-DOV and Uwe GLESSMER (ed.), *Qumran Cave 4.16. Calendrical Texts* (DJD, 21), Oxford, Clarendon, 2001,196-201; Jonathan BEN-DOV, *Head of All Years: Astronomy and Calendars at Qumran in Their Ancient Context* (STDJ, 78), Leiden, Brill, 2008, 147; Uwe GLESSMER, "The Otot-Texts (4Q319) and the Problem of Intercalations in the Content of the 364-Day Calendar", in: Heinz-Josef FABRY, Armin LANGE and Hermann LICHTENBERGER (ed.), *Qumranstudien. Vorträge und Beiträge der Teilnehmer des Qumranseminars auf dem internationalen Treffen der Society of Biblical Literature, Münster, 25-26. Juli 1993* (Schriften des Institutum Judaicum Delitzschianum, 4), Göttingen, Vandenhoeck & Ruprecht, 1996, 125-164; Sarianna METSO, *The Textual Development of the Qumran Community Rule* (STDJ, 21), Leiden, Brill, 1997, 48-54; Józef T. MILIK, *The Books of Enoch. Aramaic Fragments of Qumrân Cave 4*,

Rules I suggest that 4Q259 is "avant garde" also in a more concrete sense. Both the early dating of this manuscript (150-100 BCE) initially arrived at by MILIK [5] and subsequently elaborated by PUECH – who favours a date a little after 100 BCE [6] – as well as a number of variants between 1QS and 4Q259 that suggest scribal errors based on graphic similarities I have suggested that 4Q259 may have served as one of the *Vorlagen* used by the scribe of 1QS (100-75 BCE).[7] Given the movement associated with the site of Qumran did not settle there[8] until 4Q259 and almost certainly also 1QS were copied, the literary activity we are analysing must have taken place at a location other than the site of Qumran.[9]

1. THE MANUSCRIPT

The remains of 4Q259 span across seven fragmentary columns as well as a number of fragments. The scroll was published in two different volumes with the more familiar Community Rules material published under the siglum 4Q259 (4QS[e]) in DJD 26 and a calendrical collection that follows directly after a poorly preserved transition published under the siglum 4Q319 (Otot) in DJD 21.[10] A number of more recent editions present the entire manuscript.[11]

Oxford, Oxford University Press, 1974, 62-64 where 4Q259 is referred to as 4Q260 and James C. VANDERKAM, *Calendars in the Dead Sea Scrolls. Measuring Time*, London, Routledge, 1998, 80-84.

[5] J. MILIK *Books of Enoch*, 61 and J. MILIK, *Ten Years of Discovery in the Wilderness of Judaea*, London, SCM, 1959, 123-124.

[6] É. PUECH, "L'alphabet cryptique A".

[7] Charlotte HEMPEL, *The Community Rules from Qumran. A Commentary* (TSAJ, 183), Tübingen, Mohr Siebeck, 2020, 38-44. For the suggestion that the second hand in 1QS 7 drew on 4Q259 see É. PUECH, "Remarques sur l'écriture".

[8] See Jodi MAGNESS, *The Archaeology of Qumran and the Dead Sea Scrolls*, Grand Rapids, MI, Eerdmans, 2002, 47-72; Bruno CALLEGHER, "The Coins of Khirbet Qumran from the Digs of Roland de Vaux: Returning to Henri Seyrig and Augustus Spijkermann", in: M. FIDANZIO (ed.), *The Caves of Qumran*, 221-235 and Dennis MIZZI, "Qumran Period I Reconsidered: An Evaluation of Several Competing Theories", *DSD* 22, 2015, 1-42.

[9] See also Eibert TIGCHELAAR, "The Scribes of the Scrolls", in: George J. BROOKE and Charlotte HEMPEL (ed.), *The T&T Clark Companion to the Dead Sea Scrolls*, London, T&T Clark, 2018, 524–532, 530 and Eibert TIGCHELAAR, "Seventy Years of Palaeographic Dating of the Dead Sea Scrolls", in: Henryk DRAWNEL (ed.), *Sacred Texts and Disparate Interpretations. Qumran Manuscripts Seventy Years Later*, Leiden, Brill, 2020, 258-278.

[10] J. BEN-DOV, "4Q319 (Otot)".

[11] See Florentino GARCÍA MARTÍNEZ and Eibert J. C. TIGCHELAAR, *The Dead Sea Scrolls Study Edition*, 2 Volumes, Leiden, Brill, 1998, 532-533; Johann MAIER, *Die Qumran-Essener. Die Texte vom Toten Meer*, 2 Volumes (UTB), München, Reinhardt, 1995, Volume 2,

The thick leather is preserved in a range of colour tones that suggest different micro-conditions during the scroll's deposit, or its post-discovery treatment or storage.[12] If – as we suggested above – this scroll was brought to Qumran Cave 4 from elsewhere then the circumstances of this ancient re-location operation will also have had an impact on the condition of the fragments. In an early material reconstruction of 4Q259 Sarianna METSO's analysis of the damage patterns showed that the scroll was rolled with the beginning on the inside.[13]

2. THE SCRIPT

The script is highly unusual and a wide range of palaeographical dates have been proposed for this hand. Sarianna METSO observed the "extraordinary" and somewhat mixed script of this scribe.[14] More recently Eibert TIGCHELAAR has described the hand behind 4Q259 as representative of a group of manuscripts that attest "unique or unusual hands (e.g. 4Q259 [4QS[e]]) suggesting individual idiosyncrasy, or a different geographical provenance of the scribe."[15] An initial palaeographical dating by Frank Moore CROSS around the beginning of the 1st century BCE was noted by Józef MILIK in 1955.[16] Cross subsequently revised his opinion and dated the manuscript much later to 50-25 BCE, a date subsequently adopted by Philip ALEXANDER and Geza VERMES in the editio princeps.[17] As noted

210-213; Elisha QIMRON, *The Dead Sea Scrolls. The Hebrew Writings*, 3 Volumes, Jerusalem, Yad Ben-Zvi, 2010, Volume 1, 231-234. See also Corrado MARTONE, *La "Regola della Comunità". Edizione critica*, Turin: Silvio Zamorani, 1995, 54-80 and James Milton TUCKER, *From Ink Traces to Ideology. Material, Text, and Composition of Qumran Community Rule Manuscripts*, Doctoral Thesis, University of Toronto, 2021.

[12] On these distinctions see Mladen POPOVIĆ, "The Manuscript Collections: An Overview", in: G. BROOKE and C. HEMPEL (ed.), *Companion to the Dead Sea Scrolls*, 37-50.

[13] S. METSO, *Textual Development*, 48-51. See also Annette STEUDEL, "Reading and Reconstructing Manuscripts," in: G. BROOKE and C. HEMPEL (ed.), *Companion to the Dead Sea Scrolls*, 186-191.

[14] S. METSO, *Textual Development*, 48 and, similarly, J. MAIER, *Qumran-Essener*, Volume 2, 210.

[15] E. TIGCHELAAR, "The Scribes of the Scrolls", in: G. BROOKE and C. HEMPEL (ed.), *Companion to the Dead Sea Scrolls*, 524-532, 530.

[16] Józef T. MILIK, "Le travail d'édition des fragments manuscrits de Qumran", *RB* 63, 1956, 49-67, 61.

[17] See Frank Moore CROSS, "The Paleographical Dates of the Manuscripts", in: James H. CHARLESWORTH et al. (ed.), *The Dead Sea Scrolls. Hebrew, Aramaic, and Greek Texts with English Translations. Rule of the Community and Related Documents* (Princeton Theological Seminary Dead Sea Scrolls Project 1), Tübingen / Louisville, KY, Mohr Siebeck /

above, a significantly earlier date was suggested by MILIK (150-100 BCE) with PUECH, who has offered the most detailed palaeographical discussion to date, advocating a date around 100 BCE.[18] On MILIK's and PUECH's analysis 4Q259 constitutes one of the earliest surviving copies of the Community Rules alongside 4Q255, 4Q256 and 1QS.

Another remarkable characteristic of 4Q259 is the preservation of two short phrases ("in Israel" and "the people of [injustice]") in the Cryptic A script in 4Q259 3:3-4.[19] The cryptic letters were deciphered by MILIK, and PUECH has subsequently offered the most comprehensive analysis.[20] More details are offered in the Textual Notes below.

3. TRANSLATION

The remains of 4Q259 begin in the Penal Code with remains of a penalty prescribed for bearing a grudge without justification (cf. 1QS 7:8). The penal material is followed by an account of an emerging community referred to as the council of the community (3.2 below). This is followed, in turn, directly by the Statutes for the Maskil and the calendrical anthology published originally as 4Q319 (Otot) but widely recognised as an integral part of 4Q259.[21] The translation below does not include Otot though the analysis offered at the end of this contribution includes reflections on the significance of this part of 4Q259.[22]

Westminster John Knox, 1994, 57 and Philip A. ALEXANDER and Geza VERMES, *Qumran Cave 4.26. Serekh Ha-Yaḥad and Two Related Texts* (DJD, 26), Oxford, Clarendon, 1998, 133-134.

[18] See J. MILIK, *Books of Enoch*, 61; J. MILIK, *Ten Years of Discovery*, 123-124 and É. PUECH, "L'alphabet cryptique A", 433-435.

[19] For an overview of texts from Qumran in cryptic script as well as further bibliography see Charlotte HEMPEL, *Qumran Rule Texts in Context. Collected Studies* (TSAJ, 154), Tübingen, Mohr Siebeck, 2013, 312-317.

[20] See J. MILIK, "Le travail d'édition", 61; S. METSO, *Textual Development*, 53-54; É. PUECH, "L'alphabet cryptique A"; E. QIMRON, *Dead Sea Scrolls*, Volume 1, 225; Emanuel TOV, *Scribal Practices and Approaches Reflected in Texts Found in the Judean Desert* (STDJ, 54), Leiden, Brill, 2004, 205-206; and J. TUCKER, *From Ink Traces to Ideology*, 82-83. Cf. also C. HEMPEL, "Profile and Character of Qumran Cave 4Q", 74-80; Charlotte HEMPEL, "Bildung und Wissenswirtschaft im Judentum zur Zeit des Zweiten Tempels", in: Peter GEMEINHARDT (ed.), *Was ist Bildung in der Vormoderne?*, Tübingen, Mohr Siebeck, 2019, 229-244 and Michael E. STONE, *Secret Groups in Ancient Judaism*, Oxford, Oxford University Press, 2018, 68-71. The infrared images published by the Israel Antiquities Authority's *Leon Levy Dead Sea Scrolls Digital Library* (LLDSSDL) B-295966 and B-314657 by Shai HALEVI support the readings of J. MILIK and É. PUECH.

[21] See note 4 above.

[22] For the text and translations of the calendrical anthology that follows in 4Q259 4:9 see J. BEN-DOV, "4Q319 (Otot)" and note 11 above.

3.1 Penal Code (4Q259 1:4, 6-15; 2:3-9 // 1QS 7:8-25 // 4Q258 5:1 // 4Q261 5a-c: 1 - 6a-c: 5)

4Q259 1^{4}[for six mo]nths. [...] ^{6} [...] Whoever lies down [...And the same applies to] ^{7}the person who lea[ves] a meeting of the many with[out permission. And he who drops off up to three times ^{8}in the cour]se of a single meeting shall be punished for te[n days. But if they are standing and he leaves] ^{9}he shall be punished for thirty days. Whoever wa[lks about naked in front of his neighbour shall be ^{10}pu]nished [for s]ix mo[nths unless] there are mitigating circumstances. The person who spits into the midst of a meeting of] ^{11}the many [shall be punished for thir]ty days. [Whoever brings out] ^{12}his hand [from underneа]th [his] garment and i[t blows up and his nakedness can be seen] ^{13}shall be punished for sixty days. Whoever laughs [foolishly and ^{14}rau]cously shall be punished for thirty d[ays]. The [one who brings out his left hand] ^{15}to gesticulate with [it shall be punished for ten d]ay[s ...] 2^{3}[and he shall be sea]ted [at the back of all the people of the community.] And when he has completed ^{4}[the two years the many shall be consulted about his affairs. If they permit him to draw near he shall be enrolled according to] his [r]ank and afterwards he may be consulted ^{5}[concerning judgment. *Vacat.* But anyone who has been a member of the counci]l of the community up to completing ^{6}[ten years and his spirit turns back so as to betray the community and he departs fro]m the many in order to walk ^{7}[with a hardened heart shall never return to the council of the community again. A person from among] the people of the community who ^{8}[has dealings with him regarding his purity or his property which ... the many], his penalty shall be ^{9a}[the same: he shall be sent away.]

3.2 The Council of the Community (4Q259 2:9b-3:6 // 1QS 8:1-16 // 4Q258 6:1-8)

^{9b} In the council of the community (there shall be) twelve] (lay)people [and] three priests ^{10}[flawless concerning all that has been revealed from all of the law. They shall conduct themselves with] truth, righteousness, justice, ^{11}[devoted love and humble conduct each with his neighbour. They shall remain faith]ful in the land with a solid intellect, humility ^{12}[and a b]roken [spirit]. They shall make up for tres[passes with acts of justice and by (standing up to)] the challenge of [distress.] Their conduct with everyone ^{13}[shall adhere to the standard of] truth and the rule of [time. When these exist in] Israel the council of the community shall be established ^{14}[in truth for] eternal [judg]ment, [a holy house for Israel and] a most holy [assembly] for Aar$^{o(n)}$,^{15}witnesses of truth for judgment and choosing (God's) will [to atone for] the land [and] to [b]rin[g ba]ck upon the wicked ^{16}their reward. It shall be the tried wall, a [splendid] co[rner(stone); they shall nei]ther [shake no]r move from their place. (It shall be) ^{17}a m[o]st holy refuge for Aar[on with all of their knowledge] for the sake of the covena[nt of justice and] in order to [o]ff[er up] a soothing odour. And (it shall be) a house of ^{18}perfection and truth in [Israe]l in order to [ratify a covenant as we approach the time of] e[te]rnal [statut]es when the latter will be firmly established *Vacat.*^{19} EMPTY LINE

3[1][When the community has been founded for two years with perfect conduct they shall be set apart] as holy in the midst of the council of the peo[ple of [2]the community. And nothing that has been hidden from Israel but was fou]nd by the scholar shall the latter h[i]d[e] [3][from] these [out of fear of a] rene[gade spi]rit. [*Vacat*]

[When] these [exi]st *in Isra^{el}* they shall keep apart from the com[pa]ny of [4] the people of [injustice] and go [to] the wil[der]ne[ss to prepare the]re the way of the truth a[s] [5]it is written: ["In the wilder]ness pre[pare the way of the truth (?), make strai]ght in the desert a highway for our God." [6a]This is [the stu]d[y of the law whi]ch He has commanded through Moses.

3.3 The Statutes for the Maskil (4Q259 3:6b-4:8 // 1QS 9:12-25 // 4Q256 18:1-7 // 4Q258 7:15-8:9 // 4Q260 1:1-2)

[6b]These are the sta[tutes] [7]for the Mas[kil to walk in] them (in his dealings) with all the living according to the rule for each [time] [8]and according to the wei[ght of each person. He shall exe]cute the will of God according to everything that has been revealed [from time to time]. H[e shall acquire every insight] which has been found in previous times and the [statute] [10]of time. [He shall separate and] weigh the children of righteousness according to their sp[i]rit. [11][He shall sustain the chosen ones of the time] according to His will according to that which He has commanded. [He shall execute [12]judgment on] each person [according to his spirit.] He shall bring near each person according to the cleanness of his hands (and) acc[ording to [13]his insight allow him to approach. And equally] his [lo]ve and his hatred. He shall not [rebuke] [14]or [get into an argument with the peo]ple of destruction but conceal the coun[sel of] [15]the law [in the midst of the people of injustice.] He shall discipline with true knowledge and righteous [16]judgment the cho[sen of the way, each] according to his spirit and according to the rules of time. He shall guide them [17]with knowledge [and thus instruct them in] the wonderful mysteries. And if the way of the alliance of the community [18]reaches perfection, they shall con[duct themselves perfectly each] with his neighbours according to all that has been revealed to them. [19]This is [the time to prepare the way] in the wilderness. He shall facilitate their mastery over all 4[1][that has been found to do] at th[is] time [and] they shall keep [away from everyone who has not averted his path(s) [2]from all injustice. *Vacat*.] These are the rules of [condu]ct for the Maskil [during these times with regard to his love] [3]and [his] hatred. [(He shall direct) eter]nal [hatred] to[wards the people of destruction] with a sp[i]rit of secretiveness. He shall lea[ve] [4]to them property [and wages like a servant to his master (displaying) humility] before his ruler. He shall [be] [5]a person who is dedi[cated to the statute and rea]dy for a day of [vengeance. He shall perform the will (of God) in every]thing he do[es] [6]and in [every]thing [that is under his control (he shall comply with)] that which [...] 4Q259 4:10-7:8 AND SEVERAL FRAGMENTS FOLLOW CONTAINING A CALENDRICAL ANTHOLOGY.[23]

[23] See the discussion and note 4 above.

4. Textual Notes

4Q259 1:4 preserves the reading "[six mo]nths" of the first hand in 1QS 7:10 that was subsequently corrected with parentheses[24] before the longer penalty of "one year" was added above the line. This superlinear correction in 1QS is one of the few cases which Puech attributes to a second hand (Scribe B).[25] The original hand in 1QS likely drew on a reading like the one preserved in 4Q259. On the dating of 4Q259 proposed by Milik and Puech it is conceivable that 4Q259 was the source of the reading.[26]

4Q259 1:7 "From a meeting of (ממושׁ)" attests the preposition *min* with the accidental omission of final *bet*. 1QS 7:10 reads במושב. Long before the publication of 4Q259 Lawrence Schiffman explained the reading in 1QS as the result of an interchange of the prefixed prepositions *bet* and *mem*.[27]

4Q259 1:13 The punishment of sixty days is longer in 4Q259 1:13. 1QS 7:14 reads "thirty days." As I have argued elsewhere this may be a scribal lapse with the scribe of 1QS defaulting to the more common punishment of thirty days. A penalty of sixty days is added above the line in 1QS 7:8 in connection with not having the means to restore the losses after defrauding the community. In two copies of the Damascus Document the same offence "thirty days" is reconstructed entirely in 4Q270 (4QD[e]) 7 i 3 and partially reconstructed in 4Q266 (4QD[a]) 10 ii 11, with the preserved letters *shin yod mem* allowing for a penalty of either thirty or sixty days with the resulting line length favouring a reconstruction of sixty days.[28]

4Q259 2:4 The pronominal suffix *vav* is added above the line in "in his rank" with clear evidence of an erasure of two letters. Puech offers an original reading of *kaph he*.[29]

[24] See P. Alexander and G. Vermes, *Qumran Cave 4.26*, 134-137 and Alison Schofield, *From Qumran to the Yaḥad: A New Paradigm of Textual Development for the Community Rule* (STDJ 77), Leiden, Brill, 2009, 106-107 where the line is numbered 7:9. On the use of antisigma here and in the Dead Sea Scrolls see C. Hempel, *Community Rules*, 203 and E. Tov, *Scribal Practices*, 225. See further Emanuel Tov, *Textual Criticism of the Hebrew Bible*, 2nd ed, Minneapolis, MN / Assen, Fortress / Gorcum, 2001, 54-55 and David N. Freedman and Kenneth A. Mathews, *The Paleo-Hebrew Leviticus Scroll (11QPaleoLev)*, Winona Lake, IN, Eisenbrauns for ASOR, 1985, 36-37, 103 (Plate 3).

[25] É. Puech, "Écriture de 1QS VII-VIII", 42.

[26] See section 2 above.

[27] Lawrence H. Schiffman, *The Halakhah at Qumran* (SJLA 16), Leiden, Brill, 1975, 27-28 n. 44 and 69 n. 307.

[28] See Joseph M. Baumgarten, *Qumran Cave 4.13. The Damascus Document (4Q266 – 4Q273)* (DJD, 18), Oxford, Clarendon, 1996, 74-75, 162-163.

[29] See É. Puech, "Review of *Textual Development*", 449; P. Alexander and G. Vermes, *Qumran Cave 4.26*, 139-140 and F. García Martínez and E. Tigchelaar, *Study Edition*, 528. Cf. also E. Qimron, *Dead Sea Scrolls*, Volume 1, 222.

4Q259 2:5 The first half of this line is not preserved but allows for extra space, perhaps a *vacat* as suggested by ALEXANDER and VERMES.[30]

4Q259 2:5 reads עד "up to" ten full years where 1QS attests the preposition על "upon completing" ten full years. P. ALEXANDER and G. VERMES argue that the prepositions are interchangeable. In addition, an ethical dative לו has been added secondarily at the end of the line in 4Q259 2:5. Both *lamed* and *vav* are written slightly above the rest of the line and appear rather compressed at the end of the margin.

4Q259 2:8 The three dots in our translation of this line indicate a gap in the restoration where 1QS 7:25 is also damaged. LICHT proposes restoring "[without the consent of (לוא בעצת) the many]"[31] whereas ALEXANDER and VERMES reconstruct "[which he has pooled with the property of the many (אשר ערב עם הון הרבים)]."[32]

4Q259 2:11 The final word in this line ובענוה "and with humility" appears to have been added in a fairly compressed style. Together with the ethical dative also added secondarily at the end of the line in 4Q259 2:5 both additions represent two of the rare occasions where 4Q259 offers a longer text than 1QS. It is intriguing that in each case the plus in 4Q259 appears to be added secondarily at the end of a line.

4Q259 2:14 reads "eternal [judg]ment" where 1QS 8:5 has "eternal plant." ALEXANDER and VERMES propose a misreading from an imperfect *Vorlage*.[33] As I have argued elsewhere this is one of a series of cases where the misreading in 1QS is based on considerable graphic similarities with 4Q259.[34]

4Q259 2:14 Three letters of the name "Aaron" are added above the line. Based on the infrared image published by the Israel Antiquities Authority's *Leon Levy Dead Sea Scrolls Digital Library* (henceforth LLDSSDL) B-295972 by Shai HALEVI the superlinear remains appear to be of a damaged or partly erased *resh* followed by *resh* and *yod*.[35] There is no sign of final *nun* and superlinear *resh*(s) repeat the original *resh* in the line below. Overall this looks like a poor effort at a superlinear correction or one that has not yet been fully understood.[36]

30 P. ALEXANDER and G. VERMES, *Qumran Cave 4.26*, 139-140.

31 Jacob LICHT, *The Rule Scroll*, Jerusalem: Bialik, 1965, [Hebrew], 166.

32 P. ALEXANDER and G. VERMES, *Qumran Cave 4.26*, 139-142.

33 P. ALEXANDER and G. VERMES, *Qumran Cave 4*.26, 143.

34 See C. HEMPEL, *Community Rules*, 40-43, 222, 226-227.

35 Cf. E. QIMRON, *Dead Sea Scrolls*, Volume 1, 225.

36 See also P. ALEXANDER and G. VERMES, *Qumran Cave 4.26*, 139 and É. PUECH, "Review of *Textual Development*," 449 who read *vav nun* above the line. F. GARCÍA MARTÍNEZ and

4Q259 2:15 The translation "choosing (God's) will [to atone]" follows the reading
ובחרי רצון [לכפר] recently proposed by Sarianna METSO and James TUCKER.[37]

4Q259 2:16 The text of 4Q259 is shorter than 1QS 8:7-8 with insufficient space to accommodate the superlinear addition "its foundations" (יסודותיהו) found in 1QS. This does suggest, however, that – as elsewhere – the pre-supplemented text of 1QS corresponds to 4Q259.

4Q259 2:17 The reading "refuge" (מעוז) in 4Q259 fits the literary context of the passage well by following on from the account of stability offered by a solid wall and cornerstone, cf. Isa 28:16.[38] The reading "dwelling" (מעון) in 1QS 8:8 and 4Q258 6:2 can be attributed to a visual error given the graphic similarity between both words. 1QS and 4Q258 may have misread a *Vorlage* with a text like 4Q259 or 1QS may have drawn on 4Q258 here.

4Q259 2:17 The final *taw* in "a house of" is generously proportioned to complete the line flush with the line above. Malachi MARTIN described this phenomenon "marginal fitting."[39]

4Q259 2:18 The shorter text of 4Q259 corresponds to the first hand of 1QS 8:10 which, as PUECH has shown, was subsequently supplemented with a superlinear addition by a second hand.[40] While 4Q258 6:4-5 is broken at this point, considerations of space suggest that 4Q258 corresponds to 4Q259 and the first hand of 1QS 8:10.[41]

4Q259 2:18-19 As proposed by ALEXANDER and VERMES, the empty space at the beginning and end of this line suggests it was left blank.[42] In addition, the previous line (4Q259 2:18) also ended with a *vacat*. The translation above reflects the emphatic indication of a new beginning at

E. TIGCHELAAR, *Study Edition*, 530 read *resh*, *vav*, *nun* superlinearly and propose an erased *tav* underlying the correction.

37 See Sarianna METSO, *The Community Rule: A Critical Edition with Translation* (EJL, 51), Atlanta, SBL, 2019, 42 and J. TUCKER, *From Ink Traces to Ideology*, 75 and 79.

38 See William H. BROWNLEE, *The Dead Sea Manual of Discipline: Translation and Notes* (BASOR Supplementary Studies, 10-12), New Haven, CT, ASOR, 1951, 33; George J. BROOKE, "Isaiah in Some of the Non-Scriptural Dead Sea Scrolls", in: Florian WILK and Peter GEMEINHARDT (ed.), *Transmission and Interpretation of the Book of Isaiah in the Context of Intra- and Interreligious Debates* (BETL, 280), Leuven, Peeters, 2016, 243-260, 251-254 and Shani TZOREF, "The Use of Scripture in the Community Rule", in: Matthias HENZE (ed.), *A Companion to Biblical Interpretation in Early Judaism*, Grand Rapids, MI, Eerdmans, 2012, 203-234.

39 Malachi MARTIN, *The Scribal Character of the Dead Sea Scrolls. Two Volumes*, Louvain, Publications Universitaires, 1958, Volume 1, 109.

40 É. PUECH, "Remarques sur l'écriture", 42.

41 P. ALEXANDER and G. VERMES, *Qumran Cave 4.26*, 105-106.

42 P. ALEXANDER and G. VERMES, *Qumran Cave 4.26*, 142.

4Q259 3:1. On the translation of the preposition *lamed* in the temporal sense of "toward" ("[as we approach the time of] e[te]rnal [statut]es") see Exod 34:25. Significantly Exod 34 describes the second revelation of the law and ratification of a covenant. As in our passage the revelation of the law is expected. By describing the statutes as eternal the Community Rules resonate with the permanence of the replacement tablets that contrasts to the fleeting fate of the tablets which Moses destroyed at the foot of Mount Sinai in his rage at the idolatry with the golden calf.

4Q259 3:1 We translate the clearly marked new beginning here with "When the community has been founded for two years." For the language see the account in Ps 2:2 of kings and rulers of the world "taking counsel together (נֽוֹסְדוּ־יָ֑חַד)" against the Lord and His anointed.

4Q259 3:1 Considerations of space suggest that 4Q259 attests a shorter text than 1QS 8:10 here with one of the additions both above and below the line in 1QS lacking in 4Q259.[43]

4Q259 3:3 A form of the text shared by 4Q259 and 4Q258 6:6 was supplemented with two superlinear additions in 1QS 8:12-13. PUECH attributes both additions to a second hand.[44] The formula that is here expanded secondarily is textually fluid across the various manuscripts of the Rules of the Community.[45]

4Q259 3:3-4 Józef MILIK first deciphered the cryptic reading "in Israel," and his findings have since been confirmed more comprehensively by Émile PUECH who identified a second hand correcting an earlier unencrypted reading "in the yahad."[46] PUECH identified further letters in the Cryptic A script at the beginning of 4Q259 3:4 which read "the people of [injustice]."[47] The word "people of" opens with initial *he* rather than *aleph* in 1QS 8:13. There are philological explanations, such as the evidence of a weakening of the gutturals that may account for this.[48] It is also possible that a scribe who was not familiar with the cryptic script misread

[43] See further P. ALEXANDER and G. VERMES, *Qumran Cave 4.26*, 144-145; C. HEMPEL, *Community Rules*, 224; É. PUECH, "Remarques sur l'écriture", 41; E. QIMRON, *Dead Sea Scrolls*, Volume 1, 224 and F. GARCÍA MARTÍNEZ and E. TIGCHELAAR, *Study Edition*, 88.

[44] É. PUECH, "Écriture de 1QS VII-VIII," 42.

[45] See P. ALEXANDER and G. VERMES, *Qumran Cave 4.26*, 112-113.

[46] See J. MILIK, "Le travail d'édition", 61; S. METSO, *Textual Development*, 53-54; É. PUECH, "L'alphabet cryptique A;" E. QIMRON, *Dead Sea Scrolls*, Volume 1, 225; E. TOV, *Scribal Practices*, 205-206. Further, C. HEMPEL, "Profile and Character of Qumran Cave 4Q", 74-80; C. HEMPEL, "Bildung und Wissenswirtschaft" and M. STONE, *Secret Groups*, 68-71.

[47] É. PUECH, "L'alphabet cryptique A"; also S. METSO, *Textual Development*, 53-54 and E. QIMRON, *Dead Sea Scrolls*, Volume 1, 225.

[48] See Edward Y. KUTSCHER, *The Language and Linguisitc Background of the Isaiah Scroll (1QIsa^{a})* (STDJ, 6), Leiden, Brill, 1974, 57-60, 505-511 and E. QIMRON, *Dead Sea Scrolls*, Volume 1, 25.

the cryptic sequence *aleph nun* in a *Vorlage*, possibly 4Q259, as *he*.[49] Both the words "in Israel" and the designation "the people of [injustice]" occur in regular Hebrew script elsewhere in 4Q259.

4Q259 3:5 The introduction that builds up to the citation of Isa 40:3 in 4Q259 3:4 reads "to prepare the way of the truth" where 1QS has "the way of Him." 4Q258 6:7, which lacks the explicit quotation of Isa 40:3, is broken at this point.

4Q259 3:6 The text of 4Q259 runs on into the heading announcing the Statutes for the Maskil. By contrast, 1QS marks this new section – after a substantial plus in 1QS 8:15b-9:11 not found in 4Q259 – with an empty line and a *vacat* at the start of 1QS 9:12.[50] The plus is shared by 1QS and 4Q258 and can be identified as largely made up of elaborations of themes introduced already in the material on the Council of the Community presented in 3.2 above.[51]

4Q259 3:8 The horizontal bottom stroke of the prefix preposition *kaph* in "according to all that has been revealed" is thicker than and runs into the second *kaph*.

4Q259 3:9 reads "in previous times (לפני העתים)" where 1QS attests "according to the times" (לפי העתים).[52] The top of *nun* is clear.[53] The temporal sense for לפני adopted in the translation above is attested in the Hebrew Bible including in Neh 13:4.

4Q259 3:10 The reading "the sons of righteousness" preceded by a nota accusativi is superior to 1QS's "the sons of Zadok" (1QS 9:14). 1QS's text is likely the result of a deficient exemplar.[54] Gaster's suggestion to emend 1QS to read "the sons of righteousness" – as recorded by BROWNLEE in 1951– can now draw support from 4Q259.[55]

[49] See C. HEMPEL, *Community Rules*, 225.

[50] Although the opening lines of the Statutes for the Maskil have not survived in 4Q258, where this manuscript is preserved it shares the significant plus found in 1QS, see C. HEMPEL, *Community Rules*, 221, 233-253.

[51] See S. METSO, "The Primary Results of the Reconstruction of 4QS^{e}", *JJS* 44, 1993, 303-308 and S. METSO, *Textual Development*, 71-73. Cf. also John J. COLLINS, "The Yaḥad and 'The Qumran Community'" in: Charlotte HEMPEL and Judith LIEU (ed.), *Biblical Traditions in Transmission. Essays in Honour of Michael A. Knibb* (JSJSup, 111), Leiden, Brill, 2006, 81-96, 89; C. HEMPEL, *Qumran Rule Texts in Context*, 85-92 and C. HEMPEL, *Community Rules*, 38-44, 233-250.

[52] Cf. P. ALEXANDER and G. VERMES, *Qumran Cave 4.26*, 146 and E. QIMRON, *Dead Sea Scrolls*, Volume 1, 226.

[53] See especially PAM 43.263 as digitised on LLDSSEL B-284709, photograph by Najib Anton ALBINA.

[54] Cf. M. MARTIN, *Scribal Practices*, Volume 2, 466 and C. HEMPEL, *Community Rules*, 256, 260-261; see also 40-44.

[55] See W. BROWNLEE, *Dead Sea Manual*, 37.

4Q259 3:12 Both 1QS 9:16 and 4Q258 8:1 attest the conjunction "and according to his insight."

4Q259 3:13 A sizeable *vacat* follows the note "[And equally] his [lo]ve and his hatred" in 1QS 9:16. This is mirrored by a modest *vacat* in 4Q258 8:1. In our manuscript, by contrast, the text runs on.

4Q259 3:16 The preserved opening letters of "the cho[sen of the way" (לבח[ירי] דרך) align this reading with 4Q258 8:2. 1QS 9:17-18 reads the active participle "those who have chosen the way" (לבוחרי דרך). On either reading the description of this group suggests divine favour as well as social approval on the part of the author(s).

4Q259 3:16 reads a construct plural "the rules of time" where 1QS, 4Q256 and 4Q258 have a singular. ALEXANDER and VERMES read *vav* and suppose a scribal error in the wake of the suffix in "according to his spirit" that comes before.[56] QIMRON allows for *yod* or *vav*.[57]

4Q259 3:19 The translation "in the wilderness" is based on remains of the preposition *bet* preserved in 4Q259 particularly visible on the LLDSSDL Image B-295980 photographed by Shai Halevi.[58]

4Q259 3:19 reads the *hiphil* of משל which I have translated with "he shall facilitate their mastery over." The verb is found repeatedly in the wisdom composition 4QInstruction.[59]

4Q259 4:1 The final word "path(s)" is represented in our reconstruction as either plural (with 4Q258 8:5) or singular (with 1QS 9:20 and 4Q256 18:4). It is also possible that the suffix in 1QS and 4Q256 attests a contraction of *āw>ō*.[60]

4Q259 4:5 attests "[rea]dy (עת[י]) for a day of vengeance" and corresponds to the text of 4Q258 8:7.[61]

4Q259 4:6 As a consequence of a weakening of the gutturals the relative pronoun is spelled with initial *he*.[62]

[56] P. ALEXANDER and G. VERMES, *Qumran Cave 4.26*, 147, 149.

[57] E. QIMRON, *Dead Sea Scrolls*, Volume 1, 226.

[58] Many editions decipher the fragmentary remains as belonging to *lamed* as in 1QS 9:20, cf. P. ALEXANDER and G. VERMES, *Qumran Cave 4.26*, 145 and F. GARCÍA MARTÍNEZ and E. TIGCHELAAR, *Study Edition*, 523.

[59] See, for instance, Catherine M. MURPHY, *Wealth in the Dead Sea Scrolls and in the Qumran Community* (STDJ, 40), Leiden: Brill, 2002, 199-200 and n. 153 as well as P. ALEXANDER and G. VERMES, *Qumran Cave 4.26*, 149.

[60] See Eric D. REYMOND, *Qumran Hebrew: An Overview of Orthography, Phonology, and Morphology* (RBS, 76), Atlanta, GA, SBL, 2014, 144-145.

[61] See P. ALEXANDER and G. VERMES, *Qumran Cave 4.26*, 150-151 and E. QIMRON, *Dead Sea Scrolls*, Volume 1:226. See also Lev 16:21 where a man is to be on standby (עתי) to receive and dispatch the scapegoat into the wilderness in the context of the Day of Atonement legislation, cf. P. ALEXANDER and G. VERMES, *Qumran Cave 4.26*, 119.

[62] See LLDSSDL B-281230 (PAM 42.377), photography by Najib Anton ALBINA.

5. Analysis

5.1 From Messy to Ideal: The Penal Code Gives Way to the Vision of an Emerging Community

On the basis of the dating around 100 BCE proposed by Puech 4Q259 represents an early surviving manuscript of the Rules of the Community. Yet like 1QS (100-75 BCE), this early witness already portrays a prolonged, and at times challenging, experience of communal life. This sense of a past is particularly apparent in the provision for dealing with disloyalty on the part of a longstanding member that ends the penal code in 4Q259 2:5-9 and in 1QS. At the other end of the spectrum 4Q259 also develops an aspiration to perfection in 4Q259 2:18.[63] References to a time "when these exist in Israel" suggest that the description of the council of the community anticipates an emerging community.[64] The sequence from Penal Code (3.1) to the vision of the emerging community (3.2) is shared by 4Q259 and 1QS; 4Q258. The shorter text of 4Q259 lacks several further passages that develop the interplay between a rhetoric of perfection and serious lapses in 1QS and 4Q258.[65]

5.2 The Maskil's Place in 4Q259 and in Cosmological Salvation History

The Statutes for the Maskil offer the fullest account of the role of this communal leader whose remit spans spiritual, soteriological and cosmological realms. According to 4Q259 3:10-12 the Maskil is tasked with weighing the children of righteousness according to their spirit as well as execute judgement in line with the spiritual make-up of those who fall short. The Maskil's role is frequently associated with the judgement of the chosen (4Q259 3:15-16) as well as the day of vengeance that looms over the people of destruction (4Q259 4:4-5). The transition introducing the calendrical collection that follows in this manuscript includes a reference to the creation of the heavenly lights on the fourth day of creation (Gen 1:14) in 4Q259 4:9-11. This suggests a comparably ambitious cosmological framework both in the Maskil's remit and in the literary make-up of

[63] Cf. also the likely restoration in 4Q259 3:1.

[64] See also 4Q265 (Miscellaneous Rules) 7:7-10; Joseph M. Baumgarten, *Qumran Cave 4.25: Halakhic Texts* (DJD, 35), Oxford, Clarendon, 1999, 57-78; Charlotte Hempel, *The Damascus Texts* (CQS, 1), Sheffield, Sheffield Academic Press, 2000, 89-104; C. Hempel, *Qumran Rule Texts in Context*, 79-96.

[65] See 1QS 8:16-9:6; 4Q258 6:8-12; 7:1-7 and C. Hempel, *Community Rules*, 233-244, 247-250. On the language of perfection in 1QS 8–9 see Anja Klein, "From the 'Right Spirit' to the 'Spirit of Truth'. Observations on Ps 51 and the Community Rule," in: Devorah Dimant and Reinhard G. Kratz, *The Dynamics of Language and Exegesis at Qumran* (FAT, 35), Tübingen, Mohr Siebeck, 2009, 171-191 and Carol Newsom, *The Self as Symbolic Space. Constructing Identity and Community at Qumran* (STDJ, 52), Leiden, Brill, 2004, 159-160.

the scroll. In 4Q259 six-year cycles of priestly courses, sabbatical years and a longer cycle of forty-nine year jubilees are combined into the most ambitious calendrical calculation attested in the Qumran scrolls.[66]

6. Conclusion

By way of conclusion I offer some reflections on synergies that emerge from considering a series of material features outlined at the beginning of our discussion alongside a number of literary features that characterise 4Q259. The idiosyncratic hand penned on rather crude and thick skin in an early exemplar of the Rules of the Community coupled with the extremely learned content may take us close to the composition of the parts of the S tradition represented here. Two early papyrus manuscripts (4Q255 and 4Q257) are likely early drafts of the opening framework of what I have called the "long text" of the Community Rules as I have argued elsewhere.[67] Moreover, the graphic similarities between a number of variants attested between 4Q259 and 1QS suggest that 4Q259, or a text like it, was a *Vorlage* used by the scribe of 1QS. Our analysis of the textual evidence identified a number of occasions where 4Q259 was misread by the scribe who copied 1QS and then interpreted – by both the ancient scribe and modern scholars – in line with more familiar themes. The reading "the sons of Zadok" in 1QS 9:14 where 4Q259 3:10 reads "the sons of righteousness" comes to mind. Another example is attested in 4Q259 3:19 where the infinitive "to facilitate their mastery" (להמשילם) is read in 1QS as "to instruct" (להשכילם). It is possible that the scribe of 1QS was following a text like 4Q258 which, though copied later than 1QS, is seen by many as witnessing an earlier text form.[68] Both readings offer a cogent meaning. The graphic resemblance is again suggestive of a copying error. Moreover, a reading that may have originated as the result of a graphic misreading would, in the hands of perceptive ancient and modern readers become an equally valid reading – a kind of accidental rewriting of the tradition.[69]

[66] See J. Ben-Dov, "4Q319 (Otot)", 200-208.

[67] Cf. Charlotte Hempel, "The Long Text of the *Serekh* as Crisis Literature," *RevQ* 27, 2015, 3–24.

[68] So already J. Milik, "Le travail d'édition," 61. For discussion and bibliography see C. Hempel, *Qumran Rule Texts in Context*, 109-119.

[69] On rewriting as a deliberate process see most recently Molly Zahn, *Genres of Rewriting in Second Temple Judaism: Scribal Composition and Transmission*, Cambridge: Cambridge University Press, 2020, 3. On the fertile ground of "ambiguity" for the interpretation of the Hebrew Bible in antiquity see James Kugel, *The Bible as It Was*, Cambridge, MA, Harvard University Press, 1988, 4-5.

LUCE E SACERDOZIO IN UN FRAMMENTO DI QUMRAN NON IDENTIFICATO*

Corrado MARTONE

Pur essendo ormai da parecchio tempo pubblicati per intero, e in varia forma disponibili agli studiosi, i testi di Qumran lasciano ancora molto spazio all'interpretazione e all'identificazione.[1] Un caso particolare è quello dei frammenti di cui non è stata ad oggi ancora data una identificazione definitiva: a tal proposito sarà il caso di ricordare che un intero e non smilzo volume della serie DJD è dedicata ai frammenti non identificati.[2]

In questa breve nota intendiamo offrire una analisi del testo siglato 4Q468a-c, intitolato dal suo editore, appunto, 4QUnidentified Frgs. C a-c.

Il frammento è stato pubblicato per la prima volta nei primi anni Novanta nella edizione "non autorizzata" di B.Z. Wacholder e M. Abegg[3] e in anni più recenti nella serie "ufficiale" delle DJD per le cure di Magen Broshi.[4] Il frammento si trova nella foto PAM 43.399, e nelle meno recenti 40.609 e 42.011, col titolo 4QUnidentified D. Inoltre, il frammento è presente nell'archivio *online* della Leon Levy Scrolls Foundation col numero di serie delle foto B-473791 e B-473792.[5]

* È un piacere dedicare questa nota a Emile Puech, in segno di gratitudine per i molti anni di amicizia e insegnamenti.

[1] Su questo argomento Emile Puech ha scritto innumerevoli importanti contributi, ci limitiamo a ricordare in questa sede Émile PUECH, « Édition et reconstruction des manuscrits », *Henoch* 39 (2017) 105-125.

[2] Cfr. Dana M. PIKE, Andrew C. SKINNER, *Qumran cave 4. XXIII: Unidentified Fragments* (DJD, 33), Oxford, Clarendon, 2001; si veda anche Eibert TIGCHELAAR, « Constructing, Deconstructing and Reconstructing Fragmentary Manuscripts: Illustrated by a Study of 4Q184 (4QWiles of the Wicked Woman) », in: Maxine L. GROSSMAN (ed.), *Rediscovering the Dead Sea Scrolls: An Assessment of Old and New Approaches and Methods*, Grand Rapids, Eerdmans, 2010, 26-47.

[3] Ben Zion WACHOLDER, Martin ABEGG, *A Preliminary Edition of the Unpublished Dead Sea Scrolls*, Washington, Biblical Archaeology Society, 1991-1996, 3:379-81.

[4] Cfr. Magen BROSHI, « 468a-d. 4QUnidentified Fragments C, a-d », in: Stephen J. PFANN, Philip S. ALEXANDER, Magen BROSHI, et al. (ed.), *Qumran Cave 4. XXVI: Cryptic Texts and Miscellanea, Part 1* (DJD, 36), Oxford, Clarendon, 2000, 401-405.

[5] Si veda https://www.deadseascrolls.org.il/explore-the-archive/image/B-473791. Consultato il 4 settembre 2018. La foto, scattata il 23 agosto 2013, è ad alta risoluzione e utilissima per una migliore analisi dei particolari del frammento.

Particolarmente degno di attenzione è il fatto che alla sigla 4Q468 sono stati assegnati un discreto numero di frammenti che si trovano nella stessa foto, la già citata PAM 43.399 ma che non fanno parte né della stessa opera né dello stesso rotolo.[6]

Testo e traduzione

Si dà qui di séguito il testo in esame, (4Q468a–c [4QUnid Frgs. C, a–c]), con una resa minimalista, che limita al minimo le integrazioni:

Testo Fr. b

1 [שתי אני לנוגהו]

2 [משבצתוֹ יתהלכו כול ב◦]

3 [מ֯לך עלי ואור נגהו על ◦]

4 [ש בצאתה מזבול◦]

5 [עול ובני צד֯]ק

6 קו[ד֯ש קוד]שים

7 [יך לו]

Traduzione

1 [...]*šty* io al suo splendore [...] 2 [...] il suo castone. Andranno ogni ... [...] 3 [...] re (?) su di me, e la luce del suo splendore su ... [...] 4 [...]*š* uscendo dalla alta dimora ... [...] 5 [...] iniquità e i figli della giusti[zia ...] 6 [san]to dei san[ti ...] 7 [...]*yk lw*[...]

Osservazioni paleografiche[7]

La scrittura è ordinata e regolare anche grazie alle linee guida tracciate con uno stilo cui le lettere sono appese secondo l'uso largamente maggioritario a Qumran.[8] Le lettere sono discretamente uniformi quanto a dimensioni, e sono tracciate con più tratti di stilo, elementi questi che

[6] Cfr. Broshi, « 468a-d. 4QUnidentified Fragments C, a-d », 401.

[7] Per quanto segue ci rifacciamo allo studio classico di Frank M. Cross, « The Development of the Jewish Scripts », in: G. Ernest Wright (ed.), *The Bible and the Ancient Near East. Essays in Honor of William Foxwell Albright*, Garden City, Anchor, 1965, 170-264, ora in Id., Frank Moore Cross, « The Development of the Jewish Scripts », *in Leaves from an Epigrapher's Notebook: Collected Papers in Hebrew and West Semitic Palaeography and Epigraphy*, Winona Lake, Eisenbrauns, 2003, 3-43.

[8] Cfr. Emanuel Tov, *Scribal Practices and Approaches Reflected in the Texts Found in the Judean Desert*, Leiden ; Boston, Brill, 2004, 58-64.

indicano una grafia formale o semi-formale. Pur essendo il frammento di dimensioni ridotte è possibile rilevare la distinzione tra lettere mediane e finali (si veda la *kaf* in principio della l. 3) e la presenza di grazie in determinate lettere (*alef*, *ṣadi*, *šin* e *taw*). Questi particolari consentono di collocare questa scrittura semi-formale in epoca erodiana[9] piuttosto avanzata, come indicato in particolare dal tratto sinistro della *alef* che presenta un ripiegamento all'indietro verso destra.[10] Sulla base di questi dati si può quindi con cautela datare il nostro frammento alla prima metà del I sec. d.C. Il fatto poi che sia redatto in scrittura formale (o semi-formale) indica che si trattava di un testo di una certa importanza, copiato da uno scriba professionista.[11]

Analisi

Pur frammentario, questo testo presenta alcune interessanti caratteristiche legate a ben note, importanti tematiche della letteratura qumranica: in particolare, da un lato, il lessico legato alla luce e allo splendore e dall'altro quello legato all'ambito dell'ufficio sacerdotale.

Lin. 1

אני: Considerato che può essere dato per certo, sulla base del testo a disposizione che il nostro frammento non è un testo biblico, almeno nel senso che al termine "biblico" diamo noi oggi,[12] possiamo dire che l'uso del pronome personale di prima persona pare riportarci nell'ambito dei testi poetici e liturgici della biblioteca qumranica.[13] L'uso della prima

[9] Cfr. Ada Yardeni, *Understanding the Alphabet of the Dead Sea Scrolls: Development, Chronology, Dating*, Jerusalem, Carta Jerusalem, 2014, 30, che si rifà alla periodizzazione stabilita da Cross nello studio citato alla nota 6.

[10] Yardeni, *Understanding the Alphabet of the Dead Sea Scrolls*, 39.

[11] Sulle caratteristiche scribali che si possono evincere dai manoscritti di Qumran e degli altri siti del deserto di Giuda, oltre al già citato Tov, *Scribal Practices*, si veda da ultimo Id., « Scribal Characteristics of the Qumran Scrolls », in: Marcello Fidanzio (ed.), *The Caves of Qumran: Proceedings of the International Conference, Lugano 2014* (STDJ, 118), Leiden, Brill, 87-95; cfr. anche Emile Puech, « La paléographie des manuscrits de la mer Morte », in: Marcello Fidanzio (ed.), *The Caves of Qumran: Proceedings of the International Conference, Lugano 2014* (STDJ, 118), 96-105.

[12] Cfr. al riguardo Corrado Martone, « Biblical or Not Biblical? Some Doubts and Questions », *Revue de Qumran*, 21-3 (2004) 387-394.

[13] Sulla liturgia nei testi qumranici si veda il fondamentale studio di Bilha Nitzan, *Qumran Prayer and Religious Poetry*, Leiden ; New York, Brill, 1994; più di recente Russell

persona singolare, infatti, è ampiamente attestato nelle cosiddette *Hodayot* e in vari testi liturgici. In particolare, per quanto riguarda le *Hodayot*, non sono mancate ipotesi che hanno individuato la prima persona espressa in questi testo col Maestro di Giustizia,[14] cioè il fondatore del gruppo qumranico.[15] Nel frammento in esame il pronome è con tutta probabilità soggetto di un verbo terminante con le lettere שתי, mentre è implausibile il riferimento a 1 Sam 17,10 (הפלשתי אני). A motivo della successiva forma, introdotta dalla preposizione ל, l'editore opta per l'integrazione con un verbo di movimento: נגשתי, dalla radice נגש, il cui significato principale è quello di "avvicinarsi". La radice, in varie forme, è largamente attestata in ebraico biblico[16] e a Qumran nuovamente con una discreta presenza delle *Hodayot*.[17] La forma נגשתי, tuttavia, non è altrimenti attestata nei due *corpora*[18] e congetturare un *hapax legomenon* è metodologicamente rischioso.[19]

C. D. ARNOLD, *The Social Role of Liturgy in the Religion of the Qumran Community*, Leiden ; Boston, Brill, 2006.

[14] Si veda lo studio classico di Gert JEREMIAS, *Der Lehrer der Gerechtigkeit* (SUNT, 2), Göttingen, Vandenhoeck & Ruprecht, 1963; più di recente, sul Maestro di Giustizia cfr. Reinhard G. KRATZ, « The Teacher of Righteousness and His Enemies », in: Ariel FELDMAN, Maria CIOATĂ e Charlotte HEMPEL (ed.), *Is There a Text in This Cave? Studies in the Textuality of the Dead Sea Scrolls in Honour of George J. Brooke* (STDJ, 119), Leiden, Brill, 2017, 515–32.

[15] Cfr. al riguardo Svend HOLM-NIELSEN, « "Ich" in den Hodajoth und die Qumrangemeinde », in: Hans BARDTKE, (ed), *Qumran-Probleme. Vorträge des Leipziger Symposions über Qumran-Probleme vom 9. bis 14. Oktober 1961*, Berlin, Akademie-Verlag, 1963, 217-29; Florentino GARCÍA MARTÍNEZ, « Angel, Hombre, Mesías, Maestro de Justicia? El problemático "yo" de un poema qumránico », in: Jorge Juan FERNÁNDEZ SANGRADOR e Santiago GUIJARRO OPORTO (ed.), *Plenitudo Temporis: Miscelánea Homenaje al Prof. Dr. Ramón Trevijano Etcheverría*, Bibliotheca Salmanticensis, Salamanca, Universidad Pontifica de Salamanca, 2002, 103-131.

[16] Cfr. Gen 33,7; Exod 20,21; 34,32; 1 Sam. 7,10; 2 Sam. 3,34; 11,20f; 17,29; 1 Re 20,13; Ezr 9,1; Is 29,13; Amos 5,25.

[17] 1QS 11:13; 1QM 16:13; 19:11; 1QHa 6:18; 20:23; 4Q158 7-8:12; 4Q181 1:3; 4Q264 1:1; 4Q271 3:2; 4Q375 1 ii 7; 4Q422 2:9; 4Q429 4 ii 4; 4Q434 1 i 11; 4Q468b 1:1; 4Q491 10 ii 13; 11 ii 11; 4Q492 1:10; 4Q504 10:1; 4Q524 15-22:9; 11QT 61:15; 63:3.

[18] Per altre possibilità, purtroppo non particolarmente allettanti, si veda Ruth SANDER, Kerstin MAYERHOFER, *Retrograde Hebrew and Aramaic Dictionary* (Journal of Ancient Judaism. Supplements, 1), Göttingen, Vandenhoeck & Ruprecht, 2010, *ad loc.*

[19] Sul difficile rapporto degli studi biblici con l'arte della congettura cfr. Alessandro CATASTINI, « Da Qumran al testo Masoretico dell'Antico Testamento : spunti metodologici per la valutazione delle varianti », *Revue de Qumrân* 15 (1991) 303-313. Corrado MARTONE, « All the Bibles We Need: The Impact of the Qumran Evidence on Biblical Lower Criticism » [en ligne], in: George J. BROOKE, Daniel K. FALK, Eibert J. C. TIGCHELAAR, et al. (ed.), *The Scrolls and Biblical Traditions: Proceedings of the Seventh Meeting of the IOQS in Helsinki* (STDJ, 103), Leiden, Brill, 2012, 47-64; Bruno CHIESA, « Apologia della congettura », in:

Sia come sia, la prima persona singolare del nostro testo va riferita alla forma לנוגהו.

לנוגהו è una forma derivata dalla radice נגה che indica il risplendere della luce.[20] La radice torna alla lin. 3 del nostro frammento ed è anch'essa attestata in altri testi qumranici, tra i quali è interessante notare un testo squisitamente liturgico come 4Q286 1a iib 3.[21]

Colui che parla in prima persona, dunque, si mette in relazione "al suo splendore". Siamo quindi, come si accennava, nell'ambito di uno dei temi principali e centrali della letteratura qumranica e del gruppo di cui questa è espressione che considerava se stesso un insieme di figli della luce in contrapposizione al mondo esterno, dominio dei figli delle tenebre, come evidenziato nel manifesto di questa ideologia, la cosiddetta *Dottrina dei due Spiriti* che leggiamo nella *Regola della Comunità* (1QS 3:13 – 4:26).[22]

Lin. 2

Questa azione (forse) di avvicinamento del soggetto allo splendore può essere ulteriormente, ancorché ipoteticamente, specificata da ciò che rimane della linea 2.

Il termine משבצת è segno di un contesto sacerdotale. Il termine, non chiarissimo, ricorre nei capitoli 28 e 39 dell'Esodo[23] e indica un particolare ornamento della veste sacerdotale, quale definita direttamente da Dio, cfr. ad es. Es 28,3.11:

> parlerai a tutte le persone abili, che ho ripieno di spirito di sapienza, ed esse faranno le vesti di Aaronne per consacrarlo, perché serva a me come sacerdote ...

Edoardo BONA, Carlos LÉVY et Giuseppina MAGNALDI (ed.), *Vestigia notitiai. Scritti in memoria di Michelangelo Giusta*, Alessandria, Edizioni dell'Orso, 2012, 257-64.

[20] Cfr. 2 Sm 22,13; 23,4; Ps 18,13; Prov. 4,18; Isa 4,5; 50,10; 60,3. 19; 62,1; Ez 1,4, 13, 27f; 10,4; Gl 2,10; 4,15; Am 5,20; Ab 3,4, 11.

[21] Cfr. Bilhah NITZAN, « 4QBerakhot A-E (4q286-290): A Covenantal Ceremony in the Light of Related Texts », *Revue de Qumrân* 16 (1995) 487-506; Ead., Bilhah NITZAN, « 286. 4QBerakhot a », in Esther ESHEL, Hanan ESHEL, Carol NEWSOM, et al. (ed.), *Qumran Cave 4.VI: Poetical and Liturgical Texts, Part 1* (DJD 11), Oxford, Clarendon, 1998, 7-48; per le altre occorrenze cfr. 1QHa 14:18; 4Q184 1:8; 4Q405 20ii-22:11; 4Q429 4 i 5; 4Q468b 1:1, 3; 11Q17 7:13; 11Q22 1:2.

[22] La bibliografia sul cosiddetto dualismo qumranico è vastissima, basterà ricordare in questa sede l'importante raccolta di studi curata da Géza G. XERAVITS (ed.), *Dualism in Qumran* (Library of Second Temple Studies, 76), London ; New York, T & T Clark International, 2010.

[23] Es 28,11.13.25; 39,6.13.16.18; cfr. anche Ps 45,14.

Secondo il lavoro dell'intagliatore di pietra che incide un sigillo, inciderai le due pietre con i nomi dei figli d'Israele: li farai inserire in castoni (משבצות) d'oro.

Il termine deriva dalla radice שבץ che indica un modo di ornare il legno o il metallo (e infatti nei testi dell'Esodo è usato in riferimento al pettorale) in forma intrecciata per inserirvi le pietre preziose. La forma intrecciata rimanda insomma, probabilmente, al significato fondamentale della radice. Maimonide spiega il vocabolo in questo modo (*Mishne Torah*, *Klei HaMiqdash* 8,16):[24]

וכיצד מעשה הבגדים הכתונת בין של כ״ג בין של כהן הדיוט משבצת היתה שהיא בתים בתים באריגתה כמו בית הכוסות כדרך שעושין האורגין בבגדים הקשים ובית יד שלה נארג בפני עצמו ומחברין אותו עם גוף הכתונת בתפירה

Come sono fatti gli abiti? La tunica, sia del Sommo Sacerdote sia di un sacerdote ordinario, era intrecciata (משבצת) cioè intessuta a quadretti, analogamente alla struttura dello stomaco di un animale, nel modo in cui i tessitori fanno indumenti pesanti. La sua manica era tessuta separatamente e poi la univano cucendola al corpo della tunica.

Il tema della luce va quindi inserito in un contesto sacerdotale, confermato del resto dall'occorrenza del termine משבצות a Qumran in un testo sicuramente collegato al sacerdozio come 4Q365 (cfr. 4Q365 12b iii 11, 14).[25] Ciò che, ancora, consente di inserire il nostro frammento nella letteratura propria del gruppo qumranico che alcuni studiosi definiscono, con una punta di anacronismo, settaria.[26]

Alla luce di quanto esaminato fin qui, non pare azzardato riferire la successiva forma verbale a una funzione liturgica officiata dal sacerdozio, anche in base alla ricorrenza della forma nella letteratura qumranica in contesti di questo tipo:[27] particolarmente interessante è il passo 1QS 3:20-21, che fa parte della già menzionata *Dottrina dei due spiriti*:

[24] Testo in Eliyahu TOUGER (ed.), *Mishne Torah. A New Translation with Commentaries*, 26 vol., New York, Moznaim, 2002, *ad loc*. Per l'espressione בית הכוסות a indicare un particolare tratto dell'intestino dei ruminanti cfr. b*Hul* 42a. L'ornamento intrecciato cui fa riferimento la radice שבץ torna anche nella "casella" della scacchiera, che è uno dei significati assunti dal termine מִשְׁבֶּצֶת in ebraico moderno.

[25] Cfr. Sidnie White CRAWFORD, *Rewriting Scripture in Second Temple Times*, Grand Rapids, Mich, William B. Eerdmans, 2008; Molly M. ZAHN, « 4QReworked Pentateuch C and the Literary Sources of the "Temple Scroll": A New (Old) Proposal », *Dead Sea Discoveries* 19 (2012) 133-58.

[26] Cfr. al riguardo Corrado MARTONE, « From Universal to Sectarian: The Zadokites, Qumran, the Temple and Their Libraries », *Henoch* 40 (2018) 21-32.

[27] Cfr. CD 12:22; 19:4; 20:6; 1QS; 4:15, 18, 24; 6:2; 1QSb 3:24; 1QM 13:12; 4Q169 3-4 ii 2; 4Q257 6:2; 4Q258 2:6; 4Q263 1:2; 4Q266 5 i 15; 9 ii 8; 15:2; 4Q385a 5a-b:7; 4Q387 3:4; 4Q390 1:3, 12; 4Q418 47:3; 69 ii 3, 14; 81+81a:14; 4Q468b 1:2; 4Q495 2:4; 4Q511 1:7; 4Q525 5:9; 14 ii 15; 21:5.

20 ביד שר אורים ממשלת כול בני צדק בדרכי אור יתהלכו וביד מלאך
21 חושך כול ממשלת בני עול ובדרכי חושך יתהלכו

20 In mano del Principe delle luci sta il dominio su tutti i figli della giustizia; essi procedono su vie di luce. E in mano dell'Angelo delle 21 tenebre sta il completo dominio sui figli della menzogna; essi procedono in vie di tenebre.

Lin. 3

In questa linea troviamo ancora, rafforzato, il tema della luce: le due parole chiaramente leggibili sono infatti ואור נגהו. Della radice נגה, già incontrata alla lin. 1, si è detto. Qui è collegata al termine settario *par excellence*, frequentissimo a Qumran,[28] che indica la parte di umanità cui sono stati destinati i membri del gruppo che non a caso si autodefiniscono, come si è visto, figli della luce.[29] La terminologia del nostro frammento punta insistentemente su un contesto identitario (auto)riferito al gruppo qumranico.[30]

La prima lettera leggibile di questa linea è una *kaf* finale. Gli editori del testo danno per lettura sicura una *lamed* e, incerta, una *mem*: מלך. La ricostruzione può essere accettata: e può anzi essere considerata sicura la *lamed*, mentre della *mem* è visibile solo parte della base e del tratto superiore: che si tratti comunque di una *mem* si può dare per assodato. Una tale sequenza non ha riscontro nelle Bibbia ebraica.[31]

Lin. 4

In questa linea assistiamo al momento dell'uscita (בצאתה) di qualcosa o qualcuno dalla "alta dimora" (מזבול). La radice זבל nela Bibbia ebraica, dove ricorre cinque volte,[32] indica in buona sostanza l'abitazione di Dio

[28] Si veda l'amplissima voce dedicata alla radice in Reinhard G. KRATZ, Annette STEUDEL, Ingo KOTTSIEPER, *Band 1: Aleph – Beth, Hebräisches und aramäisches Wörterbuch zu den Texten vom Toten Meer: Einschließlich der Manuskripte aus der Kairoer Geniza* 1, Berlin, De Gruyter, 2017, 42-48.

[29] Per limitarci a un testo fondamentale del gruppo qumranico, 1QS, queste sono le occorrenze del termine אור: 1QS 1:9; 2:16; 3:3, 7, 13, 19, 24; 4:8; 11:3, 5.

[30] John J. COLLINS, « Beyond the Qumran Community: Social Organization in the Dead Sea Scrolls », *Dead Sea Discoveries* 16 (2009) 351-69; Jutta JOKIRANTA, *Social Identity and Sectarianism in the Qumran Movement* (STDJ, 105), Leiden, Brill, 2013.

[31] La sola corrispondenza nella Bibbia ebraica di una sequenza simile (solo per ך עלי) è 1Sam 1,22 (ויברך עלי), che purtroppo non è di molto aiuto nel nostro contesto.

[32] Cfr. 1 Re 8,13; 2 Cr 6,2; Ps 49,15; Isa 63,15; Ab 3,11. Su possibili paralleli in ugaritico cfr. già William FOXWELL ALBRIGHT, « Zabul Yam and Thapit Nahar in the Combat between Baal and the Sea », *JPOS* 16 (1936) 17–20. Per la ricorrenza del sintagma nel papiro di Ossirinco London, British Library, Or. 9180A si veda Pieter A. H. DE BOER, « Notes on

o comunque una residenza celeste ed è attestata anche a Qumran con il medesimo significato in testi che ci riportano ancora in un contesto liturgico e fortemente legato all'identità del gruppo, in particolare la *Regola della Comunità* e la *Regola della Guerra*.[33] In questi due testi si parla della residenza sacra degli astri e di Dio, e in particolare nella *Regola della Guerra* lo זבול è citato in un inno che aspetta e invoca l'intervento divino nella guerra escatologica tra i Figli della luce e i Figli delle tenebre:[34]

1 כיא רוב קדושים [א]לֹה בשמים וצבאות מלאכים בזבול קודשכה להֹ[ודות אמת]כֹה
ובחירי עם קודש 2 שמתה לכה ב◦[ ]◦פר שמות כול צבאם אתכה במעון קודשכה ומֹ[
]◦ים בזבול כבודכה

1 C'è infatti una quantità di santi nel cielo e schiere di angeli nella tua dimora santa per lodare il tuo nome. Gli eletti del popolo santo 2 li hai posti per te in [...] [Il li]bro dei nomi di tutte le loro schiere è con te nella tua santa dimora [...] nella dimora della tua gloria.

Lin. 5

La lin. 5 ci porta nuovamente in un contesto squisitamente qumranico: i בני עול, un sintagma che può essere tradotto letteralmente con "figli dell'iniquità", sono i membri del mondo esterno al gruppo, destinati per questo stesso fatto alla dannazione e compaiono in 1QS III 21,[35] all'interno della già più volte citata *Dottrina dei due spiriti*:

וביד מלאך 21 חושך כול ממשלת בני עול ובדרכי חושך יתהלכו

In potere dell'Angelo delle 21 tenebre sta il completo dominio sui figli della iniquità; essi procedono in vie di tenebre.

Il sintagma è di origine biblica, ma nella Bibbia ebraica non ha una particolare valenza identitaria,[36] al contrario che a Qumran dove, oltre al passo appena citato, è ampiamente attestato.[37] Così come è ampiamente attestato עול con differenti *nomina regentia* nel *corpus* qumranico per lo

an Oxyrhynchus Papyrus in Hebrew: Brit. Mus. Or. 9180 A », *Vetus Testamentum* 1 (1951) 49-57 (in particolare 51).

33 Cfr. 1QS 10:3; 1QM 12,1-2; 1QHa 11:35; 4Q256 19:1; 4Q258 8:12; 4Q260 2:2; 4Q298 3-4 i 1; 4Q403 1 i 41; 4Q405 6:2; 81:2; 4Q408 3+3a:5; 4Q468b 1:4; 4Q491 5-6:1; 11Q17 10:8.

34 Cfr. Giovanni Ibba, *La sapienza di Qumran: il patto, la luce e le tenebre, l'illuminazione*, Roma, Città Nuova, 2000.

35 Cfr. Paolo Sacchi (ed.), *Regola della comunità* (Studi biblici 150), Brescia, Paideia, 2006, *ad loc.*, che traduce icasticamente "figli del Male".

36 Cfr. 2 Sam 3,34; 7,10; 1 Cr 17,9: la traduzione usuale è «malfattori» o «malvagi».

37 Cfr. 1QS 3:21; 1QHa 13:10; 14:21; 4Q88 9:7; 4Q265 1:5; 4Q418 69 ii 8; 201:2; 4Q429 1 i 3; 4 i 5; 4Q511 1:8.

più in testi riferibili al gruppo e indica sempre una qualità negativa esterna al gruppo, e ancora maggiori sono le occorrenze di vari deverbali dalla radice עול,[38] che rimanda all'agire in maniera contraria alla giustizia.

Nel nostro frammento il termine עול è frammentario e solo l'ultima lettera è integra. Ciononostante, la ricostruzione può considerarsi certa, in quanto sono chiaramente distinguibili tracce della *waw* e il tratto superiore della *ayin*. La sola parola del tutto integra della linea è בני, seguita da tracce di una lettera in cui è agevole distinguere il braccio della *ṣadi*. In base a quanto visto fin qui è molto probabile che siano da accettare le integrazioni proposte dall'editore, che vede un riferimento, oltre che ai "figli dell'iniquità" anche ai "figli della giustizia" (בני צדק), stabilendo una contrapposizione che troviamo proprio nel già citato passo 1QS 3:20-21. Di nuovo, la terminologia usata nel nostro frammento ci riporta alla letteratura propria del gruppo qumranico e alle sue modalità di autodefinizione.[39]

Lin. 6

Le poche tracce superstiti della linea 6 fanno riferimento ancora a un contesto sacerdotale. La prima lettera leggibile è una *šin* preceduta da tracce del tratto superiore della *dalet*. Dopo uno spazio sono chiaramente leggibili le lettere קוד seguite da tracce del braccio superiore della *šin*. Il sintagma קודש קודשים è anch'esso ampiamente attestato sia a Qumran sia nella letteratura biblica e indica, con la ben nota modalità dell'ebraico biblico di esprimere il superlativo assoluto, il più alto grado di santità dell'offerta da recare in sacrificio,[40] ma indica anche la parte più interna, e più sacra, del tempio, che nella visione di Ezechiele (Ez 45,3ss), diviene il tempio stesso in quanto parte più sacra della Giudea restaurata dopo l'esilio.[41] Anche nella letteratura qumranica il sintagma ricorre, come c'era da aspettarsi, nei testi più legati alla autodefinizione del gruppo e

[38] Cfr. 1QS 3:19, 21; 5:2, 10; 6:15; 8:13, 18; 9:9, 17, 21; 11:9; 1QM 4:3; 1QHa 8:18; 9:28; 11:19; 13:26; 14:10; 17:36; 21:29; 23:36; 1Q27 f1 i 9; 4Q88 8:4; 4Q172 4:2; 4Q176 1-2 ii 3; 4Q179 1 ii 4; 4Q184 8, 10; 3:4; 4Q256 9:2, 8; 18:4; 4Q257 6:2, 3; 4Q258 1:2, 7; 6:7; 8:2, 5; 4Q259 3:4, 15; 4:2; 4Q266 3 ii 21; 4Q299 1:1; 4Q367 2a-b:13; 4Q380 1 ii 6; 4Q417 1 i 6; 2 i 7; 4Q418 43-45 i 4; 88 ii 4; 4Q418c 1:5; 4Q428 7:1; 4Q432 5:6; 4Q468b 1:5; 4Q525 28:5; 11Q5 22:7, 10; 11Q11 5:8; 11Q13 2:11.

[39] Al riguardo basterà citare in questa sede l'ormai classico studio di Carol A. NEWSOM, *The Self As Symbolic Space: Constructing Identity and Community at Qumran* (STDJ, 52), Leiden ; Boston, Brill, 2004.

[40] Cfr. Es 29,37; 30,10.29, 36; 40,10; Lv 2,3.10; 6,10.18.22; 7,1.6; 10,12.17; 14,13; 24,9; 27,28; Nm 18,9; Gd 17,3; 1 Cr 23,13; 2 Cr 31,18; Ez 43,12; 45,3; 48,12; Dan 9,24. Per la forma si veda Paul JOÜON, Takamitsu MURAOKA, *A Grammar of Biblical Hebrew* (Subsidia Biblica, 27), Roma, Editrice Pontificio Istituto Biblico, 2006, §96 Ag.

[41] Cfr. Walther D. EICHRODT, *Ezekiel: a Commentary*, London, SCM Press, 1970, 569.

al sacerdozio escatologico,[42] quali la già più volte incontrata *Regola della Comunità* e i cosiddetti *Canti dell'Olocausto del Sabato*, un'opera quest'ultima tra le più affascinanti del corpus qumranico nella quale la comunità reinterpreta se stessa come una comunità di angeli al servizio (sacerdotale) in un tempio ormai elevato a una dimensione celeste.[43]

1QS 9:5-6 sottolinea in modo inequivocabile la concezione escatologica del sacerdozio che comporta l'adesione al gruppo, con una terminologia che risuona anche nel nostro frammento:

בעת ההׄיאה יבדילו אנשי 6 היחד בית קודש לאהרון להיחד קודש קודשים ובית יחד לישראל ההולכים בתמים

in quel tempo si separeranno gli uomini della 6 comunità (come) casa santa per Aronne, per unirsi al Santo dei Santi, e (come) una casa della comunità per Israele, (per) coloro che procedono nella perfezione.

In buona sostanza costituire la comunità significa costituire un tempio col suo Santo dei Santi (קודש קודשים, appunto).[44]

Lin. 7

Nell'ultima linea del frammento sono visibili solo le ultime due lettere e le prime due lettere di due distinte parole:]יך לו[. Il nesso non è così frequente: nella Bibbia ebraica ricorre solo in Dt 10,9; 1 Re 22,18; Qo 8,12, mentre a Qumran, se escludiamo le congetture, si ritrova solo in 11Q5 22:8, uno dei cosiddetti *Salmi apocrifi*.[45] Si tratta di un passo che vale la pena di ricordare qui:

8 כמה קוו לישועתך ויתאבלו עליך תמיך לוא תובד תקותך 9 ציון ולוא תשכח תוחלתך

Come hanno sperato nella tua salvezza! Come hanno tenuto il tuo lutto i tuoi perfetti! Non si spegne la speranza di te, Sion, 9 né viene dimenticata la tua attesa.

[42] Sul sacerdozio escatologico a Qumran cfr. Corrado MARTONE, « Beyond Beyond the Essene Hypothesis ? Some Observations on the Qumran Zadokite Priesthood », *Henoch* 25 (2003) 267-75. Per le occorrenze cfr. 1QS 8:8; 9:6; 10:4; 1QSb 4:28; 4Q158 13:2; 4Q251 15:1; 4Q256 19:2; 4Q258 6:2; 9:1; 4Q259 2:14, 15; 4Q260 2:4; 4Q286 2:5; 4Q287 2:5, 7; 4Q398 9:2; 4Q400 1 i 7, 10, 12; 1 ii 6; 2:10; 4Q401 6:5; 12:1, 3; 35:2; 4Q403 1 i 11, 42, 45; 1 ii 1, 7, 27; 2:1; 3:2; 4Q404 5:1; 4Q405 6:5, 8; 7:2; 11:2; 14-15 i 2, 4, 7; 19:2, 4; 20ii-22:10; 23 ii 8; 41:3; 85:1; 4Q423 8:3; 4Q468b 1:6; 4Q502 6-10:13;; 100:2; 4Q503 15-16:2, 4 ; 23:1; 24-25:1; 27:5; 29-32:23; 11Q17 4:9; 6:5; 11Q19 35:9.

[43] Cfr. Carol A. NEWSOM, « "He has Established for Himself Priests": Human and Angelic Priesthood in the Qumran Sabbath *Shirot* », in: Lawrence H. SCHIFFMAN (ed.), *Archaeology and History in the Dead Sea Scrolls. The New York University Conference in Memory of Yigael Yadin* (JSJP.S, 8), Sheffield, JSOT Press, 1990, 101-120.

[44] Cfr. SACCHI, *Regola della Comunità*, 139, n. 5.

[45] *Editio princeps* in James A. SANDERS, *The Psalms Scroll of Qumrân Cave 11 : (11QPs*^{a}*)* (DJD, 4), Oxford, Clarendon Press, 1965.

Osservazioni conclusive

Il testo che abbiamo esaminato, pur frammentario, permette di avanzare qualche ipotesi tesa a una contestualizzazione.

Secondo un'ipotesi interessante[46] il testo citato più sopra, 11Q5 22:8, alluderebbe alla situazione di Gerusalemme dopo l'assassinio di Onia III:[47] se questa ipotesi è valida, un testo di questo tipo non stonerebbe nel nostro frammento dal momento che con tutta probabilità i disordini seguiti alla fine della dinastia sadocita sono in qualche modo legati alla nascita o al consolidamento del gruppo qumranico:[48] il frammento qui esaminato, come si è visto, bene si inserisce in un contesto di lode ed esaltazione del sacerdozio quale centro della comunità e non è escluso che potesse contenere un accenno alla situazione di Gerusalemme che ha portato alla fine del sacerdozio sadocita legittimo.[49]

[46] Cfr. Mathias Delcor, « L'hymne à Sion du Rouleau des Psaumes de la Grotte 11 de Qumrân (11 Q Ps a) », *Revue de Qumrân* 6 (1967) 71-88.

[47] Sulle complesse vicende legate a Onia III si veda ora Meron M. Piotrkowski, *Priests in Exile: The History of the Temple of Onias and Its Community in the Hellenistic Period* (SJ, 106), Berlin, de Gruyter, 2019.

[48] Cfr. al riguardo Martone, « *Beyond Beyond the Essene Hypothesis?* ».

[49] Sulla questione si veda ora Corrado Martone, « The Qumran "Library" and Other Ancient Libraries: Elements for a Comparison » [en ligne], in: Sidnie White Crawford e Cecilia Wassen (ed.), *The Dead Sea Scrolls at Qumran and the Concept of a Library* (STDJ, 116), Leiden, Brill, 2015, 55-77.

SATURATION, THAT IS, DRUNKENNESS: THE INTERPRETATION OF 1QPHAB 11:8–16 AND ITS LINGUISTIC BACKGROUND

Noam MIZRAHI*

1. BACKGROUND

The book of Habakkuk contains, towards its end (but before the psalm appended in chapter 3), a collection of five prophetic units, sometimes referred to as the "Woe Oracles" (Hab 2:5–20). Designed as dirges, they open with the interjection הוי, "woe" or "alas," but because they portray negative figures, they actually convey the expectation – or even hope – for these figures' imminent downfall.[1] Originally, these dirges may have been meant to refer to different figures. But once combined into a series, they are construed as describing different facets of a single person, introduced at the start of the series by the epithet גֶּבֶר יָהִיר, "an arrogant man" (v. 5). The ironic – or satirical[2] – dirges are then presented as the words of the nations he subjugated (vv. 5–6a). The broader context motivates the reader to identify this man with the King of the Chaldeans, who are described in some detail earlier on (1:5–11, 12–17). In contradistinction, Pesher Habakkuk does not presuppose that a single figure is being described in all the dirges. The first, second and fourth dirges are applied to the Wicked Priest; the third is interpreted as referring to the Spouter of Lies; and the fifth is understood to refer to the pagan population of Judea.

* An early version of this study was presented in the Ninth International Symposium on the Hebrew of the Dead Sea Scrolls and Ben Sira (Toronto, April 2019), and I thank the participants for their helpful comments. A Hebrew version has been published in *Meghillot* 14 (2019): 105–117. The English translation of biblical passages is usually adapted from the NRSV, and that of the Dead Sea Scrolls – from Florentino GARCÍA MARTÍNEZ and Eibert J. C. TIGCHELAAR, *The Dead Sea Scrolls: Study Edition* (2 vols.). Leiden: Brill, 1997 (in both cases, with modifications of my own).

[1] Hab 2:6b-8 ("Alas for you who heap up what is not your own!"), 9–11 ("Alas for you who get evil gain for your houses"), 12–14 ("Alas for you who build a town by bloodshed"), 15–17 ("Alas for you who make your neighbor drink"), 19–20 ("Alas for you who say to the wood, 'Wake up!'"). For some of the form-critical considerations of this series see, e.g., Robert D. HAAK, *Habakkuk* (VT.S. 44). Leiden: Brill, 1997 20–22.

[2] So Zeev WEISMAN, *Political Satire in the Bible* (Semeia Studies 32). Atlanta: SBL, 1998, 83–100.

Our concern lies with the interpretation of the fourth dirge, treated in 1QpHab 11:2–12:10. The prophetic text describes a man who gets other people drunk (v. 15a: הוֹי מַשְׁקֵה רֵעֵהוּ... וְאַף שַׁכֵּר, "alas for you who make your neighbor drink… until he is drunk"), drawing obscene satisfaction when they expose their nakedness in public (v. 15b: לְמַעַן הַבִּיט עַל מְעוֹרֵיהֶם, "in order to gaze on their nakedness").[3] The prophet asserts that the relation between the two people shall be reversed, *quid pro quo*: God will get the evil man drunk (v. 16b: שְׁתֵה גַם אַתָּה וְהֵעָרֵל תִּסּוֹב עָלֶיךָ כּוֹס יְמִין יהוה, "Drink, you yourself, and expose your shame![4] The cup in the LORD's right hand will come around to you"), so that he, who had drawn satisfaction from the shame of others (v. 16a: שָׂבַעְתָּ קָלוֹן מִכָּבוֹד, "You were sated with contempt instead of glory"), will experience his due share of shame (v. 16c: וְקִיקָלוֹן עַל כְּבוֹדֶךָ, "and shame will come upon your glory").

Pesher Habakkuk identifies the evil person with the Wicked Priest, interpreting the fourth dirge in three consecutive *pesher*-units. The first unit (1QpHab 11:2–8) identifies "his neighbor" with the Teacher of Righteousness, who is persecuted by the Wicked Priest. The second (11:8–16) and third (11:17–12:10) units describe the punishment of the Wicked Priest. Our concern here focuses on the second *pesher*-unit, which explicates v. 16:

[3] According to the MT, the passage also accuses the evil man that he adds some drug to the wine (מְסַפֵּחַ חֲמָתְךָ, "adding your poison"), presumably in order to accelerate the other person's loss of consciousness and self-control. This reading, however, may be due to textual corruption, by way of dittography, from סף חמתך (compare סַף רַעַל, in Zech 12:2) as proposed by Julius WELLHAUSEN, *Skizzen und Vorarbeiten*. 5: *Die kleinen Propheten übersetzt, mit Noten* (2nd edn). Berlin: Georg Reimer, 1893, 165. For other proposals, which I find less convincing, see Charles F. WHITLEY, "A Note on Habakkuk 2:15." *JQR* 66.3 (1976): 143–147; Meinrad STENZEL, "Habakkuk ii 15–16." *VT* 3.1 (1953): 97–99.

[4] MT's reading, וְהֵעָרֵל, is very strange. Contextually, it looks like a denominative verb derived from עָרֵל "uncircumcised," as explained by IBN EZRA: מבנין נפעל כמו: והאסף אל עמך; והטעם: תֵרָאה ערלתך, i.e., the grammatical form is derived "from the N stem, like '*and you shall be gathered* (וְהֵאָסֵף) to your kin' (Deut 32:50), and it means: so that your foreskin shall be seen" (cf. QIMHI), and ELIEZER OF BEAUGENCY further explains that such an act connotes shame and disgrace (Menahem COHEN (ed.), *Mikra'ot Gedolot HaKeter: Minor Prophets*. Ramat-Gan: Bar-Ilan University Press, 2012, ad loc.). Despite its evident difficulties, this line of interpretation still resonates in modern commentaries, e.g., William Hayes WARD, "Habakkuk," *A Critical and Exegetical Commentary on Micah, Zephaniah, Nahum, Habakkuk, Obadiah and Joel* (ICC). Edinburgh, T&T Clark, 1911, 17. However, this interpretation is forced, and the MT is probably corrupt. Critics often emend it to הֵרָעֵל, whose root means "to tremble, reel" (especially in Aramaic), thereby referring to the drunk man's physical instability. Compare Isa 35:3, "Strengthen the weak hands, and make firm the *feeble* (כֹּשְׁלוֹת) *knees*," translated by Targum Jonathan: וּרכוּבִין דְּרָעְלָן, and so also the Peshitta: ܘܒܘܪܟܐ ܕܪܬܠ; cf. Peshitta Job 4:4; 9:6; 26:11 etc. (see further below, n. 9). Incidentally, some medieval commentators tried to connect והערל to the root רעל by way of metathesis; see, e.g., the anonymous commentary of a student of Isaiah of Trani (M. COHEN, *ibid.*). For the whole matter, cf. Shmuel AHITUV, "Habakkuk," *Nahum, Habakkuk, Zephaniah* (Mikra Le-Yisrael). Tel Aviv: Am Oved & Jerusalem: Magnes, 2006 (Heb.), 48. For alternative opinions see, e.g., R. D. HAAK, *Habakkuk*, 69–70.

שבעתה 9 קלון מ<כ>בוד שתה גם אתה והרעל 10 תסוב עליכה כוס ימין יהוה וקיקלון
11 על כבודכה – 12 פשרו על הכוהן אשר גבר קלונו מכבודו 13 כיא לוא מל את
עורלת לבו וילך בדרכו 14 הרוׄיה למען ספות הצמאה וכוס חמת 15 [א]ל תבלענו
לוסיף [ק]ל[ון על ק]ל[ו]נו ומכאוב 16 [ע]ל[מכאובו]

"You are more glutted (9) with disgrace than with glory. Drink up also and get inebriated! (10) The cup of YHWH's right hand will turn against you and disgrace (11) come upon your glory" (Hab 2:16) – (12) Its interpretation concerns the Priest whose disgrace exceeded his glory (13) because he did not circumcise the foreskin of his heart *and he walked on his path* (14) *of saturation in order to annihilate the (path of) thirst*;[5] but the cup of [Go]d's (15) wrath will consume him, increasing [dis]gr[ace over his [dis]grace and pain (16) [ov]er [his pain].

The textual discrepancies between the scriptural quotation and the other textual witnesses of the Hebrew Bible have been repeatedly discussed in previous scholarship.[6] Suffice it to note that the pesherist famously alludes to two alternative readings of one keyword:

(a) The MT reads שְׁתֵה גַם אַתָּה וְהֵעָרֵל, "Drink, you yourself, and *expose your shame*!" The consonantal text of this reading, והערל, is reflected in the explication כיא לוא מל את עורלת לבו, "because he did not circumcise the foreskin of his heart," indicating that הערל was interpreted as referring to an "uncircumcised" person. The prophetic passage, then, was construed as blaming the Wicked Priest of violating an explicit Pentateuchal commandment: וּמַלְתֶּם אֵת עָרְלַת לְבַבְכֶם, "Circumcise the foreskin of your heart" (Deut 10:16), reiterated in prophetic literature: הִמֹּלוּ לַיהוה וְהָסִרוּ עָרְלוֹת לְבַבְכֶם, "Circumcise yourselves to the LORD, remove the foreskin of your hearts" (Jer 4:4).

(b) By contrast, Pesher Habkkuk quotes the scriptural text שתה גם אתה והרעל, "You should drink too and *get inebriated*."[7] This reading may

[5] I have opted here for the most literal translation possible, for reasons that will become evident in the discussion that follows. Contrast Michael WISE, Martin ABEGG and Edward COOK, *The Dead Sea Scrolls: A New Translation*. London: HarperCollins, 1996, 122: "and he lived extravagantly to bring to naught those who had but little" (but see further below, n. 18); F. GARCÍA MARTÍNEZ and E. J. C. TIGCHELAAR, *Study Edition*, 1:21: "and has walked on paths of excessiveness to slake his thirst."

[6] For the pertinent facts see especially William H. BROWNLEE, *The Text of Habakkuk in the Ancient Commentary from Qumran*. (JBL.MS 11) Philadelphia: SBL, 1959, 76–79, §§119–122; cf. Bilhah NITZAN, *The Pesher Habakkuk (1QpHab): A Scroll from the Wilderness of Judah*. Jerusalem: Bialik Institute, 1986 (Heb.), 192.

[7] Alternatively, one can translate here "stagger!" matching the conjectural emendation of the MT (above, n. 4). The translation "get inebriated" presupposes that the pesherist derived the verb from רַעַל, "poison." Admittedly, the biblical lexica do not recognize such a lexeme, translating expressions such as סַף רַעַל (Zech 12:2) and כּוֹס הַתַּרְעֵלָה (Isa 51:17, 22) as "cup/goblet of *reeling*" (e.g., BDB and HALOT s.v.). The sense of "poison," however, is easily deducible from them, and the words רעל and תרעלה are actually employed

well be reflected also in the pesherist's explication, which identifies God's "cup of (i.e., held by) the right hand" (כּוֹס יְמִין יהוה) with "the cup of God's wrath" (כוס חמת [א]ל; cf. Isa 51:17, 22), employing the word חֵמָה as an idiomatic expression for "poison" or "venom" (cf. Ps 58:5).[8] The consonantal text underlying this reading is also reflected in some of the ancient versions.[9]

The pesherist, then, explicitly quotes one reading, which differs from the MT, but explicated another reading, identical to the MT, while possibly alluding to the former as well.[10] This exegetical technique suggests that, for him – and by extension to his readership as well – the notion of the "scriptural text" was not restricted to a specific *Vorlage*, but rather is inclusive of alternative and variant readings. This conclusion is important

so in medieval Hebrew (and perhaps already in *piyyut*, the liturgical poetry of the Byzantine period). In Modern Hebrew, "poison" has become the standard sense of these words. Pesher Habakkuk suggests that this usage, so far documented only in very late sources, goes back to antiquity.

[8] Alternatively, חמה may have been introduced under the influence of an implied prooftext, i.e., Jer 4:4, in which the divine warning to follow the Deuteronomic commandment (**הִמֹּלוּ** לַיהוה וְהָסִרוּ **עָרְלוֹת לְבַבְכֶם** אִישׁ יְהוּדָה וְיֹשְׁבֵי יְרוּשָׁלָם, "*Circumcise* yourselves to the LORD, remove *the foreskin of your hearts*, O people of Judah and inhabitants of Jerusalem") is immediately followed by the threat of annihilation by God's wrath (פֶּן תֵּצֵא כָאֵשׁ **חֲמָתִי** וּבָעֲרָה וְאֵין מְכַבֶּה מִפְּנֵי רֹעַ מַעַלְלֵיכֶם, "or else *my wrath* will go forth like fire, and burn with no one to quench it, because of the evil of your doings"). This sequence echoes in our *pesher*-unit: כיא לוא מל את עורלת לבו <...> וכוס חמת [א]ל תבלענו. Incidentally, this parallel independently demonstrates that the intervening segment, marked above by the angular brackets (i.e., וילך בדרכו הרויה למען ספות הצמאה) is out of place in its present context.

[9] Note the double rendition in the Old Greek: πίε καὶ σὺ καὶ διασαλεύθητι καὶ σείσθητι, "Drink, you too, … and shake and quake!" (NETS). This is the only occurrence of διασαλεύω in the Septuagint, but the simplex σαλεύω is quite common. As it renders several Hebrew motion verbs (cf., e.g., OG Nah 1:5 [rendering רעש]; 3:12 [נוע]), the Greek translator probably read here והרעל, interpreted as "stagger!" (cf. above, n. 4). Cf. OG Zech 12:2, which translates סַף רַעַל as ὡς πρόθυρα σαλευόμενα, "as shaking doorways" (taking סף as "doorway" rather than "drinking vessel"). The second verb, σείω, is a stereotypical equivalent of Hebrew רעש, which also denotes trembling and quacking (cf., e.g., Am 9:1, וְיִרְעֲשׁוּ הַסִּפִּים, "the thresholds shall shake"). The double rendition may well result from an interpretive or stylistic expansion on the part of the Greek translator (so James A. E. MULRONEY, *The Translation Style of Old Greek Habakkuk* (FAT II.86). Tübingen, Mohr Siebeck, 2016, 85–86, 93–94), yet it testifies to the variant reading והרעל rather than והערל. Aquila renders here καρώθητι, just as in Ps 60:5 he translated תרעלה with καρώσεως; cf. AQUILA for Isa 51:17 (Field, *Origenis Hexaplorum*, 2:1006, 189, 530, respectively).

[10] For this phenomenon see Ilana GOLDBERG, "Variant Readings in Pesher Habakkuk." *Textus* 17 (1994): [9]–[24], especially [12]–[15], where previous literature is adduced. Cf. Pieter B. HARTOG, *Pesher and Hypomnema: A Comparison of Two Commentary Traditions from the Hellenistic-Roman Period* (STDJ 121). Leiden: Brill, 2017, 154–158. He further suggests (*ibid.*, 286–287) that the interchange of הרעל ~ הערל is due to an exegetical technique ("anagram").

for evaluating the thesis of the present study, namely, that the pesherist took into consideration not only the Hebrew text of Habakkuk but also its Aramaic rendition.

2. Allusion to Deut 29:18

The *pehser*-unit systematically explicates Hab 2:16 in accordance with the order of segments exhibited by the scriptural passage:

Hab 2:16	Explication
שבעתה קלון מכבוד	פשרו על הכוהן אשר גבר קלונו מכבודו
You are more glutted with disgrace than with glory.	Its interpretation concerns the Priest whose disgrace exceeded his glory,
שתה גם אתה והרעל (נ"א: והערל)	כיא לוא מל את עורלת לבו
Drink up also and stagger (*or* get inebriated; *var*. expose your shame)!	because he did not circumcise the foreskin of his heart,
—	**וילך בדרכו הרויה למען ספות הצמאה**
—	**and he walked on his path of saturation in order to annihilate the (path of) thirst;**
תסוב עליכה כוס ימין יהוה	וכוס חמת [א]ל תבלענו
The cup of YHWH's right hand will turn against you,	but the cup of [Go]d's wrath will consume him,
וקיקלון על כבודכה	לוסיף [ק]ל[ון על ק]ל[ו]נו ומכאוב [ע]ל [מכאובו]
and disgrace come upon your glory!	increasing [dis]gr[ace over his [dis]grace and pain [ov]er [his pain].

This presentation highlights the middle statement. Not being anchored in any segment of Hab 2:16, it appears like an expansion, which "disturbs the creation of full correlation between the explication and the verse."[11]

This structural anomaly is discussed below (§3), but it should first be interpreted in and of itself. In terms of content, this section alludes to a Pentateuchal warning to those entering into the covenant with God:

> (17) It may be that there is among you a man or woman, or a family or tribe, whose heart is already turning away from the LORD our God to serve the gods of those nations. It may be that there is among you a root sprouting poisonous

[11] B. Nitzan, *Pesher Habakkuk*, 100 (§56b), 193.

> and bitter growth. (18) All who hear the words of this oath and bless themselves, thinking in their hearts, "We are safe even though we go our own stubborn ways" – *so that the saturated one will sweep away the thirsty one* (לְמַעַן סְפוֹת הָרָוָה אֶת הַצְּמֵאָה) – (19) the LORD will be unwilling to pardon them, for the LORD's anger and passion will smoke against them. All the curses written in this book will descend on them, and the LORD will blot out their names from under heaven (Deut 29:17–19).

Thus, among the congregation of those accepting the covenant upon themselves, there is a person who already plans to violate it. Deuteronomy warns that such a wicked person, who is likened to a poisonous root (v. 17), will incur the curses directed against violators of the covenant (cf. Deut 28).

The enigmatic conclusion of the wicked man's thought in v. 18, לְמַעַן סְפוֹת הָרָוָה אֶת הַצְּמֵאָה, has been a notorious crux for many generations. Who or what is the "saturated one" and who or what is the "thirsty one" (both adjectives being in the feminine singular)?[12]

Sectarian literature adopted the Deuteronomic covenantal ceremony as a model for its own annual ritual of the renewal of the covenant. According to the Community Rule (1QS 2), it includes blessings uttered by the priests addressing "the people of God's lot", i.e., community members (1QS 2:2b-4a) and curses uttered by the Levites addressing the "people of Belial's lot," i.e., all outsiders (1QS 2:4b-10). Then, the priests and Levites pronounce together a special curse addressed to those present in the ceremony but secretly plan to violate their oath:

> (11) And the priests and the Levites shall continue, saying: "Cursed by the idols which his heart reveres (12) whoever enters this covenant, and places the obstacle of his iniquity in front of himself to fall over it. (13) When he hears the words of this covenant, he will congratulate himself in his heart, saying: 'I will have peace, (14) in spite of my walking in the stubbornness of my heart.' *But his thirsty spirit will be obliterated with the saturated one* (ונספתה רוחו הצמאה עם הרווה),[13] without (15) mercy. God's anger and the wrath of his

[12] See, e.g., David DAUBE, "The Extension of a Simile." Pp. 57–59 in: *Interpreting the Hebrew Bible: Essays in Honour of E.I.J. Rosenthal*. Edited by John A. EMERTON and Stefan C. REIF. Cambridge: Cambridge University Press, 1982; Cécile DOGNIEZ, "La pensée du mal selon la Septante de Dt 29,18–21." *Semitica et Classica* 4 (2011): 117–123; Jan JOOSTEN, "The Interpretation of Deuteronomy 29:17–18 in the Hellenistic Period: Septuagint, Qumran and Parabiblical Literature." Pp. 107–120, in: *The Dynamics of Language and Exegesis at Qumran* (FAT II.35). Edited by Devorah DIMANT and Reinhard G. KRATZ, Tübingen: Mohr Siebeck, 2009.

[13] Again, this is a very literal translation. Contrast M. WISE, M. ABEGG and E. COOK, *New Translation*, 128: "Surrounded by abundant water, his spirit shall nevertheless expire thirsty"; F. GARCÍA MARTÍNEZ and E. J. C. TIGCHELAAR, *Study Edition*, 1:73: "However, his spirit will be obliterated, the dry with the moist."

verdicts shall consume him for everlasting destruction. All (16) the curses of this covenant shall stick fast to him. God shall separate him for evil, and he shall be cut off from the midst of all the sons of light because of his straying (17) from following God on account of his idols and obstacle of his iniquity. He shall assign his lot with the cursed ones forever" (1QS 2:11–17).

Clearly, "thirsty" typifies the wicked person, but so also "saturated."[14] This is indicated by the fact that the particle **את** of the scriptural passage (לְמַעַן סְפוֹת הָרָוָה **אֶת** הַצְּמֵאָה) has been replaced by the preposition **עם** in the S text (ונספתה רוחו הצמאה **עם** הרווה). Evidently, **את** was interpreted as a preposition meaning "with" rather than as the accusative marker. Similarly, in 1QpHab 11:8–16, "saturated" is a feature of the Wicked Priest, paralleling the wicked man's "*thirsty* spirit" of 1QS 2:14. The sectarian interpretation Deut 29:18 was therefore strict: both thirst and saturation are taken as metaphors for the way of the wicked, extending to – and including – the Wicked Priest.

Still, the parallel between the Community Rule and Pesher Habakkuk should not be pressed too far, as the two works slightly differ in their interpretations of the Deuteronomic passage. Pesher Habakkuk takes the phrase לְמַעַן סְפוֹת הָרָוָה אֶת הַצְּמֵאָה as describing the *sin* of the one who plans to violate the covenant, moving to describing his punishment only later on ("the cup of [Go]d's wrath will consume him," etc.). The Community Rule, by contrast, integrates the allusion to Deut 29:18 into the description of the wicked man's *punishment* ("his thirsty spirit will be obliterated with the saturated one, without mercy"). The syntactic expression of this difference is found in their contradictory treatments of the particle **את** (as mentioned above): the Community Rule takes the word to be the preposition meaning "with," whereas Pesher Habakkuk considers it as the *nota accusativi*, hence its omission from the paraphrased wording **למען ספות הצמאה**, in which "the thirsty one" is clearly the (unmarked) direct object governed by the infinitival form **ספות**. Apparently, sectarian exegesis was not completely unified, allowing for various emphases and even divergent opinions.[15]

[14] The inherent exegetical difficulty posed by the proof-text of Deut 29:18 is thus matched by its confusing interpretive treatment in the Community Rule – a fact which has left not a few commentators of this work puzzling about the actual sense of the entire clause. See, e.g., Michael KNIBB, *The Qumran Community*. Cambridge: Cambridge University Press, 1987, 87.

[15] This was noted by KISTER, as cited by J. JOOSTEN, "Interpretation," 115, n. 34. For conflicting understandings of the Habakkuk passage in sectarian literature, cf. Menahem KISTER, "Biblical Phrases and Hidden Biblical Interpretations and Pesharim." Pp. 27–39 in *The Dead Sea Scrolls: Forty Years of Research* (STDJ 10). Edited by Devorah Dimant and

3. Exegetical problem, and its solution

As demonstrated above, the literary structure of the *pesher*-unit is dependent upon the scriptural passage it interprets, following it segment by segment. The conspicuous exception to this rule is the allusion to Deut 29:18, placed at the very center of the unit but with no explicit anchor in the prophetic proof-text. Why, then, was it integrated at all? And why in this particular context?

While previous commentators have naturally discussed the meaning of this section, none was able to offer a satisfactory explanation for its structural anomaly. For instance, William Brownlee suggested that it ties to the scriptural words "you are glutted… drink up (שבעתה... שתה)," assuming that the verbs denoting eating and drinking have evoked, by way of association, the reference to thirst and saturation.[16] While not impossible, this solution is evidently forced. Bilhah Nitzan similarly suggested that the problematic section was motivated by association, explaining that both passages share the theme of cursing the wicked and the figurative reference to poison.[17] But the lexical similarity between Deut 29:17–18 and Hab 2:16 is anything but clear, and it cannot sustain an associative link of the sort exemplified by her other cases.

I propose that there is another, linguistic link between the two passages enabling their association: The Hebrew participial adjective רווה/רויה, drawn from the Deuteronomic passage, was interpreted in accordance with its sense in Aramaic, which has been one of the principle vernaculars of Hellenistic-Roman Judea, alongside Hebrew and Greek. The verb *r-w-y* is commonly used in the Aramaic Targums for rendering Hebrew *š-k-r* "to be drunk." For example, וַיֵּשְׁתְּ מִן הַיַּיִן וַיִּשְׁכָּר וַיִּתְגַּל בְּתוֹךְ אָהֳלֹה,

Uriel Rappaport. Leiden: Brill & Jerusalem: Magnes, 1992, at 37–38. For the exegetical diversity within the Pesharim, see further Timothy H. Lim, *Pesharim* (Companion to the Qumran Scrolls 3). London: Sheffield Academic Press, 2002, 27–43.

[16] William H. Brownlee, *The Midrash Pesher of Habakkuk* (SBL.MS 24). Missoula: Scholars, 1979, 192.

[17] B. Nitzan, *Pesher Habakkuk*, 62 (§40), 192. Her discussion of this point is embedded in an important chapter, in which she demonstrates how *pesher*-exegesis is not focused exclusively on the interpreted passage but is also informed by various other passages that bear – thematically or verbally – on the main proof-text. Nitzan calls this phenomenon "the associative system." One may add that it applies differently to the subtypes of Pesharim literature. The continuous Pesharim thoroughly depend on the order and contents of the scriptural text being interpreted, so that the associative system reveals itself only sporadically. By contrast, the associative system plays a more decisive role in the isolated and thematic Pesharim. Cf. Liora Goldman, *Those who Hold Fast to the Ordinances: The Qumran Community and its Exegesis in Light of the Pesharim in the Damascus Document*. Jerusalem: Bialik Institute, 2019 (Heb.).

"He (Noah) drank some of the wine and *became drunk*, and he lay uncovered in his tent" (Gen 9:21), is translated by Targum Onkelos: וּשְׁתִי מִן חַמְרָא וּרְוִי וְאִתְגַּלִּי בְּגוֹ מַשְׁכְּנֵיהּ. Similarly, וְהוּא שִׁכֹּר עַד מְאֹד, "He (Nabal of Carmel) was very *drunk*" (1 Sam 25:36), is translated by Targum Jonathan: וְהוּא רָוֵי עַד לַחֲדָא. If so, the exegetical clause **וילך בדרכו הרויה** למען ספות הצמאה is nothing but an interpretation of the scriptural words **וְאַף שַׁכֵּר** in Hab 2:15. Tellingly, Targum Jonathan indeed renders the crucial word: בְּדִיל דְיִשְׁתֵּי **וְיִתְרְוֵי**, "so that he will drink *and become drunk*."[18]

This lexical usage is not restricted to Jewish Aramaic translations of the Bible. Aramaic *r-w-y* is also the standard rendition of Hebrew *š-k-r* in the Syriac Peshitta, including Hab 2:15 (ܘܡܪܘܐ ܠܗ̇). The same is true for the Samaritan Targum of the Pentateuch.[19] Furthermore, the same sense still prevails in Neo-Aramaic dialects, not necessarily the Jewish ones.[20] It can be reasonably hypothesized, therefore, that, from the point of view of a Second Temple exegete, there is indeed an verbal link that connects Deut 29:17–18 and Hab 2:15–16, but it is found not in the Hebrew text of Habakkuk but rather in its rendering into Aramaic. In other words, the sense of *r-w-y* in the passage under consideration is a calque of the cognate Aramaic lexeme.[21]

[18] This proposal was anticipated by the translation of the pertinent passage of Pesher Habakkuk in the second, revised edition of M. Wise, M. Abegg and E. Cook, *New Translation*, 87: "and he walked in the ways of *drunkenness* in order to put an end to thirst" (contrast the first edition, quoted above, n. 5). Unsurprisingly, the responsibility for this translation lies with E. Cook, a noted Aramaist (as he kindly informed me after I presented this paper in Toronto). However, it remained unexplained in the book, and, to the best of my knowledge, it left no impression on the scholarly discussion of Pesher Habakkuk.

[19] So according to MS J, which reflects the early stage of the Samaritan Targum (but not according to MS A, which reflects its late stage). See Abraham Tal, *Samaritan Targum: A Critical Edition* (3 vols.), Tel Aviv, Rosenberg School of Jewish Studies, 1980–83 (Heb.), 1:28–29 (Gen 9:21), 188–189 (Gen 43:34); 2:391 (Deut 32:42).

[20] See, e.g., David T. Stoddard, *A Grammar of the Modern Syriac Language as Spoken in Oroomiah, Persian, and in Koordistan*, London, American Oriental Society, 1855, 71; Geoffrey Khan, *The Neo-Aramaic Dialect of Barwar* (HdO I.96). Leiden, Brill, 2008, 2:1169 (I am indebted to Hezy Mutzafi for these references).

[21] While etymologically Hebrew *r-w-y* is one and the same as Aramaic *r-w-y*, synchronically they differ in their semantic scope. In Hebrew, this verb denotes being filled or full of liquids in general and water in particular, hence "be saturated" (and as such, it forms a standard word-pair with *ś-b-ʕ* "be glutted," e.g., Isa 58:11; Jer 31:14; 46:10; Lam 3:15). While this usage is also attested in Aramaic, albeit relatively marginally, the most common use of the verb in that language is for denoting the state of being sated with wine, up to the point of intoxication, hence its standard usage as rendition of Hebrew *š-k-r*. Typologically, the broad usage common to Hebrew looks earlier than the specific usage typifying Aramaic, which would be the result of semantic narrowing. Be that as it may, by the Second Temple period, each language had already established its own semantic range of this lexeme.

Scholars have previously noted that Pesher Habakkuk sometimes displays verbal contacts with Targum Jonathan.[22] Similar phenomena in other sectarian texts have been taken as potential proof for the hypothesis that an Aramaic translation of the prophetic books (a Proto-Targum of a sort) had existed as early as the late Second Temple period, be it orally or in writing.[23] Yet attractive as this hypothesis may be, most examples adduced in its support are ambiguous, and do not substantiate the existence of a continuous translation of all or parts of the prophetic books in the form of a coherent and independent literary work. As the Jewish population of Hellenistic-Roman Judea consisted of bilingual speakers of Hebrew and Aramaic, mutual coloring of both languages is to expected. By nature of the evidence, when it comes to scriptural quotations, paraphrases and allusions, Aramaic(-like) elements are most clearly discernible when comparing such texts with the Aramaic translations of the Bible.

In our case, too, the hypothesis that the pesherist had at his disposal an Aramaic translation is not impossible, but the semantic equation between Hebrew *š-k-r* and Aramaic *r-w-y*, on which the association between Hab 2:15–16 and Deut 29:17–18 is based, can be comfortably explained as resulting from an *ad hoc* rendering that reflects the bilingual background of the exegete, without necessarily resorting to the assumption of a continuous Aramaic version of Habakkuk or the Prophets.[24] In either case, though, the pesherist's exegetical notion of the scriptural text is not limited to the Hebrew text, including its variant readings; rather, it extends to the Aramaic rendition of scriptural words and phrases.[25]

[22] Robert P. GORDON, *Studies in the Targum to the Twelve Prophets. From Nahum to Malachi* (VT.S 51). Leiden, Brill, 1994, 83–95; Marcus WOOD, "Pesher Habakkuk and the Targum of Jonathan Ben Uzziel.", *JSP* 10 [19] (1999): 129–146.

[23] See, e.g., Moshe BAR-ASHER, "A Few Remarks on Mishnaic Hebrew and Aramaic in Qumran Hebrew." Pp. 12–19 in: *Diggers at the Well* (STDJ 36). Edited by Takamitsu MURAOKA and John F. ELWOLDE, Leiden, Brill, 2000; Noah HACHAM, "An Aramaic Translation of Isaiah in the *Rule of Community.*" *Leš* 67.2 (2005): 147–152 (Heb.). For the entire issue, cf. Jan JOOSTEN, "How Old is the Targumic Tradition? Traces of the Jewish Targum in the Second Temple Period, and Vice Versa." Pp. 143–159 in: *The Text of the Hebrew Bible and Its Editions: Studies in Celebration of the Fifth Centennial of the Complutensian Polyglot* (THB Supp. 1) edited by Andres PIQUER OTERO and Pablo A. TORIJANO MORALES. Leiden: Brill, 2016.

[24] For a broad perspective of the lexical and semantic processing of bilingual speakers see, e.g., J. F. KROLL and P. E. DUSSIAS, "The Comprehension of Words and Sentences in Two Languages." Pp. 169–200 in: *The Handbook of Bilingualism*. Edited by Tej K. BHATIA and William C. RITCHIE, Oxford, Blackwell, 2004.

[25] A similar phenomenon is reflected in other corpora. For instance, the Greek translators of the Hebrew Bible sometimes render words in accordance with their Aramaic rather than Hebrew usage (e.g., Jan JOOSTEN, "On Aramaising Renderings in the Septuagint." Pp. 587–600 in *Hamlet on a Hill: Semitic and Greek Studies Presented to Professor T. Muraoka on the Occasion of His Sixty-Fifth Birthday*. Edited by Marten F.J. Baasten and Wido Th. van

The calque underlying the peculiar use of *r-w-y* also explains the theological treatment of Deut 29:18 in the Community Rule. As indicated above, the adjective רוה is taken there as referring to a negative quality, characteristic of the wicked. The semantic basis for this construal is now evident: the term is understood not as in Hebrew ("saturated") but rather as in Aramaic ("being drunk"). Furthermore, Pesher Habakkuk makes clear that the charge of drunkenness stands not only for personal corruption but also for actively corrupting others. This, in turn, explains the severity of the curse that the Community Rule applies to people accused of nurturing this dangerous quality: they constitute a threat to the community as a whole, as their scheme may "poison" others' thinking as well. This runs the unforgivable risk of stripping community members of their most precious asset, namely, their unconditional adherence to the "new covenant," which ensures their survival on the pending Day of Judgment.

4. Implications

According to the proposal set above, there is indeed a verbal point of contact between the dictions of Deut 29:18 and Hab 2:15–16 that had enabled their associative linking and thus the integration of a segment alluding to the former into the exegetical treatment of the other. The keyword רוה of the Deuteronomic passage was read differently than usual, owing to an Aramaic calque, thus matching the sense of שכר in the prophecy of Habakkuk. Two implications of this explanation merit special mention.

(a) In terms of the literary structure of the relevant *pesher*-units, the allusion to Deut 29:18 is integrated into the unit discussing Hab 2:16, but it is actually construed as an interpretation of a segment of Hab 2:15. This fact argues against the common view that the hermeneutics of the Pesharim is essentially atomistic, namely, that it treats each segment of the interpreted text independently of the others, thereby enabling their explication regardless of their original order and meaning in context.[26] The case analyzed here

Peursen. Leuven: Peeters, 2003. Reprinted in Jan Joosten, *Collected Studies on the Septuagint: From Language to Interpretation and Beyond* (Tübingen: Mohr Siebeck, 2012), 53–66. And Jan Joosten, "The Aramaic Background of the Seventy: Language, Culture and History." *Bulletin of the International Organization for Septuagint and Cognate Studies* 43 (2010): 53–72.). In rabbinic literature – for which one may already assume an established tradition of an Aramaic translation of the Pentateuch and Prophets – one finds cases in which the exegetical treatment of a scriptural proof-text presupposes its Aramaic rendition rather than its Hebrew wording (e.g., Menahem Kahana, "Targum Leading to Mishnah.", in: *Talmud Studies*, 3: *Talmudic Studies Dedicated to the Memory of Professor Epraim E. Urbach* (2 vols.). Edited by Yaakov Sussmann and David Rosenthal. Jerusalem: Magnes, 2008 (Heb.), 431–437).

[26] See especially Karl Elliger, *Studien zum Habakuk-Kommentar vom Toten Meer* (Beiträge zur historischen Theologie 15). Tübingen, Mohr Siebck, 1953. But note the

demonstrates that adjacent passages can be interdependent. Although v. 15 and v. 16 are each given their own *pesher*-units (1QpHab 11:2–8a and 8b-16, respectively), a segment of the former was left with no explication in its original place, being picked up again in the following unit:

Hab 2:15	Explication
הוי משקה רעיהו	פשרו על הכוהן הרשע אשר רדף אחר מורה הצדק
Woe to anyone making his companion drunk,	Its interpretation concerns the Wicked Priest who pursued the Teacher of Righteousness
מספח חמתו	לבלעו בכעס חמתו אבית גלותו
adding his wrath (poison),	to consume him with the heat of his wrath in the place of his banishment.
אף שכר	—
or even making him drunk	—
למען הבט אל מועדיהם	ובקץ מועד מנוחת יום הכפורים הופיע אליהם לבלעם ולכשילם ביום צום שבת מנוחתם
to look at their festivals!	In festival time, during the rest of the day of Atonement, he appeared to them, to consume them and to make them fall on the day of fasting, the sabbath of their rest.
Hab 2:16	**Explication**
שבעתה קלון מכבוד	פשרו על הכוהן אשר גבר קלונו מכבודו
You are more glutted with disgrace than with glory.	Its interpretation concerns the Priest whose disgrace exceeded his glory,
שתה גם אתה והרעל (נ״א: והערל)	כיא לוא מל את עורלת לבו
Drink up also and stagger (*or* get inebriated; *var*. expose your shame)!	because he did not circumcise the foreskin of his heart,
—	וילך בדרכו הרויה למען ספות הצמאה
—	and he walked on his path of saturation in order to annihilate the (path of) thirst;

critique of B. NITZAN, *Pesher Habakkuk*, 51–58 (§§34–35), which is amplified by the discussion above.

Hab 2:16	Explication
תסוב עליכה כוס ימין יהוה	וכוס חמת [א]ל תבלענו
The cup of YHWH's right hand will turn against you,	but the cup of [Go]d's wrath will consume him,
וקיקלון על כבודכה	לוסיף [ק]ל[ו]ן על ק[ל]ו[ו]נו ומכאוב [ע]ל [מכאובו]
and disgrace come upon your glory!	increasing [dis]gr[ace over his [dis]grace and pain [ov]er [his pain].

To be sure, this fact can be interpreted in various ways. Perhaps the explication of the words ואף שכר was cut from v. 15 and mechanically pasted into the discussion of v. 16. Indeed, similar cases of transposition between consecutive *pesher*-units is attested elsewhere in the continuous Pesharim.[27] More probably, however, the structural reshuffling is meant to bolster a specific argument. The underlying rational of the relation between vv. 15–16 is that of *quid pro quo*: v. 15 describes the Wicked Priest's sin, who persecuted the Teacher of Righteousness "to consume him (לבלעו) with the heat of his wrath (חמתו)" and further attempted "to consume" the entire community (לבלעם), while v. 16 describes his due punishment by employing the same vocabulary: "the cup of God's wrath (חמת [א]ל) will consume him (תבלענו)." The transposition of a segment from the section dealing with the sin to the section dealing with the punishment reinforces the symmetry between the Wicked Priest's offence and his retribution.[28] Evidently, the pesherist did not treat every verse individually and independently from one another. On the contrary, despite splitting them between distinct *pesher*-units, he took their original literary coherence into consideration and even highlighted it for his own needs.

[27] Compare, for instance, Pesher Psalms: 4QpPs[a] (4Q171) II 23–25 fragmentarily preserves the quotation and explication of Ps 37:17–18, while the immediately following unit of 4QpPs[a] (4Q171) II 27 – III 2 discusses Ps 37:19a. The latter unit, however, includes the interpretive treatment of much of v. 18, which was quoted in the former *pesher*-unit (I owe this observation to the Master's thesis of my student, Adam LLOYD-ALFIA, "Pesher Psalms (4QpPs[a]) from Qumran: Introduction, Edition and Commentary," Tel Aviv University, 2019, 120–122). This phenomenon apparently disturbs the expected correlation between the quoted text and its explication (see Shani L. BERRIN [Tzoref], "Lemma/Pesher Correspondence in Pesher Nahum." Pp. 341–350 in: *The Dead Sea Scrolls Fifty Years after Their Discovery*. Edited by Lawrence H. SCHIFFMAN, Emanuel TOV and James C. VANDERKAM. Jerusalem: Israel Exploration Society, 2000).

[28] This point develops a comment made to me by Mehahem KISTER (personal communication).

(b) From a historical-linguistic point of view, the Aramaic calque betrays the chronolectal background of Pesher Habakkuk. The language of this work has been the focus of a recent debate regarding the extent to which it exhibits markers of Second Temple Hebrew. Ian Young argues that such features are few and sparse, thereby proving that scribes were able to produce texts in Classical Biblical Hebrew as late as the Hellenistic-Roman period.[29] Gary RENDSBURG's rejoinder identified many additional elements of Late Biblical Hebrew, demonstrating that the language of Pesher Habakkuk is replete with linguistic markers of its true age.[30] Although he does not mention cases of Aramaic influence over the semantics of Hebrew vocabulary, the present discussion indicates that such cases do exist. It may, therefore, be added to the ever-growing list of chronologically diagnostic features that reflect the historical background of the language of Pesher Habakkuk.

5. CONCLUSION

This study analyzed the literary structure and composition of a unit of Pesher Habakkuk that interprets Hab 2:16 but integrates into it an allusion to Deut 29:18. The hitherto unrecognized associative link between these two passages reflects the Hebrew-Aramaic bilingualism of the pesherist, who equated *r-w-y* of Deut 29:18 and *š-k-r* of Hab 2:15 based on the semantics of the former in Aramaic rather than in Hebrew.

This hypothesis not only solves the exegetical crux presented by the content and structure of 1QpHab 11:8–16 but also illuminates some fundamental aspects of the sectarian literature in general and the Pesharim in particular: the multifaceted textual dynamics that links the scriptural passages and their interpretive treatments, the relationship between consecutive *pesher*-units, the exegetical diversity within the dense framework of sectarian thinking, and the complex relationship between Hebrew and Aramaic in Hellenistic-Roman Judea.

[29] Ian YOUNG, "Late Biblical Hebrew and the Qumran Pesher Habakkuk." *JHS* 8 (2008): Art. 25. http://www.jhsonline.org/jhs-article.html

[30] Gary A. RENDSBURG, "The Nature of Qumran Hebrew as Revealed through Pesher Habakkuk." Pp. 133–159 in: *Hebrew of the Late Second Temple Period*. STDJ 114. Edited by Eibert TIGCHELAAR and Pierre VAN HECKE. Leiden, Brill, 2015.

OF POTS AND IMPURITY IN THE HODAYOT

Carol A. NEWSOM

Why is the term *yēṣer* so prominent in the anthropological vocabulary of the Hodayot? That simple question has bothered me since I first began working on the Hodayot, prompted by Émile Puech's publication of his reconstruction of 1QH[a] in 1988.[1] To younger scholars who have always encountered the Hodayot as it is now reconstructed it is difficult to communicate the intellectual excitement that Puech's article engendered, all the more so since his independent reconstruction matched in almost every detail that developed by Hartmut Stegemann in his unpublished dissertation.[2] At last it was possible to have a better grasp of the systemic significance of some of the features that had been noted in the columns and fragments of the earlier edition.

As I began to translate the text I puzzled over the frequency of the word *yēṣer*, how to render it, and what patterns of thought or exegetical insights had given rise to the preference for this term. In biblical texts the noun can mean either "something shaped" or "inclination," that is, the direction in which something is shaped. The noun, however, is infrequent, occurring only some nine times. In most of these the nuance has to do with mental disposition (Gen 6:5; 8:21; Deut 31:21; Isa 26:3; 1 Chr 28:9; 29:18). Only three times is it used to indicate an object that is shaped or the process of shaping (Isa 29:16; Hab 2:18; Ps 103:14). In most of those cases the verbal form is also used. In Isa 29:16 the metaphor explicitly compares God's relation to the human being to that of a potter to the pot that is shaped from clay (*ḥōmer*). Psalm 103:14 refers to the creation tradition of Gen 2:7 as a shaping of humankind like a pot from the dust (*ʿāpār*). In Hab 2:18 the reference is to an idol fashioned by humans.

In the texts from Qumran, both sectarian and non-sectarian, excluding the Hodayot, the noun occurs some twenty-four times (not counting overlapping

[1] Émile PUECH, "Quelques aspects de la restauration du Rouleau des Hymnes (1QH)," *JJS* 39 (1988): 38–55.

[2] Hartmut STEGEMANN, "Rekonstruktion der Hodajot: Ursprüngliche Gestalt und kritisch bearbeiteter Text der Hymenrolle aus Höhle 1 von Qumran" (PhD diss., Heidelberg, 1963); "The Material Reconstruction of the Hodayot," in *The Dead Sea Scrolls: Fifty Years After Their Discovery 1947–1997*, ed. L. H. Schiffman, E. TOV, J. C. VANDERKAM (Jerusalem: Israel Exploration Society, 2000), 272–84.

occurrences and the citation of Hab 2:18). Of these, in addition to two passages that are too broken to determine the nuance, eleven are in contexts that allude to the phrase "inclination of the thoughts of the heart" from Gen 6:5; 8:21 and pertain to the developing interest in the "evil *yēṣer*".[3] Three echo the phrase "steadfast disposition" (*yṣr smwk*) from Isa 26:3,[4] and four others use the term in a generally psychological or dispositional sense,[5] with an additional instance of an allusion to Ps 103:14, which may be taken either as "disposition" or as "formation" more generally (4Q508 [4QPrFêtes[b]] 2, 5). One occurrence in 4QInstruction (4Q417 1 i 17 = 4Q418 43-45 i 13) also refers to formation "according to the pattern of the holy ones." This text also preserves the distinctive phrase "inclination of the flesh" (*yṣr bśr*) in one passage (4Q416 i 16 = 4Q418 1–2c 8), an expression probably to be related to the notion of the *rwḥ bśr* in 4QInstruction. Thus it likely also has a psychological connotation, though it is notable that the psychology is articulated in terms of the materiality of the human being. Only in 4Q511 (4QŠir) 28–29 3 (*w'ny mṣrwq yṣr ḥmr*) is there a usage that is similar to that of the *Niedrigkeitsdoxologien* in the Hodayot, and 4Q511 is likely drawing on those passages.

The pattern and distribution of the noun *yēṣer* in the Hodayot is strikingly distinctive both in comparison to the pattern of usage in biblical texts and to the other texts from Qumran. Moreover, within the Hodayot, the patterns differ between the hodayot of the Teacher and those traditionally designated hodayot of the Community (or, as I prefer to call them, hodayot of the Maskil).[6] Out of a total of forty-three occurrences in the Hodayot four instances are ambiguous and might refer to "inclination" or "formation" or possibly "vessel" (14:35; 17:16; 19:23; 21:30). Leaving these aside, within the hodayot of the Teacher six of the ten examples refer to human intentions, purposes, or inclinations, and two use the phrase "steadfast disposition" from Isa 26:3. None of the examples, however, clearly evoke the phrase from Genesis 6:5 and 8:21 concerning the "inclination of the thoughts of the heart." Finally, there are two examples of the expression "vessel of clay" (11:24; 12:30), which is most similar to Isa 29:16.

[3] CD 2:16; 1QS 5:5; 1Q18 (1QJub[b]) 1-2, 3; 4Q286 (4QBer[a]) 7 ii 7; 4Q370 (4QAdmonFlood) 1 i 3; 4Q381 (4QNon-Canonical Psalms B) 76-77, 2; 4Q417 (4QInstruction[c]) 1 ii 12; 4Q422 (4QParaphrase of Gen and Exod) 1, 12; 4Q436 (4QBarkhi Nafshi[c]) 1 i a,b + ii, col. i 10; 4Q525 (4QBeatitudes) 7, 4; 11Q5 (11QPs[a]) 19:15.

[4] 1QS 4:5; 8:3; 4Q437 (Barkhi Nafshi[d]) 4, 2 (= 4Q438 [Barkhi Nafshi[e]] 4 ii 2)

[5] 4Q299 (4QMysteries[a]) 33, 2; 4Q393 (4QCommunal Confession) 1 ii 6; 4Q418 (4QInstruction[d]) 43-45 i 8; 4Q436 (Barkhi Nafshi[c]) 1a,b + ii, col. ii.

[6] See Carol A. Newsom, "A Farewell to the Hodayot of the Community," *DSD* 28 (2021):1-19.

These instances are in passages that are similar to the *Niedrigkeitsdoxologien* characteristic of the hodayot of the Maskil, where the phraseology is most at home.

In the hodayot of the Maskil in cols. 3-9 and 18-27 there are ten occurrences of "vessel of clay" (3:29; 9:23; 19:6, 20:29, 35; 21:38; 22:12; 23:13; 23:28, 25:31; cf. also "pinched off c[lay]," 18:5), five of "vessel of dust" (7:34; 8:18; 21:17, 25, 34). In four additional instances the word following *yēṣer* is broken but is probably to be restored with either "clay" or "dust" (21:11, 19, 31; 22:19). In four instances the use of *yēṣer* by itself appears to be an abbreviation of these phrases, referring to the human as a "vessel" (23:12, 14), or as an "abhorrent vessel" (23:37, 38). Two instances of *yṣr bśr* are in contexts in which it is difficult to say whether they should be translated "vessel of flesh" as a synonym for "vessel of clay/dust" or as "inclination of flesh," as a synonym for "spirit of flesh" (4:37; 5:15, 30). Although there are three instances where the word is used to mean inclination or purpose (7:26, 30; 21:29) and one instance of the Isaian phrase "stedfast disposition" (*yṣr smwk*), it is evident that the hodayot of the Maskil overwhelming use the term to refer to humans in their physicality, in sharp departure from biblical usage, non-Hodayot Qumran texts, and even the hodayot of the Teacher.

Thus the question arises as to why the hodayot of the Maskil are so invested in depicting humans as pots. As is widely recognized, the trope of the *yēṣer (hā)ḥēmar/ʿāpār* is part of the larger complex of images and exegetical interpretations associated with negative anthropology in the hodayot of the Maskil. Although this theme was identified by Heinz-Wolfgang Kuhn in his influential monograph as characteristic of the Gattungen he called *Niedrigkeitsdoxologien* and *Elendsbetrachtungen*,[7] the negative anthropology is attested also in short sentences and phrases throughout the hodayot of the Maskil and in isolated passages in the hodayot of the Teacher, though the vocabulary of vessel, clay, and dust is concentrated in the second group of Maskil hodayot in cols. 18-27.

The negative anthropology of the Hodayot is produced through a layered and complex metaphorical and exegetical process, aspects of which I have discussed elsewhere.[8] To understand how the image of the human as

[7] Heinz-Wolfgang KUHN, *Enderwartung und gegenwärtiges Heil: Untersuchungen zu den Gemeindeliedern von Qumran*, SUNT4 (Göttingen: Vandenhoeck & Ruprecht, 1966), 26–29.

[8] Carol A. NEWSOM, "Deriving Negative Anthropology Through Exegetical Activity: The Hodayot as Case Study," in *Is there a Text in This Cave? Studies in the Textuality of the Dead Sea Scrolls in Honor of* George J. Brooke, ed. A. FELDMAN, M. CIOATĂ, and C. HEMPEL, STDJ 119 (Leiden: Brill, 2017), 258–74.

pottery vessel plays a critical role in this symbolic system it is necessary to explore various interlocking systems of imagery and association. First, it is clear that the image of the human as pottery vessel is closely connected with the image of God's creating humans from the dust of the earth in Gen 2:7. This basic image schema was, of course, widespread in the ancient world and is attested also in Mesopotamian creation traditions. Indeed, one of the phrases used by Elihu to describe human creation ("pinched off from clay," Job 33:8), which also occurs in 1QH[a] 18:5, is an idiom also found in Akkadian for making humankind (*karāṣu*, *CAD* 8:209). The Hodayot, however, specifically have the creation tradition of Gen 2-3 in view, as is clear from the twelve clear allusions to Gen 2:7 and 3:19 with references to being "formed" from dust (11:22), "taken" from dust (20:27; 23:24), and "returning" to dust (18:6, 14; 19:29 [2×], 34; 22:8, 30; 23:29 [2×]). Although Genesis does not use the noun *yēṣer*, the verb *yāṣar* ("to form") does occur in 2:7. Thus it is clear how the basic image of humans as "vessels" might be derived from the passage and associated traditions. I had initially translated the noun *yēṣer* in the Hodayot as "creature" in order to capture the association between verb *yāṣar* ("create") and noun *yēṣer* ("creature"). That translation, however, is too abstract and does not adequately preserve the specificity and materiality that seems so important to the Hodayot with its insistence on "clay" and "dust." Thus "vessel" or "pot" seems better for *yēṣer*.

What that basic exegetical association does not explain, however, is the high degree of negativity that the Hodayot associate with the creation of humans as vessels from the dust. Although numerous passages could be used to illustrate, the following serves well:

> As for me, from dust [you] took [me, and from clay] I was [pin]ched off, to be a source of impurity and obscene shame, a heap of dust and a thing kneaded [with water, bread of magg]ots, a dwelling of darkness (20:27–29).

What is particularly shocking about this passage is that it suggests that it was the intention of God to create humankind from dust to be something impure, disgusting, and culpable. The imagery mostly draws on the model of the potter creating from clay, though the term for "kneaded" with water is also associated with bread making,[9] hence the restoration of the phrase "bread of maggots." Maggots are associated with rotting flesh, particularly in the dead but also sometimes on the dead flesh of a living person. It is difficult to imagine a more repugnant image of God's

[9] Jonas C. Greenfield, "The Root 'GBL' in Mishnaic Hebrew and in the Hymnic Literature from Qumran," *RevQ* 2 (1960): 156 (155–62).

creation. Here is a vision of intrinsic, inescapable moral evil grounded in human materiality. The human is created in order to be putrefaction, physically and morally.

Nothing about dust in itself, however, carries the connotation of abhorrent disgustingness in biblical tradition. The disobedience of the first humans is in no way linked to their material composition. Nor in Gen 3:19 is the "return to the dust" part of the punishment of the humans but only a marker of the duration of the time a mortal being is consigned to toil. In Ps 104:29, Job 34:15, and Qoh 3:20 and 12:7 the return to the dust is simply the decay of the material body when the life-giving breath or spirit has departed at death. Much the same is true of Sir 17:1. In Ps 103:14 a reference to creation from dust does appear to mark human frailty ("for He knows how we are formed [*yiṣrēnû*]; He is mindful that we are dust," NJPS). The image is elaborated with comparisons of human existence as ephemeral and vulnerable, like fresh grass and flowers in a dry wind (vv. 15-16), and so seems to refer to physical frailty rather than moral frailty. In the passages that employ the more developed image of God as the potter and humankind as the pot, the comparison is used to emphasize the hierarchical difference between God and humanity and to rebuke human arrogance (e.g., Isa 29:16; 45:9; Jer 18:6), though it may also serve as the basis for an appeal to God's forbearance and compassion (Isa 64:8), much as the reference to dust does in Ps 103:14.[10]

The only biblical texts that associate human materiality with moral deficiency are the three negative anthropologies articulated by Eliphaz and Bildad in Job 4:17–21; 15:14–16; and 25:4–6. References to "worms" and "maggots" in Bildad's trope evoke the disgust at putrefaction that appears in 1QH[a] 20:28, though this image is not common in the *Niedrigkeitsdoxologien*. Eliphaz's reference to humanity as "loathsome" or "abhorrent" (*nitʿāb*) in 15:16 is likely the source for the phrase "abhorrent vessel" in 1QH[a] 23:37, 38. But it is Eliphaz's first treatment of the theme in Job 4:17–21 that is most important for the imagery of the "vessel of clay" and "vessel of dust" in the Hodayot. In that passage Eliphaz develops a chain of being argument in which God exceeds the angels in righteousness

[10] Jean-Sébastien REY, however, has explored how the syntactical ambiguity of "dust" in Gen 2:7 became a key for anthropological speculation in the LXX and various Second Temple and later Jewish and Christian texts. In some cases the interpretation was positive, in some neutral, and in some negative. His examples indicate that the question of the significance of the dusty materiality of humans was one that preoccupied a wide variety of authors ("Le motif de la poussière en Gen 2,7 et sa reception dans le judaïsme du second Temple," in Anne-Laure ZWILLIG, ed., *Lire et interpreter. Les religions et leur rapports aux textes fondateurs* [Genève: Labor et Fides, 2013], 79-94).

and purity, as the angels exceed humanity, those who "dwell in houses of clay, whose foundation is in the dust." The following lines are difficult to translate but clearly refer to the disintegration of human bodies as they are "crushed" (*dk'*) and "shattered" (*ktt*). Thus the material corruption of the human mortal body serves as a symbolic index of its moral corruption as neither righteous nor pure before God (v. 17). In addition to the general similarity of imagery between Eliphaz's words and the vocabulary of the Hodayot, the *Niedrigkeitsdoxologie* that occurs in 4Q511 28-29 3 explicitly alludes to Eliphaz's imagery as the speaker makes reference to "my foundation of dust" (*swd ʿpry*).[11] Although these passages are clearly central to the development of the negative anthropology in the Hodayot and to its striking interpretation of creation traditions, they fall short of explaining why the specific image of the pottery *vessel* has such a prominent role in the Hodayot. In order to solve that conundrum it is necessary to pursue a line of inquiry that may initially appear to go in a different direction.

If one looks more closely at the *Niedrigkeitsdoxologien* and related passages, apart from the reference to humans as pottery, which is the most common complex of imagery, the next most frequent cluster consists of expressions having to do with impurity. Specifically, it is impurity associated with women. The term "fount of menstrual impurity" (*mqwr ndh*) occurs three times (5:32; 9:24; 20:28), with "obscene shame" or "genital shame" (*ʿrwt qlwn*) twice (5:32; 20:28), plus one occurrence of "foundation of genital nakedness" (*swd hʿrwh*, 9:24). Although *niddāh* by itself can be a more generalized term for impurity, the expression *māqôr niddāh* refers to the uterus as the source of menstrual impurity.[12] Moreover, the cluster of terminology in the Hodayot seems to point to Lev 20:18 and 21 as the source of the expressions, a text that forbids a man from having intercourse with his brother's wife and compares and conflates it with forbidden intercourse with a menstruant. That female impurity is the imaginative center of the imagery is evident from the passage in 1QH[a] 9:24 which refers to "a foundation of genital nakedness (*swd hʿrwh*) and a fount of impurity (*mqwr ndh*), and a crucible of iniquity" (*kwr hʿwwn*). The term *kûr* ("crucible") refers to a pottery container used for refining metals and was a metaphor for the womb as well. Thus the presumably male psalmist

[11] C. A. NEWSOM, "Deriving Negative Anthropology," 268.

[12] Hermann LICHTENBERGER, *Studien zum Menschenbild in Texten der Qumrangemeinde*, SUNT 15 (Göttingen: Vandenhoeck & Ruprecht, 1980), 84–85; Nicholas A. MEYER, *Adam's Dust and Adam's Glory in the Hodayot and the Letters of Paul: Rethinking Anthropogony and Theology*, NovTSup 168 (Leiden: Brill, 2016), 34, n. 57.

identifies himself both as a pottery vessel on the basis of Gen 2:7 and, using metaphorical expressions for the female body, as a vessel (*mqwr*, *kwr*) that contains liquids that generate impurity.

The critical nexus between the cluster of motifs concerning female impurity and the motifs of human creation is the phrase "born of woman," (*ylwd ʾšh*), one of several terms unique to the book of Job that are appropriated in the Hodayot as it develops its anthropological vocabulary.[13] This phrase occurs four times in anthropological contexts in 1QH^{a} (5:31; 21:2, 9; 23:13) and once in the generically similar Maskil psalm in 1QS 11:21. Although the phrase on its own is not intrinsically negative and appears to be a poetic expression for "human being," in biblical texts it occurs *only* in Job 14:1, 15:14, and 25:4. All three of these verses introduce negative characterizations of humanity. In 15:14–16 and 25:4–6 humans are described as guilty and abhorrent before God. In 14:1 the phrase occurs in a passage that asserts that no one can produce "a clean thing out of an unclean one," referring to humans as unclean. The proximity of the phrase "born of woman" to these descriptions of humans as guilty and polluted facilitates the transfer to the negativity to that phrase itself.

Moreover, as Nicholas Meyer has recently argued,[14] the well established analogy between the human womb and the earth as womb allows for a symbolic joining of the creation of humans from the dust of the earth in Gen 2:7 with the birth of humans from a woman. As he notes, the comparison is most common in poetic texts, including Job 1:21; Ps 139:13–16; Eccl 5:14; and Sir 40:1. Sirach 40:1 makes the connection with the Genesis traditions most explicitly: "Hard work was created for everyone, and a heavy yoke is laid on the children of Adam, from the day they come forth from their mother's womb until the day they return to the mother of all the living" (trans. NRSV). The description applied to Eve in Gen 3:20, "the mother of all the living," is here transferred to the earth itself. Similarly, the Hodayot can make a symbolic connection between the impurity associated with the birth process and the initial "birth" of humans in creation, and the authors of the Hodayot are not the first to do so.

To whom, however, does impurity attach in the birth process? According to Lev 12:2–8 the birth process rendered the parturient impure. When a woman gave birth to a male child she underwent a period of primary impurity (analogized to menstrual impurity) for seven days, followed by

[13] C. A. Newsom, "Deriving Negative Anthropology," 267–69.

[14] Nicholas A. Meyer, "Born of Woman, Fashioned from Clay: Tracking the Homology of Earth and Womb from the Hebrew Bible to the Psalms of Thanksgiving," *DSD* 28 (forthcoming).

a period of secondary impurity (referred to as "blood purification") for thirty-three days, during which time she could not enter the sanctuary or touch any consecrated thing (Lev 12:2–4). If she gave birth to a female child, her period of primary impurity was fourteen days, plus a secondary period of impurity lasting sixty-six days. No reason is specified for the difference. It is generally thought that the impurity attached to the mother but not to the child, even though it had been in contact with the birth blood and the impure mother herself. Jacob Milgrom cautions, however, that the silence of the text on this point could be interpreted either to imply that the child does not contract impurity or, conversely, "that the child's impurity is taken for granted."[15] Egyptian, Hittite, and Greek cultures assumed ritual impurity for newborns, and it is possible that ancient Israel did also, even if the matter is not explicitly treated in Leviticus.[16] The timing of the circumcision for a male infant on the eighth day might also point in this direction. It may indicate that impurity for the male infant resulting from birth was analogized to that of a man who has intercourse with a woman during her menstrual cycle and whose impurity lasts for seven days (Lev 15:24).[17] In the case of a female infant it is possible that the double period of impurity reflects the knowledge that some female infants do have a small discharge of blood after birth, though this suggestion is speculative.[18] If it is the case that Leviticus points to an assumption of impurity acquired in the birth process, then the phase "born of woman," as it appears in the Hodayot, would naturally suggest the impure state of all persons at birth. But it remains uncertain whether or not the birth process was thought to convey impurity to infants.[19]

[15] Jacob MILGROM, *Leviticus 1–16*, AB 3 (New York: Doubleday, 1991), 743. See also Jonathan MAGONET, "'But if It Is a Girl, She is Unclean for Twice Seven Days...': The Riddle of Leviticus 12:5," in *Reading Leviticus: A Conversation with Mary Douglas*, ed. John F. A. SAWYER (Sheffield: Sheffield Academic Press, 1996), 144–52.

[16] Matthew THIESSEN, "Luke 2:22, Leviticus 12, and Parturient Impurity," *NT* 54 (2012): 21 (16–29), briefly discusses the comparative evidence.

[17] MAGONET, "But if It Is a Girl," 151. Thiessen, "Luke 2:22," 23.

[18] MAGONET, "But if It Is a Girl," 151–52.

[19] 4Q266 (4QD^a) 6 ii 5-13 discusses the laws pertaining to the parturient. Lines 5-10 reproduce Lev 12:2–5 with slight reorganization. Line 11 introduces material not in Lev 12. Joseph BAUMGARTEN (DJD 18, 55–56) restores the passage to read "let her give the ch]ild to a nurse (who can nurse it) in puri[ty," (*ttn 't hy*]*ld lmnqt bṭhr*[*rh*), interpreting the passage to mandate the use of a wet nurse so that the child does not *contract* impurity from the mother, implying that the infant itself is not born with impurity. But Cecilia WASSEN (*Women in the Damascus Document*, AcBib 21 [Atlanta: Society of Biblical Literature, 2005], 56–58), has given strong arguments why this reconstruction is unlikely, since it would essentially prevent a woman from nursing, as her milk likely would have dried up by the time she had completed the days of her purification. Moreover, such a regulation would place an extraordinary logistical and economic burden on the entire society. The text is simply too broken to assess

A second line of argument, however, connects the idea of birth impurity with creation. Both Jubilees and 4Q465 (4QMiscRules) make God's creation of Adam and Eve the etiology for the laws concerning the impurity of the parturient. Jubilees 2:14 refers to Adam's creation on the sixth day of the first week, following the chronology of Gen 1. Insofar as Adam's rib was created then, Jubilees says that God created both male and female. But, harmonizing Gen 1 and 2, Jub 3:8–14 recounts God's removing the rib from Adam and showing his wife to him only in the second week of creation. Jubilees makes this timeline the etiology for the two periods of primary uncleanness for the birth of a male child and a female child in Lev 12:2–5. One week is mandated for a male because Adam was created in the first week; two weeks are mandated for a female because Eve was separated form Adam's body in the second week. Furthermore, Adam is only admitted to the holy sanctuary of Eden after forty days (the sum of the periods of primary and secondary impurity for a male child in Lev 12:4), Eve after eighty days (cf. Lev 12:5). Although Jubilees' connection between the creation account and the law of Lev 12:2-5 is implicit, it is quite clear. The halakhic text 4Q265 (4QMiscRules) makes the connection explicit. As Baumgarten reconstructs the text, it reads:

> In the fir[st] week [Adam was created, but he had nothing sacred (?) until] (12) he was brought to the Garden of Eden. And a bone [of his bones was taken for the woman, but nothing sacred (?)] (13) did she [ha]ve until she was brought to h[im in the Garden of Eden after eighty days,] (14) [for] the Garden of Eden is sacred and every young shoot which is in its midst is a consecrated thing. [Therefore a woman who bears a male] (15) shall be impure seven days, as in the days of her menstruation shall she be impure, and th[irty three days shall she remain in the blood] (16) of her purity. And if she bears a female she shall be impure [two weeks as in her menstruation, and sixty-six days] (17) [shall she remai]n in the blood of her purity. [No] consecrated thing [shall she touch, nor shall she enter the sanctuary until the completion of ...] (DSSR 1:343).[20]

But are Adam and Eve created impure? Concerning Jubilees, James VanderKam notes that Jubilees never explicitly says that Adam and Eve are impure after creation. Thus VanderKam argues that the timeline of the creation account in Jubilees serves *only* to account for the gendered

its significance for the purity or impurity of infants. Matthew THIESSEN ("Luke 2:22," 27 n. 34), however, notes that such an understanding is apparently reflected in the second-century CE Christian text, *Protevangelium of James* 5, which "claims that Mary's mother, Anna, gave birth to her but did not breastfeed her until she underwent purification." Thus it may have been considered an ideal state of affairs.

[20] For the edition of the text see Joseph M. BAUMGARTEN, DJD 35:57-78.

difference in times of impurity in Lev 12:2–5.[21] But without the implication of impurity, it is difficult to understand why there would be any delay in the first couple's entry into Eden. Thus Joseph Baumgarten and Hannah Harrington are inclined to see in Jubilees' account an assumption that the first humans are impure and can only enter the sanctuary of Eden after the time periods for primary and secondary impurity have elapsed.[22] Since Adam and Eve are analogous to the just born infants, these texts may also indicate an assumption that birth impurity affects both parturient and infant.[23] James Kugel also thinks that in its final form Jub 3:9-14 assumes that the first couple were impure, but he is troubled by the implication that "Adam and Eve were themselves *impure* at the time of their creation – how could they be? They were not *born* at all, and certainly not from a human mother."[24] But Nicholas Meyer responds that "one attuned to the symbolic coherence of earth and womb, which Lev 12:1–8 already invites, will quickly identify the earth as the primeval mother (or womb) and the source by which the newly born Adam and Eve can be inferred to acquire the same impurity infants contract from their mother."[25] Whatever the set of symbolic associations and to whomever the idea is ultimately to be attributed, in the final form of Jubilees the conclusion is nearly inescapable that creation involves impurity for the first humans. For the authors of the Hodayot it would be simple to associate the "dust" of the mother earth with the source of impurity, since they clearly draw on the formulation of Eliphaz in Job 4:17-19 to connect the materiality of dust and clay with impurity and unrighteousness.

There are, then, ample ways to understand how the authors of the Hodayot come to associate impurity both with those "born of woman" and with the beings created "from the dust" of the earth. But as a halakhic matter, impurity contracted in the birth process is easily dealt with, as Lev 12 and Jub 3 make clear. Even the tendency in the Yahad's sectarian

[21] James C. VANDERKAM, *Jubilees: A Commentary in Two Volumes* (Hermeneia. Minneapolis: Fortress, 2018), 215.

[22] Joseph M. BAUMGARTEN, "Purification after Childbirth and the Sacred Garden in 4Q265 and Jubilees," in *New Qumran Texts and Studies: Proceedings of the First Meeting of the International Organization for Qumran Studies, Paris, 1992*, ed. George J. BROOKE and Florentino GARCÍA MARTÍNEZ; STDJ 15 (Leiden: Brill, 1994), 5-6; Hannah K. HARRINGTON, *The Purity Texts*, Companion to the Qumran Scrolls (Edinburg: T&T Clark, 2004), 62.

[23] Similarly, Martha HIMMELFARB, "Sexual Relations and Purity in the Temple Scroll and the Book of Jubilees," *DSD* 6 (1999): 26 (11–36).

[24] James KUGEL, *A Walk Through Jubilees*, JSJSup 156 (Leiden: Brill, 2012), 39. Kugel attributes the implication that Adam and Eve were created impure to the interpolator of the original text of Jubilees.

[25] MEYER, "Born of Woman, Fashioned from Clay."

thinking to merge the categories of sin and impurity "into a single conception of defilement"[26] does not seem to fully account for the moral horror of the *Niedrigkeitsdoxologie* cited above. Something still seems missing in the symbolic system. This is where the critical centrality of the image of the pot, the *yēṣer*, becomes clear for the purity oriented thinking of the sectarian Yahad community.

Pottery vessels, like many other objects, can be rendered impure through contact with a conveyer of impurity. Leviticus 15 discusses the uncleanness resulting from a man with a discharge, listing the ways in which his impurity may be transmitted and the ways in which those persons and items are to be cleansed. The exception is the category of pottery vessels (*kĕli-ḥereś*). Vessels made of pottery cannot be cleansed but must be broken (Lev 15:12). So, too, in the case of a impurity from contact with the carcass of a swarming creature. Although wood, cloth, skin, or sack-cloth objects may be cleansed by washing, pottery cannot be purified and must be broken (Lev 11:32–33). It is likely that this greater susceptibility of pottery to impurity that cannot be cleansed was extended to all sources of impurity. Indeed, the presence of the pottery making facilities at Khirbet Qumran is often taken as an indication of the concern of the community for ensuring to the extent possible the purity of the pottery used there,[27] as is the presence of stone vessels, which were not susceptible to impurity except from corpses.[28]

In the imagery of the Hodayot all of humanity, created from the dust, and every individual "born of woman" enters the world in a condition of impurity. But the Hodayot radicalize this situation to create a horrifying exigency by drawing out the implications of the imagery of Gen 2:7 and related texts concerning what it means to be shaped from dust and pinched off from clay like an earthen vessel. God brings into existence a humanity contaminated by impurity, creatures who cannot by definition

[26] Jonathan KLAWANS, *Impurity and Sin in Ancient Judaism* (New York: Oxford University Press, 2000), 75.

[27] Jodi MAGNESS, *The Archaeology of Qumran and the Dead Sea Scrolls* (Grand Rapids, MI: Eerdmans, 2002), 116; Magen BROSHI, "Was Qumran, Indeed, a Monastery? The Consensus and Its Challengers, An Archaeologist's View," in *Caves of Enlightenment: Proceedings of the American Schools of Oriental Research Dead Sea Scrolls Jubilee Symposium (1947—1997)*, ed. James H. CHARLESWORTH (North Richland Hills, TX: BIBAL, 1998), 19-37. Some pottery in use at Qumran did come from Jerusalem, though of course, it is not possible to say by whom and under what conditions it was manufactured. See Joseph YELLIN, Magen BROSHI, and Hanan ESHEL, "Pottery of Qumran and Ein Ghuweir: The First Chemical Exploration of Provenience," *BASOR* 321 (2001): 65, 73 (65–78).

[28] Jonatan ADLER, "The Impurity of Stone Vessels in 11QT[a] and CD in Light of the Chalk Vessel Finds at Kh. Qumran," *DSD* 27 (2020): 78–85, 91 (66-96).

ever be purified through ritual means. Even if this is a symbolic rather than a literal assertion about the material nature of human bodies, humans in their impurity cannot come into the holy presence of God but are "abhorrent vessels" (*yṣr nt'b*, 1QH^a 23:37, 38).

The solution to this terrifying condition is that God graciously re-creates those whom God elects, by instilling God's holy spirit in them and cleansing them from impurity and from sin. The authors of the Hodayot base their understanding on an exegetical appropriation of Ezek 36:25–27. For Ezekiel, as for the Hodayot, the people's impurity exceeds the reach of the ritual system. Only God's intervention can transform the people.[29] In Ezekiel, God first purifies Israel ("I will sprinkle clean water upon you, and you will be clean"; 25a). Next comes the promise of the new heart and new spirit (26a), as the heart of stone is removed and replaced by a heart of flesh (26b). Finally, God promises "to put my spirit into your body" (27a), thus restoring the people so that they can obey the commandments of God. In the Hodayot the clean water of Ezekiel is interpreted as God's holy spirit.[30] In 1QH^a 4:38 God is blessed because "you have sprinkled your holy spirit upon your servant [and you] have cleansed his heart from [...]." Similarly, 8:30 speaks of "cleansing me by your holy spirit." That this transformation is a new creation is clearest in 23:27–29, a *Niedrigkeitsdoxologie* that uses the tropes of dust, ashes, and vessel of clay first to describe the person as originally created and then to describe the transformation by saying that "over the dust you have sprinkled [your holy] spirit" (23:29; cf. 4:29; 5:3; 8:20; 20:14-15). This cleansing is what fits the speaker to approach the sancta, "to be united with the children of heaven" (23:30), and to be among those "[who s]erve with your host" (23:34). Indeed, it is only the insight that the speaker receives from this transformation that allows him to recognize in retrospect the horror of what he was before his transformation. That is not to say that, as a mortal, embodied being the speaker is now free of the danger that his material nature constitutes. Indeed, the passage in 8:29–30, cited above, is one of the rare petitionary elements in the Hodayot in which the speaker says "I entreat you by means of the spirit you have placed in me that you make your kindness to your servant complete [for]ever, cleansing me by your

[29] "Whether Ezekiel envisions a literal purification of the people by God, or (more likely) is figuratively describing God's power of forgiveness, the fact remains that what is envisioned here is a future hope. Without God's help, the defilement of the people by sin is permanent," J. KLAWANS, *Impurity and Sin*, 31.

[30] The most extensive treatment of this motif is that of Rony KOZMAN, "Ezekiel's Promised Spirit as *adam*'s Revelatory Spirit in the Hodayot," *DSD* 26 (2019): 30-60.

holy spirit." Thus the cleansing transformation that God has initiated remains to be completed, though the psalmist can be confident of God's intentions toward him.

In a complex poetic tradition such as one finds in the Hodayot it is seldom possible to say whether the authors and hearers were consciously aware of all of the symbolic connections constructed by the diction and imagery. Given the intensive exegetical practices of the sectarian community, it is certainly plausible that they may have intentionally developed the complex of interpretive relationships among texts that I have attempted to illuminate in this essay. It is also possible that some of the associations were never explicitly intended but were established at a subconscious level. Whether by design or by poetic intuition, the emphatic image of humanity as a pottery vessel in the Hodayot served as a condensed symbol of the hopeless impurity of the human condition and the magnitude of the transformation that God provided for the elect members of the sect.

JOSÈPHE ET L'HISTOIRE DE DAVID. QUELLES SOURCES ?

Étienne NODET, O.P.

Flavius Josèphe (37-95 env.) annonce dans le prologue de son ouvrage majeur, les *Antiquités judaïques*, qu'il se propose « d'exposer toute notre histoire ancienne, ainsi que nos constitutions, le tout traduit des livres hébraïques ». Il ne dit pas « livres saints », et ailleurs il donne une liste en deux blocs : pour le premier, il indique 22 livres, et l'on reconnaît assez bien les 24 de la Bible hébraïque ultérieure, en regroupant Ruth avec Juges et Lamentations avec Jérémie (*CAp* 2:39-41). Pour le second bloc, il explique que depuis le roi perse Artaxerxès, correspondant aux récits d'Esdras-Néhémie et d'Esther, « l'histoire complète a été écrite, mais elle n'a pas été jugée digne de la même autorité que les récits précédents, faute d'une succession précise des prophètes ». Il s'agit de sources hébraïques concernant les époques hellénistique et romaine, qui sont effectivement disjointes, et que les historiens de l'époque ignoraient largement, faute d'équivalents grecs.

Josèphe explique qu'il se permet une telle entreprise grâce à un précédent bien connu, celui qui est exposé dans la *Lettre d'Aristée* : à la demande du roi Ptolémée II d'Égypte (282-246), le grand prêtre Éléazar avait accepté d'envoyer des traducteurs depuis Jérusalem, mais il avait tenu à préciser que l'opération était « contre nature » (*Lettre* § 44). Il y avait donc un tabou, comme le prouvent les hésitations de Tacite, qui écrivait nettement après Josèphe : traitant de la chute de Jérusalem en 70, il devait parler de l'origine des Juifs, selon sa coutume de présenter les peuples quand ils interféraient avec Rome. Il en ignore tout, mais après enquête, il donne six explications, dont seule la dernière a une vague ressemblance avec les récits bibliques (*Hist*. 5.2-13). C'est un des nombreux indices montrant que c'est pour les Juifs que Josèphe a écrit les *Antiquités*, et non pour les Romains en général. Josèphe ajoute même que les émissaires d'Éléazar n'avaient traduit que le Pentateuque, et qu'il se proposait de compléter ; il n'a jamais entendu dire qu'il existait déjà des traductions officielles des Prophètes et des Écrits, au sens d'exemplaires officiels et protégés, ce qui n'exclut pas des traductions privées plus ou moins partielles.

Ce que Josèphe appelle traduction n'est en fait qu'une paraphrase parfois assez lâche, et jusqu'à une époque récente on a toujours supposé qu'il s'était borné à remanier une traduction grecque antérieure, mais d'origine indéterminée ; son œuvre ne présentait donc guère d'intérêt pour la critique pour la critique biblique. L'objet de cette note est de revenir sur ce jugement : Josèphe n'a jamais consulté aucune forme de la Septante (ci-après 𝔊), et cela en toute généralité. Ensuite, si on se restreint aux livres de Samuel, il se trouve que les fragments recueillis à Qumrân montrent de remarquables contacts avec Josèphe[1], ce qui a une signification pour l'histoire du texte.

1. La Bible de Josèphe

La première alerte sérieuse invitant à regarder de plus près la Bible de Josèphe est due à A. Mez, qui observa en 1894 que sa paraphrase avait de remarquables contacts avec la forme de 𝔊[2] dite « lucianique » (ci-après 𝔏), qu'on venait de redécouvrir après une longue disparition. Vers 390, dans une préface à sa traduction des Chroniques, Jérôme signalait qu'il existait trois recensions reconnues de la Bible grecque : « Alexandrie et l'Égypte louent Hésychius comme l'auteur de leur Septante ; de Constantinople à Antioche on approuve les exemplaires du martyr Lucien ; les provinces intermédiaires lisent les livres palestiniens préparés par Origène et publiés par Eusèbe et Pamphyle[3]. » D'autres témoignages soulignaient la compétence de Lucien en hébreu[4], et Eusèbe le présentait très favorablement comme un prêtre d'Antioche martyrisé en 312 (*HE* 8.13.2). Pendant longtemps, on ignora quelles traces directes avait laissées ce texte lucianique, et ce n'est qu'à partir de 1874, grâce aux travaux sur les Hexaples d'Origène, qu'on s'aperçut que le type de texte représenté par un petit groupe

[1] Publiés par Frank M. Cross, Eugene C. Ulrich *et al.*, *Qumran Cave 4, XII: 1-2 Samuel* (DJD 17), London, Oxford University Press, 2007, en abrégé *DJD* 17.

[2] Adam Mez, *Die Bibel des Josephus, untersucht für Buch V-VII der Archäologie*, Basel, Jaeger & Kober, 1894. À sa suite, Alfred Rahlfs, *Septuaginta-Studien. Lucians Rezension der Königsbücher*, Göttingen, Vandenhoeck & Ruprecht, 1911, précisa que le travail de Lucien était tantôt de rapprocher le grec ancien du TM, tantôt de l'éloigner ; en outre, il identifia des leçons plus anciennes que Lucien, dites « proto-lucianiques ». Après les découvertes de Qumrân, Frank M. Cross, « The History of the Biblical Text in the Light of Discoveries in the Judaean Desert », *HTR* 57 (1964), p. 281-299, observa que 4QSam[a] avait des leçons proto-lucianiques, puis Emanuel Tov, « Lucian and Proto-Lucian: Toward a New Solution of the Problem », *RB* 79 (1972), p. 101-113, suggéra à bon droit que ces variantes étaient des traces d'une traduction de plein droit, combinée avec le grec ancien.

[3] Dans son *De viris inlustribus* § 77, il loue les qualités de Lucien, si remarquables que « jusqu'à maintenant certains exemplaires des Écritures sont appelés lucianiques ».

[4] Cf. les sources citées par Bruce M. Metzger, *Chapters in the History of New Testament Textual Criticism* (New Testament Tools and Studies, 4), Leiden, Brill, 1963, p. 1-41.

de manuscrits médiévaux coïncidait avec les citations de Chrysostome, de Théodoret de Cyr et d'autres Pères antiochiens[5], et même parfois avec des citations hexaplaires marquées du sigle λ (pour Λουκιανός « Lucien »).

Autrement dit, Josèphe était témoin de quelque chose de « lucianique » bien avant Lucien, mais l'autorité du Texte Massorétique (ci-après 𝔐) était telle qu'on ne parvenait pas à imaginer qu'il soit témoin d'un hébreu différent de 𝔐 ; il fallait donc conclure qu'il avait utilisé pour sa paraphrase une « Septante Protolucianique », qui devait donc être considérée elle-même comme une paraphrase de 𝔐. C'est ainsi que H. Thackeray, qui avait préparé l'édition des *Antiquités* pour la collection Loeb et beaucoup travaillé sur la Septante, alla jusqu'à conclure fermement que de 1 Samuel à 1 Maccabées Josèphe avait utilisé, à côté d'une source sémitique, probablement un targum, une Bible grecque unique de type protolucianique[6].

Avant même de rechercher les origines de ce type de texte, voici quelques cas où il est certain que Josèphe n'a pas contrôlé sa paraphrase sur le grec[7] :

– *AJ* 1:27, « au commencement Dieu créa (ἔκτισεν) le ciel etc. » et de même Gn 1,1 𝔐 ברא, mais 𝔊 met ἐποίησεν « fit, fabriqua », et de même PHILON, *Op. mundi* § 26, ce qui implique *creatio ex aliquo*, en harmonie avec le désordre primordial du v. 2, qu'on peut imaginer préexistant.

– *AJ* 1:54, « il leur parut bon de sacrifier à Dieu… Abel apporta du lait (γάλα) de ses troupeaux » ; Gn 4,4 𝔐 מחלבהם est ambigu, car on peut comprendre qu'Abel a apporté soit « de leur graisse » soit « de leur lait », de son troupeau (racines homonymes), mais 𝔊 ἀπὸ τῶν στεάτων αὐτῶν « de leurs graisses » (au pluriel, peut-être de מחלביהם) ne souffre aucune ambiguïté. Josèphe, toujours moralisateur, voulait faire d'Abel un doux et de Caïn un violent.

[5] Pour les livres historiques, les minuscules n° 19, 82, 93 et 108 de la grande édition de Robert HOLMES et James PARSONS, Oxford, 1798-1827. Après Antonio M. CERIANI, *Monumenta sacra et profana ex codicibus praesertim Bibliothecae Ambrosianae. Tom. VII : codex Syro-hexaplaris Ambrosianus*, Mediolani, typis Bibliothecae Ambrosianae, 1874, et Frederick FIELD, *Origenis hexaplorum quae supersunt sive Veterum Interpretum Graecorum in totum Vetus Testamentum Fragmenta. Tomus I : Prolegomena, Genesis–Esther*, London, Clarendon, 1875, Paul DE LAGARDE, « Semitica », *Abhandl. der Akad. der Wiss. Göttingen* 25 (1879), p. 1-48, convaincu que ce type de texte était meilleur que les grands mss classiques, ajouta aussi le ms. 118.

[6] Cf. Henry St. J. THACKERAY, *Josèphe, l'homme et l'historien*, adapté de l'anglais par Étienne NODET, Paris, Cerf, 2000 (orig. 1929), p. 85.

[7] Une étude d'ensemble a été faite par Étienne NODET, *The Hebrew Bible of Josephus* (CRB 92), Leuven / Paris, Peeters, 2018.

– *AJ* 2:322 (et jusqu'à 9:275), Josèphe rend systématiquement par « Palestiniens » (Παλαιστῖνοι) les « Philistins » de 𝔐 פלשתים, alors que 𝔊 met ἀλλόφυλοι « étrangers » non moins systématiquement, du moins à partir de Jg 3,3, car auparavant, on rencontre 13 fois Φυλιστιιμ sur un total de 252 occurrences ; Josèphe n'a jamais vu cette forme.

– *AJ* 6:157, Samuel est chargé d'aller oindre David comme roi, et il craint que Saül ne l'apprenne et le fasse mourir, mais « Dieu lui donna un moyen d'assurer sa sécurité (θεοῦ δόντος ἀσφαλείας ὁδόν) », ce qui est très vague. Selon 1 S 16,2 𝔐 Dieu lui dit de prendre עגלת בקר, ce qui va masquer la fiole d'huile, et de prétexter qu'il va faire un sacrifice à Bethléem ; 𝔊 a bien compris qu'il doit prendre δάμαλιν βοῶν « une génisse » (pour le sacrifice), mais Josèphe a interprété, d'après l'homonyme le plus fréquent, qu'il s'agissait d'un « char à bœufs », et le prétexte devient incompréhensible.

– *AJ* 8:315, Josèphe nomme Abida la mère du roi Josaphat, alors que selon 1 R 22,42 𝔐 son nom était עזובה, 𝔊 Αζουβα, Αζαεβα « Azuba ». L'explication est assez simple : ce nom un peu bizarre signifie « l'Abandonnée », peut-être un surnom, et Josèphe l'a interprété et spontanément rendu dans sa langue maternelle par l'équivalent araméen אבידה. Cela n'implique nullement qu'il ait utilisé un targum.

– *AJ* 9:96, Josèphe appelle Ὀθλία la reine Athalie, fille ou petite-fille du roi Omri ; il transcrit ainsi 2 R 8,26 𝔐 עתליהו, que 𝔊 rend par Γοθολια. Les deux transcriptions grecques sont correctes, mais elles obéissent à des systèmes indépendants et très différents. D'une façon générale, Josèphe ne rend pas ע, alors que 𝔊 met le plus souvent γ.

Par ailleurs, les copistes anciens ont eu tendance à corriger les noms propres les plus connus d'après 𝔊, qui était leur Bible. Par exemple, Gn 41,45 dit que Pharaon impose à Joseph fils de Jacob le nom de Çophnat-Panéah (צפנת פענח, 𝔊 Ψονθομφανηχ). Or, on lit en *AJ* 2:91 Ψονθονφάνηχον, avec un suffixe décliné, mais c'est un alignement sur 𝔊, car ensuite Josèphe explique exactement le sens du nom « découvreur de secrets » (κρυπτῶν εὑρετήν), ce qui est impossible avec la forme grecque.

Dans la même ligne, on pourrait ajouter les nombreux cas où Josèphe explique correctement un mot hébreu même lorsque la transcription n'est plus reconnaissable. Par exemple, en *AJ* 5:360, le femme de Pinhas fils du prêtre Éli meurt désespérée en enfantant un fils Ἰακώβην (ou Ἰοχάβην), σημαίνει δὲ ἀδοξίαν « Ikabod, ce qui signifie non-gloire », paraphrasant 1 S 4,21 אי כבוד, 𝔊-𝔏 Οὐαὶ βαρχαβωθ ; l'explication est exacte, mais le nom n'est pas identifiable en grec.

En sens inverse, mais en se limitant ici aux livres de Samuel[8], on trouve des cas où Josèphe paraît avoir consulté une traduction grecque, bien qu'il affirme en prologue qu'il n'en connaissait aucune.

– *AJ* 6:186, Goliath a demandé à David s'il était un chien pour qu'il l'attaque avec une fronde, et David répond : οὐχὶ τοιοῦτον ἀλλὰ καὶ χείρω κυνός « non pas, mais pire qu'un chien », ce qu'on retrouve en 1 S 17,43 𝔊 οὐχί, ἀλλ' ἢ χείρω κυνός, mais ni en 𝔏 ni ailleurs. Or, le comparatif χείρω « pire », fréquent chez Josèphe, est un *hapax* dans 𝔊 (traductions). Cette leçon de 𝔊 est ignorée de BHS.

– *AJ* 6:222, apprenant que David était chez Samuel, Saül envoya en vain plusieurs détachements pour se saisir de lui, « et furieux il accourut lui-même » ὀργισθεὶς αὐτὸς ἐξόρμησεν, ce qui correspond à 1 S 19,22 𝔊 ἐθυμώθη ὀργῇ Σαουλ καὶ ἐπορεύθη καὶ αὐτός alors que 𝔐 et 𝔏 n'ont que la finale וילך גם הוא « et il alla lui aussi » ; le début de 𝔊 suppose un hébreu ויחר אף שאול. Ici, le vocabulaire est ordinaire, et le contexte impose une colère de Saül ; il faut donc supposer des enjolivures indépendantes. Cette leçon de 𝔊 est signalée par BHS.

– *AJ* 6:237, Saül injurie son fils Jonathan et le traite de « fils de rebelles » (ἐξ αὐτομόλων γεγεν(ν)ημένον), comme 1 S 20,30 υἱὲ κορασίων αὐτομολούντων « fils de fillettes révoltées », alors que 𝔐 a une expression difficile בֶּן־נַעֲוַת הַמַּרְדּוּת, qu'on comprend d'après le contexte « fils d'une femme perverse de rébellion ». Il se trouve que le fragment 4QSam[b] a une forme non corrompue נערות המורדות qui donne le sens de 𝔊-𝔏 « fils de fillettes révoltées » (cf. BHS). Cependant, αὐτομολέω signifie « changer de camp » ou « déserter », d'où αὐτόμολος « déserteur », terme fréquent chez Josèphe (52 fois), alors que l'équivalent normal de 𝔊 pour מרד est ἀφιστάναι ou un dérivé.

– *AJ* 6:270, après le massacre par Saül des prêtres de Nob, David, qui l'apprit par Ébyatar, le seul survivant, « s'accusait lui-même (αὐτὸν ᾐτιᾶτο) de leur malheur ». 1 S 22,22 אנכי סַבֹּתִי בכל נפש בית אביך « je me suis tourné vers toute âme de ta maison paternelle », où le verbe est rendu ἐγώ εἰμι αἴτιος « je suis la cause » par 𝔊-𝔏 et le *targum*, comme chez Josèphe, ce que le contexte impose ; plus tard, le terme סבה signifiera simplement « cause ». On remarque en outre que αἴτιος est un *hapax* dans 𝔊-𝔏 (traductions), alors qu'il est fréquent chez Josèphe, avec le verbe αἰτιάομαι.

[8] Le texte antiochien 𝔏 est maintenant donné par Natalio FERNÁNDEZ MARCOS, José Ramón BUSTO SAIZ *et al.*, *El Texto Antioqueno de la Biblia Griega. 1-2 Samuel*, Madrid, Instituto de Filología del Consejo Superior de Investigaciones Científicas, 1989.

– *AJ* 7:15, Abner poursuivi par Asahel essaie de le convaincre d'abandonner et d'aller « prendre l'équipement d'un des soldats » ἑνὸς τῶν στρατιωτῶν ἀφέμενος τὴν πανοπλίαν. 2 S 2,21 וקח־לך את־חלצתו, 𝔊-𝔏 λαβὲ σεαυτῷ τὴν πανοπλίαν αὐτοῦ « prends-toi son équipement ». Le terme πανοπλία, fréquent chez Josèphe, est un *hapax* dans 𝔊-𝔏 (traductions).

– *AJ* 7:241, après la mise à mort d'Absalom, ils prirent son cadavre « et le jetèrent dans une fosse profonde » εἰς χάσμα βαθὺ ῥίψαντες ; on lit en 2 S 18,17 ביער אל־הפחת הגדול « dans la forêt, vers la grande fosse », mais 𝔊 et 𝔏 ont une double traduction εἰς χάσμα μέγα ἐν τῷ δρυμῷ εἰς τὸν βόθυνον τὸν μέγαν « dans *une* grande fosse dans la forêt dans *la* grande tranchée ». La première partie est semblable à ce que rend Josèphe, avec un *hapax* indéfini χάσμα ; la seconde suit 𝔐, avec l'article défini.

Ces quelques cas suggèrent que 𝔊, dont on ignore la date de composition, a pu être légèrement influencé ou retouché d'après Josèphe. Ce n'est pas intrinsèquement impossible, puisque les plus anciens mss (A, B, א) sont du IVe siècle et que pour les passages discutés il n'y a pas de citation patristique antérieure.

Quant au fait que Josèphe ait pu disposer d'une Bible hébraïque autorisée, cela ressort de ses dires : lors du triomphe conjoint en 71 de Vespasien, Titus et Domitien, les dépouilles du temple de Jérusalem défilèrent, ce que montre encore l'arc de Titus à Rome ; le dernier objet ainsi exposé était « la loi des Juifs ». Ensuite, le tout devait être exposé dans un nouveau Temple de la Paix, construit par Vespasien comme une sorte de musée[9], car il ne pouvait être question de faire un véritable sanctuaire juif à Rome. Cependant, la Bible fut déposée dans le palais impérial, c'est-à-dire soustraite aux regards (*G* 7:150-162). Plus tard, probablement après la mort de Vespasien en 79, Titus devenu empereur offrit ce trophée à Josèphe (*Vie* § 418). Il s'agissait donc d'un exemplaire très officiel, issu des archives du Temple et très utilisé pour copier ou contrôler des copies existantes. En effet, on observe des altérations caractéristiques, dont voici un échantillon :

– *AJ* 1:63, Josèphe affirme sans autre commentaire que « Lamek eut 77 fils de deux femmes, Çilla et Ada ». Cette performance antédiluvienne

[9] Commencé dès 71, il n'a peut-être été réellement achevé que sous Domitien (81-96), cf. James C. ANDERSON, « Domitian, the Argiletum and the Temple of Peace », *American Journal of Archaeology* 86 (1982), p. 101-110.

est inconnue autrement, mais on lit en Gn 4,24 שבעים יֻקַּם קין ולמך שבעתים ושבעה « Caïn sera vengé sept fois, et Lamek 77 fois ». Il suffit de supposer une petite altération de ת en בנ, de sorte que Josèphe a dû lire, en rattachant יֻקַּם à … קום שבע בנים יקם קין « Caïn engendrera 7 fils, et Lamek 77 ».

– *AJ* 1:342, Jacob enterra les idoles familiales « sous un chêne (δρῦν, de אלון) » vers Sichem, contrairement à Gn 35,4 תחת האלה « sous le térébinthe ». Josèphe a lu ou deviné ון au lieu de ה, peut être sous l'influence de Gn 12,6 « le lieu saint de Sichem, au Chêne de Moré. La même hésitation chêne/térébinthe se rencontre en 1 R 13,14 paraphrasé en *AJ* 8:218.

– *AJ* 5:58, une coalition de cinq rois se prépare à attaquer Gabaôn, « ayant établi son camp près d'une source de la ville » στρατοπεδευσαμένους ἐπί τινι πηγῇ τῆς πόλεως, ce qui développe Jos 10,5 ויחנו על גבעון « et ils campèrent sur Gabaôn (𝔊 καὶ περιεκάθισαν τὴν Γαβαων « et ils assiégèrent Gabaôn »). Josèphe a lu ou deviné ין au lieu de ל, d'où עין « source » ; de fait, Josèphe pouvait savoir qu'il y en a dans les environs, car Gabaôn est proche de Jérusalem.

– *AJ* 5:178, les Danites vont émigrer à Laïsh, proche d'une source du Jourdain, « à une journée de marche de la ville de Sidon » Σιδῶνος πόλεως ὁδὸν ἡμέρας μιᾶς, ce qui est invraisemblable, car Josèphe connaissait cette région montagneuse, et la distance à vol d'oiseau est d'au moins 50 km. Au contraire, Jg 18,17 dit que les gens de Laïsh sont « éloignés des Sidoniens » ורחקים המה מצדנים ; contrairement à son habitude, Josèphe met le nom de la ville et non celui des habitants ; il lisait donc une forme légèrement différente מצדןׄ יום « (éloignés) de Sidon, un jour », avec un ו additif *(mater lectionis)* situé au-dessus de la ligne et qu'il a mal inséré : il aurait dû le mettre après ד et non après י.

– *AJ* 5:260, les Hébreux ont fait serment de « remettre pour toujours le pouvoir » (εἰς ἀεὶ παρέχειν τὴν ἡγεμονίαν) à Jephté, contre Jg 11,11 « et le peuple le mit sur lui comme chef et comme commandant (לראש ולקצין) », avec un redoublement inutile. Il faut supposer que Josèphe a lu le second terme ולקצאין, et l'a compris comme לאין קץ « sans fin ».

– *AJ* 6:1, une fois capturée, l'Arche « resta quatre mois » chez les Philistins, mais 1 S 6,1 met שבעה חדשים « sept mois » ; comme il n'y a pas d'enjeu littéraire ou stratégique grave, il faut conclure que Josèphe a deviné ou lu ארבעה, avec אר au lieu de ש.

– *AJ* 6:110, face à une menace philistine depuis un lieu escarpé, « Jonathan encouragea son écuyer, disant : “Attaquons l'ennemi ! Et si en nous voyant ils nous disent de monter vers eux, ce sera un signe de victoire, etc." » On lit en 1 S 14,8 𝔐 ונִגְלינו אליהם « et nous nous manifesterons à eux », 𝔊-𝔏 κατακυλισθησόμεθα (= נָגֹּלֵנו) « et nous déboulerons sur eux », avec deux interprétations différentes de ונגלנו/ונגלינו (racines גלל/גלה). Le texte n'est pas très clair ; Josèphe devait lire l'une des deux formes dans le texte et l'autre en marge comme correction, et il s'est efforcé de combiner les deux sens.

– *AJ* 6:128, Jonathan est condamné pour avoir négligé l'ordre de Saül, mais les Israélites « l'arrachèrent à la malédiction de son père, et adressèrent des prières à Dieu en faveur du jeune homme ». Josèphe a combiné les deux versions de 1 S 14,45 𝔐 ויפדו את יונתן העם « et le peuple sauva Jonathan », et 𝔊-𝔏 προσηύξατο ὁ λαὸς περὶ Ιωναθαν « le peuple intercéda pour Jonathan », lisant ויפלל au lieu de ויפדו (cf. 1 S 2,25 ופללו אלהים « Dieu intercédera pour lui »), avec une petite altération de deux lettres dans 𝔐.

– *AJ* 7:98, ayant vaincu les Philistins, David prit « une grande partie de leur territoire, qu'il adjoignit à celui des Hébreux » (πολλὴν τῆς χώρας προσορίσας τῇ τῶν Ἑβραίων). 2 S 8,1 ויקח דוד את מתג האמה מיד פלשתים « enleva des mains des Philistins leur hégémonie (lit. "la bride du coude", ou "...de l'aqueduc") » ; 𝔊-𝔏 καὶ ἔλαβεν Δαυιδ τὴν ἀφωρισμένην ἐκ χειρὸς τῶν ἀλλοφύλων « et David prit la région délimitée... ». 𝔐 (confirmé par 4QSam^{a}[10]) et 𝔊 sont peu clairs ; il faut peut-être conjecturer האדמה « la terre » au lieu de האמה. Josèphe n'a pas vu le récit parallèle de 1 Ch 18,1 גת (ויקח דוד) ובנתיה « (et David prit) Gath et ses satellites ».

– *AJ* 7:108, David « consacra à Dieu tout le butin des villes et des nations conquises », mais 2 S 8,11 (הקדיש) מכל־הגוים « (consacra le butin) de toutes les nations, 𝔊-𝔏 ἐκ πασῶν τῶν πόλεων (= הערים) « de toutes les villes ». Josèphe lisait une forme dans le texte et l'autre en glose-correction marginale, et selon son habitude il n'a rien voulu perdre.

– *AJ* 7:259, après la défaite d'Absalom, « le peuple se blâmait d'avoir rejeté David et d'avoir remis la royauté à un autre » ; pour 2 S 19,10 ויהי כל־העם נדון « il arriva que tout le peuple discutait », de même 𝔊 (δια) κρινόμενος, mais 𝔏 met γογγύζοντες « murmurait » (= נלון). Pour Josèphe, ils discutaient et murmuraient, ce qui combine les deux leçons, qui ne diffèrent que d'un petit écart graphique, probablement ל altéré en ד, puis corrigé en marge.

[10] Les traductions anciennes sont confuses, cf. *DJD* 17, p. 133.

Ainsi, dans la source hébraïque de Josèphe, de menues altérations de lettres ont engendré des erreurs, surtout pour les noms propres ; il en est résulté des corrections marginales. Josèphe a voulu en tenir compte, d'où des leçons doubles. Ses parentés avec la recension lucianique signifient que celle-ci remonte, directement ou nom, à une forme spécifique de l'hébreu.

Dans de nombreux cas, Josèphe et 𝔊-𝔏 concordent contre 𝔐, et l'explication la plus simple est que 𝔐 est fautif ou remanié. Voici un échantillon :

– *AJ* 5:352 « les Philistins (Palestiniens), partis en guerre contre les Israélites, établirent leur camp... Les Israélites, venus peu après, etc. » Cela correspond à 1 S 4,1 𝔊-𝔏 « les Philistins (ἀλλόφυλοι) se rassemblèrent pour combattre Israël. Et Israël sortit », très différent de 𝔐 ויהי דבר שמואל לכל ישראל ויצא ישראל « et fut la parole de Samuel à tout Israël. Et Israël sortit ». La guerre devient une initiative d'Israël qui va être désastreuse, peut-être malgré un avertissement de Samuel (Rashi).

– *AJ* 6:135, en lançant sa campagne contre Amaleq, Saül « mit des embuscades (λόχους) dans la vallée », et de même 1 S 15,5 𝔊-𝔏 ἐνήδρευσεν, mais 𝔐 met וירב בנחל « il batailla dans la vallée » ; en fait, il suffit de considérer que וירב est une petite erreur pour ויארב, correctement rendu par les divers témoins.

– *AJ* 6:179, comme Saül craignait le défi de Goliath, David vint lui dire : « Ne laisse pas retomber ton courage. » 1 S 17,32 𝔊-𝔏 est semblable : « Que ne tombe pas le courage de Monseigneur », ἡ καρδία τοῦ κυρίου μου (= לב אדני), mais 𝔐 est différent לב אדם אל יפל « Que ne tombe le courage de quiconque (l'homme) », avec une petite erreur de lecture ם pour ני (lettres tachées).

– *AJ* 7:21, parmi les six fils des six premières épouses de David figure « Daluël d'Abigaïl » (Ἀβιγαίας Δαλουίηλος de דלויאל), la veuve de Nabal. La source est 2 S 3,3 כלאב לאביגיל, 𝔊-𝔏 Δαλουια Αβιγαιας de דלויה ; Josèphe et 𝔊-𝔏 ont deux formes parallèles mais indépendantes du même nom théophore, avec -אל et -יה, mais 𝔐, avec un nom très inhabituel Kileab, semble avoir une erreur de dittographie de לאב, avec peut-être un sens cryptique annexe « comme s'il était le père », si Abigaïl était déjà enceinte de Nabal. La généalogie de 1 Ch 3,1 met « Daniel », ce qui illustre d'un autre point de vue les accidents de transmission.

– *AJ* 7:173, après le viol de Tamar par Amnôn, « Leur père David fut très affligé (ἤχθετο), mais comme il aimait beaucoup Amnôn, son aîné, il se contraignit à ne pas le peiner ». En 2 S 13,21, 𝔐 a seulement ויחר לו מאד « et il fut très en colère », mais 𝔊-𝔏 et 4QSam[a11] ajoutent ולא עצב את רוח אמנון בנו כי אהבו כי בכורו הוא « il ne contrista pas l'esprit d'Amnôn son fils car il l'aimait car il était son aîné ». 𝔐 doit être considéré comme fautif.

– *AJ* 7:256, alors David se lamente de la mort d'Absalom, son fils rebelle, Joab le menace d'être renié par le peuple « et je rendrai ainsi plus amer et vrai (πικρότερον καὶ ἀληθὲς ποιήσω) ton deuil ». 2 S 19,8 𝔐 ורעה לך זאת מכל הרעה אשר באה עליך « et ce mal pour toi sera pire que tout le mal qui t'est arrivé », une tournure lourde ; 𝔊-𝔏 commence avec une double traduction καὶ ἐπίγνωθι (= ודעה) σεαυτῷ καὶ κακόν (= ורעה) σοι τοῦτο correspondant à une variante ודעה/ורעה, probablement issue d'une correction en glose. La menace suppose que Josèphe lisait דעה לך, qui se trouve être aussi la leçon de 4QSam[a].

2. Josèphe et les fragments de Qumrân

Les nombreux contacts de Josèphe avec le grec, lucianique ou non, contre 𝔐, pourraient suggérer qu'il avait aussi une source grecque. Cependant, dans plusieurs des cas exposés ci-dessus, ce grec concordait avec des fragments de Qumrân, et il faut rechercher si ces accords sont purement accidentels. Les grottes ont livré des fragments de quatre exemplaires distincts de 1-2 Samuel. D'après leur écriture, is ont été datés de l'époque hérodienne, soit après -50[12]. Pour la commodité de l'exposé, on met le plus important en dernier :

I. – 1QSam (1Q7), avec sept petits fragments. Trois passages ont été restaurés, 1 S 18,17-18 ; 2 S 20,6-10 et 21,16-18. Le type de texte est proche de 𝔐, mais les fautes de scribe sont nombreuses ; il n'y a pas de contact utile avec Josèphe.

II. – 4QSam[b], avec un grand fragment et sept petits. Quatre passages ont été restaurés, 1 S 16,1-11 ; 19,10-17 ; 20,26-42 ; 21,1-9 et 23,9-17. Le texte a des contacts nombreux avec 𝔊-𝔏, parfois avec 𝔊 contre 𝔐-𝔏, mais jamais avec 𝔏 seul. Une leçon plus claire que 𝔐 a été signalée plus haut (*AJ* 6:237), et un contact intéressant avec Joseph doit être indiqué :

[11] Selon la restauration de *DJD* 17, p. 149. La forme courte de 𝔐 pourrait être l'effet d'une haplographie d'homéotéleuton, car la phrase suivante (13,22) commence aussi par ולא.

[12] Avant *DJD* 17, une vue d'ensemble était donnée par Martin Abegg Jr., Peter Flint & Eugene C. Ulrich, *The Dead Sea Scrolls Bible*, Edinburgh, T&T Clark, 1999, p. 213-259.

– *AJ* 6:243, David arrivé seul à Nob expose sa mission secrète au prêtre Ahimelek et explique pourquoi il n'a pas d'escorte, puis il ajoute : « J'ai prescrit à mes serviteurs (θεράποντας προσέταξα) de me rejoindre en ce lieu-ci. » Cela correspond à 1 S 21,3 יודעתי ואת־הנערים « j'ai fait savoir aux serviteurs », avec une forme *po'el* très rare de sens *hif'il*, ce qui ressemble à une explication *ad hoc* ; 𝔊-𝔏 met τοῖς παιδαρίοις διαμεμαρτύρημαι (de העדתי) « j'ai témoigné aux serviteurs », ce qui n'est guère plus clair, mais 4QSam[b] a יעדתי « j'ai donné rendez-vous », ce qui donne le sens simple de Josèphe. C'est vraisemblablement l'original, mais on pourrait admettre que 𝔊-𝔏 résulte d'une mauvaise vocalisation de העדתי, qu'il suffirait de lire הֹעדתי comme *hif'il* de יעד (et non de עיד).

III. – 4QSam[c], avec un grand fragment donnant une partie de 1 S 25,30-31, et de nombreux petits, d'où l'on a pu reconstituer 2 S 14,7-33 et 15,1-15. Le texte, a côté de fautes de scribes, a quelques singularités et plusieurs contacts avec 𝔏 et 4QSam[a] ; une leçon utile a été signalée plus haut (*AJ* 7:173).

IV. – 4QSam[a], le plus significatif, car ses contacts avec Josèphe sont réellement impressionnants[13] :

– *AJ* 5:347, après la naissance de Samuel, sa mère Anne « se souvenant du vœu qu'elle avait fait à propos de l'enfant, le remit à Éli ; elle le confiait à Dieu pour qu'il devienne prophète ». En 1 S 1,11 𝔐 Anne a promis, si elle a un fils, de « le donner à Yhwh pour toute sa vie, et le rasoir[14] (ומורה) ne montera pas sur sa tête » ; 𝔊-𝔏 met « le donner comme "donné" (δοτόν) » et ajoute qu'il « ne boira ni vin ni boisson fermentée ». Le terme δοτόν est un *hapax* dans 𝔊-𝔏, qui avec le rasoir et l'alcool suggère fortement une consécration de *nazir* permanent[15], et c'est bien ce que montre la suite : 1 S 1,22 rapporte qu'après le sevrage de Samuel, Anne dit à son mari Elqana qu'elle veut le consacrer, et 4QSam[a] ajoute נזיר [ונתתיהו]עד עולם « et j'en ferai un *nazir*

[13] Pour une analyse détaillée, cf. Eugene C. Ulrich, *The Qumran Text of Samuel and Josephus* (Harvard Semitic Monographs, 19), Atlanta, Scholars Press, 1978, p. 165-191, mais l'auteur croit devoir conclure que Josèphe avait une source grecque semblable à 4QSam[a], ce qui crée des complications inutiles.

[14] Aquila met φόβος « crainte, peur », cf. Fridericus Field, *Origenis hexaplorum quae supersunt*, Oxford, Clarendon Press, 1875, *a. l.* Cette traduction suppose une leçon מורא, ce qui coupe tout lien avec la condition de *nazir* et rompt le parallélisme entre Samuel et Jean-Baptiste, *nazirs* permanents l'un et l'autre (cf. Lc 1,15), qui introduisent respectivement David et Jésus.

[15] Conclusion que les traducteurs ont évitée. Dans 4QSam[a], la fin de la ligne manque, et les éditeurs restaurent נזיר d'après 1 S 1,22, mais la longueur de la ligne suggère plutôt נזיר ליהוה, cf. *DJD* 17, p. 29-31 ; cela concorde mieux avec la tournure de Josèphe.

pour toujours ». Bien qu'il ne parle explicitement pas de *nazir*, c'est certainement ce que lisait Josèphe, car pour lui le vœu de *nazir* est strictement temporaire (*AJ* 4:72, conformément à Nb 6,4-21), et à propos du juge Samson, qui selon Jg 13,5 était *nazir* permanent dès le sein de sa mère, Josèphe dit seulement qu'il ne se raserait pas et ne boirait que de l'eau, et qu'il serait « prophète » (*AJ* 5:278).

– *AJ* 6:68-69, après un début controversé, le roi « Saül commença à gagner le respect de tous par la guerre contre Nahash, roi des Ammonites. En effet, celui-ci avait fait beaucoup de mal à ceux des « Juifs » qui étaient établis au-delà du Jourdain, qu'il attaqua avec une armée grande et forte. Il réduisit leurs villes en servitude… et après avoir subjugué les hommes par la violence… Aussi bien ceux qui venaient à lui sur parole que ceux qui étaient capturés selon la loi de la guerre, il leur arrachait l'œil droit. » Ce passage de Josèphe est très semblable au parallèle de 4QSam[a] ; c'est un supplément notable situé entre 1 S 10,27a et 27b, et son absence dans les textes usuels (𝔐-𝔊-𝔏) reste inexpliquée. Voici une comparaison détaillée :

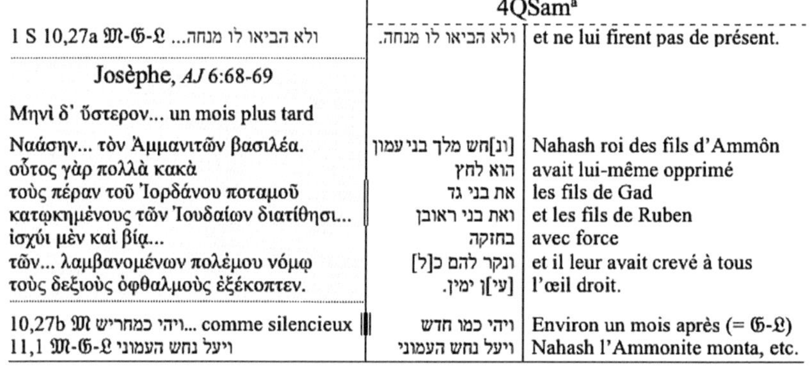

	4QSam[a]	
1 S 10,27a 𝔐-𝔊-𝔏 ...ולא הביאו לו מנחה	ולא הביאו לו מנחה.	et ne lui firent pas de présent.
Josèphe, *AJ* 6:68-69		
Μηνὶ δ' ὕστερον... un mois plus tard		
Ναάσην... τὸν Ἀμμανιτῶν βασιλέα.	[ונ]חש מלך בני עמון	Nahash roi des fils d'Ammôn
οὗτος γὰρ πολλὰ κακὰ	הוא לחץ	avait lui-même opprimé
τοὺς πέραν τοῦ Ἰορδάνου ποταμοῦ	את בני גד	les fils de Gad
κατῳκημένους τῶν Ἰουδαίων διατίθησι...	ואת בני ראובן	et les fils de Ruben
ἰσχύι μὲν καὶ βίᾳ...	בחזקה	avec force
τῶν... λαμβανομένων πολέμου νόμῳ	ונקר להם כ[ל]	et il leur avait crevé à tous
τοὺς δεξιοὺς ὀφθαλμοὺς ἐξέκοπτεν.	[עי]ן ימין.	l'œil droit.
10,27b 𝔐 ויהי כמחריש... comme silencieux	ויהי כמו חדש	Environ un mois après (= 𝔊-𝔏)
11,1 𝔐-𝔊-𝔏 ויעל נחש העמוני	ויעל נחש העמוני	Nahash l'Ammonite monta, etc.

Tableau 1. – Une notice commune à Josèphe et 4QSam[a].

La seule différence réelle entre les deux versions est que pour Josèphe l'indication « un mois plus tard », qui est perturbée dans 𝔐 mais conservée par 𝔊-𝔏, vient avant l'addition, contrairement à 4QSam[a] ; cela suggère que le passage a été une fois omis, puis mal réinséré par un copiste ultérieur, et l'erreur est probablement à situer du côté de Josèphe, car les méfaits de Nahash paraissent nettement antérieurs au récit lié à Saül. Quant à faire des tribus de Gad et de Ruben des Juifs, Josèphe a l'habitude d'identifier Hébreux, Israélites et Juifs : par exemple, en *AJ* 4:11 il parle de la révolte des Juifs contre Moïse au désert (cf. Nb 16,1s) ; en *AJ* 6:29-30, sous le prophète Samuel, il parvient à mettre les trois noms dans le même passage.

– *AJ* 6:325, les Philistins, voulant faire la guerre à Israël, convoquent leurs alliés à Regân ou Rengân (Ῥεγάν ou Ῥεγγάν). Le lieu est inconnu, mais l'action imminente va être située dans la plaine de Yizréel, non loin de Bet-Shân. Pour 1 S 28,1 le roi philistin Akish dit à David qui s'est réfugié chez lui : « Tu sortiras pour la guerre avec tes hommes. » 4QSam[a] ajoute יזרעאלה « vers Yizréel », ce qui va permettre de comprendre la forme de Josèphe, à travers une suite d'erreurs du grec. Les mss onciaux ont écrit ΕΙϹΡΕΓΑΝ, peu éloigné de ΕΙϹΡΕΛΑΝ « Yisréel » confondu avec « Israël », ce qui n'est pas rare (cf. 1 S 29,1), avec en outre une erreur banale Γ pour Λ, le suffixe directionnel ה- étant pris pour une marque de féminin ; ensuite, il faut supposer en amont une haplographie de ΕΙϹ(Ε)ΙϹΡΕΛΑΝ en ΕΙϹΡΕΛΑΝ, pour faire apparaître la préposition εἰς et la détacher[16].

– *AJ* 7:61, lorsque David arriva devant Jébus-Jérusalem, « les Jébusites lui fermèrent les portes et placèrent sur les remparts les aveugles, les boiteux et tous les estropiés pour railler le roi ; ils disaient que ces infirmes l'empêcheraient d'entrer. Cela irrita David, qui commença le siège ». Selon 2 S 5,6 les Jébusites disaient : selon 𝔐 כי אם הסירך העורים והפסחים « sauf si tu écartes les aveugles et les boiteux » ; selon 𝔊-𝔏 ὅτι ἀντέστησαν οἱ τυφλοὶ καὶ οἱ χωλοί « car les aveugles et les boiteux t'ont écarté », ce qui suppose une leçon plus courte כי הסירך. Il n'y a pas de colère de David, mais 4QSam[a] offre une leçon partielle כי הסית], qui peut être restaurée en הסית simplement (רך- et ת- sont de forme très semblable), ou encore הסיתך ou הסיתוך, ce qui introduit l'agitation de David. Josèphe lisait donc deux formes, qu'il a combinées[17] : celle de la source de 𝔊-𝔏 et celle de 4QSam[a], mais on ne peut déterminer la plus originale. Dans la suite (§ 63s), Josèphe rapporte d'exploit de Joab qui le premier a pénétré dans la ville, ce qu'indique aussi le récit parallèle de 1 Ch 11,6 (mais non 2 S 5).

– *AJ* 7:81, lorsque l'Arche arrivant à Jérusalem penchait, « Uzza avait voulu la retenir et avait tendu la main (ἐκτείναντα τὴν χεῖραν), mais lorsqu'il la toucha Dieu le fit mourir ». Pour 2 S 6,7 ויכהו שם האלהים על השל « et Dieu le frappa là pour l'irrévérence », avec un *hapax* של omis par 𝔊, et rendu par 𝔏 et Orig. ἐπὶ τῇ προπετείᾳ « pour la témérité ». Le parallèle 1 Ch 13,10 explique mieux la raison על אשׁר־שׁלח ידו על־הארון « parce qu'il avait tendu sa main sur l'Arche », ce qui rejoint Josèphe ; 4QSam[a] a conservé seulement אש על] au lieu de השל על, et la longueur de la ligne permet de restaurer d'après 1 Ch[18], ce qui est probablement l'original de 2 S.

[16] Cf. *DJD* 17, p. 95.

[17] Cf. la discussion *de DJD 17*, p. 120-121.

[18] Cf. *DJD* 17, p. 127.

– *AJ* 7:131, au moment de l'affaire de Bethsabée, David, apprenant qu'elle était enceinte, « fit revenir du front le mari de la femme, nommé Urie, qui était l'écuyer (ὁπλοφόρον "porteur d'armes") de Joab ». 2 S 11,6 𝔐-𝔊-𝔏 ignore cette haute fonction, mais 4QSam^{a} la signale, נושא כלי יואב « porteur des ustensiles de Joab », le général commandant la guerre chez les Ammonites.

Ces additions communes à Josèphe et à 4QSam^{a} sont notables. Quant aux omissions communes, on ne peut les évaluer proprement, car 4QSam^{a} est trop fragmentaire, et la paraphrase de Josèphe trop peu littérale. Outre les contacts avec des fragments de Qumrân, les derniers cas examinés font apparaître une nouvelle dimension, avec 1 Chroniques ; Josèphe peut évidemment avoir consulté ce dernier, mais il semble aussi apparaître que 4QSam^{a} pourrait avoir des contacts avec 1 Ch contre 1-2 S.

Pour l'immédiat, un examen détaillé du récit par Josèphe de l'arrivée de David à Jérusalem (*AJ* 7:61-64) paraît suivre largement 1 Ch 11, mais avec des détails qu'on ne trouve qu'en 2 S 5 et/ou 4QSam^{a} :

2 S 5:	1 Ch 11:	*AJ* 7:61-64
4-5 בן־שלשים שנה דוד... כל־ישראל	om.	om. 4QSam^{a} & *AJ*
6 וילך המלך ואנשיו ירושלם	4 וילך דויד וכל־ישראל ירושלם היא יבוס	*AJ* = 1 Ch
אל־היבסי יושב הארץ	ושם היבוסי ישבי הארץ	
ויאמר לדוד לאמר	5 ויאמרו ישבי יבוס לדויד	*AJ* = 1 Ch
לא תבוא הנה	לא־תבוא הנה	
כי אם הסירך העורים והפסחים לאמר	om.	4QSam^{a} & *AJ* הסית
לא יבוא דוד הנה	om.	*AJ* = 2 S
7 וילכד דוד את מצדת ציון היא עיר דוד	וילכד דוד את מצדת ציון היא עיר דוד	
8 ויאמר דוד ביום ההוא	6 ויאמר דויד	
כל־מכה יבסי	כל־מכה יבוסי	
ויגע בצנור	om.	4QSam^{a} יגע, om. *AJ*
	בראשונה יהיה לראש ולשר ויעל	*AJ* = 1 Ch
	בראשונה יואב בן־צרויה ויהי לראש	*AJ* = 1 Ch
ואת־הפסחים ואת־העורים שנאי נפש דוד	om.	*AJ* = 1 Ch
על־כן יאמרו עור ופסח לא יבוא אל־הבית	om.	*AJ* = 1 Ch
9 וישב דוד במצדה ויקרא־לה עיר דוד	7 וישב דויד במצד על־כן קראו־לו עיר דויד	
ויבן דוד סביב מן־המלוא וביתה	8 ויבן העיר מסביב מן־המלוא ועד הסביב	4QSam^{a} עיר = *AJ*
	ויואב יחיה את־שאר העיר	*AJ* = 1 Ch

Tableau 2. – L'arrivée de David à Jérusalem.

4QSam^{a} est mal conservé pour ce passage, mais les essais de restauration ont tous été faits à partir de 1 Ch[19].

[19] Cf. *DJD* 17, p. 119-122.

3. Josèphe, Qumrân et 1 Chroniques

1-2 Samuel et 1 Chroniques, bien que globalement parallèles, ont l'un et l'autre de nombreux passages sans parallèles. Pour les parties communes, il a été montré que 4QSam[a] a des affinités certaines avec 1 Ch, au point qu'on a d'abord cru qu'il s'agissait d'un 4QChr. Cela signifie que pour ces passages 4QSam[a] reflète une forme archaïque de 1-2 S. Cette circonstance va permettre de préciser les sources de Josèphe.

– *AJ* 7:78, après consultation, David décida de faire ramener l'Arche à Jérusalem par « ceux qui viendraient à Qiryat-Yéarim (Καριαθιάριμα) », où elle se trouvait selon Ch 13,5 להביא את ארון האלהים מקרית יערים « apporter l'Arche de Dieu depuis Qiriat-Yéarim » ; 𝔊-𝔏 traduit ἐκ πόλεως Ιαριμ « de la ville de Yarim », mais selon le parallèle 2 S 6,3 met מבית אבינדב אשר בגבעה « de chez Abinadab qui est à Gibéa (ou "sur la colline") ». 4QSam[a] est lacunaire, mais la longueur de la ligne permet de reconstituer אשר בגבעת קרית יערים « qui est sur la colline de Qiryat-Yéarim ». Il pourrait s'agit d'une correction harmonisante[20], car depuis 1 S 6,1 l'Arche revenue de chez les Philistins est restée à Qiryat-Yéarim.

– *AJ* 7:85, les prêtres transportèrent l'Arche, qui était « précédée de sept chœurs commis par le roi », correspondant partiellement à 2 S 6,13 𝔊-𝔏 ἑπτὰ χοροί (= מחלות) καὶ θῦμα μόσχος καὶ ἄρνα « sept chœurs et en sacrifice un veau et un agneau » ; Josèphe omet simplement les sacrifices d'accompagnement, mais 𝔐 est très différent et peu clair כי צעדו נשאי ארון יהוה ששה צעדים ויזבח שור ומריא « quand les porteurs eurent fait six pas (danses ?) il sacrifia un taureau et une bête grasse ». 1 Ch 15,26 met seulement ויזבחו שבעה פרים ושבעה אילים « ils sacrifièrent sept bœufs et sept béliers ». 4QSam[a], qui est lacunaire ici, mentionnait vraisemblablement les chœurs.

– *AJ* 7:121, le roi ammonite Nahash a maltraité les émissaires de David, et ses officiers comprennent « qu'un traité a été violé et qu'ils méritent une punition » ; ils doivent donc se préparer à la guerre. Pour 1 Ch 19,6 התבאשו עִם דויד « ils se sont rendus odieux à David » et de même le parallèle 2 S 10,6 נבאשו בדוד ; 𝔊-𝔏 lisait dans les deux cas comme 1 Ch, mais a cru devoir comprendre עַם דויד « peuple de David » et התבאשו a dû prendre le sens de התבישו, d'où ᾐσχύνθη λαὸς Δαυιδ « le peuple de David eut honte », ce qui n'a guère de sens ici ; en 2 S 10,6 𝔏 a tenté une correction « les serviteurs

[20] Cf. *DJD* 17, p. 128. Selon 2 S 6,4, ce sont les fils d'Abinadab qui vont conduire le chariot.

de David », ce qui répète la phrase précédente. Josèphe lisait la forme longue עִם דויד, et 4QSam[a] a pu être restauré d'après 1 Ch[21].

– *AJ* 7:121, pour préparer cette guerre, les Ammonites « envoient 1000 talents à Syros, roi de Mésopotamie ». Cela correspond à 1 Ch 19,6 וישלח חנון ובני עמון אלף ככר כסף לשכר להם מן ארם נהרים « Hanûn avec les fils d'Ammôn envoya 1000 talents d'argent pour recruter pour eux-mêmes en Aram des Deux Fleuves », semblable à 4QSam[a22] ; Josèphe ignore Hanûn fils et successeur de Nahash. 2 S 10,6 est différent וישלחו בני עמון וישכרו את ארם בית רחוב « les fils d'Ammôn envoyèrent et recrutèrent Aram de Beth-Rehob ». Il faut conclure qu'en 2 S 10,6 Josèphe lisait comme 1 Ch ou 4QSam[a].

– *AJ* 7:128, face au danger des Ammonites et de leurs alliés, David prit lui-même le commandement de toute l'armée et franchit le Jourdain, puis « il les rencontra, engagea la bataille et les vainquit ». Cela concorde avec le bref récit de 1 Ch 19,17 ויבא אלהם ויערך דויד לקראת ארם מלחמה וילחמו עמו « il vint vers eux, et il s'aligna contre eux, et David s'aligna vers Aram pour la guerre, et ils lui livrèrent bataille », avec un doublet de אלהם ויערך, de même 𝔏, mais 𝔊 échange les noms « …et Aram s'aligna vers David ». Le parallèle 2 S 10,17 est très différent, introduisant un lieu qu'ignore Josèphe ויבא חלאמה ויערכו ארם לקראת דוד וילחמו עמו « il vint à Hélam, et Aram s'aligna vers David et ils lui livrèrent bataille ».

– *AJ* 7:161, ayant vaincu les Ammonites, David « prit la couronne d'or du roi des Ammonites, qui pesait un talent et qui avait en son centre une magnifique sardoine », d'après 1 Ch 20,2 « il prit la couronne de leur roi (מלכם, 𝔊 ajoute une transcription Μελχολ), et en elle (ובה) était une pierre précieuse » ; le parallèle 2 S 12,30 omet ובה, ce qui change entièrement le sens[23].

– *AJ* 7:302, lors d'une nouvelle guerre, David envoya une armée contre les Philistins, « et son parent (ὁ συγγενὴς αὐτοῦ) Éphân se distingua : en combat singulier contre le plus courageux d'entre eux, il le tua et mit les autres en fuite ». Il s'agit d'un appendice qui revient sur les exploits de David et de ses preux, et selon 2 S 21,19, ויך אלחנן... בית הלחמי את גלית הגתי « et Elhanân… de Bethléem frappa Goliath le Gittite », ce qui ébranle l'exploit célèbre de David ; pour corriger cet effet, 𝔊 met « frappa Godolias » et 𝔏 « Elhanân… fils d'Élémi » (de אלחנן... בן הלחמי). Pour 1 Ch 20,5 ויך אלחנן... את לחמי אחי גלית הגתי « et Elhanân frappa… Lahmi

[21] Cf. *DJD* 17, p. 137.

[22] Cf. *DJD* 17, p. 137-138 où la restauration proposée לשׂכר להם מן־ארם רחוב ומן ארם מעכה suit largement 1 Ch, mais avec רחוב emprunté 2 S (devrait être בית רחוב), et on peut s'étonner que נהרים de 1 Ch n'ait pas été retenu ; c'est peut-être une simple erreur.

[23] En *DJD* 17, p. 146, le verset est reconstitué d'après 1 Ch.

frère de Goliath le Gittite ». Josèphe omet prudemment le nom du champion philistin, mais il a retenu (ou lu en glose marginale) l'indication de 1 Ch 11,26 אלחנן בן־דודו מבית לחם « Elhanân son cousin (𝔊 υἱὸς Δωδω "fils de Dodo"), de Bethléem ».

– *AJ* 7:318, David, voulant faire un recensement du peuple, « oublia les prescriptions de Moïse », qui liait tout recensement à une capitation (cf. Ex 30,12 ; Josèphe devait l'avoir expérimenté à Jérusalem). Pour 2 S 24,1, ויסף אף יהוה לחרות בישראל ויסת את דוד בהם לאמר לך מנה את ישראל ואת יהודה « la colère de YHWH recommença contre Israël, et il dévoya David contre eux, en disant : "Va dénombrer Israël et Juda" » ; au contraire, 1 Ch 21,1 a ויעמד שטן על ישראל ויסת את דויד למנות את ישראל « et Satan se dressa contre Israël, et il dévoya David pour dénombrer Israël ». Josèphe, qui n'a pas retenu la provocation divine, lisait comme 1 Ch.

– *AJ* 7:319, Joab, pour procéder au recensement voulu par David, « parcourant le pays des Israélites, nota la quantité de population… et retourna à Jérusalem », ce qui concorde avec 1 Ch 21,4 ויצא יואב ויתהלך בכל ישראל ויבא ירושלם « et Joab sortit, et il parcourut tout Israël, et il revint à Jérusalem », alors que le parallèle 2 S 24,5-7 détaille tout un parcours (Transjordanie, Gad, Galaad, Dân, Sidon, Tyr, villes cananéennes, sud de Juda) qui déborde largement le territoire d'Israël.

– *AJ* 7:320, Joab n'a pas eu le temps de recenser les tribus de Benjamin et de Lévi, car le roi s'était déjà repenti de sa faute, ce qui concorde avec 1 Ch 21,6-7, omis par 2 S 24,7-8.

– *AJ* 7:328, Dieu a envoyé en châtiment la peste, mais David intercède, disant que « lui seul, le berger méritait d'être châtié », ce qui correspond à 4QSam[a] et 2 S 24,17 𝔊 ἰδοὺ ἐγώ εἰμι ἠδίκησα καὶ ἐγώ εἰμι ὁ ποιμὴν ἐκακοποίησα « c'est moi qui ai péché, moi le berger j'ai fait le mal, et eux, le troupeau, qu'ont-ils fait ? » 𝔏 est semblable, mais omet εἰμι (soit הוא dans la reconstitution ci-après). La forme de 𝔐 se singularise, résultant d'une métathèse ער pour רע, puis d'une confusion וי pour ר. Le parallèle de 1 Ch 21,17 a perdu le jeu de mots entre les racines analogues רעה et רעע, peut-être par l'effet d'une dégradation (par la perte d'un ה).

2 S 24,17 𝔐	ואלה הצאן מה עשו	העויתי	הנה אנכי חטאתי ואנכי
2 S 24,17 source de 𝔊	ואלה הצאן מה עשו	הוא והרעה הרעתי	הנה אנכי חטאתי ואנכי
4QSam[a]	ו[...]	והרעה הרעתי	[...] נכי
1 Ch 21,17 𝔐-𝔊	ואלה הצאן מה עשו	והרַע הרעותי	אני הוא אשר חטאתי

Tableau 3. – L'intercession de David.

– *AJ* 7:330, David a reçu l'ordre de bâtir un autel chez Oronnas (Arauna), un Jébusite, et celui-ci « vannait son blé quand il vit arriver le roi et tous ses enfants (𝔊 παῖδας, peut-être "serviteurs"), et il se prosterna ». 1 Ch 21,20-21 « Ornân (Arauna) se retourna, et il vit l'ange (𝔐 המלאך, 𝔊 "le roi" de המלך) et ses quatre fils avec lui se cachant (מתחבאים, transcrit μεθαχαβιν), alors que Ornân vannait le blé ; il sortit de l'aire et se prosterna » ; « l'ange » de 𝔐, plutôt aberrant, doit être considéré comme une contamination de l'ange exterminateur du passage précédent (v. 17). 2 S 24,20 est plus court : « Arauna regarda et vit le roi et ses serviteurs (עבדיו, 𝔊-𝔏 τοὺς παῖδας αὐτοῦ) qui passaient vers lui, et Arauna sortit et se prosterna. » 4QSam[a] précise מתחבאים בשקים « cachés dans des sacs », détail ignoré de Josèphe (ou omis car trop incongru), qui autrement concorde avec 1 Ch. Ici, 4QSam[a] offre un cas de synthèse, additionnant tous les détails pour former un long verset très redondant[24] :

וירא את המלך דויד ואת ארבעת בניו עמו מתחבאים בשקים וארנא דש חטים ויבא דויד עד ארנא
וירא את המלך ואת עבדיו עברים עליו מתכסים בשקים באים אליו ויצא ארנא ארצה וישתחו לדויד על אפיו

Les éléments combinés sont : quatre enfants cachés, ajoutant les sacs (1 Ch) ; serviteurs du roi cachés de même (2 S) ; vanner le blé (1 Ch) ; arrivée du roi (2 S). Voici une comparaison des récits parallèles de 2 S et 1 Ch, qui montre que Josèphe a fait une combinaison, mais ce n'est pas celle de 4QSam[a] :

2 S 24	1 Ch 21	*AJ* 7:329-334
20 וישקף ארונה	20 וישב ארנן	4QSam[a] -*AJ* ארנא
וירא את־המלך	וירא את־המלאך	*AJ* = 2 S
ואת־עבדיו עברים עליו	וארבעת בניו עמו מתחבאים	*AJ* = 2 S
	וארנן דש חטים	*AJ* = 1 Ch
	21 ויבא דויד עד־ארנן	*AJ* = 1 Ch
	ויבט ארנן וירא את־דויד	*AJ* = 1 Ch
ויצא ארונה	ויצא מן־הגרן	*AJ* = 1 Ch
וישתחו למלך אפיו ארצה	וישתחו לדויד אפים ארצה	
21 ויאמר ארונה מדוע בא אדני־המלך אל עבדו	om.	*AJ* = 2 S
ויאמר דוד לקנות מעמך את־הגרן	22 ויאמר דויד אל־ארנן תנה־לי מקום הגרן	
לבנות מזבח ליהוה	ואבנה־בו מזבח ליהוה	
	בכסף מלא תנהו לי	*AJ* = 1 Ch
ותעצר המגפה מעל העם	ותעצר המגפה מעל העם	
22 ויאמר ארונה אל־המלך יהוה אלהיך ירצך	om.	*AJ* = 2 S

Tableau 4. – L'arrivée de David chez Arauna le Jébusite.

[24] Reproduit d'après la discussion de *DJD* 17, p. 194, cf. Zipora TALSHIR, « The Relationship between Sam-MT, 4QSam(a) and Chr, and the Case of 2 Sam 24 », dans : Kristin DE TROYER, T. Michael LAW, & Marketta LILJESTRÖM (eds.), *In the footsteps of Sherlock Holmes*, Leuven / Paris, Peeters, 2014, p. 273-298 ; Jason K. DRIESBACH, *4QSamuel[a] and the Text of Samuel* (VTSup, 171; Leiden / Boston: Brill, 2016), p. 321-329.

CONCLUSION

Il n'existe pas de type de texte pur, car les copistes, outre leurs propres erreurs ou corrections, avaient coutume de croiser leurs sources, suivant un exemplaire principal et le complétant (ou contrôlant) lorsque la lecture était difficile. Il en était de même pour les traducteurs, avec en outre l'obligation de comprendre, c'est-à-dire d'interpréter ou de corriger ; dans son prologue, le traducteur de Ben Sira se lamente vers -132 des traductions insatisfaisantes de la Loi, des Prophètes et des livres associés. Le cas de la Bible est spécial, car elle a été copiée, citée et traduite un nombre incalculable de fois par des copistes ou traducteurs de compétence variable.

À cet égard, la Bible hébraïque traditionnelle 𝔐, très stable, constitue une exception, comme si elle avait été révisée et établie par des libraires minutieux, à la manière du travail des lettrés d'Alexandrie sur les œuvres d'Homère ; cependant, elle doit être considérée comme une édition rabbinique établie au IIe siècle : vers 120, au temps de Rabbi Aqiba, un pilier de cette tradition, il fut requis de rejeter les livres « anciens » et de s'en tenir à cette nouvelle forme (*b.Pesahim* 112a). Ainsi, un exemplaire déposé à la cour du Temple était considéré comme impropre pour le culte public (*m.Kelim* 15:6), ce qui fait penser à l'exemplaire hébreu utilisé par Josèphe.

Les livres 1-2 Chroniques, qui courent de la Création au décret de Cyrus, combinent deux types de sources : les unes lui sont propres, et en particulier les généalogies de 1 Ch 1–9 ; les autres correspondent à des passages parallèles de 1-2 Samuel et 1-2 Rois.

Parmi ces derniers, il est certain que certains récits sont réécrits pour honorer une justice divine méticuleuse. Ainsi, le roi Manassé, un pécheur extrême, a eu un règne scandaleusement long, et 2 Ch 33,13s explique qu'en réalité il a été capturé par les Assyriens, et qu'en exil il s'est converti, d'où son retour providentiel et sa conduite devenue exemplaire. En sens inverse, son petit-fils Josias, vénéré comme grand réformateur, est mort stupidement à Megiddo, ce qui paraît injuste, mais 2 Ch 36,22s prend la peine de dire qu'il avait péché en n'écoutant pas l'ordre de Dieu. La coexistence dans le Bible de récits contradictoires pose des questions qui n'intéressent surtout pas Josèphe, qui se veut historien à la manière de Thucydide, rapportant des faits et s'interdisant de rechercher des significations cachées, ce qui rend sa prose assez boursouflée. Dès le Pentateuque, il s'efforce d'unifier les récits et les lois, n'hésitant pas à omettre ou à enjoliver ce qui lui paraît inconvenant.

Mais on ne peut généraliser sur les réécritures rassurantes de 1-2 Ch : pour l'histoire de David, les contacts de 1 Ch avec 4QSam[a] (et Josèphe) contre 1-2 S (surtout 𝔐) indiquent un état antérieur du texte de 1-2 S, et il faut considérer 𝔐 comme le plus tardif des témoins, surtout avec l'affaiblissement du profil de Samuel, qui n'est plus vraiment un *nazir* permanent. Mais 𝔐, composé avec le plus grand soin, est aussi celui dont le sens littéral est le plus difficile, c'est-à-dire aussi celui pour lequel l'invitation à rechercher d'autres significations est la plus forte, sous les apparence du récit agité d'un roitelet ambitieux. Par exemple, l'épisode final de l'arrivée de David chez le Jébusite Arauna pour y bâtir un autel, mêlé à une affaire d'ange exterminateur, résiste à une lecture trop plate.

COMMENT DIT-ON « BAʿLU ʾUGĀRIT » EN HOURRITE ?

Histoire d'un joint malvenu de deux fragments de tablettes découverts à Ras Shamra en 1929

Dennis PARDEE

La réponse à la question posée dans notre titre n'est pas difficile. Il s'agit de deux noms propres : un théonyme désignant le dieu de l'orage, et un toponyme désignant le nom de l'ancienne ville correspondant au Ras Shamra moderne. Or, on connaît le nom hourrite du dieu de l'orage, /teššob/, qui s'écrit {tṯb} en écriture alphabétique[1], et la graphie du toponyme ne montre pas de variation en écriture alphabétique en passant d'une langue à une autre[2]. Ainsi la forme hourrite du nom *baʿlu ʾugārit* en écriture alphabétique devait s'écrire {tṯb ůgrt(w)}[3]. Certes, mais il est toujours utile de disposer de la preuve formelle d'une hypothèse, même si celle-ci paraît évidente. Cette étude de deux fragments de la première campagne de fouilles à Ras Shamra-Ougarit a pour objectif de porter une réponse, certes pas nouvelle mais passée inaperçue par les spécialistes de la religion ougaritaine, à cette question.

Le théonyme composite qui s'écrit {bʿl ůgrt} dans le système alphabétique cunéiforme d'Ougarit est attesté plus de vingt fois dans une dizaine de textes rituels livré par les fouilles archéologiques de Ras Shamra entre 1931 et 1961[4]. En revanche, la version hourrite du théonyme n'est attestée

[1] Voir Emmanuel LAROCHE, « Documents en langue hourrite provenant de Ras Shamra », dans Jacques-Claude COURTOIS (éd), *Ugaritica* V. *Nouveaux textes accadiens, hourrites et ugaritiques des archives et bibliothèques privées d'Ugarit, commentaires des textes historiques (première partie)* (Mission de Ras Shamra XVI ; Bibliothèque Archéologique et Historique LXXX), Paris, Imprimerie Nationale et Geuthner, 1968, 447-544, 539 (liste des attestations dans les textes hourrites en écriture alphabétique de Ras Shamra) ; idem, *Glossaire de la langue hourrite*, *Revue Hittite et Asianique* 34-35 (1976-1977), 263-264 ; Daniel SCHWEMER, *Die Wettergottgestalten Mesopotamiens und Nordsyriens im Zeitalter der Keilschriftkulturen. Materialien und Studien nach den schriftlichen Quellen*, Wiesbaden, Harrassowitz, 2001, 443-587.

[2] E. LAROCHE, *Ugaritica* V, 539 (liste des attestations dans les textes hourrites en écriture alphabétique de Ras Shamra) ; idem, *Glossaire*, 277.

[3] Le morphème {-w} du génitif n'est pas toujours représenté dans l'orthographe : E. LAROCHE, *Ugaritica* V, 531. Nous remercions Joseph LAM d'avoir ajouté un témoignage plus récent confirmant cet aspect de la grammaire hourrite (communication personnelle).

[4] La liste des attestions se trouvera chez Dennis PARDEE, *Les textes rituels* (Ras Shamra–Ougarit XII), Paris, Éditions Recherche sur les Civilisations, 2000, 1125.

qu'une fois et, dans ce cas, il n'est que partiellement conservé, le premier signe ayant disparu : on lit {[...]⸢ṯ⸣b . ủgrt} à la troisième ligne du petit fragment RS 1.031, et la restitution {[... t]⸢ṯ⸣b . ủgrt} ne présente aucune difficulté. La lecture du deuxième signe et la restitution du premier étaient proposées dès 1963 dans le premier corpus des textes ougaritiques[5] ; mais la bonne lecture de RS 1.031:3′ est passée inaperçue des spécialistes et l'existence du théonyme *tṯb ủgrt* n'a pas été reconnue[6]. L'oubli dans lequel cette lecture est tombée s'explique par deux faits : (1) entre 1930 et 1963 la proposition erronée de joint entre ce fragment et RS 1.008 a obscurci la situation textuelle, et (2) quelques années après la publication du *Corpus* d'A. Herdner, cette collection a été remplacée sur le métier de nombreux ougaritisants par une collection plus ample sortie en 1976, augmentée en 1995 et 2013 par les textes nouvellement découverts entretemps, et la lecture de RS 1.031:3′ comporte une erreur dans les trois éditions qui a eu pour effet d'obscurcir la bonne lecture d'A. Herdner[7]. Ainsi les avan-

[5] Andrée HERDNER, *Corpus des tablettes en cunéiformes alphabétiques découvertes à Ras Shamra-Ugarit de 1929 à 1939* (Mission de Ras Shamra X ; Bibliothèque Archéologique et Historique LXXIX), Paris, Imprimerie Nationale et Geuthner, 1963, 265 (texte 175:3) – désormais *CTA*.

[6] La lecture/restitution d'A. Herdner n'a été reconnue ni par E. LAROCHE, *Ugaritica* V, 539 ; idem, *Glossaire*, 263-264 ; ni par D. SCHWEMER, *Die Wettergottgestalten* : RS 1.031 est cité dans la note 1774, p. 255, mais le théonyme composé à la l. 3′ ne figure pas dans la discussion. David M. CLEMENS, *Sources for Ugaritic Ritual and Sacrifice. Vol. I: Ugaritic and Ugarit Akkadian Texts* (AOAT 284/1), Münster, Ugarit-Verlag, 2001, 1067, cite, avec point d'interrogation, le texte fautif de *CAT* 7.43:4 (à propos de cette nouvelle lecture, voir la suite de cette introduction et, plus loin, le commentaire de RS 1.031) après la formule logo-syllabique {^{d}IŠKUR ša KUR.ú-ga-ri-it} (RS 88.2158:15-16 [RSO XIV 1 : Sylvie LACKENBACHER, « Une lettre d'Égypte », dans Marguerite YON, Daniel ARNAUD (éd.), *Études ougaritiques I. Travaux 1985-1995* (Ras Shamra – Ougarit XIV), Paris, Éditions Recherche sur les Civilisations, 2001, 239-48]), la bonne lecture de *CTA* n'étant pas mentionnée ; apparemment D. Clemens ne voyait pas de rapport directe entre les deux formules, car, à la p. 1076, il cite de nouveau le texte fautif de *CAT* 7.43:4 après la formule très différente {DINGIR.MEŠ URU.KI} (RS 92.2004:27 [RSO XIV 22A : Daniel ARNAUD, « Textes administratifs religieux et profanes », ibid, p. 323-32, 323-26]), qui correspond à {[...]⸢-⸣t} dans le texte ougaritique RS 24.643:40, vraisemblablement à restituer sous la forme {[ỉl q]⸢r⸣t} (voir D. PARDEE, *Les textes rituels*, 796, 803).

[7] M. DIETRICH, O. LORETZ et J. SANMARTÍN, *Die keilalphabetischen Texte aus Ugarit einschließlich der keilalphabetischen Texte außerhalb Ugarits*. Teil 1 *Transkription* (AOAT 24/1), Kevelaer, Butzon & Bercker ; Neukirchen-Vluyn, Neukirchener Verlag, 1976, 422 (RS 1.031 = texte 7.43:4 « [ ]x*ṯb .ugrt* ») ; idem, *The Cuneiform Alphabetic Texts from Ugarit, Ras Ibn Hani and Other Places (KTU : second, enlarged edition)* (ALASP 8), Münster, Ugarit-Verlag, 1995, 523 (de même) ; idem, *Die keilalphabetischen Texte aus Ugarit, Ras Ibn Hani und anderen Orten. Dritte, erweiterte Auflage. The Cuneiform Alphabetic Texts from Ugarit, Ras Ibn Hani and Other Places. Third, Enlarged Edition. KTU*^{3} (AOAT 360/1), Münster, Ugarit-Verlag, 2013, 653 (de même). Ces trois éditions, parce qu'elles portent trois titres différents, seront désignés ici à la suite par les acronymes *KTU*, *CAT* et *KCAT*. Nous verrons que la bonne lecture se trouve en fait dans *KCAT*, mais, assez bizarrement,

tages évidents d'une collection en un volume de tous les textes disponibles à un moment donné ont eu le contre-effet malheureux de faire tomber en obscurité l'ouvrage d'A. Herdner, dont les lectures sont parfois, plus souvent que l'on ne l'admet généralement, supérieures à celle des collections qui l'ont remplacé. Dans le cas actuel, un effet du mauvais joint a perduré, malgré son abandon général dès 1963, jusqu'au dernier corpus en date (voir la suite de cette présentation historique).

Voici les principales étapes de l'histoire de l'étude de RS 1.008 et RS 1.031.

– 1929 : Charles Virolleaud, avec une rapidité exemplaire, présenta un échantillon des textes découverts pendant la première campagne de fouilles à Ras aš-Šamra (site qui ne portait pas encore le double nom de « Ras Shamra – Ougarit » parce que l'identification du tell avec l'ancienne ville/royaume de ce nom n'était pas encore établie[8]). Cette fouille a commencé le 9 mai 1929 et les premières tablettes sont sorties de terre déjà le 14[9]. Ces textes furent présentés sous forme de copies seulement, car le système d'écriture, inconnu auparavant, n'était pas encore déchiffré, et dans l'ordre de l'inventaire, de sorte que RS 1.008 et RS 1.031 se trouvaient, comme de raison, sur deux planches distinctes de cette publication[10].

– 1930 : Hans Bauer, dans son premier ouvrage sur le déchiffrement de la nouvelle écriture a présenté le huitième texte et le trente-et-unième comme fragments d'une seule et même tablette, avec cette remarque : « Nr. 31 läßt sich an Nr. 8 unten rechts derart anpassen, daß Zeile 1 von Nr. 31 die Zeile 10 von Nr. 8 fortsetzt »[11].

dans une reprise erronée de la tablette créée par le faux joint des deux fragments qui sont l'objet de cette étude, cette nouvelle transcription figurant, pour cette raison, au bas du texte 1.45 (voir plus bas, la comparaison des transcriptions de *CTA* 175, *KTU* 7.43 et *KCAT* 1.45:11-18).

[8] La proposition d'identification, déjà émise comme hypothèse par W. F. ALBRIGHT (« The Syro-Mesopotamian God Šulman-Ešmûn and Related Figures », *AfO* 7 [1931-32] 164-69, 165 n. 9), fut confirmée par des textes sortis du sol de Ras Shamra dès la troisième campagne (voir Ch. VIROLLEAUD, « Note complémentaire sur le poème de Môt et d'Aleïn », *Syria* 12 [1931] 350-57, 351-52 ; F.-A. Claude SCHAEFFER, « Note additionnelle », *Syria* 13 [1932] 24-27, où il est indiqué, p. 26 : « M. Émile Forrer, le premier, m'avait suggéré ce rapprochement il y a tantôt deux ans »).

[9] F.-A. SCHAEFFER, « Les fouilles de Minet-el-Beida et de Ras Shamra (campagne du printemps 1929). Rapport sommaire », *Syria* 10 (1929) 285-303. C'était René Dussaud qui a suggéré que la fouille passe du port de Minet el-Beida au tell marquant la ville que ce port devait servir (voir p. 293-94).

[10] Charles VIROLLEAUD, « Les inscriptions cunéiformes de Ras Shamra », *Syria* 10 (1929) 304-10, pl. LXI-LXXX. La copie de RS 1.008 a paru à la planche LXVII, celle de RS 1.031 à la planche LXXIII.

[11] Hans BAUER, *Entzifferung der Keilschrifttafeln von Ras Schamra*, Halle/Saale, Niemeyer 1930, 39. La présentation est conservée dans le travail mûr du même auteur où une traduction

– 1931 : Le troisième des grands savants de l'époque qui ont proposé chacun son déchiffrement de cette écriture, P. Dhorme, a admis le joint proposé par Bauer, et l'a incorporé dans sa « première traduction » de ces textes[12].

– 1936 : En revanche, l'auteur de la première traduction des textes ougaritiques en hébreu moderne, H. L. Ginsberg, a présenté les deux textes séparément, tous les deux comme en langue ougaritique ; dans une note de bas de page, il a explicitement repoussé le joint proposé par Bauer[13].

– 1941 : Dans un survol des études du peuple et de la langue hourrites, R. de Vaux était le premier à citer la raison dirimante pour dissocier les deux fragments : RS 1.031 était « peut-être » hourrite (alors qu'il n'y a jamais eu de doute sur l'identification de la langue de RS 1.008 comme étant ougaritique)[14].

– 1942 : L'un des savants de l'époque qui a exercé une grande influence sur l'évolution des études ougaritiques, jusqu'à proposer un système de numération des textes ougaritiques par lequel son auteur voulait mettre fin à l'absence de système suivi pour la citation de ces textes, Otto Eißfeldt, a admis le joint proposé par Bauer dans la première de ces tentatives[15].

est normalement jointe à la transcription, mais pas pour ce texte composite : *Die alphabetischen Keilschrifttexte von Ras Schamra* (Kleine Texte für Vorlesungen und Übungen 168) Berlin, De Gruyter, 1936, III, 10-11. On rencontre à la p. 11 du dernier ouvrage la remarque suivante, qui semble indiquer que ce grand savant commençait à avoir des doutes : « Da die Bruchstücke nicht ineinandergreifen, ist die Zeilenführung nicht ganz sicher. »

[12] P. DHORME, « Première traduction des textes phéniciens de Ras Shamra », *RB* 40 (1931), p. 32-56, traduction avec de brèves remarques p. 45.

[13] H. L. GINSBERG, *ktby ʾū^{w}gryt* (*The Ugarit Texts*), Jérusalem, Bialik 1936, 87 (RS 1.008), 125 (RS 1.031), avec note 1 à la p. 87. Voir aussi plus bas, la note 15.

[14] R. de VAUX, « Études sur les Ḫurrites », *Vivre et Penser* 1 [= *RB* 50] (1941) 194-211, 202.

[15] O. EISSFELDT, « Bestand und Benennung der Ras-Schamra-Texte », *ZDMG* 96 (1942) 507-39, 526. Dans le tableau représentant les divers systèmes de numérotation des textes ougaritiques l'auteur indique que H. L. Ginsberg admet le joint de ces fragments à la suite de Bauer ; dans le corps de l'article, il cite l'article de H. L. GINSBERG, « Baʿl and ʿAnat », *Or n.s.* 7 (1938) 1-11, où, en effet H. L. Ginsberg admet le système proposé par H. Bauer. C'était pourtant passer trop rapidement d'un principe de numérotation à un cas spécifique, car le cas de RS 1.008 et RS 1.031 ne figure pas dans la brève prise de position de H. L. Ginsberg, et, dans *ktby ʾū^{w}gryt* (voir plus haut, note 13), il a explicitement repoussé ce détail précis du système de H. Bauer. Un autre auteur de l'époque, Robert DE LANGHE porte l'identification de Bauer dans son tableau de la numérotation des textes d'après Eißfeldt en indiquant qu'il s'agit du système de numérotation aussi de Ginsberg (*Les textes de Ras Shamra-Ugarit et leurs rapports avec le milieu biblique de l'Ancien Testament* [Universitas Catholica Lovaniensis, Dissertationes ad gradum magistri in Facultate Theologica vel in Facultate Iuris Canonici consequendum conscriptae, Series II, Tomus 35], Gembloux, Duculot ; Paris, de Brouwer, 1945, I, 139 (voir p. 134 pour l'indication que le système est celui d'O. Eißfeldt) ;

– 1947 : Dans la deuxième de ses quatre ouvrages présentant la langue ougaritique, augmentés et corrigés progressivement au fur et à mesure de la publication des textes, Cyrus H. Gordon a classé RS 1.031 parmi les textes dont l'écriture était alphabétique alors que la langue représentée était hourrite, mais avec point d'interrogation[16].

– 1963 : Dans son corpus des textes en cunéiforme alphabétique découverts à Ras Shamra avant la deuxième guerre mondiale, A. Herdner a présenté le texte de chacun des fragments comme indépendant l'un de l'autre et, fait essentiel, comme rédigé chacun dans sa propre langue, RS 1.008 sous le numéro 27, texte ougaritique, RS 1.031 sous le numéro 175, texte hourrite, avec, pour chacun, une note de bas de page repoussant le joint malvenu[17].

par ailleurs il prend position lui-même en affirmant qu'il s'agit de « deux fragments d'une même tablette » (I, 170) et il cite la présence du toponyme {ủgrt} en indiquant le numéro de ligne dans le texte composite (I 36 n. 4 ; II 41). La présentation de M. DIETRICH et O. LORETZ, *Konkordanz der ugaritischen Textzählungen* (AOAT 19), Kevelaer, Butzon & Bercker ; Neukirchen-Vluyn, Neukirchener Verlag, 1972, reflète mieux la position de H. L. Ginsberg en portant dans leurs listes uniquement les sigles utilisés explicitement par cet auteur ; ainsi, aux p. 4 et 10, la colonne « Gins[berg] » est vide en face de *CTA* 27 et 175.

[16] C. H. GORDON, *Ugaritic Handbook. Revised Grammar, Paradigms, Texts in Transliteration, Comprehensive Glossary* (Analecta Orientalia 25), Rome, Pontificium Institutum Biblicum, 1947, 200. Dans la version suivante, on lit : « Hurrian text (unless associated with 8) » (*Ugaritic Manual. Newly Revised Grammar, Texts in Transliteration, Cuneiform Selections, Paradigms – Glossary – Indices* [Analecta Orientalia 35], Rome, Pontificium Institutum Biblicum, 1955, 192) ; dans la dernière : « Text with names of Hurrian gods », c'est-à-dire sans mention de joint possible avec RS 1.008 (*Ugaritic Textbook: Grammar, Texts in Transliteration, Cuneiform Selections, Glossary, Indices* [Analecta Orientalia 38], Rome, Pontificium Institutum Biblicum, 1965, 258). Ces trois éditions sont désignées par les acronymes *UH*, *UM* et *UT*. Dans sa traduction d'un échantillon de textes ougaritiques parue entre *UH* et *UM* (*Ugaritic Literature. A Comprehensive Translation of the Poetic and Prose Texts*, Rome, Pontificium Institutum Biblicum, 1949, 56), il a traduit RS 1.008 sans la moindre allusion à RS 1.031.

[17] A. HERDNER, *CTA*, 106 (texte 27 des documents rédigés en langue ougaritique), 264-65 (texte 175, dans la section consacrée au textes hourrites). Dans la note 1, p. 264, elle affirme explicitement l'identification hourrite du texte 175, et elle cite Bauer comme à l'origine du faux joint, C. H. Gordon, R. de Vaux (références ici plus haut) et Ch. Virolleaud (« communication personnelle ») pour l'avis contraire. Puisque la première présentation explicite de l'argument contre le joint faisant appel à la rédaction de chacun des deux textes en langue différente était celle d'Herdner, soit dit une fois pour toutes ici que, en théorie, rien ne s'oppose à la restitution d'une tablette portant des textes, voire des passages ou des formules, en hourrite et en ougaritique – il existe d'assez nombreux textes bilingues hourro-ougaritique (les textes rituels de se type se trouveront dans notre réédition des textes rituels [voir plus haut, la n. 4]). Il n'est pourtant pas possible d'admettre cette identification de RS 1.008 et RS 1.031 car, comme nous le verrons plus bas, le faux joint place des fins de lignes en langue hourrite en face de débuts de lignes d'un texte en ougaritique, et les deux textes sont de genre littéraire différent. Le joint des deux fragments a en fait créé un monstre linguistique et littéraire.

– 1976, 1995 : dans les deux premières éditions de leur collection des textes en cunéiforme alphabétique, M. Dietrich, O. Loretz et J. Sanmartín ont suivi A. Herdner dans son identification de RS 1.008 et RS 1.031 comme fragments provenant de tablettes différentes et du second comme étant en langue hourrite : les deux textes sont numérotés, respectivement, 1.45 et 7.43[18]. Une erreur de lecture s'est pourtant glissée dans ces collections, comme nous l'avons mentionné en introduction et comme il sera indiqué en détail plus bas dans une remarque textuelle, qui a ramené sur la lecture de la ligne 3′ l'obscurité qui régnait avant le travail d'A. Herdner : « [ ]xṯ*b* . *ugrt* » pour {[…]ṯb . ůgrt}, qui se lit sur la tablette et qui se trouve dans la transcription de *CTA*.

– 2013 : La double indication que le joint des deux fragments était fautif est répétée dans la troisième édition de cette collection[19]. Malgré cette indication explicite, la transcription de *KCAT* 1.45 comporte une étourderie qui laissera pantois le lecteur qui a suivi les étapes de l'histoire jusqu'ici : ce texte y est représenté comme comportant dix-huit lignes, et la partie droite des lignes 11-18 consiste en une nouvelle transcription de RS 1.031. Il paraît probable que la personne qui est revenue à la lecture de la « tablette » créée par le faux joint ne connaissait pas l'histoire dressée ici et qu'elle ne s'est pas rendu compte que la partie droite de *KCAT* 1.45:11-18 correspondait au fragment porté dans le même recueil sous le numéro 7.43, car la transcription de *KCAT* 1.45:11-18 comporte plusieurs lectures différentes de celles qui sont indiquées pour *KCAT* 7.43, y compris la bonne lecture de RS 1.031:3′, c'est-à-dire celle qui a motivé l'étude actuelle. En effet, à *KCAT* 1.45:13 on lit « [xxx xx]ṯ*b* . *ugrt* », alors que, à *KCAT* 7.43:4, on trouve « [ ]xṯ*b* . *ugrt* » (corps italique dénote lecture certaine, corps romain signe abîmé) – voir plus bas les remarques textuelles à propos de RS 1.031 où les deux transcriptions sont portées vis-à-vis. On conclura qu'un membre de l'équipe chargée de préparer la nouvelle édition de cette collection s'est trouvé en face d'une photographie de la « tablette » reconstituée (voir paragraphe suivant) et s'est mis à déchiffrer le fragment inférieur. On s'étonne que cette erreur de débutant a pu passer inaperçue des auteurs dont les noms sont indiqués sur la couverture, mais le fait est là.

Enfin, étape essentielle, mais que l'on n'est pas en mesure de placer avec précision dans ce récit chronologique : quelqu'un qui connaissait la

[18] *KTU*, 78-79 (RS 1.008 = texte 1.45, avec note de bas de page indiquant que le joint de ce fragment avec RS 1.031 était « irrtümlich »), 422 (RS 1.031 = texte 7.43. avec note de bas de page à contenu similaire) ; *CAT*, 82 (RS 1.008 : « incorrectly … joined »), 523 (RS 1.031 : « erroneously … joined »).

[19] *KCAT*, 83, 653 (les mêmes termes que dans *CAT* sont employés pour qualifier la valeur du joint).

proposition de H. Bauer a créé une fausse tablette en rapprochant les deux fragments au point où ce joint est envisageable. Vu l'exiguïté de la surface de part et d'autre où les deux fragments se touchaient, il fallait créer un encadrement de plâtre pour les fixer en place. Ainsi, on ne peut pas dire que les fragments ont été véritablement recollés parce que l'étendue de la surface de part et d'autre est insuffisante pour un joint normal : voir la photographie portée dans la figure 2, où les deux fragments d'avant recollage sont rapprochés pour illustrer le « joint » avant sa consolidation avec du plâtre. Ce travail n'a pas été effectué tout de suite après l'arrivée des tablettes de la première campagne au musée du Louvre parce que chacun porte son propre numéro d'inventaire au Département Oriental (RS 1.008 = AO 12.034, RS 1.031 = AO 12.025[20]) et que les photographies publiées dans *CTA* et conservées dans les Archives Schaeffer montrent les fragments individuels. Voir les photographies reproduites ici : figure 1, les deux fragments ; figure 2, les deux fragments rapprochés pour illustrer ce sur quoi le restaurateur travaillait ; figure 3, le résultat de ce travail de « restauration », autre photographie des Archives Schaeffer ; figure 4, l'objet tel qu'il était encore visible lorsque nous l'avons photographié pour la dernière fois en 2009. En revanche, les fragments réunis sont enregistrés au musée d'Alep sous un seul numéro (l'ancien cote A2741 a été transformé en M3355 lors d'une refonte entière du système d'enregistrement au siècle dernier[21]), ce qui permet de supposer – mais une supposition n'est qu'une supposition – que la « restauration » de la tablette ait eu lieu au Louvre avant le réintégration de la moitié des tablettes de Ras Shamra en Syrie après la guerre.

Réédition des deux fragments

RS 1.008 (copie de l'auteur fig. 5)
= M3358 = *UT* 8 = *CTA* 27 = *KTU*/*CAT*/*KCAT* 1.45

Dimensions : hauteur 65 mm ; largeur 68 mm ; épaisseur 21 mm.

État : partie supérieure de tablette, reconstituée elle-même de plusieurs fragments ; le *recto* et la tranche gauche sont assez bien conservés, aussi

[20] *CTA*, 106, 264 ; données confirmées *de visu* par Pierre Bordreuil et Dennis Pardee, *La trouvaille épigraphique de l'Ougarit* (Ras Shamra – Ougarit V,1), Paris, Éditions Recherche sur les Civilisations, 1989, 16. Voir la photographie composite des fragments réunis (fig. 4), où l'on voit encore sur la tranche gauche de RS 1.008 et sur la tranche droite de RS 1.031 le numéro du musée du Louvre porté en encre claire sur la terre cuite et noircie par l'incendie du bâtiment où ces tablettes étaient rangées.

[21] Seuls les anciens numéros sont cités dans *KTU*. Le travail était encore en cours lorsque nous travaillions au musée d'Alep en 1980-1981.

bien que quelques signes le long de la marge gauche au *verso*. La surface est assez bien conservée, de sorte que l'on arrive à lire la plupart des signes.

Caractéristiques épigraphiques : main ferme et appuyée ; le déroulement des signes à clous horizontaux superposés est de bas en haut, et le clou supérieur est effectué avec pivotement du calame vers le haut de sorte que ce clou est plus grand que les autres (voir le {r}, l. 2, {ph}, l. 3) ; le clou de droite des signes à clous verticaux multiples montre moins l'effet du pivotement du calame, pour ces signes vers la droite ; les clous du {h} sont longs et fins, ceux du {ỉ} un peu plus courts ; la pointe inférieure du clou central du {š} s'étire vers le bas et ce clou était gravé avant le clou de gauche, car il est déformé par ce dernier[22], et les clous latéraux sont de forme oblique et posés de manière symétrique, la pointe gauche du clou de gauche relevé à peu près au même niveau que la pointe droite du clou de droite ; le {ʿ} montre la forme relativement rare où le bord gauche est presqu'à la verticale ; {ṯ} à six pointes, effectué par la pose d'un clou horizontal sur un clou oblique.

Lieu de trouvaille : Acropole, Maison du grand prêtre[23].

Editio princeps : Ch. VIROLLEAUD, *Syria* 10 (1929), pl. LXVII (copie seule) ; *editio secunda* : A. HERDNER, *CTA* (1963), p. 106, n° 27 (la copie, fig. 72, est celle de Virolleaud ; photographie pl. XXXV).

Principales études et traductions[24] :

[22] À propos de la variabilité dans l'ordre de pose des trois clous du {š}, voir John Lee ELLISON, *A Paleographic Study of the Alphabetic Cuneiform Texts from Ras Shamra/Ugarit*, thèse, Harvard University, 2002, 373-91 ; le signe dans cette main correspond à son type « C » (p. 385-87, fig. 1647-1667) ; « D » (p. 387-88, fig. 1668-1680) montre aussi cet ordre de pose, mais avec un *ductus* différent (l'étude de ce signe se trouve aux p. 773-818 de la version commercialisée par ProQuest, où les illustrations sont intégrées dans le texte principal, les photographies étant pourtant peu lisibles). Dans notre expérience, il est rare de trouver des exemples aussi nets que ceux de cette tablette des déformations que peut subir le clou central du signe par la gravure du clou de gauche lorsque l'autre clou était déjà en place.

[23] Si le lieu de découverte des tablettes de la première campagne est connu de manière générale (voir P. BORDREUIL et D. PARDEE, *La trouvaille*, 15), l'inventaire officiel et le carnet de fouilles sont perdus, de sorte que les détails concernant les objets individuels le sont aussi.

[24] Les travaux les plus importants sont indiqués ici en l'ordre alphabétique des auteurs, avec titre abrégé de l'ouvrage aussi bien que l'année de publication pour permettre au lecteur de situer rapidement dans le temps la contribution en question ; si plus bas un spécialiste est cité par seulement son nom, la référence est aux données indiquées ici. On trouvera chez D. CLEMENS, *Sources*, 1168, un précis des études et des descriptions brèves de ce texte par treize spécialistes, entre 1931 et 1999.

BAUER, *Die alphabetischen Keilschrifttexte* (1936) 10-11[25].
CLEMENS, *UF* 33 (2001) 65-116[26].
DHORME, *RB* 40 (1931) 45.
GASTER, *Religions* 18 (1937) 27-28, 36 n. 53[27].
GINSBERG, *ktby ʾū^{w}gryt* (1936) 87.
GORDON, *UL* (1949) 56.
KUTTER, *nūr ilī* (2008) 49-52[28].
RENDSBURG, *JNSL* 8 (1980) 82-84[29].
RIN et RIN, *ʿ^{a}lī^{y}lō^{w}t hāʾēlī^{y}m* (1968) 269-70[30].
— *Haṭṭū^{w}r haššᵊlī^{y}šī^{y}* (1979) 75[31].
— *Haṭṭū^{w}r haššᵊlī^{y}šī^{y}*, deuxième édition (1992) 105[32].
— *ʿ^{a}lī^{y}lō^{w}t hāʾēlī^{y}m*, deuxième édition (1996) 399-400[33].

Texte

Recto

1) b[34] yn . ỉš[- - -]⸢ỉ⸣lnr
2) spr . ⸢--⸣ḥ⸢-⸣k . šbʿt
3) ghl . ph . ṯmnt
4) nblůh . špš ⸢.⸣ ym⸢-⸣

[25] Seul le texte est donné ; comme il a été remarqué plus haut (note 11), à la différence de la présentation des autres textes de ce recueil, ce texte n'est pas traduit, aucune remarque portant sur l'interprétation n'est proposée, et les remarques en notes de bas de page sont d'ordre uniquement épigraphique.

[26] David M. CLEMENS, « KTU 1.45 and 1.6 I 8-18, 1.161, 1.101 », *UF* 33 (2001) 65-116.

[27] Theodor H. GASTER, « New Light on Early Palestinian Religion : More Texts from Ras Shamra », *Religions* 18 (1937) 7-36.

[28] Juliane KUTTER, *nūr ilī. Die Sonnengottheiten in den nordwestsemitischen Religionen von der Spätbronzezeit bis zur vorrömischen Zeit* (AOAT 346), Münster, Ugarit-Verlag, 2008 : texte, traduction et commentaire, le tout suivant de près l'étude de CLEMENS, *UF* 33.

[29] Gary RENDSBURG, « Hebrew *ʾšdt* and Ugaritic *ʾišdym* », *JNSL* 8 (1980) 81-84.

[30] Svi RIN et Shifra RIN, *ʿ^{a}lī^{y}lō^{w}t hāʾēlī^{y}m. kol šī^{y}rō^{w}t ʾū^{w}gārī^{y}t mᵊtoʿ^{o}tāqō^{w}t mᵊšuktābō^{w}t ū^{w}mᵊpōrāšō^{w}t* (*Acts of the Gods. The Ugaritic Epic Poetry Transliterated, Transcribed and Interpreted*), Jérusalem, Inbal, 1968.

[31] Idem, *Haṭṭū^{w}r haššᵊlī^{y}šī^{y} laʿ^{a}lī^{y}lō^{w}t hāʾēlī^{y}m. paršegen kol šī^{y}rō^{w}t ʾū^{w}gārī^{y}t* (*The Third Column of The Acts of the Gods. A Hebrew Paraphrase of the Ugaritic Epic Poetry*), Philadelphia, Inbal, 1979.

[32] Idem, *Haṭṭū^{w}r haššᵊlī^{y}šī^{y} laʿ^{a}lī^{y}lō^{w}t hāʾēlī^{y}m. paršegen kol šī^{y}rō^{w}t ʾū^{w}gārī^{y}t mah^{a}dū^{w}rā^{h} ḥ^{a}dāšā^{h} mᵊtuqqenet ū^{w}mᵊnuqqedet* (*The Third Column of The Acts of the Gods. A Revised Paraphrase of the Ugaritic Epic Poetry with Tiberian Vocalization*), Philadelphia, Inbal, 1992.

[33] Idem, *ʿ^{a}lī^{y}lō^{w}t hāʾēlī^{y}m. kol šī^{y}rō^{w}t ʾū^{w}gārī^{y}t. mah^{a}dū^{w}rā^{h} ḥ^{a}dāšā^{h} bᵊdū^{w}qā^{h} ū^{w}morḥebet* (*Acts of the Gods. The Ugaritic Epic Poetry. A Revised and Expanded Edition*), Philadelphia, Inbal, 1996.

[34] Ce {b} se trouve sur la tranche gauche face au premier signe se trouvant sur la face principale, donc sans doute ajouté secondairement : voir notre copie, la photographie de la tranche gauche et, plus loin, la remarque textuelle et le commentaire.

5) hlkt . tdrq . [-]⸢-⸣[…]
6) špš . bʿdh . t[-]⸢--⸣[…]
7) ảṯr . ảṯrm[…]
8) ảṯr . ảṯr⸢m⸣[…]
9) ỉšdym . t[…]
10) bk . mlả . ⸢š⸣[…]
11) ủdmʿt . d[…]
12) [ ]⸢-⸣ . bn . ⸢-⸣[…]
13) [ ]⸢- . -⸣[…]

....

Verso

....

14′) ⸢-⸣[…]
15′) ⸢-⸣[…]
16′) ⸢-⸣[…]
17′) š[…]
18′) ⸢-⸣[…]

Remarques textuelles

1) Aucun de nos prédécesseurs n'a remarqué le {b} gravé sur la tranche gauche. On connaît d'autres cas d'un signe omis par erreur qui a ensuite été gravé à gauche de la marge gauche du texte, par exemple la lettre RS 18.134 (*KTU* 2.44), où, ligne 3, le {ḥ} du mot *tḥm*, « message », est situé à la marge gauche, et le {t} se trouve à gauche de ce signe, sur la tranche.

Le signe dont la partie gauche est perdu dans la lacune centrale est {h,ỉ} (avec A. Herdner, contre les auteurs de *KTU*/*CAT*/*KCAT*, qui indiquent un {h} certain). Ceci dit, on remarque qu'il est possible que le bord de la lacune ait suivi le côté droit du clou inférieur de {ỉ}.

2) Sur le bord gauche de la lacune, nous n'avons trouvé qu'une trace de clou, l'angle supérieur gauche d'un clou plutôt vertical qu'horizontal, bien que la trace soit trop petite et trop mal conservée pour permettre la certitude (l'éditeur a dessiné deux traces infimes de clous horizontaux – pourtant la photographie de la tablette prise avant le joint avec RS 1.031 et l'ajout de plâtre pour consolider l'ensemble montre cette zone de la tablette dans le même état de conservation qu'aujourd'hui). Au-dessous de cette trace, il est possible que la cassure ait suivi le bord gauche de la tête d'un clou horizontal, et, plus loin et au même niveau, on voit peut-être l'angle inférieur gauche d'un autre clou de ce signe et, ensuite, ce qui semble être une partie du bord inférieur d'un long clou horizontal. La situation de ce clou, sensiblement plus haut que les traces possibles de clous inférieurs qui viennent d'être évoquées, indique que le premier signe serrait

{b,d} plutôt que {r}, et que ce {b,d} aurait été suivi d'un long clou horizontal, {t} ou à la rigueur, le clou de droite de {å,n,k}. Plus loin, l'éditeur a dessiné ce qu'A. HERDNER a pris pour la partie inférieure d'un {ḥ} ; ces restes sont bien conservés, bien qu'emplis de plâtre aujourd'hui de sorte qu'ils sont passés inaperçus des auteurs de *KTU/CAT/KCAT*. Ainsi, le nombre de signes partiellement conservés ici monte vraisemblablement à trois (avec A. HERDNER). À droite de la lacune, on voit la pointe d'un clou horizontal à gauche du {k} bien conservé ; puisqu'une trace de cette forme ne peut pas faire partie d'un {ḥ}, il faut augmenter d'un le nombre de signes indiqués par les auteurs de *KTU/CAT/KCAT* entre le clou séparateur à gauche et le {k} à droite (quatre au lieu de trois).

On voit un petit séparateur après le {k} (nouvelle lecture de *CTA*, adoptée dans *KTU/CAT/KCAT*).

3) La lecture du premier signe comme un {g} paraît certaine, car il consiste certainement en un seul clou vertical dont l'arête centrale est conservée sur presque toute sa longueur sans rupture, aussi bien qu'une bonne partie du bord droit, sans trace de la rupture que la pose de tête de clou inférieur aurait produit (avec la copie de Ch. VIROLLEAUD, contre H. BAUER qui pensait à {ḫ})[35].

4) Le deuxième signe comporte sans aucun doute deux clous inférieurs : sur sa copie, Ch. VIROLLEAUD a représenté la forme produite par les deux fissures qui traversent ce signe (l'un, vaguement vertical, suit le côté gauche du signe, l'autre, horizontal, suit l'arête centrale des deux clous inférieurs) comme un seul grand clou horizontal – ce qui se comprend, l'écriture n'ayant pas encore été déchiffrée lorsqu'il préparait cette copie. A. HERDNER, toute en reproduisant la copie de son maître, a transcrit sans commentaire le signe comme un {b} abîmé, alors que la lecture est portée comme certaine dans *KTU/CAT/KCAT*. On doit admettre le bien-fondé de cette dernière évaluation de la lecture, car, bien que l'intérieur des clous ait souffert, des traces importantes des bords de ces clous sont conservées, y compris les deux angles de la tête du deuxième clou.

CH. VIROLLEAUD a porté sur sa copie un trait séparateur entier après {špš} que l'on ne retrouve pas sous cette forme entière. La photographie de l'objet effectuée avant le joint avec RS 1.031 montre que la lacune entre le fragment central et celui de droite avait la même largeur qu'aujourd'hui. On voit au bord gauche de la lacune une forme triangulaire moins large

[35] Parmi ceux qui ont étudié l'original, l'avis est unanime que le signe ne comporte qu'un clou vertical, et il faut se méfier de la proposition de corriger {ghl} en {ṣhl} (C. H. GORDON, *UT*, § 19.2149 [p. 473] ; admis comme lecture valable par G. RENDSBURG, *JNSL* 8, p. 82-83) dans un texte dont l'interprétation est difficile de tous les points de vue.

que le séparateur typique de ce texte et aux bords émoussés : il s'agit vraisemblablement soit du séparateur entier mais abîmé, soit de la partie gauche d'un séparateur à l'origine plus large, interprétation épigraphiquement plus satisfaisante.

La partie inférieure du dernier signe à disparu, et il s'agit donc de {p,h,ỉ} (Ch. VIROLLEAUD a porté deux clous entiers sur sa copie, sans indiquer que la cassure a enlevé la partie inférieur du clou inférieur, et comparer l'ancienne photographie montre que la tablette n'a pas détérioré en cet endroit depuis cette époque ; on trouve {⸢p⸣} dans *CTA* et *KTU*, {p,ẓ} dans *CAT*/*KCAT*, mais le deuxième terme de cette alternative est à éliminer puisque la pointe du clou supérieur est conservée et le clou inférieur l'est presque jusqu'à la pointe). L'état assez bien conservé de la partie supérieure droite de ce signe élimine aussi la lecture préférée de D. CLEMENS, celle d'un {k} mal conservé (p. 92, 95-97). Ce signe était certainement le dernier de la ligne, car la surface est conservée à droite des deux clous dont il vient d'être question, et l'on y verrait au moins la partie supérieure d'un signe gravé là (contre l'indication dans *KTU*/*CAT* d'une lacune de largeur indéfinie et celle dans *KCAT* d'une lacune de la largeur d'un signe).

5) La lecture de la dernière lettre du deuxième mot comme un {q} paraît certaine (la copie de l'éditeur représente la partie gauche d'un {š} ; A. HERDNER ne propose pas de lecture ; un {q} certain est indiqué dans *KTU*/*CAT*/*KCAT*).

Sous le dernier signe de la ligne précédente et un peu à droite, on voit le bord supérieur d'un clou horizontal précédé d'un peu du bord supérieur d'un premier clou horizontal, le tout partiellement empli de plâtre (nouvelle lecture). Ce signe était gravé en pente montante de sorte qu'il aurait presque touché la pointe du clou inférieur du dernier signe de la ligne précédente si celui-ci était {h}.

6) On croit voir les traces d'écriture dessinées par l'éditeur comme se trouvant sur le petit pan de surface sous les signes {q .} à la ligne précédente ; ces traces ont pourtant été partiellement emplies de plâtre lors de la reconstitution de la fausse tablette résultant du joint de RS 1.008 et de RS 1.031, de sorte qu'on n'arrive pas à déterminer aujourd'hui s'il s'agit de clous horizontaux ou verticaux ; les deux traces semblent pourtant ne pas se toucher (ces traces ne sont pas enregistrées dans *KTU*/*CAT*/*KCAT*)[36].

[36] Quoi qu'en soit la bonne lecture, ces traces sont trop rapprochées l'une de l'autre pour correspondre aux signes {ṯb} de la restitution {t[ṯ]b}, « s'assied », proposée une fois par Ch. VIROLLEAUD, « Le roi Kéret et son fils (II K) (*Troisième partie*) », *Syria* 23, 1942-

9) L'absence du {t} avant la cassure dans la transcription de *KTU/CAT* était sûrement une coquille, car ce signe est indiqué dans *KCAT*.

10) La disposition des restes du dernier signe partiellement conservé est plutôt celle de {š} (ce que présuppose la copie de l'éditeur) que de celle de {ḏ} (indiqué comme lecture certaine dans *KTU/CAT/KCAT* ; A. HERDNER remarque en note de bas de page qu'elle ne distinguait pas le {š} que la copie « suggère » – remarque que l'on ne comprend pas puisque les traces sont claires sur la photographie de l'époque). Le clou central est bien à la verticale, et le clou de gauche, rempli de dépôt, présente l'angle des autres {š} dans ce texte (normalement, lorsque le clou de droite de {ḏ} est à la verticale, le clou de gauche est plus couché qu'ici).

11) Comme il est indiqué plus haut, le texte de RS 1.031 est à tort transcrit dans *KCAT* comme la partie droite de cette ligne et les suivantes.

12) Il semble que les auteurs de *KTU/CAT* aient suivi *CTA* ici, car des petits restes tels que ceux que l'on trouve à gauche et à droite des signes {. bn .} ne sont pas normalement enregistrés par A. HERDNER dans sa transcription : ces auteurs aussi transcrivent par {. bn .}, alors que les restes dessinés par l'éditeur de part et d'autre de ces trois signes sont parfaitement visibles sur la tablette. Le signe à gauche semble avoir été {ṭ, ḥ}, alors que, à droite, on ne voit que l'angle supérieur gauche d'un clou horizontal (la lecture dans *KCAT* d'un {ṯ} ne convient point à ce reste typique d'un clou horizontal, et ce signe n'est évidemment pas suivi de l'écriture conservée à RS 1.031:2′).

13) On retrouve des restes des deux signes dessinés par l'éditeur (les auteurs de *KTU/CAT* n'enregistrent qu'un signe ici – et cette lecture est abandonnée dans *KCAT*, où rien n'est indiqué à cette ligne avant les signes se trouvant sur RS 1.031:3′). En plus de ces restes de signes à gauche et à droite, on croit voir des restes d'un clou séparateur entre ces signes.

14′-18′) Aucun de nos prédécesseurs n'a enregistré les quelques restes du texte gravé au *verso* de la tablette, dont aucun signe n'est conservé en entier, seulement un suffisamment conservé pour en permettre la lecture certaine. Le texte se terminait certainement par la dernière de ces lignes.

1943, 1-20, 9, et admise par M. DAHOOD, « The Linguistic Position of Ugaritic in the Light of Recent Discoveries », dans J. COPPENS, A. DESCAMPS, É. MASSAUX (éd), *Sacra Pagina. Miscellanea biblica Congressus Internationalis Catholici de re biblica. Volumen Primum* (BETL 12), Gembloux, Duculot, 1959, 267-79, 276-78. En effet, l'angle supérieur droit d'un {ṯ} ne devrait pas être tout près de l'angle supérieur gauche d'un {b}, comme c'est le cas de ces deux traces. En revanche, l'espace étroit entre ces traces semble aussi éliminer la lecture du signe comme un {l} (D. CLEMENS, *UF* 33, 96 ; cf. p. 95 n. 158, où la copie de Virolleaud est citée en faveur de la lecture de deux têtes de clou vertical).

Traduction

Recto

1) DANS/PAR le vin ’IŠ[---]⸢’I⸣LNR
2) COMPTER/RÉCITER ⸢--⸣Ḥ⸢-⸣K les sept
3) retentissements$^{?}$ de sa bouche, ses huit
4) flammes. *Šapšu* pendant$^{?}$ un jour
5) a marché, AVANCER [-]⸢-⸣[…]
6) *Šapšu*, après lui/elle, elle [-]⸢--⸣[…]
7) à la suite, à la suite[…]
8) à la suite, à la suit[e …]
9) ’IŠDYM T[…]
10) PLEURER PLEIN ⸢Š⸣[…]
11) larmes D[…]

………………

Commentaire

Il y a peu à redire sur l’étude de ce texte par D. Clemens[37], qui remarque à juste titre que ce texte a été l’objet de peu d’études et que, dans celles qui existent, on rencontre énormément de variété, autant dans l’interprétation des termes et des formules que dans l’analyse littéraire. Lui non plus n’a proposé d’interprétation qui tiendrait compte de l’ensemble du texte, se contentant de signaler plusieurs recoupements avec l’histoire de l’ensevelissement de *Ba‘lu* d’après les cinquième et sixième tablettes du Cycle de *Ba‘lu*, avec un autre texte où figure *Ba‘lu* (RS 24.245 [*KTU* 1.101]) et avec le rituel funéraire pour l’avant-dernier roi d’Ougarit (RS 34.126 [*KTU* 1.161])[38].

Ligne 1. La lecture d’un {b} bien conservé sur la tranche gauche en face de cette ligne entraîne forcément une nouvelle interprétation de la ligne ; pourtant, celle-ci est trop mal conservée pour permettre d’apprécier

[37] Plusieurs des remarques présentées sous forme d’étude du texte de RS 1.008 dans *UF* 33 ont été anticipées dans la thèse du même auteur, soutenue en 1999 et parue en édition en 2001 (*Sources*, 83 n. 382, 88 n. 416, 140 n. 666, 446 n. 1531, 536-37 [à propos du lien, non admis, avec RS 1.031], 554 n. 2093, 556-57, 883, 918-19 n. 1392, 985, 1123) ; on trouvera p. 1168, sous forme de liste en ordre alphabétique des auteurs, l’identification du genre littéraire proposée par divers ougaritisants.

[38] La liste des passages comparables se trouve dans le paragraphe de conclusion (*UF* 33, 113). Sans vouloir éliminer la valeur de ces rapprochements, on se sent tout de même dans l’obligation de stipuler que l’identification du genre littéraire de ce texte ne peut découler de la mention du dieu *Ba‘lu* dans ce texte (G. del Olmo Lete, *Mitos y leyendas de Canaan según la tradición de Ugarit*, Madrid, Ediciones Cristiandad, 1981, 86), car ce théonyme ne s’y rencontre pas (cf. H. L. Ginsberg, « Interpreting Ugaritic Texts », *JAOS* 70, 1950, 156-60, 159 : « … no. 8 doesn’t even mention Baal or Anath »).

pleinement cette nouveauté. Cette lettre jointe aux lettres suivantes ne donne pas un mot connu, et il paraît nécessaire de prendre ce premier signe pour la préposition *b*, qui transforme {yn . ỉš[---]} en formule adverbiale, « Dans le vin-X ». Le mot qui qualifie le vin est communément restitué depuis l'édition de l'un des fragments dits « des Rephaïm » d'après la formule *yn ỉšryt* à RS 2.[024]:19′ (*KTU* 1.22)[39]. Du point de vu purement épigraphique, la restitution est possible ; mais le {r}, dont la longueur est variable dans cette main, devait être l'un des plus courts. Le sens du mot *ỉšryt* est débattu, inconnu déjà dans le texte mieux conservé – type de vin ou lieu d'origine ?[40] – et le mauvais état du texte examiné ici signifie que la présence même du mot est incertaine. Dans l'autre texte, ce vin figure parmi plusieurs denrées dont un festin des *Rapaʾūma* est approvisionné, ce qui permet au moins de déduire qu'il s'agit d'un vin de qualité paraissant seulement sur les tables les plus raffinées. L'autre texte est aussi important pour l'interprétation de celui-ci du fait que, à la fin de la description du festin, au septième jour de son déroulement, *Baʿlu* lui-même arrive – mais c'est là que la tablette est cassée, de sorte que l'objectif de cette apparition ne peut que se déduire de l'explication globale du texte[41]. Au moins ce texte rapproche le vin-ʾIŠRYT des *Rapaʾūma* et du grand dieu qui fraie le plus avec eux.

H. L. GINSBERG était le premier à proposer que les quatre derniers signes pouvaient signifier « dieu de la lumière », lecture préférée par RIN et RIN, aussi bien que par RENDSBURG. RIN et RIN citent la formule *nrt ỉlm*, « lumière des dieux », épithète de *Šapšu*, mais sans affirmer explicitement qu'il s'agirait d'une autre manière de désigner la déesse solaire, c'est-à-dire en exprimant sa nature divine sans allusion au fait que, pour les ougaritains, cette divinité était féminine. Pour D. CLEMENS, identifier *ỉl nr* et *nrt ỉlm* serait difficile, comme le serait l'explication d'après *nyr* en RS 34.126:19 (*KTU* 1.161)[42], où la formule par laquelle *Šapšu* et interpellée est en fait double : *nyr rbt*, « ô source de lumière, ô la Grande » (nom commun de genre masculin suivi d'un adjectif substantivé marqué pour le féminin). En plus de l'ambiguïté quant à l'identification de la divinité ainsi qualifiée,

[39] Ch. VIROLLEAUD, « Les Rephaïm : fragments de poèmes de Ras-Shamra », *Syria* 22 (1941) 1-30, 26. Il s'agit de la première colonne du texte qui résulte de notre proposition selon laquelle les trois fragments en question proviendraient d'une seule et même tablette : D. PARDEE, « Nouvelle étude épigraphique et littéraire des textes fragmentaires en langue ougaritique dits "Les Rephaïm" (*CTA* 20-22) », *Or* n.s. 80 (2011) 1-65, 37.

[40] D. CLEMENS, *UF* 33, p. 103-4 n. 197, fournit l'historique des propositions d'interprétation de ce texte-ci à la lumière du texte mieux conservé.

[41] Cf. D. PARDEE, *Or* 80, 57, 63-64.

[42] *UF* 33, p. 104.

la lecture elle-même ne va pas sans difficultés : le premier signe n'est pas certainement un {ỉ}, et, si l'on admet la lecture, ce serait le seul cas de deux mots distincts sans séparateur entre les deux. Et l'ambiguïté s'accroît par l'incertitude du sens précis du qualificatif : désignerait-il la « lumière » ou la « flamme » qui fait naître la lumière ? Il s'agit là des deux principales champs sémantiques que la racine *mediae infirmae* N(W/Y)R exprime dans les langues sémitiques. S'il s'agit de « flamme », l'identification de la divinité avec *Ba'lu* est au moins envisageable, car le qualificatif pourrait faire allusion aux éclairs qu'il projette (*brqm* en RS 24.245:3 [*KTU* 1.101]), alors que l'on ne s'attend pas à ce que ce dieu soit identifié comme source importante de simple « lumière ». Enfin, lire les signes {ỉlnr} comme un seul mot laisserait entendre qu'il s'agit d'un anthroponyme (ainsi P. DHORME), analyse qui ne semble pas convenir aux formules suivantes[43].

Ligne 2. La présence des signes {spr} constitue l'une des difficultés principales de ce texte, car le nom commun *spr* /sipru/, « document », est caractéristique du genre administratif, et, plus particulièrement du genre épistolaire, et il est attesté, avec ce sens de « document » au début du rituel funéraire en forme poétique RS 34.126 (*KTU* 1.161) : *spr dbḥ ẓlm*, « Document du/des sacrifice(s) des mânes ». Comme attestation certaine dans un texte mythologique (nous ne comptons pas {spr} dans les colophons du scribe *'Ilîmilku*, situés toujours en fin de texte, le plus souvent sur la tranche gauche de la tablette), on ne peut citer que la première tablette du Cycle de *Ba'lu*, col. v, ligne 24′ (*KTU* 1.1 ii 24), passage encore plus abîmé que celui-ci, où l'analyse de la forme est aussi incertaine qu'ici mais où il s'agit peut-être de la récitation d'un message. Si la forme est en faite verbale ici, l'état du texte nous empêche de distinguer entre le sens propre à la comptabilité (« compter » ou « établir un compte »[44]) et le sens développé de « raconter ».

[43] Anticipant sur le commentaire suivant, on pourrait prendre les signes en question comme anthroponyme et traduire : « Sous l'effet du vin-'IŠRYT, *'Ilînūru* a raconté : En le fils du *ḥātiku* sont les sept retentissements de sa bouche, ses huit feux ». On se demande pourtant pourquoi le tonnerre et la foudre sont décrites comme étant « en » le dieu de l'orage. Sans doute vaudrait-il mieux lire {⸢dt⸣ ḥ⸢t⸣k} « Du *ḥatūki* sont ... » ; mais prendre *ḥtk* seul pour une épithète permettant l'auditeur de saisir qu'il s'agit du dieu de l'orage est plus difficile que d'admettre cette fonction pour les deux épithètes complexes /'ilu nūri/ et /binu ḥātiki/. Voir le commentaire qui suit, où cette seconde interprétation est avancée.

[44] Il s'agit certainement d'un verbe dans le mémorandum épistolaire RS 16.264 (*KTU* 2.25), où, aux lignes 17-18, l'auteur royal ordonne à son correspondant de fournir un compte des quantités de « bois », vraisemblablement des troncs d'arbre, qu'il va recevoir, le verbe SPR étant probablement au schème-D (*w l 'ṣm tspr* « et pour les troncs tu établiras un compte »). Rien n'appuie la traduction de {spr} à RS 1.008:2 par le verbe « envoyer », figurant dans une identification du texte comme lettre (P. DHORME, *RB* 40, 45 ; T. H. GASTER, *Religions* 18, 27).

Bien que très abîmés, les restes d'écriture au milieu de la ligne permettent tout de même quelques identifications. Pour deux signes la lecture est certaine : le {k} final est entièrement conservé, et les restes du {ḥ} sont assez typiques pour éliminer toute autre lecture. L'espace occupé par le signe entre les deux dont il vient d'être question est assez étroit pour éliminer un {r} normal dans cette main, et même un {k} serait un peu serré – il s'agit donc probablement de {t,ȧ,n}. Du signe à gauche du {ḥ}, on ne voit qu'une partie du bord inférieur d'un clou horizontal, cet espace aussi étant assez réduit. Nous avons vu dans la remarque textuelle que le premier signe aussi est très mal conservé, mais que l'on retrouve peut-être des restes de ce qui serait un {b} plutôt qu'un {d}. On remarque enfin que le {k} final doit correspondre à une lettre radicale, car l'analyse comme pronom de la 2e personne du singulier, masculin ou féminin, est éliminée par les formes alentour. Ainsi, il doit s'agir d'une racine ḤxK, où le deuxième signe n'est pas long et se terminant par un clou horizontal. Seul ḤTK paraît conforme à ces exigences épigraphiques. Pourtant, cette conclusion ne mène pas loin, car la forme employée ici n'est pas évidente. Les attestations de formes dérivées de cette racine ne sont pas nombreuses ; mais on rencontre néanmoins des formes exprimant l'exercice du pouvoir au sens large[45], aussi bien que trois termes homographes, tous les trois en rapport avec l'autorité paternelle : (1) *ḥtk* en parallèle avec *ȧb*, « père », (2) *ḥtk* qui tient lieu de *bn*, « fils », et (3) *ḥtk* désignant l'ensemble de la « famille », donc, en traduction littérale, « le gouverneur », « le gouverné », et « le siège de la gouvernance »[46]. De cet éven-

[45] On ne connaît qu'un passage où la racine paraît sous forme assez clairement verbale : RS 2.[009]⁺ vi 45-50 (*CTA* 6) : *špš* (46) *rpỉm tḥtk* (47) *špš tḥtk ỉlnym* (48) *ʿdk ỉlm hn mtm* (49) *ʿdk kṯrm ḥbrk* (50) *w ḫss dʿtk* « Ô *Šapšu*, tu gouvernes les *rapaʾūma*, / Ô *Šapšu*, tu gouvernes les êtres divins. // Avec toi (sont) les divins voici défunts, / avec toi *Kôṯaru* ton allié, / avec toi *Ḫasīsu* ton intime ». Bien que d'autres formes de la racine expriment le rapport père – fils (et fils – père), le fait que la déesse solaire gouverne le séjour des morts montre que la définition de base ne comporte pas la notion de la *patria potestas*, comme on l'affirme parfois. Le nom commun exprimant le sens de base de « pouvoir » est attesté dans une série de termes qui paraît deux fois, et qui illustre le sens de base du mot : *ʿz* … *ḏmr* … *lản* … *ḥtk* … *nmrt*, « la force, la protection, la puissance, la gouvernance, la splendeur divine » (RS 24.252:21′-25′ [*KTU* 1.108]). Voir O. LORETZ, « Ugaritische Lexikographie », *SEL* 12 (1995) 105-20, 114-15, qui présente très bien la diversité d'usage. La distribution sémantique est assez clairement a : b, a′ : b′, c (où les « a » désignent la puissance de base, les « b » des variétés de la puissance (celle qui protège, celle qui gouverne), et « c » la manifestation visible de la puissance divine. Il va sans dire que ces deux textes et ceux qui seront cités dans la note suivante mériteraient commentaire ; mais l'espace imparti ne le permet pas.

[46] Le premier usage se rencontre deux fois dans le texte de la première tablette du Cycle de *Baʿlu*, les deux passages fort abîmés mais de reconstitution vraisemblable, chaque fois dans un message du dieu *ʾIlu*, le premier adressé au dieu artisan *Kôṯaru-wa-Ḫasīsu*, le second à la déesse *ʿAnatu* (RS 3.361 iv 5′-6′, v 17′-18′ [*CTA* 1 III, II – ordre de lecture inverse !]).

tail assez large d'acceptions pour si peu d'attestations réelles, seul l'un de ces termes utilisés dans une formule nouvelle servant de qualificatif du « dieu de la flamme » paraît plausible, peut-être *bn ḥtk*, « fils du gouverneur (paternel) », avec renvoi assez clair à la formule bien connue *bn dgn* et la variante *ḥtk dgn* – renvoi assez clair par sa vocalisation /binu ḥātiki/, car, dans la formule *ḥtk dgn*, le premier mot présentait sans doute la forme /ḥatūku/, « le gouverné ». Si la lecture est admissible, il s'agirait d'une épithète nouvelle de *Baʿlu*, et sa fonction dans le passage aurait été d'identifier le « dieu de la flamme », épithète à vrai dire passablement surprenante, vu le nombre de fois que des formes de la racine N(W/Y)R servent pour qualifier la déesse *Šapšu* (voir plus haut, commentaire de la ligne 1).

Ligne 3. La lecture du premier signe comme un {g} paraissant claire, on est obligé d'admettre la présence ici d'un mot {ghl}, pour lequel on ne trouve pas de parallèle précis, c'est-à-dire en même temps phonétique et sémantique, dans les langues sémitiques : voir le long commentaire historique de D. Clemens (p. 78-86), qui finit par accepter la dérivation de la racine *mediae infirmae* GYL, bien attesté en hébreu avec le sens de « se réjouir », interprété dans ce passage comme « éclats (de voix) ». Ce spécialiste a cité le verbe GHR, qui exprime un éclat de voix (RS 92.2014:11 [RSO XIV 52][47]) en ougaritique aussi bien qu'en hébreu biblique[48], parmi les « less plausible cognate roots » (p. 83) ; pourtant, si l'« échange » de /l/ et /r/ n'est pas fréquent en ougaritique[49], le nombre de cas est plus important lorsque l'on élargit la perspective à l'échelle du sémitique comparé,

Le deuxième n'est attesté qu'une fois, dans l'un des textes où *Baʿlu* est le sujet principal mais qui ne s'insère pas facilement dans le Cycle de *Baʿlu* : à RS 3.362⁺ iii 34 (*CTA* 10) on rencontre la formule *ḥtk dgn*, qualificatif de *Baʿlu* qui semble remplacer *bn dgn*. L'usage de *ḥtk* pour désigner la famille n'est attesté que dans la première colonne de la première tablette portant l'histoire de *Kirta*, d'abord sous la forme *ḥtkn* // *mknt* (on ne sait si {ḥtkn} constitue un schème nominal variant ou l'usage du *n*-enclitique), plus loin *ḥtk* // *ḥtk* // *ṯbt* : « la famille » // « l'établissement » … « la famille » // « la famille » // « le siège » (RS 2.[003]⁺ i 10-11, 21-23 [*CTA* 14]) – la famille en question était constituée sans doute des frères de *Kirta* avec leur progéniture, car *Kirta* n'avait encore ni de femme, ni d'enfants. Les trois termes pouvaient être prononcés /ḥātiku/ (participe actif), /ḥatūku/ (participe passif), et /ḥatku/ (forme nominale de base) ; le quatrième terme, celui qui signifie « la gouvernance » (cité à la note précédente), pouvait présenter la forme /ḥutku/, le schème /qutl/ étant typique des noms communs exprimant l'abstrait.

[47] Pierre Bordreuil et Dennis Pardee, « Une incantation », dans Marguerite Yon, Daniel Arnaud (éd.), *Études ougaritiques I. Travaux 1985-1995* (Ras Shamra–Ougarit XIV), Paris, Éditions Recherche sur les Civilisations, 2001, 387-92.

[48] Madadh Richey, « The Thunder of the Prophets : Elijah and Elisha's גה״ר (1 Kgs 18:42; 2 Kgs 4:34–35) », *ZAW* 131 (2019) 235-43.

[49] Josef Tropper, *Ugaritische Grammatik. Zweite, stark überarbeitete und erweiterte Auflage* (AOAT 273), Münster, Ugarit-Verlag, 2012, 155 (§ 33.135.4-5).

surtout aux époques archaïques[50]. Cela dit, on ne voudrait pas simplement faire appel dans ce cas au principe de l'échange de ces deux consonnes, car le nombre d'attestations des deux racines est trop réduit – il est sans doute plus prudent de penser à deux racines verbales distinctes mais dont le champ sémantique est similaire.

Ligne 4. Le sens de *nblủh* en ougaritique semble être établi par un passage du Cycle de *Baʿlu* où il est question des flammes par lesquelles passent des métaux précieux qui en sortent comme des matériaux propres à la construction du palais du dieu de l'orage, le mot paraissant plusieurs fois sous forme féminine (*nblảt*) et toujours en parallèle avec *ỉšt*, « feu ». Les objets qui sortent du feu sont désignés dans le texte comme des « briques » d'argent et d'or (*lbnt* en RS 2.[008] vi 35 [*CTA* 4]). Le parallélisme de *ỉšt* et *nblảt* dans ce dernier texte permet d'établir un lien avec RS 1.008 et la deuxième tablette du Cycle de *Baʿlu*, où les messagers de *Yammu* se présentent sous la forme « d'un feu, deux feux » (*ỉšt ỉštm*), la langue un glaive tranchant (*ḥrb lṭšt*) (*CTA* 2 iv 32-33 [ordre de lecture des colonnes inverse !]). L'identification des messagers de ce texte comme envoyés de *Yammu* est claire ; mais cela ne nous sert guère pour identifier le *ỉl nr* de RS 1.008, qui, lui, est seul, comme le montre le pronom suffixe *-h*, ce qui permet de conclure que la divinité en question n'est pas un simple messager, qu'il agit soit à son propre compte, soit comme plénipotentiaire d'un groupement divin. L'orthographe avec {ủ} de la forme masculine *nblủh* en RS 1.008 indique qu'il s'agit d'un nominatif, sans doute le sujet d'une phrase nominale. Cette analyse grammaticale oblige à prendre *ỉl nr* comme le référent du pronom suffixe, ce qui, vu le lien possible entre ce texte et RS 24.245 (*KTU* 1.101), où le dieu des foudres ne peut qu'être *Baʿlu*, indiquerait que ce dieu de la flamme est aussi *Baʿlu*. Ici c'est le dieu de la flamme qui raconte l'activité de *Šapšu*, avec peut-être des allusions à la recherche par *Šapšu* de la dépouille mortelle de *Baʿlu* – il s'agirait donc de *Baʿlu* qui raconte son propre passage par le domaine de la mort.

Il paraît nécessaire de lire le dernier mot de la ligne {ym˹h˺}, car on ne comprend ni {ym˹p˺}[51], ni {ym˹ỉ˺}. L'usage du suffixe adverbialisant *-h* est rare avec fonction temporelle : mais on ne voit ce que signifierait l'analyse de *ymh* comme « son jour », puisque la déesse solaire règne sur tous les jours.

[50] Michael P. Streck, « Eblaite and Old Akkadian », dans Stefan Weninger *et al.* (éd.), *The Semitic Languages. An International Handbook* (Handbücher zur Sprach- und Kommunikationswissenschaft 36), Berlin, De Gruyter, 2011, 340-59, 343.

[51] D. Clemens mentionne l'analyse du dernier signe comme un {p} pris pour la conjonction, ajoutant en note de bas de page : « It is difficult to find analogies for post-position of *p* as would be the case here » (p. 92 n. 142).

Ligne 5. *hlkt* étant marqué pour le genre féminin, il s'agit soit du perfectif (/halakat/), soit du participe (/hālik(a)tu/). En revanche, *tdrq* est connu en ougaritique comme nom commun, et on peut voir ici soit un nouvel exemple de ce mot, soit la première attestation de la racine sous forme de verbe qui pourrait être au schème-G ou D à l'imperfectif (l'analyse comme schème-tD au perfectif, 3e personne du masc. sing., avec nuance de répétition, obligerait d'admettre que le sujet du verbe ne soit pas identique à celui de *hlkt*)[52].

Ces diverses lectures et analyses permettent une reconstitution hypothétique de la première partie du texte sous la forme suivante :

(1) *b yn ỉš[ryt]*	Sous l'influence du vin ʾIŠRYT,
˹*ỉ*˺*l nr* (2) *spr*	le dieu de la flamme raconte,
˹*bn*˺ *ḥ*˹*t*˺*k*	le fils de celui qui gouverne ;
šbʿt (3) *ghl ph*	sept (sont) les retentissements de sa voix,
ṯmnt (4) *nblủh*	huit ses feux :
špš ym˹*h*˺ (5) *hlkt*	Pendant? le jour *Šapšu* marche,
tdrq [-]˹-˺[…]	d'un pas pressé …

Ligne 6. Étant donnée la distribution des formes de la particule *bʿd* en ougaritique, il paraît nécessaire d'admettre la notion du passage par une ouverture du type qui peut ensuite être fermée (voir, en particulier, RS 24.244:70-71 [*KTU* 1.100], où il s'agit d'une porte, et RS 2.002:70-71 [*CTA* 23], où il s'agit d'une brèche dans une clôture). Et, *Šapšu* étant le personnage principal nommé aux lignes 4-6, l'identifier comme le référent du pronom suffixe paraît logique, sans être certain, vu l'état du texte.

Lignes 7-8. Contrairement à ce que l'on trouve dans tel ou tel dictionnaire, il n'existe pas de passage en ougaritique où ʾṮR fonctionne certainement comme verbe, et il est sans doute préférable de voir ici un usage particulier soit de la préposition signifiant « derrière, après » (avec D. Clemens, p. 99), soit du nom commun signifiant « endroit », rare en ougaritique, bien que largement attesté en sémitique. Avec la première identification lexicale, le *-m* de *ảṯrm* serait nécessairement la particule enclitique. Avec l'identification comme nom commun, l'état du texte fait que l'on hésite devant l'analyse comme morphème du pluriel (« endroit des endroits »), du duel (« un endroit, deux endroits »), ou enclitique (« endroit, endroit = tout endroit = n'importe quel endroit »). L'attestation la plus claire du nom commun se rencontre dans une lettre : ˹*ả*˺*dm* (34) *ảṯr ỉṯ bqṯ* (35) *w štn ly* « Un homme, dans quelque endroit qu'il soit, cherche(-le) et fais-le moi

[52] D. Clemens préfère l'analyse comme verbe (p. 94) ; mais l'état du texte interdit de trancher.

parvenir » (RS 18.038 [*KTU* 2.39]). En revanche la préposition *ảṯr* s'emploie dans le mythe de *Baʿlu* pour exprimer le fait de descendre dans les entrailles de la terre après *Baʿlu* aussi bien que dans le rituel en forme poétique de la mise en tombe de l'avant-dernier roi d'Ougarit, ce langage étant certainement choisi en imitation du texte mythologique (CLEMENS évoque évidemment ces passages, de première importance pour son interprétation de RS 1.008 : voir *UF* 33, 97-100).

Ligne 9. Sans contexte, l'interprétation de {ìšdym} ne peut qu'être sujet de conjecture (voir D. CLEMENS, pp. 102-3).

Lignes 10-11. Le mot *ủdmʿt*, entier et bien conservé, désigne sans aucun doute les « larmes », et toute l'interprétation du texte comme en rapport avec les lamentations pour *Baʿlu* défunt découle de ce mot. À ce jugement, on peut ajouter que l'interprétation de *bk*, ligne 9, comme forme de BKY, « pleurer », convient facilement à cette façon de voir le passage, car on n'a rencontré aucun exemple de morphème de la 2e personne dans ce texte, et prendre le {b} pour la préposition présente par conséquent peu d'attrait.

CONCLUSION

Rien n'est facile dans l'interprétation de ce texte dont le support est fâcheusement abîmé, car les termes ou formules que l'on peut entrevoir comme faisant allusion à des passages que l'on comprend mieux sont en fait différents, au point que l'on se sent obligé de déplorer le véritable état de notre compréhension du texte.

RS 1.031 (copie de l'auteur fig. 6)

= M3358 = *CTA* 175 = *UT* 31 = *KTU/CAT/KCAT* 7.43

Dimensions : hauteur 50 mm ; largeur 34 mm ; épaisseur 19 mm.

État : partie inférieure droite de tablette dont seulement le *recto* est conservé ; l'angle inférieur droit a disparu, mais la courbe de la partie inférieure de la tranche droite marque le tournant vers cette tranche.

Caractéristiques épigraphiques : la main n'est pas identique à celle de RS 1.008. L'espacement des lignes sur les deux fragments n'est pas identique, le texte de RS 1.008 étant plus serré que celui du petit fragment. Bien que peu de signes soient conservés sur le petit fragment RS 1.031, on remarque que les clous de ce dernier texte ont souvent l'air plus fin que ceux de RS 1.008 (par exemple, les clous du {k}, premier signe de RS 1.031, sont plus fins que dans les signes de ce type de l'autre texte, de sorte qu'il existe un espace assez important sur le plan vertical entre les deux premières têtes de clou). Les clous verticaux des {b} de RS 1.031 étaient plus longs que d'habitude de sorte que la pointe de ces clous est visible sous le bord inférieur des clous horizontaux (ce n'est pourtant pas le cas ni du {ủ}, l. 3′, ni du {d}, l. 4′) ; les deux clous inférieurs et le dernier clou du {r} à la ligne 5′ font marches d'escalier, chacune des pointes étant visible ; le {ṯ} est composé d'un clou vertical et d'un clou qui doit être qualifié d'oblique, car, bien que le bord inférieur soit presqu'à la horizontale, le bord gauche est penché plus à droite que ne l'est ce bord d'un clou horizontal typique. Une caractéristique commune aux deux mains est celle de la pose de bas en haut des clous de signes composés de clous horizontaux superposés (voir surtout le {ỉ} à la ligne 6′).

Lieu de trouvaille : Acropole, Maison du Grand-prêtre.

Editio princeps : Ch. VIROLLEAUD, *Syria* 10 (1929), pl. LXXIII (copie seule) ; *editio secunda* : A. HERDNER, *CTA* (1963), p. 264-65, nº 175 (la copie, fig. 254, est celle de Virolleaud ; photographie pl. LXXXIII).

Texte

Recto

1′) [...]klm
2′) [...]tṯb
3′) [...]⸢ṯ⸣b . ủgrt
4′) [...]nbdgn
5′) [...]⸢ḫ⸣mrbn
6′) [...   ]. ỉn
7′) [...   ]⸢ả⸣⸢ṯ⸣⸢tḫ⸣n
8′) [   ]n
9′) [...   ]
10′) [...   ]n
....

REMARQUES TEXTUELLES

Nous reportons au début de ces remarques les deux transcriptions fondées sur l'examen de l'original, suivies de celle de *KCAT* 1.45 pour marquer le contraste entre ce texte et le texte indiqué pour 7.43[53] :

[53] À l'exception de l'usage de trois points pour indiquer la lacune à gauche de largeur inconnue (au lieu d'un grand espace blanc de largeur variable), nous portons les deux textes ici avec les normes de transcription des auteurs : (1) espace avant et après le point de séparation dans *CTA*, aucun espace dans *KTU* ; (2) les trois alif notés par l'alif à gauche de la voyelle dans *CTA*, par simple voyelle dans *KTU* ; (3) signes abîmés suivis d'astérisque dans *KTU*.

CTA 175	*KTU* 7.43[54]	*KCAT* 1.45:11-18
1) [...]		
1) [...]*klm*	2) [...]klm	11) u*dmʿt* . *d klm*
2) [...]*ṯṯb*	3) [...]nṯb	12) [xxx] . *bn* . ṯ*ṯb*
3) [... *t*]*ṯb* . *ʾugrt*	4) [...]xṯ*b.ugrt	13) [xxx xx]ṯ*b* . *ugrt*
4) [...]*nbdgn*	5) [...]nbgdn	14) [xxx xxx]*nbdgn*
5) [...]*ḫmrbn*	6) [...]ḫmrbn	15) [xxx xxxx]*zmrd*
6) [...]. *ʾin*	7) [...].in	16) [xxx xxx xx]. *in*
7) [...]ṯm*n*	8) [...].ṯtgn	17) [xxx xxx xx]ṯ*tt* . *ḥn*
8) [...]*n*	9) [...]x	18) [xxx xxx xxx]*n*[55]
9) [...]*n*	10) [...]n*	
11) [...]		

On ne voit pas pourquoi les auteurs de *KTU/CAT/KCAT* indiquent une ligne dont aucun reste n'est conservé avant celle qu'A. Herdner a numéroté comme la première – le seul effet du procédé, qui n'est nullement typique de ces collections, est de créer un décalage inutile dans la numérotation des autres lignes par rapport à *CTA*. Nous citerons le texte selon le nombre de lignes en fait conservées sur la tablette, en accord avec *CTA* pour les lignes 1′ à 8′.

2′) L'identification du premier signe comme un {t} nous paraît certaine (avec *CTA*, contre *KTU/CAT/KCAT*, où est enregistré un {n} certain – ici la personne responsable de la nouvelle transcription de *KCAT* 1.45 a vu juste) : devant le long clou horizontal qui, à l'exception de son angle supérieur gauche, est très bien conservé, on ne trouve aucune trace des autres

[54] La lecture des signes est inchangée dans *CAT /KCAT* 7.43 (à l'exception de la correction de la coquille à la ligne 5 : la bonne lecture de {nbdgn} est indiquée à *KCAT* 7.43:5 aussi bien qu'à *KCAT* 1.45:14 – voir ici la colonne de droite). La méthode de présentation est pourtant modifiée : la tentative de représenter l'alignement vertical des signes le long de la cassure à gauche par un espace blanc de largeur variable est abandonnée en faveur de l'indication d'un vide à longueur invariable (l'ancienne méthode est retenue dans la transcription de *KCAT* 1.45:11-18 comme on le verra ici à la colonne de droite, avec, en plus, des « x » pour indiquer avec précision le nombre de signes que l'auteur de la nouvelle transcription estime être tombés), un espace est ajouté avant et après le point de séparation et les signes bien conservés sont portés en corps italique, les signes abîmés en corps romain.

[55] Il s'agit certainement du signe transcrit par « x » dans *KTU/CAT/KCAT*, qui est en fait un {n} bien conservé, pas du signe bien rendu par {n} à la ligne 10 de *KTU/CAT/KCAT* 7.43. Le {n} à la ligne que nous portons comme la dixième dans notre transcription (voir plus bas, la remarque textuelle à propos de l'espace entre les lignes 8′ et 10′) est visible sur la photographie des Archives Schaeffer et sur les nôtres ; il est sans doute moins clair sur la photographie dont disposait la personne qui a créé ce nouveau texte. Comme cette personne ne s'est pas rendu compte qu'il s'agissait en fait de RS 1.031 (voir plus haut, histoire de l'étude des deux fragments), elle n'a pas consulté la copie de Ch. Virolleaud et l'édition d'A. Herdner, où deux lignes se terminant chacune par un {n} bien conservé sont indiquées.

angles inférieurs d'un {n} qui devraient y être visible s'il s'agissait de ce signe, au moins le premier en comptant de droite à gauche.

3′) La cassure traverse verticalement le {ṯ}, et par conséquent le « x » de *KTU/CAT/KCAT* ne peut correspondre qu'à un reste d'écriture se trouvant sur RS 1.008 (comme l'a vu l'auteur de la nouvelle transcription de *KCAT* 1.45). La copie de Ch. VIROLLEAUD reflète ce fait, et A. HERDNER a indiqué {[...]ṯb} dans sa transcription, bien que seulement la pointe inférieure droite du premier signe soit bien conservée.

4′) {nbgdn} dans *KTU/CAT* n'est qu'une coquille, corrigée dans *KCAT*[56].

Nous avons cru au premier examen que ce {g}, aussi bien que celui à la ligne suivante, montraient la forme archaïque qui consiste à être composée de deux clous. On voit bien deux têtes à ce premier exemple, mais l'agencement de ces clous n'est pas celui du {g} ainsi composé[57]. En effet, on voit nettement ici un petit clou vertical, mais trop petit pour être le clou principal d'un {g}, et, posé sur la partie droite de ce clou, un grand clou, ces deux clous pivotés un peu dans le sens inverse des aiguilles d'une montre au lieu d'être bien à la verticale comme le {g} à la ligne suivante. Il paraît donc que le scribe ait gravé un petit clou vertical, peut-être dans son esprit un clou séparateur et penché à gauche comme le séparateur plus à gauche dans cette ligne (contre cette identification doit pourtant compter le peu d'espace entre le signe précédent et le petit clou, et il s'agit peut-être donc d'une première tentative de graver le {g}, jugé trop petit, et pour raison). Ensuite il aurait corrigé cette erreur en posant un clou de taille normale pour un {g} sur la partie droite de ce petit clou, avec le même angle de pose, sans essayer préalablement d'effacer le premier clou.

5′) Nous n'indiquons pas le {ḫ} comme une lecture certaine car, si le scribe avait laissé un peu d'espace entre les deux rangées d'un {y}, on ne verrait pas trace de cette première rangée – la lecture de {ḫ} est pourtant indiquée par le sens du texte (voir commentaire). La nouvelle lecture de {zmrd} de *KCAT* 1.45:15 est tout simplement hors de propos : le premier signe comporte certainement trois clous, comme l'ont bien vu tous les témoins oculaires, l'avant-dernier signe, bien qu'un peu abîmé, ne comporte certainement que quatre clous, et le {n} final est bien conservé. Il est sans doute nécessaire de postuler que ce dernier signe n'est pas visible

[56] Voir déjà M. DIETRICH, O. LORETZ, *Word-List of the Cuneiform Alphabetic Texts from Ugarit, Ras Ibn Hani and Other Places (KTU : second, enlarged edition)* (ALASP 12 : Münster : Ugarit-Verlag, 1996), p. 225.

[57] À ce sujet, voir D. PARDEE, « {g} as a Palaeographic Indicator in Ugaritic Texts », dans E. DEVECCHI (éd.), *Palaeography and Scribal Practices in Syro-Palestine and Anatolia in the Late Bronze Age. Papers Read at a Symposium in Leiden, 17-18 December 2009* (PIHANS 119), Leiden, Nederlands Instituut voor het Nabije Oosten, 2012, p. 111-26.

sur la photographie dont disposait l'auteur de cette transcription, comme, d'ailleurs, sur celle de la planche LXXXIII de *CTA*, sans doute effet de la manipulation du négatif en vue de l'impression, car le signe est parfaitement visible sur la même photographie conservée sous forme de négatif dans les Archives Schaeffer (reproduite ici plus bas, figure 1).

7′) Au bord de la lacune à gauche on voit un angle de clou qui n'est pas assez bien conservé pour permettre de déterminer avec certitude s'il s'agit de la pointe d'un clou horizontal ou de l'angle supérieur droit d'un clou vertical (la copie de Virolleaud fait penser à la seconde identification ; la trace est portée comme séparateur dans les transcriptions de *KTU*/*CAT*/*KCAT*, comme l'angle supérieur droit d'un {ṯ} dans la nouvelle transcription de *KCAT* 1.45). Pourtant, à regarder de près, il semble que le bord supérieur suit un angle montant, ce qui fait préférer l'identification comme clou horizontal. Ensuite, on se rend compte que la pointe des signes se terminant par un clou horizontal est située haut par rapport au signe suivant : la comparaison avec {tṯ}, l. 2′ est particulièrement significative, car la pointe du {t} se situe par rapport au {ṯ} comme ici, un peu plus bas que l'angle supérieur gauche du {ṯ}.

La lecture du ou des signe(s) suivant le {ṯ} est tout sauf certaine ; il s'agit soit de {m} (*CTA*), soit de {t⸢g⸣} (*KTU*/*CAT*/*KCAT* – rien n'appuie la lecture de {. ḫ} de la nouvelle transcription de *KCAT* 1.45), soit de {t⸢z/ḫ⸣}. La partie inférieure du clou de droite est assez bien conservé, alors que toute la partie supérieure est abîmé. Dans la partie inférieure, on croit voir un angle de clou à droite et à la hauteur de ce qui serait la tête du clou inférieur de {z,ḫ} (voir notre copie). Le mot hourrite *ảṯtḫ*, « féminin » étant attesté trois fois sous trois formes différentes ({ảṯtḫ[n]}, {ảṯtḫnm} et {ảṯtḫ}) dans le paragraphe XVI (l. 54-59) du texte hourrite en écriture alphabétique RS 1.004 (*CTA* 166, *KTU* 1.42), on est attiré vers la lecture ici de {⸢ả⸣ṯ⸢t⸣ḫ⸣n} « les féminins », vraisemblablement précédé de *ỉn*, c'est-à-dire « les divinités féminines », comme à RS 1.004:55, en opposition avec *ỉn trḫn*, « les dieux masculins »[58].

8′-10′) L'espace entre les deux signes visibles paraît suffisant pour permettre d'envisager la présence sur la tablette originale d'une ligne d'écriture supplémentaire (Herdner, suivie par les auteurs de *KTU*/*CAT*/*KCAT*, n'a compté que deux lignes ici ; comme il a été remarqué en commentant dans la note 55 la nouvelle transcription de *KCAT* 1.45, le signe à la ligne 8′ est un {n} bien conservé, et on ne comprend pas la transcription par « x » dans *KTU*/*CAT*/*KCAT* 7.43:9).

[58] Voir l'exégèse de ce texte par LAROCHE, *Ugaritica* V, 447-544, 518-27.

Commentaire

N'ayant pas de compétences en hourrite, nous nous limitons à quelques observations de dilettante. Il est évident que la plupart des termes assez bien conservés pour en permettre l'interprétation correspondent à des théonymes : *Teṯṯob* (l. 2′), [*Te*]*ṯṯob* d'Ougarit (l. 3′), *Nubadig* (l. 4′)[59], [*Ḫebat*] de l'édifice cultuel-*ḫamri* (l. 5′)[60], ou aux nom communs « dieu(x) » (l. 6′)[61] et « déesses » (l. 7′)[62]. Aucun des théonymes ne porte le morphème {-d} marquant au singulier le datif en hourrite, forme courante dans les textes sacrificiels hourro-ougaritiques où des offrandes sont attribuées aux divinités nommées, et par conséquent il s'agit vraisemblablement d'un autre genre de texte. Les signes {klm} étant isolés après la cassure à la ligne 1′, on ne peut être certain qu'il s'agisse d'un mot entier ; mais, cela dit, il pourrait correspondre au mot *klm* attesté à RS 1.004:2 (*CTA* 166, *KTU* 1.42) dont l'interprétation n'est pas parfaitement établie[63]. Les recoupements entre ce texte et RS 1.004 se limitent à ce mot *klm* et la mention de théonymes, en particulier les *åṯṯḫn* « divinités féminines » (si la lecture est admise), peut-être aussi les « dieux masculins », indices trop ténus pour

[59] Laroche, *Glossaire*, 186. Le théonyme se rencontre dans quatre textes hourro-ougaritiques en écriture alphabétique (Pardee, *Les textes rituels*, 1184). Vu l'association de cette divinité avec le toponyme anatolien *Bibita*, il paraît légitime d'entrevoir un rapport entre ce dieu hourrite et le dieu sémitique *Rašap* dont la demeure principale, selon la tradition ougaritique, était fixée en ce lieu (voir M. Barré, « dLAMMA and Rešep at Ugarit: The Hittite Connection », *JAOS* 98, 1978, 465-67).

[60] Laroche, *Glossaire*, 92 ; Schwemer, *Die Wettergottgestalten*, 255 n. 1774. D'après une photographie gros plan (projet PhoTEO, Mission de Ras Shamra) de la tranche gauche, partie centrale, de RS 1.004 (*CTA* 166, *KTU* 1.42), la lecture à la ligne 60 de {ḫbt . ḫmr'b'n}, postulée par Schwemer (contre « ḫbt ḫmr xb*n » de *KTU*, retenue dans *CAT*, devenue « *ḫbt ḫmr* [x]b*n* » *KCAT*), paraît plausible : la pointe du dernier clou du {r} a disparu dans la lacune, mais rien ne s'oppose à la restitution de ce clou avec longueur suffisante pour éliminer la nécessité de restituer un signe entier dans cette lacune. En tout cas, l'indication dans *KCAT* que le signe « x » serait à restituer entièrement est sans aucun doute préférable à celle d'un signe partiellement visible dans les éditions précédentes, car on ne retrouve trace de signe entre le {r}, à gauche de la fente, et la pointe du deuxième clou inférieur du {b} à droite.

[61] Puisque ce nom au singulier est le plus souvent « suivi d'épithètes ou de génitifs » (Laroche, *Glossaire*, 80 ; voir les exemples attestés dans les textes sacrificiels hourro-ougaritiques chez Pardee, *Les textes rituels*, 1114-15), il s'agit peut-être ici du pluriel en rapport de manière inconnue avec les théonymes peuplant le texte tel qu'il est conservé. D'après la nouvelle lecture de la ligne suivante, il pourrait s'agir des « dieux masculins », *ỉn trḫn*, comme en RS 1.004:55 – le scribe aurait réparti la formule sur deux lignes parce que l'espace était insuffisant pour les quatre signes du deuxième mot.

[62] Voir plus haut, la remarque textuelle.

[63] Laroche, *Glossaire*, 142-43 ; Joseph Lam, « A Reassessment of the Alphabetic Hurrian Text RS 1.004 (KTU 1.42) : A Ritual Anointing of Deities ? », *JANER* 11 (2011) 148-69, 163-64.

permettre de proposer que les deux textes appartiennent au même genre littéraire ; mais la possibilité qu'il s'agisse d'un texte rituel non-sacrificiel se trouve quelque peu appuyée par ces menus points de comparaison. Vu l'absence de tout mot ougaritique et les points communs avec RS 1.004, il faut au moins privilégier l'identification comme texte entièrement hourrite.

Le seul indice possible de la largeur de la tablette originale s'identifie aux lignes 6′-7′, où l'on pense à restituer {[…] . ỉn (7′) [trḫ̮n . ỉn .] ⸢ả⸣ṯ⸢ḫ̮⸣n} à l'instar de RS 1.004:55. La restitution est certes plausible mais loin d'être certaine. Elle permettrait d'estimer la largeur de la tablette comme étant d'environ 55 mm, hauteur inconnue, donc tablette environ la moitié plus petite que RS 1.004, qui mesure 155 mm de haut et 111 mm de large[64]. La tranche inférieure et le *verso* du fragment étant détruits, on a perdu tout indice de la longueur du texte original, qui pourtant, si l'estimation approximative de la taille de la tablette qui vient d'être suggérée est admise, ne pouvait guère dépasser, si toute les surfaces étaient inscrites, environ trente-cinq lignes, chacune comportant en général pas plus de quinze signes (séparateurs inclus).

Conclusion

RS 1.031 est sans doute à identifier comme un fragment de texte hourrite monolingue dont principalement des théonymes sont conservés. Le texte ne comporte pas les marqueurs du datif typiques des textes sacrificiels hourrites, ce qui semble obliger à l'identifier comme appartenant à un autre genre de rituel.

[64] Herdner, *CTA*, p. 255 ; Lam, *JANER* 11, 150. Les dimensions « 130 × 101 » indiquées dans P. Bordreuil et D. Pardee, *La trouvaille épigraphique*, 16, sont manifestement fausses.

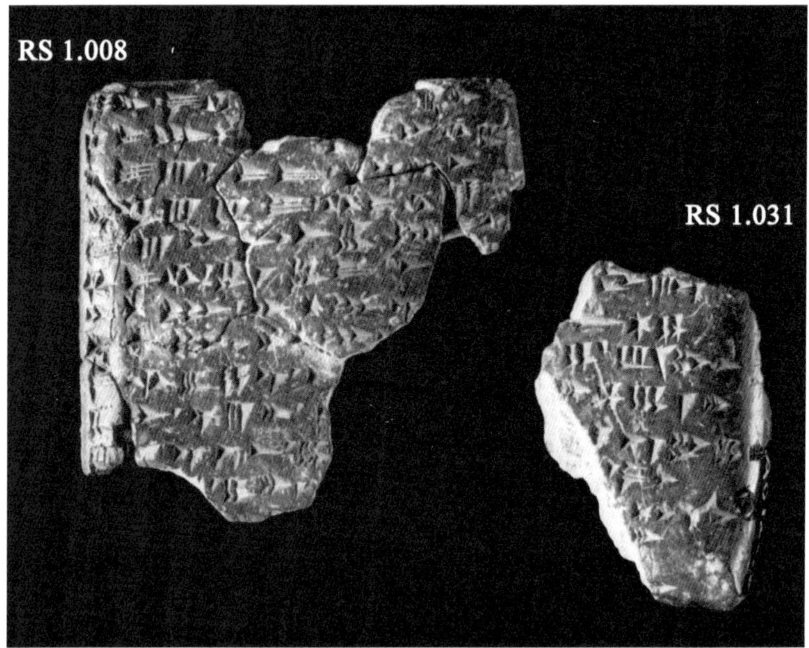

Figure 1: Les fragments RS 1.008 et RS 1.031
(photographie Archives Schaeffer)

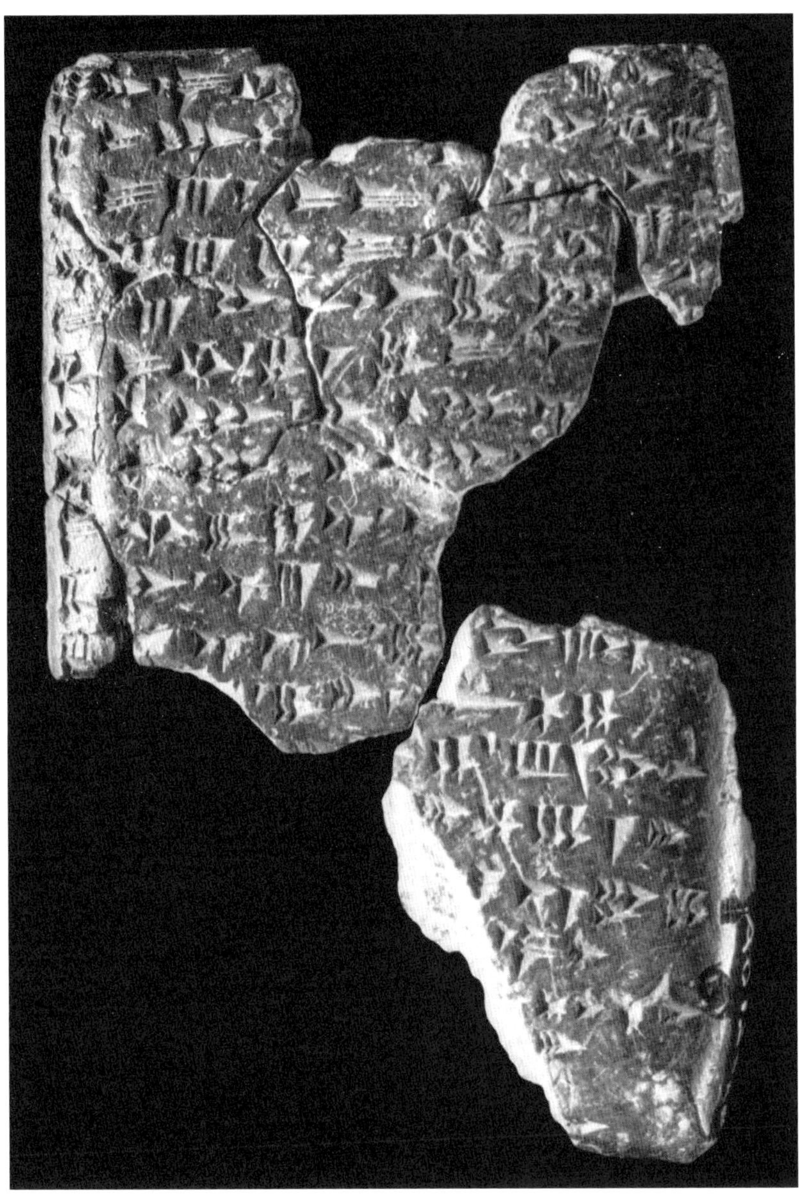

Figure 2: Les deux fragments de la figure 1 rapprochés pour illustrer le joint malvenu

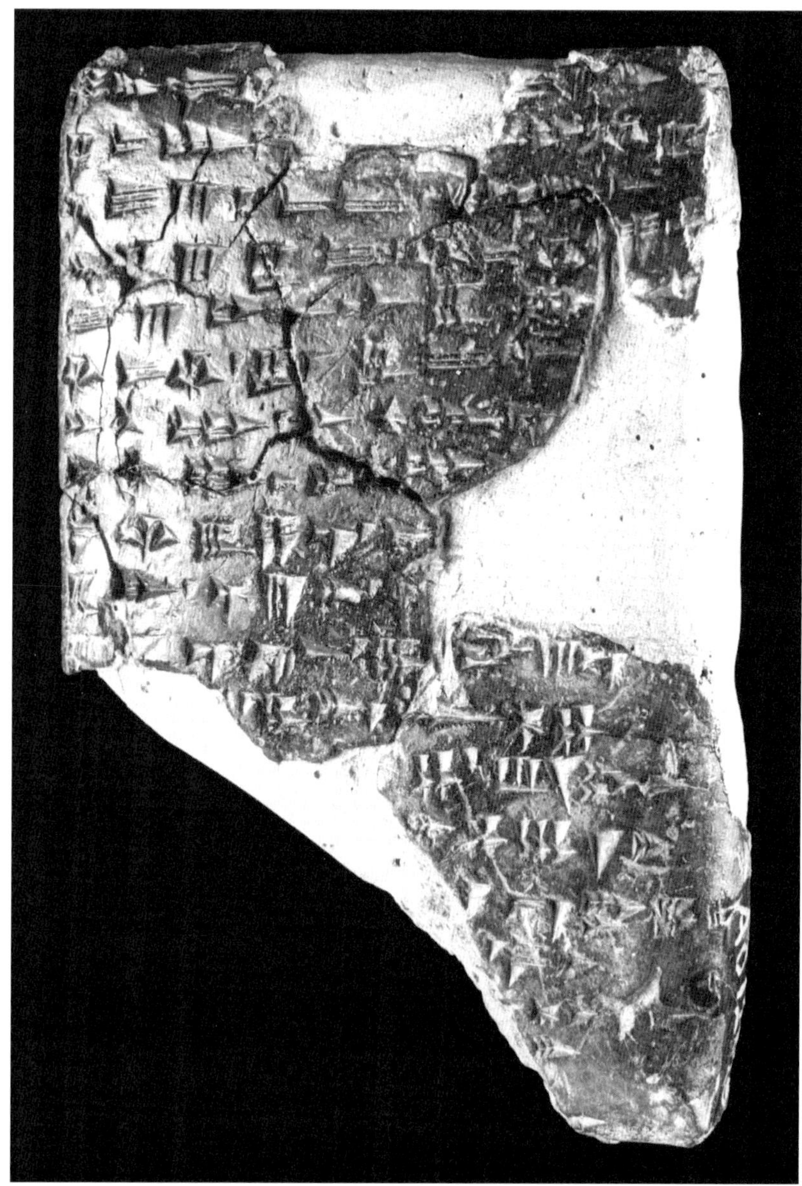

Figure 3: Le joint malvenu des deux fragments
(photographie Archives Schaeffer)

Figure 4: Le joint malvenu des deux fragments
(photographie de l'auteur, 2009)

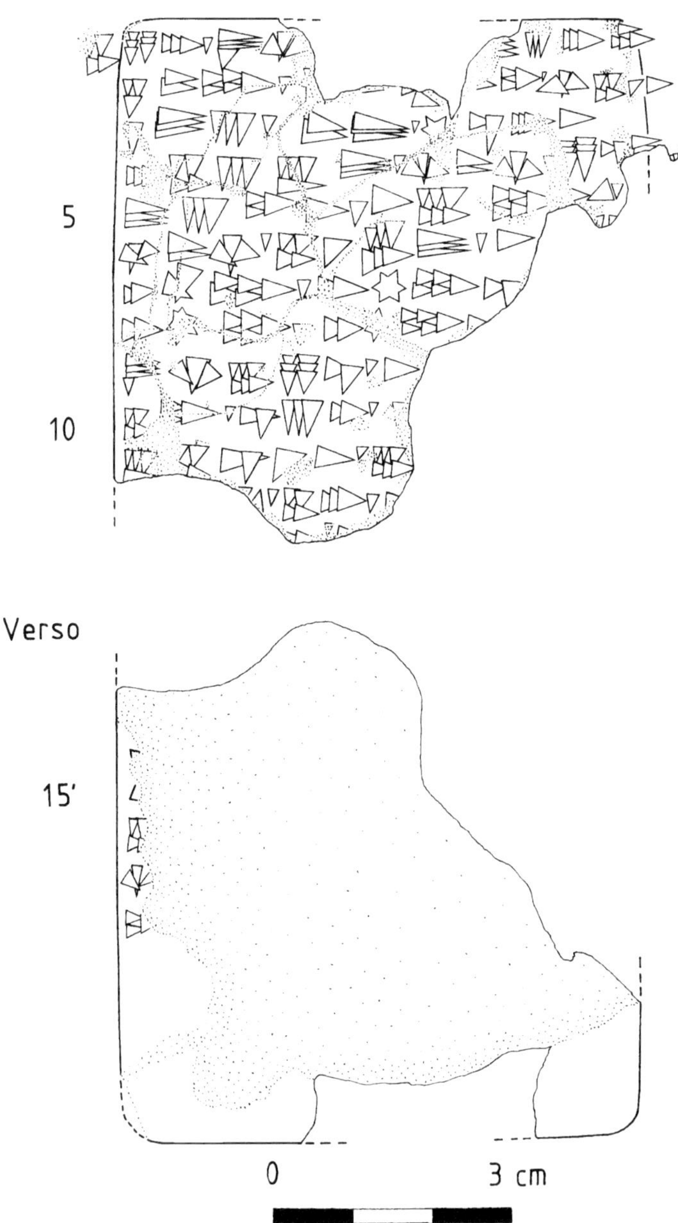

Figure 5: RS 1.008 (copie de l'auteur)

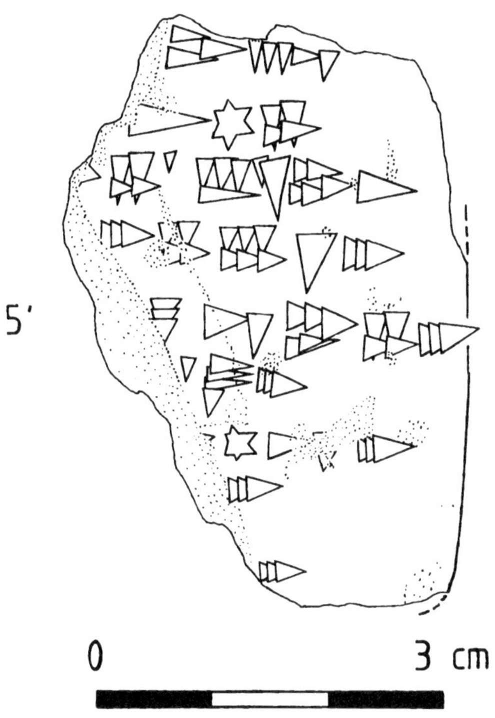

Figure 6: RS 1.031 (copie de l'auteur)

"NUVOLA DI FANGO" OPPURE "PEGNO"? UNA PSEUDO-VARIANTE DI AB 2,6

Massimo Pazzini

1. Ab 2,6 in alcune traduzioni italiane

Nell'ambito della *critica textus* Ab 2,6[1] è un versetto complesso, specialmente nella prima parte, mentre le parole finali non sembrano sollevare problemi particolari tra gli esegeti.

Le traduzioni della Bibbia in lingua italiana, edite dalla Conferenza Episcopale Italiana (CEI) nel 1974 e nel 2008, traducono il versetto in maniera quasi identica:

Bibbia CEI 1974: "Forse che tutti non lo canzoneranno, non faranno motteggi per lui? Diranno: Guai a chi accumula ciò che non è suo, – e fino a quando? e si carica di pegni!".

Bibbia CEI 2008: "Forse che tutti non lo canzoneranno, non faranno motteggi per lui? Diranno: «Guai a chi accumula ciò che non è suo, – e fino a quando? – e si carica di beni avuti in pegno!»".

Le due versioni italiane differiscono solo nelle ultime parole del versetto ma senza evidenziare problemi testuali: "si carica di pegni!" (1974) e "si carica di beni avuti in pegno!" (2008). La Bibbia CEI 2008 cerca di chiarire ulteriormente ciò che, di per sé, è già abbastanza chiaro.

Anche le versioni in lingua italiana provenienti dall'ambiente evangelico propongono una traduzione simile della parte finale del versetto: "Guai a chi si carica di pegni" (Nuova Riveduta) e "Guai… a chi si carica di pegni" (Nuova Diodati)[2].

Le versioni italiane sopra menzionate sono dunque concordi nel tradurre "pegno" e non evidenziano alcun problema testuale.

[1] Dominique Barthélemy, *Critique textuelle de l'Ancien Testament*. 3. Ezéchiel, Daniel et les 12 prophètes (Orbis Biblicus et Orientalis 50), Éditions Universitaires; Vandenhoeck & Ruprecht: Fribourg-Suisse; Göttingen 1992, 846-847. Per il testo ebraico si veda Anthony Gelston (ed.), *The Twelve Minor Prophets* (*Biblia Hebraica Quinta editione cum apparatu critico novis curis elaborato*, 13), Deutsche Bibelgesellschaft, Stuttgart 2010.

[2] Citato da http://www.laparola.net/. [Consultato *online* il 18/3/2019]

2. Ab 2,6 nelle versioni antiche

La Peshiṭta e la Vulgata, a differenza della Septuaginta[3] e del Targum[4], hanno una traduzione fra loro simile dell'ultima parte del versetto la quale non corrisponde al Testo Masoretico (TM) e potrebbe fare pensare a una diversa *vorlage* ebraica.

Peshiṭta: *m'šn 'lwhy 'nn' dsyn'* (*ma'šen 'lawhy 'nōnō' dasyōnō'*), cioè "addensa su di sé una nuvola di fango".

Questa traduzione ci fa intendere che la Peshiṭta divide la parola ebraica *'aḇṭîṭ* "debito/pegno" in due parti, cioè *'aḇ* "nuvola" e *ṭîṭ* "fango", ottenendo due nuovi termini che significano "una nuvola di fango". Quindi il TM "Si carica di pegni/debiti" diventa, nella Peshiṭta, "addensa su di sé una nuvola di fango"[5].

Vulgata: *et adgravat contra se densum lutum*, " e appesantisce (accumula) a proprio danno denso fango".

Come la Peshiṭta anche la Vulgata scompone la parola ebraica *'aḇṭîṭ* in due parti che però sono costituite dalle stesse consonanti e dalle medesime vocali della parola intera. Differisce lievemente dalla siriaca in quanto interpreta il nome ebraico *'aḇ* nel senso di "denso" o "spesso"[6].

La lezione delle due versioni appena ricordate è condivisa dal rotolo dei Profeti minori proveniente dal Naḥal Ḥever nel deserto di Giuda (8HevXIIgr) dove si legge: *páchos pēloû*[7] "spessore di fango", espressione che deriva anch'essa dalla medesima divisione di *'aḇṭîṭ* in due parti.

[3] La LXX traducendo "appesantisce fortemente il suo collare" trasmette l'immagine del debito come collare o giogo che stringe il collo dello sfruttatore. Si veda in proposito Sandro Paolo Carbone–Giovanni Rizzi, *Abaquq, Abdia, Nahum, Sofonia: secondo il testo ebraico masoretico, secondo la versione greca della LXX, secondo la parafrasi aramaica targumica* (Lettura ebraica, greca e aramaica, 4), EDB, Bologna 1997, 116-117. La lezione della LXX può essere supportata filologicamente dalla lettura variante di *'ālāw* (scritta *defective* come nel *Pesher* di Abacuc a Qumran) interpretata come *'ullô* "il suo giogo". Si veda in proposito Dominique Barthélemy, *Les devanciers d'Aquila*. Première publication intégrale du texte des fragments du Dodécaprophéton trouvés dans le désert de Juda, précédée d'une étude sur les traductions et recensions grecques de la Bible réalisées au premier siècle de notre ère sous l'influence du rabbinat palestinien (Supplements to "Vetus Testamentum" 10), Brill, Leiden 1963, 188-190.

[4] Il Targum traduce: "(fino a quando) tu aggraverai su di te la forza dei peccati/debiti?". Passa dalla terza alla seconda persona, ma mantiene l'idea del debito o peccato grave che pesa sul colpevole. Si veda la discussione in S.P. Carbone–G. Rizzi, *Abaquq*, 116-117.

[5] Gillian Greenberg (ed.), *The Book of the Twelve Minor Prophets According to the Syriac Peshitta Version with English Translation*, english translation by Donald M. Walter, Gillian Greenberg; text prepared by George A. Kiraz, Joseph Bali, (The Antioch Bible), Gorgias Press, Piscataway 2012, XXXV.

[6] Come avviene in Es 19,9: "Ecco, io sto per venire verso di te in una *densa* nube..." (lett.: "nella densità della nube").

[7] D. Barthélemy, *Les devanciers d'Aquila*, 189; Emanuel Tov, *The Greek Minor Prophets Scroll from Naḥal Ḥever* (8HevXIIgr). The Seiyâl Collection I (Discoveries in the Judaean Desert 8), Clarendon, Oxford, 1995, 53.

L'accordo così evidente fra queste tre versioni potrebbe fare pensare a una diversa *vorlage* ebraica. In realtà non ci sono elementi sufficienti per sostenere questa suggestiva ipotesi per i motivi riportati qui di seguito.

3. Una libera interpretazione di Peshiṭta, Vulgata e 8HevXIIgr

La parola ebraica *'aḇṭîṭ*, intera o divisa in due parti, contiene le stesse consonanti e le medesime vocali, cioè *'aḇ* e *ṭîṭ*. Dunque l'interpretazione delle versioni non implica un cambiamento nella loro fonte. Possiamo, però, chiederci quali siano gli elementi che hanno indotto gli antichi traduttori a questa scelta.

Da un lato la parola ebraica *'aḇṭîṭ* è un *hapax* nell'AT, quindi il significato del sostantivo mantiene un certo margine di incertezza. Invece le parole *'aḇ* e *ṭîṭ* sono più frequenti – rispettivamente 31 e 13 volte – anche se non compaiono mai insieme. Forse la rarità del termine ebraico ha aperto la porta ad una diversa e suggestiva interpretazione basata sulla divisione in due parole meglio conosciute. L'immagine plastica che ne scaturisce rende assai bene la gravità della situazione.

D'altra parte può essere illuminante il ricorso al verbo *'āḇaṭ* "prendere in prestito, prendere un pegno" (6 volte)[8] e al sost. *'ăḇôṭ* "pegno" (4 volte). Questi termini, appartenenti alla stessa radice, a mio avviso chiariscono a sufficienza il senso di *'aḇṭîṭ* nel nostro contesto.

Infine non è da sottovalutare la tendenza o libertà delle antiche versioni – nel nostro contesto Peshiṭta, Vulgata e 8HevXIIgr – a spiegare termini difficili o rari in forma midrashica e dotta.

Per questi motivi si deve parlare di pseudo-variante e non di variante vera e propria. La scelta operata da Peshiṭta, Vulgata e 8HevXIIgr è da considerarsi una libera interpretazione suggestiva e, in un certo senso, anche motivata, che però non procede da una variante del testo ebraico.

[8] Il verbo compare due volte al Qal "prendere un pegno" (Dt 24,10 e 15,6); una volta al Piel "contorcere" (Gl 2,7: "non contorceranno (= smarriranno) la loro strada"); tre volte all'Hifil "prestare contro pegno" (Dt 15,6.8).

I HAVE ENGRAVED YOU ON THE PALMS OF THE HANDS. ISA 49:16

Łukasz POPKO, O.P.

1. IT IS ABOUT AN IMAGE

In one of the restoration poems of the so-called *Book of Consolation*, Isa 49:14-21, YHWH speaks directly to the personified feminine Zion[1]. She is speaking of YHWH in the 3rd person, which presumes a certain virtual absence of God, or at least it rhetorically expresses his remoteness.

14. Zion has said:

"He has abandoned me, YHWH. And my Lord **has forgotten** me"

In the following lines, God speaks to Zion as to a mother bereaved of her family. It is less clear if YHWH sees himself as her husband (in deed the title אֲדֹנָי in v. 14 may suggest it). In v. 15, YHWH takes over the last verb from her complaint, "he has forgotten" (שׁכח), to refute it three times.

15. Can a woman **forget** her infant? From her womb, a son of her belly?
Even **they can forget**, but I, I shall **not forget**.
16. Behold:

On the palms [of hands] I have engraved you.
Your walls are before me all the time.
הֵן עַל־כַּפַּיִם חַקֹּתִיךְ חוֹמֹתַיִךְ נֶגְדִּי תָּמִיד
17. Your sons have hurried! Your destroyers and devastators will depart…

Since the restored Zion is further, in v. 21, depicted as a mother with numerous children, the comparison with a woman forgetting her baby creates a direct contrast between human and divine fidelity: human memory can be helpless, YHWH's memory is effective and life-bringing.

[1] For the discussion concerning the placement of this pericope in the overall structure of the book see Ulrich BERGES, *Jesaja 49-54* (HthKAT), Freiburg im Breisgau, Herder Verlag, 2015, 27-29. He sees here the beginning of a larger unit, 49:14 – 52:12. This can be further divided into three parts: 14-21 ended with a *petuhah*; 22-23 with a *setumah*, and 24-26 again with a *setumah*. See also: Rosario Pio MERENDINO, "Jes 49,14-26: Jahwes Bekenntnis zu Sion und die Neue Heilszeit", *RB* 89 (1982) 321-369.

Verse 16, which is the object of our present study, serves as a turning point of the poem[2]. In a way of a rhetorical enthymeme (הֵן – *Behold!*), YHWH seems to be showing something to the Lady Zion, something on the palms of his hands. This demonstration is to convince her of his long-lasting and saving remembrance. Subsequently, v. 17 and the following verses will speak only about the renewal and reconstruction of the city.

The direct context makes it clear what the v. 16a should mean: YHWH's act shows that he did not and could not forget Zion. Any explanation of His gesture must take into account this fundamental association with memory and remembrance. Although the term *zikkaron* does not appear here, we are dealing clearly with the semantic field of remembrance, and YHWH's act can be therefore be understood as a kind of memorial.

The brief phrase עַל־כַּפַּיִם חַקֹּתִיךְ was sometimes explained as an idiomatic, fixed expression, a type of proverbial saying without any reference to any actual image or custom. For example, Charles Torrey wrote that this verse is "undoubtedly a long-familiar figure of speech, this and nothing more"[3]. The very concept of "this and nothing more" seems to me to be something very foreign to poetry and foreign to any tradition-based literature. My point in this paper will be, on the one hand, to deal with this text as with a true "living" metaphor; i.e. a new and creative expression which affects our understanding and which was created for the sake of this poem. On the other hand, I will try to point to some parallel phenomena from the ancient culture which should shed light on this potent and complex message conveyed in this Isaianic line.

2. What did YHWH do?

If the deictic particle הֵן intends to bring Lady Zion's attention to something to be seen, a kind of display, we should ask: what is to be seen? A brief review of the history of interpretation should demonstrate that we have not yet *seen* it clearly.

[2] The poem is composed of two regular 7-line cantos: 14-18 and 19-21. V. 16, together with v. 17, creates a 2-line pivotal centre of the first strophe. See: Pieter van der Lugt, "Form, Context and Meaning of Isa 49,14-21", in: Stefan M. Attard, Marco Pavan (ed.), *"Canterò in eterno le misericordie del Signore" (Sal 89,2). Studi in onore del prof. Gianni Barbiero in occasione del suo settantesimo compleanno* (AnBib.S, 3), Roma, Gregorian & Biblical Press, 2015, 121-141, 124-126.

[3] Torrey Charles Cutler, *The Second Isaiah. A New Interpretation*, New York, Charles Scribner's Sons, 1928, 386. It is telling that Torrey does not quote any other occurrence of this presumed well-known idiom.

2.1. On the palms of hands

The first notable difficulty is how to interpret the prepositional phrase עַל־כַּפַּיִם or to what exact body part the noun כַּף refers to. The fact that MT does not mention the owner of כַּפַּיִם, is relatively easy to overcome. The dual כַּפַּיִם makes it sufficiently clear that one is speaking of the two hands of the same person and there is simply no better candidate than YHWH Himself. There are only two persons mentioned in this context, and YHWH cannot possibly show Zion her own hands. It just would not make much sense[4].

Some Biblical texts suggest that the noun כַּף can be more precisely specified as a cupped hand so that one could place in it a sacrificial gift, as in Lev 14:15-17. On the other hand, in Isa 49, the inside part of the palm of the hand seems to be less probable, if we are to interpret this image as something that is "before me always". First of all, the inside part of the palm is not a place of display, or at least is less so than the outside of the hand. Secondly, if one would consider it as a tattoo, the palm hand is virtually never used. The inside palm is one of the most sensitive parts of the body, so "engraving" anything there means a very painful process and that is why it is virtually never done. Moreover, the palm is one of the worst places on the human body to paint or draw anything, for a tattoo or an incision made there vanishes much quicker and fades faster than on any other part of the body, and that goes against the main function of 'engraved palms' in Isaiah since they are to serve as a permanent reminder.

2.2. Interpretation of the Verb חָקַק

These last two difficulties can be dismissed if we agree that the body of YHWH can have qualities different from the human flesh. The use of the verb suggests that the author does not have in mind a *human* tattoo. The discussion on the body part cannot be detached from the considerations concerning the meaning of the verb חָקַק. As it often happens, we can find the range of interpretations already in the ancient translations. We can list them beginning with the literal meaning of חָקַק up to its more metaphorical uses, where what is important are not the material aspects of this action, but its results:

[4] To my knowledge only John Goldingay and David Payne considered the rendering: "on your palms I have engraved you [with my name]". Yet even they did not develop this possibility. See: John GOLDINGAY and David PAYNE, *A Critical and Exegetical Commentary on Isaiah 40-55*, vol. 2, (ICC), New York, London, T & T Clark, 2006, 186.

1) the physical aspect of the action: 'to cut in', 'to engrave'; see: hewing a tomb in Isa 22:16. This connotation was expressed by Symmachos (following Theodoret[5]): ἐπὶ τῶν χειρῶν μου ἐχάραξα (from χαράσσω) σε καὶ τα τείχη σου διὰ παντός ἄντικρυς κεῖται ἐμοῦ.
2) the physical result of the action: 'to draw', 'to delineate'; e.g. the image of Jerusalem in Ezek 4:1. Also in other occurrences, the object of the verb seems to be an architectural project: Prov 8:27: "when he delineated a circle on the face of *tehom*"; Prov 8:29: "to trace the foundations". This is also the choice made by the LXX: ἰδοὺ ἐπὶ τῶν χειρῶν μου ἐζωγράφησά σου τὰ τείχη καὶ ἐνώπιόν μου εἶ διὰ παντός ("Behold on my hands I depicted your walls and you are always before me"). The LXX rendered this Hebrew verb in the same manner in Ezek 23:14. According to the commentary by Theodoret of Cyr, Theodotion also translated: ἐπὶ τῶν χειρῶν μου διέγραψα (from διαγράφω).
3) the result of the action is an inscription: 'to inscribe' – i.e. with the use of letters in a book, like the divine judgments in Isa 30:8. There the verb expresses both the durability and the importance for the future. This was also the translation chosen by Aquila: ἐπι ταρσῶν ἠκρίβωσεν (from ἀκριβόω 'to ascertain') σε τείχη σου ἔναντι ἐμοῦ ἐνδελεχῶς.
4) a technical legal meaning: 'to decree', 'to make an order' derives from the above; see Isa 10:1[6].

Other ancient versions made some wise translation choices, for the corresponding cognate verb in Syriac has virtually the same set of connotations as the Hebrew חָקַק. Jerome's rendering *ecce in manibus meis descripsi te* loses the connotation of 'hewing' but otherwise the verb *describere* preserves a similar range of direct objects: an image, a writing, or a written law. It is therefore clear that any further specification of the meaning of the verb חָקַק must depend on the presumed object of inscription.

2.3. To Incise an Image?

The exact meaning of the 2nd fem. sing. suffix in חַקֹּתִיךְ raises the question of what exactly was "hewn" on God's palms. Probably the oldest solution can be found in the LXX, which presumes that it was the image of the walls of Zion. The translator divided the text differently than the MT and seems to have altogether omitted the suffix. It resulted in the

[5] In contrast, Procopius of Gaza attributes the meaning 'to engrave' (διεχάραξα) to Theodotion. See: Joseph ZIEGLER, *Isaias* (Septuaginta: Vetus Testamentum Graecum, 14), Göttingen, Vandenhoeck & Ruprecht, 1939, 308. This discrepancy of sources does not change anything for our argument.

[6] For the study of the legal connotations of this root see: Richard HENTSCHKE, *Satzung und Setzender: Ein Beitrag zur israelitischen Rechtsterminologie* (BWANT, 83), Stuttgart, Verlag W. Kohlhammer, 1963.

rendering ἐζωγράφησά σου τὰ τείχη "I have depicted your walls". The LXX presumes that an image was inscribed and not a script. The Targum to Isaiah, with a different phrasing, expresses the same idea: "Behold, *as* on *hands* you *are portrayed before me* (צירא); your walls are continually before me"[7].

Following the identification of the direct object with the walls of Jerusalem, the commentators on the LXX developed the interpretation of God as an architect. Thus, for example, Theodoret of Cyr wrote: "He predicts the reconstruction and teaches that He himself like an architect traces (οἷόν τις ἀπρχιτέκτων διαγράφει) the plan of the reconstruction"[8]. The direct context speaks about the reconstruction, and this fact further resulted in the conviction that the presumed image must have presented the future walls of the reconstructed Jerusalem[9].

A certain variant of this exegesis identified the rebuilt walls of Zion with her eschatological restoration[10]. This interpretation is not out of place in the context of the Book of Isaiah. As Franz Delitzsch noted, because the walls of Jerusalem are written on the palms of God, even if the city remains destroyed down below, she has a share with His eternal and heavenly existence[11].

Several commentators identified YHWH's inscription with the walls of Jerusalem, mostly because of the presumed synonymous parallelism with the following phrase and because of the lack of any better solution[12].

[7] Bruce D. CHILTON, *The Isaiah Targum* (ArBib, 11), Collegeville, MN, The Liturgical Press, 1987, 97.

[8] THÉODORET de Cyr, *Commentaire sur Isaïe. Sections 14-20*, (ed. Jean-Noël GUINOT, SC 315), Paris, Cerf, 1984, 90.

[9] In fact, this was also the main point of the spiritual interpretation by Eusebius and Cyril of Alexandria: whereas the Jews were the cause of Jerusalem's demise, the new Jerusalem, i.e. the Church, is rebuilt on faith in Christ; *ibid.*, 91, n. 2.

[10] We can find this interpretation already in 2 Bar. 4:2, where the Lord seems to refuse any connection between the earthly, sinful and therefore doomed, Jerusalem, and the heavenly construction which was prepared before the creation of Paradise. See: Judyta PUDEŁKO, "*Sulle palme ti ho scolpito...*: l'uso di Isaia 49,16a nel 2 Baruch 4,2", *BibAn* 4 (2014) 313-329. A similar intuition of a heavenly Jerusalem was followed also by T. K. CHEYNE, *The Prophecies of Isaiah*. vol. 2 (5th edition), London, Kegan Paul, 1888, 17.

[11] Franz DELITZSCH, *Commentary on the Old Testament*, vol.7 Isaiah, T&T Clark, Edinburgh, 1866-1891, 475-476; first published as *Biblischer Commentar über den Propheten Jesaia*, (BCAT 3/1), Leipzig, Dorffling & Franke, 1867.

[12] For example, it has been noted that the verb חָקַק is never used with names; see: J. GOLDINGAY and D. PAYNE, *Isaiah 40-55*, 186. Similarly also: Jan Leunis KOOLE, *Isaiah III. vol. 2: Isaiah 49-55* (HCOT), Leuven, Peeters, 1998, 56. Duhm followed the LXX because according to him, the MT disrupted the feminine imagery; Bernhard DUHM, *Das Buch Jesaia* (HKAT, 3:1), Göttingen, Vandenhoeck & Ruprecht, 1922[4], 374. For a review of the older scholarship see: KOOLE, *Isaiah III*, 56.

Some scholars also interpreted Isa 49:16 as the reversal of the dire scene from of Ezek 4, where the same verb חָקַק is used to speak of a blueprint of the city engraved on a mudbrick. Some pointed to the ancient royal iconography where the city founder can be seen offering a blueprint of the city to a patron divinity (Gudea of Lagash)[13]. We can add here a closer example from the Stele of Nebuchadnezzar II where the king is depicted next to the architectural scheme as an "architect" of Etemenanki, holding the "broken reed"; i.e. a measuring rode[14]. This iconographic parallel also suits very well Isa 49 and its message of reconstruction.

Nevertheless, there is a major flaw in this interpretation which imagines an architectural project: it is the very idea of inscribing a blueprint on the architect's body. Additionally, the main aim of this act was to help God's own memory; i.e. it must connect YHWH also with the past and not just with the future. That is why already David Kimchi identified the presumed image in YHWH's hand with the destroyed walls of Jerusalem; i.e. those which still expect reconstruction[15].

3. To Inscribe a Name

The second major interpretative line, which we will consider now, is to interpret the pronominal suffix in חַקֹּתִיךְ as referring to the name of Jerusalem, and hence to interpret it as some kind of inscription on YHWH's palms.

3.1. The "hands of Ishtar"

In the Assyriological literature, one can encounter references to the curious artefacts named by the contemporary scholars in a rather misleading way as "hands of Ishtar"[16]. They are made of clay, in a form of a hand,

[13] Burkard M. Zapff, *Jesaja 40-55* (NEB.ATE, 36), Würzburg, Echter Verlag, 2001, 303; and: Joseph Blenkinsopp, *Isaiah 40-55: A New Translation with Introduction and Commentary* (AB, 19A), New York, Doubleday, Anchor Books, 2002, 311.

[14] For more on the figure of the royal architect and the public display of the king as an architect see Natalie N. May, "Text and Architecture: YBC 5022 and BM 15285 as 'Manuals of an Architect'", in: Pascal Attinger, Antoine Cavigneaux, Catherine Mittermayer (et al.), *Text and Image. Proceedings of the 61e Rencontre assyriologique internationale, Geneva and Bern, 22-26 June 2015* (OBO.SA, 40), Peeters, 2018, 255-269, 259.

[15] See: www.sefaria.org. Similarly also: Antoon Schoors, *I Am God Your Saviour: A Form-critical Study of the Main Genres in Is. XL-LV* (VT.S, 24), Leiden, Brill, 1973, 106; Pierre-E. Bonnard, *Le second Isaïe: Son disciple et leurs éditeurs. Isaïe 40-66* (EB, 60), Paris, Gabalda, 1972, 225.

[16] See examples: BM 140430 or BM 90976 (www.britishmuseum.org), or MET 324624 (www.metmuseum.org).

or more precisely – a clenched fist turned upwards. The quality of the form varies a lot: sometimes the fingernails are individually delineated and sometimes not. The fingers are rendered identically, with no special indication of a thumb. Behind the fingers, the "hands" are broken in the section which was left rough and would have functioned as a shank to be inserted into the wall in regular intervals. One-third of them bears inscriptions, allowing for precise dating and establishing the place of origin. Yet, since most of them do not bear any inscription, the writing seems to be an inessential and secondary development.

Paul-Emile Botta, who first found those artefacts in Khorsabad, thought them to be architectural elements introduced to support ceiling beams. But since the material used is too weak for this function, he later thought that they held the tops of the sculptured slabs. But, in fact, neither can they serve as consoles supporting an upper architectural member because the clay fist presents no smooth surface suitable for such a purpose[17]. Since even this function seemed to be too demanding for this type of material, others speculated that the "hands of Ishtar" were simply to make a decorative cornice to visually separate the slabs from the paintings above. Indeed, they were found in the rooms with the bas-reliefs.

Although their exact function remains unresolved for modern scholars, they were likely employed as decorative architectural corbels, probably in connection with window ledges or timber roof beams. There were also a few bronze sheathing exemplars found, similar to the clay ones. They were hollow and probably covered an underlying wooden structure, such as the end of a roof beam[18]. By contrast, the clay hands were displayed with a purely decorative function, as a sort of replica of those which had a constructive role in the building. As they served no structural purpose their function must have been non-practical: and therefore possibly ideological or religious.

The particular shape of the hand incited, of course, some interpretations. For some, the clay hands may have been connected with an apotropaic meaning and served to protect the space of the palace from evil spirits[19]. But they were not only found by the windows and it is difficult to associate them with a specific deity. Furthermore, the connection

[17] E. Douglas VAN BUREN, *Symbol of Gods. Symbols of the Gods in Mesopotamian Art* (AnOr, 23), Roma, Pontificio Istituto Biblico, 1945, 58.

[18] Eleanor GURALNICK, "Assyrian Clay Hands from Khorsabad", *JNES* 67 (2008) 241-246.

[19] Edgar J. PELTENBURG, "Assyrian Clay Fists", *OrAnt* 7 (1968) 57-62. He rightly noted that in Northern Syria they were first functional and decorative. He was also right that they not seem to have been a symbol of a specific deity.

with the so-called Phoenician hand of Tanit or *hamsa*[20] is only distant and superficial.

The earliest such forms must probably be associated with the endings of the roof-supporting beams from the building facades which can be traced as early as Middle Bronze age Syria[21]. It is a form analogous to the triglyph in Doric architecture, which, besides representing in stone the wooden beam, also gives the impression of an ideological meaning[22]. The clay hands seem always to appear just below the ceiling, marking a typical style in monumental and temple architecture. It is not known why at a certain moment those decorative elements became clearly shaped like hands. We are left to our speculations. Are they shaped into the supernatural beings supporting the roof? Or is it rather an artistic manner of embodying the power of the king as the builder of the mighty royal palace[23]?

At this stage, the inscriptions preserved on one-third of them can bring us some help both in interpreting the form of the „hand of Ishtar" and in directing us towards the appropriate interpretation of Isaiah. All examples of the inscriptions (except one from Asshur) come from Nimrud or Nineveh. The Assyrian inscriptions are written only on one side of the hand, on the fingers, or, once, on two adjacent sides of the arm. Some inscriptions would be viewed upside down[24]. Mostly the inscriptions are simply „labels" indicating ownership, such as the following:

> Palace of Ashurnasirpal, great king, mighty king, king of the world, king of Assyria,
> son of Tukulti-Ninurta, king of the world, king of Assyria,
> son of Adad-Nirari, also king of the world, king of Assyria.
> **Property** of the city of Kalhu.[25]

The inscriptions record the name of the king, his genealogy and titles (variously developed) and sometimes they state that they belong to, or were from the palace (of Nimrud), the temple of Ishtar of Nineveh or the

[20] VAN BUREN, *Symbol of Gods*, 58-59.

[21] See the well-documented study in: Sebastiano SOLDI, "Assyrian Clay Hands in the Architecture of the Ancient Near East", *Metropolitan Museum Journal* 52 (2017) 8-23.

[22] It should be noted that this commonly accepted origin of the triglyph brings some serious difficulties: its shape and regular intervals simply do not correspond to the practice of the wooden architecture. It is highly probable that in the case of this typical Doric element also, the triglyph has more ideological functions. See: Mark WILSON JONES, "Tripods, Triglyphs, and the Origin of the Doric Frieze", *AJA* 106 (2002) 353-390.

[23] SOLDI, "'Assyrian Clay Hands'", 19.

[24] Grant FRAME, "Assyrian Clay Hand", *BaM* 22 (1991) 335-381, 343-344.

[25] Inscription H in: FRAME, "Assyrian Clay Hand", 350.

temple of Ninurta in Nimrud. It must be noted that similar inscriptions are found on clay cones and bricks. The label marks first of all the property of kings or gods; e.g. "Property of the temple of the goddess Ishtar'[26]. In some cases, the inscription bears only the name of the owner, or the name of the building and the word 'property of' does not appear at all.

There are some significant differences between the inscribed Assyrian clay hands and the image transmitted by Isa 49:16. The Assyrian clay hands cannot be understood as hands of a god, because nobody signs his hand to mark that it belongs to him. The *hand of Ishtar* is a misnomer; it is not a divine hand. Whereas in Assyria it is the building which is inscribed with the name of the owner or builder, in Isaiah it is YHWH who is inscribed with the name or some symbol of the construction; i.e. Jerusalem.

The inscription does not refer only to the particular clay hand but rather is a label placed on the whole building. The function of the inscription cannot be purely informative. They are not anything precious that should be marked for protection's sake. Any person entering the temple or the palace could have no doubts in identifying the whole building. One should, therefore, seek for some different reason for its existence.

The inscriptions indicate the builder, restorer, or „owner" of the construction. Notably, some of them, as with most of the royal inscriptions, were not placed in easily readable positions[27]. Therefore, the intended addressee of these inscriptions were not necessarily humans but gods and other supernatural beings. The royal name seems to work also as a **dedication** of the royal palace to a divinity, which means placing it under his/her **protection**. They seem to work as **votive objects and votive inscriptions**.

The inscriptions still do not explain the hand-shape of the artefact. Yet, if the hands are not divine, we can see here that the temple or royal palace has hands! They look like an interesting expression of a model or parallel between a building and a human body[28].

[26] In the sumerograms: NÍG.GA É [d]INANNA. See inscription C, line 4 in: FRAME, "Assyrian Clay Hand", 346. The signs NÍG.GA correspond to the Akkadian *makkūru* with the generic meaning: treasures, valuables, property, assets, estate; also referred to slaves; CAD 10/II, 136.

[27] FRAME, "Assyrian Clay Hand", 356.

[28] The reader may find it useful to note a particular imagery of the feminine body and the building, for which see: Meir MALUL, "Woman-Earth Homology in Biblical *Weltanschauung*", *UF* 33 (2000) 339-363 and Silvia SCHROER, "Frauenkörper als architektonische Elemente: zum Hintergrund von Ps 144,12", in: Susanne BICKEL (Hrsgb.), *Bilder als Quellen. Studies on Ancient Near Eastern Artefacts and the Bible Inspired by the Work of Othmar Keel* (OBO.S), Fribourg, Academic Press Fribourg, 2007, 425-450.

3.2. Commemorative Inscriptions

The context of Isa 49:16, where the verb 'to forget' and 'not to forget' so often occurs, suggests that YHWH's hewing on his own palms can be associated with an inscription and the first function of an inscription is precisely commemoration. In Isa 56:5, the phrase referring to a 'hand' also refers to a memorial: יָד וָשֵׁם . Another hint that in Isa 49:16 YHWH plays on the dedicatory inscription comes from the preposition נֶגֶד: 'your walls are ever in front of me, in my sight'. It comes from the common practice of placing the dedicatory inscriptions 'in front of' the holy place, in the sight of the deity, as the case of YHWH's temple in Samaria proves[29]. Although the placement of an inscription could be connected with some significant offering, it belongs not so much to the logic of *do ut des*. Rather, its function is explicitly to remind the beholder of the relationship and preserve it.

The earliest form of the inscription was only a name; actually, the Sumerian term for an inscription is MU SAR.RA which literally means "written name". The first inscriptions claimed the ownership of, or presence in, the inscribed object or place[30]. The inscriptions on the Assyrian hands seem to have something in common with the two types of inscriptions. The first one addresses first of all gods, the second one humans. Since the inscription is made on a body part, it can be classified as a votive text; it "inscribed monuments which were to be placed in temples"[31]. In the Mesopotamian context, inscriptions were placed most often on the votive statues of a ruler and his family. The votive figurines and objects had a similar role in the relationship with gods. When they were left in a temple, they were to remind the divinity of the person who offered it. Votive statues filled the temples; the worshiper's statue is presented and inscribed with the sponsor's prayer.

In the Biblical context, Aaron's stones of remembrance from Exod 28:9-12 should be understood as a type of a votive object[32]. The *ziqqaron* stones

[29] Several inscriptions use the analogous preposition *qdm* 'before'. See: Anne Katrine DE HEMMER GUDME, "A Lingering Memory: Materiality and Divine Remembrance in Aramaic Dedicatory Inscriptions", *ARAM.P* 29 (2017) 89-104, 96.

[30] The Sumerian term MU SAR.RA appears most often in the context of curses where the inscription refers to itself while cursing anyone who would attempt to efface it. From this earliest practice originated royal literature, such as the triumphal texts. These were not placed in a temple but in a subjugated territory, where they also were to commemorate the victorious king and his god. See: Sandra L. RICHTER, *The Deuteronomistic History and the Name Theology:* lesakken semô sam *in the Bible and the Ancient Near East* (BZAW, 318), Berlin, de Gruyter, 2002, 130-138.

[31] S. L. RICHTER, *The Name Theology*, 136.

[32] A certain connection with this text was proposed in: Edward J. KISSANE, *The Book of Isaiah*, vol. 2: *XL-LXVI*, Dublin, Browne and Nolan Limited, 1943, 132.

of the high priest are to be worn whenever the priest enters the sanctuary. They bore the inscriptions with the names of the twelve tribes of Israel which were to serve as a physical memorial of Israel's existence. Here the intention of the memorial does not presume that the Lord has forgotten them. Because the memory of God is never neutral or passive, the *ziqqaron* is to "secure His favorable attentiveness"[33]. The stones are like a silent prayer entreating God. Jeffrey H. Tigay noted that because of the names inscribed, the stones have "seal-like character" and compared them with the votive seals, which were placed on a deity's statue. They are easy to distinguish because such seals were designed to be read directly and not from their impressions. This makes them even closer to any votive inscription[34].

Mesopotamian culture knew the custom of placing the inscribed votive objects on a statue of a god. The great difference with the text of Isaiah is the fact that the support of this "memorial" is nothing less than His own body.

The second category of commemorative inscriptions which are meaningful for the interpretation of Isa 49:16 are building inscriptions. The longest list of artefacts belongs to this category: bricks, foundation deposits, pivot-stones, and clay nails. In this case, the inscriptions themselves declare to be addressing the future generations[35]. Especially the inscriptions found in the foundation deposits usually mention the future destruction or the need for restoration. Correspondingly, they are addressed to "the future prince".

Let us remind ourselves that in the context of the second part of Isaiah, there simply was no possibility of placing any votive inscriptions because of the temple remained in ruins and the place itself remained inaccessible to the worshippers. The people could fear that YHWH forgot them not because he was particularly forgetful. Rather, it was they who could not be assured of the divine remembrance in a traditional way. Isaiah 49:16

[33] Jeffrey H. TIGAY, "The Priestly Reminder Stones and Ancient Near Eastern Votive Practices", in: Moshe BAR-ASHER, Dalit ROM-SHILONI, Emanuel TOV (et al. ed.), *Shai le-Sara Japhet: Studies in the Bible, Its Exegesis and Its Language*, Jerusalem, The Bialik Institute, 2007, 339*-355*, 340*. According to Tigay, this custom could be seen as a background for the pleading of the bride in Song 8:6; see also further.

[34] TIGAY, "The Priestly Reminder Stones", 342*– 343*. He notes that sometimes the votive inscriptions bear only the name of the founder (p. 349*) and that there are some west Semitic seals written in a positive (i.e. and not as a mirror-image negative designed to give a positive inscription when the seal is used), but there is no proof that they were designed as votive (p. 354*).

[35] The model inscription contains: the name of the divinity to whom the building was dedicated, the name of the ruler, verb, and the name of the construction; RICHTER, *The Name Theology*, 142-144.

claims the contrary: there is an inscription, god-made, ineffaceable and effective. An inscription "on a god" is suggestive of a temple: yet here it is God himself who bears the traits of a temple. However unusual it may sound, we find an explicit statement in Isa 8:14 where, in the context of announcing the Assyrian invasion, we can read:

> It is the LORD of hosts whom you should regard as holy (אֹתוֹ תַקְדִּישׁוּ).
> And He shall be your fear, And He shall be your dread.
> v. 14. Then He shall become a sanctuary (וְהָיָה לְמִקְדָּשׁ)...

There is much to learn from this cultural context for the interpretation of Isaiah. YHWH made an inscription on himself to address his memory but also to show it to humans. YHWH shows to the Lady Zion his palms with an inscription or some kind of sign to reassure her of his lasting memory. But this memory is not just a passive spontaneous thought in the divine mind but contains an active element, and is something that provokes recalling and is a trigger to action[36]. What follows immediately after the recollection of Zion is the announcement of her impending restoration.

The building metaphor and the family metaphor are here so intrinsically connected that it is impossible to disentangle them. Zion is rebuilt because she will again have her children back. That is why it is virtually impossible to decide whether in v. 17 we should read בָּנָיִךְ 'your sons' as in the MT, or בֹּנַיִךְ 'your builders' following the LXX. The divine inscription/remembrance will make the sons/builders return[37].

4. To Write on a God?

Probably the most straightforward cultural background which can be associated with the divine body is a stone or metal statue of a divinity. Indeed, one such attestation of the verb חָקַק outside of the Bible is the Aramaic royal inscription from the Syrian-Anatolian context, which was actually engraved on a god. The king of Sam'al, Panamuwa I placed a lengthy inscription on a monumental, 4 m. high, figure of the god Hadad in Gerçin. It is quite precisely datable between 770 and 780 BC. It has survived complete, lacking only legs and possibly also a base. The arms are broken off but the inscription begins only at the waist downwards. So, in fact, we do not have any inscription preserved on Hadad's hands here.

[36] This active quality is common in the notion divine memory see: Hermann Eising, "זָכַר *zākhar*", TDOT IV, 64-82.

[37] Let us add that the engraving made by YHWH on his own hands has a parallel in v. 18, in another self-referential act, where YHWH pronounces an oath formula by His name.

The inscription has a form of a royal testament. After a summary of his successful reign, king Panamuwa lists the duties and some norms of conduct for his successors. In the end, he lists the series of dire consequences for an impious successor, in the case when his instructions are not followed. In this context, we read in line 34: *tḥq ʿlyh*. The verb is commonly recognised as the form of *ḥqq* with the same meaning as the Hebrew "to inscribe". In this threatening context, it must, therefore, mean something like "you shall make a decree against him"[38]. Through an inscription made on his god Hadad, the king Panamuwa asks him to "inscribe", or "to make a decree against" a wicked successor.

On Hadad's monumental body, we find by way of a *mise en abyme*, written on a god, an inscription demanding that this same god should "inscribe", i.e. make a ruling, against the wicked king. The very literary genre of will and testament is particularly interested in the durability of the text since it addresses a god and future human readers. Like the "inscribed palms" in Isaiah 49, the placement of this message is to guarantee its long-lasting efficiency.

Yet, there are also some fundamental differences between Hadad and YHWH. In the case of Hadad's monument, it was a human, even if it was a human king, placing his inscription on Hadad's stone body. Second, the inscription was not found on his hands, which seems to be an important detail for Isa 49. Three, Isaiah does not state clearly that what YHWH inscribed was an inscription.

The use of the unusual verb חָקַק with the reference to the palms of YHWH has something in common with the work of the human smiths shaping their iron gods with axes and hammers. In contemporary Christian and Jewish theology, God is understood as a purely spiritual being, i.e. without a body. This is also the interpretation that is spontaneously imposed equally on all Old Testament texts. In consequence, all references to the corporeal members of God have been usually explained away as unavoidable anthropomorphic figures of speech, metaphors or symbols. Indeed, body and body parts have frequently non-literal meanings, as is also the case in human bodies[39]. Nevertheless, the question is more complex than that.

[38] From Josef Tropper's rendering: "du sollst eine Bestimmung(?) gegen ihn erlassen". See: Josef TROPPER, *Die Inschriften von Zincirli: Neue Edition und vergleichende Grammatik des phönizischen, sam'alischen und aramäischen Textkorpus* (ALASP, 6), Münster, UGARIT-Verlag, 1993, 54-58, and the discussion on 97.

[39] E.g.: Marc GIRARD, *Symboles bibliques, langage universel: pour une théologie des deux Testaments ancrée dans les sciences humaines*, Paris, Montréal, Médiaspaul, DL, 2016, 1183-1629.

Whether we follow the notion of the fluidity of divine bodies proposed by Benjamin Sommer or the model of the three types of divine bodies by Mark Smith[40], some reference to the divine body occurs more than once in Isa 40-55. YHWH the Creator places himself and his body in contrast with the bodies of idols which are produced by human creators, the craftsmen. Deutero-Isaianic texts repeatedly face the reader with the question, who has made whom? In this contrasting frame, we should see the cosmic body of YHWH[41] contrasted with the metal or wooden figures which remain at human disposal. In a manner of a rhetorical apophasis, YHWH declares his incomparability with idols, but in fact He does compare Himself with the works of "engraver and refiner" חָרָשׁ וְצֹרֵף working in gold and silver (Isa 40:18-20). Furthermore, in Isa 44:12 the idol maker is an ironsmith, and in 46:6 again he is a goldsmith.

And yet, the real craftsman is YHWH, He "who stretches out the heavens like a curtain" (Isa 40:22). YHWH's body must be of cosmic dimensions because with his hand he can measure the earth (Isa 40:12). His body is, therefore, clearly inaccessible for human beings, only YHWH himself can touch it, only He is able... to engrave it.

The use of the verb חָקַק "to hew" presumes that YHWH's divine body is spoken of as if made of some hard and resisting material, like stone or metal. Quite the opposite of the ethereal and cloudy spirits. We can find the traces of this idea of a metal body in the visions of cherubim or other beings belonging to the divine sphere, like the *cherubs* in Ezek 1:7 and 40:3 where their legs are said to be "gleaming like polished brass". In Dan 10:6 also the arms of the divine messenger "looked like burnished bronze". Indeed, in ancient Egypt, divine bodies were imagined to be made of precious minerals: their flesh was gold, their bones were silver, their hair lapis lazuli, because like those minerals they never changed or grew old. Even when chopped in pieces like the Osiris body, they did not decompose or rot[42]. In every stage, the reader should be mindful that it is not a usual body that is spoken of in Isa 49:16.

[40] See especially: Esther J. HAMORI, *"When Gods Were Men." The Embodied God in Biblical and Near Eastern Literature* (BZAW, 384), Berlin, New York, de Gruyter, 2008; Benjamin SOMMER, *The Bodies of God and the World of Ancient Israel*, Cambridge, New York, Melbourne, Cambridge University Press, 2009; Mark S. SMITH, *Where the Gods Are. Spatial Dimensions of Anthropomorphism in the Biblical World* (AYBRL), New Haven, CT, London, Yale University Press, 2016, 21-27.

[41] Smith defines thus the body of YHWH in Isa 40:12 and 66:1 as "God's cosmic mystical body" because it cannot be found in this world but rather is placed somewhere beyond it. See: SMITH, *Where the Gods Are*, 21-27.

[42] Dimitri MEEKS and Christine FAVARD-MEEKS, *The Daily Life of the Egyptian Gods*, Cornell University Press, 1996, 57.

5. Branding of a Slave

The placement of the sign gains a whole new importance when we interpret YHWH's gesture in the light of Isa 44:5 where the actions of the returning Israelites are described[43]:

> This one will say, I am the LORD's (לַיהוָה אָנִי);
> And this one will call on the name of Jacob;
> And this one will write *on* his hand, *Belonging* to the LORD, (יִכְתֹּב יָדוֹ לַיהוָה)
> And will name Israel's name with honour.

For our study of Isa 49:19, the phrase "he will write *on* his hand" is of particular interest. The syntax of the phrase יִכְתֹּב יָדוֹ לַיהוָה needs a bit of explication, for the lack of a preposition before יָדוֹ makes it more ambiguous. Jerome in his Vulgate understood "his hand" as an instrumental case, *manu sua* "with his hand". But one only ever writes with a hand, so it makes poor sense unless we take it in a modal manner "he will sign *himself* as", that is, "out of his own will". The most common solution is to interpret יָדוֹ as a locative: "*on* his hand"[44]. This meaning is presumed also in the LXX by the prefix ἐπι- in the verb ἐπιγράψει, 'to put a mark' on oneself by inscribing on one's own hand[45].

Since Isa 43:1, YHWH repeatedly has been addressing Jacob as "my slave", עַבְדִּי. In this context, therefore, seeing a self-imposed slave mark in 44:5 is very appealing[46]. The branding of slaves is attested since the Hammurabi Code (§ 226) and was practiced by the Israelites themselves in their colony in Elephantine[47]. The particular image of individuals branded as the property of a divinity, here of YHWH, is also perfectly

[43] Thus also: Shalom M. PAUL, *Isaiah 40-66. Translation and Commentary* (ECCo), Grand Rapids, MI, Cambridge, Eerdmans, 2012, 228.

[44] In his commentary, Jerome associates this tattoo with the rite performed on a man when he joined the Roman legions; this practice seems to be common since the fourth century AD; see: Marc ADRIAEN (ed.), *S. Hieronymi presbyteri opera. Pars I,2: Opera exegetica, Commentariorum in Esaiam libri XII-XVIII* (CC.SL 73) 497.

[45] Jan Leunis KOOLE, *Isaiah III. vol. 1: Isaiah 40-48* (HCOT), Leuven, Peeters, 1997, 364-365.

[46] Thus: Ulrich BERGES, *Jesaja 40-48* (HthKAT), Freiburg im Breisgau, Herder Verlag, 2008, 324. Berges emphasises here an individual and free decision of a branded person and a well-established theology in which YHWH owns his people; cf. Deut 14:2 (סְגֻלָּה). See the same interpretation in: John HUEHNERGARD and Harold LIEBOWITZ, "The Biblical Prohibition against Tattooing", *VT* 63 (2013) 59-77, 71.

[47] See the document B33 "Apportionment of Slaves" in: Bezalel PORTEN, J. Joel FARBER, Cary J. MARTIN, et al., *The Elephantine Papyri in English: Three Millennia of Cross-Cultural Continuity and Change* (DMOA, 22), Leiden, Brill, 1996, 200. For example, in the case when slaves were shared between brothers: "And behold this is the share which came to you as a share, you, Jedaniah: Petosiri by name, his mother Tabi, a slave *mšnt [mšunnat] 'l ydw bymyn šnt qry'tw 'rmyt kk lmbtḥyh* branded on his right hand (with) a brand reading (in)

understandable in the ancient context, because a great number of slaves belonged to the temples, especially in the Neo-Babylonian context.

Significantly, it was usually a divinity him- or herself marking humans as is expressed in this exemplary formula: "The one whom (the goddess) Nana has branded or marked with a star *kakkabtum*". The mark was branded on the slave's wrist, or perhaps on the back of the hand with a hot iron. In other cases, a tattoo mark was applied – in addition to a star, for the Eanna slaves. The mark was called in Akkadian *arru* or rather in plural *arrātu*; i.e. 'curses'[48]. It seems that sometimes the marking was limited to attaching a wooden or metal tag[49].

For the exilic context, it is important to note that in the Neo-Babylonian times the prisoners of war were usually turned into temple slaves. (Later, Persians used them mostly for the construction works of the state). The second source of temple slaves was the piety of the private owners and their vows in which they offered some part of their property to the temple[50]. It looks, therefore, that in Isaiah, the use of the recurring motif of "Israel, my servant/slave" is first of all about YHWH reclaiming his property from Babylon and her gods. This was also the function of the signs marking the slaves: they served to claim the property of run-away slaves or slaves abducted by others.

A fortunately surviving sixth century BC Babylonian cuneiform tablet provides us with an illuminating example of how the hand mark worked. We learn that the slave woman Nanaya-hussinni and her son appeal to the Babylonian court to establish their true proprietor. They used to belong to a certain man called Nurea. In the court, Nurea witnessed that he bought the woman a long time ago and that only when she ran away from him she drew on her hand a star and wrote an inscription "for (the goddess) Nanaya". The slave woman rejected his version of events and claimed that she always belonged to Ištar. The Mesopotamian scribes (trained in the cuneiform script) called a specialist for help, a *sēpiru*, i.e. a scribe of the alphabetic writing. This case is worth a quote:

> Les juges, ayant entendu leurs déclarations, firent venir un *sēpiru* et, la main de Nanaya-hussinni, après avoir expertisé, il déclara : « D'une inscription

Aramaic like this: "(Belonging) to Mibtahiah". See also the papyrus: B39 "Testamentary Manumission" and B42 "Adoption".

48 CAD I/2, 305.

49 Muhammad A. DANDAMAEV, *Slavery in Babylonia. From Nabopolassar to Alexander the Great (626-331 BC)* (revised edition), DeKalb, IL, Northern Illinois University Press, 1984, 488-489.

50 DANDAMAEV, *Slavery*, 472.

ancienne, d'il y a longtemps, « Pour Nanaya », sa main est inscrite et une seconde inscription, sous l'inscription précédente, porte « Pour Ištar d'Uruk ».[51]

The woman appears to have on her hand not one but two alphabetic marks proving her belonging to the goddess. To the Babylonian court, it was clear that Nurea possessed those slaves illegally.

Daniel Arnaud argued that the slave woman appealed to the court out of her initiative because she was counting on a relatively better situation for the temple slaves. We have therefore a proof that in sixth century BC Babylon, one could find of a slave who would like to put on his or her hand an inscription marking him or her as a property of a divinity.

Greek examples were noted a long time ago by exegetes[52]. Similar self-branding is mentioned also a century later, in the Persian period, by Herodotus, but this time in a context more corresponding to the free-will self-dedication presumed by Isaiah. Herodotus wrote about a sanctuary in the mouth of the Nile, the Canopic mouth, where any person, free or slave, by self-branding could dedicate oneself for a god and thus find protection:

> Now there was (and still is) on the coast a temple of Heracles; if a servant (οἰκέτης – household slave) of any man takes refuge there and is branded with certain sacred marks (ἐπιβάληται στίγματα ἱρά), delivering himself to the god (ἑωυτὸν διδοὺς τῷ θεῷ), he may not be touched. This law continues today the same as it has always been from the first.[53]

The late witness of Lucian of Samosata in his *De Dea Syria* from the second century AD, states simply that bearing some kind of a mark was popular among the devotees:

> All people are marked (στίζονται), some on their wrists and some on their necks. For this reason, all Assyrians carry a mark (στιγματηφορέουσιν).[54]

There are some studies which try to connect the Jewish custom of wearing the phylacteries with other parallel Egyptian customs of wearing armbands with the names of gods and pharaoh[55]. Marking oneself with a

[51] Daniel ARNAUD, "Un document juridique concernant les oblats", *RA* 67 (1973) 147-156.

[52] E.g. already in : Augustin CALMET, *Commentaire littéral sur tous les livres de l'Ancien et du Nouveau Testament. Le Prophète Isaïe*, Paris, Emery, Saugrain et Martin, 1713, 527.

[53] HERODOTUS, II, 113, in: A. D. GODLEY (ed.), vol. 1; (LCL, 117), Cambridge, Harvard University Press, 1920, 403.

[54] *De dea Syra* 59 in: Harold W. ATTRIDGE and Robert A. ODEN (ed.), *The Syrian Goddess (De Dea Syria) attributed to Lucian* (SBL.TT. Graeco-Roman Religion Series, 1) Montana, Scholars Press, 1976, 59.

[55] Othmar KEEL, "Zeichen der Verbundenheit: Zur Vorgeschichte und Bedeutung der Forderungen von Deuteronomium 6,8f und Par.", in: Pierre CASETTI, *Mélanges Dominique*

name or a symbol of one's god is perfectly understandable in the ancient context.

What makes Isa 49:16 exceptional is the fact that it is not a human but rather a divinity branding himself for the sake of humans! It looks therefore as a great reversal of the ancient social and religious customs. Here YHWH speaks about his devotion and piety towards Zion. It is He who binds himself forever with his people. The branding creates a bond of belonging which is not based on the paternal relationship, and nevertheless, its effects are not less important because this mark truly makes one a member of the household. The mark on a hand is a sign of slavery but also of perpetual belonging. Surprising as it is, Isaiah does speak elsewhere about the *enslaved* God:

> You have bought Me no sweet cane with money,
> And with the fat of your sacrifices you have not inebriated Me;
> Rather you have enslaved Me (הֶעֱבַדְתַּנִי) with your sins,
> You have wearied Me with your iniquities. (Isa 43:24)

The same Hiphil verb עָבַד is used, for example, in Exod 1:13 and 6:5 where Egyptians enslave the Israelites, or in 2 Sam 12:31 where David forces the conquered nations to hard labour, without wages (see also Ezek 29:18); last but not least, this verb describes the state of Judeans in Babylon (Jer 17:4).

In Isaiah, YHWH announces not only that Jacob belongs to Him, that Jacob is His slave, but in surprising reciprocity, YHWH demonstrates that He is also bound to the people. Whereas in Isa 43:24, the enslavement is more explicit but also imposed on YHWH by the sinful nation, the self-branding of YHWH from 49:19 has something much more of a deliberate, as much as passionate, free act of God. Indeed, YHWH is precise in reminding that he did this "inscription" for Himself and not as a reminder for Zion. If it is the slavery of God, it is a freely chosen state.

6. Seal of lovers

The simile to the relationship between a mother and her child also suggests that those freely chosen bonds can be easily associated with the relationship based on love. This understanding of our passage is explicated most briefly by the following dialogue between the personified feminine

Barthélemy. Études bibliques offertes à l'occasion de son 60e anniversaire (OBO, 38), Fribourg, Éditions universitaires de Fribourg / Universitätsverlag Freiburg, 1981, 159-240, 212-213.

Congregation of Israel and God, as imagined by R. Berekhiah in the Babylonian Talmud (*Ta'anit* 4a):

> And further she (the Congregation of Israel) asked (God) in an inappropriate manner. She said before him, 'Lord of the world, "Set me as a seal upon your heart, as a seal upon your arm" (Song 8:6). Said to her the Holy One, blessed be he, 'My daughter, you have petitioned for something that sometimes can be seen and sometimes cannot be seen. But I will make of you something that can be seen all the time: "Behold, I have graven you upon the palms of my hands".[56]

Later commentators wrote even about YHWH's gesture as the one of the lover who makes himself a tattoo with the name of his beloved woman; unfortunately, they did not give any ancient examples of similar custom[57]. Their intuition has some merits but does not do justice to the whole range of serious social and religious consequences of bearing someone's name or symbol.

7. Conclusions

7.1. Divine Anamnesis

There is no single background that would explain the expression used in Isa 49:16. There is no proof that it could be seen as a stereotypical expression or an idiom. On the linguistic level, it is, rather, a truly unique metaphor. When one tries to grasp the meaning of these words *via* the study of the applied imagery, it must be concluded that although some parallels can be indicated, the image conveyed by Isa 49:16 remains unique and should be uniquely treated. It is a living metaphor, created for this particular context, which in a condensed and creative manner brings together formerly distant ideas. Additionally, it has a strong evocative power by bringing to the reader's mind strong emotions and memories.

The use of the verb חָקַק corresponds more to the material of stone or metal than flesh. It could suggest a particular nature of the imagined divine body of YHWH but maybe also we can take it as a word-play suggesting that this "hewing" on divine palms will render perennial his judgements and plans concerning Zion. Ultimately it is He who is the "inscriber/ lawgiver" of Israel, his מחקק (Isa 33:22).

[56] Jacob NEUSNER, *The Babylonian Talmud*. vol. 7, *Tractate Ta'anit; Tractate Megillah; Tractate Mo'ed Qatan; Tractate Hagigah: A Translation and Commentary*, Peabody, MA, Hendrickson Publishers, 2005, 14. Accoding to Neusner's division the quotation comes from: Ta'anit II.9, K.

[57] Paul VOLZ, *Jesaia II. Kapitel 40-66* (KAT, 9/2), Leipzig, A. Deichertsche Verlagsbuchhandlung D. Werner Scholl, 1932, 193; or: PAUL, *Isaiah 40-66*, 335.

The ambiguity of the engraved shape can be also intended: we cannot be sure if the walls or the name of Zion are suggested. YHWH's divine body can be an object only for YHWH Himself, and thus it remains in strong contrast to the passive, human-made idols.

In a subversive way, YHWH reverses the image of the temple bearing the name of a god. Here the God of Israel bears on his hands the sign of Zion! In the context of the destroyed temple where there was no physical space to place a memorial, it is YHWH's own body that takes over this function. His own body becomes a bearer of a votive inscription, He takes over some functions of the temple.

The common ancient custom of slave branding adds an aspect of personal dedication. YHWH is not just saying that the relationship between Him and his people is simply reciprocal, but it is created and reinforced by this initiative. The bond thus created goes beyond the natural familial relationship. It is still a real bond within the household model of relationship. It also adds, as we have seen, some less positive connotations, scandalous even, if one attributes them to a divinity: toil, dependence, and suffering. Literal 'hewing' on one's palms of hands combines in a quite oxymoronic manner the intimacy (palms) with suffering ('hewing').

7.2. Old Testament Intertextuality

The gesture of Isa 49:16 is unique, but in the perspective of the whole Old Testament, we can nevertheless point to another memorial which YHWH prepared for himself, namely his bow which he placed in the clouds after the flood. Eising was right that even though the term זִכָּרוֹן "memorial" does not appear here, the cognate verb is used twice in this context, making clear that the function of the "bow" is analogous: it "will be seen in the clouds" (Gen 9:14), and then YHWH "will remember" his covenant with every living creature, v. 15. 9:16 repeats again "I will look upon it, to remember". The bow of YHWH in the clouds is not here called זִכָּרוֹן but "the sign of the covenant" (אוֹת־הַבְּרִית), as if the clouds were an interface between the earth and the God in heaven. Maybe this was also the inspiration for Sa'adiah Ga'on who explained "the palms of hands" from Isaiah as "like clouds"[58].

[58] After David Kimchi: "The interpretation of the blessed memory Sa'adiah: like clouds, and when he rose his heart to his palms of hands"; see: www.sefaria.

7.3. Christian Intertextuality

The study of the cultural context of this gesture brought us to see in YHWH's address to Zion from Isa 49:16 a curious mixture of images and sometimes seemingly opposed connotations. It looks like **violence** self-inflicted on one's own **body**, which intended to confirm the relationship. It is a **freely** chosen sign of **slavery** and an expression of belonging, **love,** and devotion. It is a troubling reversal in which God marks himself with a human sign as if turning his hands into a perennial **votive** offering to himself and thus making of his body a **temple** for his temple-less people. It is a memorial that will not allow Him to forget, a sign which is to trigger restoration.

Yet, there are still some questions that remain unanswered, such as, for example, why the two palms? One would be perfectly enough, to fulfil the abovementioned functions. At this stage, a Christian reader is almost compelled to think about the famous meeting of the Risen Jesus with Thomas in J 20. There the apostle, who had been absent on the first evening after the resurrection, exclaimed that he has to "see the mark of the nails τὸν τύπον τῶν ἥλων" (v. 25). Accordingly, a week later Jesus came once more and says to him "See my hands! ἴδε τὰς χεῖράς μου... Believe!" (v. 27).

SIX LISTS IN ARAMAIC OSTRACA FROM ELEPHANTINE

Bezalel PORTEN

It is with great pleasure that we pen these few lines in honor of Émile Puech, who has contributed so much to the advancement of paleography and epigraphy.

It took just under 100 years for the French to publish the more than 300 Aramaic ostraca that they had found on the island of Elephantine at the beginning of the twentieth century.[1] Among these were six lists of names, five of which may be dated because they contain names that appear in dated papyri. With one exception, none bear informative captions.

1. This ostracon (No. X_{11}) begins with the demonstrative אלה ("these") that introduces lists of names in the Hebrew Bible (Gen 6:9, 10:20, 31-32, 11:10, 25:16, 36:19; Ru 4:18) and in the Aramaic papyri introduces the Words of Ahiqar (TAD C1.1: [restored]),[2] the warriors of Darius in the Bisitun text (TAD C2.1:74 [restored]), and the witnesses and boundaries in contracts (TAD B1.1:15; 2.7:13, 3.4:7, 3.7:5). In the ostracon, it introduces "Jews/Judeans[3] who took allotment" (יהודיא זי לקחו פרס). The term יהודי/\א occurs as both noun ("Jew/Judean who is in the fortress of Elephantine of the detachment of PN" [e.g. TAD B2.2:3]) and adjective, as in חילא יהודיא ("the Jewish/Judean troop" [TAD A4.1:1; C3.15:1]). As members of a military troop, the Jews/Judeans received a regular "allotment" "given" (יהב/נתן) to them monthly (TAD B4.2:6) and which may be "taken" (יתלקח) anywhere (TAD A2.3:8). Below the caption there follow three and a half lines, the bottom break cutting out the praenomen of the fourth name. The caption itself appears on two lines, and the end of the second line appears to have been erased. It seems to have contained the beginning of the first name – מכי בר, written on a separate line, as were the following three+ names. The name Makki appears once in the

[1] Hélène LOZACHMEUR, *La collection Clermont-Ganneau. Ostraca, épigraphes sur jarre étiquettes de bois* (MAI 35), Paris, Boccard, 2006, 2 vols.

[2] TAD = Bezalel PORTEN and Ada YARDENI, *Textbook of Aramaic Documents from Ancient Egypt, Newly Copied, Edited and Translated into Hebrew and English.* Jerusalem. Department of the History of the Jewish People, 1986-1999, vols. 1-4 (A-D).

[3] Are they Judeans, having come from the state of Judah, or are they Jews, as are the יהודים in the book of Esther?

Hermopolis letters as hypocoristicon of Aramaic Makkibanit ("Who is like Banit?" [TAD A2.2:1 etc.]), once as father of the witness צפניה (TAD B5.1:11), several times on pre-exilic inscriptions[4], and as father of the spy Geuel of the tribe of Gad (Num 13:15 [though spelled with initial *qamatz* {Machi}]). The other six names were well known in the Elephantine papyri, but none is of a known person – גמריה the father of מכי, ידניה בר מכיה, ענניה בר הושעיה, and PN son of שלמם. Notice that both מכיה and שלמם are spelled *defectiva*.

2. If this list tagged some four Jews/Judeans, a second list, an opisthograpic palimpsest, tagged some eight persons (No. X_2). Two of these also appear in the papyri: גדול בר משלם and ישביה בר מתן. The first appears in the Collection Account dated in the fifth year at the end of the century (TAD C15:25 [Gaddul son of Meshullam son of Mibtahiah]). The second is related to a party in a fragmentary contract, Mattan son of Yashobiah, who is uniquely labelled ארמי סונכן ("Aramean, Syenian") (TAD B5.2:1). So our Jashobiah son of Mattan would be either the son or father of Mattan son of Yashobiah in the contract.

As son, he would be Yashobiah son of Mattan son of Yashobiah; as father he would be Mattan son of Yashobiah son of Mattan.

In either case, Yashobiah would date to the same year as Gaddul son of Meshullam son of Mibtahiah, that is 400, and Mattan to a generation earlier, say 425. The usual ethnicon was ארמי זי סון ("Aramean of Syene"), but both the noun and adjective form were used to describe Jews/Judeans (e.g. TAD A4.10:6; B2.1:2).

3. A third list, also an opisthograph (No. X_4), tagged some twenty persons. It is unique in that it has an equal number of feminine and masculine names and listed two people as "his brother," that is, of the preceding name. One of the female persons is the three generation אצול ברת אושע בר קצירי ("Aṣṣul daughter of Osea son of Qaṣiri"), the first name being both male and female. It is a phonetic variant of הצול (cf. TAD B3.8:44 and C3.15:29-30 [400 BCE]), hypocoristicon of הצליה ("YH has delivered"[5]). The grandfather's name resembles קצרי ("Qoṣri" ["Shorty"]), a witness in a loan contract of ca. 487 (TAD B4.2:13), and timewise possibly the same person as our grandfather. The person on our list who is definitely the same as

[4] Rainer Albertz and Rüdiger Schmitt, *Family and Household Religion in Ancient Israel and the Levant*, Winona Lake, IN, Eisenbrauns, 2012, 575.

[5] Ran Zadok, *The Pre-Hellenistic Israelite Anthroponymy and Prosopography* (OLA 28), Leuven, Peeters, 1988, 114.

one on a papyrus list dating about the same time as the list above is נתן בר נריה (see TAD C4.4:6 [ca. 420 BCE]).

4. A fourth list, a one-sided seven-line ostracon (No. 96), of about the same period, whose first name on the last line is in dispute, has two names that appear elsewhere. The disputed name was read דליה by the editor, Lozachmeur, but גלית by the reviewer André Lemaire,[6] who followed Arthur Cowley and André Dupont-Sommer, both of whom read a *taw* and not a *he*. Based on the name of the Philistine giant, this would have been something of a nickname for a very tall person, as the name in the above ostracon was for a short person.[7] The two names appearing in dated papyri were פלטי בר יאוש and יסלח בר גדול.

The former appears in four texts: (1) the recipient of a letter from Hoshaiah son of Natan (TAD A3.6), (2) and twice appears together with him as witness to a contract of 404, both signing their own name (TAD B3.10:24-25); (3) as father of daughter Yaḥmol in the Collection List of 400 BCE (C3.15:92); (4) and together with Yislaḥ in a list of those who did/made *ḥmy* (TAD D3.17:8-9).

Yislaḥ, on the other hand, appears in five texts: (1) together with Pilṭi on the above list (TAD D3.17:8-9); (2) as creditor in 407 (TAD B4.5); (3) as witness to a deed of marriage in 420 (TAD B3.8:43-44), (4) and to a deed of withdrawal, signing his own name, in 416 (TAD B2.10:19); (5) and as a single name on an ostracon (TAD D9.6). So, this ostracon, too, would have been written in the last quarter of the century.

5. A fifth list, an opisthograph with ten lines on each side (No. J9) has four names that appear elsewhere in the papyri and suggests a date in the early part of the century: גדול בר יגדל, בעדי בר גדול, גמריה בר אחיו and זכור בר משלם. By the way, each of the latter two names appears twice in the list. (1) Gaddul and Gemariah appear one after the other as witness to a contract in *464* (TAD B2.2:18); (2) Gemariah is also scribe and debtor on a contract of 487 (TAD B4.2:16) and is recipient of a GIFT in an ostracon of the first quarter century (TAD D7.9:2);

(3) Baadi must be the same as Baadiah grandfather of מנחם בר גדול בר בעדיה, who is witness in a contract of 416 (TAD B2.10:18), yielding the four-generation genealogy

מנחם בר גדול בר בעדי[ה] בר גדול

[6] *Transeuphratène* 34 (2007), 180.

[7] See Tal ILAN, *Lexicon of Jewish Names in Late Antiquity, Part II, Palestine 200-650* (Texts and Studies in Ancient Judaism 148), Tübingen, Mohr Siebeck, 2012, 77.

and placing Baadi(ah) son of Gaddul about the same time as Gaddul and Gemariah, that is *464*.

(4) If the fourth person, Zakkur son of Meshullam were the father of Tamet's master Meshullam son of Zakkur, who had a son named Zakkur (TAD B3.3:2, 3.6:2, 12; 3.8:2, 3.9:2), that would yield another four-generation genealogy,

Zakkur son of Meshullam son of ZAKKUR SON OF MESHULLAM.

6. A sixth list, containing five lines (No. 177) and only two names intact, may have one of them as witness on a contract. Even the intact name is cut off at the left edge – אושע בר פטחנ[ום]. This may be paralleled by the witness הושע בר פטחנום in the same contract of 464 (mentioned above) where Gaddul and Gemariah were witnesses (TAD B2.2:17-18). He may be the same one as אושע בר פט[...] who wrote about the same time from Migdol to his son Shelomam (TAD A3.3:14).

So the five lists that have persons appearing in dated papyri show three from the end of the century (Nos. 2-4) and two from ca 464 (Nos. 5-6). Only one has a caption (No. 1) and it contains no datable persons. Most striking, however, is the large number of names that have no parallels in the papyri. Clearly, the ostraca provide a valuable source for the colony's demography.

MESSAGE ON A BOTTLE: THE TELL SIRAN INSCRIPTION REVISITED

Matthieu RICHELLE

1. ONE TEXT, MANY TRANSLATIONS

While relatively brief, the Ammonite text engraved on the Tell Siran bottle, found in 1972 in Amman and dated ca. 600 B.C.E.[1], has aroused the curiosity of many scholars[2]. In spite of all their efforts, there exists

[1] Most scholars agree that the inscription should be paleographically dated to ca. 600 B.C.E. and that the Amminadab mentioned in line 3 is probably the same person as *Am-mi-na-ad-bi šarru mat bit am-ma-na* mentioned by Assurbanipal in cylinder C ca. 667 B.C.E. Indeed, this Amminadab may also be mentioned in two seals:

L'DNPLṬ ʿBD ʿMNDB (CAI 17 = WSS 858)

LʿDNNR ʿBD ʿMNDB (CAI 40 = WSS 859)

The paleography of these seals seems less developed than that of the Tell Siran inscription, notably because the tops of the heads of B and ʿ are closed, whereas they are open on the bottle, and this corresponds to a diachronic development in the Ammonite script, under the influence of the Aramaic script. This development is clearly attested in the seal script (Larry G. HERR, «Aramaic and Ammonite Seal Scripts», in Jo Ann HACKETT, Walter A. AUFRECHT [eds.], *"An Eye for Form". Epigraphic Essays in Honor of Frank Moore Cross*, Winona Lake, Eisenbrauns, 2014, 185) and in the cursive script (Christopher A. ROLLSTON, "Northwest Semitic Cursive Scripts of Iron II", in *ibid.*, 223; Matthieu RICHELLE, "Revisiting the Ammonite Ostraca", *MAARAV* 22.1-2 [2018] 72-73). Unfortunately, the first seal is unprovenanced, so its authenticity is uncertain, but the second was found in a tomb in Amman during excavations.

[2] Henri O. THOMPSON, Fawzi ZAYADINE, "The Tell Siran Inscription", *BASOR* 212 (1973) 5-11; Frank M. CROSS, "Notes on the Ammonite Inscription from Tell Sīrān", *BASOR* 212 (1973) 12-15; Oswald LORETZ, "Die Ammonitische Inschrift von Tell Siran", *UF* 9 (1973) 169-172; Javier TEIXIDOR, "Bulletin d'épigraphie sémitique", *Syria* 51 (1974) 317-18; H. O. THOMPSON, F. ZAYADINE, "Tell Siran", *RB* 81 (1974) 80-85; Paul-Emile Dion, "Notes d'épigraphie ammonite", *RB* 82 (1975) 24-33; J. TEIXIDOR, "Bulletin d'épigraphie sémitique", *Syria* 52 (1975) 262-63; Charles R. KRAHMALKOV, "An Ammonite Lyric Poem", *BASOR* 223 (1976) 55-57; William H. SHEA, "The Siran Inscription. Amminadab's Drinking Song", *PEQ* 110 (1978) 107-12; Robert B. COOTE, "The Tell Siran Bottle Reconsidered", *BASOR* 240 (1980) 93; Massimo BALDACCI, "The Ammonite Text from Tell Siran and North-West Semitic Philology", *VT* 31 (1981) 363-68; Bob BECKING, "Zur Interpretation des Ammonitischen Inschrift vom Tell Sīrān", *BiOr* 38 (1981) 273-76; John A. EMERTON, "The Meaning of the Ammonite Inscription from Tell Siran", in Wilhelmus C. DELSMAN (ed.), *Von Kanaan bis Kerala: Festschrift für Prof. Mag. Dr. J. P. M. van der Ploeg O. P. zur Vollendung des siebzigsten Lebensjahres am 4 Juli 1979* (AOAT, 211), Neukirchen-Vluyn, Neukirchener Verlag, 1982, 367-77, reprinted in Graham DAVIES and Robert GORDON

no consensus as to its meaning (see a non-exhaustive list of translations in Appendix). To summarize, one may distinguish between two main interpretations:

1. A commemorative inscription

This is the interpretation offered in the *editio princeps*[3]. Typical is the translation in Aḥituv's handbook[4]:

(eds.), *Studies on the Languages and Literature of the Bible. Selected Works of J.A. Emerton* (VTSup, 165), Leiden, Brill, 2015, 398-409; H. O. THOMPSON, F. ZAYADINE, "The Tell Siran Bottle. An Additional Note", *BASOR* 249 (1982) 87-89; Kent P. JACKSON, *The Ammonite Language of the Iron Age* (HSM, 27), Chico, Scholars Press, 1983, 54-68; Gösta W. AHLSTRÖM, "The Tell Siran Bottle Inscription", *PEQ* 116 (1984) 12-15; Emile PUECH, "L'inscription de la statue d'Amman et la Paléographie Ammonite", *RB* 92 (1985) 12; Erasmus Johannes SMIT, "The Tell Siran Inscription. Linguistic and Historical Implications", *Journal for Semitics* 1 (1989) 108-17; H. O. THOMPSON, F. ZAYADINE, "The Ammonite Inscription from Tell Siran", in H. O. THOMPSON (ed.), *Archaeology in Jordan*, New York, Peter Lang, 1989, 159-93; Ulrich HÜBNER, *Die Ammoniter. Untersuchungen zur Geschichte, Kultur und Religion eines Transjordanischen Volkes im 1. Jahrtausend v. Chr.* (ADPV, 16), Wiesbaden, Harrassowitz, 1992, 26-30; André LEMAIRE, "Epigraphy, Transjordany", *ABD* 2, 561-68; Klaus BEYER, "The Ammonite Tell Siran Bottle Inscription Reconsidered", in Ziony ZEVIT, Seymour GITIN and Michael SOKOLOFF (eds.), *Solving Riddles and Untying Knots. Biblical, Epigraphic, and Semitic Studies in Honor of Jonas C. Greenfield*, Winona Lake, Eisenbrauns, 1995, 389-91; Hans-Peter MÜLLER, "Kohelet und Amminadab", in Anja A. DIESEL, Reinhard G. LEHRMANN, Eckart OTTO, Andreas WAGNER (eds.), *"Jedes Ding hat seine Ziet…". Studien zur israelitischen und altorientalischen Weisheit Diethelen Michel zum 65. Geburtstag* (BZAW, 241), Berlin/New York, de Gruyter, 1996, 149-65; Walter E. AUFRECHT, "The Tell Sīrān Inscription", in William HALLO, K. Lawson YOUNGER (eds.), *The Context of Scripture* II. *Monumental Inscriptions*, Leiden/Boston/Köln, Brill, 2000, 139-40; Joseph AZIZE, "The Ammonite Bottle and Phoenician Flasks", *ANES* 40 (2003) 62-79; Dirk KINET, "Die Bronze-Flasche aus Tell Siran", in Friedbert Ninow (ed.), *Wort und Stein. Studien zur Theologie une Archäologie. Festschrift für Udo Worschech* (Beiträge zur Erforschung der antiken Moabitis [Ard el-Kerak], 4), Frankfürt, Peter Lang, 2003, 133-44; Ingo KOTTSIEPER, "Zur Inschrift auf der Flasche vom Tell Sīrān und ihrem historischen Hintergrund", *UF* 34 (2003) 353-62; idem, "Eine ammonitische Inschrift des ʿMNDB von Ammon", in Bernd JANOWSKI, Gernot WILHELM (eds.), *Texte aus der Umwelt des Alten Testaments, Neue Folge* II. *Staatsverträge, Herrscherinschriften und andere Dokumente zur politischen Geschichte*, Gütersloh, Gütersloher Verlagshaus, 2005, 314; Giovanni GARBINI, *Introduzione all'epigrafia semitica* (Studi sul Vicino Oriente antico, 4), Brescia, Paideia Editrice, 2006, 105; Shmuel AḤITUV, *Echoes from the Past. Hebrew and Cognate Inscriptions from the Biblical Period*, Jerusalem, Carta, 2008, 363-67; Douglas J. GREEN, *"I Undertook Great Works". The Ideology of Domestic Achievements in West Semitic Royal Inscriptions* (FAT, II.41), Tübingen, Mohr Siebeck, 2010, 266-81; Walter E. AUFRECHT, *A Corpus of Ammonite Inscriptions*, Lewinston, Edwin Mellers, 2018², 356-65 [1st edition 1989].

[3] H. O. THOMPSON, F. ZAYADINE, "The Tell Siran Inscription".

[4] Sh. AḤITUV, *Echoes*, 363.

line	text	Aḥituv's translation
1	MʿBD ʿMNDB MLK BN ʿMN	The works of ʿAmmînāḏāḇ, king of the Ammonites,
2	BN HṢL'L.MLK BN ʿMN	the son of Hiṣṣil'ēl, king of the Ammonites,
3	BN ʿMNDB MLK BN ʿMN	the son of ʿAmmînāḏāḇ, king of the Ammonites:
4	HKRM.WH.GNT.WH'TḤR[5]	the vineyard and the garden and the tunnel/channel(?)
5	W'ŠḤT	and the reservoir.
6	YGL WYŠMḤ	May he rejoice and be happy
7	BYWMT RBM WBŠNT	for many days and in years
8	RḤQT	far off.

According to a variant of this translation, defended by Coote[6] and Aufrecht[7], the first word of the inscription is explicited in lines 4-5 and is the subject of the verbs in line 6. Here is Aufrecht's translation:

(1) May the produce of ʿAmmīnadab king of the Ammonites,
(2) the son of Haṣṣil'il king of the Ammonites,
(3) the son of ʿAmmīnadab king of the Ammonites
(4) – the vineyard and the garden(s) and the hollow (5) and cistern –
(6) cause rejoicing and gladness (7) for many days (to come) and in years (8) far off.

2. A poem

Krahmalkov[8] suggested translating the first word of the inscription into "poem" and that lines 4-8 constituted the poem in question:

The poem of Amminadab, king of the Ammonites,
the son of Hassel'el, king of the Ammonites,
the son of Amminadab, king of the Ammonites:
"To the vineyard and the orchard! Or shall I be left behind and destroyed?"
He (who says this) rejoice and be happy that life is long and there are years yet unlived.

[5] The reading of this letter has been debated; it appears on the base of the bottle. Most published images of the bottle only offer a front view and do not enable one to correctly see the letter. The images on Inscriptifact leave no doubt that it must be read R.

[6] R. B. Coote, "Tell Siran Bottle", 93.

[7] W. E. Aufrecht, "Tell Sīrān Inscription", 139-40.

[8] C. R. Krahmalkov, "Ammonite", 56.

Krahmalkov commented his translation as follows: "The lyric seems to be antiphonal in character. In a feigned plaint the fear of being delayed and cut off in the pursuit of life's pleasures and contentments is given expression; haste is urged to the vineyard and orchard[9]." Shea[10], Loretz[11] and Emerton[12] adopted this interpretation with a few differences. Essential to this line of interpretation is the notion that lines 4-5 should not be regarded as a list of four building works, but as two pairs of words: a reference to a vineyard and an orchard, followed by two verbs used to ask rhetorical questions. This line of interpretation has influenced even some scholars whose overall interpretation is that of a commemorative inscription but who regard the last of the four words in lines 4-5 as a verb[13].

In the end, although most scholars follow one of the two main lines of interpretation presented above, there is a profusion of competing translations. What is frustrating is that many scholars adopt one of the two main interpretations without really discussing the philological reasons they have to reject the other. Against this background, the purpose of the following is not to add yet another interpretation of an inscription that is already subject to so many speculations, but to bring some clarity to the debate. I shall attempt to show that certain philological considerations, a neglected feature of the inscription, and some Ancient Near Eastern parallels, render the second line of interpretation unlikely. To this end, I will briefly review the analysis of the most debated parts of the text: the first word of line 1; the two last words of lines 4-5; lines 6-8.

2. The meaning of the first word of the inscription

No fewer than seven different translations of the first word have been proposed (see Table 1).

Table 1: Analyses of MʿBD

	translation	**analysis**	**scholars**
1	Works	Susbtantive masc. pl., root ʿBD Cf. מַעְבָּדֵיהֶם (Job 34:25), מַעֲבָדוֹהִי (Dan 4:34)	Thompson and Zayadine; Teixidor; Dion; Baldacci; Lemaire; Hübner; Müller; Kottsieper; Garbini

[9] C. R. Krahmalkov, "Ammonite", 56.
[10] W. H. Shea, "Siran Inscription".
[11] O. Loretz, "Die Ammonitische Inschrift von Tell Siran".
[12] J. A. Emerton, "Meaning".
[13] B. Becking, "Interpretation"; I. Kottsieper, "Inschrift".

	translation	**analysis**	**scholars**
2	Work	Susbtantive masc. sing., root ʿBD	Jackson
	Product; produce		Coote; Aufrecht
	Crop yield		Becking
3	Object		Loretz
4	Poem		Krahmalkov (1976); Emerton
5	From the cultivation of	Preposition M + (passive?) participle	Shea
6	That which… has laid out	Proclitic M + verb	Ahlström; Beyer
7	Pious	Adjective masc. sing. Cf. ʿBD "to serve, worship"	Azize

Proponents of the hypothesis of a commemorative inscription assume that the word MʿBD is a substantive, with the preformative M and the root ʿBD. The most widely accepted meaning is "work(s)" on the basis that ʿBD means "to work" in Aramaic.[14] Now "work" is a very general term and a few scholars have attempted to render it more specifically in view of the context and of possible parallels in Biblical Hebrew for the root ʿBD, hence the proposals "product", "produce" and "crop yield". The underlying assumption is that the word refers to the contents of the bottle. Actually a botanical analysis of the contents showed that it mainly consisted of wheat and barley, but radiocarbon dating yielded a date later than that of the inscription by at least a century[15], so it may be a case of secondary usage. In any case, the weakness of the "contents" approach to the term MʿBD is that it would be a surprisingly general choice of word

[14] Most scholars prefer to regard the word as a plural because of their interpretation of the text (e.g. the "works" in question could be the building works mentioned in lines 4-5). Indeed, it is clear from the expression BN ʿMN, "sons of Ammon", in line 1-3, that the masculine plural is not marked in Ammonite (cf. W. Randall GARR, *Dialect Geography of Syria-Palestine, 1000-586 B.C.E.*, Philadelphia, University Press, 1985, 91).

[15] The result was 450 or 400 +- 50 B.C.E. depending on the calculation method (H. O. THOMPSON, F. ZAYADINE, "Additional Note", 88). Since there was no king in Ammon in the 5th or 4th centuries B.C.E (it was part of the Persian empire), the appropriate conclusion is not to reject the paleographical dating in the late Iron Age, as approximate as it may be, but to admit that the contents of the bottle results from a secondary usage.

to refer to perfume or cereals.The occurrences of ʿBD in the Biblical Hebrew that are alleged in order to support their cases are no solid ground. Some scholars also refer to various occurrences of עשה, but this seems to me a tenous basis. It is not because ʿBD is sometimes used to designate some work in an agricultural context (Gen 2:15; Deut 28:39) that we can "import" this acception into any new context, lest we commit an "illegitimate totality transfer", to borrow James Barr's expression. We would need very solid contextual reasons in the text under scrutiny to propose such a translation. "Works" would be a more appropriate designation of the realities mentioned in lines 4-5 if they were "vineyard", "garden", perhaps "canal" and "reservoir", as many scholars argue. The same objection holds true for the translation "object": why not use a word meaning "bottle"[16]? Moreover, it is just an *ad hoc* translation with no clear semantic basis linked to the root ʿBD[17].

In reality, the main alternative proposal to "work(s)" is "poem". It is based on two considerations. First, lines 4-8 constitute a poem according to these scholars, which is debatable, as we shall see. Second, MʿBD is explained by an analogy with מַעֲשֶׂה in Psalm 45:2, which Krahmalkov renders as "poem"[18]. However, unless we commit, again, an "illegitimate totality transfer", we cannot argue from this occurrence that the word מַעֲשֶׂה bears *in itself* the extremely rare meaning "poem", so it does not allow us to import this meaning into any other context; we would need very solid contextual reasons for that. All the more so when it comes to import this meaning for another word (MʿBD) in another language (Ammonite), even if we admit that it is the Aramaic (and Ammonite) equivalent of מַעֲשֶׂה[19].

[16] Objection made by D. J. GREEN, *"I Undertook"*, 273 fn. 27.

[17] In spite of LORETZ's claims, neither Job 34:25 not Dan 4:34 are grounds for this hypothesis.

[18] C. R. KRAHMALKOV, "Ammonite", 56. Emerton also refers to דבר in Prov 30:1; 31.1, which does not seem helpful: while it is unsurprising that a term that usually means "word" can sometimes mean "composition," it is a completely different matter to say that a word based on a root meaning "to make" can sometimes mean "poem."

[19] In fact, what prompted Krahmalkov and Emerton to go to such lengths to find a new meaning of MʿBD is some supposed problems with the translation "work(s)." Notably, there would be no connection between the building works referred to in the word MʿBD, and listed in lines 4-5, on the one hand, and the bottle on which it is engraved, on the other (C. R. KRAHMALKOV, "Ammonite", 55). Yet the same problem obtains with the translation "poem," because the only possible connection between the poem (in both Krahmalkov and Emerton's translations) and the flask is that the latter is the medium on which the former is inscribed. Why did Amminadab have such a poem engraved on a bottle? Moreover, I suggest

Other analyses must be mentioned. Shea thinks that M is the preposition "from" and ʿBD a participle, and he translates the word as "from the cultivation of"[20]. As Emerton has pointed out, Shea's analysis is somewhat fuzzy and the resulting translation problematic since he needs to postulate that "The wine in this vessel comes" is implied before the beginning of the text. Also, it is doubtful that the quantity of wine that this bottle, be it a good bottle of *Bordeaux*, could contain would be able to make somebody drunk. More interestingly, Ahlström and Beyer[21] regard M as a proclictic particle meaning "that which", hence "that which he has made" or "that which he has laid out". There are instances of a similar construction in Biblical Hebrew[22] and in epigraphy[23], so this seems possible. Finally, Azize regards MʿBD as an adjective meaning "pious", on the grounds that ʿBD often means "to serve, to worship" in Hebrew and Phoenician[24]. Yet this semantic deduction seems a bit of a stretch, and Azize does not offer any detailed justification for the formation of the word MʿBD.

To sum up, at face value, the most plausible translations of MʿBD seem to be "work(s)" and "that which...", while the translation "poem" would need to be supported by strong contextual reasons. This leads me to lines 4-5.

3. The two last the words in line 4-5

The two first words in line 4 are only rarely disputed as regards their meaning; what is debated is their function in the context. It really depends on the interpretation of the last word of line 4 (H'TḤR) and the word on line 5 ('ŠḤT).

No fewer than eight different translations of the last word of line 4 have been proposed (see Table 2), and five for the word in line 5 (see Table 3).

there may have been a connection between the bottle and the building works of lines 4-5: maybe the (original) contents of the bottle were products made thanks to these agricultural installations. This hypothesis does not depend on the notion that MʿBD refers to the bottle or its content; the very fact that this bottle contained such products was sufficient.

[20] W. H. Shea, "Siran Inscription", 108.

[21] K. Beyer, "Ammonite", 390.

[22] *IBHS* §18.3d.

[23] *DNWSI*, 600.

[24] J. Azize, "Ammonite", 70-71.

Table 2: analyses of H'TḤR

	root	grammatical details	translation	proponents
1	ḤWR	Noun with prothetic ' and infixed T	tunnel	Dion; Baldacci; Aḥituv ("tunnel/ channel")
2	ḤRR	Idem; cf. South-Arabian ḤRT ("canal"), Akkadian ḫarāru and ḫerû ("to dig")	canal	Lemaire; Garbini
3		Idem; cf. חֹר in Num 33:32	hollow	Aufrecht
4	'ḤR	verbal adjective, Gt or Dt with a passive sense ("what was kept")	stock	Becking
5	'ḤR	Interrogative particle H + imperfect Dt, 1st pers. sing. Cf. Arabic *ta'aḫḫara* ("to be delayed; to be left behind")	shall I be left behind? > shall I vex myself?	Krahmalkov Emerton
6		Idem but Gt	should I stay behind?	Loretz
7	ḤRH	Interrogative particle H + imperfect Dt, 1st pers. sing.	shall I inflamme myself?	Shea
8	?	Imperfect Gt, 3rd pers. sing.	he dedicated	Azize

Table 3: analyses of 'ŠḤT

	root	grammatical details	translation	proponents
1	ŠWḤ	sing. or pl. noun with prothetic ' cf. 'ŠWḤ on the Mesha stele; שׁוּחָה ("pit" in Jer 2:6); שַׁחַת ("pit"; Ezek 19:4); ("reservoir"); אשיח Ben Sira 50:3)	cistern(s); pools; reservoir(s)	Thompson and Zayadine; Teixidor; Dion; Baldacci; Lemaire; Beyer; Aufrecht; Smit; Hübner; Müller; Kinet; Garbini; Aḥituv
2	ŠḤT	imperfect N-stem; 1st pers. sing.	shall I be destroyed?	Krahmalkov; Shea
3		Imperfect G-stem; 1st pers. sing.	shall I destroy?	Becking
4	ṢḤ	unclear; cf. Arabic "to be in good health"	he recovered	Azize
5	'Š + ḤT	substantive 'Š ("man") or relative pronoun + adjective cf. חַת (1 Sam 2:4)	those who are scared	Kottsieper (2003)

There are several problems with the interpretations that take these words as verb forms. First, most of these interpretations (more precisely, #5-8 in Table 2 and #4-5 in Table 3) are based on tenuous philological foundations. Regarding the last word in line 4 ('TḤR), Krahmalkov's interpretation (cf. #5 in Table 2) relies on the notion that the root 'ḤR is "well attested in common Semitic in the intensive stem [D] with the meaning 'to be delayed, late, to tarry; to be left behind' (intransitive) and 'to delay, postpone; to hinder; to leave back' (transitive)"[25]. Yet for the Dt stem, which he takes on for the word under scrutiny, he is only able to mention the Arabic form 5 (= Dt) with the meaning "to be delayed" or "to be left behind". In fact, I failed to find solid evidence of the meaning "to be left behind" in any stem in West Semitic languages, and it seems precarious to argue that it would exist in Ammonite. The derived meaning "to be vexed", put forward by Emerton (see, again, #5 in Table 2), is even more conjectural. Moreover, Krahmalkov's analysis requires that a metathesis of T and the first radical (>'TḤR) occurs in the Ammonite Dt stem, but it is not very likely since among the other Semitic languages this metathesis occurs only in Akkadian[26]. Loretz's interpretation (#6 in Table 2) postulates a Gt stem, but, even assuming that this stem existed in Ammonite[27], the meaning "to stay behind" corresponds to the D stem or Dt stem in other languages, as far as I can see. Shea's proposal (#7 in Table 2) presupposes an elision of the final radical H, which does not happen in Hebrew, and we have no ground to assume that it happens in Ammonite[28]. As for Azize's proposal (#8 in Table 2), it is even more problematic since no precise root is suggested.

With regard to the word in line 5 ('ŠḤT), Azize's interpretation (#4 in Table 3) is based on a comparison with ṢḤ in Arabic, which is hardly convincing. As for Kottsieper's idea (#5 in Table 3) to break 'ŠḤT into 'Š + ḤT, it is more astute than compelling. Note in particular that the Ammonite relative pronoun is not 'Š but Š[29].

[25] C. R. KRAHMALKOV, "Ammonite", 56.

[26] Edward LIPIŃSKI, *Semitic Languages. Outline of a Comparative Grammar* (OLA, 80), Leuven, Peeters, 2001², 406. The exception, of course, is when the first radical is a sibilant in Hebrew, Phoenician and Aramaic.

[27] There is no evidence for this; see Ill-Sung Andrew YUN, "The Transjordanian Languages during the Iron Age II", *UF* 37 (2005) 757.

[28] As noted by B. BECKING, "Interpretation", 274.

[29] Matthieu RICHELLE, Michael WEIGL, "Hisban Ostracon A1. New Collation and New Readings", *ADAJ* 53 (2009) 133; RICHELLE, "Notes épigraphiques sur l'ostracon n°3 de Tell el-Mazar", *Semitica* 54 (2012) 139; idem, "Revisiting", 56; *pace* W. R. GARR, "Dialect Geography", 85; I.-S. A. YUN, "Transjordanian Languages", 751.

Second, these interpretations strike me as improbable as regards the resulting meaning of the text. For instance, Krahmalkov translates: "To the vineyard and the orchard! Or shall I be left behind and destroyed?", which I find far from poetic. The same with Loretz's translation: "O Weinberg, o Kelter, und ich soll zurückbleiben und verderben?" As for Shea's proposal: "Shall I inflame myself (with it) and be ruined?", it is inspired by the idea that the king might be "inflamed" by wine as in Isaiah 5:11, but the verb used in the latter verse is דָּלַק, whereas the metaphorical use of חָרָה concerns anger (e.g. Psalm 37:1), not inebriation.

Third, I would like to draw attention to a feature of the text that has been neglected by most scholars and that leads me to regard the "poem" interpretation as unlikely. What is rarely noted by commentators is that the engraver took care that the layout of the engraved text followed the inner logic of the contents. Thus each of the three first inscribed lines follows the parallel construction of the text and ends by "king of the sons of Ammon":

(1) MʿBD of Amminadab, king of the sons of Ammon,
(2) the son of Hiṣṣal'el, king of the sons of Ammon,
(3) the son of Amminadab, king of the sons of Ammon

It is not just because there was no space after the words "sons of Ammon" that the engraver started a new line: line 4 shows that he was able to go even more to the left if he wanted to do so. Similarly, the engraver started a new line after the word of line 5 and after the two words of line 6, whereas in both cases there was plenty of space left. The only possible explanation is that the layout of the inscription corresponds somewhat to its literary structure, or its syntactical components. Thus line 6 stops relatively early because of the poetical structure of the clauses in line 6 ("May he rejoice and be glad") on the one hand, and in lines 7-8 on the other ("for many days and years far off"), both of which contain a pair of nearly synonymous expressions. Apparently, only space contraints prevented the scribe from writing the entire second clause on the same line.

(6) May he rejoice and be glad
(7) for many days and years
(8) far off.

This concern for the correspondance between the layout and the structure of the contents is very unusual in North-West Semitic epigraphy as far as continuous texts are concerned; it happens with lists, but I failed to find a parallel when it comes to royal inscriptions or letters. This is a fascinating feature of this inscription. It means either that the engraver understood what he was writing (contrary to Thompson and Zayadine's view[30]) or that he was reproducing a layout prepared by a scribe.

In my view, this observation renders the "poetic" interpretation unlikely. If lines 4-5 really comprised two different clauses, as argued by Krahmalkov, Shea, Loretz and Emerton (see their translations in the Appendix), then I submit that the convention followed by the engraver in the rest of the inscription would have led him to start a new line after the second word of line 4. The corresponding layout would have been the following:

HKRM.WH.GNT.
WH'TḤR.W'ŠḤT

In my view, the layout writing of lines 4-5 encourages us to read the word in line 5 (W'ŠḤT) as the direct continuation of the previous sentence[31], so lines 4-5 constitutes one sentence (or, alternatively, the end of a longer sentence).

Fourth, the literary genre of inscriptions commemorating the building works of a king is well attested in the Ancient Near East, the only peculiarity of the present inscription being its medium, a bottle. The same cannot be said in favor of the "poem" interpretation. Moreover, many scholars[32] have noted the similarity of the text with Qoheleth 2: 4-5:

> I made great works; I built houses and planted vineyards for myself; I made myself gardens and parks, and planted in them all kinds of fruit trees. I made myself pools from which to water the forest of growing trees.

It is not, of course, that the Biblical passage and the inscription belong to the same literary genre, but they are based on the same royal rhetoric which exalts the building and botanical works of a king.

So I find various weaknesses in the "poem" interpretation. By contrast, the only difficulties with the "commemorative text" interpretation are the analysis of the last word in line 4 (H'TḤR), and the absence of a definite article before the word in line 5 ('ŠḤT). Yet plausible explanations have

[30] H. O. THOMPSON, F. ZAYADINE, "Tell Siran Inscription", 5; idem, "Ammonite", 162. This view was based on the anomalous presence of the separator in WH.GNT in line 4.

[31] It is even tempting to hypothesize that line 6 marks the beginning of a new sentence, since it is so neatly separated from what precedes. This would rule out the translations of COOTE, AUFRECHT, KOTTSIEPER and GARBINI. However, I would refrain from reasoning in such a way because we see in lines 6-7 that the engraver started a new line in the middle of a sentence.

[32] See e.g. H.-P. MÜLLER, "Kohelet und Amminadab".

been put forward for the former, based on the roots ḤWR or ḤRR with an infixed T[33] (#1-3 in Table 2), and all of them leads to more or less the same interpretation: a tunnel, a canal or a reservoir, perhaps a hollow, that is, some water system. This fits the context very well. As for the absence of definitive article in line 5, it does not seem to me an insuperable difficulty; maybe it was just an oversight or an aural error.

4. Lines 6-8

Finally, lines 6-8 are less debated, although there exist some variations. The majority interpretation regards it as a self-contained sentence bearing a general wish: "May he [= the king Amminadab] rejoice and be happy for many years and in years far off". But some scholars argue that the subject of the verbs in line 6 (YGL and YŠMḤ) is no other than the works mentioned in lines 4-5[34] or the wine supposedly contained in the bottle[35]. As already mentioned, Coote and Aufrecht even propose that the entire text contains only one sentence, the first word being explicited in lines 4-5:

> May the produce of ʿAmmīnadab (…) – the vineyard and the garden(s) and the hollow and cistern – cause rejoicing and gladness for many days (to come) and in years far off.

In my view, these proposals do not render justice to the fact that this text contains a well attested topos of Levantine inscriptions[36], whereby a king expresses his wish that his life (and his reign) last as long as possible. Green gathers various parallels, in Yehimilk (KAI 4), Elibaal (KAI 6), Shipitbaal (KAI 7), Kilamuwa II (KAI 25), Tell Fekherye and the royal inscription from Ekron[37]. The typical sentence is: "May DN lengthen the days of PN [the king] and his years over his kingdom"[38]. It strains

[33] See E. Lipiński, *Semitic Languages*, 227.

[34] K. Beyer, "Ammonite", 390-91.

[35] W. H. Shea, "Siran Inscription", 110.

[36] There are also good parallels for "may he rejoice and be glad", since the pair of verbs occurs several times in the Hebrew Bible (Isa 25:9; 66:10; etc.), and for "for many days and years far off" (Ezek 12:27: לְיָמִים רַבִּים וּלְעִתִּים רְחוֹקוֹת). Yet what we find on the bottle is a combination of both, and the best parallel for this is to be found in some royal inscriptions.

[37] D. J. Green, *"I Undertook"*, 272.

[38] Strictly speaking, the wish does not concern the lengthening of the king's life, but his enjoyment during that life (line 6). Usually, one encounters some form of the verb ʾRK ("to lengthen"); here, it is the verbs YGL and YŠMḤ that convey the wish. Yet this does not mean that the king takes for granted that he will have a long life; to wish that one may rejoice during numerous days is also a way of wishing that one will have numerous days in the first

credulity to believe that the resemblance between lines 6-8 and this topos is a coincidence, and this constitutes, in my view, yet another reason to regard the inscription as a commemorative text. Interestingly, the Tell Siran inscription deviates from the well-established pattern in that it does not mention any deity. While I can accept that the deity is left unmentioned (perhaps only implied) because the text is "king-centered", as argued by Green[39], I find it doubtful that the deity would be replaced by building works as the source of the well-being and long reign of the king, as Coote and Aufrecht's interpretation requires[40]. In addition, the initial position of the verbs (YGL and YŠMḤ) is a good fit for their jussive function in a new sentence[41].

CONCLUSION

The classical interpretation of the Tell Siran bottle inscription as a commemorative text has been challenged by another interpretation that reads it as a poem. While this second line of interpretation was based on astute reasoning and has appealed to various scholars, it is unlikely for several reasons: the philological basis of the corresponding translations are tenuous, it does not fit the careful layout of the text and it misses important parallels in Ancient Near Eastern documentation. The most recent interpretation of an inscription is not necessarily the best.

It is a great honor and pleasure to offer this study to Professor Emile Puech as a modest token of admiration and friendship. The work of this distinguished epigrapher has marked many areas in the field of West-Semitic epigraphy; the Ammonite corpus, to which the Tell Siran bottle belongs, is no exception and I remember how, when studying this corpus, I found myself constantly returning to Emile Puech's article on Ammonite paleography[42].

place. The phrasing is a subtle way to wish both a good quality (line 6) and great quantity (lines 7-8) of life (D. J. GREEN, *"I Undertook"*, 273).

39 D. J. GREEN, *"I Undertook"*, 277.

40 Note also that the identification of the topos rules out M. BALDACCI's translation: "May he be gratified and may he be congratulated after many days and long years" ("Ammonite", 364).

41 See, for Classical Biblical Hebrew poetry, Jan JOOSTEN, *The Verbal System of Biblical Hebrew. A New Synthesis Elaborated on the Basis of Classical Prose* (Jerusalem Biblical Studies, 10), Jerusalem, Simor, 2012, 433.

42 É. PUECH, "L'inscription de la statue d'Amman"; see also É. PUECH and A. ROFÉ, "L'inscription de la Citadelle d'Amman", *RB* 80 (1973) 531-546. In particular, my own direct examination of Hisban ostracon A1 (also named Ostracon IV) has led me to conclude that the Ammonite relative pronoun is not 'Š but Š (as already noted above). I was struck by the

APPENDIX: VARIOUS TRANSLATIONS OF THE TELL SIRAN INSCRIPTION

Author	Lines 1-3	Lines 4-5	Lines 6-8
Thompson and Zayadine 1973	The works of Amminadab, king of the Ammonites, the son of Hiṣṣal'el, king of the Ammonites, the son of Amminadab, king of the Ammonites,	a vineyard and the gardens and the *ʾtḥr* and cisterns.	May he rejoice and be glad for many days and long years.
Dion 1975	Travaux d'Amminadab roi des Ammonites, Fils de Hiṣṣīl'ēl, roi des Ammonites, Fils d'Amminadab, roi des Ammonites:	la vigne et les jardins et les tunnel (?) et citerne (?).	Qu'il se réjouisse et qu'il soit heureux en des jours nombreux et des années prolongées!
Khramalkov 1976	The poem of Amminadab, king of the Ammonites, the son of Hassel'el, king of the Ammonites, the son of Amminadab, king of the Ammonites:	"To the vineyard and the orchard! Or shall I be left behind and destroyed?"	He (who says this) rejoice and be happy that life is long and there are years yet unlived.
Shea 1978	(The wine in this vessel comes) From the cultivation of Amminadab, king of the sons of Ammon, the son of Hiṣṣal'el, king of the sons of Ammon, the son of Amminadab, king of the sons of Ammon,	of the vineyard and the garden, and shall I inflame myself (with it) and be ruined? (No!)	It shall make glad and bring joy for many days and long years.
Loretz 1978	Gegenstand Amminadab, Königs der Ammoniter, Sohn des Hiṣṣal-El, Königs der Ammoniter, Sohn des Amminadab, Königs der Ammoniter.	O Weinberg, o Kelter, und ich soll zurückbleiben und verderben?	Er möge jubeln und sich freuen viele Tage und lange Jahren!
Coote 1980	May the product of Amminadab, king of the Ammonites, the son of Hiṣṣil-'el, king of the Ammonites, the son of Amminadab, king of the Ammonites	– the vineyard and the orchard and the park and <the> pools –	give pleasure for many days and for years far off.

fact that this confirmed Emile Puech's drawing of the ostracon ("L'inscription de la statue", 17, Fig. V): before Š, he had correctly read the letter W instead of ʾ read by other scholars. And yet his reading was not based on the meaning of the text, only on his impressively accurate "eye".

Author	Lines 1-3	Lines 4-5	Lines 6-8
Baldacci 1981	Work of ʿmndb, king of ʿAmmon, son of hṣl'l, king of ʿAmmon, son of ʿmndb, king of ʿAmmon.	the vineyards and the orchards and the tunnel and a cistern.	May he be gratified and may he be congratulated after many days and long years.
Becking 1981	Ernteertrag des Amminadab, des Königs der Ammoniter, des Sohnes des Hiṣṣal'el, des Königs der Ammoniter, des Sohnes des Amminadab, des Königs der Ammoniter.	Den Weinberg, den Garten(/die Gärten) und den Vorrat: soll ich (diese) vernichten?	Lass ihn Freude und Fröhlichkeit verbreiten während vieler Tage und in fernen Jahren.
Emerton 1982	The poem of Amminadab, king of the Ammonites, the son of Hassel'el, king of the Ammonites, the son of Amminadab, king of the Ammonites.	O Vineyard and garden: (or: in the vineyard and garden). Shall I vex myself and destroy myself?	Let a man rejoice and be glad for many days and far-off years.
Smit 1989	The works of Amminadab, king of the Ammonites, the son of Hissil'el, king of the Ammonites, the son of Amminadab, king of the Ammonites,	the vineyard, and then the gardens, and the trough, and (many) cisterns.	May he rejoice and be glad for many days and years far away.
Lemaire 1991	Deeds of Amminadab king of the Ammonites, the son of Hizzilel king of the Ammonites, the son of Amminadab king of the Ammonites:	the vineyard and the gardens(s?) and the *canal* and the reservoir(s?).	May he rejoice and be glad for many days and long years.
Beyer 1995	That which Amminadab, the king of the Ammonites, the son of Hessilel, the king of the Ammonites, the son of Amminadab, the king of the Ammonites, has laid out are	the vineyard, the garden, the orchard and cisterns.	May they cause joy and pleasure for many days and in far off years.
Müller 1996	Die Werke Amminadabs, des Königs der Ammoniter, des Sohnes des *Haṣṣil'ils*, des Königs der Ammoniter, des Sohnes Amminadabs, des Königs der Ammoniter:	der Weinberg und die Gärten und das Reservoir (?) und Zisternen.	Er juble und freue sich viele Tage und ferne Jahre lang.

Author	Lines 1-3	Lines 4-5	Lines 6-8
Aufrecht 1989; forthcoming	May the produce of ʿAmmīnadab king of the Ammonites, the son of Haṣṣil'il king of the Ammonites, the son of ʿAmmīnadab king of the Ammonites	– the vineyard and the garden(s) and the hollow and cistern –	cause rejoicing and gladness for many days (to come) and in years far off.
Kottsieper 2003	Werke des ʿMNDB, des Königs der Ammoniter, des Sohnes des HṢL'L, des Königs der Ammoniter, des Sohnes des ʿMNDB, des Königs der Ammoniter,	sind der Weinberg und der Garten und der/die/das *'tḥr/n*. Und (so) sollen/ werden die, die verschreckt/entmutigt sind,	jubeln und sich freuen für viele Tage und ferne Jahre.
Azize 2003	Pious is Amminadab, king of the sons of Ammon, son of Hassal'il king of the sons of Ammon, son of Amminadab king of the sons of Ammon,	He (dedicated?) the cultivated field and the garden, and he (recovered?)	May he rejoice and be glad for many days and in years far off.
Kinet 2003	Die Werke des Amminadab, des Königs der Ammoniter, des Sohnes des Hissal'el, des Königs der Ammoniter: des Sohnes Amminadab, des Königs der Ammoniter:	der Weinberg und die Obstgärten und die Teiche (?) und die Zisternen	Er möge jubeln und sich erfeuen während zahlreicher Tage und Jahre langer
Garbini 2006	Le opere di Amminadab re degli Ammoniti, Figlio di Hasalel re degli Ammoniti, Figlio di Amminadab re degli Ammoniti,	(e cioè) la vigna, il giardino, il canale (?) et la cisterna	diano letizia e gioia per molti giorni e per lunghi anni.
Aḥituv 2008	The works of ʿAmmînāḏāḇ, king of the Ammonites, the son of Hiṣṣil'ēl, king of the Ammonites, the son of ʿAmmînāḏāḇ, king of the Ammonites:	the vineyard and the garden and the tunnel/channel(?) and the reservoir.	May he rejoice and be happy for many days and in years far off.

LATE EGYPTIAN WISDOM AND THE COMPOSITION OF PROVERBS 10:1–15:33

Bernd U. SCHIPPER

For decades the so-called "Solomonic collection" of the book of Proverbs (10:1–22:16) has been seen as a collection of highly disparate proverbs. In his 1984 commentary, Otto Plöger, for example, argued that Prov 10 does not have a continuous theme.[1] Rather, it should be seen like the other chapters of Prov 10–22 – a simple collection of sayings without a meaningful structure. The same was stressed by other scholars for the Solomonic proverbs in general. The variegated chapters of Prov 10:1–22:16 have been taken primarily as a collection of individual proverbs and not as a planned and coherent composition.[2] As a result, scholarship has tended to inquire into the formal aspects of the combination of the individual sayings, such as through key words or phonetic similarities.[3]

In this article I shall argue that Prov 10 as well as the unit Prov 10–15 should be regarded as masterful compositions and not as collections of individual proverbs. My thesis can be summarized easily: A clear compositional strategy is found not only in the first chapter of the so-called Solomonic collection, Prov 10, but also in Prov 10–15. By contrasting different perspectives of a wisdom grounded in life experience, a chain of arguments is created that leads to a fundamental theological statement.

I will start with a brief look at Egyptian wisdom literature from the first millennium BCE, followed by a more detailed discussion of the compositional strategy of Prov 10–15. The final section will summarize the main arguments.

[1] Otto PLÖGER, *Sprüche Salomos (Proverbia)* (BKAT, 17), Neukirchen-Vluyn, Neukirchener, 1984, 122.

[2] See also Claus WESTERMANN, "Weisheit und praktische Theologie", *Praktische Theologie* 79 (1990) 515–16, and Leo G. PERDUE, *Proverbs* (IBC), Louisville, Westminster John Knox, 2000, 163–64.

[3] See the overview by Roger N. WHYBRAY, *The Book of Proverbs: A Survey of Modern Study* (History of Biblical Interpretation Series, 1), Leiden, Brill, 1995, 34–61, and Ruth SCORALICK, *Einzelspruch und Sammlung: Komposition im Buch der Sprichwörter Kapitel 10–15* (BZAW, 232), Berlin, Walter de Gruyter, 1995, 127–29, 161–81.

1. The Phenomenon of Discursive Wisdom in Late Egyptian Wisdom Literature

Not only classical wisdom instructions from ancient Egypt such as the Instruction of Any or the Instruction of Amenemope are important for the interpretation of the book of Proverbs, but also late Egyptian wisdom texts.[4] The late hieratic Instruction of Papyrus Brooklyn 47.218.135[5] and the demotic wisdom books of Ankhsheshonqi and of Papyrus Insinger share striking similarities with passages from Proverbs. Since the hieratic instruction from Papyrus Brooklyn and the aforementioned demotic instructions can be dated to the late Twenty-Sixth Dynasty, that is, the sixth century BCE, we have parallel Egyptian wisdom texts from the historical period when most parts of the book of Proverbs were written.[6]

Two aspects are important when comparing the demotic instructions with the wisdom literature from Pharaonic Egypt. First, the demotic instructions as well as the hieratic Papyrus Brooklyn 47.218.135 refer directly to the canonical wisdom literature from the Middle and New Kingdom. We have quotations and allusions in the late texts that can be explained by the use of the older wisdom literature in the scribal schools of Late Period Egypt.[7] And second, when looking at the chain of arguments, the wisdom texts from the Late Period expand on subjects that already appear in the classical texts. This can be seen, for example, in the Instruction of Any. The famous instruction from the New Kingdom begins with the paradigmatic phrase:

> "Behold, I give you these useful counsels for you to ponder in your heart;
> Do it and you will be happy, all evils will be far away from you" (B 15:1).[8]

[4] For the following paragraph see Bernd U. Schipper, *Proverbs 1–15* (Hermeneia), Minneapolis, Fortress, 2019, 17–21. An overview of the classical Egyptian instructions of life and Old Testament wisdom can be found in Nili Shupak, "The Contribution of Egyptian Wisdom to the Study of Biblical Wisdom Literature," in: M.R. Sneed (ed.), *Was There a Wisdom Tradition?* (AIL, 23), Atlanta: SBL, 2015, 265–304.

[5] See Richard Jasnow, *A Late Period Hieratic Wisdom Text (P.Brooklyn 47.218.135)* (SAOC, 52), Chicago, Oriental Institute of the University of Chicago, 1992.

[6] Current scholarship agrees that the formation of the book of Proverbs took place in the Persian and probably early Hellenistic period, see Bernd U. Schipper, *Proverbs 1–15,* 39, and James A. Loader, *Proverbs 1–9* (HCOT), Leuven et al., Peeters, 2014, 9.

[7] See J. Houser Wegner, *Cultural and Literary Continuity in Demotic Instructions* (Dissertation Yale University), 2001, and Bernd U. Schipper, "The Phenomenon of 'Textual Coherence' in Egyptian and Israelite Wisdom Literature", in: R. Müller, J. Pakkala (ed.), *Insights into Editing in the Hebrew Bible and the Ancient Near East* (CBET, 84), Leuven, Peeters, 2017, 100–26.

[8] The translation follows Joachim F. Quack, *Die Lehren des Ani: Ein neuägyptischer Weisheitstext in seinem kulturellen Umfeld* (OBO, 141), Fribourg, Presses Universitaires,

Unlike the classical wisdom instructions, this text ends with a dialogue between father and son in which the son raises objections to the father's instruction. The son states that the instruction is too long and too difficult for him, that "each man is led by his nature" (*r jwn=f*), and that a "youth" (*'ḏd*) is not yet able to grasp the instruction.[9] The dispute ends with the statement that humans are "companions of the god" (*sn.nw n nṯr*) and that it is ultimately the deity who ensures that humans are on the right path.

This religious dimension of sapiential knowledge is also found in the Instruction of Amenemope. This Ramesside-period instruction, which is paralleled by Prov 22:17–24:22, emphasizes the religious dimension of sapiential knowledge.[10] This emphasis can be seen for example in Am 19:16–17, where the sapiential author of the instruction states:

> "On one side are the words that people say; on the other is what the god does."[11]

Similar thoughts are found in Am 20:5–6; 22:5–6, and 24:10–11, 24:20.

When moving to the demotic Instruction of Khasheshonqi (usually referred to as the Instruction of Ankhsheshonqi)[12] and the Great Demotic Wisdom Book of Papyrus Insinger, important evidence emerges. On the one hand, we have the aforementioned theological dimension, on the other, the composition of the instruction itself combines single sayings in a distinct way.

The so-called Instruction of Khasheshonqi contains a framing narrative that describes the fate of the wise priest Khasheshonqi, who is wrongly imprisoned and instructs his son from there.[13] Since he is not allowed to use papyrus, he writes his instruction on potsherds, which he then sends to his son. Egyptologists have explained this framing narrative as resulting

1994, 121–23. See also Miriam LICHTHEIM, *Ancient Egyptian Literature: Vol II: The New Kingdom*, 2nd edition, Berkeley, University of California Press, 2006, 138.

[9] See also Günter BURKARD, Heinz-Josef THISSEN, *Einführung in die ägyptische Literaturgeschichte II: Neues Reich* (EQÄ, 6), Berlin, LIT, 2008, 104–7.

[10] The parallels between the Instruction of Amenemope and Prov 22:17–23:11 were discovered by Adolf ERMAN, "Eine ägyptische Quelle der 'Sprüche Salomos'", *SPAW* 15 (1924), 86–93. See also Michael V. FOX, "From Amenemope to Proverbs: Editorial Art in Proverbs 22,17–23,11", *ZAW* 126 (2014), 76–91, and Bernd U. SCHIPPER, "Die Lehre des Amenemope und Prov 22,17–24,22: Eine Neubestimmung des literarischen Verhältnisses", *ZAW* 117 (2005), 53–72, 232–48.

[11] Translation according to Vincent Pierre-Michel LAISNEY, *L'Enseignement d'Aménémopé* (StPohl, 19), Rome, Pontifical Bible Institute, 2007. Vincent Pierre-Michel LAISNEY, "Amenemope, Lehre des", *Wissenschaftliches Bibellexikon im Internet*, Stuttgart, Deutsche Bibelgesellschaft, 2009, https://www.bibelwissenschaft.de/ stichwort/66897/.

[12] See Joachim F. QUACK, *Einführung in die altägyptische Literaturgeschichte III: Die demotische und gräko-ägyptische Literatur* (EQÄ, 3), Berlin, LIT, 2009, 128.

[13] For the following see the overview in J. QUACK, *Einführung*, 128–38.

from the fact that the instruction itself does not have a clear structure but instead contains a variety of individual proverbs, some of which appear more than once.[14] These proverbs generally stand alone, although they are sometimes part of a thought that is developed over several lines. A similar phenomenon can be found in the wisdom instruction from Papyrus Insinger, also called the "Great Demotic Wisdom Book."

This wisdom instruction from Late Period Egypt bears the title "The Way of Knowing Knowledge." It consists of twenty-five thematic units that are numbered in the demotic text.[15] These units reflect an interesting connection between a thematic pattern and individual proverbs. As was already noted, there is no longer the thematically-oriented structure of "maxims" found in the classical wisdom instructions, but a combination of different sayings appears within each chapter.[16]

The text is characterized by the contrast between the wise person and the fool or between the pious person (the "man of god") and the wicked person. In some cases, the antitype of the wise person is also referred to as the "hothead", the "stupid person", or as the "wicked one".[17] The instruction addresses officials, who are expected to find their place within the social hierarchy. The religious dimension of the instruction has been noted since the time of its discovery.[18] Although the author is confident that the wise and pious person will be rewarded by the deity, he also emphasizes the deity's free will and the limits of sapiential education.[19]

The eighth instruction provides an example of this thinking. This chapter about wealth and poverty includes classical sapiential sayings, for example, the fool is greedy (5:18), and it is better to have less than to want too much (7:6). The end of the chapter surprisingly questions classical sapiential thought (7:15–17):[20]

[14] See Friedhelm HOFFMANN, Joachim F. QUACK, *Anthologie der demotischen Literatur* (EQÄ, 4), 2nd edition, Berlin, LIT, 2018, 272–73.

[15] See J. QUACK, *Einführung*, 113–25.

[16] See F. HOFFMANN, J. QUACK, *Anthologie*, 272–73. See also Miriam LICHTHEIM, *Late Egyptian Wisdom Literature in the International Context: A Study of Demotic Instructions* (OBO, 52), Fribourg, Presses Universitaires, 1983, 138.

[17] See Fragment Ricci IV, line 5 (F. HOFFMANN, J. QUACK, *Anthologie*, 276), for the "hothead" see Papyrus Insinger, l. 4,5.

[18] See François LEXA, *Le Papyrus Insinger. Les enseignements moraux d'un scribe égyptien du premier siècle après J.-C. Texte démotique avec transcription, traduction française, commentaire, vocabulaire et introduction grammaticale et littéraire*, Paris, P.Geuthner, 1926, 27.

[19] See Heinz-Josef THISSEN, "Achmim und die demotische Literatur", in: A. EGBERTS, B. P. MUHS, J. VAN DER VLIET (ed.), *Perspectives on Panopolis. An Egyptian Town from Alexander the Great to the Arab Conquest*, Leiden, Brill, 2002, 249–60, 259 (with discussion of the Demotic term *sḫn*).

[20] The translation follows F. HOFFMANN, J. QUACK, *Anthologie*, 283.

It is not necessarily a frugal wise person who finds a fortune,
It is not necessarily a squanderer who comes to poverty.
It is god who gives riches abundantly.

When looking at the composition of the Great Demotic Wisdom Book, a principle can be found in which classical sapiential rules are put into question and the divine dimension is emphasized. So, for example, at the end of the tenth instruction we read (Papyrus Insinger 9:16–19):[21]

There is one who has not been taught, yet he knows how to instruct another.
There is one who knows the instruction, yet he does not know how to live by it.
It is not necessarily a true son who accepts instructions so as to be taught. It is the god who gives the heart, gives the son, and gives the good character.

The limits of sapiential knowledge are expressed in a characteristic way. The formulae "there is" (*wn*) and "there is not" (*mn*) introduce ideas that oppose or negate what comes beforehand. As Joachim Friedrich Quack notes, this serves "to reflect the inscrutability of the world in which the deity can decide a person's fate."[22]

A similar thought is found at the end of the seventh instruction (Papyrus Insinger 5:3–6):[23]

There is one wise in heart, but his life is hard.
There is one who is satisfied by his fate, there is he who is satisfied by his wisdom.
It is not necessarily the wise in character who lives by it.
It is not necessarily the fool as such whose life is hard.

What we have here is a critical reflection on the foundations of sapiential thought, that is life experience. This critique of empirical wisdom is connected to a theological perspective (5:11):

The fate and the fortune that come – it is the god who sends them.

It would go beyond the scope of this article to speak in detail about the differences between the versions of the Great Demotic Wisdom Book. However, to give just one example from the textual history, a characteristic reduction of the contradictory statements can be seen in Papyrus Carlsberg.[24]

[21] For the translation see J. QUACK, *Einführung*, 115, and Miriam LICHTHEIM, *Ancient Egyptian Literature: Vol III: Late Period*, Berkeley, University of California Press, 1980, 192.

[22] See J. QUACK, *Einführung*, 115 ("die Unerforschlichkeit der Welt darzustellen, in der Gott über das Schicksal schalten kann").

[23] The English translation follows F. HOFFMANN, J. QUACK, *Anthologie*, 281; see also M. Lichtheim, *Late Egyptian Wisdom Literature*, 11, 200–1.

[24] See J. QUACK, *Einführung* 116 and for a different perspective M. Lichtheim, *Late Egyptian Wisdom Literature*, 116. For Papyrus Carlsberg 2 see AKSEL VOLTEN, *Kopenhagener*

Later scribes understood the contradictory statements as a problem requiring resolution.

Another important characteristic of the demotic instruction on Papyrus Insinger is its general composition. Even though each of the twenty-five chapters of the instruction has its own subject, the individual proverbs are thematically interconnected. Some proverbs that in fact belong in one specific chapter because of their thematic focus also appear elsewhere in the text. These cross-references provide the work with an overarching internal coherence. A particular theme is raised in one place by an individual proverb but discussed in detail only in another chapter.[25] This is the case, for example, with the subjects of wealth and poverty. The first subject – wealth – is the topic of chapter 3, but it is also found in individual sayings in other chapters, such as in 4:7; 15:21; 16:12; or 19:3. Another topic is the relationship to women, which appears in individual sayings spread throughout the instruction (3.16; 5:22; 7:11; 8:14–15; 11:15; 18:22).[26]

In sum, the demotic instruction of Papyrus Insinger is characterized by a masterful composition. On the one hand, the instruction is composed in such a way that individual sayings are combined, and on the other hand, this combination presents different perspectives. We have the composition principle of "discursive wisdom" in which different, and sometimes contradictory positions are placed side-by-side.[27] All of this is done to pave the way for a rather theological definition of wisdom. Or to restate the point with the aforementioned quote from the tenth chapter of Papyrus Insinger:

> "It is the god who gives the heart, and the son and good."

2. Discursive Wisdom in Prov 10–15

When looking at Prov 10–15 in light of the demotic instruction of Papyrus Insinger, the nature of the composition of the so-called Solomonic Wisdom

Texte zum demotischen Weisheitsbuch (AnAeg, 1), Copenhagen, Munksgaard, 1940; Aksel Volten, *Das Demotische Weisheitsbuch: Studien und Bearbeitung* (AnAeg, 2), Copenhagen, Munksgaard, 1941, and Joachim F. Quack, "Ein neues Berliner Fragment des großen demotischen Weisheitsbuches (Papyrus Berlin 29007)," *Enchoria* 28 (2002/2003), 85–88, Taf 11.

[25] See J. Quack, *Einführung*, 115.

[26] See Jacco Dieleman, "Fear of Women? Representations of Women in Demotic Wisdom Texts", *Studien zur altägyptischen Kultur* 25 (1998), 7–46.

[27] For the concept of "discursive wisdom" see B. Schipper, *Proverbs 1–15*, ch. 4.4 ("From Practical Knowledge to Discursive Wisdom") and pp. 354–56.

appears in a different light. In the following I will develop the thesis that we find in Prov 10–15 the same compositional strategy as in demotic instructions. (1) A combination of different perspectives that lead to a theological dimension, and (2) individual sayings on particular subjects that create thematic connections between the different chapters. I will start with some observations on Prov 10, which serves as an introduction of Prov 10:1–22:16, then highlighting the main compositional principles of Prov 10–15.

The problem of the literary structure of the so-called Solomonic Wisdom in the book of Proverbs has already been seen by scholars from the nineteenth century. In his commentary from 1898, Wilhelm Frankenberg, for example, stressed that Prov 10–22 is characterized by the "selbständigem Zweizeiler, der keine Verbindung mit dem folgenden kennt" ("independent two-liners that have no connection with what follows").[28] A different position can be found in Franz Delitzsch's commentary on Proverbs from 1873. He summarized, regarding the line of thought in Prov 10: "the progressive unfolding follows no systematic scheme, but continuously wells forth."[29] In the same context, Delitzsch stated in contrast to previous research:

> "The succession of proverbs here is nevertheless not one that is purely accidental or without thought; it is more than a happy accident when three of the same character stand together; the collector has connected together proverb with proverb according to certain common characteristics."[30]

Delitzsch pointed to literary evidence that is important for our investigation of the composition of Prov 10–15. When comparing the subjects mentioned in Prov 10 with the subjects of the following chapters, it turns out that Prov 10 introduces the main themes:[31]

[28] Wilhelm FRANKENBERG, *Die Sprüche* (HKAT, II/3,1), Göttingen, Vandenhoeck & Ruprecht, 1895, 8.

[29] Franz DELITZSCH, *Biblical Commentary on the Proverbs of Solomon*. Trans. M.G. Eaton (Biblical Commentary on the Old Testament), Edinburgh, T&T Clark, 1874, 208. The original German wording is: "Die Fortbewegung folgt keinem systematischen Schema, sondern ist wellenartig." Franz DELITZSCH, *Salomonisches Spruchbuch* (Biblischer Commentar über das Alte Testament, 4/3), Leipzig, Dörffling und Franke, 1873, 160.

[30] F. DELITZSCH, *Biblical Commentary*, 208. The German wording is: „Indes ist die Aneinanderreihung der Sprüche auch hier keine rein zufällige und gedankenlose; es ist mehr als die Folge eines glücklichen Wurfs, wenn Gleichartiges beisammensteht; der Samler hat Spruch um Spruch nach gewissen gemeinsamen Merkmalen zusammengeordnet." F. DELITZSCH, *Spruchbuch*, 160.

[31] See Bernd U. SCHIPPER, "From Epistemology to Wisdom Theology: The Composition of Prov 10", in: S. C. JONES, C. ROY-YODER (ed.), "*When the Morning Stars Sang": Essays in Honor of Choon-Leong Seow* (BZAW, 500), Berlin, Walter de Gruyter, 2017, 145–57, 153.

(1) Wealth and poverty (10:1–5 ~ 11:28–30; 14:31; 17:5; 20:4; 22:1–2)
(2) The consequences of hard work (10:4 ~ 12:24; 13:11)
(3) The consequences of false speech and wrong communication (10:6–11 ~ 11:9–15; 12:13–23; 17:7–15; 18:1–9)
(4) Expectations and their fulfillment connected to the inner person (10:23–30 ~ 11:23–27 / 13:12–19; 14:19–24)

Starting with Prov 10, a network of connections can be detected that runs to Prov 15 and extends to Prov 16–22. This network is characterized by a combination of different perspectives on display in Prov 10. The chapter starts in vv. 1–5 with the subject of wealth and poverty, presenting contradictory positions.[32]

1 A wise son (בֵּן חָכָם) makes a[33] father rejoice,
but a foolish son (בֵּן כְּסִיל) is his mother's grief.
2 Treasures of wickedness (רֶשַׁע) are of no use,
but righteousness (צְדָקָה) saves from death.
3 Yhwh does not let the appetite of a righteous person (צַדִּיק) starve,
but he rebuffs the craving of the wicked ones (רְשָׁעִים).
4 Poor is the one who works with a lax hand,[34]
but the hand of the diligent makes rich.
5 One who gathers in summer is an intelligent son (בֵּן מַשְׂכִּיל),
one who sleeps[35] at harvest time is a shameful son (בֵּן מֵבִישׁ).

The five verses have a double concentric structure.[36] The outer frame, which consists of vv. 1 and 5, is marked by the contrast of the two sons (expressed by the keyword בֵּן), while the inner frame in vv. 2a and 4b is linked by the subject of "wealth". According to the outer frame in vv. 1 and 5, a wise son is diligent, whereas a foolish son is lazy. This is specified in v. 4, which states that the diligent person becomes rich, and the lazy

[32] For the following see Thomas KRÜGER, "Komposition und Diskussion in Proverbia 10", *ZTK* 92 (1995), 413–33 and B. SCHIPPER, "From Epistemology to Wisdom Theology", 145–57.

[33] Some scholars add a masculine suffix "his father," but this is no more than a hypothesis without textual witnesses; see Bruce K.WALTKE, *The Book of Proverbs: Chapter 1–15* (NICOT), Grand Rapids, Eerdmans, 2004, 447 with n. 3, and Michael V. FOX, *Proverbs 10–31: A New Translation with Introduction and Commentary* (AB, 18B), New Haven, Yale University Press, 2009, 510.

[34] Lit. "Whoever works with a lazy hand will become poor." Cf. F. DELITZSCH, *Biblical Commentary*, 210–11, followed by Knut M. HEIM, *Like Grapes of Gold Set in Silver: An Interpretation of Proverbial Clusters in Proverbs 10:1–22:16* (BZAW, 273), Berlin, Walter de Gruyter, 2001, 111.

[35] The Hebrew word רדם expresses that the shameful son sleeps soundly, cf. Christine ROY-YODER, *Proverbs* (AOTC), Nashville, Abingdon, 2009, 119.

[36] Cf. Knut M. HEIM, "Coreferentiality, Structure and Context in Proverbs 10:1–5", *JTT* 6 (1993), 199–203; ROY-YODER, *Proverbs*, 118–19.

person becomes poor. The wording of the Hebrew text underlines that wealth and poverty are in a person's "hands." Thus, the moral of the text is that the wise and diligent person will receive respect and wealth, whereas the foolish and lazy person comes into poverty.[37]

In contrast to this, vv. 2–3 present a different view. Only righteousness can save from death because the treasures of wickedness are not useful (לֹא־יוֹעִילוּ). This is connected to what God gives: "[God] does not let the appetite of a righteous person starve" (v. 3).

The two perspectives in vv. 1–5 create a critical dialogue:[38] vv. 2–3 relativize the positive view of wealth in vv. 4–5 insofar as wealth is only legitimate if it is not connected to wickedness. What is presented in vv. 4–5 as general wisdom appears almost naïve in light of vv. 2–3. The hand of the diligent not only brings wealth (v. 4b) but also a *specific type* of wealth. Only if wealth is connected to righteousness (צְדָקָה) can it lead to a successful life before YHWH.

When we move from Prov 10:1–5 to the subsequent chapters of Prov 11–15, an interesting chain of argumentation appears. On the one hand, we have the phenomenon of discursive wisdom, presenting different perspectives on the very same subject. On the other hand, there is an overarching structural dimension that connects individual chapters into a meaningful composition (Prov 10–15).[39]

This connection can already be found in Prov 11. The chapter reaches back to Prov 10 and applies its general sapiential principles to a specific topic: ethically correct behavior in the economic sphere and toward one's neighbor, whether someone of low social status or a trading partner.[40] In this way, chap. 11 seems like a learned interpretation of 10:2: "Treasures of wickedness are of no use, but righteousness delivers from death" (cf. 11:4).[41]

Here, two levels of meaning converge: the benefits for oneself and the benefits for others. Wealth can be good as long as it is obtained by just means (chap. 10), but personal wealth is legitimate only when the socially disadvantaged are kept in mind (11:24–26).[42]

[37] See Arndt MEINHOLD, *Die Sprüche 1–15* (ZBK, 16.1), Zürich, TVZ, 1991, 165–68.

[38] See T. KRÜGER, "Komposition", 421–22.

[39] The following paragraph presents a rather systematic perspective on observations also found in the first part of my commentary on Proverbs: B. SCHIPPER, *Proverbs 1–15*, 359–513.

[40] See B. SCHIPPER, *Proverbs 1–15*, 413.

[41] For the connection between Prov 11:4 and 10:2 see Knut M. HEIM, *Poetic Imagination in Proverbs: Variant Repetitions and the Nature of Poetry* (BBRS, 4), Winona Lake, Eisenbrauns, 2013, 213–217 (set 27).

[42] See also Raymond VAN LEEUWEN, *Proverbs* (NIB, 5), Nashville, Abingdon, 1995, 117.

This thought is connected with a perspective that underlines the divine dimension of wisdom in the very first verse:

11:1	Balances of deceit are an abomination to Yhwh, but a complete weight is his favor.	מֹאזְנֵי מִרְמָה תּוֹעֲבַת יְהוָה וְאֶבֶן שְׁלֵמָה רְצוֹנוֹ

This theological dimension is connected to a critical perspective on classical sapiential thought, constructed by a phrase in Hebrew similar to the Egyptian *wn*, "there is this" (יֵשׁ):

11:24	There is one who distributes (freely) and is given even more, and another who saves in excess, (but it leads) only to lack.	יֵשׁ מְפַזֵּר וְנוֹסָף עוֹד וְחוֹשֵׂךְ מִיֹּשֶׁר אַךְ־לְמַחְסוֹר

In his studies on Ecclesiastes, Diethelm Michel discusses the use of יֵשׁ in Proverbs and Ecclesiastes (Eccl 1:10; 2:21; 4:8, 9; 5:12; 6:1, 11; 7:15; 8:6, 14; 9:4; 10;5).[43] In contrast to the meaning "property/wealth" (Prov 8:21) or as a particle of existence (Prov 3:28; 19:18; 23:18; 24:14), יֵשׁ in the books of Proverbs and Ecclesiastes can also mean "es kommt vor" ("in some cases"). The word introduces "a reflection on some opposing situation or paradox" as Agustinus Gianto recently demonstrated.[44] Therefore, the passage in Prov 11:24 could also be translated as: "There is this: one who distributes freely and is given even more, and another who saves in excess, (but it leads) only to lack."

By introducing the whole statement, the particle יֵשׁ points to a paradox.[45] There is some life experience that stands in contrast to what was previously stated.[46] Similarly constructed paradoxical statements can be found in Prov 12 and 13. In 12:18 an opposing perspective on the effects of speech is made, whereas 13:7 presents a reflection on wealth and poverty:[47]

[43] Diethelm MICHEL, *Untersuchungen zur Eigenart des Buches Qohelet* (BZAW, 183), Berlin, de Gruyter, 1989, 184–85. See also Hans-Jürgen HERMISSON, *Studien zur israelitischen Spruchweisheit* (WMANT, 28), Neukirchen-Vluyn, Neukirchener, 1968, 148.

[44] Agustinus GIANTO, "On יֵשׁ of Reflection in the Book of Proverbs", in: S. C. Jones, C. Roy-Yoder (ed.), *"When the Morning Stars Sang": Essays in Honor of Choon-Leong Seow* (BZAW, 500), Berlin, Walter de Gruyter, 2017, 158–62, 158. See also Agustinus GIANTO, "Some Notes on Evidentiality in Biblical Hebrew", in: A. GIANTO (ed.), *Biblical and Oriental Essays in Memory of Willian L. Moran* (BibOr, 48), Rome, Ponfiticio Istituto Biblico, 2005, 133–53.

[45] For Prov 11:24 see A. MEINHOLD, *Sprüche 1–15*, 198.

[46] See A. GIANTO, "On יֵשׁ of Reflection in the Book of Proverbs", 159.

[47] For Prov 12:18 see Crawford H. TOY, *The Book of Proverbs* (ICC), Edinburgh, T&T Clark, 1899, 253.

12:18	There is this: gossip like knife stabbings, but the tongue of the wise (brings) healing.	יֵשׁ בּוֹטֶה כְּמַדְקְרוֹת חָרֶב וּלְשׁוֹן חֲכָמִים מַרְפֵּא
13:7	There is this: some pretend to be rich but possess nothing; some claim to be poor but have great fortune.	יֵשׁ מִתְעַשֵּׁר וְאֵין כֹּל מִתְרוֹשֵׁשׁ וְהוֹן רָב

Already in Prov 12, the compositional principle of Prov 10–15 can be seen. The reference to a contradictory life experience is connected with an emphasis on the theological dimension:

12:2	A good person will attain favor from Yhwh, but a man of (treacherous) plans he declares as wicked.	טוֹב יָפִיק רָצוֹן מֵיְהוָה וְאִישׁ מְזִמּוֹת יַרְשִׁיעַ
12:22	An abomination to Yhwh are lying lips, but those who act truthfully (find) his favor.	תּוֹעֲבַת יְהוָה שִׂפְתֵי־שָׁקֶר וְעֹשֵׂי אֱמוּנָה רְצוֹנוֹ

Following chap. 11, in Prov 12 the author describes a way of acting that is required for a successful life before God.[48] This is expressed by the meaningful placement of the two Yhwh-sayings, one in the introduction of the chapter (vv. 1–4) and the other in the paragraph on the central subject of right and wrong speech (vv. 13–25).[49]

When moving from ch. 12 to Prov 13, a different concept appears.[50] There are no Yhwh-Proverbs in the entire chapter. In contrast v. 14 takes on a normative quality in expressing the benefits of sapiential thought:

13:14	The *torah* of the wise person is a fountain of life for avoiding the snares of death.	תּוֹרַת חָכָם מְקוֹר חַיִּים לָסוּר מִמֹּקְשֵׁי מָוֶת

What we have here is an example of a twice-told proverb. The same wording appears in 14:27, but with a significant difference:[51]

14:27	The fear of Yhwh is a fountain of life for avoiding the snares of death.	יִרְאַת יְהוָה מְקוֹר חַיִּים לָסוּר מִמֹּקְשֵׁי מָוֶת

[48] See R. VAN LEEUWEN, *Proverbs*, 128–29.

[49] See B. SCHIPPER, *Proverbs 1–15*, 416–17. 12:22 is chiastically connected to vv. 17 and 19, see A. MEINHOLD, *Sprüche 1–15*, 209.

[50] For the thematic connections between Prov 12 and Prov 14–16 see B. WALTKE, *Proverbs 1–15*, 518 and the overview in Ryan O'DOWD, *Proverbs* (The Story of God Bible Commentary), Grand Rapids, Zondervan, 2017, 216.

[51] K. HEIM, *Poetic Imagination*, 353–58 (set 51). See also R. VAN LEEUWEN, *Proverbs*, 133.

Both verses are identical apart from the grammatical subject. Whereas the fear of Yhwh (יִרְאַת יְהוָה) stands in the center in Prov 14:27, in Prov 13:14 the "Torah of the wise person" (תּוֹרַת חָכָם) is a fountain of life. The use of the word "torah" (תּוֹרָה) is not accidental. Unlike in chaps. 10–12, the concept of wisdom in chap. 13 takes on a clearly normative character. The striking reference to the "*torah* of the wise" (תּוֹרַת חָכָם, v. 14) indicates the authoritative nature of the knowledge conveyed by the wisdom teacher.[52] Through its stark contrast with wickedness (רִשְׁעָה, v. 6) and injustice (מִשְׁפָּט בְּלֹא, v. 23), *torah*-wisdom is characterized as the only correct way. Only the skills acquired through discipline can lead to happiness and wealth, which are important for many different aspects of life. In this respect, the *torah*-wisdom of chap. 13 need not refer explicitly to Yhwh since it is itself a "fountain of life" (v. 14). What can be found in Prov 13 is the concept of normative wisdom. It is one of the few cases in the book of Proverbs where the word "torah" does not have a nomistic dimension that points to the book of Deuteronomy.[53]

This contrast between normative wisdom and a theological perspective illustrates the aforementioned principle. In short, Prov 13 reflects a different concept of wisdom from the one found in chaps. 10–12. While chaps. 10–12 make frequent reference to Yhwh, chap. 13 seems to argue in favor of the benefits of wisdom as an independent entity. Such wisdom, which is bestowed upon the prudent as knowledge (v. 16), can lead to a successful life.[54] By presenting such a conception of normative sapiential instruction, Prov 13 serves as a transitional chapter within chaps. 10–15. It builds on what precedes and at the same time prepares for what follows.

This can be seen in the wording of Prov 14:27, which puts the "fear of Yhwh" into focus. A contrast between normative wisdom and a theological perspective is created through the same wording in 13:12 and 14:27.

The new perspective of Prov 14 becomes clear already in the first two verses of the chapter:

[52] See also R. O'Dowd, *Proverbs*, 219. See also M. Fox, *Proverbs 10–31*, 567 with interesting observations on the metaphors of the couplet and its "striking tonality".

[53] See Bernd U. Schipper, *The Hermeneutics of Torah. Proverbs 2, Deuteronomy and the Composition of Proverbs 1–9* (AIL, Atlanta: SBL, 2021), ch. 5.2.4. For the use of תּוֹרָה in the book of Proverbs, see also William P. Brown, "The Law and the Sages: A Reexamination of Tôrâ in Proverbs," in: J. T. Strong, S.S. Tuell (ed.), *Constituting the Community: Studies on the Polity of Ancient Israel in Honor of S. Dean McBride Jr.*, Winona Lake, IN: Eisenbrauns, 2005, 251–80.

[54] See B. Schipper, *Proverbs 1–15*, 459–60.

14:1	The wisdom of women has built her house, but folly tears it down with her hands.	חַכְמוֹת נָשִׁים בָּנְתָה בֵיתָהּ וְאִוֶּלֶת בְּיָדֶיהָ תֶהֶרְסֶנּוּ
14:2	One who walks in his uprightness fears Yhwh, but one who is devious (in) his ways despises him.	הוֹלֵךְ בְּיָשְׁרוֹ יְרֵא יְהוָה וּנְלוֹז דְּרָכָיו בּוֹזֵהוּ

What wisdom has built is torn down by folly.[55] Proverbs 14 presents a critical perspective on traditional wisdom combined with an emphasis on the divine dimension. Wisdom is only valuable if it is connected to Yhwh and should not be presented as a secular principle. This fundamental critique of the foundations of a wisdom grounded in life experience is made explicit in v. 12. This verse is constructed by the same phrase "there is" (יֵשׁ).

14:12	There is a way (that seems) right before a man, but (at) its end are ways to death.	יֵשׁ דֶּרֶךְ יָשָׁר לִפְנֵי־אִישׁ וְאַחֲרִיתָהּ דַּרְכֵי־מָוֶת

Similar to the other statements constructed with יֵשׁ, a contradictory life experience is stressed:[56] What function does human knowledge serve? According to v. 12, such knowledge is necessarily limited. Although a particular behavior may seem useful to someone, it turns out to be completely wrong. This insight is combined in v. 13 with an interesting thought:

14:13	Even in laughter the heart can be in pain, and the end of joy is grief.	גַּם־בִּשְׂחֹק יִכְאַב־לֵב וְאַחֲרִיתָהּ שִׂמְחָה תוּגָה

V. 13 describes the deeply subjective nature of human perception.[57] Although one is able to perceive one's own feelings as no one else can, one's perception of the world has clear limits.

In sum, Prov 14 contains a fundamental critique of sapiential knowledge. One of the basic insights of wisdom is that humans are able to recognize

[55] See A. MEINHOLD, *Sprüche 1–15*, 230 and Tremper LONGMAN III, *Proverbs*, (Baker Commentary on the Old Testament. Wisdom and Psalms) Grand Rapids, Baker Academic, 2006, 296. In contrast, Roland E. MURPHY, *Proverbs*, (Word Biblical Commentary), Nashville, Thomas Nelson, 1998, 193 argues that Wisdom and Folly are personified here.

[56] See A. MEINHOLD, *Sprüche 1–15*, 235, who translates accordingly "das gibt es", and C. Toy, *Proverbs*, 239. The wording of 14:25 appears also in 16:25, see K. HEIM, *Poetic Imagination*, 304–15 (set 45).

[57] See Hans Ferdinand FUHS, *Das Buch der Sprichwörter: Ein Kommentar* (FB, 95), Würzburg, Echter, 2001, 231.

orderly patterns through empirical observation. This is questioned in v. 13 in a way that resembles the book of Ecclesiastes (cf. Eccl 2:2).[58]

This position prepares the ground for Prov 15. Chap. 15 connects thematically to chap. 14 but takes the sapiential discourse of chaps. 10–14 a decisive step further.[59] The problems raised by "critical wisdom" in chap. 14 are answered in the reference to Yhwh in chap. 15: sapiential knowledge is legitimate only if it is connected to Yhwh. Within the whole unit of Prov 10–15, chap. 15 contains nine Yhwh-sayings, more than any preceding chapter.[60] In this way, Prov 15 identifies Yhwh as the final authority for sapiential thought.[61] Although one's father and mother are important for instruction (v. 5 refers to the father, and v. 20 refers to the father and mother), they only represent "discipline" (מוּסָר) and are not the ultimate source of wisdom, which is Yhwh alone.

In short, the nine Yhwh sayings prove to be a key for understanding chap. 15 as a whole. Unlike chaps. 10–14, which simply state that human behaviors have consequences for one's relationship to God, chap. 15 describes these consequences in detail. Proverbs 15 also addresses the question of communication with the deity, whether through ritual (sacrifice, v. 8a) or prayer (vv. 8b, 29).[62] This train of thought is connected with the subject of wealth from Prov 10, which now clearly receives a theological dimension:[63]

15:16	Better is a little in the fear of Yhwh than much treasure and dismay with it.	טוֹב־מְעַט בְּיִרְאַת יְהוָה מֵאוֹצָר רָב וּמְהוּמָה בוֹ

3. From Discursive Wisdom to Sapiential Theology

When looking back at the argument of this article, three aspects can be summarized:

(1) Starting with Prov 10, the unit of Prov 10:1–15:33 presents a compositional strategy in which different positions are placed side-by-side. One the one hand, we have classical sapiential ideas like, for example, that a lazy person will stay poor, while a diligent person becomes rich.

[58] See also R. van Leeuwen, *Proverbs*, 141 who also points to Qoh 7:1–5.

[59] See B. Schipper, *Proverbs 1–15*, 487.

[60] See A. Meinhold, *Sprüche 1–15*, 247 and R. O'Dowd, *Proverbs*, 237 who stressed that the divine name appears in "36 percent of the verses" of Prov 15.

[61] Richard J. Clifford, *Proverbs: A Commentary* (OTL), Louisville, Westminster John Knox, 1999, 155.

[62] See R. O'Dowd, Proverbs, 236.

[63] See T. Longman III, *Proverbs*, 318.

On the other hand, as can be seen in the first part of Prov 10, traditional ideas from the world of wisdom are contrasted with the divine dimension. It is God who gives wealth. Or to say it in the words of Prov 10:22: "The blessing of Yhwh, it makes rich, and (one's own) effort adds nothing to it."

(2) The same principle can be found in late Egyptian wisdom literature. In the demotic instruction of Papyrus Insinger, sapiential life experience is contrasted with contradictory life experience like, for example, in chapter 5:

> "It is not necessarily a frugal wise person who finds a fortune,
> It is not necessarily a squanderer who comes to poverty."

Within the demotic instruction these different perspectives placed side-by-side turn out to be a compositional principle. In light of a critique of the foundations of sapiential thought, that is epistemology, the theological dimension is emphasized: "It is god who gives riches abundantly."

(3) The same compositional strategy is found in Prov 10–15. By means of phrases constructed similar to the Egyptian *wn* "there is" (in Hebrew יֵשׁ), the author refers to life experiences that call general sapiential thought into question. What we have in both literatures, ancient Egyptian and the book of Proverbs, is discursive wisdom in which different and sometimes paradoxical positions are brought together. This composition principle is introduced in the first chapter of the so-called Solomonic collection, Prov 10 and developed further in the subsequent chapters. What we find in Prov 10–15 is not only a masterful composition of the individual chapters, but also a deeper dimension of the overarching structure of this unit. By underlining sapiential rules in one chapter, as can be seen in Prov 13, and questioning it in the following one (Prov 14), the theological dimension of sapiential thought is emphasized. Similar to demotic instructions, the compositional principle of discursive wisdom serves a clear goal. By presenting positions grounded in life experience, that is epistemology, the way is paved for a theological definition of wisdom. Therefore, the last verse of Prov 15 marks a first climax within the composition of Prov 10–22 when its states:

> 15:33 The fear of Yhwh is discipline for wisdom, and before honor (comes) humility.

A SONS OF LIGHT REWORKING IN THE SCROLLS FROM QUMRAN

Annette STEUDEL

Sons of Light is a self-designation of the Qumran community, that evokes the colourful picture of dualistic thinking.[1] Appearing almost out of darkness and again disappearing into it, the term Sons of Light leaves impressive, though limited traces in Qumran literature. Although well-known, the designation is merely found in a couple of compositions, among them the three rule texts Serekh ha-Yachad (S), Damascus Document (D), and the War Rule (M). In all three the Sons of Light strikingly occur in the incipits of these works. This raises questions on the role of this term in the development of the world view of the community, which we can access via the development of the community's literature. Observations on the Sons of Light might exemplarily serve as a window into the history of Qumran literature, that is still known to us only in bits and pieces.

With the title of this article I am taking up Jean Duhaime's "A Dualistic Reworking in the Scrolls from Qumran", who already in 1987 exemplarily showed that the compositions S, D, and M underwent a dualistic reworking.[2] My observations on the redaction of the incipits of these three compositions evolved independently of Jean Duhaime's article, while intensively studying the rule texts with our Göttingen group. The more I am happy that they seem to ask similar questions.[3]

[1] Speaking about Qumran and the community, I use these terms in a broad sense, being aware that the community consisted of many different communities, which were spread much more widely than at Qumran and its surrounding and existed and developed over a long period of time.

[2] Jean DUHAIME, Dualistic Reworking in the Scrolls from Qumran, *CBQ* 49/1, 1987, 32-56.

[3] Other terms that also occur in dualistic contexts have to be studied separately and might have had a development on its own. The first, most extensive analysis of dualism in the history of Qumran literature was written by Peter VON DER OSTEN-SACKEN, Gott und Belial. Traditionsgeschichtliche Untersuchungen zum Dualismus in den Texten aus Qumran, Studien zur Umwelt des Neuen Testaments 6, 1968. His still precious study deserves a future fresh discussion on the basis of our current knowledge about the Qumran compositions and manuscripts.

1 Preliminary Considerations on a History of Qumran Literature

A thorough study of the literary development of each single Qumran composition leads to an increase in understanding of the history of Qumran literature in general.[4] Thus, such analyses of single works are the starting point that is needed, if we want to find out in which sequence main Qumran compositions came into being.[5]

Most of the Qumran compositions consist of different literary layers, that is, they grew over time. Each composition has its own way in achieving its fullest literary form. In some cases, it is easier to find out how this development went on, in others it is more complicated to trace. An advantage in the literary analysis of the Qumran compositions is that they are known to us often via more than one copy per work. Furthermore, in many cases vacats and graphical marks in the margin give hints to former divisions of the text. Sometimes, like in the case of the Hodajot and the Damascus Document, all copies seem to preserve (almost) the same text,[6] in other cases, like the War Rule and Serekh ha-Yachad, different forms of texts are handed down. The explanation for this can be different: The deviating versions of a composition could present various stages of literary growth, or they could originate from different contemporary communities, or might reflect different purposes of usage, like e.g. a short form being a didactic summary. Thus, the abundance of possible interpretations has to be handled with care in a literary analysis, and every composition has to be treated on its own. Observations have to be collected, evaluated and

[4] In this article I focus on "genuine" Qumran compositions, those works which seem to be the literary product of the so-called Qumran community, but the same holds true of course for a broader perspective.

[5] Especially the images of the Leon-Levy-Digital-Library enhance the understanding of the Dead Sea Scrolls immensely. This will hopefully soon multiply our knowledge also about long known Qumran texts. Promising recent studies that combine the profound analysis of single (parts of) compositions with a comparison to other (parts of) works from Qumran are e.g. that of Arjen Bakker, Sages and Saints: Continuous Study and Transformation in Musar le-Mevin and Serekh ha-Yaḥad, In: Hindy Najman/ Jean-Sébastien Rey/ Eibert Tigchelaar (eds.), Tracing Sapiential Traditions in Ancient Judaism, Supplements to the Journal for the Study of Judaism 174, Leiden/Boston 2016, 106-118, and Meike Christian, The Literary Development of the "Treatise of the Two Spirits" as Dependent on Instruction and the Hodayot, in: Jutta Jokiranta/ Molly Zahn (eds.), Law, Literature and Society in Legal Texts from Qumran, Studies on the Texts of the Desert of Judah 128, Leiden/Boston 2016, and the forthcoming printed dissertations of both of them.

[6] The Text of CD B (Col. XIX-XX), although ancient, is not attested among the preserved D-manuscripts at Qumran. The text of the Hodajot is consistent, but larger and smaller collections of its hymns are handed down in its different copies.

conclusions not to be drawn to early. Most of this research is not yet done, although there are first attempts since long and the potential is vast.

Qumran Compositions can usually be dated only relatively to each other, e.g. in observing a development in thought,[7] in terminology[8] or in exegetical instruments that they use,[9] as well as the addition of biblical quotations in order to give more strength to an idea[10]. Very rarely there is an indication for the absolute date of a text by the mentioning of historical names, as e.g. of king Jonathan in 4Q448,[11] or of the kings in Pesher Nahum,[12] or the Kittim (= the Romans) in Pesher Nahum and Habakuk. In cases like these, the youngest historical event gives us the terminus post quem for the composition.[13] The terminus ad quem, of course, is given by the age of the written manuscript, i.e. a composition cannot be younger than its oldest manuscript. Furthermore, it has always to be kept in mind, that the youngest manuscript of a composition does not necessarily preserve the youngest version of a text.

A small number of Qumran compositions is unanimously relatively dated (e.g. the Damascus Document is older than Pesher Habakuk), while the sequence of others is still disputed (e.g. the Anglo-American tradition assumes that the Damascus Document is older than the Serekh ha-Yachad, the German speaking tradition supposes that S is older than D), and the time of emergence of most compositions, like e.g. the Hodajot, is still unknown.

Difficulties and differences in dating texts may occur on the basis of methodological presuppositions that are made (e.g. the more theological version of a text is older than the less theological one, or vice versa, or the shorter text is older than the longer, or vice versa). Some problems may be limited, if we refrain from comparing whole literary compositions with

[7] See e.g. the upcoming interest in eschatology, cf. Annette STEUDEL, Dating Exegetical Texts from Qumran, In: Devorah DIMANT/ Reinhard KRATZ (eds.), The Dynamics of Language and Exegesis at Qumran, FAT 35, Tübingen, 2009, 39-53.

[8] See e.g. the development of the term דורש התורה, cf. A. STEUDEL, Dating, 49-50.

[9] E.g. fullier developed forms of quotation-/interpretation-formulas, cf. Steudel, Dating, 50-51.

[10] See e.g. CD 3:21-4:1, stressing the role of the Sons of Zadoq in the community by taking up 1QS V:2 (versus the S-versions represented by 4Q256 frg. 9:2-3 and 4Q258 frg. 1:2, both have הרבים instead of בני צדוק) and adding explicitly the quotation of Ezek 44:15.

[11] In this case there are two options, it could be either Alexander Janaios, see E. ESHEL/ H. ESHEL/A. YARDENI, 4Q448, in DJD XI, Oxford 1998, 403-4015, or Jonathan the Maccabee, see Emile Puech, Jonathan le prêtre impie et les débuts de la communauté de Qumrân. 4QJonathan (4Q523) et 4QpsAp (4Q448), RdQ 17, 1996, 241-270, and most recently Psaume et Prière pour le roi Jonathan (4Q448) revisités, *RdQ* 32, 2020, 279-291, cf. also A. STEUDEL, Dating, 41 with note 5.

[12] Demetrius, king of Greece (probably Demetrius III) and Antiochus (probably Antiochus IV Epiphanes), 4QpNah frg. 3-4 i:2.

[13] Cf. A. STEUDEL, Dating, 47-48.

each other. Instead it is often far more adequate to compare smaller units of texts with each other (e.g. unit 1 of text A depends on unit 2 of text B) and allow for the possibility of mutual literary influence of texts on each other (i.e. unit 3 of text B depends on unit 4 of text A).[14]

2 Observations on the Sons of Light Occurrences

The term בני אור is completely preserved in eleven passages among the findings from Qumran (1QS I:9; II:16; III:13; III:24; III:25; 1QM I:1; I:3; I:9; I:11; I:13; MidrEschat b 4Q177 frg. 10-11:7 בני האור; frg. 12-13:7). In further five cases it is very probable to complete the remaining letters of this term (MidrEschat a 4Q174 frg. 1-2:9; MidrEschat b 4Q177 frg. 12-13:11; 4Q266 frg. 1a-b:1; 4Q280 frg. 2:1 בני האור, and 4Q510 frg. 1:7).[15] It might very well have occurred also in the lacuna after the mentioning of the Sons of Darkness in 1QM XIII:16.[16]

In three instances, the Sons of Light appear right at the beginning of a composition, that is in 1QM I, in the long first sentence in 1QS, in I:9, and in the first line of 4QD a (4Q266).[17] Similarly, it occurs at the beginning of a literary unit, namely in 1QS III,13 (beginning of the Treatise of the Two Spirits), and in 4Q510. In the latter two cases the appearance of the Sons of Light is connected with the use of the word משכיל, which is probably also to be completed at the very beginning of 1QM,[18] and is usually restored in analogy at the beginning of 1QS and 4QD a.[19] Although

[14] Cf. e.g. Reinhard Kratz, Der Penal Code und das Verhältnis von Serekh ha-Yachad (S) und Damaskusschrift (D)," *RdQ* 25, 2011, 199-227, and A. Steudel, The Damascus Document (D) as a Rewriting of the Community Rule (S)," *RdQ* 25, 2012, 605-620.

[15] A completion in 11Q13 II:8 (see e.g. DJD XXIII) might be slightly too long, and the reading בני אל, assumed by É. Puech, e.g. in Notes sur le manuscrit de XIQMelkîsédeq, Revue de Qumrân 12, 1987, 483-513, and others, seems to fit better.

[16] Among the Aramaic texts the well-known evidence of the בני נהורא is preserved in the Visions of Amram 4Q548 1ii-2:16. It obviously relates to the Hebrew Sons of Light texts and its role in the literary history deserves further considerations.

[17] Peter Porzig/James Tucker, Between Artefacts, Fragments, and Texts: An Analysis of 4Q266 Column I, Dead Sea Discoveries 25/3, 2018, 335-358, think that the Sons of Light are a supralinear addition in 4Q266. For material reasons, I am not yet fully convinced about their observation. Anyhow, if they are correct, this would also speak for a Sons of Light redaction at the beginning of 4Q266. In this case an older beginning of D (the main text of the first lines) which already seems to refer to the Treatise of the Two Spirits (see l. 2 corresponding with 1QS III:18) would have been completed by the term Sons of Light, reflecting perhaps literary developments within the Treatise of the Two Spirits itself, which might have led to different stages of dualistic reworking of the beginning of D.

[18] The remains of the first two letters can best be read as למ.

[19] In S and in D משכיל is often used in the title of literary units, see e.g. 4QSb (4Q256) frg. 9:1 (par 1QS V:1 has a different title), 1QS IX:12, CD XII:21, and CD XIII:22. Notice the similar use of משכיל plus בני שחר ("Sons of Dawn") in the title of 4Q298.

not the same, this reminds of Dan 12:3 "And the Maskilim shall shine as the brightness of the firmament, and they that turn many to righteousness as the stars for ever and ever".[20]

In almost all of the other cases where the term Sons of Light does not occur at a beginning of a composition or a literary unit, it is part of a ritual, namely a ritual of blessings and curses at the annual covenant ceremony (cf. Dtn 29)[21] in 1QS II, 4Q280, and also 4Q510 might be understood in this context (as a kind of appendix to the blessings and curses).[22]

It remains to explain the occurrences in 4Q174 + 4Q177, where the Sons of Light occur in an eschatological midrash.[23] Here it is the motive of כשל and the help by an angel that links these passages to 1QS III,24-25 and at the same time to Dan 11,33-35 and Dan 12,1.

3 The Sons of Light in the History of Qumran Literature

To start with the end: A rather clear and negative observation can be made if we look at the final phase in the production of Qumran literature which is represented by the pesharim, especially pHab and pNah. There the Sons of Light do not occur, but rather the Teacher terminology and

[20] Cf. on the Maskil Carol NEWSOM, The Self as Symbolic Space. Constructing Identity and Community at Qumran, STDJ 52, Leiden/Boston 2004, 189: "[He] is a figure who can be described not only as an apotheosis of sectarian selfhood but of the sect itself". Similar to Dan 12:3 is the self-designation בני צדק "Sons of Righteousness" that appears also in the broader Sons of Light contexts in Qumran, see for certain in the Treatise of the Two Spirits, 1QS III:20.22.

[21] With tribes instead of Sons of Light.

[22] See Esther ESHEL, "Apotropaic Prayers in the Second Temple Period," In: Esther CHAZON (ed.), Liturgical Perspectives: Prayer and Poetry in Light of the Dead Sea Scrolls; Proceedings of the Fifth International Symposium of the Orion Center for the Study of the Dead Sea Scrolls and Associated Literature, 19–23 January 2000, Studies on the Texts of the Desert of Judah 48, Leiden 2003, 69–88 (esp. 83–84). On further thoughts about 4Q510 see Joseph ANGEL, Maskil, Community, and Religious Experience in the Songs of the Sage (4Q510-511), Dead Sea Discoveries 19/1, 2012, 1-27.

For further studies of the literary history of Qumran it might be of interest, that the corresponding ritual described at the end of the Damascus Document, the expulsion ceremony (4Q266 11,5-16a) does not use the Sons of Light/Darkness terminology, cf. A. STEUDEL, Rewriting, 616. One might perhaps assume that the passage in D represents an earlier phase in the literary history than the more dualistic one in 1QS II-III (and perhaps the above mentioned other ritual Sons of Light texts).

In 1QM XIII,16 we might expect the Sons of Light in the lacuna (after the mentioning of the Sons of Darkness), in a kind of hymnic appendix (XIII:7-16, cf. the Treatise of the Two Spirits in S) to the blessing and curses ritual in XII:end (lost)-XIII:6 (cf. the blessing and curse ritual in S), cf. above on 4Q510.

[23] On 4Q174 + 4Q177 cf. Annette STEUDEL, Der Midrasch zur Eschatologie aus der Qumrangemeinde (4QMidrEschata.b). Materielle Rekonstruktion, Textbestand, Gattung und traditionsgeschichtliche Einordnung des durch 4Q174 („Florilegium") und 4Q177 („Catena A"), Studies on the Texts oft he Desert of Judah 13, Leiden 1994.

other sobriquets are used to speak about the community.[24] The last composition where we find the Sons of Light might be the Midrash on Eschatology (4Q174+177) which is formally a rather late development on the way towards the Pesharim, knowing e.g. as well D as S.[25] Together with the Melchisedek-Midrash it belongs to the few compositions that reflects the world of thought that is find in the incipits of 1QS, 1QM, and 4QDa. The Midrash on Eschatology does not seem to know the Romans in the land.[26] That means, the usage of the term Sons of Light probably had stopped somewhen before the Romans entered Jerusalem in 63 BCE. The Sons of Light make their earliest appearances in the manuscript 1QS, which is paleographically dated to around 100 BCE or slightly later. That is, at latest at the beginning of the first century BCE the term Sons of Light was already in use – a point in history where the major rule texts from Qumran, S and mainly also D, had both developed their fullest/final forms. Since the incipits of the compositions S and D, the units where the Sons of Light occur, belong in both compositions to the young literary stages, there was a phase of so far unknown length in the history of the Qumran Community, where the Sons of Light had not been a designation for the community, but terms like היחד (S) and e.g. designations with ברית (S, D) prevailed. The fact that also 1QM has a Sons of Light beginning and an earlier literary history without them,[27] might indicate that in all three compositions, S, D, and M, the Sons of Light incipits were added more or less at the same period of time by the same group of people. That would have consequences for the date of M, which then as S and D would have received its incipit at latest around 100 BCE.[28] It seems that the reception of the book of Daniel has played a major role in the Sons of Light reworking of Qumran compositions. The influence of Dan 11-12 has been observed since long mostly for 1QM I,[29] but it seems to have had an impact on the incipits of S and D as well (also on 4Q510).[30]

[24] E.g. "the Teacher of Righteousness and the members of his party" (1QpHab IX:9-10), and "Judah" (4QpNah frg. 3-4 iii:4).

[25] See A. STEUDEL, Dating, 46-52.

[26] The same holds true for the Melkisedek-Midrash, but it is too poorly preserved to be sure about it.

[27] The oldest literary stage is found in 1QM II-IX.

[28] Other reworkings of the War Rule would have been possible still later on; the manuscript 1QM, which handed down the fullest version of M, stems from Herodian times.

[29] See e.g. Hanna VANONEN, The Textual Connections between 1QM 1 and the Book of Daniel", In: Hanne VON WEISSENBERG/ Juha PAKKALA/ Marko MARTTILA (eds.), Changes in Scripture: Rewriting and Interpreting Authoritative Traditions in the Second Temple Period (BZAW 419) Berlin 2011, 223-246.

[30] See above part 2 (Observations on the Sons of Light Occurences). Of course, there were other influences like e.g. Gen 1, Isa 45,7 (cf. Isa a XXXVIII:12-13 with its even

The author of the Midrash of Eschatology (4Q177), who uses the term the Sons of Light is (together with 11QMelch) the first one who explicitly quotes Daniel,[31] and could belong to the circles, that created the beginnings of S, D, and M. But perhaps more likely the Midrash on Eschatology reflects its ongoing usage or might have taken up the term Sons of Light and the kind of world view connected to them at a time shortly before it was no longer used (Pesharim).

These preliminary observations are intended first of all to inspire a more detailed literary analysis and further questions, like: Which circumstances might have caused the emergence of the term Sons of Light somewhen in the second half of the second century BCE? What made this dualistic and eschatological concept so important that it became the reading lens for at least three major texts of the community?[32] Does it perhaps intend to broaden (again) the narrower priestly Sons of Zadoq perspective, that earlier on had itself initiated a redactional layer?[33] And why was its usage stopped somewhen in the first half of the first century BCE? Or had there always been Qumran groups that did not accept the Sons of Light perspective?[34] I leave these questions unanswered so far and do look forward to critical reflections and further discussion, not least with my teacher and friend Emile Puech, who has been studying these texts like nobody did before.

stronger dualistic reading than in the MT, written by the same scribe as 1QS), and the Book of Jubilees (e.g. Jub 10). On the development of the Treatise of the Two Spirits in the context of S see recently Peter PORZIG, The Place of the "Treatise of the Two Spirits" (1QS 3:13–4:26) within the Literary Development of the Community Rule, In: Jutta JOKIRANTA, Molly ZAHN (eds.), Law, Literature, and Society in Legal Texts from Qumran: Papers from the Ninth Meeting of the International Organisation for Qumran Studies, Leuven 2016, STDJ 128, Leiden/Boston 2019, 127-152.

[31] 4Q174 frg. 1-3 ii:3, 11Q13 2:18.

[32] It is not excluded that also other compositions received a similar Sons of Light reworking at its beginning. Possible candidates might be the Hodajot and Instruction (Musar le-Mevin).

[33] See note 9.

[34] A manuscript like 4Q258 (4QS d) which definitely lacks the first four (Sons of Light) columns of 1QS, might in principal be explained in such a way, but a number of other possibilities exist.

UN COMPLEXE SCIENTIFIQUE À QUMRÂN LE DISQUE DE PIERRE, LES CLEPSYDRES ET LES *MIŠMAROT*

Paul TAVARDON, O.C.S.O.

1. LE DISQUE DE PIERRE

En 1954 le P. Roland de Vaux trouve à Qumrân dans le *locus 45* ce qu'il nomme « *un disque de pierre* ». La fiche de fouille porte le numéro 1229. L'objet est déposé aujourd'hui au Musée d'Israël[1]. Il s'agit d'un disque de calcaire de 150 mm de diamètre. Ce disque se caractérise par une surface concave sur laquelle sont tracés des cercles et des sillons concentriques et un certain nombre de marques en creux ou en plein[2] (figure 1).

Sans hypothèse préconçue nous avons effectué un ensemble de mesures en utilisant le calcul statistique absolument nécessaire vu l'état de l'objet et compte tenu des zones manquantes. Ces méthodes statistiques sont plus ou moins complexes, mais elles permettent des mesures correctes.

Ne présumant pas d'un gnomon ni de son épaisseur, nous définissons des coordonnées cartésiennes qui permettront des mesures de longueur et d'angles.

[1] Sur le locus 45 voir Roland de VAUX, Jean-Baptiste HUMBERT, Alain CHAMBON, *Fouilles de Khirbet Qumrân et de Aïn Feshkha I : Album de photographies. Répertoire du fonds photographique. Synthèse des notes de chantier du Père Roland de Vaux OP,* – Fribourg Pérolles 42 : Éditions universitaires de Fribourg / Universitätsverlag Freiburg, 1994, (Novum Testamentum et Orbis Antiquus [NTOA] Series Archaeologica, Vandenhoeck & Ruprecht, 1994), 168, 170, 307-308. *Le cadran est enregistré comme objet n° 1229, actuellement au Sanctuaire du Livre),* Musée d'Israël, Jérusalem. (Israel Antiquities Authority, Accession number: 97.74 [134]

[2] U. GLESSMER, M. ALBANI, An Astronomical Measuring Instrument from Qumran In: Parry DONALD W, Ulrich Eugene CHARLES (éd.), *The Provo International Conference on the Dead Sea Scrolls* (Studies on the Texts of the Desert of Judah 30) Leiden, Brill 1999, 407-442. M. ALBANI & U. GLESSMER., « Un instrument de mesures astronomiques à Qumrân », *RB* 104 (1997) 89-115. G.M. HOLLENBACK, "The Qumran Roundel: An Equatorial Sundial?", (DSD 7, 2000), 123-129. B. THIERING, "The Qumran sundial, as an odometer using fixed lengths of hours", (DSD 9, 2002), 347-363. Paul TAVARDON, *Le disque de Qumrân*, (CRB 75) Paris, Gabalda, 2010.

Jonathan BEN-DOV, "The Qumran Dial: Artifact, Text, and Context," in *Qumran und die Archäologie* (ed. J. FREY, C. CLAUSSEN, and N. KESSLER, (WUNT 278) Tübingen: Mohr Siebeck, 2011, 211-237.

On se reportera à la figure 1. L'origine des coordonnées est placée en O au centre du disque. L'axe des abscisses (x) reliant le point O au signe en forme de Φ couché, coupe la limite du disque en E pour x positif et en W pour x négatif. L'axe des ordonnées (y) est perpendiculaire en O à l'axe des abscisses, il coupe la limite du disque en S pour y négatif et en N pour y positif. Le signe Φ est posé comme origine des mesures angulaire ($\Phi = 0°$). Les angles sont comptés dans le sens inverse des aiguilles d'une montre, dit sens direct.

On peut voir sur la figure 1 que *le disque* est composé d'un ensemble de couronnes et de sillons concentriques. Les couronnes sont en plein et les sillons en creux.

1.1. Les couronnes et leur gradations

On peut compter sept couronnes numérotées C_1, C_2, C_3, C_4, C_5, C_6, C_7.

Ces couronnes peuvent être classées en deux catégories. Les couronnes C_4, C_6, C_7 portent des marques en creux orientées vers le centre du disque.

Les couronnes C_2, C_3, C_5 portent des marques en plein dont l'orientation vers le centre est moins stricte (figure 2). Ces couronnes portent par ailleurs d'autres marques qu'il faudra décrire (figure 1).

1.1.1. *Les marques en creux*[3]

Les marques en creux des couronnes C_4 et C_6 sont totalement différentes de celles de la couronne C_7.

a-Couronnes C_4 et C_6

Couronne C_4 : 37,5 mm $\leq R \leq$ 41,25 mm
Couronne C_6 : 48,75 mm $\leq R \leq$ 56,25 mm

Ces marques en creux peuvent être estimées à 72 pour chaque couronne, soit une suite de divisions de 5° en 5°. Les graduations des deux couronnes sont en décalage de 2,5°[4]. Ainsi les deux couronnes C_4 et C_6 permettent une division du cercle en 144 divisions de 2,5°.

[3] *Voir*. la représentation du disque figure 1. Couronne C_4, C_6, C_7 et la figure 2.

[4] Pour le détail des mesures basées sur des méthodes statistiques compte tenu de l'endommagement du disque Voir Paul TAVARDON, *Le disque de Qumrân*, pour la couronne C_4, 21 -26, pour la couronne C_6, 26-30. On calcule ici une courbe de tendance et un coefficient de détermination pour chacun des échantillons : pour C_4, deux échantillons, 0° à 92,4°, 120° à 154,9°. Dans le cas de C_6, un échantillon, 3° à 92°. Dans les trois cas nous avons une fonction de forme $y = ax + b$, avec a = 5° et un coefficient de détermination $R^2 = 0,9 \approx 1$.

b-Couronne C_7 60 mm $\leq R \leq$ 63,75 mm

Cette couronne offre deux particularités qui la distinguent des couronnes C_4 et C_6. Elle n'est pratiquement pas séparée de la couronne C_6 dont elle se présente, à première vue, comme une continuation, mais son plan est très différent de celui des autres couronnes. Il fait un angle de plus de 45° avec l'horizontal. Les marques sont en creux comme pour C_4 et C_6, l'évaluation du nombre en est plus complexe vu le mauvais état de la couronne. Ont été retenus quatre échantillons a = 0° à 40,8°, b = 55° à 85,3°, c = 110,4° à 177,9°, d = 222,6° à 269°.[5] L'étude statistique plus fine basée sur l'écart-type est développée dans notre étude[6].
Une première analyse des quatre groupes (a, b, c, d) de graduations de la couronne C_7, par régression linéaire[7] a montré que l'espacement des graduations ne suit pas une même progression arithmétique comme dans le cas des couronnes C_4 et C_6. L'hypothèse tendant à chercher une relation avec le déplacement de l'ombre d'un gnomon ou d'un bec triangulaire ne donne aucun résultat pour cette couronne[8]. L'étude statistique conduit à un nombre de graduations n compris entre : 79 et 92. $79 \leq n \leq 92$.

En appelant k (en degré) la valeur d'un espacement des graduations de C_7, on peut écrire : $3{,}91° \leq k \leq 4{,}56°$.

Une différence fondamentale se fait jour dans la distinction des trois couronnes portant des marques en creux. Dans le cas de C_7, les mesures des espacements ne présentent pas de cohérence. En revanche dans le contexte de Qumrân, le nombre de 91 graduations peut aisément être rapporté aux 364 jours du calendrier essénien. (91*4 = 364)

Couronnes	***R***	**espacement**	**Nombre de graduations**	**Fonction**
C_4	37,5 mm $\leq R \leq$ 41,25 mm	5°	72	$y = 5x$
C_6	48,75 $R \leq$ 56,25 mm	5°	72	$y = 5x$
C_7	C_7 60 $\leq R \leq$ 63,75 mm	*Non déterminé*	91	$y = 3{,}956x$

Tableau 1 : Couronnes C_4, C_6, C_7

[5] Rappelons que les angles sont comptés à partir de $\Phi = 0°$.
[6] P. Tavardon, *Le disque de Qumrân*, 124 et suiv.
[7] P. Tavardon, *disque*, 30-34.
[8] *Ibid.* 123.

1.1.2. *Les marques en saillie*

Ces marques apparaîtront avec l'étude complète du disque, comme l'élément essentiel et original de cet objet, bien qu'elles ne soient pas facilement observables. Elles n'apparaissent pas sur tous les clichés et la maquette du *Musée d'Israël* ne permet pas de les distinguer. En revanche sur le modèle original du *Musé*e et avec un bon éclairage ainsi que sur les photos de qualité elles apparaissent très nettement[9].

On note en premier lieu que ces marques en saillie ne sont présentes que sur la partie comprise entre 0° et 90° de notre croquis, avec une exception, réservée à un autre usage. Trois couronnes sont concernées, C_2, C_3, C_5, (C_2, 15 mm $\leq R \leq$ 26,25 mm ; C_3, 30 mm $R \leq$ 37,5 mm ; C_5, 41,25 mm $\leq R \leq$ 45 mm.) Pour chaque couronne on mesure l'angle que fait chacune des marques en saillie avec l'axe des abscisses. Cet angle est noté *a'* (Pour une raison que le développement explicitera, on crée une colonne avec *a* = (270° - *a')*. Cela revient à prendre, pour origine des mesures de l'angle α, le point S sur la figure 1, avec S = 0°[10].

C_2	*a'*	*a*	C_3	*a'*	*a*	C_5	*a'*	*a*
– 1	– 6°	276°	– 1	– 6°	276°			
1	+ 9°	261°	1	+ 17°	253°	1	10°	260°
2	+ 17°	253°	2	+ 27°	243°	2	19°	251°
3a	+ 34°	236°	3	+ 34°	236°	3	31°	239°
3b	+ 42°	228°	4	+ 46°	224°	4	42°	228°
4	+ 54° °	216°	5	+ 53°	217°	5	49°	221°
5	+ 59° °	211°	6a	+ 55°	215°	6	53°	217°
			6b	+ 57°	213°	7	59°	211°
			7	+ 59°	211°			

Tableau 2 : Couronnes C_2, C_3, C_5

[9] Par exemple elles apparaissent très visiblement dans la première photo. Voir PAM 42.683 objet 1229 trouvé dans le locus 45, J.-B. HUMBERT, A. CHAMBON, R. DE VAUX, *fouilles*, 307-308.

[10] Sur la couronne C_2 la graduation en saillie (n° 3) n'est pas dans l'axe du centre du disque. Sa base (3a) sur C2 intérieure fait un angle *a* de 34° avec le signe Φ couché alors que son sommet (3b) sur C_2 extérieure fait un angle de 42°, soit une différence de 8°. Le même phénomène se constate sur la couronne C3 avec 6a (+ 55°) et 6b (+ 57°).

Si l'on exclut la marque $a' = -6^{\circ}$ (au-dessous de l'axe des x), on peut constater que :

$$9^{\circ} \leq a' \leq 59^{\circ}, \text{ soit } 276^{\circ} \geq a \geq 211^{\circ}.$$

Peut-on faire apparaître une relation entre les valeurs de a' ou a ? A partir du tableau 2 il est possible d'émettre une hypothèse sur la signification des marques en saillie des couronnes C_2, C_3 et C_5.

Indépendamment du fait de savoir encore si *le disque* avait une fonction astronomique, on peut relever une correspondance entre la valeur α des marques indiquées sur *le disque* sur les couronnes C_2, C_3, C_5 et les azimuts du Soleil donnés par les *Ephémérides de l'IMCCE*[11].

Prenons comme exemple le 9 février an 0, à 2 h vraies, l'azimut[12] du Soleil donné par les Ephémérides est de 215,9° (≈ 216°), ce qui correspond à un angle α' = 54,1° (≈ 54°) (voir en note les paramètres utilisés et les résultats du calcul)[13]. Nous voyons dans le tableau 2 (figure 2) qu'il existe une marque en saillie : la marque n° 4 située sur la couronne C_2. Cette marque $a' = (270^{\circ} - a)$ correspond à l'azimut du Soleil à 2 h vraies le 9 février de l'année 0. Certes, cette correspondance ne peut constituer à elle seule une preuve. Il reste alors à généraliser la méthode pour l'ensemble des marques en saillie.

L'analyse permet d'obtenir de manière systématique le résultat suivant :

Du 9 février au 21 mai de l'an 0 à la longitude et latitude de Qumrân les marques indiquant la valeur de l'azimut à 2 h vraies sont distribuées comme suit sur la couronne C2.

[11] *Cf.* Site de l'IMCCE, http://www.imcce.fr (Institut de Mécanique Céleste et Calcul des Ephémérides).

[12] L'azimut du Soleil est compté positivement depuis le méridien Sud vers l'Ouest de 0° à 180° et négativement vers l'Est de 0° à -180°. Voir Denis SAVOIE, *La gnomonique*, Les Belles Lettres, 2007, 11.

[13] http://www.imcce.fr # Miriade.ephemcc.results

Request:

targetType: Star, targetNumber: 11, targetName: Sun, Diameter: 1392000.00 km, Orbital period: 0.00000000E+00 d, Time_Scale: TT, Planetary_Theory: DE406/LE406, Coordinates: Dedicated to the observation, frameType: Apparent (true equator; equinoxe of the date), frameCentre: Topocenter, Location_Name: userLocation, Location_Coordinates: 2h 21m 50.064s E ; 31d 44m 26.880s N ; 0.00m

Sun, Date, année, mois, jour, heure, minute, seconde, 0-02-09T 11:55:30.00, heure vraie 2h 0m 0.02, Déclinaison : -15 30 15.99, azimut (d, m, s) 215° 52′ 8.06″, hauteur : +34 41 7.58.

N° des marques sur C_2	$a' = (270° – a)$	a	Dates
4	54°	216°	9 février
3	34°	236°	11 avril
2	17°	253°	21 mai

Tableau 3 : Couronnes C_2 et azimuts du Soleil

Les mêmes mesures effectuées sur la couronne C_5 donnent le tableau 4[14] :

Sur le tableau 4 on voit qu'il existe une marque en saillie : la marque n° 3 située sur la couronne C_5. Cette marque $a' = (270° – a) = 31°$ correspond à l'azimut du Soleil 239° à 2 h vraies le 28 août an 0.

N° des marques sur C_5	$a' = (270° – a)$	a	Dates
1	10°	260°	7 juillet
2	19°	251°	3 août
3	31°	239°	28 août
6	53°	217°	31 octobre
7	59°	211°	16 décembre

Tableau 4 : Couronne C_5 et azimuts du Soleil

L'étude des marques en saillie des couronnes C_2 et C_5 toutes rassemblées sur le premier quart du disque entre 0° et 90 établit avec certitude une finalité d'ordre astronomique pour *le disque* de Qumrân. Cette finalité se fonde sur la correspondance des valeurs angulaires des marques et des azimuts du Soleil pour une seule et même heure, 2 h vraie (2h du Soleil).[15]

Il faut encore se demander si ces dates et cette distribution ont une fonction particulière, car elles ne peuvent être l'effet du hasard compte tenu de l'heure semblable pour toutes les marques à savoir : 2h vraies. On

[14] Relevé des résultats donnés par les Ephémérides de l'IMCCE pour le 28 août.

Request:

targetType: Star, targetNumber: 11, targetName: Sun, Diameter: 1392000.00 km, Orbital period: 0.00000000E+00 d, Time_Scale: TT, Planetary_Theory: DE406/LE406, Coordinates: Dedicated to the observation, frameType: Mean of the date, Framecentre: Topocenter, Location_Name: userLocation, Location_Coordinates: 2h 21m 50.064s E ; 31d 44m 26.880s N ; 0.00m

Sun, 0-08-28T11:38:07.00, 12.30406, 12 1 17.91, -00 8 40.48, 2h 0m 0.23s, +10 40 32.57, 239 26 12.72, +55 12 18.69,

[15] Le fait qu'une seule partie du disque soit graduée, échappe totalement tant à U. GLESSMER and M. ALBANI, "An Astronomical…", qu'à J. BEN-DOV, "The Qumran Dial: Artifact" qui n'ayant pas remarqué les marques en saillie écrit, "In the Qumran dial, however, the entire circle is graduated. Moreover, there are no markings on the circle that would indicate the parts actually covered by the shadow", 219.

examinera à cet effet trois dates : 9 février, 7 juillet, 31 octobre pour chacune de ces marques relevées dans les tableaux 3 et 4 l'heure du Soleil comme nous l'avons vérifié, est de 2 h. (Angle horaire H = 2h). Quelle est pour chacune de ces marques l'heure du calendrier compté en Temps moyen, *TM* ou heure du méridien origine ?

- Le 9 février[16], *TM* = 11h 55m 30s, et en rajoutant la longitude de Qumrân : 2h 21m 50s, le *TM* de Qumrân est de 14 h 17m 20s pour un Temps vrai du Soleil, *TV* = 14h. En posant *Hv* = heure vraie du Soleil et *Hm* = heure moyenne des montres, des calendriers, des sabliers ou des clepsydres on a pour le 9 février : *Hm* = *Hv* + 17 m ou *Hv* = *Hm* - 17m.
- Le 7 juillet : *Hm* = *Hv*
- Le 31 octobre, *Hm* = *Hv* – 13,8 m ou *Hv* = *Hm* + 13,8m[17].

Ces mesures précisent le rôle des marques en saillie. Elles indiquent l'azimut du Soleil à 2 heures vraies, heure qui diffère du temps régulier des calendriers. Le principe de cette différence est étudié sous le nom *d'équation du temps E*[18]. Le temps solaire est irrégulier, le temps de nos montres, le temps des éphémérides ou le temps des sabliers et des clepsydres est un temps moyen et régulier, un temps mathématique construit. Ce phénomène était connu des anciens astronomes et l'on en trouve un développement important dans *la Composition Mathématique* de Claude Ptolémée[19].

Ainsi après vérification, on obtient un tableau complet des marques relevées sur les couronnes C_2 et C_5 et des relations entre E (équation du temps) et l'azimut du Soleil à 2 h vraies

	9/02	**11/04**	**21/05**	**7/07**	**3/08**	**28/08**	**31/10**	**16/12**
H_v	2 h	2 h	2 h	2 h	2 h	2 h	2 h	2 h
H_m	2 h 17,5 m	2 h	1 h 52,6 m	2 h	2 h 2,9 m	2 h	1 h 46,6 m	2 h
a	215,9°	235,6°	253,4°	259,6°	251°	239,4°	216,9°	211,2°
a'	54,1°	34,37°	16,59°	10,43°	19,03°	30,58°	53,08°	58,8°

Tableau 5 : Azimuts du Soleil à 2 h vraies et équation du temps

[16] Voir la note 11.

[17] http://www.imcce.fr (IMCCE). On pratique comme dans le cas du 9 février.

[18] Pour l'équation du temps D. SAVOIE, *La gnomonique*, 41-62. L'auteur donne en particulier un tableau des valeurs de *E* entre – 1000 et 2000, 51. *Ibid*, 455 : « calcul de l'équation du temps ».

[19] Claude PTOLÉMÉE, *Composition mathématique*, trad. de M. HALMA suivie de notes de M. DELAMBRE, Henri Grand, Paris, 1813, 1968, 206-210. Voir O. NEUGEBAUER, *A History of Ancient Mathematical Astronomy*, Part one, "Equation of Time", 61-68.

Une fois relevées ces marques significatives, on peut procéder à l'examen de la totalité des marques du tableau 2 des trois couronnes C_2, C_3, C_5. Toutes sans exception indiquent un azimut du Soleil pour 2 h vraies[20].

La correspondance des marques du disque entre *l'équation du temps* et les azimuts du Soleil à 2 h vraies autorisent maintenant à tirer quelques conclusions touchant l'utilisation de cet objet.

a – La finalité du disque est bien d'ordre astronomique, ce qu'atteste la représentation de l'équation du temps par des azimuts particuliers du Soleil distribués autour de 2h dans le premier quart du disque. L'équation du temps ne peut figurer qu'en contexte astronomique. Elle n'a pas d'autre usage.

b – Les graduations en saillie indiquent un autre point important du fonctionnement du disque. Parlant d'instrument astronomique, de marque des azimuts et des heures, il s'agit alors d'une forme de cadran solaire. Si, de plus, ces graduations sont relatives à des heures et à des azimuts et cela en même temps (tous les azimuts sont relevés pour 2 h), alors la question d'un gnomon doit être reformulée.

On ne peut baser une analyse de départ sur un « gnomon », ou un style droit de 8 mm de diamètre comme on le trouve chez J. Ben-Dov, mais encore dans des représentations du *Musée d'Israël*[21]. Partant de *l'a priori* d'un gnomon de 8 mm, on conclut à l'impossibilité de parler d'un instrument astronomique, les graduations et les espacements étant trop fins pour le gnomon dont on a posé par avance la largeur[22]. Il est clair alors que l'argument peut se renverser, des graduations fines nous conduisent à un style d'un diamètre proportionnel et adéquat.

Mais ces marques dès lors appelées gradations qui sont relatives à des heures (2h par exemple) mais aussi à des azimuts permettent de traiter plus efficacement de la question du style porté par *le disque*.

Il est maintenant possible d'orienter la figure 1. La ligne des ordonnées (y), doit se confondre avec le méridien du lieu à savoir de Qumrân, N indiquant le Nord et S le Sud. La marque en forme de Φ couché indique

[20] Voir P. TAVARDON, *Le disque de Qumrân,* 108, 111-112, 121

[21] Voir J. BEN-DOV, "The Qumran Dial" 213, "It contains a non-penetrating socket in its center, probably meant for a gnomon (8 mm in diameter). The dial is of a slightly concave form, like a saucer, but the concavity is not nearly as deep as in the Greek hemispherical or conical dials".

[22] *Ibid.* 219, "It should be pointed out at this stage that several material traits of the dial do not conform to its use as a sundial. The following problems merit special attention: 1. The graduation marks are very fine and too close to each other when compared with the width of the gnomon".

l'Est et l'origine de la mesure des angles. Elle se situe sur l'axe des abscisses. (x). Toutes les graduations en saillie sont rassemblées sur le 1er quart situé après midi vrai, N.

Parler de gradations marquant les azimuts du Soleil, suppose l'existence d'un style droit. Mais avec l'indication des heures, on doit aussi admettre l'existence d'un style polaire[23]. Ainsi les graduations en saillie des couronnes C_2, C_3, C_5, qui articulent azimuts et heures, nous conduisent à poser l'existence d'un style triangulaire (figures 3 et 4).

1.1.3. *Les sillons (figures 1 et 2)*

Les sillons se répartissent en quatre catégories.

S_1 et S_2 : sillons larges et profonds (figure 8).
S_3 et S_4 : simples marques dessinées sur la surface du disque.
S_5 : sillon légèrement plus large et profond que S_3 et S_4.

Enfin, S_6 constitue la base de la couronne C_7 qui, elle-même, fait un angle de 45° avec le plan horizontal.

Les sillons modifient la régularité de la surface du disque. Leurs tracés, par le constructeur, ne sont certainement pas accidentels et l'on peut déjà émettre l'hypothèse qu'ils répondent comme les couronnes à une finalité à découvrir. Les sillons permettent de distinguer pour chaque couronne une limite intérieure plus proche du centre et une limite extérieure. Ainsi pour la couronne C_2 on distingue C_{2int} et C_{2ext}. Les sillons S_1 et S_2 marquent les limites de la couronne.

1.2. Mesure du style triangulaire (figures 3 et 4)

Jonathan Ben-Dov signale, sans en tirer toutes les conséquences, la concavité du disque[24]. L'hypothèse de l'eau servant à orienter et à caler l'instrument est certes possible, mais elle n'est ni première ni fondatrice, bien que non contradictoire avec notre hypothèse[25]. Là encore l'absence de mesure conduit à des approximations.

La concavité du disque est très précise. Il s'agit d'un cône renversé dont on peut mesurer les dimensions. Un moulage exécuté sur l'original a permis d'obtenir des mesures précises et déterminantes. En théorie, on peut

[23] Voir D. SAVOIE, *La gnomonique*, 131-138.

[24] Voir J. BEN-DOV, *Dial*, 213, "The dial is of a slightly concave form, like a saucer."

[25] De même. "*Glessmer* and *Albani* (Henceforth:GA) plausibly suggested that the form of a saucer was intended to contain water, used for horizontal adjustment of the object when laid on a flat surface."

dire que la surface du disque est un cône de révolution. Il peut être généré simplement par la rotation d'une droite OK passant par O autour d'un axe ON différent de OK. La génératrice du cône est d'une longueur de 75 mm et fait un angle fixe de valeur = 76,43° avec l'axe de rotation. L'inclinaison par rapport à l'horizontale constitue un angle ω d'une valeur de 13,57°[26].

1.2.1. *Le style droit*[27].

En posant $\varphi = 31{,}5^\circ$ (latitude de Qumrân), $\varepsilon = 23{,}7^\circ$ (obliquité de l'écliptique année 0), $\omega = 13{,}57^\circ$ (inclinaison du disque) et R = apothème du cône = 75 mm, on obtient :

L = hauteur du style droit = 68,27 mm

1.2.2. *Le style polaire*

fait un angle égal à la latitude du lieu avec la ligne de midi, c'est-à-dire avec le méridien. Il pointe vers le nord géographique[28].

1.2.3. *Les ombres hyperboliques (figure 7).*

La concavité du disque présente comme autre conséquence celle de la forme des ombres sur sa surface. Les ombres d'un style oblique sur un plan sont des droites, mais ici il s'agit d'ombres sur une surface conique (intérieur d'un cône). Ces ombres comme nous le montrons sont des branches d'hyperboles (figure 3)[29].

La forme conique du disque et les couronnes expliquent l'absence totale d'inscriptions, question que pose Jonathan Ben-Dov : « A serious question remains: how were full hours measured? »[30]

Le détail du mouvement de l'ombre et l'indication des heures nécessiteraient une étude détaillée dont on ne donne ici que le principe[31]. L'heure

[26] Voir P. TAVARDON, *disque*, 40-43. En posant h_1 hauteur du Soleil au solstice d'hiver. h_2 hauteur du Soleil à l'équinoxe, h_3 hauteur du Soleil au solstice d'été, nous avons $\text{tg}\,\omega = 2[(\text{tg}h_2)/2 - 2\,\text{tg}h_1]$. Et $L = R\,[\text{th}h_1 \cos\omega) + \sin\omega]$ avec R = 75mm. On pourra encore déduire la hauteur du style en fonction de φ la latitude du lieu et ω l'inclinaison de l'écliptique : $L = R\,[(\cos\omega)/(\,\text{tg}(\varphi + \omega)) + \sin\omega]$

[27] *Ibid.*

[28] Voir D. SAVOIE, *gnomonique*, 131. Le bec triangulaire sera composé du style oblique PN coupant le style droit ON à son sommet N et de la base OP rejoignant la base du style droit O à la base du style oblique P. Nous aurons $\text{OPN} = \varphi + \omega = 45{,}07^\circ$. $\text{PNO} = 90^\circ - \varphi = 58{,}5^\circ$. $\text{NOP} = 90^\circ - \omega = 76{,}43^\circ$.

[29] Voir P. TAVARDON, *disque*, 66-67. L'équation de la projection de l'ombre dans le plan horizontal :

$L^2\,[1 - (\text{tg}\,\varphi / L\,\text{tg}\,\beta)x + (\text{tg}\,\varphi / L)y]^2 = (x^2 + y^2)\,\text{tg}^2\,\omega$. Ces ombres sont dépendantes de L, la hauteur du style, de φ la latitude du lieu et de ω, l'inclinaison.

[30] Voir J. BEN-DOV, "The Qumran Dial" 232.

[31] Voir P. TAVARDON, *disque*, 65-73.

est indiquée par le point de tangence de l'ombre des hyperboles et de chacune des couronnes intérieures ou extérieures. Mais ceci n'est possible que par le fait que les ombres sont hyperboliques[32]. Si l'on appelle β l'angle que fait l'ombre avec l'axe des y, axe du méridien (axe de midi vrai), nous avons des relations différentes pour une surface plane et une surface conique telle qu'on l'a décrite.

Avec R = apothème du cône ω : inclinaison, L : hauteur du style droit φ = latitude du lieu, H = angle horaire.

Surface plane	Surface conique
$\text{tg}\,\beta = \sin\varphi\,\text{tg}\,H$	$\text{tg}\,\beta = -y/x$ avec $y = R'^2\,\text{tg}\,\varphi / (\pm R'\,\text{tg}\,\omega - L)$ $\text{tg}\,\varphi\,(R'^2/y) = \pm R\,\text{tg}\,\omega - L$
$\text{tg}\,H = \text{tg}\,\beta / \sin\varphi$	$x^2 = R'^2 - y^2 \rightarrow x = (R'^2 - y^2)^{1/2}$ et $\omega = 13{,}57°$ $L = 68{,}27$ mm $\varphi = 31{,}5°$ $R' = R\cos\omega$ $\text{tg}\,H = \text{tg}\,\beta / \sin\varphi$

Le tableau suivant montre la correspondance entre le rayon des couronnes et l'angle horaire H. (Les étapes du calcul, R_x, R'_x, $\beta°$, H en degré et H en heure sont indiqués).

Ainsi quand l'ombre de l'hyperbole est tangente à C_3int. il est 2 h vrai au Soleil.[33]

Couronnes	***R_x (mm)***	***R'_x (mm)***	***β °***	***H°***	***H (h)***
C_{2int}	15	14,58	7,93	14,93	1 h
C_{3int}	30	29,16	16,97	30,28	2 h
C_{4int} Eq.	37,5	36,45	22,06	37,8	2 h 30
C_{5ext}	45	43,74	27,68	45,11	3 h
C_{7int}	60	58,33	42,2	60,05	4 h
C_{8ext} S.h.	75	72,91	61,84	74,38	4 h 58

Tableau 6 : Angles horaires indiqués par les couronnes

32 Voir figure 7.

33 *Int.* et *Ext.* désigne le coté intérieur (le plus près du centre, plus petit rayon) et le coté extérieur de la couronne (plus grand rayon).

L'ombre se déplace sur la surface conique en coupant successivement les sillons et les couronnes. On a réalisé une étude du mouvement de l'ombre aux environs de 2 h (heure remarquable du disque) sur une maquette 3D du disque adaptée aux coordonnées et aux variations de paramètres du fait des 2000 ans écoulés (figure 4). On a pu relever ceci :

L'ombre oblique traverse la couronne C_2 en 45 min. À 1 h 45 min elle est tangente à C_{2ext} (R = 26,25 mm, R' = 25,5 mm). Elle entre dans le sillon S_2 et y demeure 15 min. Elle coupe C_3 en deux points M et N. La longueur du segment brisé, MN diminue progressivement et à 2 h (R = 30 m, R' = 29,2 m) l'ombre est tangente à C_{3int}. (figure 8)

On souligne trois points :

Les indications données par *le disque*, aux environs du méridien, sont les moins entachées d'erreur d'observation, en particulier pour la zone de pénombre du style[34]. On a avec les deux couronnes (C_1, C_2) et les deux sillons (S_1, S_2), des indications de temps précises : 15 min (S_1 et S_2), 30 min (C_1), 45 min (C_2).

Enfin et surtout, l'alternance des sillons (ombres brisées) et des couronnes (ombres droites) permet une plus juste appréciation de la lecture exacte des heures. Ainsi s'éclaire la fonction des sillons gravés sur *le disque* et la profondeur remarquable de S_2 (figure 8).

Il est ainsi possible de définir sur *le disque* un ensemble entièrement destiné à donner la différence entre le temps régulier et le temps solaire. Les trois couronnes C_2, C_3, C_5 qui donnent les indications de l'ombre d'un bec triangulaire sur une surface conique, à savoir les azimuts du Soleil relatifs au maximum et minimum de l'équation du temps pour une heure donnée : 2 h. Les azimuts particuliers étant marqués par des graduations en saillie et les heures par les points de tangence des ombres avec les couronnes ou les sillons. Le système couronnes-sillons avait pour finalité une lecture plus précise du mouvement de l'ombre.

Mais une question s'impose. Comment fonctionnait ce système et quelle était sa finalité ? Quand les graduations en saillie correspondent toutes à des points remarquables de l'équation du temps de l'époque. Il faut supposer que les valeurs étaient connues et relevées. Ainsi le 9 février année 0 à 2h (ombre hyperbolique), le style droit indique une gradation en saillie, un azimut de 216°. Graduation remarquable sur les quatre indiquées sur la couronne C_2. Le fait que cette graduation ait été marquée implique que sa signification était connue. Ce jour-là, il y avait une différence de 17,5 mm entre le Soleil vrai et le Soleil moyen.

[34] Voir D. Savoie, *gnomonique*, pour l'étude de la pénombre dans les cadrans solaires, 481-490.

$$T_m = T_v + E$$

Pour 2h au Soleil le temps régulier était de 2h 17,5 min. Si cela est significatif aujourd'hui entre temps du Soleil et temps de nos montres, quel était le sens de cette distinction et son utilité dans le contexte de Qumrân ?

Les graduations en saillie distribuées selon les valeurs de l'équation du temps suffisent à établir l'utilisation d'une correction du temps solaire vrai. Si l'on se reporte à la description précise qu'en donne Ptolémée dans la *Syntaxe mathématique* au chapitre VIII du livre III[35], nous retrouvons ce que nous savons aujourd'hui de l'équation du temps. Seul est réel le temps irrégulier du Soleil. Le temps moyen est basé sur le déplacement à vitesse constante d'un Soleil fictif au cours de l'année. C'est donc un temps construit. Si l'on ne peut établir que les gens de Qumrân connaissaient le principe de l'équation du temps, la présence de l'instrument atteste cependant qu'ils en connaissaient l'utilisation. Ptolémée indique précisément le seul usage de l'équation du temps : *Cette différence négligée pour le Soleil et les autres astres ne nuirait pas sensiblement aux observations ; mais si on la négligeait pour la Lune, elle deviendrait bientôt considérable, 3/5 d'un degré, à cause de la célérité de son mouvement*[36]. Ce qui est aujourd'hui encore clairement exprimé par Denis Savoie[37].

Il est certain que le seul usage possible de l'équation du temps portait sur le mouvement de la Lune, ce qui, comme on le verra, est bien en accord avec la littérature astronomique retrouvée à Qumrân.

1.3. Le calendrier

On a considéré jusqu'ici les possibilités du disque de corriger le temps solaire. Si l'instrument était susceptible d'indiquer les variations de l'équation du temps pour tous les jours de l'année, il faut supposer qu'il était en mesure d'indiquer aussi de quel jour de l'année il s'agissait. Là encore ce

[35] PTOLÉMÉE, *Syntaxe mathématique*, édition Halma, 206.

[36] PTOLÉMÉE, *Syntaxe*, 209.

[37] D. SAVOIE, « L'aspect gnomonique de l'œuvre de Fouchy : La méridienne de temps moyen », *Revue d'histoire des sciences*, 2008/1 (Tome 61), p. 41-62. Et Edward S. KENNEDY, '*Two medieval approaches to the equation of time*', *Centaurus*, 31 (1988), 1-8. *L'usage de l'équation du temps dans l'Antiquité, puis pendant l'âge d'or des sciences arabes répond à un besoin essentiel : réduire un intervalle de temps exprimé en temps solaire vrai en temps solaire moyen. Si un astronome observe une éclipse ou l'instant du passage au méridien d'une étoile, il mesure les instants du phénomène en temps solaire vrai, indiqué par les cadrans solaires. Pour utiliser par la suite son observation dans la construction d'une théorie du mouvement de l'astre, il faut convertir l'instant exprimé en temps vrai en temps moyen. Pratiquement, cela n'est vraiment important que pour la Lune : l'équation du temps atteignant au maximum 17 minutes en valeur absolue, la variation de longitude du Soleil ou des planètes est négligeable pendant cet intervalle.*

sont les graduations en saillie qui conduisent à poser la nécessité d'un calendrier fixe.

Revenons à la couronne C_7 et aux les valeurs statistiques trouvées plus haut pour k et n

$$3{,}91^o \leq k \leq 4{,}56^o$$
$$79 \leq n \leq 92$$

On a[38] pour $n = 91$, $k = 3{,}956^o \approx 3{,}96^o$. Dans cette hypothèse chaque intervalle n'a de sens que par sa valeur ordinale[39]. Dans l'optique de Qumrân,[40] les 91 intervalles de la couronne C_7 peuvent représenter trois mois d'un calendrier de 364 jours, deux mois de 30 jours et un mois de 31 jours. L'inclinaison prononcée de la couronne pouvait faciliter la fixation d'une marque que l'on déplacerait manuellement chaque jour. Une année ferait quatre tours complets soit 364 jours.

Quand on connaît les calendriers perpétuels ou les calendriers fixes ont perçoit facilement dans ce calendrier essénien un calendrier de ce type. Une année de 364 jours compte exactement 52 semaines. Il peut ainsi débuter toujours le même jour et les fêtes et autres événements peuvent être placés toujours le même jour de l'année. *1 Hénoch LXXI, 12*[41].

L'année solaire tropique étant d'environ 365,25 jours, peut-on trouver sur *le disque* une correspondance entre ce calendrier de 364 jours et le mouvement annuel du Soleil ? Les équinoxes et solstices permettent un repère fixe par rapport à l'année solaire[42]. Pour traiter de la marque des

[38] Rappelons que k (en degré) = la valeur d'un espacement entre les graduations de la couronne C_7 et n = nombre de graduations.

[39] Si la couronne C_7 avait été tracée avec précision, elle comporterait 91 intervalles de 3,956° chacun très précisément. Mais du fait que seul le nombre des intervalles a valeur, l'imprécision du tracé ne prête pas à conséquence.

[40] A. Jaubert, *La date de la Cène : Calendrier biblique et liturgie chrétienne*, Études bibliques, Gabalda, Paris, 1957, et *D.B.Sup*, Qumrân, Mathias Delcor, *Les calendriers*, col. 958-960. Pour le calendrier perpétuel voir Paul Couderc, *Le calendrier*, Que sais-je, PUF, Paris, 2000, 100.

[41] On se référera à *l'Introduction* de l'édition *du livre d'Hénoch* dans l'édition de la Pléiade : *Le Soleil et les astres produisent des années exactes conformes entièrement à leur position, éternellement, sans avance ni retard d'un seul jour. Ils changent l'année avec une exactitude rigoureuse. Chaque année est de trois cent soixante-quatre jours (soit) pour trois ans, mille quatre-vingt-douze jours, pour cinq ans, mille huit cent vingt jours, si bien que huit ans comptent deux mille neuf cent douze jours.* André Caquot, Marc Philonenko, *La Bible Ecrits intertestamentaires, Introduction générale*, Bibliothèque de la Pléiade, Gallimard, Paris, 1987,. LXVII, voir *1 Hénoch*, LXXIV, 12-13, 558-559. Voir *ibid.*, Psaumes pseudo-davidiques, XXVII, 4-6, 330-331 : *Et il écrivit des psaumes (au nombre de trois mille six cents ; et des chants à chanter devant l'autel pour l'holocauste du sacrifice perpétuel pour chaque jour, pour tous les jours de l'année (au nombre de) trois cent soixante-quatre.*

[42] P. Tavardon, *disque, « la marque des équinoxes »*, 139.

équinoxes sur la surface du disque, il faut revenir à la graduation en saillie notée 3, (3a-3b) dans le tableau 2[43].

La graduation en question est la graduation 3b de C_2. L'azimut du Soleil : (figure 2, indiquée par un signe + de couleur noir)

$$a \text{ est de } 228° (\rightarrow a' = 42°, a'' = 48°).$$

Le 22 mars était le jour de l'équinoxe de printemps[44]. On peut voir que pareillement, pour le 25 septembre, jour de l'équinoxe d'automne, le 24 juin jour du solstice d'été et le 22 décembre jour du solstice d'hiver des graduations en saillie indiquent l'azimut du Soleil pour 2h[45].

La marque de l'équinoxe de printemps se trouve renforcée et confirmée par une autre indication, celle de la date de Pâques. On se reportera plus haut, à la liste des graduations en saillie[46]. La première graduation est indiquée sur le tableau 2, couronne C_2 : $-6° \rightarrow a = 276°$. On la retrouve sur la couronne C_3. Ces deux graduations ne figurent pas dans les graduations qui sont fonction de l'équation du temps. Enfin, cette même marque se retrouve tangente au signe Φ de la couronne C_4. (Figure 2)

Plus significatif encore, au niveau de la couronne C_6, (où l'on ne trouve que des graduations en creux, fonctions de l'azimut du Soleil), on peut cependant remarquer un signe en forme de « *N* » reliant les graduations indiquant $-6°$ et $-10°$, ou si l'on préfère : $a = 276°$ et $a = 280°$ (figure 2)[47]. Il se trouve que cette valeur de 276° correspond à l'azimut du coucher du Soleil le 4 avril 41. Si on pose le jour de l'équinoxe de printemps le 22 mars comme 1er jour du 1er mois, le 4 avril correspond bien au 14e jour du 1er mois : jour qui, dans le calendrier essénien correspond à la Pâque. La marque en forme de « *N* » indiquerait le 15 du mois de Nisan[48].

[43] *Cf. supra*. Tableau 2.

[44] C'est cette graduation fortement inclinée en 3a-3b de la couronne C_2 qui permet de repérer la marque de l'équinoxe. Il s'agit de deux graduations en une seule. Pour les années : – 135, 0, 135, les Ephémérides donnent les dates suivantes pour les équinoxes de printemps : Printemps 23 mars – 135 à 23 h 6 m UT, Printemps 22 mars 0 à 15 h 52 m UT, Printemps 22 mars 135 à 9 h 0 m UT, Pour chacune des trois dates de cette période le Soleil, à 2 h à Qumrân, atteindra un azimut de : (Année – 135 : $a = 227°\ 30'$, Année 0 : $a = 227°\ 37'$, Année 135 : $a = 227°\ 47'$). Compte tenu des limites de précision de l'instrument on peut dire que l'azimut observé était de 228°. C'est cette valeur qui est indiquée sur la couronne C_2 par la graduation 3b.

[45] P. TAVARDON, *disque*, 139-140. 25 septembre, gradation n° 4, couronne C_5. 24 juin, graduation n° 1, couronne C_2. 22 décembre, la graduation en saillie $a' = 59°$ figure sur C_5, C_3 et C_2.

[46] Voir Tableau 2.

[47] Voir figure 2, le *N* est entouré d'un cercle blanc.

[48] Voir P. TAVARDON, *disque*, 137. On peut en effet vérifier que l'angle situé entre la marque de l'équinoxe (couronne C_2, marque 3b, 42°) et la marque de la date de Pâque ($C_2 = -6°$) atteint une valeur totale de 48°. En comptant 3,96° pour un intervalle de C_7, nous

1.3.1 *Dérive et mise à jour*

Ainsi apparaissent clairement les articulations du calendrier essénien et du calendrier solaire. La couronne C_7 porte les 364 jours d'un calendrier perpétuel. Le 22 mars 41 (équinoxe de printemps) est un mercredi et il correspond au 1er jour d'un premier mois dans le calendrier essénien, le 1er de Nisan. Le calendrier essénien, comptant 364 jours, une dérive était alors à prévoir par rapport au mouvement du Soleil. Si pour l'année 41, le 1er jour du premier mois d'une année d'un calendrier vague de 364 jours correspond avec l'équinoxe de printemps, il n'en sera plus de même pour les années suivantes de sorte que par exemple pour l'année 48, le mercredi 1/I, premier jour de l'année, tomberait alors le 13 mars, soit 9 jours avant l'équinoxe. Il suffisait de faire correspondre les deux calendriers : le solaire et l'essénien au moyen d'une correction.

Cela est mathématiquement possible en intercalant un jour blanc non compté entre le 31 du mois XII et le 1er du premier mois et deux jours blancs non comptés tous les 4 ans. On rattraperait ainsi le décalage entre 364 jours et 365,25 jours.

Cela se pratiquait-il ? Il est difficile de le savoir. Mais il est certain en revanche que si cela ne se faisait pas, l'instrument serait devenu très vite inutilisable du fait d'une dérive de l'ensemble des valeurs des graduations en saillie. Sans un accord entre le calendrier de 364 jours et le mouvement du Soleil les valeurs fonctions de l'équation du temps et par conséquent du mouvement du Soleil noté sur les couronnes subiraient un décalage progressif quant à leurs dates. Aussi c'est encore l'utilisation de l'équation du temps qui nous conduit à poser la correction annuelle du calendrier de 364 jours.

1.4. Signes particuliers

D'autres signes peuvent encore être mis en évidence sur *le disque*. Pour mention, on renvoie le lecteur à notre publication. Ces signes viennent consolider notre hypothèse sur plusieurs de ses aspects.

1.4.1. *Le bec triangulaire*

On peut relever une marque en creux sur la couronne C_5 qui ne comporte que des marques en saillie. Cette marque en creux se situe exactement sur

sommes dans le 13e intervalle à compter du premier jour de l'année. Les deux barres « / / » du signe *N* indiquent par conséquent le 14 et le 15 de Nisan le jour de la Pâque (le jour étant compté à partir du coucher du Soleil).

l'axe du méridien (axe des *y*)[49] plein sud. Cette marque permet de supposer une sous-stylaire : correspondant à la projection d'un style oblique sur *le disque*. Dans le même sens, on remarque une marque tangente au sillon S_2 sur la gauche du disque qui peut très bien correspondre à l'encrage du style[50]. (Figure 1).

1.4.2. *Les « rayures »*

Un examen plus fin de la couronne C_2 révèle une autre catégorie de « rayures » en apparence plus désordonnées, gravées et plus fines. (Figure 2)[51]. Elles n'apparaissent que sur la couronne C_2 et sont tracées à partir de C_{2int} vers C_{2ext}. Précisons (cela peut se calculer) que l'ombre hyperbolique est tangente à C_{2int} à 1h[52]. Les *rayures* de la couronne C_{2int} ne peuvent correspondre à des marques d'azimut. Elles s'étendent sur les quarts I et IV du disque et sont sans relation avec les deux couronnes indiquant les azimuts, couronnes C_4 et C_6. De plus les orientations des *rayures* sont diverses. Ce qui importe en revanche, c'est le point qu'elles indiquent sur la couronne C_{2int}. De 0 h à 1h, l'ombre hyperbolique coupe en deux points cette couronne. Aussi nous en concluons (après mesures) que ce parcours de l'ombre de 0h à 1h se trouve être divisé en petite unité de temps de 4 min. La présence d'un style oblique reste la seule explication de ces rayures qui relèvent de coordonnées horaires et non horizontales. S'il reste difficile de justifier la nécessité de ces petites quantités de temps, on en verra plus loin toute l'importance.

1.4.3. *L'analemme*[53]

Cette étrange marque sur le bord du disque n'est pas accidentelle. Elle constitue une entaille soigneusement tracée et sur laquelle est dessiné un double triangle. Il s'agit certainement d'une indication de fabrique de l'instrument et surtout d'un descriptif de ses proportions et qui en rendait possible la duplication. L'analemme permet de connaître la profondeur du disque ω et la hauteur du style L ainsi que le tracé des couronnes pour la latitude du lieu. On peut en conclure à la possible existence d'autres exemplaires du même format.

[49] A 270° du signe en forme de Φ soit 180° de midi du Soleil.
[50] Voir figure 1.
[51] Voir figure 2, les rayures sont indiquées par des * noires.
[52] *Cf. supra.*
[53] Voir P. TAVARDON, *disque*, 175.

1.4.4 *La marque du temps, le « ע »*[54]

Sur le dos du disque. En ce qui concerne la datation de la gravure, on reprendra la conclusion de l'analyse d'Émile Puech « *Autant qu'on puisse en juger par une seule lettre incisée au dos du "disque", il me paraît que ce tracé du ע est certainement antérieur à la fin du 1er siècle avant Jésus-Christ : il peut être attribué à l'époque hasmonéenne ou début hérodienne au plus tard.*»[55]. On reviendra sur l'importance de cette datation.

1.4.5. *En résumé*

« *Le disque de pierre* » apparaît comme un petit cadran ayant pour finalité de déterminer la différence entre le temps vrai du Soleil et le temps moyen d'un Soleil fictif se déplaçant d'un mouvement régulier. La petite taille de l'objet confirme la thèse qu'il ne s'agit pas d'un cadran visant à calculer les déclinaisons et les hauteurs du Soleil. Dans ce cas le cadran serait plus grand. De plus il est possible de le déplacer. Le calendrier de la colonne C_7 et la marque des équinoxes, des solstices et de la Pâque permettent de fixer les jours. L'ombre oblique du style donne les heures et le style droit les azimuts du Soleil. Tout est centré sur 2 heures du Soleil à Qumrân, temps pour lequel sont tracées en saillie, sur le premier quart du disque, des graduations donnant le mouvement de l'équation du temps.

Trois questions vont ouvrir la seconde partie de cette étude.

Comme l'avait préconisé Ptolémée, l'équation du temps ne fut utilisée dans l'antiquité et le moyen âge qu'en vue de travaux sur le mouvement de la Lune compte tenu de la vitesse de cet astre[56]. La validité du cadran est comprise entre 5h vraie avant midi et 5h vraie après-midi. Jonathan Ben-Dov en conclut qu'il était trop petit de rayon pour un usage

[54] *Ibid.* 164.

[55] La lettre ע nous permet de faire une relation avec le terme עת (le temps). Ce mot est utilisé par exemple vingt-six fois à la suite dans le livre de Qohéleth (3:2 et suivants) pour indiquer ce temps qui se succède égal à lui-même. Qoh 3:2 *un temps (עת) pour enfanter et un temps (עת) pour mourir…* Le terme est aussi utilisé pour caractériser les temps mystérieux scrutés par les astrologues - astronomes de l'époque : dans le *livre d'Esther* 1,13 : *Alors le roi s'adressa aux sages qui avaient la connaissance des temps* (עתים). On trouve aussi assez souvent le terme עת dans la littérature de Qumrân. On relève un passage de l'*Ecrit de Damas*, X, 14-17, qui met en relation le mouvement du Soleil, l'observation et le sabbat : *Au sujet du sabbat, qu'on l'observe selon l'ordonnance le concernant. Qu'on ne fasse aucun ouvrage le sixième jour à partir du moment (עת) où le disque du Soleil est éloigné en sa plénitude de la porte où il se couche ; car c'est ce qu'il a dit : Observe le jour du sabbat pour le sanctifier. Cf. Ecrits intertestamentaires*, 171.

[56] Ptolémée, *Syntaxe mathématique*, édition Halma, 206.

astronomique[57]. En effet pour le solstice d'été[58], le Soleil se lève à 6h 57m (*H*) et se couche à 7h 3m (*H* =heure vraie). Ce qui fait 7h environ avant et après midi. Les ombres hyperboliques ne peuvent indiquer que de – 5h à + 5h compte tenu du rayon du disque. On dira donc que le Soleil se couche deux heures après la validité du cadran. Pour le solstice le coucher du Soleil est à 4 h 55m ≈ 5h.

Mais ceci n'infirme pas l'usage astronomique du disque, mais seulement son usage en vue du calcul des heures du lever et du coucher du Soleil. Car son fonctionnement portait essentiellement sur 2h (toujours éclairé le jour) et sur les azimuts du Soleil à cette heure. Il pouvait ensuite indiquer l'heure jusqu'à seulement 5h vraie. Mais l'important se jouait entre 0h et 1h pour les graduations de 4 en 4 degrés et à 2 h pour les azimuts des points remarquables.

Cependant le fait que *le disque* ait pour finalité une correction de temps vrai en temps moyen et qu'il se limite dans son fonctionnement à + ou – 5 h, pose la question de la conservation du temps. Comment pouvait-on mesurer l'heure d'un quelconque phénomène avant 5h du matin et après 5h du soir. Si l'on pense à un usage destiné au mouvement de la Lune, comment mesurer les levers et les couchers de la Lune, leurs relations au Soleil.

C'est alors que peut se poser l'hypothèse de l'existence de clepsydres susceptibles de conserver le temps[59]. Hypothèse qui est exigée par l'ensemble de ce que nous révèle *le disque*.

2. Les clepsydres à *conduit d'écoulement*

2.1. Description et situation des jarres

Si le « disque de pierre » fut découvert en 1954 par Roland de Vaux[60], durant la campagne de fouilles de 1953, ce dernier, rapportait dans *la Revue Biblique*[61] qu'il trouva dans ce même *locus 45* une jarre qu'il classe

[57] J. Ben-Dov, "The Qumran Dial": *The dial is too small. Its size would render it inefficient for the detection of the compass points and the cardinal days of the year...*, 219.

[58] Voir Site de l'IMCCE, http://www.imcce.fr

[59] Avant l'invention de l'horloge mécanique, deux sortes d'instruments sont utilisés pour mesurer le temps. D'un côté, gnomons et cadrans solaires donnent *l'heure qu'il est*, l'heure des astres. De l'autre, sabliers et clepsydres (ou horloges à eau) servent à compter le temps qui passe, le temps qui s'écoule.

[60] *Cf. supra.*

[61] R. de Vaux, « Fouilles au Khirbet Qumrân », *RB* 61 (1954), 206-256. L'auteur parle : *d'une sorte de jarre entonnoir, dont le fond a un goulot d'écoulement...*, 217.

sous le N° de fouille 800, elle est décrite comme suit : *Grande jarre large ouverture, sans col, lèvres retroussée, deux anneaux annulaires sur l'épaule, base arrondie percée d'un conduit d'écoulement. Terre rouge, grise à la section, couverte blanche à l'extérieur*[62]. C'est l'absence de col et le *conduit d'écoulement* qui constituent pour nous l'originalité et l'intérêt de cette forme de jarre trouvée à proximité du disque. (A1 figure 5).

Quand en 2007, Yitzhak Magen et Yuval Peleg publient un rapport préliminaire des fouilles de Qumrân entre 1993 et 2004[63], ils donnent une photo d'une autre jarre comportant un *conduit d'écoulement.* (A3 figure 5)

Dans le rapport final [64] sont donnés les détails concernant cet objet et sa provenance : *un locus au sol en plaque de tessons déjà trouvés par de Vaux..... Sous le sol se trouvaient beaucoup de poteries et de récipients, dont un pichet intact trouvé dans la partie sud-est dans le coin de la pièce: une grande jarre avec une ouverture à la base a été trouvée à l'ouest de la pièce.*[65]

Irina Eisenstadt dans ce même rapport consigne que l'on a trouvé trois jarres entières avec *conduit d'écoulement* dans les *locii 45* et *63*[66]. A savoir : celle découverte par de Vaux (A1 figure 5), et sous le sol plâtré deux découvertes par la mission Y. Magen et Y. Peleg (A3, A4 figure 5) et les fragments d'une autre dans la grotte 13 à 2 km du site[67] (A2, figure 5). La jarre découverte par R. de Vaux et celle de la grotte 13 sont de la même période. Cette dernière ayant été cachée au moment de la catastrophe de 68. Ces deux jarres présentent d'ailleurs un *conduit d'écoulement* semblable, terminé par un rebord plus large comme le montre la figure 5, A1-A2. Les deux autres jarres mises à jour par les Israéliens, sous le sol plâtré, sont de ce fait antérieures. Elles présentent aussi des *conduits d'écoulement* mais différents de ceux de la dernière période.

[62] R. DE VAUX, J.-B. HUMBERT, A. CHAMBON ; *Fouilles de Khirbet Qumrân.* Je remercie É. Puech de m'avoir signalé ces objets uniques, les clepsydres que l'étude du disque laissait prévoir.

[63] Yitzhak MAGEN et Yuval PELEG, *The Qumran Excavations 1993-2004, Preliminary ra*pport, (Staff Officer of Archaeology – Civil Administration of Judea and Samaria Jerusalem 2007).

[64] Y. MAGEN, Y. PELEG *et alii*, *Back to Qumran: Final Report (1993-2004), Judea and Samaria Publications*, Volume: 18, (Published by: Israel Antiquities Authority, Staff Officer of Archaeology – Civil Administration of Judea and Samaria, 2018).

[65] *Ibid.*, L9059, [160].

[66] Irina EISENSTADT, "Qumran Pottery" in Y. MAGEN, Y. PELEG et alii, *Back to Qumran: Final Report (1993-2004).* Q-SJ10B, [187].

[67] Joseph PATRICH, Benny ARUBAS," A Juglet Containing Balsam Oil (?) from a Cave near Qumran", *Israel Exploration Journal,* (1989) vol. 39, p. 43-59.

2.2. L'hypothèse des clepsydres à sable.

L'hypothèse repose sur trois points. Premièrement le fonctionnement général du disque conduit à la nécessité d'un outil susceptible de conserver le temps. Il se trouve que ces jarres qui peuvent fonctionner comme des clepsydres ont été trouvées à proximité du disque. Enfin comme le constate Irina Eisenstadt on en connaît que trois, plus celle qui s'ajoutera avec la grotte 13. Enfin il n'a pas été émis d'hypothèse sérieuse concernant ces jarres à *conduit d'écoulement*.

Mais si l'on pose l'hypothèse d'une clepsydre, une autre question surgit : clepsydre à eau ou clepsydre à sable (sablier). David Brown, John Fermor et Christopher Walker développent longuement la question de l'utilisation de clepsydres en Mésopotamie[68]. Nos auteurs nous préviennent qu'ils n'ont aucune attestation archéologique de ces clepsydres,[69] mais qu'ils se basent sur des textes décrivant les calculs et les mesures données par un instrument nommé *Maltaktum*, dont ils discutent l'étymologie[70]. L'instrument est bien lié à la mesure du temps, incluant la notion de poids : « *peser le temps* ». Mais l'utilisation de l'eau n'est pas impérative et Von Soden a soutenu la possibilité d'horloges à sable[71].

Nous avons des attestations claires de l'usage du sable au Moyen-Âge pour des travaux astronomiques. Dans un de ses traités, Al Bīrūnī aborde l'usage de la clepsydre dans le cas d'une éclipse de Lune. Il souligne que la pureté de l'eau n'est pas constante et qu'elle dépend des sources, dont elle provient. Il montre aussi que le contact de l'eau et de l'air a une incidence sur la régularité de la clepsydre, aussi finit-il par énoncer sa préférence pour l'utilisation du sable[72].

Il faut cependant préciser que la différence ne consiste pas uniquement dans l'utilisation du sable plutôt que de l'eau. Clepsydre et sablier n'obéissent pas aux mêmes lois. Dans une clepsydre la vitesse d'écoulement varie avec la hauteur de l'eau restante : le débit n'est donc pas constant, plus rapide au début, plus lent à la fin. Le sablier quant à lui est plus stable que la clepsydre, car sa vitesse d'écoulement constante le rend plus pratique pour mesurer les durées intermédiaires entre deux événements.

[68] David BROWN, John FERMOR and Christopher WALKER, "The Water Clock in Mesopotamia" *Archiv für Orientforschung*, Bd. 46/47 (1999/2000), pp. 130-148.

[69] *Ibid.* 130.

[70] *Ibid.* 132.

[71] *Ibid.*

[72] Voir Al Bīrūnī, *Kitāb Taḥdīd Nihāyāt al-Amākin, The determination of the Coordinates of Positions for the Correction of Distances between Cities*, Beirut 1967, reprinted Frankfurt: Institute for History of Arabic-Islamic Science, 1992, Islamic Geography vol. 26, 155, l. 11…

La clepsydre obéit à la loi de Torricelli[73]

$$D = \sqrt{2gh}\ \pi\ R^2 \text{ ou simplement } V = \sqrt{2gh}.$$

Si P est la pression au bas de la colonne, P est proportionnel à la hauteur h, et la vitesse est proportionnelle à $\sqrt{P}$. La vitesse augmente donc avec la pression au bas de la colonne.

Le sablier ou « clepsydre à sable » ou pour toute substance granulaire obéit à la loi de Beverloo. La hauteur de sable est sans influence sur la vitesse d'écoulement[74]. On obtient[75]

$$D = \sqrt{g}\ R^{\frac{5}{2}} \text{ ou } \sqrt{g\ R}\ R^2$$

Si la formule de Torricelli et celle de Beverloo ne se distinguent que par h et R, il est clair que h varie tout au long de la vidange, alors que R est constant.

2.2.1. *Etude de la jarre à* conduit d'écoulement *(Fouille 1953 du P. de Vaux) : A1 (sur la figure 5)*

On donnera l'ensemble des méthodes de calcul appliquées à la jarre qu'on nommera par facilité (Jarre – R. de Vaux, A1 sur la figure 5). En vue de savoir si cette jarre peut fonctionner comme une clepsydre à sable, on en calculera le volume.

Calcul intégral via une interpolation numérique.

Dans cette méthodologie on partira d'une coupe longitudinale de la jarre, *cf.* figure 6. Sachant que la jarre mesure 56 cm de hauteur en réalité, la figure 6 est à l'échelle ¼. Comme la jarre est un volume de révolution, il faut commencer par déterminer l'équation du profil longitudinal. Pour cela on interpole 9 points en mesurant l'abscisse x et l'ordonnée y de chacun d'eux. Le tableau 7 reprend les coordonnées des différents points.

[73] Pour le détail voir le site *Formules de Physique* : http://www.formules-physique.com/search et *Formulaire de physique* : https://www.sciences.be/ressource/formulaire-de-physique/ D = débit d'écoulement, g = accélération de la pesanteur, h = hauteur de la colonne d'eau. R = rayon du trou d'échappement. Dans la seconde expression V = vitesse d'écoulement. Il existe une relation entre le débit volumique et la vitesse d'écoulement $V= D/S$. *(En respectant les unités,* D en $m^3.s^{-1}$, S en m^2, V en $m\ s^2$*).*

[74] Pour comprendre cette loi : il suffit de regarder la 2ᵉ formule donnant D où l'on a séparé R^2 et $\sqrt{R}$. La loi de Beverloo est similaire à celle de Toricelli, sauf que la hauteur totale h a été remplacée par le rayon R du trou.

[75] En faisant la gravité g (unité : m/s^2) le rayon R (unité : m) du trou. D le débit (unité : m^3/s), on aura un coefficient lié au sable.

On encode d'abord ces coordonnées dans le logiciel GeoGebra[76]. Ensuite, on utilise la fonction polynôme en lui passant les coordonnées des 9 points comme argument afin qu'il détermine le polynôme qui passe par ceux-ci. Soit *h* ce polynôme[77]. Or, comme le montre la figure 6, le profil est relativement régulier.

Points	**X1**	**X2**	**X3**	**X4**	**X5**	**X6**	**X7**	**X8**	**X9**
X[cm]	E	F	G	H	I	J	K	L	M
Y[cm]	0	4,01	12,21	17,56	28,2	37,74	46,41	53,03	56
Points	1,33	9,05	15,28	16,54	17,88	18,75	18,51	11,26	6.45

Tableau 7 : Encodage du profil de la jarre A1 sur Geogebra

Pour calculer le volume de révolution, il suffit d'utiliser la formule suivante :

$$V = \int_0^{0,56} \pi f^2 (x)dx$$

Dans Geogebra on pose *V*=Intégrale (π* *h***h*, 0, 56) (*h* désignant le polynôme d'interpolation).

On obtient le volume de la jarre (Jarre -R de Vaux) :

$$V = 44,9 \text{ soit} \approx 45 \text{ l}$$

2.2.2. *Loi de Beverloo*

La loi de Beverloo va permettre de calculer le débit $v_s(r)$ (*en kg/s*) de la jarre (et de tout récipient) à sable (ou à grains) grâce à la relation suivante :

$$v_s(r) = C\rho\sqrt{g(r - rm)^{5/2}}$$

Avec :

C = constante de compacité[78] elle varie de 0,5 à 0,6 pour le sable

[76] GeoGebra est un logiciel de géométrie dynamique en 2D/3D. Il permet de manipuler des objets géométriques et de voir immédiatement le résultat. https://www.geogebra.org/?lang=fr

[77] A ce stade il est important de garder à l'esprit qu'il faut choisir les points de façon à ce qu'ils ne soient ni trop nombreux ni pas assez. D'une part, si on prend trop de points, le degré du polynôme d'interpolation devient élevé et la courbe oscille de plus en plus fort entre les points. D'autre part, si on ne prend pas suffisamment de points, il est évident que la courbe géométrique ne sera pas correctement représentée.

[78] La *compacité* indique le rapport entre la quantité de grain dans un volume donné et le volume total du matériau granulaire. Soit *C* la compacité du milieu granulaire: *C* = volume des grains/volume total. En supposant que les grains sont des billes de même diamètre,

ρ = masse volumique, pour le sable 1400 à 1600 kg/m^3
g =9.81ms^2= constante gravitationnelle
r =0.009 m= rayon du trou de vidange en m dans le cas de notre jarre (9mm)
r_m =0,0005 m= rayon de 1 grain

L'intérêt de cette formule consiste dans le fait que le débit du sable est indépendant de la hauteur de sable restant dans la jarre. Une fois la vitesse obtenue, nous pouvons déterminer la masse de sable qui a été évacué grâce à la relation[79] :

$$M = v_s(r)\Delta t(r) = constante$$
$$V = 1000M/.\rho$$

Le tableau 8 donne le choix des différentes constantes pour V = 45 l.

V	**45**	l
C	0,6	l
ρ	1565	kg/m^3
g	9,81	m/s^2
rm	0,0005	m

Tableau 8 : Tableau des constantes (Loi de Beverloo) pour un volume de sable V = 45l

On peut maintenant faire varier le rayon r de l'orifice de vidange pour relever l'effet entraîné sur le débit de vidange de la jarre. On note la masse de sable écoulée. Les résultats sont intéressants à relever :

l'entassement des billes le plus étroitement possible conduit à une structure cubique à faces centrées ou bien à un réseau hexagonal c= $\frac{\pi\sqrt{2}}{6}$=74%. C'est la valeur maximale que l'on peut obtenir avec des billes de même diamètre. Si l'empilement est aléatoire et statique, cas du sable, on montre que la compacité qui correspond à l'empilement le plus dense (Random-Close Packing) est: c = 0,635.

Voir pour l'ensemble de la question des sabliers, le cours de Mécanique des matériaux granulaires de Ghilhem Mollon : http://guilhem.mollon.free.fr/Telechargements/Mecanique_des_Materiaux_Granulaires.pdf

Ghilhem Mollon, *Mécanique des matériaux granulaires*, INSA, (Institut des Sciences Appliquées, Lyon, 2014-2015).

[79] $\Delta(r)$ est le temps de vidange qui est fonction du rayon r. Finalement, le volume est obtenu en divisant la masse M par la densité du sable et en multipliant par 1000 pour passer de m^3 à dm^3, c-à-d. en litres.

V	45	45	45
M [kg]	70,42	70,42	70,42
r[m]	0,009	0,00693	0.005977
vs [kg/s]	0,019561	0,009736	0,006519
Δt [s]	3600,24	7233,54	10802,44
Δt [h]	1h	2h	3h

Tableau 9 : Tableau des relations du temps de vidange Δt [h] et du rayon de l'orifice *r*[m]

On constate que pour un rayon de 9 mm la jarre de 45 litres qui contient 70,42 kg de sable aux caractéristiques données (C = 0,6 et ρ = 1565kg/m^3), mettra 1 heure pour se vider, 2 h pour un rayon de 0,00693 $\simeq$ 7 mm, 3 h pour un rayon de 0.005977 $\simeq$ 6 mm.

(On trouve 5 h pour un rayon de 5 mm).

En retenant le fonctionnement de cette jarre, compte tenu de sa proximité d'avec *le disque de pierre* à usage astronomique, l'hypothèse d'une clepsydre à sable devient tout à fait vraisemblable.

2.2.3. *Hypothèse de fonctionnement.*

La clepsydre conserve le temps alors qu'un cadran donne le temps solaire. Il faut donc suposer une relation entre ces deux instruments de mesure. Si l'on se fie au fonctionnement des clepsydres babyloniennes, on peut voir que la correspondance entre l'eau ou le sable et le temps se faisait par le poids. Le liquide ou le sable écoulé étaient pesés et le temps correspondant à l'écoulement était proportionnel au poids de liquide ou de sable échappé de la clepsydre[80].

C'est à ce niveau qu'on peut tenter un rapprochement entre *le disque de pierre* et la jarre à *conduit d'écoulement.* Dans le cas de la clepsydre (Jarre – R. de Vaux, avec r = 9 mm) on peut établir la relation entre le temps et le poids du sable écoulé. En prenant dans le tableau 9, la colonne correspondant à 1 h d'écoulement, on a :

[80] Voir D. Brown, J. Fermor and C. Walker, "The Water Clock", 132, *However, although Mul-Apin specifies weights when describing day and night lengths, the fact is that it gives the daily change in day length in terms of time units, which also means that the weight and time units were thought of as being in direct proportion. Cf. aussi : a mastaktum may have been understood as a wooden weighing device. Since it seems also to have measured time, this was perhaps done by weighing the fluid involved, hence the minas and shekels we see in Mul.Apin, EAE 14 and the like.*

70,42 kg de sable = 45 l = 1h
Soit M [kg] = 0,019561 [kg/s] * Δt [s]

Ainsi 1,17366 kg de sable correspondront (dans notre système d'unités) à un temps d'1 min.

Si l'on revient maintenant aux « rayures »[81] de la couronne C2 avec une division du temps en unité de 4min pour 1h, on obtiendrait le relevé suivant :

***M* [kg]**	**Δt [m]**
4,70	4
9,40	8
14,1	12
18,8	16
23,51	20
28,2	24
32,9	28
37,6	32
42,3	36
47	40
51,7	44
56,4	48
61,1	52
70,42	59,9

Tableau 10 : Tableau donnant le poids de sable écoulé pour 4 min de temps.

Ainsi à 4,7 kg de sable correspondront 4 m de temps et 1 intervalle entre deux rayures sur la couronne C_2. La mise à l'heure de la clepsydre est alors relativement facile par cette correspondance entre le temps, le poids et le débit constant des substances granulaires selon la loi de Beverloo.

On relève que pour ces jarres-clepsydres, il faut considérer deux constantes propres à la jarre elle-même, son volume (V) et le rayon de l'orifice d'écoulement (r) et trois variables appartenant à la substance

[81] *Cf. supra*. Signes particuliers. Voir *Astronomical Diaries and Related Texts from Babylonia*, Abraham SACHS and Hermann HUNGER (eds.), Wien, Austrian Academy of Sciences, *cf. Time mesurement :* « Les intervalles de temps plus courts qu'un jour sont mesurés dans les agendas par l'unité UŠ, ce qui correspond à 4 de nos minutes ».

granulaire : le coefficient de compacité (C), la masse volumique de la substance granulaire utilisée (ρ) et le rayon d'un grain (r_m).

Prenons pour la même jarre un autre sable avec (C = 0,6 ρ = 1480, r_m = 1 mm) :

On obtient un débit de 0,0208 kg/s, une masse de 66,6 kg et un temps de vidange de 53,4 min, soit pour 20 min, 24,9 kg contre 23,51kg avec le sable du tableau 10. Les variations de masse sont faibles, mais la mise à l'heure de la clepsydre était facile et possible aisément en changeant la substance granulaire. La couronne C_2 et les divisions en 4 min permettaient cette adaptation.

On peut examiner ce qu'il en est des deux autres clepsydres. A3 et A4.

Clepsydre A3.

Selon la même méthode, nous trouvons un volume de

$$V = 54{,}42\text{l soit} \approx 54{,}5\text{ l}$$

La loi de Beverloo permet de calculer le débit $v_s(r)$ (*en kg/s*) de la clepsydre A3 grâce à la relation suivante :

$$v_s(r) = C\rho\sqrt{g(r - rm)^{5/2}}$$
$$\text{Soit } M\text{ [kg]} = 0{,}015721\text{ [kg/s]} * \Delta t\text{ [s]}$$

Ainsi 0,94681 kg de sable correspondront (dans notre système d'unités) à un temps d'1 min.

Soit 3,8 kg pour 4min indiqué sur la couronne C_2.

On donnera simplement les résultats obtenus sur la clepsydre A4 présentant le même orifice que A3.

$$V = \int_{5{,}05}^{006} \pi f^2\ x\ (dx)$$
$$V = \approx 41{,}7\text{ l}$$
$$M\text{ [kg]} = 0{,}018127\text{ [kg/s]} * \Delta t\text{ [s]}$$

La clepsydre A4 a un *conduit d'écoulement* semblable à A3. Son orifice de vidange est estimé à 0,0084 m (8,4 mm) de rayon (A4 appartient à la même période que A3 qui est différente des jarres A1 et A2 postérieures et présentant des *conduits d'écoulement* de formes différentes.)

Si l'on prend un sable caractérisé par C= 0,6, ρ = 1565, mais d'un grain plus fin r_m = 0,00016 mm la clepsydre se videra en 1 h. Nous aurons une vidange de 4,35 kg de sable en 4 min.

Il faut rajouter qu'a été trouvé à côté de cette jarre un couvercle percé d'un trou. (Figure 5, A4)[82]. Ce dispositif confirme l'hypothèse de la clepsydre à sable[83].

Comme on le voit, le fonctionnement de ces clepsydres à sable se révèle relativement simple. Les trois jarres sont bien de volumes différents (45 l, 54,5 l, 41,7 l), mais cela n'influe pas sur les mesures. Seul influent la qualité du sable (ou de la substance granulaire) avec ses trois coefficients (C, ρ, r_m) et le rayon de l'orifice de la jarre (r). C'est là qu'intervient l'harmonisation entre *le disque* et les clepsydres.

Indépendamment de la hauteur de sable, *le disque* donne un intervalle de temps solaire Δt de 4 min ou tout autre temps mesurable correspondant à une quantité de sable écoulé et pesé M [kg] pour ce temps Δt. M [kg] = vs [kg/s] * Δt [s].

La vitesse d'écoulement est une constante vs [kg/s].= $\frac{M\ [kg]}{\Delta t\ [s]}$.

3. Les *mišmarot*[84]

La question qui se pose maintenant est assez classique dans la littérature de l'astronomie ancienne. Les auteurs des écrits astronomiques de Qumrân se ont-ils procédé à des observations authentiques ou bien ont-ils accompli un simple travail de copiste ou tout au plus de rédacteur à partir de sources documentaires ? On a de bons exemples de cette tournure d'esprit avec de grands noms comme Théon d'Alexandrie (335-405) reprenant de manière scolaire le travail de Ptolémée[85] avec plus tard celui de Stéphane

[82] Irina Eisenstadt, *Qumran Pottery*, Q-SJ10B, [187]. Et 5a planche 6 [227], [226] Jar knob.

[83] Voir site de physique expérimentale de l'Université Paris Diderot : *Sablier Intermittent*.
http://www.msc.univ-paris-diderot.fr/~phyexp/pmwiki.php/Main/HomePag
http://www.msc.univ-paris-diderot.fr/~phyexp/pmwiki.php/Sablier/SablierInte

Le sablier présente plusieurs régimes : Un régime continu : écoulement régulier du sable du compartiment supérieur au compartiment inférieur du sablier. Un régime de blocage : Absence de tout écoulement. Un régime intermittent : écoulement avec un flux régulier (couplage des deux régimes : stationnaire et bloqué).

Lors de l'écoulement de petits grains, l'écoulement peut brusquement s'arrêter. Étant donné que les grains sont petits, il existe donc moins d'espace entre chaque grain. Le sablier composé de petits grains est donc moins perméable à l'air. Lorsque se produit une dépression dans la chambre supérieure, une arche de sable stable empêche l'air de remonter vers la chambre supérieure. Ainsi la pression n'augmente pas donc pas d'écoulement. Dans le cas des jarres, le couvercle A5, servait à bloquer l'écoulement en fermant le trou dont il était percé.

[84] Tous les calculs sont réalisés à partir des données *du* site de l'IMCCE, http://www.imcce.fr (Institut de Mécanique Céleste et Calcul des Ephémérides).

[85] Voir Anne Tihon, « Le calcul de l'éclipse de Soleil du 16 juin 364 p.C. et le Petit Commentaire de Théon », (Bulletin de l'Institut historique Belge de Rome), 46-47 (1976-1977) 40.

de Constantinople[86] et dans le monde arabe al-Fargāni faisant connaître et initiant aux méthodes de *l'Almageste* par son *Compendium*[87]. (*Kitāb fī Jawāmi' 'Ilm al-Nujūm* vers 833).

Dans le cas présent on part d'un fait très concret, rare dans l'histoire, on possède un ensemble d'instruments dont on décrit les possibilités et la finalité. Notre méthode d'approche consistera à voir en quoi ces instruments '(disque et jarres) s'accordent avec les textes astronomiques trouvés à Qumrân, mais aussi à d'autres possibilités non attestées par des écrits découverts à ce jour.

Comme cela est bien attesté par l'ensemble des chercheurs, les travaux d'astronomie de Qumrân restent largement tributaires de l'astronomie babylonienne[88].

3.1. Théories de la Lune : *Lunar six* et *Lunar three*

Mathieu Ossendrijver souligne que la réalisation la plus remarquable de l'astronomie mathématique babylonienne concerne sans doute le calcul du « Lunar Six », qui sont des intervalles de temps entre le lever ou le coucher de la Lune et celui du Soleil autour de Nouvelle Lune ou de la Pleine Lune[89].

1. NA_1 – Temps entre le coucher du Soleil et le coucher de la Lune le soir, première visibilité de la Lune, la conjonction.

2. SU – Temps entre le coucher de la Lune et le lever du Soleil, heure à laquelle la Lune se couche pour la dernière fois avant le lever du Soleil, juste avant la pleine Lune.

Anne TIHON (éd.), *Le Grand Commentaire de Théon d'Alexandrie aux Tables Faciles de Ptolémée*, Livre I, Cité du Vatican, 1985. Anne TIHON (éd.), *Le Grand Commentaire de Théon d'Alexandrie aux Tables Faciles de Ptolémée*, Livre II, III, (Cité du Vatican, 1991). Barlaam de Séminara, *Traités sur les éclipses de Soleil de 1333 et 1337*. Histoire des textes, éditions critiques, traductions et commentaires par Joseph MOGENET et ANNE TIHON avec la collaboration de Daniel DONNET, ed. Peeters, 1977.

[86] Voir Jean LAMPIRE, « Un manuel d'astronomie attribué à Stéphanos (VIIe s.). Un texte héritier de l'enseignement scientifique d'Alexandrie », *Forum Romanum Belgicum*, 2014, article 6.

[87] *Cf.* Régis MORELLON, « L'astronomie arabe orientale entre le VIIIe et le XIe siècle », 39, dans Histoire des Sciences arabes, Tome I, Le Seuil, 1997.

[88] *Cf.* Jonathan BEN-DOV, *Head of All Years, Astronomy and Calendars at Qumran in their Ancient Context*, Series: Studies on the Texts of the Desert of Judah, Volume: 78, Brill, 2008.

[89] Mathieu OSSENDRIJVER, *Babylonian Mathematical Astronomy:Procedure Texts*, (Springer New York Heidelberg Dordrecht London, 2012), 113. Voir OTTO NEUGEBAUER, *A History of Ancient Mathematical Astronomy*, part One, 538. O. NEUGEBAUER, *Astronomical Cuneiform Text*, 3 vols, London, Lund Humphries, 1955, N° 201, 226.

3. NA$_{30}$ – Le temps entre le lever du Soleil et le coucher de la Lune, lorsque la Lune se couche pour la première fois après le lever du Soleil (juste après la pleine Lune).

4. ME – Temps du lever de la Lune au coucher du Soleil, lorsque la Lune se lève pour la dernière fois avant le coucher du Soleil (juste avant la pleine Lune).

5. GE$_6$ – Le temps entre le coucher du Soleil au lever de la Lune, lorsque la Lune se lève pour la première fois après le coucher du Soleil (juste après la pleine Lune).

6. KUR – La date et l'heure du lever de la Lune au lever du Soleil, lorsque la Lune est visible pour la dernière fois avant la conjonction.

Ces intervalles révèlent à la fois une astronomie mathématique, mais aussi une astronomie d'observations, fondement de son aspect calculatoire, le tout se situant dans une finalité de prédiction des événements, technique que l'on nomme depuis Abraham J. Sachs[90] : « Goal-Year ».

Ainsi pour la Lune les textes babyloniens relevant de cette méthode utilisent une période de 18 ans. Les textes mentionnés comprennent les éclipses, mais aussi des *informations sur la durée séparant le coucher de la Lune du coucher du Soleil. Et ainsi de suite et divers moments importants du mois*[91].

Abraham J. Sachs a nommé « Lunar Three »[92] un ensemble de texte reposant uniquement sur KUR, NA$_1$ et NA$_{30}$. C'est précisément ce « Lunar-Three » qui structure les *mišmarot* comme le montre Jonathan Ben-Dov. Après une étude minutieuse, il peut conclure que les phénomènes lunaires rapportés dans les *mišmarot* reflètent les techniques de l'astronomie babylonienne non mathématique à savoir de « Lunar Three », modifiées à Qumrân afin de correspondre au calendrier de 364 jours[93]. Les déductions reposent sur l'examen de 4Q320 et 4Q321. L'auteur donne une interprétation pertinente de *X* et de *dwq* dans les textes de Qumrân qui sont liés

[90] Abraham J. SACHS, "A Classification of Babylonian Astronomical Tablets of the Seleucid Period", *Journal of Cuneiform Studies* 2, 1948, 271–90. *Cf.* aussi pour "Goal-Year", J.M.K. GRAY, J. M. STEELE, "Studies on Babylonian goal-year astronomy I: a comparison between planetary data in Goal-Year Texts, Almanacs and Normal Star Almanacs". *Archive for History of Exact Sciences 62*: 2008, 553–600. Dans la traduction française de James EVANS, *Histoire et pratique de l'astronomie ancienne*, Paris, Les Belles Lettres, 2016 : « Naissance de la prédiction : les textes babyloniens pour « année-objectif » (Goal-Year), 348.

[91] J. EVANS, *Histoire et pratique*, 353.

[92] A. J. SACHS, *Classification.*, §16.

[93] Voir J. BEN-DOV, *Dial,* 242.

au couple babylonien NA et KUR de « Lunar Three ». X (Qumran) = KUR (Babylone) = dernière visibilité matinale de la Lune à la fin de la lunaison. *dwq* (Qumrân) = NA (Babylone) = premier coucher de la Lune après le lever du Soleil, le lendemain de la pleine Lune[94].

Il faut aussi noter une influence déterminante de l'astronomie babylonienne sur *l'Hénoch araméen*. Henryk Drawnel[95] établit une comparaison éclairante entre les tables publiées par F. Al-Rawi et A. R. George[96] et le *livre araméen* en question[97].

Ces mesures relatives au coucher et au lever de la Lune et du Soleil permettent un ensemble de connaissances et de calculs portant sur le mouvement de la Lune, ce qui conduisait à la fixation d'un calendrier et à une prévision des phénomènes astronomiques : pleine Lune, nouvelle Lune, éclipses.

Que l'on soit en « Lunar Six » ou en « Lunar Three », le système repose sur des mesures de positions de la Lune et du Soleil par rapport à l'horizon, technique largement développée dans toutes ses implications par Otto Neugebauer et Mathieu Ossendrijver. Comment ces mesures sont-elles possibles ? C'est là que la présence du disque et des clepsydres à sable permet de voir se dessiner une astronomie d'observation.

À cinq heures *le disque* n'était plus utilisable, l'ombre étant extérieure à sa surface. Toutes les mesures effectuées sur l'horizon au coucher du Soleil ne pourront l'être en aucune façon par un cadran et son ombre. La clepsydre (jarre à *conduit d'écoulement*) sera alors utilisée selon ce qui a été expliqué plus haut. À une quantité de sable correspondra un temps donné. C'était la seule manière de conserver le temps et d'effectuer des mesures sur les intervalles de temps Lune-Soleil. Mais il faut encore ajouter que *le disque* pouvait être utilisé pour donner les azimuts des levers et couchers de la Lune et du Soleil. (Azimuts des couchers et des levers, couronnes C_4 et C_6).

[94] *Ibid.* 236. 4Q210, 4Q209.

[95] H. DRAWNEL, *op. cit*, 302.

[96] Farouk AL-RAWI and Andrew GEORGE, "Enuma Anu Enlil XIV and Other Early-Astronomical Tables," *AfO* 38–39 (1991–92). Il s'agit de quatre tables lunaires : (A) durée de la visibilité de la Lune au cours du mois équinoxial, tradition du Nippour ; (B) durée de la visibilité de la Lune dans le mois équinoxial, tradition de Babylone ; (C) variation saisonnière de la longueur du jour et de la nuit ; (D) variation mensuelle de la visibilité de la Lune à la nouvelle lune et de son invisibilité à la pleine lune.

[97] H. DRAWNEL, *op. cit*, 303, 304, 306. *Cf.* appendix III, IV, 425-428.

3.2. Les vents et les portes du livre d'Hénoch.

L'Hénoch astronomique araméen[98] va ouvrir une autre possibilité du disque et des clepsydres. Il s'agit de la division de l'espace en « portes » et en « vents ». *La rose des vents* composée de douze *vents* répartis sur quatre directions cardinales divise le cercle de l'horizon (360°) en douze parties symétriques de 30° chacune[99].

Mais comme le souligne Henryk Drawnel[100] à la suite de Paul V. Neugebauer et Ernst F. Weidner, cette division n'est pas d'ordre uniquement géographique, elle s'enracine dans une division du ciel héritée de Babylone[101]. Dans cette perspective nous comprenons mieux pourquoi les couronnes C_4 et C_6 sont graduées sur 360°, et non pas seulement entre les valeurs extrêmes des azimuts du Soleil pour la latitude de Qumrân. Dans cette optique *le disque* et ses graduations azimutales constituent un système de coordonnées de la voûte céleste. Cela nous conduit à rapprocher une autre conclusion de Paul V. Neugebauer et Ernst F. Weidner d'un aspect du disque de Qumrân. Nos auteurs ont également noté en effet que dans l'éclipse lunaire *omina*[102], la surface de la Lune est divisée en quadrants correspondant aux quatre régions du ciel, comme cela se présente dans le Texte MUL-APIN[103]. Et comme le conclut Henryk Drawnel : *L'interprétation des directions cardinales et des vents latéraux par Neugebauer et Weidner semble trouver sa confirmation dans les observations astronomiques des éclipses lunaires, où les vents sont davantage subdivisés afin de décrire correctement le mouvement de l'ombre de l'éclipse à la surface de la Lune. La rose des vents selon le livre d'Hénoch imite cette subdivision des directions cardinales et la transpose dans la terminologie araméenne.*

C'est alors que ces divisions en saillie des couronnes C_2, C_3, C_5, qui permettent de convertir le temps vrai en temps moyen viennent renforcer l'hypothèse de l'observation d'éclipses à Qumrân. On peut le soutenir parce que cette forme de correction dans toute l'histoire de l'astronomie

98 Henryk DRAWNEL, *The Aramaic Astronomical Book from Qumran*, Oxford University Press, 2011.

99 *Ibid.*, 320.

100 *Ibid.*, Thus, calculating the position of the stars according to MUL.APIN II i 68- 71, one finds the following azimuth for the cardinal directions: north: 0°; east: 90°; south: 180°; west: 270°. 341.

101 Voir Paul V. NEUGEBAUER et Ernst F. WEIDNER, "Die Himmelsrichtungen bei den Babyloniern" *AfO* 7: 1932, 269-71.

102 Richard A PARKER, *A Vienna demotic papyrus on eclipse- and lunar-omina*, Brown University Press, 1959.

103 H. DRAWNEL, *Astronomical Book*, 342.

ancienne ne s'applique que dans le cas de calculs portant sur le mouvement de la Lune et encore plus spécialement sur les intervalles de temps séparant les éclipses.

Ptolémée précisant qu'il tient ses méthodes des anciens c'est-à-dire des Babyloniens affirme que les observations doivent se faire sur les éclipses de Lune du fait de l'absence de parallaxe : *En conséquence, pour chercher généralement quels sont les lieux vrais de la Lune, on dira qu'il ne faut pas se servir des autres observations des lieux qui s'y montrent à la vue des observateurs, mais seulement de celles des éclipses de Lune*[104]. La surface du disque avec ses divisions azimutales et avec sa possibilité de conversion d'un temps irrégulier en temps régulier (semblable à celui des clepsydres) permettait de déterminer le temps entre deux éclipses[105]. L'erreur sur la différence du temps vrai et du temps moyen peut atteindre 30 min si les mesures ont été effectuées en février et novembre, périodes où E atteint ses plus grandes valeurs positives en février et négatives en novembre.

Mais l'on doit encore noter que la notion de « vent » est aussi liée aux éclipses de Soleil et cette fois sur le plan météorologique, le vent et sa direction font partie des descriptions d'éclipses solaires. De même pour les comètes et les météores[106].

3.3. Les portes

La question des « portes » dans l'astronomie du *Livre d'Hénoch* constitue un sujet difficile qui a suscité bon nombre d'interprétations. Notre propos ne consiste pas a en proposer une nouvelle, mais plutôt de voir comment le matériel astronomique découvert à Qumrân et qui a été décrit peut éclairer la problématique des « portes » et cela indépendamment des interprétations particulières.

Dès les travaux de Sylvain Grebaut, il est question du nombre de jours pendant lesquels la Lune se lève et se couche à travers l'une des six portes

[104] PTOLÉMÉE, *Syntaxe mathématique*, édition Halma, Livre IV, chap. 1.

[105] Comme nous l'avons signalé chez Ptolémée, Ptolémée, *Syntaxe mathématique*, édition Halma, 206. Il se trouve que sur la période que nous étudions un grand nombre d'éclipses de Lune totale furent visibles sur Qumrân. Soit 82 entre – 98 et 68. *Voir* NASA, Eclipse Web Site : https://eclipse.gsfc.nasa.gov/lunar.html

[106] Voir *Astronomical Diaries and Related Texts from Babylonia*, Abraham SACHS and Hermann HUNGER, c) Eclipses et 4) Meteor, Comets, etc.... *Keeping Watch in Babylon The Astronomical Diaries in Context* Series: Culture and History of the Ancient Near East, Volume: 100 Editors: Johannes HAUBOLD, John STEELE and Kathryn STEVENS. Voir (Description d'une éclipse de Soleil, Février 133 BCE), 63.

à son lever et à travers l'une des six portes à son coucher. Grebaut rapportait ces portes à des coordonnées [2]écliptiques c'est-à-dire au Zodiaque. Otto Neugebauer quant à lui va rejeter toute interprétation zodiacale[2] des « [2]portes »[107]. Lorsque Milik publie les fragments araméens de l'AAB[108], il paraît évident qu'ils contiennent le système des six portes entendu comme les lieux du lever et du coucher de la Lune similaire à ce qui a déjà été connu de *1Hénoch* et du Livre de *la Révolution des Luminaires Célestes*. L'explication de Neugebauer sur les portes avait remplacé, semble-t-il, la précédente sur le zodiaque. Cependant plusieurs chercheurs ont récemment affirmé que les portes du *Livre d'Hénoch* pouvaient être considérées comme une projection des signes zodiacaux à l'horizon[109]. Pour Francis Schmidt les portes sont chacune divisées en 30 petites ouvertures pour le lever et le coucher du Soleil[110] quotidiens.

On peut alors poser la question de la relation du disque de pierre et de cette astronomie. Il apparaît clairement, comme le dit H. Drawnel, que la finalité du système des portes consiste en la synchronisation du mouvement du Soleil et de la Lune[111]. Mais cette synchronisation n'était pas simple. H. Drawnel remarque que les références aux portes araméennes apparaissent de manière assez aléatoire et ne visent pas à communiquer le nombre de jours que la Lune passe dans une porte[112].

Déterminer l'heure des levers et couchers de la Lune est une opération complexe du fait de la grande irrégularité du mouvement de la Lune. Et l'on comprend qu'une approche purement arithmétique par un travail de scribes devait fatalement se révéler assez éloignée de la réalité.

Si des écrits comme le *livre d'Hénoch* indiquaient une méthode de travail, il était certainement nécessaire de revenir à l'observation, c'est ce que *le disque* et les jarres peuvent laisser supposer. Dans le cas des « portes », il fallait déterminer les lieux des levers et couchers du Soleil et de la

[107] Otto NEUGEBAUER, « Notes on Ethiopic Astronomy[2] », *Orientalia*, NS 33: 49-71. *Cf.* H. DRAWNEL, *Astronomical Book.*, 293.

[108] Joseph MILIK, *The Books of Enoch: Aramaic Fragments of Qumran Cave 4*. Oxford: Clarendon, 275-278.

[109] BRACK-BERNSEN, Lis et HUNGER, Hermann, « The Babylonian Zodiac: Speculations on its invention and significance », *Centaurus* 41 (1999), 280–292.

[110] Ces petites ouvertures sont appelées חרתין dans *le livre astronomique araméen*, et simplement «portes» – «שערים» – dans le rouleau de calendrier hébreu, 4Q503, qui numérote les portes 1 à 30 selon le jour du mois. *Cf.* Francis SCHMIDT, "Le calendrier liturgique des prières quotidiennes (4Q503). En annexe : l'apport du verso (4Q512) à l'édition de 4Q503," dans *Le temps et les temps dans les littératures juives et chrétiennes au tournant de notre ère* (JSJSup 112; eds. C. GRAPPE and J.C. INGELAERE, Leiden: Brill, 2006), 55–83.

[111] H. DRAWNEL, *Astronomical Book*, 297.

[112] *Ibid*. 293.

Lune à savoir leurs azimuts respectifs. L'azimut des couchers et levers est donné par la relation Arc cos $\alpha = \frac{sin\delta}{cos\varphi}$ (Avec δ = déclinaison de l'astre et φ = latitude du lieu). Si la déclinaison du Soleil est relativement facile à trouver au moyen d'un cadran à ombre comme *le disque* et s'il est possible d'en suivre la progression sans recours à l'observation par une méthode calculatoire, ce n'est pas le cas de la Lune.

Cette dualité de l'observation et du calcul en ce qui concerne la Lune se laisse bien voir dans une tentative de synchronisation selon laquelle la Lune et le Soleil se lèveraient dans la même porte à savoir auraient même azimut[113].

L'existence des deux couronnes du disque C_4 et C_6 permettait alors de comparer l'azimut du lever du Soleil par exemple en C_4 à celui de la Lune en C_6. Les deux couronnes avec un décalage de 2,5° pouvaient trouver là une application expérimentale des méthodes calculatoires exposées dans les *mišmarot* et le *livre d'Hénoch*.

Conclusion

Les trois entités analysées, le « disque de pierre », les jarres à *conduit d'écoulement* et les *mišmarot* et l'*Hénoch araméen* prennent cohérence et sens dans la mise en évidence de leurs interrelations.

Mais prises individuellement des questions difficiles se posent.

Ainsi, la finalité astronomique du *disque de pierre* a été contestée[114]. La principale lacune des publications qui y furent consacrées consiste dans l'absence totale d'une analyse mathématique fine reposant sur une méthodologie de statistique adaptée à cet objet archéologique endommagé.

De même, les *jarres à conduit d'écoulement*, considérées en elles-mêmes ne permettaient pas d'y voir quelques objets à finalité scientifique. Irina Eisenstadt parle d'un *d'une utilisation qui n'est pas claire* et émet sans conviction l'hypothèse *d'une fonction de filtre pour la purification de*

[113] H. Drawnel, *Astronomical Book*, 270. *However, the Aramaic scribe bases his notes on the rising of the moon on the arithmetical calculation that he follows, not on actual observation. This interpretation of verse 4b is confirmed by the rest of the arithmetical calculation in 4Q208 and 4Q209, and by verse 4c, which states that the moon is visible during the day ('on that day'). Also, verse 4d suggests the same interpretive approach, because it synchronizes moonrise with sunrise on the same day and in the same gate.* Texte : Ethiopic text and English translation of 1 Enoch 7 3 :4-, (a) And it rises in this way: (b) Its head which is in the east emerges on the thirtieth day, (c) and on that day it is seen, (d) and becomes for you the beginning of the month on the thirtieth day with the sun, in the gate where the sun emerges, *ibid.*

[114] J. Ben-Dov, "The Qumran Dial", 235.

l'argile servant à la fabrication des poteries du site[115]. La question est renouvelée du fait de la proximité du lieu de leur découverte. *Le disque* et ces jarres très particulières se trouvent au même endroit. De plus et surtout, le disque destiné à fonctionner le jour ouvre la possibilité et même la nécessité de *conserver* le temps : c'est la fonction des clepsydres. Or il se trouvait que si on possède de belles descriptions des « water-clock » babyloniennes, il ne semble pas que l'on ait pu en mettre à jour quelque exemplaire. Cela est dû à une fixation sur la seule possibilité d'un fonctionnement à l'eau. Or, les descriptions babyloniennes ouvrent la possibilité de l'utilisation du sable. Et l'on a pu voir qu'il s'agissait là de deux principes physiques différents (loi de Torricelli, loi de Beverloo). Le sablier se présente comme un instrument de mesure plus fiable et facilement utilisable.

Enfin les textes astronomiques trouvés à Qumrân pouvaient-ils avec certitude être rattachés à une activité scientifique locale ? Pouvait-on parler, d'observations ? Ce qui impliquait, disons-le, une compréhension préalable des textes, une formation en un mot une école. La présence du « disque » à finalité astronomique, son origine locale, son utilisation sur plusieurs générations qui couvrent la Période II de R. de Vaux (en accord avec la datation du ע)[116] donne une épaisseur historique à une science essénienne. Enfin la proximité des jarres à *conduit d'écoulement*, instrument complémentaire du disque permettent une réponse positive.

Ces textes se sont concrétisés dans un matériel qui en certifie et la compréhension et certainement une finalité de vérification en vue d'une adaptation locale. C'est d'ailleurs là un processus classique de l'histoire de l'astronomie, tant à Alexandrie qu'à Constantinople et plus tard à Bagdad, à Tabriz et Samarkand : tradition, observation, adaptation.

[115] I. EISENSTADT, *Qumran Pottery*, Q-SJ10B, [187]. Hypothèse suivie par J.-B. Humbert qui parle de jarre-filtre. Voir *Khirbet Qumrân et Aïn Feshkha : fouilles du P. Roland de Vaux. III A, L'archéologie de Qumrân : reconsidération de l'interprétation : les installations périphériques de Khirbet Qumrân*, Jean-Baptiste Humbert o.p. et Alain CHAMBON ; notice de Hervé Monchot : *Qumran terracotta oil lamps* / Jolanta MLYNARCZYK. – Göttingen ; Bristol (Conn.) : Vandenhoeck & Ruprecht, cop. 2016. jarre 800, locus 45a, planche 16 (4 photos).

[116] *Cf. supra* 1.4.4. *La marque du temps*, le « ע ».

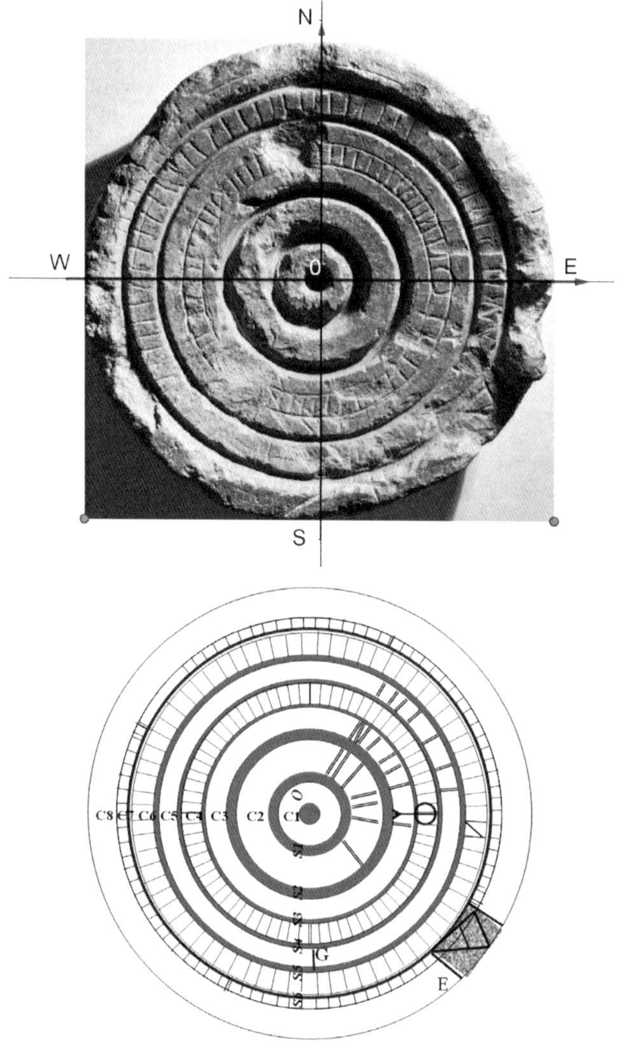

O : Cavité centrale
C1 à C8 : Couronnes concentriques
S1 à S6 : Sillons concentriques
— : Traits entaillés dans les couronnes, C4, C6 et C7
═ : Traits en saillie sur les couronnes, C2, C3, C5
Φ : Couché au niveau de la couronne C4
Z : Traits reliés sur la couronne C6
E : Entaille au niveau des couronnes C7 et C8
G : Trait entaillé à − 90° (270°) du Φ couché

Figures 1 : le disque de pierre

Figure 2 : le disque de pierre, détail des couronnes

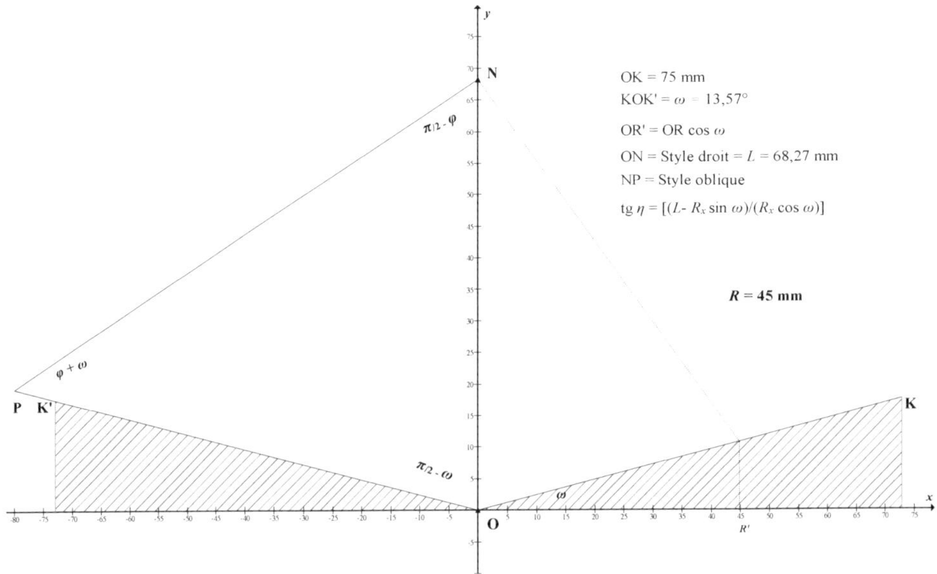

Figure 3 : Le style triangulaire du disque

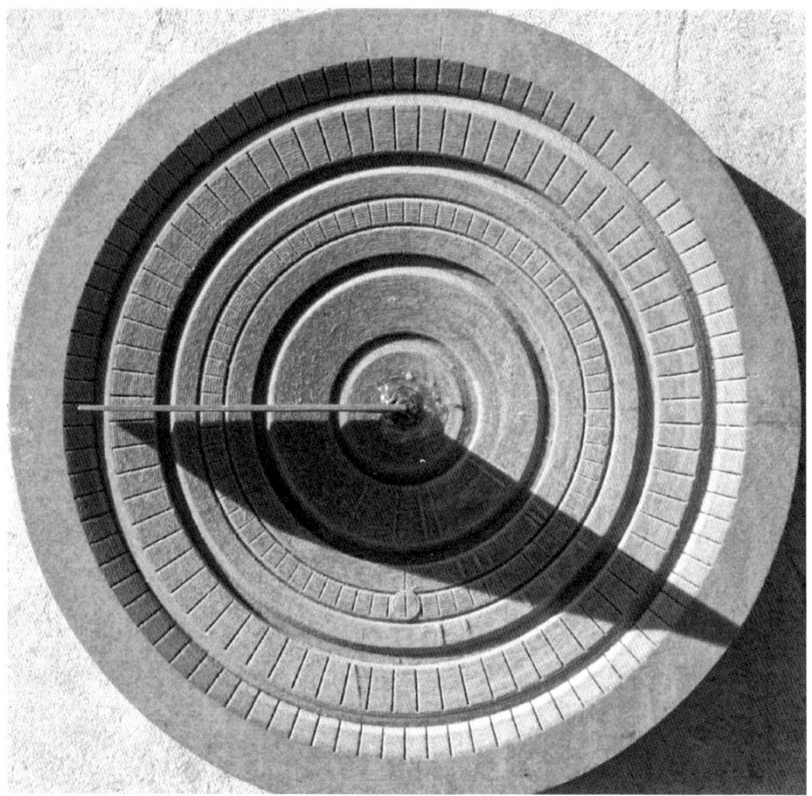

Figure 4: Reconstitution 3D du disque
Ombre du style à 2h vraies

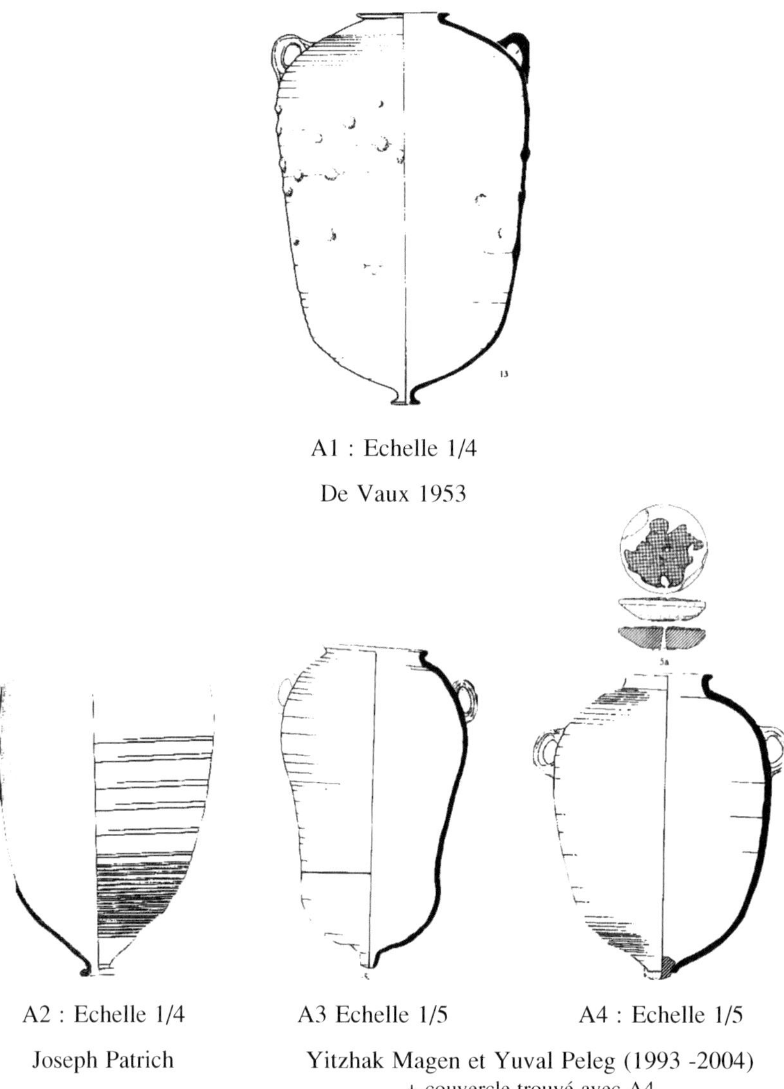

A1 : Echelle 1/4
De Vaux 1953

A2 : Echelle 1/4 — Joseph Patrich

A3 Echelle 1/5 — A4 : Echelle 1/5

Yitzhak Magen et Yuval Peleg (1993 -2004)
+ couvercle trouvé avec A4

Figure 5 : Les jarres à conduit d'écoulement

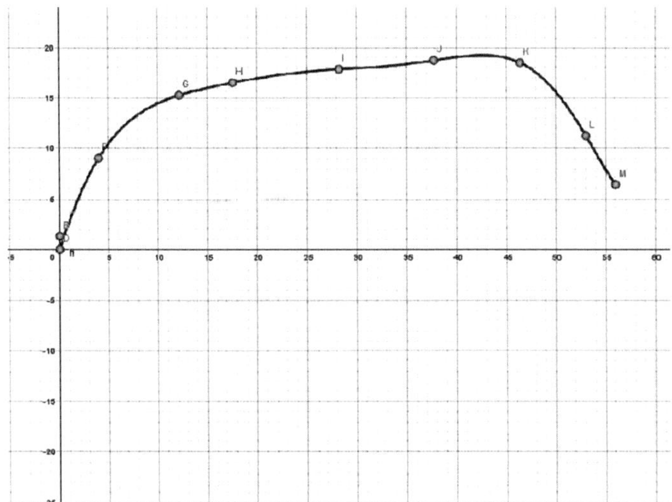

Figure 6 : Courbe du profil de la jarre A1 (GeoGebra)

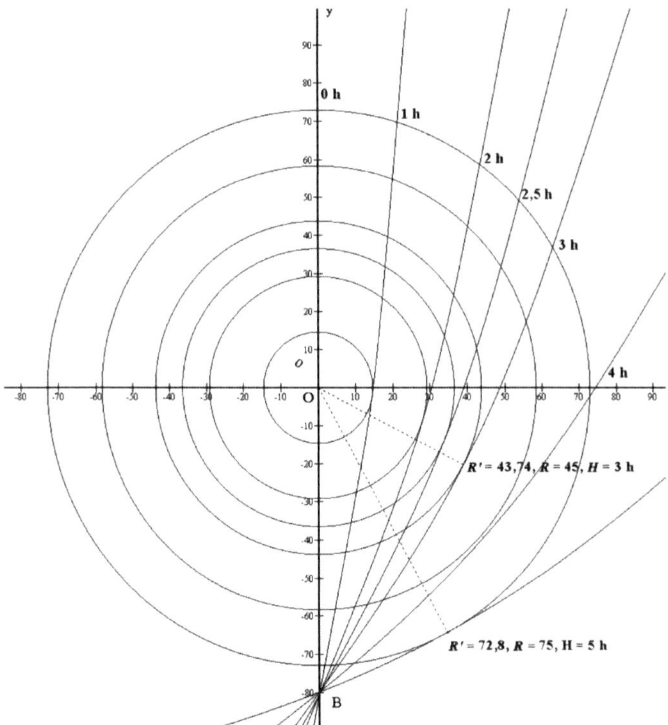

Figure 7 : Projections virtuelles des ombres du style oblique

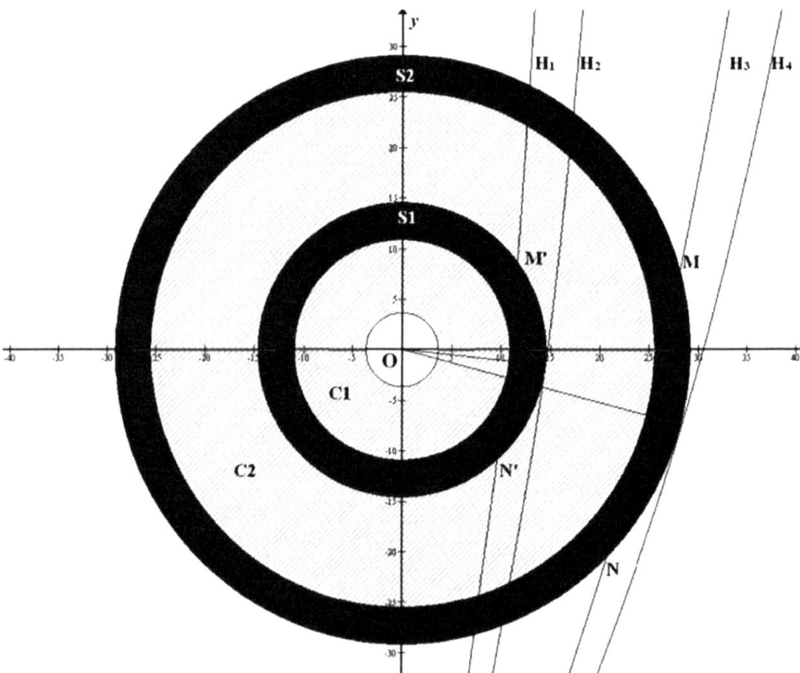

Figure 8 : Projection des ombres sur les sillons et couronnes.

NOTES ON TWO MASADA SCRIPTURE MANUSCRIPTS: MAS1 (MASGEN) AND MAS1F (MASPS[B])

Eibert TIGCHELAAR

Emile Puech's contributions to the fields of North West Semitic and Dead Sea Scrolls epigraphy are not limited to his many own editions of texts and artefacts in books and articles. Often overlooked, but equally impressive are his numerous reviews, generally consisting of scores of perceptive comments as well as corrections of the readings of other scholars, often presented in lapidary fashion. In this token of friendship and of acknowledgment of Emile's keen eye for details, I offer some observations on two Masada scripture manuscripts, taking into account Emile's own comments in his review article of the final edition of the Hebrew and Aramaic Masada manuscripts.[1]

1. THE MASADA GENESIS FRAGMENT (MAS1; MASGEN; MAS 1039-317)

Shemaryahu Talmon published a small fragment with remnants of Gen 46:7-11 in five lines as follows[2]

1 ובנות בניו וכול זרעו הביא אתו] מצרים vac
2 ואלה שמות בני ישראל הבאים מצרי]ם את יעקוב
3 אביהם בכור יעקוב ראובן] ו̇[בנ]י ראובן חנוך
4 ופלוא וחצרון וכרמי ובני שמעון ימ]ו̇אל וימין
5 ואוהד ויכין וצוהר ושאול בן הכנענית] ו̇בנ̇י לוי

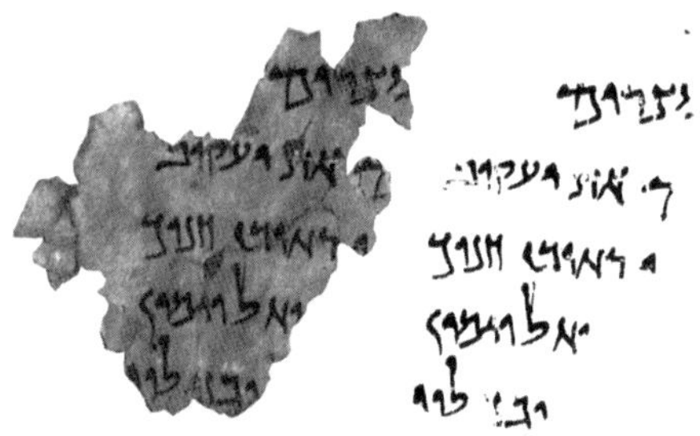

Fig. 1. MasGen photo of fragment (photo Shai Halevi) and digitized version (digitized by Maruf Dhali)

[1] Shemaryahu TALMON, *Masada VI: The Yigael Yadin Excavations 1963-1965 Final Reports*, Jerusalem, Israel Exploration Society, 1999; Emile PUECH, "Recension de *Masada VI*", *RevQ* 22/81 (2003) 125-28.
[2] S. TALMON, *Masada VI*, 31-35, 34.

In the edition, Talmon called attention the presumed *vacat* at the end of line 1, creating a "break [which] dovetails with the masoretic section-divider (*parašah*) after Gen 46:7", discussed at length the variant reading את in line 2, and reconstructed, with reference to Jub. 44:11, the variant הבאים מצרים את יעקוב אביהם, instead of the "awkward MT phrase" הבאים מצרימה יעקב ובניו.[3]

Correctly, Puech referred to traces of a line above line 1, and, more importantly, to the fact that line 1 does not end with a *vacat*, but with a gap.[4] He also proposed that some of the small pieces should be joined differently, but I prefer to follow Talmon except for the placement of the small fragment. Puech thought he could read remnants of letters on both sides of the gap, i.e., וֺ[אל]הֺ at the end of line 1, but neither the old photograph IAA-302374, nor the new IAA photograph by Shai Halevi can confirm this. Yet, Puech is absolutely right that for the reconstruction of the lines it is more likely that ואלה was at the end of line 1 than at the beginning of line 2. At the same time, he is reluctant to accept Talmon's emendation without support of אביהם, and prefers to read with MT ובניו. Nonetheless, Puech emphasizes that the absence of the *parashah*, the twofold מצרים instead of מצרימה, and the variant את, show that the text is not a witness to the Masoretic Text.

Puech's rejection of Talmon's emendation of אביהם as without support seems too strict in my opinion. While there is no epigraphic support of this emendation, there is ample textual evidence. The starting point is the close correspondence between Gen 46:8, Exod 1:1, and Jub. 44:11

Gen 46:8 ואלה שמות בני ישראל הבאים מצרימה יעקב ובניו בכר יעקב ראובן
Exod. 1:1 ואלה שמות בני ישראל הבאים מצרימה את יעקב איש וביתו באו

Gen 46:8	These were the names of the Israelites who came to Egypt. Jacob and his descendants: Reuben, Jacob's firstborn …
Exod 1:1	These were the names of the sons of Israel who came to Egypt with Jacob, each with their family
Jub. 44:11	These were the names of the sons of Jacob who came to Egypt with their father Jacob

Talmon simply suggested that MasGen and Jub. 44:11 attest to a variant in the text of Gen 46:8 which read הבאים מצרימה את יעקב אביהם. The textual relationships are more complex, though. A range of LXX

[3] S. TALMON, *Masada VI*, 33-34.

[4] Cf., similarly, Eugene ULRICH, "Two Perspectives on Two Pentateuchal Manuscripts from Masada", in Shalom M. PAUL et al. (ed.), *Emanuel: Studies in Hebrew Bible, Septuagint, and Dead Sea Scrolls in Honor of Emanuel Tov* (VTS, 94), Leiden, Brill, 2003, 453-64; reprinted with some additions as "The Masada Scrolls", in *The Dead Sea Scrolls and the Developmental Composition of the Bible* (VTS, 169), Leiden, Brill, 2015, 251-63.

manuscripts reads in Gen 46:8 ἅμα Ἰακὼβ τῷ πατρὶ αὐτῶν, which would seem to support the assumption that MasGen and Jubilees are witnesses of a well-known textual variant. However, in all those cases (MasGen, Jubilees, LXX mss) the variant may also have been influenced by Exod 1:1.[5] In MT and SP, Exod 1:1 has the preposition את before יעקב but lacks אביהם. Yet, in Exod 1:1 both the LXX (ἅμα Ἰακὼβ τῷ πατρὶ αὐτῶν) and 4Q13[6] (preserved are from this verse the four words את יעקוב אביהם איש) read there אביהם, thus attesting to a text which could have influenced the scribes of MasGen and Jubilees.

While it is possible that the text of MasGen is simply a matter of assimilation to the variant text of Exod 1:1 with the phrase את יעקב אביהם (LXX, 4Q13) replacing יעקב ובניו (MT/SP), it may also have been part of a more thorough revision of this section of Genesis which suffers from difficulties with regard to the counting of the persons in the list.[7] The MT wording יעקב ובניו may have been intended to include Jacob in the total number of seventy given in MT/SP Gen 46:27. This leads us, however, into the field of literary criticism,[8] and the evidence of MasGen is simply too limited to determine whether the textual variant of את could have been part of a version distinct from MT, or simply an ad hoc "assimilation"[9] or a "memory variant",[10] as found frequently in the Dead Sea Scrolls scriptural manuscripts. I would therefore transcribe

]○[
1 [ובנות בניו וכול זרעו הביא אתו] מצרים [ואלה]
2 [שמות בני ישראל הבאים מצרי]ם את יעקוב
3 [אביהם *vac* בכור יעקוב ראובן ובנ]י ראובן חנוך
4 [ופלוא וחצרון וכרמי ובני שמעון ימ]ואל וימין
5 [ואוהד ויכין וצוהר ושאול בן הכנענית] ובני לוי

[5] This is most likely in the LXX, given the relatively rare use of ἅμα in both Exod 1:1 and the variant in Gen 46:8.

[6] See the edition of 4Q13 (4QExod[b]) by Frank Moore CROSS in *Qumran Cave 4. VII: Genesis to Numbers* (DJD, 12), Oxford, Clarendon, 1994, 79-95, esp. 83-84 who lists a range of variants where 4Q13 stands with LXX.

[7] On Jubilees' text as an attempt to deal with the MT consistencies, see the discussion in James C. VANDERKAM, *Jubilees: A Commentary* (Hermeneia), Minneapolis, Fortress, 2018, 1095-1102.

[8] Cf., e.g., Itamar KISLEV, "The Census of the Israelites on the Plains of Moab (Numbers 26): Sources and Redaction", *VT* 63 (2013) 236-60.

[9] *General Introduction and Megilloth* (BHQ, 18), Stuttgart, Deutsche Bibelgesellschaft, 2007, lxxxix.

[10] David CARR, "Torah on the Heart: Literary Jewish Textuality Within its Ancient Near Eastern Context", *Oral Tradition* 25 (2010); reprinted in Werner H. KELLER and Paula A. SANDERS (ed.), *Oral-Scribal Dimensions of Scripture, Piety, and Practice: Judaism, Christianity, Islam*, Eugene, OR, Cascade Books, 2016, 21-48.

In his preliminary description, Yadin stated that "the script resembles, on the whole, that of the Isaiah scroll A", even though the particular form of the *kaph* of חנוך seems to be "somewhat later, i.e., from the beginning of the first century B.C.E."[11] Probably, Yadin's first impressions were based on the medial-like form of this final *kaph*, since several other letters have forms entirely different from those of 1QIsa[a]. Talmon commented on what he called the semi-cursive and irregular writing, and stated it seemingly resembles the script of 1Q19, an assessment which should be dismissed.[12] Puech does not comment on the script. The published image in *Masada VI* is barely legible, but the photographs[13] enable one to recognize the script as similar to the round or rustic semi-formal early Herodian script. One of the features of this script is the characteristic pressed and curved lower part of *lamed* which induced Ada Yardeni to assign a range of manuscripts from Qumran, as well as the Masada Joshua Apocryphon (Mas11), to one single prolific Qumran scribe.[14] However, though most of the manuscripts assigned by Yardeni to this one scribe do share a common style, the many variations in the forms of other letters preclude attributing them to one and the same scribe. Groningen digital palaeographic research assigns only eight or so of those manuscripts to one individual hand, and did not match the Masada Joshua Apocryphon confidently to the scribes of the Qumran manuscripts in the round semi-formal script.[15] In fact, in spite of the rounded *lamed*, the script of the Masada Joshua Apocryphon is quite different from most of the manuscripts listed by Yardeni. In contrast, most forms of letters of MasGen are closer to some of the manuscripts recorded by Yardeni, such as 4Q166. However, the complete set of preserved letters does not fully match that of any Qumran manuscript (especially the narrow *ḥet* is atypical for most of these so-called round semiformal manuscripts), and the scribe may have been one of many individuals who used this specific style.

However, if one takes the Qumran manuscripts inscribed in this round semiformal style as the closest comparanda to MasGen, then one can make a few observations which could shed light on MasGen. First, the use of this curvilinear style is most common in nonbiblical Hebrew manuscripts,

[11] Yigael YADIN, *The Excavation of Masada 1963/64: Preliminary Report* (IEJ, 15), Jerusalem, Israel Exploration Society, 1965, 104.

[12] S. TALMON, *Masada VI*, 32 and n. 3.

[13] See both the old photograph I-302374 (https://www.deadseascrolls.org.il/explore-the-archive/image/B-299507) and the new photographs made by Shai Halevi (not yet uploaded).

[14] Ada YARDENI, "A Note on a Qumran Scribe", in Meir LUBETSKI (ed.), *New Seals and Inscriptions: Hebrew, Idumean, and Cuneiform* (HBM, 8), Sheffield, Sheffield Phoenix, 2007, 289-98.

[15] Cf. PhD work of Gemma HAYES (University of Groningen, ERC project "The Hands that Wrote the Bible").

and used rarely in biblical manuscripts, many of which are written in a formal more rectilinear style (especially in the Herodian period).[16] Second, virtually all those manuscripts display a non-MT orthography (extensive use of *waw* for not only long, but also short /o/ and /u/; use of *he* as mater lectionis for final /ā/, both where MT has final /ā/ without mater lectionis, and in specific cases where MT lacks final /ā/ altogether). This holds true not only for non-biblical manuscripts, but also for the biblical ones, notably 4Q27, 4Q38, and 4Q38a. Third, the few biblical manuscripts in this script display a range of variants vis-à-vis MT, some shared with other witnesses, and others unique. The least one can say is that the manuscripts written in this script are neither characterized by formal writing, nor by a conservative MT-like orthography, or a close similarity to a specific textual tradition. Though an amount of eleven preserved words in MasGen, some of which only partially preserved, is too small for any firm statement, the few preserved variants do point at a profile very similar to those Qumran biblical manuscripts.

2. The Masada Psalm 150 fragments (Mas1f; MasPs^b; Mas 1103-1742)

Mas1f consists of two fragments, frag. a, which preserves most words of Ps 150:1-3, and frag. b, with extensive remains of Ps 150:4-6. Talmon placed frag. a above frag. b, in one and the same column, with one line missing in between.[17]

Fig. 2. MasPs^b fragments aligned frag. a above frag. b (photo Shai Halevi; alignment Talmon)

[16] See Drew Longacre, "Disambiguating the Concept of Formality in Palaeographic Descriptions: Stylistic Classicification and the Ancient Jewish Hebrew/Aramaic Scripts", *COMSt Bulletin* 5 (2019) 101-28, for introducing the aspects of rectolinearity and curvilinearity in relation to the so-called formal and semi-formal styles.

[17] S. Talmon, *Masada VI*, 91-97.

Fragment b has the remnants of two columns, and at the left side of the fragment the end of the sheet. While the left column has Ps 150:4-6, Talmon interpreted the few letters of the right column as the remains of Ps 147:18-19. On that basis, he calculated the scroll to have had ca. 44 lines, which would mean that Mas1f once was a large Psalms scroll. Eva Jain even proposed an alternative calculation according to which the scroll could have had 61 lines a column.[18] Puech correctly saw that Talmon's reading of the few letters of the right column of frag. b as רו[חו and ח[קיו should be dismissed, and in stead proposed הללו[הו resp. מל[אכיו, from Ps 148:1-2. Puech's rejection of Talmon's reading is correct. The reading רו[חו is clearly wrong. The headbar which extends to the left of the left downstroke rules out *khet*, and a reading הו with *he* rather than *khet* is necessary. As for Talmon's ח[קיו, the *qop* might not be entirely impossible, but the remaining traces are different from those of the other *qofs*. Puech's own proposal, מל[אכיו requires a form of *kap* unlike that of כרב in this manuscript. I propose one can better read *taw*, for which see the *taw* in בתקע. These readings fit well with an alternative placement of the fragments. Rather than one above the other, the fragments can be placed side to side, with frag. b joining to frag. a, both physically and textually. The tear separating the two fragments runs vertically through the left leg of the second *he* of line 2 הללוהו.[19] This join is also supported by the ruling lines: on both fragments the ruling line of line 2 is clear and thick, while the ruling lines of lines 3 and 4 are thinner and fainter, and that of line 1 least legible of all.

Fig. 3 MasPs^{b} fragments joined to one another (join Tigchelaar)

[18] Eva JAIN, *Psalmen oder Psalter? Materielle Rekonstruktion und inhaltliche Untersuchung der Psalmenhandschriften aus der Wüste Juda* (STDJ, 109), Leiden, Brill, 2014, 211-16.

[19] This is difficult to see on the infra-red images produced here, but the two halves of the downstroke are clearly visible on the IAA colour image of Museum Plate X81. It seems that when the fragments were torn, part of the lower layer of the parchment remained on frag. b and the corresponding upper part of the layer on frag. a.

A transcription of the two columns would then be:

[הלל]הו בתף ו[מ]חול הללהו	1	[הללו י]ה̊]
ב̇[מ]נ̇ים ועוגב הללהו בצלצלי	2	הללו אל בקדשו הללוהו
שמע הללהו בצלצלי תרועה	3	ברקיע עזו הללה[ו בגבר]ת̇יו
כל הנ̇[שמה]ת̇הלל[יה]	4	הללהו כרב גדלו [הללהו]
[הללויה]	5	ב̇תקע שפ̇ר̊[הללהו בנבל]
	6	[וכנור

Materially, this placement of the fragments gives the best explanation of the straight left and top edges of frag. b: they are the top left horizontal and vertical edges of the sheet. There is no need to speculate on intentional damage resulting in these lines.[20]

The distance between the top edge and the first ruling line is identical to the distance in between the horizontal ruling lines (4 mm).[21] In comparison to the ruling of the other lines, the ruling line of line 1 is very vague, and only recognizable in a few spots. As in the so-called post-Herodian manuscripts, the letters do not hang from the guiding lines, but are written beneath them. However, the distance between ruling lines and the tops of the letters increases in the bottom lines. This might suggest that the ruling was not made for this text, and that the scribe ignored the pre-existing ruling, as in 1QpHab and other manuscripts.

The writing on the lines suggests a total height of the inscribed text in these columns of six lines, or even five, if וכנור would have fitted in col. 1 line 5. It is unlikely that a scribe would have left a large piece of parchment below these six lines unwritten. One may hypothesize that this text was written on a small piece of parchment, perhaps a left-over of an already ruled sheet. This hypothesis rules out Jain's assumption of a substantial or even complete Psalms scroll.[22] In contrast, it is even possible that the original artefact contained only Psalm 150.

Talmon erroneously dated the fragment palaeographically to the late Hasmonaean or early Herodian period, which Puech corrected to the first century CE.[23] The hand has some of the ornamentation usually ascribed

[20] See such speculations in S. TALMON, *Masada VI*, 91-92, who had to offer an explanation for the straight edge in the middle of his reconstructed column.

[21] This size of 0.4 cm is smaller than any of those recorded by Emanuel TOV, *Scribal Practices and Approaches Reflected in the Texts Found in the Judaean Desert* (STDJ, 54), Leiden, Brill, 2004, 99-103.

[22] E. JAIN, *Psalmen*, 216.

[23] Virtually none of Talmon's palaeographic datings are correct. See for several corrections Puech's review.

to so-called late Herodian and post-Herodian calligraphic hands,[24] but it lacks the forward leaning direction of the later post-Herodian calligraphic hands. Characteristic of this specific manuscript is the cutting of the nib of the pen, resulting in very thin top-right-to-bottom-left diagonal strokes, not attested in this extreme and consistent manner in other preserved manuscripts from this period.

The very light colour of the parchment is rare among the Dead Sea Scrolls. Comparable examples are 4Q91 (4QPs^{j}), and, perhaps to a lesser extent, Mur3 (MurIsa) and 3Q9 (3QSectarian Text), all of which can be dated palaeographically to the first century CE.

In this manuscript, the single stichs are separated by uninscribed spaces, but, contrary to a traditional stichographic layout, the individual stichs do not begin on a new line. Hence, this layout has been called "a hybrid of 'prose-' and stichographic layout."[25]

The new join of the two fragments changes our perspective on the manuscript. The two fragments are not part of the last column of a large scroll of the Psalter ending with Ps 150, and one should therefore be cautious to use this fragment to argue for a specific sequence of Psalms. Rather, these fragments are the remnants of a probably small sheet of parchment which contained only one separate text, Ps 150.

One can only guess why this artefact was produced, how it would have functioned, and why it was found at Masada. The artefact could have been an exercise in calligraphic writing, written from memory in an irregular defective spelling of הללהו, and in an uncommon stichographic layout. Subsequently, it might have functioned as an individual's religious object carried along to Masada.

[24] On the kind of ornamentation, see the descriptions in Ada YARDENI, *The Book of Hebrew Script: History, Palaeography, Script Styles, Calligraphy and Design*, London, The British Library, 2002, 182.

[25] Anna KRAUSS and Friederike SCHÜCKING-JUNGBLUT, "Stichographic Layout in the Dead Sea Psalms Scrolls: Observations on its Development and its Potential", in Bradford A. ANDERSON (ed.), *From Scrolls to Scrolling: Sacred Texts, Materiality, and Dynamic Media Cultures* (JCITTT, 12), Berlin, De Gruyter, 2020, 13-34, 18. On the relationship between very narrow columns and stichometric arrangement, see Kipp DAVIS, "Structure, Stichometry, and Standardization: An Analysis of Scribal Features in a Selection of the Dead Sea Psalms Scrolls", in Mika S. PAJUNEN and Jeremy PENNER (ed.), *Functions of Psalms and Prayers in the Late Second Temple Period* (BZAW, 486), Berlin, De Gruyter, 2017, 155-84.

3. Character and Provenance of the Masada Scripture Manuscripts

Very soon after Talmon's publication of the Masada materials, Emanuel Tov launched the hypothesis that the Masada nonbiblical literary texts were brought there from Qumran, and the biblical ones by "groups which adhered to one single biblical text, probably the Jerusalem central text."[26] Tov has reiterated with some nuances this view up to the present day, consistently contrasting the corpus of scripture manuscripts found in the Qumran caves with a "group of twenty-five Scripture texts large enough for analysis" found at other sites in the Judaean Desert, all of the latter agreeing "with the consonantal framework of the medieval Masoretic text, even though they derive from very different periods."[27]

This hypothesis has been gently challenged by Ulrich, who argued, at least for the first century CE, for a broader spectrum of textual variety in Judaean scripture manuscripts,[28] implicitly by Puech in his review who questioned MasGen's alignment with MT and emphasized the heterogeneity of the manuscripts, and rejected by Mladen Popović who cautioned that the archaeological context of the textual finds at Masada does not support Tov's reference to two collections.[29] Overall, Tov's interpretive framework goes back to much earlier stages of scholarship, which posited clear but anachronistic contrasts between the Qumran sect and protorabbinic normative Judaism. For example, Tov's assertion that the Masada rebels followed the guidance of protorabbinic spiritual centers in religious matters is likely based on Yadin's interpretation of the *miqva'ot*, which has more recently been disputed as anachronistic.[30]

[26] Emanuel Tov, "A Qumran Origin for the Masada Non-biblical Texts?" *Dead Sea Discoveries* 7 (2000) 56-72, 61.

[27] Emanuel Tov, "The Background and Origin of the Qumran Corpus of Scripture Texts", in Henryk Drawnel (ed.), *Sacred Texts and Disparate Interpretations: Qumran Manuscripts Seventy Years Later: Proceedings of the International Conference Held at the John Paul II Catholic University of Lublin, 24-26 October 2017*, (STDJ, 133), Leiden: Brill, 2020, 51-65, 51. See 51 n. 1 for literature discussing the evidence for this claim. Similarly, E. Tov, "The Myth of the Stabilization of the Text of Hebrew Scripture", in Elvira Martín-Contreras and Lorena Miralles-Macía (ed.), *The Text of the Hebrew Bible: From the Rabbis to the Masoretes* (JAJ Sup, 13), Göttingen, Vandenhoeck & Ruprecht, 2015, 37-45, 44, in almost the same words.

[28] E. Ulrich, "Two Perspectives."

[29] Mladen Popović, "Qumran as Scroll Storehouse in Times of Crisis? A Comparative Perspective on Judaean Desert Manuscript Collections", *JSJ* 43 (2012), 551-94, 567-68.

[30] Yigael Yadin, *Masada: Herod's Fortress and the Zealot's Last Stand*, London, Weidenfeld and Nicholson, 1966, 164-67, "the defenders of Masada were devout Jews, so that

However, while one should always be critical of scholars' interpretive frameworks, a main weakness in Tov's and others' claim of the proto-Masoretic character of the Masada scriptural manuscripts is methodological.[31] One problem is that the proto-Masoretic character of some Masada manuscripts is emphasized (and the similarities in some cases exaggerated[32]), and contrasted to the average Qumran manuscript where even so-called MT-like manuscripts would have less agreement with the MT.

As Puech already noted, one can hardly consider MasGen to be MT-like, a problem which Tov brushes away by qualifying it as not large enough for analysis, and Young by excluding it as being not a Genesis but a Jubilees fragment.[33] Another case is Mas1a (MasLev[a]), a small fragment with about sixty words from Lev 4:3-9. It differs textually only once from the main witnesses of the MT, namely in the orthographic variant ישפוך against MT ישפך, while it has a few variants vis-à-vis the SP and the LXX.[34] But with what should one compare this manuscript? Ulrich argues that in this section of Leviticus, MT, SP, and LXX only differ in tiny details, and that one may not be able to assess the nature of MasLev[a]

even here, on dry Masada, they had gone to the arduous lengths of building these ritual baths in scrupulous conformity with the injunctions of traditional Jewish law" (167). But cf. Stuart S. MILLER, "Stepped Pools and the Non-Existent Monolithic 'Miqveh'", in Douglas R. EDWARDS and C. Thomas MCCOLLOUGH (ed.), *The Archaeology of Difference: Gender, Ethnicity, Class and the "Other" in Antiquity* (*Festschrift Eric M. Meyers*), Boston, American Schools of Oriental Research, 2007, 215-34; Yonathan ADLER, "The Myth of the *'ôṣār* in Second Temple Period Ritual Baths: an Anachronistic Interpretation of a Modern-Era Innovation", *JJS* 65 (2014), 263-83.

[31] Tov considers Ian YOUNG, "The Stabilization of the Biblical Text in the Light of Qumran and Masada: A Challenge for Conventional Qumran Chronology?" *DSD* 9 (2002), 364-90, to have provided evidence for this hypothesis.

[32] E. TOV, "Qumran Origin", 73, the "agreement between MasLev[b] and the medieval text pertains to the smallest details of orthography, including details in which the orthography ad loc. goes against the conventions elsewhere in the book." But the examples referred to by TOV, and taken from S. TALMON, *Masada VI*, do not demonstrate this. Leviticus MT uses three times the form תמימם (once, perhaps twice, also in MasLev[b]) against once תמימים, and one cannot simply oppose the defectively written *wayyiqtol* וַיַּקְרִבוּ (twice in Leviticus) to the plene *yiqtol* form יַקְרִיבוּ (four times in Leviticus). Neither in these cases, nor in Talmon's other examples of remarkable correspondence, does the shared MasLev[b]-MT orthography go against the conventions in the book.

[33] I. YOUNG, "Stabilization", 371; slightly more cautious, but still unwilling to draw any conclusions from this fragment, I. YOUNG, "The Contrast Between the Qumran and Masada Biblical Scrolls in Light of New Data", in Shani TZOREF and Ian YOUNG (ed.), *Keter Shem Tov: Essays on the Dead Sea Scrolls in Memory of Alan Crown* (Perspectives on Hebrew Scriptures and Its Contexts, 20), Piscataway, Gorgias, 2013, 113-19.

[34] See overviews and discussion in S. TALMON, *Masada VI*, 36-39, esp. 38; E. ULRICH "Two Perspectives", 458-60; summative E. TOV, "Qumran Origin", 72-73.

by comparing them to these witnesses.[35] Young, however, compared the proportion of non-orthographic variants (vis-à-vis MT) of the Masada scripture manuscripts with those of the Qumran manuscripts of the same works.[36] The two Masada Leviticus manuscripts have no non-orthographic variants from the MT (Leningrad Codex), all the Qumran Leviticus manuscripts (except for the tiny 6Q2) have some or many nonorthographic variants. Young admits that 1Q3 (1QpaleoLev) and 4Q25 (4QLev[c]) have only a minimal amount of variants, in contrast to 4Q24 (4QLev[b]) and 11Q1 (11QpaleoLev[a]). Nonetheless, he argues that the overall evidence "puts the Masada corpus in strong contrast to the Qumran corpus."[37]

However, if one does not compare corpora (in the case of Masada this is certainly an artificial term), but individual manuscripts, then the difference between Mas1a (no variant on 61 total words, in Young's counting; and one orthographical variant) and 4Q25 (two variants on 111 total words, in Young's counting; and no orthographical variant at all) is minimal. Young does not record which two variants of 4Q25 he includes, but probably Lev 4:14 (4Q25 3 5 reading אתה for MT אתו) and Lev 5:12 (4Q25 5 2 reading היא, with SP, for MT *ketiv* הוא, *qere* היא). Since none of these MT הִוא cases ever corresponds to a Qumran or other Judaean Desert manuscript with הוא,[38] perhaps this should not be included as a variant, leaving only the אתו/אתה variant left.[39] Compared with one another, there are no grounds at all to contrast 4Q25 and Mas1b, or to dissociate the Mas1b fragment from the Qumran manuscripts.

The Masada Psalm 150 manuscript is yet another example. Its variants have been discussed by Talmon and Ulrich: five times the unique הללהו versus הללוהו of MT; שפר versus שופר in MT; and ועוגג with 11Q5 and MT[L] versus MT[A]. Quite rightly, Ulrich observes that with respect to orthography these fragments do not correspond as closely to the MT tradition as some other manuscripts do. Ulrich does acknowledge that the fragment attests to the MT version of the Psalter, with Ps 150 at its very end, as against the LXX of 11Q5 with additional material. The correct join presented in this article, however, suggests a small scroll, plausibly even a

[35] E. ULRICH, "Two Perspectives", 459.

[36] I. YOUNG, "Stabilization", 374-75. Note that the reliability of such proportions is smaller when the preserved text is limited.

[37] I. YOUNG, "Stabilization", 375.

[38] In Mas1b 3:21 (Lev 10:17) and 4:9 (Lev 11:6) one might read either הוא or היא.

[39] Note that 4Q25 frag. 3 may have been incorrectly assigned to 4Q25. Contrast the script and the amount of spacing between the words.

small piece of parchment with only Ps 150. On that basis we can say nothing about a collection, MT, or 11Q5, or LXX-like.

While some of the Masada scriptural manuscripts are very close to the MT consonantal text, more so than the majority of the Qumran scriptural manuscripts, there is no ground to contrast individual manuscripts, like MasGen, MasLev[a], or MasPs[b], with manuscripts from Qumran. In fact, a hypothesis which holds that some Masada manuscripts might have been brought there from Qumran, should also consider that these could have included MasGen, MasLev[a], or MasPs[b]. However, there is no cogent reason, neither literary, nor palaeographically, nor orthographically, that any of the Masada manuscripts need to have been brought there from Qumran, and, as Emile has showed in many of his publications, careful epigraphic work should precede broad interpretive speculation.[40]

[40] Images: Courtesy of The Leon Levy Dead Sea Scrolls Digital Library; Israel Antiquities Authority, photos: Shai Halevi. The author is also a research associate of the University of Pretoria.

THE CHRONOLOGY OF JACOB'S LIFE IN JUBILEES AND RELATED SOURCES

James C. VanderKam

1. Introduction: Chronological Information in Genesis and Exodus

Chronology was a subject of interest to ancient readers of Genesis and other scriptural books. We have texts by several authors who tried to establish an absolute chronology from creation to whatever endpoint interested them. Genesis includes a set of interlocking year numbers that allow a reader to reconstruct much of the chronology underlying the narratives. There are different chronologies at some points in the MT, SP, and LXX so that, depending on the copy of Genesis that a later writer used, the systems derived from them might differ in significant ways. As expected, early chronologists were not troubled by matters such as source divisions in the text. Genesis furnished a single account for them so that they could use all chronological data in the book to establish their timelines.

The genealogy in Genesis 5 offers a set of related dates – most helpfully, the age of the father when his first son was born – so that from the list one can infer a running chronology from Adam's first year to the time of the flood. The genealogy in Gen 11:10-26 supplies similar numbers permitting the chronology to continue to the time of Abra(ha)m. The stories involving him report his age at the time of key events, including when he left Haran (75 years of age, Gen 12:4) and when Ishmael and Isaac were born (86 and 100 years, respectively, 16:16 and 21:5). Later one learns that Isaac was 60 years old when he became the father of Esau and Jacob (25:26). So far, so good.

With the lifetime of Jacob problems arose for chronologers. Virtually no event in his early life is dated; Gen 26:34 is an exception but only by implication from his twin Esau's age (40 years). The notices about the births of his first eleven sons and one daughter lack indications of his age when they were born (Gen 29:31–30:24), although the time when he would have become their father is circumscribed by other notices. The only son of Jacob whose birth can be fixed to an exact year in his lifetime is Joseph. According to Gen 37:2 (MT SP LXX), Joseph was 17 years of age when he had the fateful encounter with his brothers that eventuated in his being sold and transported to Egypt. When Joseph stood before Pharaoh and interpreted his dreams, he was, says Gen 41:46 (MT SP LXX), thirty years old. There followed the seven years of plentiful harvests and two of famine before his father Jacob and the family arrived in Egypt. At that time, when Joseph was 39 (note that he tells his brothers there were five years of famine remaining, 45:6 MT SP LXX), Jacob told Pharaoh that he was 130 years (Gen 47:9 MT SP LXX). If he was 130 when Joseph was 39, Joseph was born when Jacob was 91.[1] Ten sons and one daughter were born before Joseph's birth, although Genesis does not divulge how long before. It may be that the text locates the births in the second seven-year span that Jacob worked for his wives – since he married them after his first seven years of labor – and before the six years of extra service (see the sequence in Gen 29:20–30:24, and the divisions of the full twenty-year period in 31:41).[2] If so, the others were born in the years when Jacob was 84-90 or 91.[3] The 20 years with Laban would then have coincided with years 77 to 97 of Jacob's life. These appear to be straightforward inferences from Genesis.

The dearth of helpful dates in the birth notices of Jacob's children continues in subsequent generations traced in the Book of Exodus. The

[1] See, for example, Chaim MILIKOWSKY, *Seder Olam. Critical Edition, Commentary, and Introduction*, vol. 2 *Commentary*, Jerusalem, Ben-Zvi, 2013, 30; William ADLER and Paul TUFFIN, *The Chronography of George Synkellos. A Byzantine Chronicle of Universal History from the Creation*, Oxford, Oxford University Press, 2002, 149 n. 5, for writers who drew the inference. Syncellus wrote about the scriptural implications of the ages of Jacob and Joseph at an earlier time in their lives: "Now it can be shown from scripture that Joseph was born in the 91st year of Jacob, seeing that it was in his father's 120th year that he, in his 30th year was elevated to the rule of Egypt" (W. ADLER and P. TUFFIN, *The Chronography of George Synkellos*, 166; cf. 160). Syncellus also worked back from Jacob's age of 91 at Joseph's birth, allotting one year for each birth, so that Reuben, the eldest, was born when Jacob was 80 and Levi, the third son, when he was 82 (e.g. 161). This approach yields a period of twelve years for the births of twelve children, as in Jubilees (see below).

[2] Victor P. HAMILTON, *The Book of Genesis Chapters 18-50* (The New International Commentary on the Old Testament), Grand Rapids, Eerdmans, 1995, 264.

[3] Note the comment of R. Aibu in *Ber. R.* 70.18 regarding Gen 29:21 where Jacob demands "my wife" from Laban after his first seven years of labor: "Even the most dissolute does not use such language! It was this, however, that he said: 'The Holy One, blessed be He, has decreed that I am to produce twelve tribes. I am now eighty-four years old, and if I do not beget them now, when will I do so?'" (*Midrash Rabbah Genesis*, vol. 2, translated by H. FREEDMAN, 3rd ed., London/New York, Soncino, 1983, 649). Or, in 68.5, where Hezekiah is commenting on Gen 28:10 (Jacob's going out from his home to Haran): "Our father Jacob was sixty-three years old when he received the blessings; and he spent another fourteen secluded in the Land and studying under Eber; a further seven years were spent by him in working for the matriarchs. Thus he married at age eighty-four, whereas Esau married at the age of forty" (618).

short genealogical list in Exod 6:14-25 deals with the sons of Jacob's three oldest – Reuben, Simeon, and Levi. When it reaches Levi, it follows his line, the priestly family, over several generations. For the leading figure in each generation it supplies his age at death (the numbers preceding the parentheses are the same in MT SP LXX, with exceptions indicated):

Levi	137 (6:16)
Kohath	133 (6:18; LXX 130)
Amram	137 (6:20; SP 136; LXX 132).

Amram was the father of Moses[4] and of Aaron who, with his sons, would serve as priests in the wilderness sanctuary. The problem for chronographers here was that in no case does the list specify how old the father was when his son was born. In the absence of such information, the ability to continue the exact chronology from Genesis was compromised.

2. Later Chronologies

The data in Genesis served as the basis for chronologies developed by several ancient writers or by the schools they may have represented. A very early example is the third-century BCE chronographer Demetrius,[5] parts of whose work were preserved by the first-century BCE writer Alexander Polyhistor and from him by Eusebius in *Preparation for the Gospel* 9. For the dates in Jacob's life that are of interest for this paper Demetrius gives the following:

Event	Jacob's Age
Jacob to Haran	77[6]
Jacob marries	84
Children born	84-91
Levi born	87
Joseph born	91
Jacob to Egypt	130
Jacob dies	147

[4] We learn about Moses's age at various points in his life (e.g. Exod 7:7) but not about his father's age when he was born.

[5] For a discussion of when Demetrius was active, see Carl R. Holladay, *Fragments from Hellenistic Jewish Authors*, vol. 1 *Historians* (SBL T&T 20, Pseudepigrapha series 10), Chico, CA, Scholars Press, 1983, 51-52.

[6] He gives 75, 77, and 80 in different places, but his other calculations assume the age of 77 for the journey (C. Holladay, *Fragments from Hellenistic Jewish Authors*, 1.80 n. 4).

These ages correlate precisely with the implications of the verses in Genesis that were summarized above. They represent careful, sensible exegesis of scriptural numbers.

The Book of Jubilees, a second century BCE work[7] that offers a running chronology from creation, includes a fairly extensive sequence of dates for the period it covers – from creation to the Exodus (and entry into Canaan) – and hence for the life of Jacob. The givens in Jubilees are a bit strange because, despite the frequency of dates for events in his life, they raise a number of problems and, at times, conflict with what Genesis has to say.

Jubilees' chronology for Jacob contains several cases in which numbers are inconsistent and others that are internally contradictory. According to Jub 19:13 the twins Esau and Jacob were born to Rebekah and Isaac in the year of the world 2046, or, in its terms, jubilee 42 (see 19:1), week 6, year 2. The next passage that correlates his age and the year of the world is 25:1, 4, where, in the year 2109 (jubilee 44, week 1 [see 24:21], year 2), Jacob was 63 years of age when his mother blessed him. The two numbers harmonize (2046 and 2109 are 63 years apart).[8] However, when Joseph was born (2134 [sixth year of the fourth week in jubilee 44 (see 27:19)]), a time when Jacob should have been 91 according to the calculations from Genesis noted above, he was, if Jacob was born in 2046, 88 years of age. Jubilees dates Isaac's death at age 180 to the year 2162 (36:1, 18). If Isaac became a parent of the twins when he was 60, Jacob should have been 120 years at the time, but in Jubilees' chronology he is only 116 (2046 to 2162).

These kinds of inconsistencies involve inferences from numbers in Jubilees; they are not explicit in the text. But in other cases conflicts are explicit. When Jacob arrived in Egypt, he told Pharaoh that he was 130 years (Gen 47:9// Jub 45:6). Jubilees 45:1 puts the event in the year of the world 2172 (jubilee 45 [see 41:1], week 3, year 2) when Jacob would have been 126 (2046 to 2172). When Jacob died, his age was 147 (Gen 47:28// Jub 45:13); Jubilees dates his passing to the year of the world 2188, when he would have been 142 (2046 to 2188).

[7] Dates ranging throughout much of the second century BCE have been proposed by contemporary scholars. For a survey, see James VANDERKAM, *Jubilees 1. A Commentary on the Book of Jubilees Chapters 1-21* (Hermeneia), Minneapolis, Fortress, 2018, 28-37.

[8] In the same context Jacob charges that his brother Esau had been quarreling with him for 22, years, trying to persuade him to marry a sister of his two wives. Since Esau married them when he (and thus his twin Jacob) was 40 years old (Gen 26:34), he had filled the time between the marriages and Jacob's meeting with his mother in Jubilees 25 with such enticements.

One of the surprising dates in the book is Jacob's age when he went to Haran. We saw that fairly simple calculations from Genesis strongly favored an age of 77 for him when he fled from Esau, precisely the age given by Demetrius. Jubilees dates his journey to the year of the world 2115 (27:19 [jubilee 44, week 2, year 1]). With a birthdate in 2046, he would have been 69 at the time. In the book's chronology, the birthdates of the children extend from when Jacob was 76 to when he was 88, with Leah bearing Levi when Jacob was 81 (28:14)[9] and Rachel giving birth to Joseph when Jacob was 88 (28:18). These are strange numbers, especially 69 years of age for the flight to Laban; it has no parallel in the sources, all of which give a higher age.

The figures in Jubilees are close to what is expected, always within 3-5 years of being correct, apart from the date for Jacob's flight which is eight years off. If one considers the system the author of Jubilees employed to date events – jubilees, weeks, years – it is understandable that mistakes could seep in. Also, the book's long history of translation and hand-copying would have provided ample opportunities for slips in reproducing the numbers.[10] We have manuscript evidence for some variations. Just a few examples are:[11]

Hebrew: 4Q219 (4QJub^{d}) II 25, Jub 22:1, indicates the jubilee number was 43, not 44 as in the Ethiopic copies.

Latin: at 28:20, where the Ethiopic puts the birth of Gad in week 3, year 5, Latin puts it in year 3, week 4

[9] According to the Aramaic Levi Document, Levi was 48 years when the family entered Egypt. Since his father was 130 years at that time, Levi would have been born when Jacob was 82 (Jonas GREENFIELD, Michael STONE, and Esther ESHEL [eds.], *The Aramaic Levi Document. Edition, Translation, Commentary* [SVTP 19], Leiden, Brill, 2004, 98-99; 12:8 in their enumeration of chapters and verses). The Greek T. Levi 12:5 puts his age at 40 years when he entered Egypt, meaning Jacob was 90 when he became his father. Testament of Judah 12:12 says that Judah was 46 when they descended to Egypt; hence Leah would have given birth to him when Jacob was 84 (83 according to Jub 28:15). Reuben died two years after Joseph (who died at age 110) and at his death was 125 years (T. Reub. 1:1-2). He was thus thirteen years older than Joseph (Levi was eight years older; see T.Levi 12:7). In other words, in the Testaments of the 12 Patriarchs, the span of time in which the births of the eleven sons and one daughter took place was twelve years (C. MILIKOWSKY, *Seder Olam*, 2.31).

[10] Some of the symbols or letters used to represent numbers in Hebrew could be confused, but in all the instances of numbers in the Qumran fragments of Jubilees they are spelled out as words, not represented by letters or symbols. The words for *three* (שלש) and *six* (שש) are candidates for confusion and could account for some instances in which the year numbers are off by three.

[11] For these and the other dates in Jubilees according to all the versions of the book, see J. VANDERKAM, "Studies in the Chronology of the Book of Jubilees" pp. 522-44, especially pp. 528-32, in VANDERKAM, *From Revelation to Canon. Studies in the Hebrew Bible and Second Temple Literature* (JSJSupp 62), Leiden, Brill, 2000.

Syriac Chronicle: at 12:12, where Abram is 60 in the Ethiopic copies, a Syriac citation reads 56.

How should one account for Jubilees' unexpected year numbers for Jacob's trip to Haran and the births of his children? We have seen how they are surprising in light of the data in Genesis that are reflected by Demetrius. We can compare them with other timelines for Jacob's life to reinforce the point.

Event	Seder Olam	Syncellus
Jacob to Haran	77	73[12]
Jacob marries	84	80
Children born	84-91	80-91
Levi born	87	82[13]
Joseph born	[91]	91
Jacob to Egypt	130	130

The numbers that are explicit and those than can be inferred from information in Seder Olam are the same as the ones Demetrius furnished. This is noteworthy because the two texts come from rather different times and places in the Jewish world. Their agreement can be explained by their shared reliance on the chronological information in Genesis. The numbers in Syncellus are a few years lower than those in Demetrius and Seder Olam in the first four lines above and agree in the last two. Syncellus's lower numbers are a product, not of exegesis, but of his assumption that a year was assigned for the birth of each of the eleven sons.[14]

Jubilees' numbers diverge from those of Demetrius and Seder Olam especially for Jacob's age when he fled to Haran (69 as against 77 [Demetrius], 73 [Syncellus]); for the other numbers it diverges by the 3-5 years noted above. Perhaps it is significant that *69* in Jubilees' system of jubilee periods, weeks, and years would differ from *77* by one unit in each of the weeks and years columns.

[12] Syncellus considered Africanus's suggestion of 77 impossible (W. ADLER and P. TUFFIN, *The Chronography of George Synkellos*, 149). He arrived at the age of 73 for Jacob's flight by working back from Joseph's birth in Jacob's 91st year and "allotting one year for each child, as is suggested by the words of scripture" (129), that is, when Jacob was 80 to 91. If the births began when Jacob was 80, he arrived in Haran seven years earlier when he was 73.

[13] Since Levi is the third of the children and one year was reserved for each child, he was born when Jacob was 82.

[14] Seder Olam 2.8-9 says that each of the twelve pregnancies during the seven years of childbearing lasted seven months. Hence, no pregnancy overlapped with any other. On the passage, see C. MILIKOWSKY, *Seder Olam*, 2.30-32.

3. 4Q559 (4QpapBiblical Chronology ar)

Cave 4 at Qumran yielded a very poorly preserved text that seems to contain chronological numbers for the period we are examining. Thirteen fragments have been grouped under the rubric 4Q559. The editor and our honoree, Émile Puech, published the official edition in his erudite, precise, and learned fashion. He dates the copy to the first half of the first century BCE and believes the chronology in it derives from priestly sources that are several centuries older.[15] Although he produced the official edition in the DJD series, Puech was not the first to treat the text. Michael Wise devoted a lengthy essay to it,[16] and in the same year W. Nebe contributed a shorter analysis.[17] Hans Rapp later examined the data from 4Q559 in a wider study of chronological information in texts regarding Jacob.[18]

The remains of the manuscript, while supplying specific bits of information, are too meager in most spots to divulge exactly what the text says. The placement of the fragments relative to one another is debatable, no complete line has survived, and the letters and numbers at the edges of the fragments can be challenging to decipher. As a result, each of the scholars who has edited the text has added words and phrases around the preserved pieces in order to suggest a context for what is legible. The supplements from the experts, though learned, are hypothetical and are understandably dependent not only on details in Genesis but also on ones in texts such as the Aramaic Levi Document, the Visions of Amram, Jubilees, and others.

The focus here will be on the information in 4Q559 as it may relate to the issues raised above in connection with the chronology of Jacob's life. The first three fragments of 4Q559 (that is, the ones numbered frgs. 1-3 in Puech's edition) appear to cover some of the same stretches of time and may, given the many affinities between Jubilees and other texts found in

[15] Émile Puech, "559. 4QpapChronologie biblique ar", in Puech (ed.), *Qumrân Grotte 4 XXVII. Texts araméens, deuxième partie* (DJD 37), Oxford, Clarendon, 2009, 266, 267. The photograph is Planche XV. The complete edition of the text occupies pp. 263-89.

[16] Michael Wise, "To Know the Times and the Seasons: A Study of the Aramaic Chronograph 4Q559", *JSP* 8/15 (1997), 3-51. For an earlier edition, see Robert A. Eisenman and Michael Wise, T*he Dead Sea Scrolls Uncovered. The First Complete Translation and Interpretation of 50 Key Documents Withheld for Over 35 Years*, Shaftesbury, Element, 1992, 92-93.

[17] W. Nebe, "4Q559 'Biblical Chronology'", *ZAH* 10 (1997), 85-88.

[18] Hans A. Rapp, *Jakob in Bet-El. Gen 35, 1-15 und die jüdische Literatur des 3. und 2. Jahrhunderts* (Herders Biblische Studien 29), Freiburg, Herder, 2001, 160-63. The fourth chapter in the third part of his book, where these pages appear, is entitled "Chronologien und Genealogien" and treats some of the texts used in the present essay.

the Qumran caves, cast some light on the situation in Jubilees. Or perhaps Jubilees will cast some light on 4Q559.

4Q559 Fragments 1-3

It is useful to preface the treatments below with a rather minimal presentation of the text that survives on frgs. 1-3:[19]

Fragment 1

1 י]שחק יעק[ב
2]5 בא[רע
3]לח שנין [

Fragment 2

2 [בר ש]נין 20[
3 [ויש]חק ב[ר שנין
4 [בר שני]ן 65[
5 [ ]חנו[ך

Fragment 3

7 [ולוי בר שני]ן[ ]4 א[ולד
8 [בר שנין]5 אולד ית עמ[ר]ם ועמ[רם בר שנין
9 [אולד] ית אהרון ואהר[ו]ן נפק ממצ[רין
10 [ ] אלן 11 לף 536 [

For these sections of the text, we should see what the scholars who have read and supplemented them have proposed. We will take them up in the chronological order in which their publications appeared.

Wise (pp. 10-12)

By combining what he numbered as frgs. 3 (= Puech 1) and 10 (= Puech 9) into his col. 1, Wise translated:

Column 1 [7] … after I]saac [blessed him,] Jac[ob fled] [8] [and entered, at the age of fifty-]five the la[nd of the sons of] the Ea[st.] [9] [… he s]erved [fo]urteen years for [Leah] [10] [and Rachel …]*l*[ ]*vacat*

He combined his frgs. 1 (= Puech 2) and 2 (= Puech 3) to form col. 2 and translated as:

[19] The text is cited from Donald W. PARRY and Emanuel TOV (eds.), *Exegetical Texts* (The Dead Sea Scrolls Reader 2), Leiden, Brill, 2004), 136-39. They furnish editorial expansions, as evident here, but not on the scale one finds in the other editions. PARRY and TOV represent the number symbols in the text by Arabic numerals. H. RAPP (*Jakob in Bet-El*, 160-61) also presents an only slightly expanded text and places the fragments in the order 2, 1, 3 (as Nebe does; see below).

Column 2 [3] [… Abraham was] nin[ety-nine ye]ars old [4] [when he fathered Isaac. And Is]aac was [sixty years o]ld [when he fathered] [5] [Jacob. And Jacob was] sixty-five y[ears old when he fathered Levi.] [6] [He gave to Levi the book of the words of] Enoch [to preserve and give] [7] [to his (own) descendants. And Levi was thirty-f]ive when he fa[thered Kohath.] [8] [And Kohath was twenty-ni]ne when he fathered Am[r]am. And Amr[am was] [9] [one hundred and twenty-three when he fathered] Aaron. And Aaro[n[left Egy[pt] [10] [with the priests;] these [totaled] eleven thousand, five hundred and thirty-six. *vacat*

Nebe (pp. 86-87)

Nebe, arranged and interpreted the fragments differently.[20] He put in the first place his frg. 1 (= Puech 2) and rendered it as:

[1] [und Isaaq nahm sich als] 4[0-jäh]riger [Rebeqqa [2] zur Frau, und Isa]aq [zeugte als 60-jäh]riger [den [3] Jaqob, und er war] ein 65-[jäh]riger, [als Abraham [4] seine Kinder rief …,] um [ihnen]mitzuteilen […].

Frg. 2 (= Puech 1), with frg. 6 added in the last line (= Puech 9?)

[1] [und] Isaaq [schickte] Jaqob [nach Mesopotamien (?) [2] und Jaqob wohnte 6]9 [Jahre] im Lan[de Kanaan [3] und er d]iente 14 Jahre dem [Laban [4] für Lea und Rahel]

Frg. 3 (= Puech 3)

[1] [und Levi zeugt]e als 3]5-[jähriger den Qahat, und Qahat] zeugte [2] als 2[9-jähriger] den Amram, und Am[ram [3] zeug]te [als … -jähriger] den Aaron. Und Aar[on] brach auf aus Ägypt[en, er und seine ganze Familie, [4] und]diese waren 11536.

Puech (pp. 268, 271, 273-74)

Puech produced the following translation:

Frg. 1

0. … *Et après qu'*
1. *Ésau vit qu'*I]saac[*l'avait béni,*] Jac[ob *fuit devant lui/son frère*
2. *demeurer* à l'âge de 5]5 [ans] au p[ays *des fils de l'orient;*
3. *(et) Joseph fils de Jacob* avait se]rvi 30 années au[pays d'Égypte *lorsque*
4. *descendit Jacob* âge de] 100 [+ 30 (= 130) an]s[*auprès de lui*

[20] The sequence of frgs. 1-2 defended by Puech and Wise presupposes that 4Q559 first gave several dates in Jacob's life and then moved back to a chronology that begins with Abraham (Wise) or Nahor (Puech). See Rapp's comments about Wise's ordering of the fragments (*Jakob in Bet-El*, 161-62). In the sequence defended by Nebe and Rapp, that problem is avoided.

Frg. 2 (+ 3 = col. i)

01… Et Nahor
1. engendra Térah, et Térah à l'âge de]7[0 ans engendra Abram,
2. (*-c'est Abraham-,*) et Abraham à l'âge de]9[9 a]ns
3. engendra Isaac de Sarah, et Isa]ac à l'ä[ge de 60 ans engendra
4. Jacob, et Jacob à l'âge de] 65 [an]s [engendra Lévi,
5. Et il donna à Lévi *tous* les livres d']Hénoch[*pour qu'il les garde et (les) transmette*

Frg. 3 Puech thinks the bottom extension of a final letter at the top of the fragment is from the final *kaph* in חנוך in the preceding line (frg. 2 line 5).[21] Hence, he repeats that line in his translation of frg. 3 (as his alternative line numbering in the edition shows, these would be lines 6-10 of the column).

1. et il donna à Lévi tous les livres d'Héno]ch[pour qu'il les garde et (les) transmette
2. à tous ses fils. Et Lévi à l'âge de] 20[+ 20 + 10] + 4 (= 54) [an]s en[gendra Qahat
3. et Qahat à l'âge de 24 +] 5 (= 29) ans engendra Am[ra]m, et Amra[m à l'âge de
4. 115 ans engendra] Aaron, et Aar[o]n sortit d'Égyp[te
5. avec les fils de Lévi, tous] ceux-ci: 11 mille 536. *vac* (?)[Et à

The arguments formulated below build upon the proposals found in these studies and are meant to offer another perspective – to suggest some reasons to be hesitant about accepting key placements of fragments and important supplements of lines proposed by their authors.

The extant bits of text presented above allow us to recognize that at least Isaac, Jacob, Enoch, Amram, and Aaron play a part in it. These are the names that survive fully or fully enough to identify. Other names must be supplied, some with a high degree of certainty (e.g. Qahat), others less so. Also, the third fragment offers a priestly genealogy. It would be reasonable, then, to inquire whether frgs. 1-2 also trace a family line but from an earlier point in it. Wise, Nebe, and Puech have concluded that they do.[22] If so, one would have helpful information for reconstructing frgs. 1-2. If the text mentions, in genealogical sentences, Isaac as the father of Jacob and later notes that Amram begat a son, it would be sensible to think that in the intervening but missing text Jacob's fathering Levi and Levi's begetting Amram were mentioned.

So, there is evidence in the text (frg. 3) that it contains a genealogy of priests, but the first three fragments of 4Q559 do not consist exclusively

[21] Wise interprets the stroke in the same way ("To Know the Times and the Seasons", 19).

[22] H. Rapp (*Jakob in Bet-El*, 163) appears to do so as well.

of genealogical lines. They contain other content such as the reference to Enoch (if the name is read correctly) and the one to the Exodus from Egypt. The most intriguing and challenging feature of the text is the set of numbers it includes. Some of these are preserved fully, others only partially. There are two that should be treated in this context:

Fragment 1 line 2: the number *5*, with the possibility, in fact the strong likelihood, that one or more larger numerals preceded it.[23] The small blank space to the right of the five strokes makes it highly probable that the ending number was just *5* and not some other digit from *6-9*.[24] Isaac and Jacob are named in the preceding line.

Fragment 2 line 4: all symbols for *65* – *20*, *20*, *20*, and *5* – are present, with a space both before and after them indicating that they constitute the entire number.

The Two Numbers

Wise and Puech conclude that the number ending in -*5* refers to Jacob's age at the time of his flight to Laban and *65* designates Jacob's age when he became the father of Levi.[25] They work from the latter inference by subtracting ten years from *65*, Jacob's age when Levi was born. Those ten years included the first seven-year period that Jacob served Laban plus three more until the birth of his third son, assuming that the sons were born in consecutive years. They thus arrive at *55* for the first number. I think the conclusion is questionable.[26] If 4Q559 puts the flight to Haran when Jacob was 55, it would be far from his expected age and certainly, as they recognize, without parallel in early chronologies.

In order to evaluate their arguments, we should examine the contexts for the numbers. Both Wise and Puech arrange the fragments such that a small piece (Puech's frg. 1) gives the partial number -*5*. Then the small frg. 2, which has the number *65*, is placed by both scholars in close proximity to the larger frg. 3 on the grounds that they are continuous in content – both are parts of a genealogy in which the order of names is known from Genesis. Wise and Puech think, as we have seen, that they follow directly on each other – the bottom tip of a final letter at the top of frg. 3 is the end of the final *kaph* in חנוך in the last line of frg. 2.

[23] NEBE adds four strokes to the five that can be read to produce the number *9*, part of *69*, the age of Jacob when he fled from Esau according to Jubilees ("4Q559 'Biblical Chronology'", 86). See the next note.

[24] As the representation of *six* at the end of the number 11,536 in frg. 3 line 5 shows, all the strokes representing the number are grouped together, with no space between them.

[25] M. WISE, "To Know the Times and the Seasons", 14-17; É. PUECH, "559. 4Qpap-Chronologie biblique ar", 269, 273.

[26] So also H. RAPP, *Jakob in Bet-El*, 161 n. 82.

The argument from the lower end of a final letter is, of course, not strong. The short stroke at the top of frg. 3 could be from a final *kaph* in the last line of frg. 2, but it could as well be from a final letter in another word. The argument from genealogical context has more force and should be addressed. If frgs. 1-3 are structured as a genealogy, it would be very helpful for placing them and interpreting the words and numbers preserved. But do frgs. 1-2 take the form of a genealogy?

Wise and Puech recognize that there is no genealogy evidenced on frg. 1. They supplement the five visible strokes on line 2 to yield *55* by inserting the figures for *20*, *20*, and *10* before it. As they note, the context is not a genealogical statement because the accusative particle ית does not separate the name of the son (Jacob in line 1) from that of the father (Isaac) as it does in the preserved genealogical lines. Both of them conclude that the context deals with Jacob's age of 55 when he went to Haran.

As for frg. 2, Wise and Puech interpret it as genealogical in content, although they do not agree on the generation with which it begins. Wise thinks the first lines deal with Abraham's fathering Isaac and Isaac begetting Esau and Jacob. Puech thinks they record Terah siring Abram and Abram becoming the father of Isaac. But they agree that according to line 4 Jacob was 65 years of age when Levi was born. Though his name is not preserved, Levi would be a good choice for the son in light of frg. 3 which definitely contains genealogical sentences tracing the priestly family from Qahat through Amram to Aaron.

It is the case, nevertheless, that the legible letters on frg. 2 give little support to the hypothesis that it contains a genealogy. One could make a case, and Wise and Puech have done so, that *65* is the age of someone in a genealogy. In line 1 there is apparently the symbol for *20* (marked by Puech with a supralinear circlet), in line 2 there is a plural ending (probably of שׁנין) followed by a number, in line 3 there are the last two consonants of what is likely to be the name *Isaac* followed by what could be the first letter of בר, a standard term in expressions for the age of a person (X was a son of Y years when he became the father of Z), and then the number *65*, possibly preceded by the last letter of שנין. The next line, however, is not genealogical, if the preceding readings are correct, because the preserved letters are those of the name *Enoch* (so Puech and Wise). The reading is not certain but possible. Wise and Puech understand the line to refer to Jacob's giving the ancestral books to Levi, as in Jub 45:16, which, however, does not single out Enoch but mentions only the books of the ancestors as a group. So, the thesis that frg. 2 should be read as a genealogy from Abraham (or Terah) to Levi has no secure basis; only the letter ב in line 4 could be cited in support if it is part of the word בר. How distant frg. 2 was from frg. 3, which is genealogical, is unknown.

The lack of evidence for lines that take the form of genealogies in frgs. 1-2 encourages caution in interpreting the numbers *-5* and *65*, since the context for neither of them is at all clear. We have seen above that other ancient chronographers date Jacob's flight from Esau to a time when he was older (69, 73, 77), ages that are considerably more plausible and more in tune with data in Genesis. Why should one think that the number in frg. 1 line 2 is *55* and that it is Jacob's age when he left his home and went to Haran?

As we have seen, Wise and Puech have drawn their inference from the number *65* in frg. 2 line 4. But how do we know that the latter number specifies Jacob's age upon becoming the father of Levi? Their hypothesis assumes the context is genealogical, but it is far from certain that it is. An entire genealogical statement has to be reconstructed around it to yield the result. Moreover, in all the other ancient chronologies Jacob is much older when Leah bears Levi. The possible reference to Enoch in line 5 could be an indication that here Jacob is giving all the books of his ancestors to Levi, but no ancient text specifies Enoch as the ancestor whose books Jacob bequeathed to Levi.

We should grant that Wise and Puech, who are both fully aware of the evidence from other chronologies for Jacob's life, may be correct in their interpretations of the numbers. In my estimation, however, it is safer to conclude that the full form of the number *-5* in frg. 1 is too uncertain to identify as Jacob's age when leaving his parents. Perhaps, and this is only a guess, it is part of the number *15*, the number of years that Abraham, Isaac, and Jacob lived together in the land. As for the fully preserved number *65*, its referent is also unknown. Jubilees mentions that Jacob was 63 when he and his mother discussed marriage and she blessed him (this is his age in Seder Olam when Isaac blessed him). By implication, Jubilees puts his departure for Haran at age 69. Perhaps the number refers to an event that happened between the two.[27]

[27] W. Nebe, "4Q559 'Biblical Chronology'", 86 n. 14) thinks it designates Isaac's age when Abraham summoned his children. Jubilees 20:1 places the event in the year of the world 2052. The book does not name the year when Isaac was born but sets Sarah's pregnancy in 1987 (16:15), 65 years before Abraham instructed his sons. H. Rapp (*Jakob in Beth-El*, 161-62) favors his interpretation and notes that in Jubilees 20 Isaac receives his inheritance from Abraham.

PUBLICATIONS D'ÉMILE PUECH

1971

Articles de revues

- « Sur la racine SLḤ en hébreu et en araméen », *Semitica* 21, 5-19.

1973

Articles de revues

- « L'inscription de la citadelle d'Amman », *Revue Biblique* 80, 531-546 (en collaboration avec A. ROFÉ).

1974

Articles de revues

- « L'inscription du tunnel de Siloé », *Revue Biblique* 81, 196-214.

1975

Recensions

- J.B. PECKHAM, The Development of the Late Phoenician Scripts, Cambridge Mas., 1968, *Revue Biblique* 82, 446-452.
- R. DEGEN, Altaramäische Grammatik, Wiesbaden, 1969, *Revue Biblique* 82, 614-615.

1976

Articles de revues

- « Deux nouveaux sceaux ammonites », *Revue Biblique* 83, 59-62.
- « Le rite d'offrande de cheveux d'après une inscription phénicienne de Kition, vers 800 avant notre ère », *Rivista di Studi Fenici* 4, 11-21.

Article de dictionnaire

- « L'inscription de la citadelle d'Amman, revue », dans : *The Interpreter's Dictionary of the Bible, Supplementary Volume*, Nashville, 1976, *Inscriptions*, figure 2, 433.

1977

Articles de revues

- « Milkom, le dieu ammonite, en Amos I 15 », *Vetus Testamentum* 27, 117-125.
- « Documents épigraphiques de Buseirah », *Levant* 9, 11-20.
- « L'acte de vente d'une maison à Kafar Bébayu en 135 de notre ère », *Revue de Qumrân* 34, 213-221.
- « L'inscription phénicienne du trône d'Aštart à Séville », *Rivista di Studi Fenici* 5, 85-92.

Recensions

- P.E. Dion, La langue de Ya'udi, Waterloo, 1974, *Revue Biblique* 84, 446-447 et *Revue d'Assyriologie* 71, 183-185.
- *Encyclopaedia biblica. Thesaurus rerum biblicarum alphabetico ordine digestus, ed. Institutum Bialik et Museum Antiquitatum Judaicarum*, VII, Qaat ad Shelishia, Hierosolymis, 1976, *Revue Biblique* 84, 128-129.

1978

Articles de revues

- « Remarques sur la colonne XXXVIII de 11QtgJob », *Revue de Qumrân* 35, 401-407 (en collaboration avec F. García Martínez).
- « Un ivoire de Bît - Guši (Arpad) trouvé à Nimrud », *Syria* 55, 163-169.
- « Fragments du Psaume 122 dans un manuscrit hébreu de la grotte IV », *Revue de Qumrân* 36, 547-554.

Revue de vulgarisation

- « Les Esséniens et la vie future », *Le Monde de la Bible* 4, 38-40.

Recensions

- B. Jongeling - C.J. Labuscagne - A.S. van der Woude, Aramaic Texts from Qumran with Translations and Annotations, Leiden, 1976, *Revue de Qumrân* 36, 589-591.
- J. Hoftijzer - G. van der Kooij, Aramaic Texts from Deir 'Alla, *Documenta et Monumenta Orientis Antiqui*, Leiden, 1976, *Revue Biblique* 85, 114-117.

1979

Articles de revues

- « Remarques sur l'écriture de 1QS VII-VIII », *Revue de Qumrân* 37, 35-43.
- « Remarques sur quelques inscriptions phéniciennes de Chypre », *Semitica* 29, 19-43.
- « Remarques sur quelques inscriptions christo-palestiniennes de Kh. es-Samra », *Liber Annuus* 29, 259-269.

Recensions

– R. DE VAUX - J.T. MILIK, I Archéologie, II Tefillim, Mezuzôt et Targums (4Q128-4Q157), *Discoveries in the Judaean Desert* VI, Oxford, 1977, *Revue Biblique* 86, 275-277.
– J. POUILLY, La règle de la communauté de Qumrân, Paris, 1976, *Revue de Qumrân* 37, 1979, 103-111.
– J.B. PRITCHARD, Recovering Sarepta. A Phoenician City. Excavations at Sarafand, Lebanon, 1969-1974, Princeton, 1978, *Revue Biblique* 86, 279-281.

1980

Article dans des ouvreages collectifs

– J. BRIEND, J.B. HUMBERT assistés de E. PUECH, *Tell Keisân (1971-1976). Une cité phénicienne en Galilée* (Orbis Biblicus et Orientalis, Series archaeologica I), Fribourg-Göttingen-Paris, 1980, 392 pp. - 142 pls et un dépliant. (« niveaux 9c à 11 », 216-234 et Pl. 67 à 80, 130 et 132 ; « mise à jour du catalogue des monnaies (Fulco *Revue Biblique*) », 235-241 et Pl. 133 ; « timbre amphorique », 254-255 et Pl. 87 et 135 ; « glyptique : sceaux inscrits et tessons gravés », 296-299, voir 286, note 1, et Pl. 89-90 et 136 ; « inscriptions et incisions, poids », 301-310 et Pl. 91-94, 136-137 ; « ivoires », 327-329 et Pl. 101).

Articles de revues

– « Fragments d'un rouleau de la Genèse provenant du Désert de Juda (Gen 33,18-34,6) », *Revue de Qumrân* 38, 163-166.
– « Abécédaire et liste de noms propres hébreux du début du IIe s. A.D. », *Revue Biblique* 87, 118-126.
– « Une inscription éthiopienne ancienne au Sinaï (Wadi Hajjaj) », *Revue Biblique* 87, 597-601.

1981

Article dans des ouvreages collectifs

– « Athalie, fille d'Achab, et la chronologie des rois d'Israël et de Juda », dans : R. AGUIRRE, García LOPEZ (éd.), *Escritos de Biblia y Oriente. Miscelanea commemorativa del 25e aniversario del Instituto Biblico y Arqueologico (Casa de Santiago) de Jerusalén* (Biblioteca Salmanticensis, 28), Salamanca – Jerusalén, 117-136.

Articles de revues

– « Remarques sur quelques inscriptions phéniciennes de Byblos », *Rivista di Studi Fenici* 9, 153-168.
– « L'ivoire inscrit d'Arslan Tash et les rois de Damas », *Revue Biblique* 88, 544-562.

Recensions

– R. MOOREY and P. PARR (éd.), Archaeology in the Levant. Essays for Kathleen Kenyon, Warminster, 1978, *Revue Biblique* 88, 93-96.

- F. Bron, Recherches sur les inscriptions phéniciennes de Karatepe, Genève – Paris, 1979, *Revue Biblique* 88, 96-98.
- R.S. Tomback, A Comparative Semitic Lexicon of the Phoenician and Punic Languages (SBL Dissertations Series, 32), Missoula, 1978, *Revue Biblique* 88, 99-101.
- S. Segert, A Grammar of Phoenician and Punic, Munich, 1976, *Revue Biblique* 88, 268-269.
- M. Kochavi - A.F. Rainey - I. Singer - R. Giveon - A. Demsky, Aphek - Antipatris 1974-1977, The Inscriptions, Tel Aviv, 1978, *Revue Biblique* 88, 1981, 269-270.
- M. Heltzer - M. Ohana, The Extra-Biblical Tradition of Hebrew Personal Names, From the First Temple Period to the End of the Talmudic Period (*'ivrît*), Haifa, 1978, *Revue Biblique* 88, 270-272.
- E.Y. Kutscher, Studies in Galilean Aramaic, Translated from the Hebrew Original and Annoted with Additional Notes from the Author's Handcopy, by M. Sokoloff, Ramat Gan, 1976, *Revue Biblique* 88, 272-273.
- J.A. Fitzmyer - D.J. Harrington, A Manual of Palestinian Aramaic Texts (Second Century B.C. - Second Century A.D.), Rome, 1978, *Revue Biblique* 88, 273-274.
- G.R. Driver, Semitic Writing. From Pictograph to Alphabet, Oxford, [3]1976, *Revue Biblique* 88, 461.

1982

Articles de revues

- « Note sur la particule accusativale en Phénicien », *Semitica* 32, 51-55.
- « Note d'épigraphie latine palestinienne. Le dieu *Turmasgada* à Césarée Maritime », *Revue Biblique* 89, 210-221.
- « Les nécropoles juives palestiniennes au tournant de notre ère », *Les Quatre Fleuves* 15-16, 35-55.
- « Les inscriptions araméennes I et III de Sfiré : nouvelles lectures », *Revue Biblique* 89, 576-587.
- « Ossuaires inscrits d'une tombe du Mont des Oliviers », *Liber Annuus* 32, 355-372.
- « Couvercle de jarre inscrit », *Estudios Biblicos* 40, 347-352.

1983

Articles dans des ouvrages collectifs

- « Quelques remarques sur l'alphabet au deuxième millénaire avant J. C. », dans : S.F. Bondì (ed.), *Atti del I congresso internazionale di studi fenici e punici - Roma, 5-10 Novembre 1979* (Collezione di Studi Fenici, 16/2), Rome, 1983, 563-581.

Articles de revues

- « Présence phénicienne dans les îles à la fin du IIe millénaire. A propos de deux coupes inscrites », *Revue Biblique* 90, 365-395.

– « Notes d'onomastique christo-palestinienne de Kh. es-Samra », *Annali del Instituto Orientale di Napoli*, 43, 505-526.
– « Inscriptions funéraires palestiniennes : tombeau de Jason et ossuaires », *Revue Biblique* 90, 481-533.
– « La racine *šhyt - šh't* en araméen et en hébreu. A propos de Sfiré I A 24, 1QH[a] III 30 et 36 (= XI 31 et 37) et Ezéchiel », *Revue de Qumrân* 43, 367-378.

Recensions

– A. ABOU ASSAF - P. BORDREUIL - A.R. MILLARD, La statue de Tell Fekherye et son inscription biblingue assyro-araméenne, Paris, 1982, *Revue Biblique* 90, 594-596.
– J.A.L. LEE, A Lexical Study of the Septuagint of the Pentateuch, Chico, 1983, *Revue Biblique* 90, 606.

1984

Article dans des ouvreages collectifs

– « Les poids », dans : A. CHAMBON, *Tell el-Far'ah I, L'âge du Fer* (Editions Recherches sur les Civilisations, Mémoire, 31), Paris, 1984, pp. 79-84, 242-243, pl. 67.

Articles de revues

– « Un emploi méconnu de *wl'* en araméen et en hébreu », *Revue Biblique* 91, 88-101.
– « La "Crainte d'Isaac" en Gn 31,42 et 53 », *Vetus Testamentum* 34, 356-361.
– « Courtes inscriptions de la région de Qumrân », *Revue de Qumrân* 44, 525-535.
– « L'inscription christo-palestinienne d''Ayoun Mousa (Mont Nebo) », *Liber Annuus* 34, 319-328.
– « L'inscription christo-palestinienne du monastère d'el-Quweismeh », *Liber Annuus* 34, 341-346.

Revue de vulgarisation

– « Los Esenios y la vida futura », *El Mundo de la Biblia* 4, 38-40.

Recensions

– Traductions hébraïques des Évangiles rassemblées par J. CARMIGNAC : I - The Four Gospels Translated into Hebrew by W. GREENFIELD in 1831, Introduction par J. CARMIGNAC, Turnhout, 1980 ; II - Évangiles de Matthieu et de Marc traduits en hébreu en 1668 par GIOVANNI BATTISTA IONA retouchés en 1805 par THOMAS YEATES, introduction par J. CARMIGNAC, Turnhout, 1981 ; III - Évangiles de Luc et de Jean traduits en hébreu en 1668 par GIOVANNI BATTISTA IONA retouchés en 1805 par THOMAS YEATES, Turnhout, 1982, introduction par J. CARMIGNAC, *Revue Biblique* 91, 124-125.
– M. STONE, Scriptures, Sects and Visions. A Profile of Judaism from Ezra to the Jewish Revolts, Oxford, 1982, *Revue de Qumrân* 44, 591-593.

- J. Murphy O'Connor, Guide archéologique de la Terre Sainte, Paris, 1980, *Le Monde de la Bible* 32, 59-60.

1985

Articles dans des ouvrages collectifs

- « L'inscription sur plâtre de Tell Deir 'Alla », dans : J. Amitai (éd.), *Biblical Archaeology Today. Proceedings of the International Congress on Biblical Archaeology, Jerusalem April 1984*, Jerusalem, Israel Exploration Society, 354-365.

Articles de revues

- « L'inscription de la statue d'Amman et la paléographie ammonite », *Revue Biblique* 92, 5-24.

Recensions

- J.W. Betlyon, The Coinage and Mints of Phoenicia. The Pre-Alexandrine Period, *Harvard Semitic Monograph* 26, Chico, 1982, *Revue Biblique* 92, 285-289.
- K.P. Jackson, The Ammonite Language of the Iron Age (Harvard Semitic Monograph 27), Chico, 1983, *Revue Biblique* 92, 289-290.
- M.J. Fuentes Estañol, Vocabulario fenicio, *Bibliotheca. Fenicia* 1, Barcelona, 1980, *Revue Biblique* 92, 290-293.
- A.F.L. Beeston - M.A. Ghul - W.W. Müller - J. Ryckmans, Sabaic Dictionary (English-French-Arabic) - Dictionnaire sabéen (anglais-français-arabe), Louvain la Neuve – Beyrouth, 1982 et J. Copeland Biella, Dictionary of Old South Arabic, Sabaean Dialect (Harvard Semitic Monograph 25), Chico, 1982, *Revue Biblique* 92, 293-294.
- La Biblia, versio dels textos originals i commentari pels monjos de Montserrat, XII, Saviesa, versio de Dom M.M. Estradé, Ecclesiàstic, versio de Dom J.M. Bruguera, commentari de Dom R.M. Diaz, Montserrat, 1982, *Revue Biblique* 92, 307.
- R. McClive Good, The Sheep of his Pasture. A Study of the Hebrew Noun 'Am(m) and its Semitic Cognates, Chico, 1983, *Revue Biblique* 92, 307-308.
- E.Y. Kutscher, The Language and Linguistic Background of the Isaiah Scroll (IQIs[a]). Indices and Corrections by E. Qimron, Introduction by Sh. Morag, Leiden, 1979, *Revue Biblique* 92, 308-309.
- H.W. Attridge and R.A. Oden, Philo of Byblos. The Phoenician History. Introduction, Critical Text, Translation, Notes, Washington, 1981, *Revue Biblique* 92, 312-313.
- Th. Fischer, Silber aus dem Grab Davids ? Jüdisches und Hellenistisches auf Münzen des Seleukidenkönigs Antiochos VII. 132-130 v. Chr., Bochum, 1983, *Revue Biblique* 92, 313-314.
- R.S. Hanson, Tyrian Influence in the Upper Galilee, Cambridge Mas., 1980, *Revue Biblique* 92, 314.
- V. Cottini, La vita futura nel Libro dei Proverbi. Contributo alla storia dell'esegesi, Gerusalemme, 1984, *Revue Biblique* 92, 435-438.
- P. Figueras, Decorated Jewish Ossuaries, Leiden, 1983, *Revue Biblique* 92, 577-581.

1986

Articles de revues

– « The Tell el-Fûl Jar Inscription and the *Netînîm* », *Bulletin of the American Schools of Oriental Research* 261, 69-72.
– « Ta droite assiste mon épée », Note sur le Ps XVIII, 36, par B. Couroyer, Note paléographique, par É. Puech, *Revue Biblique* 93, 38-51.
– « Origine de l'alphabet. I - Documents en alphabets linéaire et cunéiforme du IIe millénaire », *Revue Biblique* 93, 161-213.
– « Les inscriptions phéniciennes d'Amrit et les dieux guérisseurs du sanctuaire », *Syria* 63/3-4, 327-342.
– « Une inscription syriaque palestinienne », *Liber Annuus* 36, 309-316.
– « *In memoriam* : l'Abbé Jean Carmignac », *Revue de Qumrân* 47, 323-324.

Revues de vulgarisation

– « La stèle de Mésha : un roi de Moab proclame ses victoires sur Joram d'Israël », *Le Monde de la Bible* 46, 28-29.
– « L'inscription de Deir 'Alla: Admonitions de Balaam, l'homme qui voit les dieux », *Le Monde de la Bible* 46, 36-39.
– « Penuel - Jacob – Israël », *Le Monde de la Bible* 46, 40.

Recensions

– J.A. Hackett, The Balaam Text from Deir 'Alla, Chico, 1984, *Revue Biblique* 93, 285-287.
– Studi in onore di Edda Bresciani, publicati a cura di S.F. Bondi, S. Pernigotti, F. Serra e A. Vivian, Pisa, 1985, *Revue Biblique* 93, 446.

1987

Articles dans des ouvrages collectifs

– « Le texte "ammonite" de Deir 'Alla. Les admonitions de Balaam (première partie) », dans : *La vie de la Parole. De l'Ancien au Nouveau Testament. Etudes d'exégèse et d'herméneutique bibliques offertes à Pierre Grelot professeur à l'Institut Catholique de Paris*, sous la responsabilité du Département des Études Bibliques de l'Institut Catholique de Paris, Paris, Desclée, 1987, 13-30.

Articles de revues

– « Notes sur le manuscrit de 11Qmelkîsédeq », *Revue de Qumrân* 48, 483-513.
– « Notes sur le manuscrit des Cantiques du Sacrifice du Sabbat trouvé à Masada », *Revue de Qumrân* 48, 575-583.
– « The Canaanite Inscriptions of Lachish and Their Religious Background », *Tel Aviv* 13-14(1986-87), 13-25.
– « *In memoriam* : Père Pierre Benoit », *Revue de Qumrân* 48, I-II.

Recensions

– L. Mildenberg, The Coinage of the Bar Kokhba War, Frankfurt am Main – Aarau – Salzburg, 1984, *Revue Biblique* 94, 440-442.

– A. TAL, The Samaritan Targum of the Pentateuch. A Critical Edition. Part III: Introductio, Tel Aviv, 1983, *Revue Biblique* 94, 442-444.
– C. NEWSOM, Songs of the Sabbath Sacrifice: a Critical Edition, Atlanta, 1985, *Revue Biblique* 94, 604-608.
– R. WEIS, The Aramaic Targum of Job, Tel Aviv, 1979, *Revue Biblique* 94, 633-634.

1988

Ouvrage collectif

– *Mémorial Jean Carmignac. Etudes Qumrâniennes*, sous la direction d'Émile PUECH et Florentino GARCÍA MARTÍNEZ, *Revue de Qumrân* 13, Paris.

Articles dans des ouvrages collectifs

– « Les Écoles dans l'Israël pré-exilique : données épigraphiques », dans : *Supplements to Vetus Testamentum* 40, ed. by J. EMERTON, Leiden, 189-203.
– « Quelques aspects de la restauration du rouleau des Hymnes (1QH) », *Symposium on the Manuscripts from the Judaean Desert, Institute of Jewish Studies of University College London, June 11-12 1987*, ed. by G. VERMES (Journal of Jewish Studies, 39), 38-55.

Articles de revues

– « Avant-propos », *Revue de Qumrân* 13, VII-IX.
– « Biographie de Jean Carmignac », *Revue de Qumrân* 13, 1-7.
– « Un Hymne essénien en partie retrouvé et les Béatitudes. 1QH V 12-VI 18 (= col. XIII - XIV 7) et 4QBéat. », *Revue de Qumrân* 13, 59-88.
– « Une inscription syriaque palestinienne. Note additionnelle », *Liber Annuus* 37, 349-352.
– « Une inscription syriaque sur mosaïque », *Liber Annuus* 38, 267-270.
– « Les inscriptions christo-palestiniennes de Khirbet el-Kursi – Amman », *Liber Annuus* 38, 383-389.
– « Quarante ans de découvertes au Désert de Juda » (Procès verbaux des séances de la Société des Lettres, Sciences et Arts de l'Aveyron, XLV/2), 244-259.

Revue de vulgarisation

– « Les inscriptions d'Arad », *Le Monde de la Bible* 54, 38-40.
– « Aux sources de la Prière du Seigneur », *Le Monde de la Bible* 55, 38-40.

Recensions

– H. ROUILLARD, La péricope de Balaam (Nombres 22-24). La prose et les «Oracles», Paris, 1985, *Revue d'Histoire des Religions* 205/3, 299-301.
– C. GIANOTTO, Melchisedek e la sua tipologia, Tradizioni giudaiche, cristiane e gnostice (sec. II a. C. - sec. III d. C.), Brescia, 1984, *Revue Biblique* 95, 113-114.

- G. LÜDERITZ, Corpus jüdischer Zeugnisse aus der Cyrenaika, mit einem Anhang von Joyce M. Reynolds, Wiesbaden, 1983, *Revue Biblique* 95, 140-141.
- M.A. FRIEDMAN, Jewish Marriage in Palestine. A Cairo Geniza Study. Vol. I, The *Ketubba* Traditions of Eretz Israel. II, The *Ketubba* Texts, Tel Aviv - New York, 1980-1981, *Revue Biblique* 95, 141-142.
- Traductions hébraïques des Évangiles rassemblées par J. CARMIGNAC, 4, Die vier Evangelien ins Hebräische übersetzt von FRANZ DELITZSCH (1877-1890-1902). Introduction par J. CARMIGNAC, Kritischer Apparat der zwölf Auflagen von H. KLEIN, Turnhout, 1984, *Revue Biblique* 95, 145.
- M. BAILLET, Qumrân grotte 4. III (4Q482-4Q520) (Discoveries in the Judaean Desert VII), Oxford, 1982, *Revue Biblique* 95, 404-411.
- D.A. BERTRAND, La Vie Grecque d'Adam et Ève. Introduction, texte, traduction et commentaire, Paris, 1987, *Revue Biblique* 95, 584-585.
- J. NAVEH - SH. SHAKED, Amulets and Magic Bowls. Aramaic Incantations of Late Antiquity, Jerusalem, 1985, *Revue Biblique* 95, 585-588.
- J.M. LINDENBERGER, The Aramaic Proverbs of Ahiqar, Baltimore and London, 1983, *Revue Biblique* 95, 588-592.
- N. AVIGAD, Hebrew Bullae from the Time of Jeremiah. Remnants of a Burnt Archive, Jerusalem, 1986,
- N. AVIGAD, *Bwlwt 'brywt mymy yrmyhw. 'wdym mwslym m'rkywn t'wdwt*, Jerusalem, 1986, *Revue Biblique* 95, 592-594.

1989

Articles dans des ouvrages collectifs

- « Une inscription araméenne sur un couvercle de sarcophage », *Mémorial Yigael Yadin, Eretz Israel* 20, 161*-165*.
- « Hazor once again in new Mari Documents », par A. MALAMAT, « *Addendum* » par Émile PUECH, dans : M. LEBEAU et Ph. TALON (éd.), *Reflets des Deux Fleuves. Volume de mélanges offerts à André Finet* (Akkadica, Supplementum VI), Leuven, 117-118.

Articles de revues

- « Notes en marge de 11QpaléoLévitique. Le fragment L, des fragments inédits et une jarre à manuscrits de la grotte 11 », *Revue Biblique* 96, 161-183.
- « 4QEz[a] : note additionnelle », *Revue de Qumrân* 53, 107-108.
- « *In memoriam* : l'Abbé Jean Starcky », *Revue de Qumrân* 53, 3-6.
- « Nouvelle inscription en alphabet cunéiforme court à Sarepta », *Revue Biblique* 96, 338-344.
- « Une inscription sur jarre en christo-palestinien à Umm er-Rassas (Jordanie) », *Liber Annuus* 39, 268-270.

Revue de vulgarisation

- « La synagogue judéo-chrétienne du Mont Sion », *Le Monde de la Bible* 57, 18-19.
- « Abbé Jean Starcky (1909-1988). Le savant », *Le Monde de la Bible* 58, 54.

Recensions

- GEORGE E. MENDENHALL, The Syllabic Inscriptions from Byblos, Beirut, 1985, *Orientalia* 58, 134-138.
- M. WEINFELD, The Organizational Pattern and the Penal Code of the Qumran Sect. A Comparison with Guilds and Religious Associations of the Hellenistic-Roman Period, Fribourg-Göttingen, 1986, *Revue de Qumrân* 53,147-148.
- SAUL M. OLYAN, Asherah and the Cult of Yahweh in Israel, Atlanta 1988, *Revue Biblique* 96, 584-588.
- P. BORDREUIL, Catalogue des sceaux ouest-sémitiques inscrits de la Bibliothèque Nationale, du Musée du Louvre et du Musée Biblique de Bible et Terre Sainte, Paris, 1986, *Revue Biblique* 96, 588-592.

1990

Articles dans des ouvrages collectifs

- « Ben Sira 48,11 et la résurrection », dans : H.W. ATTRIDGE, J.J. COLLINS, Th.H. TOBIN (éd.), *Of Scribes and Scrolls. Studies on the Hebrew Bible, Intertestamental Judaism, and Christian Origins, presented to John Strugnell on the occasion of his sixtieth birthday* (College Theology Society Resources in Religion, 5), Lanham-New York-London, 1990, 81-90.
- « Notes sur des inscriptions phéniciennes de Kition et Kato-Paphos », dans : *Hommages à Maurice Sznycer II*, *Semitica* 39, 99-109.
- « Qumrân », dans : J.-L. VESCO (éd.), *L'Ancien Testament. Cent ans d'exégèse à l'Ecole Biblique* (Cahiers de la Revue Biblique 28), Paris, pp. 199-214.
- « La glyptique de Tell Keisan (1971-1976) », par O. KEEL, avec une contribution de E. PUECH, dans : Othmar KEEL / Menakhem SHUVAL / Christoph UEHLINGER (éd.), *Studien zu den Stempelsiegeln aus Palästina/ Israel*, Band III - *Die Frühe Eisenzeit. Ein Workshop* (Orbis Biblicus et Orientalis, 100), Freiburg-Göttingen, pp. 163-260 (248-253, édition revue et augmentée de 1980).

Articles de revues

- « 11QPsAp[a] : un rituel d'exorcismes. Essai de reconstruction », *Revue de Qumrân* 55, 377-408.

Revues de vulgarisation

- « Un culte lunaire ? », *Le Monde de la Bible* 65, 14.
- « L'Ecole Biblique de Jérusalem a cent ans », *Le Monde de la Bible* 66, 58-59.
- « Le iscrizioni di Arad, *Il Mondo della Bibbia*, 4/agosto - ottobre, 38-40.
- « Alle sorgenti della preghiera del Signore », *Il Mondo della Bibbia*, 5/nov.-dic., 38-40.

Traduction française et mise à jour

- M. PEARLMAN, *Les rouleaux de la mer Morte dans la Maison du Livre*, traduit de l'anglais et mis à jour par E. PUECH, Jérusalem.

1991

Ouvrage collectif

- *Mémorial Jean Starcky*, I, sous la direction de É. PUECH et F. GARCÍA - MARTÍNEZ, *Revue de Qumrân* 15.

Articles dans des ouvrages collectifs

- « Capitolo X - Giudaismo A. C. », « Capitolo XI – Qumrân », dans : Jean-Luc Vesco (a cura di), *Cent'anni di esegesi. I. L'antico Testamento. L'École biblique di Gerusalemme* (Supplementi alla Rivista Biblica 25), Bologna, Associazione Biblica Italiana, 189-203.
- « Approches paléographiques de l'inscription sur plâtre de Deir 'Alla », dans : J. HOFTIJZER and G. VAN DER KOOIJ (éd.), *The Balaam Text from Deir 'Alla Re-evaluated. Proceedings of the International Symposium held at Leiden 21-24 August 1989*, Leiden, Brill, 221-238.
- « Les premières émissions byblites et les rois de Byblos à la fin du Ve siècle avant J. C. », dans : E. ACQUARO (ed.), *Atti del II congresso internazionale di Studi Fenici e Punici, Roma, 9-15 Novembre 1987* (Collezione di studi fenici 30), Rome, Consiglio Nazionale delle Richerche, 1991, pp. 287 - 298.
- « La tablette cunéiforme de Beth Shemesh, premier témoin de la séquence des lettres du Sud-Sémitique », dans : Cl. BAURAIN - C. BONNET - V. KRINGS (éd.), *Phoinikeia Grammata, Lire et écrire en Méditerrannée. Actes du Colloque de Liège, 15-18 novembre 1989* (Studia Phoenicia XIII), Namur, Société des Études Classiques, 1991, 33-47.

Articles de revues

- « Jean Starcky 1909 - 1988 (biographie) », *Revue de Qumrân* 15, 1-9.
- « Bibliographie de Jean Starcky », *Revue de Qumrân* 15, 11-20.
- « Le Testament de Qahat en araméen de la grotte 4 (4QTestQah) », *Revue de Qumrân* 15, 23-54.
- « 4Q525 et les péricopes des Béatitudes en Ben Sira et Matthieu », *Revue Biblique* 98, 1991, 80-106.
- « Les fragments non identifiés de 8KhXIIgr et le manuscrit grec des Douze Petits Prophètes », *Revue Biblique* 98,161-169.

Revue de vulgarisation

- « La sinagoga giudeo-cristiana del Monte Sion. In questo edificio di tipo sinagogale diversi elementi indicano un luogo di culto giudeo-cristiano », *Il mondo della Bibbia* 7, 18-19.

Recensions

- SABATINO MOSCATI (éd.), Les Phéniciens, Paris, 1989, *Revue Biblique* 98, 436-439.
- ROBERT S. MERRILLEES, Alashia Revisited, Paris, 1987, *Revue Biblique* 98, 600-602.

– OTHMAR KEEL - MENAKHEM SHUVAL - CHRISTOPH UEHLINGER, *Studien zu den Stempelsiegeln aus Palästina/ Israel*, Band III, *Die Frühe Eisenzeit. Ein Workshop*, Freiburg – Göttingen, 1990, *Revue Biblique* 98, 602-605.

1992

Ouvrage collectif

– *Mémorial Jean Starcky*, II, sous la direction de É. PUECH et F. GARCÍA - MARTÍNEZ, *Revue de Qumrân* 59, 1992.

Articles dans des ouvrages collectifs

– « Les traités araméens de Sfiré », dans : J. BRIEND avec la collaboration de R. LEBRUN et É. PUECH, *Traités et serments dans le Proche Orient ancien* (Suppléments au Cahier Evangile 81), Paris, pp. 88-107, 115.
– « Fragments d'un apocryphe de Lévi et le personnage eschatologique. 4QTestLévi[c-d] (?) et 4QAJa », dans : J. TREBOLLE BARRERA, L. VEGAS MONTANER (éd.), *The Madrid Qumran Congress. Proceedings of the International Congress on the Dead Sea Scrolls, Madrid 18 - 21 March 1991* (STDJ 11,2), Leiden - Madrid, Brill – Universidad Complutense, 449-501.
– « Les deux derniers Psaumes davidiques du rituel d'exorcisme 11QPsAp[a] IV 4 - V 14 », dans : D. DIMANT, U. RAPPAPORT (éd.), *The Dead Sea Scrolls. Forty Years of Research. Papers read at a Symposium sponsered by Yad Izhak Ben-Zvi at The University of Haifa and at Tel Aviv University, March 20-24, 1988* (STDJ 10), Leiden - Jerusalem, Brill – Magness, 64-89.

Articles de revues

– « Fragment d'une apocalypse en araméen (4Q246 = Pseudo-Dan[d]) et le "royaume de Dieu" », *Revue Biblique* 99, 98-131.
– « La stèle de Bar-Hadad à Melqart et les rois d'Arpad », *Revue Biblique* 99, 311-334.
– « La Pierre de Sion et l'autel des holocaustes d'après un manuscrit hébreu de la grotte 4 (4Q522) », *Revue Biblique* 99, 676-696.
– « Une apocalypse messianique (4Q521) », *Revue de Qumrân* 60, 477-524.
– « Notes en marge de 8KhXIIgr », *Revue de Qumrân* 60, 585-595.

Articles de dictionnaire

– « Fear of Isaac », dans : D.N. FREEDMAN (ed.), *Anchor Bible Dictionary* II, New York: Doubleday, 779-780.
– « Palestinian Funerary Inscriptions », dans : D.N. FREEDMAN (ed.), *Anchor Bible Dictionary* V, New York: Doubleday, 126-135.

Recensions

– AHARON KEMPINSKI, Megiddo. A City-State and Royal Centre in North Israel, Bonn, 1989, *Revue Biblique* 99, 753-755.

1993

Monographies

– *La croyance des Esséniens en la vie future : Immortalité, Résurrection, vie éternelle ? Histoire d'une croyance dans le Judaïsme ancien.* Tome I - *La résurrection des morts et le contexte scripturaire.* Tome II - *Les données qumrâniennes et classiques.* Préface d'A. Caquot, Membre de l'Institut, Professeur au Collège de France (Etudes Bibliques : Nouvelle Série, 21-22), Paris, Gabalda.

Articles dans des ouvrages collectifs

– « The Collection of Beatitudes in Hebrew and in Greek (4Q525 1-4 and Mt 5,3-12) », dans : F. MANNS - E. ALLIATA (éd.), *Early Christianity in Context. Monuments and Documents. Essays in Honour of Emmanuel Testa* (Studium Biblicum Fransciscanum Collectio Maior, 38), Jerusalem, 353-368.
– Une nouvelle amulette samaritaine, dans : M. HELTZER, A. SEGAL, D. KAUFMAN (éd.), *Studies in the Archaeology and History of Ancient Israel in Honour of Moshe Dothan*, Haïfa, Haïfa University Press, 153-162.
– « The École Biblique et Archéologique Française. The First Hundred Years », dans : A. BIRAN - J. AVIRAM (éd.), *Biblical Archaeology Today. Proceedings of the Second International Congress on Biblical Archaeology, Jerusalem, June - July 1990*, Jerusalem, Israel Exploration Society, 9-12.

Articles de revues

– « Le vocable d'*'Athtart Hurri - 'shtrt hr* à Ugarit et en Phénicie », *Ugarit-Forschungen* 25, 327-330.

Revue de vulgarisation

– « A-t-on redécouvert le tombeau du grand-prêtre Caïphe ? », *Le Monde de la Bible* 80, 42-47.

Recensions

– R. GONEN, Burial Patterns and Cultural Diversity in Late Bronze Age Canaan, Winona Lake, 1992, *Revue Biblique* 100, 429-430.
– E. BLOCH-SMITH, Judahite Burial Practices and Beliefs about the Dead, Sheffield, 1992, *Revue Biblique* 100, 430-434.
– W. VAN DEN HORST, Ancient Jewish Epitaphs. An introductory survey of a millennium of Jewish funerary epigraphy (300 BCE - 700 CE), Kampen, 1991, *Revue Biblique* 100, 434-436.

1994

Monographie

– *Les manuscrits de la mer Morte. Aux origines du Christianisme*, éditions Lafon, Dijon.

Articles dans des ouvrages collectifs

- « Les Esséniens et le temple de Jérusalem », dans : Jean-Claude PETIT (éd.) avec la collaboration d'André CHARRON et André MYRE, *"Où demeures-tu ?" (Jn 1,38) : la maison depuis le monde biblique. En hommage au professeur Guy Couturier à l'occasion de ses soixante-cinq ans*, Montréal, 263-287.
- « Un'iscrizione in cristo-palestinese », dans : M. PICCIRILLO - E. ALLIATA (éd.), *Umm al-Rasas - Mayfa'ah. I Gli scavi del complesso di Santo Stefano* (Studium Biblicum Franciscanum Collectio Maior, 28), Gerusalemme, 289-290.
- « Inscription de Deir 'Alla : Admonitions de Bala'am », dans : J. ASURMENDI (éd.), *Prophéties et oracles dans le Proche-Orient ancien* (Supplément au Cahier Évangile 88), Paris, 92-95.
- « Messianism, Resurrection and Eschatology at Qumran and in the New Testament », dans : J. C. VANDERKAM - E. ULRICH (éd.), *Community of the Renewed Covenant, Notre Dame Conference on the Dead Sea Scrolls, 26-28 April 1993* (Christianity and Judaism in Antiquity Series 10), Notre Dame: University of Notre Dame Press, 235-256.

Articles de revues

- « Un cratère phénicien inscrit : rites et croyances (Pls. VI-XI) », *Transeuphratène* 8, 47-73.
- « La stèle araméenne de Dan : Bar Hadad II et la coalition des Omrides et de la Maison de David », *Revue Biblique* 101, 215-241.
- « Notes sur le fragment d'apocalypse 4Q246 - "le fils de Dieu" », *Revue Biblique* 101, 533-558.
- « Préséance sacerdotale et Messie - Roi dans la Règle de la Congrégation (1QSa ii 11-22) », *Revue de Qumrân* 63, 351-365.
- « L'image de l'arbre en 4QDeutéro-Ézéchiel (4Q385 2,9-10) », *Revue de Qumrân* 63, 429-440.
- « La "Forteresse des Pieux" et Kh. Qumrân. A propos du papyrus Murabba'ât 45 », *Revue de Qumrân* 63, 463-471.

Revues de vulgarisation

- « Des esséno-zélotes chrétiens de Judée ! Une position originale sur les manuscrits de la mer Morte », dans : *Les manuscrits de la mer Morte. Aux origines du Christianisme* (Les Dossiers d'archéologie, 189), 97-101.
- « Déchiffreur de manuscrits », *Le Monde de la Bible* 86, 9-11.
- « Les manuscrits de la mer Morte et le Nouveau Testament », *Le Monde de la Bible* 86, 34-40.
- « Où il est question de crucifixion », *Le Monde de la Bible* 86, 41.
- « Pétra et les manuscrits de la "grotte aux lettres" », *Le Monde la Bible* 88, 10.
- « Jean Baptiste était-il essénien ? Le retour d'Élie », *Le Monde de la Bible* 89, 7-8.

Recensions

- J.A FITZMYER and S.A KAUFMAN with the Collaboration of ST.F. BENNETT AND E.M. COOK, An Aramaic Bibliography. Part I. Old, Official, and Biblical Aramaic, Baltimore and London, 1992, *Revue Biblique* 101, 582-588.

- J.H. Charlesworth with R.E. Whitaker, L.G. Hickerson, S.R.A. Starbuck, L.T. Stuckenbruck, Graphic Concordance to the Dead Sea Scrolls, Tübingen, 1991, *Revue Biblique* 101, 588-590.
- G. Vermes and M.D. Martin, The Essenes According to Classical Sources, Sheffield, 1989, *Revue Biblique* 101, 590-593.

1995

Articles dans des ouvrages collectifs

- « Note de lexicographie hébraïque qumrânienne (*m-sw/yrwq, mhshbym, swt*) », dans : Z. Zevit, S. Gitin, and M. Sokoloff (ed.), *Solving Riddles and Untying Knots. Biblical, Epigraphic, and Semitic Studies in honor of Jonas C. Greenfield*, Winona Lake, Eisenbrauns, 181-189.
- J. Briend, R. Lebrun y E. Puech (éd.), *Tratados y Juramentos en el Antiquo Oriente proximo* (Documentos in torna a la Biblia, 23). Estella, Verbo divino.
- « Qumran et les manuscrits de la mer Morte », dans : *Itinéraires en Terre Sainte*, Guides Gallimard, Paris (traduit en espagnol, Madrid 1995, et en italien en 1996).
- « Présence arabe dans les manuscrits de "La grotte aux lettres" du Wadi Khabra », dans : H. Lozachmeur (éd.), *Présence arabe dans le Croissant fertile avant l'Hégire. Actes de la Table ronde internationale organisée par l'Unité de Recherche Associée 1062 du CNRS, Études sémitiques, au Collège de France, le 13 novembre 1993*, Paris, Éditions Recherche sur les Civilisations, 37-46.

Articles de revues

- « A propos de la Jérusalem Nouvelle d'après les manuscrits de la mer Morte », *Semitica 43-44*, 87-102.
- « Restauration d'un texte hymnique à partir de trois manuscrits fragmentaires : 1QH[a] xv 37- xvi 4 (vii 34 - viii 3), 1Q35 (H[b]) 1,9-14 et 4Q428 (H[b] 7,1-10) », *Revue de Qumrân* 64, 543-558.
- « Un autre manuscrit de la Genèse récemment identifié dans les fragments de la grotte 4 (4QGn[n]) », *Revue de Qumrân* 64, 637-640.
- « Des fragments grecs de la Grotte 7 et le Nouveau Testament ? 7Q4 et 7Q5, et le Papyrus Magdalen Grec 17 = P[64] », *Revue Biblique* 102, 570-584.

Articles de dictionnaire

- « Lel *ll* », dans : K. van der Toorn, B. Becking and P. W. van der Horst (éd.), *Dictionary of Deities and Demons in the Bible*, Leiden - New York – Köln, 950-956.
- « Lioness *lb't* », dans : K. van der Toorn, B. Becking and P. W. van der Horst (éd.), *Dictionary of Deities and Demons in the Bible*, Leiden - New York – Köln, 981-983.
- « Milkom *mlkm* », dans : K. van der Toorn, B. Becking and P. W. van der Horst (éd.), *Dictionary of Deities and Demons in the Bible*, Leiden - New York – Köln, 1076-1080.

Revue de vulgarisation

- « Surprenante révélation à Dan : Aram contre la maison de David », *Le Monde de la Bible* 90, 38-40.
- « L'attente des morts », *Le Monde de la Bible* 91, 16.

1996

Ouvrages collectifs

- G. BROOKE, J. COLLINS, T. ELGVIN, P. FLINT, J. GREENFIELD, E. LARSON, C. NEWSOM, E. PUECH, L.H. SCHIFFMAN, M. STONE, J. TREBOLLE BARRERA, *Qumran Cave 4 · XVII. Parabiblical Texts, Part 3* (Discoveries in the Judaean Desert XXII), Oxford, Clarendon Press.
- *Hommage à Józef Tadeusz Milik*, sous la direction de F. GARCÍA MARTÍNEZ et É. PUECH, *Revue de Qumrân* 17.

Articles dans des ouvrages collectifs

- « 4Q246 » et « 4QApocryphe de Daniel ar », dans : G. BROOKE, J. COLLINS, T. ELGVIN, P. FLINT, J. GREENFIELD, E. LARSON, C. NEWSOM, E. PUECH, L.H. SCHIFFMAN, M. STONE, J. TREBOLLE BARRERA, *Qumran Cave 4 · XVII. Parabiblical Texts, Part 3* (Discoveries in the Judaean Desert XXII), Oxford, Clarendon Press, 165-184, 350-51, Pl. XI.
- « La prière de Nabonide (4Q242) », dans : K.J. CATHCART, M. MAHER (éd.), *Targumic and Cognate Studies. Essays in Honour of Martin McNamara* (Journal for the Study of the Old Testament, Supplement Series, 230), Sheffield, Sheffield Academic Press, 208-227.
- « Deux amulettes palestiniennes, une en grec et une bilingue grec - christo-palestinien », dans : H. GASCHE et B. HROUDA (ed.), *Collectanea Orientalia. Histoire, arts de l'espace et industrie de la terre. Études offertes en hommage à Agnès Spycket* (Civilisations du Proche-Orient ; Série I. Archéologie et environnement, vol. 3), Neuchâtel, Paris, 299-310.
- « Du bilinguisme à Qumrân ? », dans : F. Briquel Châtonnet (éd.), *Mosaïque de langues, mosaïques culturelle. Le bilinguisme au Proche Orient Ancien. Table ronde de l'URA 1062, Institut d'Études sémitiques, Collège de France, 18 nov. 1995* (Antiquités sémitiques 1), Paris, Maisoneuve, 171-189.

Articles de revues

- « Józef Tadeusz Milik (biographie) », dans : *Hommage à Józef Tadeusz Milik, Revue de Qumrân* 17, 5-10.
- « Jonathan le Prêtre Impie et les débuts de la Communauté de Qumrân. 4QJonathan (4Q523) et 4QPsAp (4Q448) », dans : *Hommage à Józef Tadeusz Milik, Revue de Qumrân* 17, 241-270.
- « Notes sur les fragments grecs du manuscrit 7Q4 = 1 Hénoch 103 et 105 », *Revue Biblique* 106, 592-600.

Article de dictionnaire

- « Siloé (L'inscription du tunnel de) », dans : J. BRIEND and É. COTHENET (ed.), *Supplément au Dictionnaire de la Bible*, Fasc. 71 - Vol. XII, Paris, Letouzey, 1341-1352.

Revues de vulgarisation

- « Une conquête de Jérusalem, il y a trois mille ans », dans : *Les 3000 ans de Jérusalem* (Sources vives 67), 25-32.
- « Die Erwartung der Toten », *Welt und Umwelt der Bibel. Archäologie und Geschichte* 1/1, 16.
- « Petra e i manoscritti della "grotta delle lettere" », *Il mondo della Bibbia* 31, 10
- « L'attesa dei morti », *Il mondo della Bibbia*, 32, 16.

1997

Articles dans des ouvrages collectifs

- « I frammenti greci della grotta 7 e il Nuovo Testamento ? 7Q4 e 7Q5, e il papiro Magdalen greco 17 = P64 », dans : J. O'CALLAGHAN - C. P. THIEDE - M. BAILLET - C. FOCANT - H.-U. ROSENBAUM - É. PUECH - M.-É. BOISMARD - P. GRELOT, *Postfazione di* G. SEGALLA, F. DALLA VECCHIA (éd.), *Ridatare i Vangeli ?* (Giornale di Teologia n. 247), Brescia, Queriniana, 127-147.
- « Osservazioni sui frammenti greci del manoscritto 7Q4 = *1 Enoc* 103 e 105 », dans : J. O'CALLAGHAN - C. P. THIEDE - M. BAILLET - C. FOCANT - H.-U. ROSENBAUM - É. PUECH - M.-É. BOISMARD - P. GRELOT, *Postfazione di* G. SEGALLA, F. DALLA VECCHIA (éd.), *Ridatare i Vangeli ?* (Giornale di Teologia n. 247), Brescia, Queriniana, 149-161.
- « Les manuscrits de la mer Morte et le Nouveau Testament », dans : E.-M. LAPERROUSAZ (éd.), *Qumrân et les manuscrits de la mer Morte, un Cinquantenaire*, Paris, Cerf, 253-313.
- « Les Esséniens croyaient-ils à la résurrection ? », dans : E.-M. LAPERROUSAZ (éd.), *Qumrân et les manuscrits de la mer Morte, un Cinquantenaire*, Paris, Cerf, 409-440.
- « Les fragments du plus ancien exemplaire du Rouleau du Temple (4Q524) », dans : M. BERNSTEIN, F. GARCÍA MARTÍNEZ and J. KAMPEN (éd.), *Legal Texts and Legal Issues. Proceedings of the Second Meeting of the International Organization for Qumran Studies Cambridge 1995, Published in Honour of Joseph M. Baumgarten* (STDJ 23), Leiden, Brill, 19-64.
- « Biographie intellectuelle du R. P. B. Couroyer », dans : M. SIGRIST (éd.), *Études égyptologiques et bibliques à la mémoire du Père B. Couroyer, Jérusalem 7 mars 1994.* (Cahiers de la Revue Biblique, 36), Paris, Gabalda, 9-28.

Articles de revues

- « Notes sur 11Q19 LXIV 6-13 et 4Q524 14,2-4. À propos de la crucifixion dans le *Rouleau du Temple* et dans le Judaïsme ancien », *Revue de Qumrân* 69, 109-124.
- « Quelques résultats d'un nouvel examen du Rouleau de cuivre (3Q15) », *Revue de Qumrân* 70, 163-190.
- « Messianisme, eschatologie et résurrection dans les manuscrits de la mer Morte », *Revue de Qumrân* 70, 255-298.
- « Sept fragments grecs de la *Lettre d'Hénoch* (1 Hén 100, 103 et 105) dans la grotte 7 de Qumrân (= 7QHéngr) », *Revue de Qumrân* 70, 313-323.

- « Les manuscrits de la mer Morte, cinquante ans après », *Bulletin du Centre de Recherche Français de Jérusalem* 1, 18-23.

Revues de vulgarisation

- « Les convictions d'un savant (entretien réalisé par F. Mébarki) », *Le Monde de la Bible* 107, 51-57.
- « Des documents chrétiens à Qumrân ? », *Le Monde de la Bible* 107, 58.
- « Sauvetage et dernières révélations (en collaboration avec N. Lacoudre) », *Le Monde de la Bible* 107, 60-62.
- « La crucifixion et la tradition juive ancienne », *Le Monde de la Bible* 107, 69-71.
- « Les manuscrits de la mer Morte : 50 ans après », *Archéologia* 339, 6-7.
- « Decifrare i manoscritti », *Il Mondo della Bibbia* 38, 11-13.
- « I manoscritti del Mar Morto e il Nuovo Testamento », *Il Mondo della Bibbia* 38, 36-41.
- « La questione della crocifissione », *Il Mondo della Bibbia* 38, 43.

Audio-visuel

- Participation au film documentaire *Corpus Christi* - ARTE (réalisé par Gérard Mordillat - Jérôme Prieur).

1998

Monographies

- *Qumrân Grotte 4 · XVIII. Manuscrits hébreux (4Q521-528, 4Q576-579)* (Discoveries in the Judaean Desert XXV), Oxford, Larendon Press, XVIII- 230 in fol., XV Planches et 2 figures.

Articles dans des ouvrages collectifs

- A. MALAMAT, « Hazor Once Again in New Mari Documents », *Addendum* par E. PUECH, dans : A. MALAMAT (ed.), *Mari and the Bible* (Studies in the History and Culture of the Ancient Near East 12), Leiden, Brill, 41-44.
- « Inscriptions araméennes du Golfe : Failaka, Qala'at al-Bahreïn et Mulayha (ÉAU) », dans : *Recherches pluridisciplinaires sur une province de l'empire achéménide. Mélanges offerts à Jacques Briend, I-II, Transeuphratène* 16, 31-55.
- « Les apparitions dans la littérature péritestamentaire », dans : M. I. Alves (ed.), *Actas do congresso internacional de Fátima. Fenomenologia e teologia das aparições (9-12 de outubro de 1997)*, Fátima, Santuário de Fátima, 575-89.

Articles de revues

- « The necropolises of *Khirbet* Qumrân and 'Ain el-Ghuweir and the Essene belief in afterlife », *Bulletin of the American Schools of Oriental Research* 312, 21-36.
- « L'alphabet cryptique en 4QS[e] (4Q259) », *Revue de Qumrân* 71, 429-35.
- « In memoriam : l'abbé Maurice Baillet », *Revue de Qumrân* 71, 339-41.

Revues de vulgarisation

- « La thèse infondée du témoin oculaire (à propos de C.P. THIEDE et M. D'ANCONA, *Témoin de Jésus, La preuve matérielle que l'Évangile selon saint Matthieu est un témoignage oculaire écrit par des contemporains du Christ*, Paris 1996, et de C.P. THIEDE, *Jésus selon Mathieu. La nouvelle datation du papyrus Magdalen d'Oxford et l'origine des Évangiles. Examen et discussion des dernières objections scientifiques*, Paris 1996) », *Le Monde de la Bible* 109, 44-45.
- « Esenios : en los márgenes del antiguo Israel », *Nueva Revista de politica, cultura y arte* 57, 65-81.
- « Textes de Qumrân », *Version Originale. Le trimestriel de réflexion* (édition française et américaine). *Moyen Orient : la paix est-elle possible ?*, Cahier n° 7, 306-311.
- « Überzeugungen eines Gelehrten, Interview mit Emile Puech », *Welt und Umwelt der Bibel, Archäologie - Kunst - Geschichte* 9/3, 55-61.
- « Christliche Schriften in Qumrân ? », *Welt und Umwelt der Bibel, Archäologie - Kunst - Geschichte* 9/3, 62.
- « Die Kupferrolle - Konservierung und neue Erkenntnisse (mit N. Lacoudre) », *Welt und Umwelt der Bibel, Archäologie - Kunst - Geschichte* 9/3, 64-66.
- « Die Kreuzigung und die altjüdische Tradition », *Welt und Umwelt der Bibel, Archäologie - Kunst - Geschichte* 9/3, 73-75.
- « Markus und Matthäus : Irrwege und falsche Datierungen ? » *Welt und Umwelt der Bibel, Archäologie - Kunst - Geschichte* 10/3, 44-45.
- « Les manuscrits de Qumrân », *La vie en marche, A l'écoute* (oct.-nov. 1998), *Fondation des orphelins apprentis d'Auteuil*, 29-31 (propos recueillis par A. Perrot).
- « Rencontre avec Émile Puech. Un Français à Qumrân (propos recueillis par F. Mébarki) », *Le journal du CNRS*, 101, 23.

Recensions

- L. CANSDALE, Qumran and the Essenes: A Re-Evaluation of the Evidence, Tübingen, 1997, *Revue de Qumrân* 71, 437-41, et *Revue Biblique* 105, 281-85.
- J.H. CHARLESWORTH with F.M. CROSS, J. MILGROM, L.H. SCHIFFMAN, L.T. STUCKENBRUCK, AND R.E. WHITAKER, The Dead Sea Scrolls. Hebrew, Aramaic, and Greek Texts with English Translations. Volume I: Rule of the Community and Related Documents, Tübingen – Louisville, 1994, *Revue de Qumrân* 71, 441-45.
- F. GARCÍA MARTÍNEZ & E. J. C. TIGCHELAAR, The Dead Sea Scrolls Study Edition. Volume I. 1Q1-4Q273, Leiden, New York, Köln, 1997, *Revue de Qumrân* 71, 446-47.
- S. METSO, The Textual Development of the Qumran Community Rule, Leiden, New York, Köln, 1997, *Revue de Qumrân* 71, 448-53.

1999

Articles dans des ouvrages collectifs

- « Le grand prêtre Simon (III), fils d'Onias III, le Maître de Justice ? », dans : B. KOLLMANN, W. REINBOLD und A. STEUDEL (éd.), *Antikes Judentum und*

Frühes Christentum. Festschrift für Hartmut Stegemann zum 65. Geburtstag (Beihefte zur Zeitschrift für die neutestamentliche Wissenschaft, 97), Berlin, De Gruyter, 137-158.
- « Un anneau inscrit du Bronze Récent à Megiddo », dans : R. CHAZAN, W.W. HALLO, L.H. SCHIFFMAN (éd.), *Ki Baruch hu: Ancient Near Eastern, Biblical, and Judaic Studies in Honor of Baruch A. Levine*, Winona Lake, Eisenbrauns, 51-61.
- « Le "fils de Dieu" en 4Q246 », in *Frank Moore Cross Volume* (Erets Israel, 26), Jerusalem, 143*-152*, 236*.
- « Le livre de Ben Sira et les manuscrits de Qumrân », dans : N. CALDUCH et J. VERMEYLEN (éd.), *Treasures of Wisdom. Studies in Ben Sira and the Book of Wisdom. Festschrift M. Gilbert* (Bibliotheca Ephemeridum Theologicarum Lovaniensium, 143), Louvain, Peeters, 411-26.
- « Some Remarks on 4Q246 and 4Q521 Texts and Qumran Messianism », dans : D. W. PARRY and E. C. ULRICH (éd.), *The Provo International Conference on the Dead Sea Scrolls, Technological Innovations, New Texts, and New and Reformulated Issues,* (STDJ 30), Leiden, Brill, 545-565.
- « Qumrân e il Libro dei Proverbi », dans : G. BELLIA, A. PASSARO (éd.), *Il Libro dei Proverbi. Tradizione, redazione, teologia,* Casale Monferrato, Edizione Piemme, 169-189.
- « Mesianismo, escatología y resurrección en los manuscritos del Mar Muerto », dans : J. TREBOLLE BARRERA (éd.), *Paganos, judíos y cristianos en los textos de Qumrán* (Biblioteca de ciencias bíblicas y orientales, 5), Madrid, Trotta, 245-286.
- « L'esprit saint à Qumrân », dans : *Colloquium Study on the Holy Spirit, Jerusalem, 30th April - 2nd May 1998, Liber Annuus*, 49, 283-297.
- « Inscripción de Deir 'Alla : advertencias de Bala'am » dans : J. M. ASURMENDI RUIZ (éd.), *Profecias y oráculos*, Estella, Verbo divino, 92-95.

Articles de revues

- « Les fragments 1 à 3 du *Livre des Géants* de la Grotte 6 (6Q8 1-3) », *Revue de Qumrân* 74, 227-38.
- « Un nouveau manuscrit de la Genèse de la grotte 4 : 4Q483 = pap4Qgenèse », *Revue de Qumrân* 74, 259-60.
- « Une nouvelle copie du *Livre des Jubilés* : 4Q484 = pap4Qjubilés[j] », *Revue de Qumrân* 74, 261-64.
- « Note sull'identificazione di 7Q5 con Mc 6,52-53 », *Ho Theológos* 17, 73-84.

Revue de vulgarisation

- « Les langues de Palestine vues par les inscriptions », *Les Dossiers d'Archéologie* n° 240, 150-53.
- « Zwoje znad Morza Martwego (= Les manuscrits de la mer Morte) » (Interview D. Dlugosz), *Nasza rodzina* 656-657, 13-14.
- « Wywiad z ks. Emilem Puechem » (Interview de D. Dlugosz), *Buch Biblijny i Liturgiczny* 52/3, 258-61.
- « The Treasures of the Dead Sea: the Copper Scroll », *The XFactor, Cover-ups, Paranormal, Mysteries. Ufos* 56, 1550-54.

2000

Articles dans des ouvrages collectifs

– « 4Q522 - Ps 122 in 4QProphecy of Joshua », dans : E. ULRICH *et alii* (éd.), *Qumran Cave 4 XI. Psalms to Chronicles* (Discoveries in the Judaean Desert XVI), Oxford, Clarendon Press, 169-170.
– « Les manuscrits de la mer Morte et le Nouveau Testament », dans : P. GEOLTRAIN (éd.), *Aux origines du christianisme*, Paris, Gallimard et Le Monde de la Bible, 157-167.
– « Jean-Baptiste était-il essénien ? », dans : P. GEOLTRAIN (éd.), *Aux origines du christianisme*, Paris, Gallimard et Le Monde de la Bible, 171-176.
– « Józef Tadeusz Milik et Cinquantenaire de la découverte des manuscrits de la mer Morte de Qumrân », dans : D. DLUGOSZ, H. RATAJCZAK (éd.), *Józef Tadeusz Milik, éditeur des manuscrits de la mer Morte*, Varsovie, Centre scientifique de l'Académie Polonaise des Sciences à Paris, 31-36.
– « Abbé Maurice Baillet (1923-1998) », dans : D. F. FALK, F. GARCÍA MARTÍNEZ and E. M. SCHULLER (éd.), *Sapiential, Liturgical and Poetical Texts from Qumrân.* in *Proceedings of the Third Meeting of the International Organization for Qumrân Studies. Published in Memory of Maurice Baillet* (STDJ, 35), Leiden, Brill, ix-xiii.
– « Bibliographie de Maurice Baillet », dans : D. F. FALK, F. GARCÍA MARTÍNEZ and E. M. SCHULLER (éd.), *Sapiential, Liturgical and Poetical Texts from Qumrân.* in *Proceedings of the Third Meeting of the International Organization for Qumrân Studies. Published in Memory of Maurice Baillet* (STDJ, 35), Leiden, xiv-xx.
– « Les Psaumes davidiques du rituel d'exorcisme (11Q11) », dans : D. F. FALK, F. GARCÍA MARTÍNEZ and E. M. SCHULLER (éd.), *Sapiential, Liturgical and Poetical Texts from Qumrân.* in *Proceedings of the Third Meeting of the International Organization for Qumrân Studies. Published in Memory of Maurice Baillet* (STDJ, 35), Leiden, 160-181.
– « Qumrân et le texte de l'Ancien Testament », dan : A. LEMAIRE, M. SAEBØ (éd.), *Congress Volume, Oslo 1998* (Supplements to Vetus Testamentum, 80), Leiden, Brill, 437-64.
– « Les langues et les écritures dans les manuscrits de la mer Morte », dans : R. VIERS (éd.), *Des signes pictographiques à l'alphabet. La communication écrite en Méditerranée. Actes du Colloque, 14-15 mai 1996, Villa grecque* Kérylos. *Fondation Théodore Reinach* (Beaulieu sur Mer), Paris, Karthala, 175-211, + figures 27-34b.
– « Immortality and Life After Death », dans : L. H. SCHIFFMAN, E. TOV, and J. C. VANDERKAM (éd.), *The Dead Sea Scrolls. Fifty Years After Their Discovery. Proceedings of the Jerusalem Congress, July 20-25, 1997*, Jerusalem, Israel Exploration Society, The Shrine of the Book, 512-520.
– « Some Results of the Restoration of the Copper Scroll by ÉDF *Mécénat* », dans : L. H. SCHIFFMAN, E. TOV, and J. C. VANDERKAM (éd.), *The Dead Sea Scrolls. Fifty Years After Their Discovery. Proceedings of the Jerusalem Congress, July 20-25, 1997*, Jerusalem, Israel Exploration Society, The Shrine of the Book,889-94.

- « Les pointes de flèches inscrites de la fin du IIe millénaire en Phénicie et Canaan », dans : Maria-Eugenia AUBET, Manuela BARTHÉLEMY (éd.), *Actas del IV Congreso internacional de estudios fenicios y púnicos, Cádiz, 2 al 6 octubre 1995*, Cádiz, Servicio de Publicaciones, Universidad de Cádiz, pp. 251-269.

Articles d'encyclopédie

- « Death », dans : J. C. VANDERKAM - L. H. SCHIFFMAN (éd.), *Encyclopedia of the Dead Sea Scrolls*, Oxford, Oxford University Press, 2000, 183-86.
- « Elect of God », dans : J. C. VANDERKAM - L. H. SCHIFFMAN (éd.), *Encyclopedia of the Dead Sea Scrolls*, Oxford, Oxford University Press, 2000, 240-41.
- « Hodayot », dans : J. C. VANDERKAM - L. H. SCHIFFMAN (éd.), *Encyclopedia of the Dead Sea Scrolls*, Oxford, Oxford University Press, 2000, 365-69.
- « Messianic Apocalypse », dans : J. C. VANDERKAM - L. H. SCHIFFMAN (éd.), *Encyclopedia of the Dead Sea Scrolls*, Oxford, Oxford University Press, 2000, 543-44.
- « Milik », dans : J. C. VANDERKAM - L. H. SCHIFFMAN (éd.), *Encyclopedia of the Dead Sea Scrolls*, Oxford, Oxford University Press, 2000, 552-54.
- « Rock of Sion », dans : J. C. VANDERKAM - L. H. SCHIFFMAN (éd.), *Encyclopedia of the Dead Sea Scrolls*, Oxford, Oxford University Press, 2000, 783-84.
- « Starcky », dans : J. C. VANDERKAM - L. H. SCHIFFMAN (éd.), *Encyclopedia of the Dead Sea Scrolls*, Oxford, Oxford University Press, 2000,891-92.

Articles de revues

- « Une lampe byzantine inscrite de Dayr al-Qattar al-Byzanti (Jordanie) », *Revue Biblique* 107, 558-560.
- « Le livre de Qohélet à Qumrân », *Ho Theológos* 18, 109-114.
- Note additionnelle sur le fragment paléo-hébreu, *Revue de Qumrân* 75, 449-51.
- « Sur la dissimilation de l'interdentale ∂ en araméen qumranien. A propos d'un chaînon manquant », *Revue de Qumrân* 76, 607-616.
- « Un nouveau fragment du manuscrit[b] de l'Ecclésiaste (4QQohélet[b] ou 4Q110) », *Revue de Qumrân* 76, 617-621.
- (avec A. Steudel) « Un nouveau fragment du manuscrit 4QInstruction[c] (XQ7 = 4Q417-4Q418) », *Revue de Qumrân* 76, 623-627.
- « Les songes des fils de Semihazah dans *le Livre des Géants* de Qumrân », *Comptes Rendus de l'Académie des Inscriptions et Belles Lettres*, janvier - mars, 7-26.

Revues de vulgarisation

- « The Mysteries of the "Copper Scroll" », *Near Eastern Archaeology - The World of the Bible* 63, pp. 152-153.
- « The Convictions of a Scholar. Interview with Émile Puech », *Near Eastern Archaeology - The World of the Bible* 63, pp. 160-163.

Recensions

- J. C. VANDERKAM, Calendars in the Dead Sea Scrolls: Measuring time, London, 1998, *Revue Biblique* 107, pp. 110-13.

- S. M. OLYAN, A Thousand Thousands Served Him. Exegesis and the Naming of Angels in Ancient Judaism, Tübingen, 1993, *Revue de Qumrân* 75, 457-59.
- L. T. STUCKENBRUCK, The Book of Giants from Qumran. Texts, Translation, and Commentary, Tübingen, 1997, *Revue de Qumrân* 76, 635-638.
- S. ENSTE, Kein Markustext in Qumran. Eine Untersuchung der These: Qumran-Fragment 7Q5 - Mk 6,52-53, Fribourg-Göttingen, 2000, *Revue de Qumrân* 76, 639-640.

2001

Monographie

- *Qumran Grotte 4 XXII. Textes araméens première partie (4Q529-4Q549)* (Discoveries in the Judaean Desert XXXI), Oxford, Clarendon Press.

Articles dans des ouvrages collectifs

- « Qohelet a Qumran », dans : G. BELLIA, A. PASSARO (éd.), *Il Libro del Qohelet Tradizione, redazione, teologia* (Cammini nello Spirito sez. Biblicam 44), Milano, Paoline, 144-170.
- « La crucifixion comme peine capitale dans le judaïsme ancien », dans : S. MIMOUNI (éd.) en collaboration avec F. STANLEY JONES, *Le Judéo-Christianisme dans tous ses états. Actes du colloque de Jérusalem, 6-10 juillet 1998* (Lectio Divina, hors série), Paris, Cerf, 41-66.
- « Un nouvel autel à encens de Palmyre », dans : P. M. M. DAVIAU, J. W. WEWERS and M. WEIGL (éd.), *The World of the Arameans II. Studies in History and Archaeology in Honour of Paul-Eugène Dion* (Journal for the Study of the Old Testament Supplement Series, 325), Sheffield, Sheffield Academic Press, 243-256.

Articles de revues

- « Essénisme et christianisme. Les manuscrits de la mer Morte et Jésus », Œuvres & Critiques 26/2, 153-173.
- « Notes d'épigraphie christo-palestinienne cisjordanienne », *Revue Biblique* 108, 61-72.
- « Identification de nouveaux manuscrits bibliques : *Deutéronome* et *Proverbes* dans les débris de la grotte 4, » *Revue de Qumrân* 77, 121-127.
- « Un autre fragment du Psaume 122 en 4Q522 (4Q522 26) », *Revue de Qumrân*, 77, 129-132.
- « Dieu le Père dans les écrits péritestamentaires et les manuscrits de la mer Morte », *Revue de Qumrân* 78, 287-310.

2002

Ouvrage collectif

- F. MÉBARKI et E. PUECH, avec la participation de G.J. BROOKE, M. BROSHI, F. GARCÍA MARTÍNEZ, A. STEUDEL et E.C. ULRICH, *Les manuscrits de la mer Morte*, Rodez, Éditions du Rouergue.

Articles dans des ouvrages collectifs

- « La escatología en el Antiguo Testamento y en el Judaísmo antiguo », dans : C. IZQUIERDO, J. BURGRAFF, J. L. GUTIÉRREZ y E. FLANDES (éd.), *Escatología y vida cristiana, XXII Simposio Internacional de Teología de la Universidad de Navarra (Pamplona, 25-27 de abril de 2001)* (Simposios Internacionales de Teología, 22), Pamplona, Servicio de Publicaciones de la Universidad de Navarra, 249-270.
- « Some Results of a New Examination of the Copper Scroll (3Q15) », dans : G. J. BROOKE, Ph. R. DAVIES (é.d), *Copper Scroll Studies* (Journal for the Study of the Pseudepigrapha, Supplement Series, 40), Sheffield, Sheffield Academic Press, 58-89.

Articles de revues

- « Notes sur quatre inscriptions proto-sinaïtiques », *Revue Biblique* 109, 5-39.
- « Le Testament de Lévi en araméen de la Geniza du Caire », *Revue de Qumrân* 80, 511-556.
- « A propos de l'ossuaire de Jacques, le frère de Jésus », *The Polish Journal of Biblical Research* 2/1, 7-23.

Encyclopédie

- « Qumrân (Manuscritos de) », dans : *Verbo. Enciclopédia Luso-Brasileira de Cultura* 24 (Ediçâo Século XXI), Lisboa, Sâo Paulo, col. 665-673.

Revues de vulgarisation

- « I rotoli dei Figli della Luce. Intervista esclusiva a Emile Puech di Francesco Garufi », *Hera* 29, Maggio, 22-26.
- « È l'ossario di Giacomo il Giusto ! Intervista a Emile Puech e André Lemaire di Francesco Garufi », *Hera* 36 diecembre 2002, 38-45.

Recensions

- R. DEUTSCH and A. LEMAIRE, Biblical Period Personal Seals in the Shlomo Moussaieff Collection, Tel Aviv, 2000, *Revue Biblique* 109, 426-28.
- J.H. CHARLESWORTH (ed.) The Dead Sea Scrolls : Hebrew, Aramaic, and Greek Texts with English Translations, vol. II : Damascus Document, War Scroll and Related Documents, Tübingen, 1995, *Revue de Qumrân* 80, 593-97.
- Sh. PAUL, M. STONE and A. PINNICK (éd.), 'Al kanefei Yonah. Collected Studies of Jonas C. Greenfield on Semitic Philology, Jerusalem, 2001, *Revue de Qumrân* 80, 597.

2003

Ouvrages collectifs

- F. MÉBARKI e E. PUECH con testi di G.J. BROOKE, M. BROSHI, F. GARCÍA MARTÍNEZ, A. STEUDEL, E.C. ULRICH, *I manoscritti del Mar Morto*, edizione italiana a cura di Gianfranco RAVASI, Milano.

Articles dans des ouvrages collectifs

- « (Dan) Surprenante révélation à Dan : Aram contre "la Maison de David" », dans : Jacques BRIEND (éd.), *La terre Sainte. Cinquante ans d'archéologie, I-II*, Paris, Bayard, 103-105.
- « (Qumrân) Déchiffreur de manuscrits », dans : Jacques BRIEND (éd.), *La terre Sainte. Cinquante ans d'archéologie, I-II*, Paris, Bayard, 442-46.
- « (Qumrân) Sauvetage et dernières révélations », dans : Jacques BRIEND (éd.), *La terre Sainte. Cinquante ans d'archéologie, I-II*, Paris, Bayard,505-509.
- « (Stèle de Moab) Un roi proclame ses victoires », dans : Jacques BRIEND (éd.), *La terre Sainte. Cinquante ans d'archéologie, I-II*, Paris, Bayard, 629-31.
- « (Jérusalem) A-t-on redécouvert le tombeau du Grand-Prêtre Caïphe ? », dans : Jacques BRIEND (éd.), *La terre Sainte. Cinquante ans d'archéologie, I-II*, Paris, Bayard, 1291-98.
- « (Arad) Les inscriptions d'Arad », dans : Jacques BRIEND (éd.), *La terre Sainte. Cinquante ans d'archéologie, I-II*, Paris, Bayard, 1720-24.
- « Les inscriptions syriaques au-dessus de l'accès aux grottes funéraires 37 et 38 », dans : Marie-Joseph STEVE, avec la collaboration de C. HARDY-GUILBERT, C. et F. JULLIEN, E. SMEKENS, F. GAFFARY, E. HAERINCK, E. PUECH et A. ROUGEULLE, édité par H. GASCHE, *L'île de Khârg. Une page de l'histoire du golfe persique et du monachisme oriental* (Civilisations du Proche-Orient, Série I - Archéologie et Environnement 1, Recherches et Publications), Neuchâtel, 49-50.
- « L'inscription funéraire judéo-araméenne de la tombe 25 », dans : Marie-Joseph STEVE, avec la collaboration de C. HARDY-GUILBERT, C. et F. JULLIEN, E. SMEKENS, F. GAFFARY, E. HAERINCK, E. PUECH et A. ROUGEULLE, édité par H. GASCHE, *L'île de Khârg. Une page de l'histoire du golfe persique et du monachisme oriental* (Civilisations du Proche-Orient, Série I - Archéologie et Environnement 1, Recherches et Publications), Neuchâtel, 59-67.
- « L'épitaphe en arabe de la galerie nord de l'église », dans : Marie-Joseph STEVE, avec la collaboration de C. HARDY-GUILBERT, C. et F. JULLIEN, E. SMEKENS, F. GAFFARY, E. HAERINCK, E. PUECH et A. ROUGEULLE, édité par H. GASCHE, *L'île de Khârg. Une page de l'histoire du golfe persique et du monachisme oriental* (Civilisations du Proche-Orient, Série I - Archéologie et Environnement 1, Recherches et Publications), Neuchâtel, 103-106.
- « The Names of the Gates of the *New Jerusalem* (4Q554) », dans : Sh.M. PAUL, R.A. KRAFT, L.H. SCHIFFMAN and W.W. FIELDS, with the assistance of E. BEN-DAVID, *Emanuel. Studies in Hebrew Bible, Septuagint, and Dead Sea Scrolls in Honor of Emanuel Tov*, Leiden, Boston, Brill, 379-392.
- « L'inscription christo-palestinienne du Ouadi Rajib-Ajloun et de nouvelles inscriptions christo-palestiniennes de Jordanie », dans : G. C. BOTTINI, L. DI SEGNI and L. D. CHRUPCALA (éd.), *One Land - Many Cultures. Archaeological Studies in Honour of Stanislas Loffreda OFM* (Studium Biblicum Franciscanum, Collectio Major, 41), Gerusalemme, 517-525.
- « Apports des textes apocalyptiques et sapientiels à l'eschatologie du judaïsme ancien », dans : F. GARCÍA MARTÍNEZ (éd.), *Wisdom and Apocalypticism in the Dead Sea Scrolls and in the Biblical Tradition. Colloquium Biblicum Lovaniense,*

Journées Bibliques de Louvain LI, July 31 - August 1-2, 2002 (Bibliotheca Ephemeridum Theologicarum Lovaniensium, 168), Leuven, Peeters, 133-170.

Articles de revues

– « La requête d'un moissonneur dans le sud-judéen à la fin du VIIe s. av. J.-C. », *Revue Biblique* 110, 5-16.
– (en collaboration avec J. ZIAS) « Le tombeau de Zacharie et Siméon au monument funéraire dit d'Absalom dans la Vallée de Josaphat », *Revue Biblique* 110, 321-335.
– « La conception de la vie future dans le Livre de la *Sagesse* et les manuscrits de la mer Morte : un aperçu », *Revue de Qumrân* 82, 209-232.
– « Notes sur le *Testament de Lévi* de la grotte 1 (1Q21) », *Revue de Qumrân* 82, 297-310.
– « Un autre manuscrit du *Lévitique* », *Revue de Qumrân* 82, 311-313.
– « Notes sur le manuscrit des *Juges* 4Q50^a », *Revue de Qumrân* 82, 315-319.
– « James the Just, or just James? The 'James Ossuary' on Trial », *Bulletin of the Anglo-Israel Archaeological Society*, 21, 45-53.

Revues de vulgarisation

– « L'eschatologie du judaïsme ancien et les textes de Qumrân : la croyance à la résurrection, - 1ère Partie », *Bulletin de l'Association* Bible et Terre Sainte, Numéro 6 - Septembre, 2-10.
– « Quand on retrouve le Livre des Géants », *Le Monde de la Bible* 151, juin, 25-27.
– « James the Just, or Just James? The Epigrapher's Trail », *Minerva* January/February 14/1, 4-5.
– « Czy znaleziono ossuarium Jakuba, brata Jezusa ? », *Verbum Vitae* 3, 269-276.
– « L'ossuaire de Jacques, le frère de Jésus ? », *Kephas* 5, 41-46.
– « Yad Absalôm hayah qedosh kebar beméah lanôtzerîm », *Haaretz* 22-08-2003, 1.7a.
– « Yad Absalom was holy to the Christians already in the 4th c. », *Ha'aretz*, 22-08-03, 1.2.
– « Yôm 'ehad ha'otiôt yits'û », *Môsaf ha'aretz*, 01-08-03, 38-42.
– « One day the letters emerged », *Haaretz Magazine*, August 1/2003, 18-21.
– « Inscription discovery links Jerusalem tomb to Jesus », *Reuters Kobra*, 22-08-03, 1-2.
– « Revealing the word », *Reuters, Taipei Times - Archives*, 23-08-03, 1-5.
– « Luck reveals Inscription on ancient Tomb », *The Associated Press*, 24-08-03, 1-3.
– « Scholars Discover Parts of New Testament », *The Associated Press*, 23-11-03, 1-2.
– « Gospel inscription discovered on Jerusalem tomb », *The Jerusalem Post*, 23-11-03

– « Grave Discovery », *Jerusalem Post Supplement,* December 12/2003, 10-11.
– « Descoberta a tumba do sacerdote Zacarias », *Resposta fiel*, 3/9, 20-23.

Recensions

– CH. R. KRAHMALKOV, Phoenician - Punic Dictionary, Leuven, 2000, *Revue Biblique* 110, 265-267.
– A. PINNICK, The Orion Center Bibliography of the Dead Sea Scrolls (1995-2000), Leiden, Boston, Köln, 2001, *Revue de Qumrân* 81, 119.
– D. GOODBLACK, A. PINNICK & D. R. SCHWARTZ (éd.), Historical Perspectives from the Hasmoneans to Bar Kokhba in Light of the Dead Sea Scrolls. Proceedings of the Fourth International Symposium of the Orion Center for the Study of the Dead Sea Scrolls and Associated Literature, 27-31 January, 1999, Leiden, Boston, Köln, 2001, *Revue de Qumrân* 81, 120-121.
– A. YARDENI, Textbook of Aramaic, Hebrew and Nabataean Documentary Texts from the Judaean Desert and Related Material. Volume A : The Documents. Volume B : Translation, Palaeography, Concordance, Jerusalem, 2000, *Revue de Qumrân* 81, 121-124.
– SH. TALMON With Contributions by C. NEWSON AND Y. YADIN, Masada VI. Yigael Yadin Excavations 1963-1965, Final Reports. Y. YADIN With Notes on the Reading by E. QIMRON and Bibliography by F. GARCÍA MARTÍNEZ, Hebrew Fragments from Masada, The Ben Sira Scroll from Masada., Jerusalem, 1999, *Revue de Qumrân* 81, 125-128.
– P. C. BEENTJES, The Book of Ben Sira in Hebrew. A Text Edition of All Extant Hebrew Manuscripts and a Synopsis of All Parallel Hebrew Ben Sira Texts, Leiden, New York, Köln, 1997, *Revue de Qumrân* 81, 128-129.
– E. D. HERBERT, Reconstructing Biblical Dead Sea Scrolls. A New Method Applied to the Reconstruction of 4QSam^{a}, Leiden, New York, Köln, 1997, *Revue de Qumrân* 81, 129-132.
– A. FINCKE, The Samuel Scroll from Qumran. 4QSam^{a} restored and compared to the Septuagint and 4QSam^{c}, Leiden, Boston, Köln, 2001, *Revue de Qumrân* 81, 130-132.
– C. KÖRTING, Der Schall des Schofar. Israels Feste im Herbst, Berlin, New York, 1999, *Revue de Qumrân* 81, 132-133.
– J. K. LEFKOVITS, The Copper Scroll 3Q15: a Reevalutation. A New Reading, Translation, and Commentary, Leiden, Boston, Köln, 2000, *Revue de Qumrân* 81, 133-135.
– D. M. GROPP, Wadi Daliyeh II: The Samaria Papyri from Wadi Daliyeh, M. BERNSTEIN, M. BRADY, J. CHARLESWORTH, P. FLINT, H. MISGAV, S. PFANN, E. SCHULLER, E. TIGCHELAAR, J. VANDERKAM, Qumran Cave 4: Miscellanea, Part 2 (Discoveries in the Judaean Desert XXVIII), Oxford, 2001, *Hebrew Study*, 44, 275-280.
– A. STEUDEL *ET ALII*, Die Texte aus Qumran II. Hebräisch/Aramäisch und Deutsch mit masoretischer Punktuation, Übersetzung und Anmerkungen, Darmstadt, 2001, *Revue de Qumrân* 82, 325-326.
– G. BRIN, The Concept of Time in the Bible and the Dead Sea Scrolls., Leiden-Boston-Köln, 2001, *Revue de Qumrân* 82, 326-327.

– M.L. GROSSMAN, Reading for History in the Damascus Document: a Methodological Study, Leiden, 2002, *Revue de Qumrân* 82, 328-329.

2004

Monographie

– FARAH MÉBARKI, EMILE PUECH, avec la collaboration de G. BROOKE, M. BROSHI, F. GARCÍA MARTÍNEZ, A. STEUDEL, E. ULRICH, *Les Manuscrits de la mer Morte* (Livre de Poche).

Ouvrages collectifs

– B. BIOUL, avec la participation de M. BELLIS, A. CAQUOT, P. DONCEEL-VOÛTE, H. ESHEL, N. GOLB, K. GALOR, Y. HIRCHFELD, J.-B. HUMBERT, E. PUECH, J. VANDERKAM, *Qumrân et les manuscrits de la mer Morte. Les hypothèses, le débat*, Paris, De Guibert.

Articles dans des ouvrages collectifs

– « Apocalíptica esenia: la vida futura », dans : J. Vázquez ALLEGUE (éd.), S. AUSÍN, M. BROSHI, P. FRAILE YÉCORA, F. GARCÍA MARTÍNEZ, F. JIMÉNEZ BEDMAN, M. PÉREZ FERNÁNDEZ, E. PUECH, I. RODRÍGEZ TORNÉ, A. ROITMAN, J.M. SÁNCHEZ CARO, F. SEN MONTERO, J. TREBOLLE BARRERA, *Para comprender los manuscritos del Mar Muerto*, Estella, Verbo Divino, 85-102.
– « El mesianismo », dans : J. Vázquez ALLEGUE (éd.), S. AUSÍN, M. BROSHI, P. FRAILE YÉCORA, F. GARCÍA MARTÍNEZ, F. JIMÉNEZ BEDMAN, M. PÉREZ FERNÁNDEZ, E. PUECH, I. RODRÍGEZ TORNÉ, A. ROITMAN, J.M. SÁNCHEZ CARO, F. SEN MONTERO, J. TREBOLLE BARRERA, *Para comprender los manuscritos del Mar Muerto*, Estella, Verbo Divino, 119-141.
– « La croyance à la résurrection des justes dans un texte qumranien de sagesse : 4Q418 69 ii », dans : Ch. COHEN, A. HURVITZ, Sh. PAUL (éd.), *Sefer Moshe: The Moshe Weinfeld Jubilee Volume. Studies in the Bible and the Ancient Near East, Qumran, and Post-Biblical Judaism*, Winona Lake, Eisenbrauns, 427-444.
– « La escatología del judaísmo antiguo y los textos de Qumrân: la creencia en la resurrección », dans : R. LÓPEZ ROSAS (éd.), *Comer, beber y alegrarse. Estudios bíblicos en honor a Raúl Duarte Castillo* (Estudios Bíblicos Mexicanos, 1), México, Coedición Qol y Departamento de Publicaciones de la Universidad Pontifica de México, 2004, 91-118.
– « Le fils de Dieu, le fils du Très-Haut, messie roi en 4Q246 », dans : *Le jugement dans l'un et l'autre Testament. I Mélanges offerts à Raymond Kuntzmann*, Postface de Mgr Doré (Lectio Divina, 197), Paris, Cerf, 271-286.
– « Il Libro della Sapienza e i manoscritti del Mar Morto : un primo approccio », dans : G. BELLIA, A. PASSARO (éd.), *Il Libro della Sapienza. Tradizione Redazione Teologia. 3º Convegno di Studi Biblici, Palermo 22-23 marzo 2002*, Roma, Facoltà Teologica di Sicilia, 131-155.

Articles de revues

– « Morceaux de sagesse populaire en araméen : 4QProverbes araméens (= 4Q569), *Revue de Qumrân* 83, 379-386.

– « Le fragment 2 de 4Q377 *Pentateuque apocryphe* B : l'exaltation de Moïse », *Revue de Qumrân* 83, 469-475.
– « Le Tombeau de Siméon et Zacharie dans la Vallée de Josaphat (avec J. ZIAS) », *Revue Biblique* 111, 563-77.

Revues de vulgarisation

– « L'eschatologie du judaïsme ancien et les textes de Qumrân : la croyance à la résurrection, 2ème partie », *Bulletin de l'Association Bible et Terre Sainte*, Numéro 7 - Janvier, 2-12.
– « Les tombeaux de Zacharie et Syméon », *Le Monde de la Bible* 157, 55.

Recensions

– O. MULDER : Simon de hogepriester in Sirach 50 (à compte d'auteur) 2000, paru depuis lors sous le titre Simon the High Priest in Sirach 50. An Exegetical Study of the Significance of Simon the High Priest as Climax to the Praise of the Fathers in Ben Sira's Concept of the History of Israel, Leiden, 2003, *Revue Biblique* 111, 90-92.
– E.J.C. TIGCHELAAR, To Increase Learning for the Understanding Ones. Reading and Reconstructing the Fragmentary Early Jewish Sapiential Text 4QInstruction. Leiden, Boston, 2001, *Revue de Qumrân* 84, 652-655.
– J. UN-SOK RO, Die sogennante "Armenfrömmigkeit" im nachexilischen Israel, Berlin, New York, 2002, *Revue de Qumrân* 84, 655-656.
– J. MAGNESS, The Archaeology of Qumran and the Dead Sea Scrolls, Grand Rapids, 2002, *Bulletin of the Anglo-Israel Archaeological Society*, 22, 60-67.

2005

Articles dans des ouvrages collectifs

– « The Essenes and Qumrân, the Teacher and the Wicked Priest, the Origins" dans : G. BOCCACCINI with J.H. ELLENS and J.A. WADDELL (éd.), *Enoch and Qumran Origins. New Light on a Forgotten Connection*, Grand Rapids, Michigan, Cambridge, U.K., Eerdmans, 298- 302, 317-326.
– « The Book of Wisdom and the Dead Sea Scrolls: an Overview », dans : A. PASSARO and G. BELLIA (éd.), With an Introduction by J.J. COLLINS, *The Book of Wisdom in Modern Research. Studies on Tradition, Redaction, and Theology* (Deuterocanonical and Cognate Literature. Yearbook 2005), Berlin, New York, De Gruyter, 117-141.
– « Les inscriptions proto-sinaïtiques 346 et 357 », dans : A.S. GIAMMELLARO (éd.), *Atti del V Congresso Internazionale di Studi Fenici e Punici, Marsala-Palermo, 2-8 ottobre 2000, Volume I*, Palermo, 2005, 27-41.

Articles de revues

– « Le Diable, homicide, menteur et père du mensonge en Jean 8,44 », *Revue Biblique* 112, 215-252.
– « Les fragments eschatologiques de 4QInstruction (4Q416 1 et 4Q418 69 ii, 81-81a et 127) », *Revue de Qumrân* 85, 89-119.

– (en collaboration avec J. ZIAS) « The Tomb of Absalom Reconsidered », *New Eastern Archaeology,* 68/4, 148-165.
– « In memoriam André Caquot », *Revue de Qumrân* 85, 3-5.

Articles d'encyclopédie

– « Arad », 178-179, « Calendrier hébreu au Ier millénaire av. J.-C. », 388-389, « Qohélet », 1854, « Qoumrân », 1854-1856, « Résurrection (Bible) », 1886, « Satan/ Bélial », 1964, dans : J. LECLANT (éd.), *Dictionnaire de l'Antiquité*, Paris, PUF.

Revue de vulgarisation

– « Qumran, grottes de lumière ou cavernes à rendre baba ? » *Christianisme aujourd'hui* 11, déc., 38 (interview de Paul Ohlott).

Recensions

– J.H. CHARLESWORTH et alii, The Dead Sea Scrolls. Hebrew, Aramaic, and Greek Texts with English Translations. Pseudepigraphic and Non-Massoretic Psalms, Tübingen, 1997, *Revue de Qumrân,* 85, 131-34.
– J.H. CHARLESWORTH et alii, The Dead Sea Scrolls. Hebrew, Aramaic, and Greek Texts with English Translations. Angelic Liturgy: Songs of the Sabbath Sacrifice, Tübingen, 1999, *Revue de Qumrân* 85, 134-36.
– J.H. CHARLESWORTH et alii, The Dead Sea Scrolls. Hebrew, Aramaic, and Greek Texts with English Translations. Pesharim, Other Commentaries, and Related Documents, Tübingen, 2002, *Revue de Qumrân* 85, 136-39.
– U. DAHMEN, Psalmen- und Psalter-Rezeption im Frühjudentum. Rekonstruktion, Textbestand, Struktur und Pragmatik der Psalmenrolle 11QPs[a] aus Qumran, Leiden-Boston, 2003, *Revue de Qumrân* 86, 279-81.
– C.H.T. FLETCHER-LOUIS, All the Glory of Adam. Liturgical Anthropology in the Dead Sea Scrolls, Leiden, Boston, Köln, 2002, *Revue de Qumrân* 86, 281-85.
– T. ILAN, Lexicon of Jewish Names in Late Antiquity. Part I - Palestine 330 BCE-200 CE, Tübingen, 2002, *Revue de Qumrân,* 86, 285-87.
– T. MURAOKA -J.F. ELWOLDE (eds), Diggers at the Well. Proceedings of a Third International Symposium on the Hebrew of the Dead Sea Scrolls and Ben Sira, Leiden, Boston, Köln, 2000, *Revue de Qumrân* 86, 287-89.
– C. M. MURPHY, Wealth in the Dead Sea Scrolls and in the Qumran Community, Leiden, Boston, Köln, 2002, *Revue de Qumrân* 86, 289-91.
– K. P. SULLIVAN, Wrestling with Angels. A Study of Relationship between Angels and Humans in Ancient Jewish Literature and the New Testament, Leiden, Boston, 2004, *Revue de Qumrân* 86, 291-94.
– J.A. FITZMYER, Tobit, Berlin, New York, 2003, *Revue de Qumrân* 86, 294-96.

2006

Ouvrage collectif

– Daniel BRIZEMEURE, Noël LACOUDRE EDF, Émile PUECH, CNRS, EBAF, *Le rouleau de cuivre de la Grotte 3 de Qumrân (3Q15). Expertise - Restauration - Épigraphie, Volume I – Texte. Volume II – Planches* (STDJ, 55 I-II), Leiden, Brill.

Articles dans des ouvrages collectifs

- « Les manuscrits 4QJuges[c] (= 4Q50[a]) et 1QJuges (= 1Q6) », dans : P.W. FLINT, E. TOV, J.C. VANDERKAM, *Studies in the Hebrew Bible, Qumran, and the Septuagint Presented to Eugene Ulrich* (Supplements to Vetus Testamentum, 101), Leiden, Boston, Brill 184-202.
- « Resurrection: the Bible and Qumran », dans : J. H. CHARLESWORTH (éd.), *The Bible and the Dead Sea Scrolls. The Princeton Symposium on the Dead Sea Scrolls.* Volume II: *The Dead Sea Scrolls and the Qumran Community*, Baltimore, Baylor University Press, 2006, 247-81.
- « Jesus and Resurrection Faith in Light of Jewish Texts », dans : J. H. CHARLESWORTH (éd), *Jesus and Archaeology,* Grands Rapids, Cambridge, Eerdmans, 639-59.
- « Apports des manuscrits de Qoumrân à la croyance à la résurrection dans le judaïsme ancien », dans : A. LEMAIRE, S.C. MIMOUNI (éd.), *Qoumrân et le Judaïsme du tournant de notre ère, Actes de la Table ronde, Collège de France, 16 novembre 2004* (Collection de la Revue des Études juives), Paris, Louvain, Dudley, Peeters, 81-110.

Articles de revues

- « Les manuscrits de la mer Morte et le Nouveau Testament, 'la tierra, las gentes, el libro' », *Estudios Bíblicos* 64, 337-68.
- « Le mausolée de saint Etienne à Khirbet Jiljil - Beit Jimal », *Revue Biblique* 113, 100-126.
- « In memoriam Józef Tadeusz Milik (1922-2006) », *Revue de Qumrân*, 87, 335-39.

Revue de vulgarisation

- « 60 tonnes d'or cachées dans ce texte ? », *Science & Vie Junior,* 198, mars, 64-5 (interview de Emmanuel Deslouis).
- « Joseph Milik (Disparitions) », *Le Monde* dimanche 22 - Lundi 23 janvier, 25.

Recensions

- J.-M. VAN CANGH et A. TOUMPSIN, L'Evangile de Marc : un original hébreu ? Brussels, 2005, *Catholic Biblical Quarterly* 68, 556-57.
- M. BAR-ASHER, D. DIMANT, Meghillot. Studies in the Dead Sea Scrolls, III, *Rivista Biblica* 54, 240-244.

2007

Ouvrage Collectif

- A. HILHORST, E. PUECH, E. TIGCHELAAR (éd.), *Flores Florentino: Dead Sea Scrolls and Other Early Jewish Studies in Honour of Florentino García Martínez* (Journal for the Studies of Judaism Supplements, 122), Leiden, Boston, Brill.

Articles dans des ouvrages collectifs

- L'ostracon de Khirbet Qumrân (KhQ1996/1) et une vente de terrain à Jéricho, témoin de l'occupation essénienne à Qumrân, dans : A. HILHORST, E. PUECH,

E. TIGCHELAAR (éd.), *Flores Florentino: Dead Sea Scrolls and Other Early Jewish Studies in Honour of Florentino García Martínez* (Journal for the Studies of Judaism Supplements, 122), Leiden, Boston, Brill, 1-29.
- « Une nouvelle amulette en araméen christo-palestinien », dans : A. MAMAN, S.E. FASSBERG, and Y. BREUER (éd.), *Sha'rei Lashon. Studies in Hebrew, Aramaic and Jewish Languages Presented to Moshe Bar-Asher*, *Volume II* : *Rabbinic Hebrew and Aramaic*, Jerusalem, Bialik, p.71*-84*.

Articles de revues

- « What can the Dead Sea Scrolls teach us about the belief in the resurrection in Ancient Judaism », *Canon & Culture* 2, 43-88.
- « Aramaic Scribal Exercices of the Hellenistic Period from Maresha: Bowls A and B(en collaboration avec E. Eshel et A. Kloner) », *Bulletin of the American School of the Oriental Research*, 345, 39-62.
- « Une amulette judéo-palestinienne bilingue en argent », dans : M. BAR-ASHER, E. TOV (éd.), *A Festschrift for Deborah Dimant. Studies in the Dead Sea Scrolls, Meghillot* V-VI, 177*-186*.

Revue de vulgarisation

- « La soi-disant tombe perdue de Jésus », *Biblia* 59, 44-45.
- « La conception de la vie future chez les Esséniens », *Trajets* 3 - avril-mai-juin, 58-66.

2008

Articles dans des ouvrages collectifs

- « Les identités en présence dans les scènes du jugement dernier de *4QInstruction* (4Q416 1 et 4Q418 69 ii) », dans : F. GARCÍA MARTÍNEZ and M. POPOVIĆ (éd.), *Defining Identities: We, You, and the Others in the Dead Sea Scrolls, Proceedings of the Fifth Meeting of the IOQS in Groningen* (STDJ, 70), Leiden, Boston, Brill 147-173.
- « Ben Sira and Qumrân », dans : A. PASSARO, G. BELLI (éd.), *The Book of Wisdom in Modern Research. Studies on Tradition, Redaction, and Theology* (Deuterocanonical and Cognate Literature, 1), Berlin, New York, De Gruyter, 79-118.
- « Bala'am and Deir 'Alla », dans : G. VAN KOOTEN, J. VAN RUITEN (éd.), *The Prestige of the Pagan Prophet Balaam in Judaism, Early Christianity and Islam* (Themes in Biblical Narrative, 10), Leiden, Brill, 25-47.
- « 4QSamuel^{a} (4Q51). Notes épigraphiques et nouvelles identifications », dans : H. AUSLOOS, B. LEMMELIJN, M. VERVENNE, *Florilegium Lovaniense. Studies in Septuagint and Textual Criticism in Honour of Florentino Garciía Martínez* (Bibliotheca Ephemeridum Theologicarum Lovaniensium CCXXIV), Leuven, Paris, Dudley, Peeters, 373-386.

Articles de revues

- « Le *Testament de Lévi* araméen, *Cambridge A-B et F. Corrigenda et addenda* », *Revue de Qumrân* 92, 543-561.

Revue de vulgarisation

– « Les manuscrits de Qumrân et Jésus », *Képhas*, 27 juillet – septembre 2008, 23-31.

Recensions

– M.G. ABEGG, with J.E. BOWLEY & E.M. COOK in consultation with E. TOV, The Dead Sea Scrolls Concordance. Volume One: The Non-Biblical Texts from Qumran [Part One and Two] Leiden, Boston, 2003, *Revue de Qumrân* 92, 569-72.
– L. DITOMMASO, The Dead Sea New Jerusalem Text. Contents and Contexts, Tübingen 2005, *Revue de Qumrân* 92, 572-74.

2009

Monographie

– *Qumrân grotte 4 · XXVII. Textes araméens, Deuxième partie. 4Q550-4Q575a, 4Q580-4Q587 et Appendices* (Discoveries in the Judaean Desert XXXVII), Oxford, Clarendon Press, 2009.

Ouvrages collectifs

– *Les manuscrits de la mer Morte* (nouvelle édition actualisée), en collaboration avec F. MÉBARKI, Rodez, 240 p., avec illustrations.
– *Los Manuscritos del Mar Muerto*, con 172 reproducciones en color, nueva edición revisada (avec F. MÉBARKI), traducción S. Rostom Maderna (Serie arqueología, objetos y sociedad, ed. SB), Buenos Aires.

Articles dans des ouvrages collectifs

– « L'inscription phénicienne du pithos d'Amathonte et son contexte », dans : J. D. SCHLOEN (éd.), *Exploring the* Longue Durée. *Essays in Honor of Lawrence E. Stager*, Winona Lake, 391-401.
– « L'identité d'Israël à Qumrân », dans : Olivier ARTUS et Joëlle FERRY (éd.), *L'identité dans l'Écriture. Hommage au Professeur Jacques Briend* (Lectio Divina), Paris, Cerf, 277-94.
– « Manuskrypty znad Morza Martwego a Nowy Testament. Mistrzowie i nadzieje » [Les manuscrits de la mer Morte et le Nouveau Testament : les Maîtres et les espérances], dans : HENRYK DRAWNEL, ANDRZEJ PIWOWAR (éd.), *Qumran pomiędzy Starym a Nowym Testamentem* (Analecta Biblica Lublinensia, 2), Lublin, 187-203.
– « Manuskrypty znad Morza Martwego a Nowy Testament. Nowy Mojżesz czyli o kilku praktykach Prawa » [Les manuscrits de la mer Morte et le Nouveau Testament : le Nouveau Moïse, de quelques pratiques de la Loi], dans : Henryk DRAWNEL, Andrzej PIWOWAR (éd.), *Qumran pomiędzy Starym a Nowym Testamentem* (Analecta Biblica Lublinensia, 2), Lublin, 205-225.

Articles de revues

– « 4Q173a : note épigraphique », *Revue de Qumrân* 94, 287-90.
– « Los Manuscritos del Mar Muerto y el Nuevo Testamento. El Nuevo Moisés: algunas practícas de la Ley », *Revista Antiguo Oriente* 7, 219-54.

2010

Articles dans des ouvrages collectifs

– « André Caquot et le Rouleau du Temple », dans : JEAN RIAUD, MARIE-LAURE CHAIEB (éd.), *L'Œuvre d'un orientaliste. André Caquot 1923-2004* (Bibliothèque d'Études Juives, 41, Série Histoire 36), Paris, 139-49.
– « Quelques observations sur le 'canon des Écrits' », dans : M. Popović (éd.), *Authoritative Scriptures in Ancient Judaism. The Contribution of the Dead Sea Scrolls and Related Literature, 28-29 April 2008, Groningen* (STDJ, 141), Leiden-Boston, Brill, 117-41.
– « Le volume XXXVII des *Discoveries in the Judaean Desert* et les manuscrits araméens du lot Starcky », dans : D. STÖKL BEN EZRA, K. BERTHELOT (éd.), *Aramaica Qumranica : Proceedings of the Conference on the Aramaic Texts from Qumran at Aix en Provence 30 June-2 July 2008* (STDJ, 94), Leiden, Boston, Brill, 2010, 47-61, 123, 143, 179, 220, 273, 297, 373, 401-02, 513, 542-43, 562-63.
– « Le témoignage des épigraphistes », dans : Laurent HÉRICHER et alii (éd.), *Qumrân. Le secret des manuscrits de la mer Morte, Catalogue de l'exposition à la Bibliothèque Nationale de France,* Paris, 91.
– « Esséniens et interprétations », dans : Laurent HÉRICHER et alii (éd.), *Qumrân. Le secret des manuscrits de la mer Morte, Catalogue de l'exposition à la Bibliothèque Nationale de France*, Paris, 135-36.

Articles de revues

– « L'ostracon de Khirbet Qeyafa et les débuts de la royauté en Israël », *Revue Biblique* 117, 162-84.
– « In Memoriam. *Pierre Grelot* (1917-2009) », *Henoch* 32/1, 233-35.
– « In memoriam. *Henri Cazelles* (1912-2009) », *Henoch* 32/1, 236-38.
– « L'épigraphie de Qumrân : son apport à l'identification du site (Mémorial John Strugnell : EBAF 31 mars 2009) », *Revue de Qumân* 95, 433-40.
– « Secrétariat de la *Revue de Qumrân* », *Revue de Qumân* 96, 515-16.
– « Notes sur le manuscrit 4Q201 = 4QHénoch. À propos d'un livre récent », *Revue de Qumân* 96, 627-49.

Revue de vulgarisation

– « Czy Jesus byl essénczykiem ? », *Biblia krok po kroku* 15, 22-24.
– « Le Messie attendu par les Esséniens », *Sources vives*, 155, 17-19.

Recension

– M. LANGLOIS, Le premier manuscrit du Livre d'Hénoch. Étude épigraphique et philologique des fragments araméens de 4Q201 à Qumrân (LD hors série), Paris, 2008, 615 p., *Revue Biblique* 117, 435-39.

2011

Articles dans des ouvrages collectifs

– « La sagesse dans les béatitudes de Ben Sira. Étude du texte de Si 51,13-30 et de Si 14,20-15,10 », dans : J.-S. REY, J. JOOSTEN (éd.), *The Texts and*

Versions of the Book of Ben Sira. Transmission and Interpretation (SJSJ, 150), Leiden, Boston, Brill, 2011, 297-329.
- « Notes d'épigraphie christo-palestinienne de Jordanie », dans : Cl. DAUPHIN and B. HAMARNEH (éd.), *In Memoriam: Michele Piccirillo*, ofm (1944-2008). *Celebrating his life and work* (BAR International Series, 2248), Oxford, Archeopress, 75-94, 205-236.
- « L'hymne de la glorification du Maître de Justice de 4Q431 », dans : J. PENNER, K.M. PENNER, C. WASSEN (éd.), *Prayer and Poetry in the Dead Sea Scrolls and Related Literature. Essays in Honor of Eileen Schuller on the Occasion of Her 65th Birthday* (STDJ, 98), Leiden, Brill, 367-397.

Articles de revues

- « Khirbet Qumrân et les Esséniens », *Revue de Qumrân* 97, 63-102.
- « Un nouveau fragment 7a de 4QGn-Ex[a] = 4QGn-Ex 1 et quelques nouvelles lectures et identifications », *Revue de Qumrân* 97, 103-111.
- « 4Q530 9-10 – Addenda et corrigenda », *Revue de Qumrân* 97, 127-131.
- « La lettre de Jacques et Qumrân », *Rivista Biblica* 59, 29-55.
- « Inscriptions d'un hypogée de Sha'fât et du tombeau des rois », *Revue Biblique* 118, 321-330.

Recensions

- J. GUNNEWEG, A. ADRIAENS, J. DIK (éd.), Holistic Qumran. Trans-Disciplinary Research of Qumran and the Dead Sea Scrolls. Proceedings of the NIAS-Lorentz Center Qumran Workshop, 21-25 April 2008, Leiden, Boston, 2010, *Revue de Qumrân* 97,140-43.
- EUGENE ULRICH, The Biblical Scrolls. Transcriptions and Textual Variants, Leiden, Boston, 2010, *Revue de Qumrân* 97, 143-46.
- U. SCHATTNER-RIESNER, L'araméen des manuscrits de la mer Morte, I. Grammaire, Belfort, 2004, *Revue de Qumrân* 97, 146-55 et *Dead Sea Discoveries* 18, 264-73.
- A. LANGE, Handbuch der Textfunde vom Toten Meer. Band 1: Die Handschriften biblischer Bücher von Qumran und den anderen Fundorten, Tübingen, 2009, *Revue de Qumrân* 97, 155-56.
- H. VON WEISSENBERG, 4QMMT. Reevaluating the Text, the Function, and the Meaning of the Epilogue, Leiden, Boston, 2009, *Revue de Qumrân* 97, 159-60.
- L.H. SCHIFFMAN and SH. TZOREF (éd.), The Dead Sea Scrolls at 60. Scholarly Contributions of New York University Faculty and Alumni, Leiden, Boston, 2010, *Revue de Qumrân* 98, 327-331.
- GIOVANNI GARBINI, Introduzione all'epigrafia semitica (Testi sul Vicino Oriente antico, 4), Brescia, 2006, *Rivista Biblica*, 59, 428-435.

2012

Articles dans des ouvrages collectifs

- « Criticism and the Dead Sea Scrolls », dans : A. PIQUER OTERO, P. TORIJANO MORALES, *Studies in Honour of Julio Trebolle Barrera: Florilegium Complutense* (JSJS, 175), Leiden, Brill 277-302.

– « L'épilogue de *4QMMT* revisité », dans : E.F. MASON, S.I. THOMAS, A. SCHOFIELD, E. ULRICH (éd.), *A Teacher for All Generations: Essays in Honor of James VanderKam,* (JSJS, 153 I/II), Leiden, Brill, 309-339.
– « Qumran Research Contribution of the École Biblique et Archéologique Française de Jérusalem », dans : D. DIMANT (éd.), *The Dead Sea Scrolls on Scholarly Perspective* (STDJ, 99), Leiden, Brill, 403-32.

Articles de revues

– « La constitution de groupements de livres normatifs à Qumrân », *Revue Biblique* 119, 45-57.
– « L'inscription cananéenne en alphabet cunéiforme sur un ivoire de Tirynthe », *Revue Biblique* 119, 321-30.
– « Synthèse des observations de la nécropole de *Khirbet* Qumrân. Tombes d'Esséniens et tombes de bédouins », *Revue de Qumrân* 99, 335-368.
– « Jérusalem dans les manuscrits de la mer Morte », *Revue de Qumrân* 99, 423-438.
– « Un 'bol' de bois des grottes de Qumrân », *Revue de Qumrân* 99, 439-444.
– « Nouvelles identifications des manuscrits bibliques dans la grotte 4. 4QRois[a] (4Q54[a]) et 4QRois[b]- 4Q54[b] (?) ou 4QIs[c]-4Q69[c] », *Revue de Qumrân* 99, 467-472.
– « Addendum 4QSm[a] IX 2-4 », *Revue de Qumrân* 99, 479-480.
– « Los Manuscritos del Mar Muerto y el Nuevo Testamento. Los Maestros y las Esperanzas », *Revista Bíblica*, 72, 5-27.
– « Quelques exemples d'apports des manuscrits à l'étude du judaïsme ancien (Mémorial John Strugnell, EBAF 31 mars 2009 », *Revue Biblique* 119, 543-563.
– « Cruche magique en araméen babylonien », *Semitica et Classica*, 5, 249-259.
– « Une nouvelle amulette en araméen christo-palestinien », *Liber Annuus* 62, 303-317.
– « La *Première Épître de Pierre* et Qumrân. Quelques observations sur le milieu judéo-chrétien de l'Épître », *Rivista Biblica* LX, 493-525.

Recensions

– J. FREY, C. CLAUSSEN und N. KESSLER (éd.), Qumran und die Archäologie. Texte und Kontexte, Tübingen, 2011, *Revue de Qumrân* 99, 483-491.
– SH.L. BERRIN, The Pesher Nahum Scroll from Qumran. An Exegetical Study of 4Q169, Leiden, Boston, 2004, *Revue de Qumrân* 99, 493-499.

2013

Articles dans des ouvrages collectifs

– « Family Relationships in 4Qinstruction », dans : Angelo PASSARO (éd.), *Family and Kindship in the Deuterocanonical and Cognate Literature, Conference of the International Society of Deuterocanonical and Cognate Literature* (Deuterocanonical and Cognate Literature Yearbook 2012/13), Berlin, Boston, De Gruyter, 2013, 377-404.

– « 'Les oeuvres de la Loi' : mariage et divorce à Qumrân et dans les lettres de Paul », dans : JEAN-SÉBASTIEN REY (éd.), *The Dead Sea Scrolls and Pauline Literature* (STDJ, 102), Leiden, 2013, 143-169.
– « Presentacion », dans : *La Bíblia. Ancian Testament. Letras d'òc. La Bíblia occitana*, Pau, 8-10.

Articles de revues

– « L'œuvre de Jean Starcky », *Bulletin de l'Association Bible et Terre Sainte* 25, 2-17.
– « L'inscription araméenne du linteau de Saint-Pierre en Gallicante », *Revue Biblique* 120, 481-90.
– « Addendum 4Q Sam[a] = 1 S 5,8b », *Rivista Biblica* 60, 195-196.
– « 4Q225 revisité : un midrash essénien ? », *Revue de Qumrân* 102, 169-209.
– « 4Q252 : "Commentaire de la Genèse A" ou "Bénédictions patriarcales" », *Revue de Qumrân* 102, 227-251.
– « 4Q226 7 revisité », *Revue de Qumrân* 102, 284-290.
– « Une stèle funéraire araméenne de Tayma' », *Liber Annuus* 63, 339-342, 488.
– « In memoriam : Jerome Murphy-O'Connor, OP (1935-2013) », *Revue de Qumrân* 102, 141-144.

Recensions

– J.-S. REY, 4QInstruction : sagesse et eschatologie, Leiden, Boston, 2009, *Revue de Qumrân* 101, 135-39.
– T. MURAOKA, A Grammar of Qumran Aramaic, Leuven, Paris, Walpole, 2011, *Rivista Biblica* 61, 567-571.

2014

Articles dans des ouvrages collectifs

– « Abraham dans les manuscrits de la mer Morte », dans : A. PASSARO, A. PITTA (éd.), *Abramo tra storia e fede* (Ricerche Storico-Bibliche, 1-2), Bologna, EDB, 205-233.

Articles de revues

– « Inscriptions en araméen christo-palestinien du Wadî Hajjaj (Sinaï) », *Liber Annuus 64* (*Dedicated to Giovanni Claudio Bottini, ofm, on the Occasion of His 70th Birthday*), 591-601 et 660.
– « Les inscriptions hébraïques de Kuntillet 'Ajrud (Sinaï) », *Revue Biblique* 121, 161-19.
– « Un quatrième manuscrit du livre de Job dans la grotte 4 de Qumrân (4Q101[a] - 4QJob[d]) », *Revue de Qumrân* 103, 431-33.
– « Un nouveau fragment du manuscrit 4Q27 - 4QNb[b] 18a », *Revue de Qumrân* 103, 435-37.
– « Note sur 4Q200 fragment 8 », *Revue de Qumrân* 103, 453-54.
– « Un Hymne d'action de grâce pour les merveilles de Dieu (4Q427) », *Rivista Biblica* 62, 441-74.

Articles de vulgarisation

– « Los Esenios pudieron reconocer en Jesus al Mesias, interview de F. Garufi », Monografico Ano/Cero, 64-69.

Recension

– ELISHA QIMRON, The Dead Sea Scrolls. The Hebrew Writings, Volume Two, Jérusalem, 2013, *Revue de Qumrân* 104, 631-38.
– T. MURAOKA, A Grammar of Qumran Aramaic, Leuven, Paris, Walpole, 2011, *Journal for the Studies of Judaism* 45, 133-138.

2015

Monographie

– *The Copper Scroll* (STDJ, 112), Leiden, Boston, Brill.

Articles dans des ouvrages collectifs

– « Cruche magique ornée de malédictions écrites en araméen babylonien, dans : JACQUES CHARLES-GAFFIOT, ALAIN DESREUMAUX (éd.), *Grandes Heures des Manuscrits Irakiens. Une collection dominicaine inconnue de manuscrits orientaux (xiie-xxe siècles). VIIIe Centenaire de la fondation de l'Ordre des Prêcheurs par Saint Dominique*, Paris, 2015, 232-33.
– « Aux sources de l'alphabet : de quelques anciens témoignages en écriture alphabétique », dans : C. RICO, C. ATTUCCI (éd.), *Origins of the Alphabet. Proceedings of the First Polis Institute Interdisciplinary Conference,* Newcastle on Tyne, 2015, 73-123.
– « Yahweh et son ashérah dans les inscriptions de l'époque du Fer II », dans : J. LUIS D'AMICO, C. MENDOZA (éd.), *La Palabra. Está muy cerca de ti, en tu boca y en tu corazón… Dt 30,14. Homenaje a Fray Gabriel Nápole, OP 1959-2013* (Suplementos a la Revista Bíblica, 1), Buenos Aires, 141-155.
– « Ricordo del prof. Émile Puech », dans : M. PASSINI (éd.), *La vita come viaggio. Ricordando Pietro Alberto Kaswalder*, Milano, 65-71.

Articles de revues

– « L'inscription 3 de Khirbet el-Qôm revisitée et l'*'ashérah* », *Revue Biblique* 122, 5-25.
– « La tablette RS 24.258 = KTU 1.114, 14-15 revisitée », *Revue Biblique* 122, 284-89.
– « La Lettre essénienne *MMT* dans le manuscrit 4Q397 et les parallèles », *Revue de Qumrân* 105, 99-135.
– « L'inscription grecque de la cuve baptismale à Tabgha », *Liber Annuus* 65, 483-491.
– « Les copies du livre de Josué dans les manuscrits de la mer Morte : 4Q47, 4Q48, 4Q123 et XJosué », *Revue Biblique* 122, 481-506.

Recensions

– B. PORTEN AND A. YARDENI, Textbook of Aramaic Ostraca from Idumea, Vol. 1, Winona Lake, 2014, *Revue Biblique* 122, 297-301.

– Corine Bonnet et Herbert Niehr, La religion des Phéniciens et des Araméens, Dans : le contexte de l'Ancien Testament, Genève, 2014, *Revue Biblique* 122, 609-617.

2016

Articles dans des ouvrages collectifs

– M. Fidanzio, E. Puech, « Identification d'un nouveau manuscrit de la Grotte 11 : 11Q23 - 11QcryptA Lv[c], La grotta 11 di Quman : Archeologia e frammenti monoscritti », dans : M. Crimella, G.C. Pagazzi, S. Romanello (éd.), *Extra Ironiam nulla salus. Studi in onore di Roberto Vignolo in occasione del suo LXX compleanno* (Biblica 8), Milano, Glossa, 927-948.
– « Les Esséniens et la croyance à la résurrection : de l'eschatologie zoroastrienne aux notices de Josèphe et d'Hippolyte », dans: J. Baden, H. Najman, E. Tigchelaar (éd.), *Sibyls, Scriptures and Scrolls: John Collins at Seventy* (JSJSup, 175/1-2), Leiden, Boston, Brill, 1068-1095.
– « La paléographie des manuscrits de la mer Morte », dans: M. Fidanzio (éd.), *The Caves of Qumran. Proceedings of the International Conference, Lugano 2014* (STDJ, 118), Leiden, Boston, Brill, 96-105.
– « Glanures épigraphiques », dans: *Eretz-Israel. Archaeological, Historical and Geographical Studies. Joseph Naveh Volume* (Eretz Israel, 32), Jerusalem, 71*-78*.

Articles de revues

– « Le *Cantique des Cantiques* dans les manuscrits de Qumrân : 4Q106, 4Q107, 4Q108 et 6Q6 », *Revue Biblique* 123, 29-53.
– « Les inscriptions hébraïques du domaine de Sainte Anne de Jérusalem », *Revue Biblique* 123, 230-238.
– « Les manuscrits de Qumrân inspirés du livre de *Josué* : 4Q378-4Q379, 4Q175, 4Q522, 5Q9 et Mas 1039-211 », *Revue de Qumrân* 107, 45-116.

Revues de vulgarisation

– « Qu'es aquò que foguèt realament descobèrt a Qumrân ? », *Lo Bornat*, abriu, mai, junh, 2016/2, 11-14 (a segre).
– « L'ouragan vient de la mer Morte », *Le Figaro Hors-Série* décembre 2016, 116-119.

Recensions

– Jo Ann Hackett and Walter E. Aufrecht (éd.), « An Eye for Form ». Epigraphic Essays in Honor of Frank Moore Cross, Winona Lake, 2014, *Revue Biblique* 123, 125-129.
– J. Duhaime et P.W. Flint (éd.), Célébrer les manuscrits de la mer Morte. Une perspective canadienne, comprenant vingt-cinq contributions par des spécialistes des manuscrits de la mer Morte et de la littérature connexe, Montréal, Paris, 2014, *Science et Esprit*, 68, 421-25.
– Per Jarle Bekken, The Lawsuit Motif in John's Gospel from New Perspectives: Jesus Christ, Crucified Criminal and Emperor of the World, Leiden, Boston, 2015, *Revue Biblique*, 123, 621-25.

- ELISHA QIMRON, The Dead Sea Scrolls. The Hebrew Writings, Volume Three, Jerusalem, 2014, *Revue de Qumrân* 108, 287-95.
- KARL JAROŠ, Zeugen auf Stein und Ton. Inschriften des Heiligen Landes und seiner Nachbarregionen aus vier Jahrtausenden, Wiesbaden, 2014, Syria : HTTP://SYRIA.REVUES.ORG/4367
- WOLFGANG RÖLLIG, Die aramäischen Texte aus Tall Šēḫ Ḥamad / Dūr-Katlimmu / Magdalu, Wiesbaden, 2014, Syria : HTTP://SYRIA.REVUES.ORG/4371

2017

Articles dans des ouvrages collectifs

- « L'ostrakon di Khirbet Qeyafa rivisitato e gli inizi della monarchia in Israele », dans : G. PAXIMADI - M. FIDANZIO (éd.), *Terrasancta II. Ricerche storiche e filologiche. Atti dei convegni 2012-2014* (ISCAB.SA, 2), Lugano, 2017, 28-55.
- « Ricostruire i manoscritti », dans : G. PAXIMADI - M. FIDANZIO (éd.), *Terrasancta II. Ricerche storiche e filologiche. Atti dei convegni 2012-2014* (ISCAB.SA, 2), Lugano, 2017, 88-107.
- « Un nouveau manuscript de Daniel : 4QDn^f = 4Q116^a », dans : A. FELDMAN, M. CIOATA, Ch. HEMPEL (éd.), *Is There a Text in This Cave? Studies in the Textuality of the Dead Sea Scrolls in Honour of George J. Brooke* (STDJ 119), Leiden, Brill, 2017, 123-132.

Articles de revues

- « Édition et reconstruction des manuscrits », *Henoch* 39, 105-25.
- « Les fragments de papyrus 7Q6 1-2, 7Q9 et 7Q7 = pap7QLXXDt », *Revue de Qumrân* 109, 119-127.
- « Le livre des Juges dans les copies qumraniennes (4Q559 4-6, 1Q6, 4Q49-50-50a) », *Revue Biblique* 124, 342-368.
- « Élie et Élisée dans l'Éloge des Pères: Sira 48,1-14 dans le manuscrit B et les parallèles », *Revue de Qumrân* 110, 205-218.

Revues de vulgarisation

- « Qu'es aquò que foguèt realament descobèrt a Qumrân ? (Partida III) », *Lo Bornat* (janvier-mars 2017), 17-22 (a segre).
- « Qu'es aquò que foguèt realament descobèrt a Qumrân ? (partida IV - bis) » *Lo Bornat* (janvier-març 2018), 23-28 (a segre)

Recensions

- LA BÍBLIA. Novèl Testament. Revirada occitana de JOAN ROQUETA-LARZAC, Pau, 2016, *Revue Biblique* 124 (2017) 146-147.
- M.S. PAJUNEN AND H. TERVANOTKO (ÉD.), Crossing Imaginary Boundaries. The Dead Sea Scrolls in the Context of Second Temple Judaism, Helsinki, 2015, *Revue Biblique*, 124, 595-598.
- E. TOV, K. DAVIS and R. DUKE (Ed.), Dead Sea Scrolls Fragments in the Museum Collection, Leiden, Boston, 2016, *Revue de Qumrân* 109, 153-156.
- J.-B. HUMBERT, A. CHAMBON et J. MŁYNARCZYK, Khirbet Qumrân et Aïn Feshkha. Fouilles du P. Roland de Vaux, IIIA – L'archéologie de Qumrân, reconsideration

de l'interprétation, Corpus of the Lamps, Göttingen, 2016, *Revue de Qumrân* 110, 287-314.
- M PHILONENKO, Histoire des religions et exégèse (1955-2012), Vol. 1 et 2, Paris, 2015, *Revue Biblique* 124, 625-626.

2018

Articles de revues

- « Le cantique d'action de grâce du pauvre à Dieu sauveur en 4Q491 11 et les parallèles », *Revue de Qumrân* 112, 235-64.
- « La Lettre de Jude et la Deuxième Lettre de Pierre et Qumrân. Quelques observations sur les sources et les techniques de composition », *Rivista Biblica* LXVI, 631-663.
- « L'inscription alphabétique sur un cuveau dans une tombe d'Alassa (Chypre) », *Folia Phoenicia* 2, 2018, 413-419.
- « La tablette cunéiforme de Tell Ta'anak », *Revue Biblique* 125, 120-123.
- « Deux graffiti témoins de destructions au palais d'Hérode lors de la première révolte juive », *Revue Biblique*, 125, 262-268.
- « L'attente du retour d'Élie dans l'Ancien Testament et les écrits péritestamentaires : 4Q558 et 4Q521 », *Revue de Qumrân*, 111, 3-26.
- « La préséance du messie prêtre en 1QSa II 11-22 », *Revue de Qumrân*, 111, 85-89.

Recensions

- BEZALEL PORTEN, ADA YARDENI with the assistance of MATT KLETZING, EUGEN HAN, Textbook of Aramaic Ostraca from Idumea, Vol. 2. Winona Lake, Indiana, 2016, *Revue biblique* 125 (2018) 443-47.
- J. STARR, Classifying the Aramaic Texts from Qumran. A Statistical Analysis of Linguistic Features, London, Oxford, New York, New Delhy, Sydney, 2017, *Revue Biblique* 125, 610-612.

2019

Articles dans des ouvrages collectifs

- « Nouveaux menus fragments de la Grotte 11Q (P1344, P1345 et P 1348B) », dans : M. FIDANZIO, J.B. HUMBERT (éd.), *Khirbet Qumrân and Aïn Feshkha. IVa - Qumrân Cave 11Q. Archaeology and New Scroll Fragments* (Novum Testamentum et Orbis Antiquus, Series Archaeologica, 8a), Göttingen, Vandenhoeck and Ruprecht, 2019, 203-229.
- « Nouveaux menus fragments de la Grotte 11Q (boîte 1032A/1), » dans : M. FIDANZIO, J.B. HUMBERT (éd.), *Khirbet Qumrân and Aïn Feshkha. IVa - Qumrân Cave 11Q. Archaeology and New Scroll Fragments* (Novum Testamentum et Orbis Antiquus. Series Archaeologica. 8a), Göttingen, Vandenhoeck and Ruprecht, 2019, 245-247.

Articles de revues

- « Les manuscrits des livres de Samuel dans les grottes 1 et 4 de Qumrân : 1Q7, 4Q51-52-53, et l'Apocryphe de Samuel - 4Q160 », *Revue Biblique* 126, 5-51.

– « Le sceau de Miqnêyaw, serviteur de YHWH, revisité », *Revue Biblique* 126, 109-112.
– « "Les peuples, fils de Seth" en 4Q417 1 i 15 », *Revue de Qumrân*, 113, 135-143.
– « Fragments des livres de *Josué* et des *Chroniques* dans la Grotte 4, *4Q47*[a] et *4Q418* 2-3 ? », *Revue de Qumrân* 114, 303-305.

Revues de vulgarisation

– « Qu'es aquò que foguèt realament descobèrt a Qumrân ? » *Lo Bornat* (janvier, febrier, març 2019), 30-32 (a segre).
– « Qu'es aquò que foguèt realament descobèrt a Qumrân ? » *Lo Bornat* (abriu, mai junh 2019), 17-19 (a segre).

Recensions

– E. Lipiński, Studies in Aramaic Inscriptions and Onomastics IV, Leuven, Paris, Bristol, 2016 et E. Lipiński, Peuples de la Mer, Phéniciens, Puniques. Études d'épigraphie et d'histoire méditerranéenne, Leuven, Paris, Bristol, CT, 2015, *Revue Biblique* 126, 113-117.
– C.D. Elledge, Resurrection of the Dead in Early Judaism 200 BCE-CE 200 (Oxford: Oxford University press, 2017), *Revue Biblique* 126, 299-302.
– G. Geiger, Introduzione all'aramaico biblico, Milano, 2018, *Revue Biblique* 126, 626-627.

2020

Articles dans des ouvrages collectifs

– « La stèle et le fragment phéniciens de Nora en Sardaigne et Tarsis », dans : S. Celestino Pérez, E. Rodríguez González (éd.), *Un viaje entre el Oriente y el Occidente del Mediterraneo. A Journey between East and West in the Mediterranean. Actas/Proceedings. IX Congreso Internacional de Estudios Fenicios y Púnicos, IX International Congress of Phoenician Studies, 22-26 Octobre 2018 Mérida (Extremadure, España)*, Volumen I (MYTRA monografias y trabajos de arqueología. 5), Mérida, Instituto de Arqueología, 2020, 317-325.
– « Destructions dans la ville haute au début de la première révolte juive », dans : A. Giambrone (éd.), *Rethinking the Jewish War : Archaeology, Society, Tactics, and Traditions, Symposium EBAF October 30-November 1 2018* (Études Bibliques, Nouvelle Série, 84), Leuven, Peeters, 2020, 63-71.
– « La stèle araméenne de Dan revisitée et le fragment de stèle d'Afis », dans : Innocent Himbaza, Clemens Locher (éd.), *Études textuelles et littéraires offertes en hommage à Adrian Schenker à l'occasion de ses quatre-vingts ans* (Cahiers de la Revue Biblique, 95), Leuven, Paris, Bristol, Peeters, 2020, 331-345.
– « "YHWH vient de Téman" et le monothéisme en Israël et Juda », dans : Uri Gabbay, Jean-Jacques Pérennès (éd.), *Du polythéisme au monothéisme, Mélanges Marcel Sigrist* (Études Biblique, Nouvelle Série, 82), Paris, Leuven, Peeters, 2020, 71-106.

– « L'inscription en araméen christo-palestinien de ʿAbûd (Samarie) », dans : *Mélanges Eugenio Alliata* (Studium Biblicum Fransciscanum Collectio Maior), 2020, 329-336.

Articles de revues

– « L'inscription de Ḥorvat ʿUza, un document sapientiel », *Revue Biblique* 127, 321-337.
– « Exercices de deux scribes à Khirbet Qumrân : KhQ 161 et KhQ 2207 », *Revue de Qumrân* 115, 43-56.
– « Le targum de Job de la grotte 4 : 4Q157 = 4QtgJob », *Revue de Qumrân* 115, 135-141.
– « L'ostracon araméen/hébreu de Tell Keisân », *Revue Biblique* 127, 607-610.

Recensions

– T. ELGVIN, The Literary Growth of the Song of Songs during the Hasmonean and Early-Herodian Periods, Leuven, Paris, Bristol, 2018, *Revue Biblique,* 127, 136-140.
– S.J. JOSEPH, Jesus, the Essenes, and Christian Origins. New Light on Ancient Texts and Communities, Waco, 2018, *Revue Biblique,* 127, 451-453.
– H. ESHEL, Exploring the Dead Sea Scrolls. Archaeology and Literature of the Qumran Caves, edited by Sh. TZOREF, B. LEVI SELAVAN, Göttingen, 2015, *Revue Biblique* 127, 618-621.

À paraître

– « La stèle funéraire araméenne de Ḥayan, roi de Samʾal, à Ördekburn », *Revue Biblique*, 2021.
– « L'inscription en araméen christo-palestinien », dans : C. DAUPHIN (éd.), *Une ferme ecclésiastique byzantine en Galilée occidentale : le domaine agricole de Shelomi* (BAR International Series), Oxford.
– « Le sceau-moule bilingue en araméen christo-palestinien et en arabe de ʿAïn al-Maʿamoudiyeh », dans : Bertrand RIBA (éd.), *Rapport de la fouille de ʿAïn al-Maʿamoudiyeh.*
– « Le Livre de Job », dans : A. PASSARO, G. BELLIA (éd.), *Il Libro di Giobbe. Tradizione, redazione, teologia, 7-8 aprile 2006, Facoltà Teologica di Sicilia "San Giovanni Evangelista" – Palermo.*
– Préface au Recueil des articles de J. Murphy O'Connor sur les manuscrits de la mer Morte.
– « Le livre de *Josué* dans les manuscrits de la mer Morte », dans : *IX Convegno di Studi biblici, Palermo 2015.*
– « Les attentes du retour d'Elie dans l'Ancient Testament et les écrits péritestamentaires », *Journée d'études Autour de saint Jean-Baptiste: cultes et traditions*, IFPO – EBAF, *Syria.*
– « Les manuscrits des *Livres de Samuel* à Qumrân », dans : *I libri di Samuele. Tradizione, redazione, teologia. Convegno di studi biblici 7-8 aprile 2017,* Pontificia Facoltà teologica di Sicilia, Palermo.
– « Les *Livres des Chroniques* et les manuscrits de Qumrân : les Apocryphes 4Q118 et 4Q381 et la Prière de Manassé », *Colloquio biblico. Il Libro delle Cronache, Facoltà teologica di Palermo, 23 Marzo 2018, Rivista Biblica* (2020).

- « Les *Livres des Rois* à Qumrân : *4Q54, 5Q54a* (?), *5Q2* et *6Q4* », dans : A. PASSARO, G. BELIA (éd.), *I Libri dei Rei. Tradizione Redazione Teologia, XI convegno di studi biblici, Pontificia Facoltà teologica di Sicilia, 12-13 aprile 2019.*
- « Une inscription palmyrénienne sur une plaque de marbre d'un cimetière romain », dans : VINCENZO FIOCCHI NICOLAI, L'ERMA DI BRETSCHNEIDER (éd.), *La basilica di papa Marco sulla via Ardeatina a Roma (scavi 1993-1996)*, Roma, 333-334.
- « Anse de jarre gravée à ʿAyun Musa », dans : F.M. BENEDETTUCCI (éd.), *Excavations at Ayun Musa (M. Nebo – Jordan).*
- « Les Livres des Maccabées, Flavius Josèphe et les Assidéens-Esséniens dans les manuscrits de Qumrân », dans : A. PASSARO (éd.), *Colloquio biblico. I Libri dei Maccabei. Tradizione Redazione Teologia, XI convegno di studi biblici, Pontificia Facoltà teologica di Sicilia, 3 aprile 2020.*
- « Les Inscriptions 10 et 7 de Ḥorvat ʿUza : deux documents administratifs », dans : *Ada Yardeni Volume, Eretz Israel.*
- « Les ostraca de Lakish et le prophète Jérémie », dans : Paolo Garuti, Jean Jacques Pérennès, Martin Staszak (éd.), *In Memoriam Francolino Goncalves (1943-2017)* (Études Biblques, Nouvelle Série), Leuven.
- « Fragments des livres de Josué et des Chroniques dans la grotte 4, 4Q47^{a} et 4Q118 2-3 », *Revue de Qumrân.*
- « Les ostraca et les inscriptions de Machéronte », *Liber Annuus.*
- « Le manuscrit *4QPseudoDaniel^{c} - 4Q245* revisité », *Revue Biblique.*
- « Psaume et Prière pour le roi Jonathan (4Q448) revisité », *Revue de Qumrân.*
- « Inscription cananéenne sur une jarre de Lakish », *Revue Biblique.*
- « Un grafitte nord-arabique dans la catacombe romaine des martyrs Marcellin et Pierre », dans : VINCENZO FIOCCHI NICOLAI, L'Erma DI BRETSCHNEIDER (éd.), *La basilica di papa Marco sulla via Ardeatina a Roma (scavi 1993-1996)*, Roma.
- « La jarre inscrite de Tel Arad et *grgr* – olive », *Revue Biblique.*
- « Notes sur l'inscription du sarcophage d'Aḥirom, roi de Byblos », *Revue Biblique,* 2021.
- « La stèle funéraire araméenne de Ḥayan, roi de Sam'al, à Ördekburn », *Revue Biblique*, 2021.

Recensions

- T. MURAOKA, A Biblical Aramaic Reader with an Outline Grammar, Leuven, Paris, Bristol, Ct, 2015, *Revue Biblique.*
- A. B. PERRIN, K. S. BAEK, D. K. FALK (éd.), Reading the Bible in Ancient Traditions and Modern Editions. Studies in Memory of Peter W. Flint, Atlanta, 2017, *Revue Biblique.*
- E. ANDREA, P. XELLA, IN COLLABORATION WITH U. LIVADIOTTI, V. MELCHIORRI (éd.), *Encyclopaedic Dictionary of Phoenician Culture I : Historical Characters*, Leuven, Paris, Bristol, CT, 2018, *Revue Biblique.*
- ANTHONY PERROT (éd.), Les manuscrits de la mer Morte au lendemain de leur 70e anniversaire. Actes de la journée d'étude HET-PRO, St-Légier (Suisse), 2019, *Revue Biblique.*

- B. Porten, A. Yarden, Textbook of Aramaic Ostraca from Idumea, Vol. 3, Pennsylvania, 2018, *Revue Biblique*.
- B. Porten and A. Yardeni, Textbook of Aramaic Ostraca from Idumea, Volume 4, Pennsylvania, 2020, *Revue Biblique*.
- Marc Abou-Abdallah, L'histoire du royaume de Byblos à l'âge du Fer 1080-333, Leuven, Paris, Bristol, CT, 2018, *Revue Biblique*.
- Hélène Sader, The History and Archaeology of Phoenicia, Atlanta, 2019, *Revue Biblique*.
- Sarianna Metso, The Community Rule. A Critical Edition with Translation, Atlanta, 2019, *Revue de Qumrân - Revue Biblique*.
- Silvio Barbaglia, Il tempio di Eliopoli e i rotoli del Mar Morto. Nuova ipotesi sulle origini di Qumran, Torino, 2020, *Revue Biblique*.

TABLE DES MATIÈRES

PRINTED ON PERMANENT PAPER • IMPRIME SUR PAPIER PERMANENT • GEDRUKT OP DUURZAAM PAPIER - ISO 9706

N.V. PEETERS S.A., WAROTSTRAAT 50, B-3020 HERENT